THE CONSERVATION ATLAS
OF
TROPICAL FORESTS
ASIA
AND THE PACIFIC

Contributors

Jesus B. Alvarez, Jr. Quezon City, Philippines

Paul Anspach IUCN, Vientiane, Laos

Ishak bin Ariffin WWF–Malaysia

J. Axelssson Lao/Swedish Forestry Co-operation Programme, Vientiane, Laos

Pallava Bagla Indian Institute of Public Administration, Dehli, India

Henry Barlow Malayan Nature Society, Kuala Lumpur, Malaysia

Sultana Bashir University of Cambridge, UK

Steve Bass Rockefeller Foundation, New York, USA

Dr Elizabeth Bennett WWF–Malaysia

Dr Russell H. Betts WWF, Bogor, Indonesia

Dr John Blower Environmental Consultant, Guernsey

Guido Broekhaven IUCN

Professor Eberhardt Bruenig World Forestry Institute, Hamburg, FRG

Peter Burgess Suffolk, UK

Cartographic Publishing House Beijing

Barney Chan Sarawak Timber Association, Kuching, Sarawak

Graham Chaplin Oxford Forestry Institute, UK

Cheong Ek Choon Forestry Department, Kuching, Sarawak

Dr Chin See Chung Department of Botany, University of Malaya

Dr Marcus Colchester Survival International, London, UK

Dr Richard T. Corlett University of Hong Kong

Eric B. Cowell BP International Ltd, London, UK

Roger Cox Environmental Consultant, London, UK

The Earl of Cranbrook Saxmundham, Suffolk, UK

Dr Arthur Dahl UNEP, Nairobi, Kenya

Dr Jack Dangermond ESRI, California, USA

Dr James Davie Queensland National Park, Rockhampton, Australia

Steve Davis IUCN, Kew, UK

Alexandra M. Dixon Zoological Society of London, UK

Peter Eaton University of Brunei Darussalam

Christopher Elliott WWF-International, Gland, Switzerland

J. Fidloczky Lao/Swedish Forestry Co-operation Programme, Vientiane, Laos

Michel Fromaget ORSTOM, New Caledonia

Dr Michael J. B. Green WCMC

Oscar Gendrano AsDB Manila, Philippines

Sompon Tan Han Royal Forest Department, Thailand

Dr Tim Hatch Horticultural Consultant, Kuching, Sarawak

Dr Jan Van Der Heide Institute of Soil Fertility, Gröningen, Netherlands

U Saw Hahn Rangoon, Myanmar

Professor Vernon Heywood IUCN, Kew, UK

Dinh Hiep Forest Department, Hanoi, Vietnam

Daniel Hiong Sabah Forest Department

G. Hindsen Lao/Swedish Forestry Co-operation Programme, Vientiane, Laos

William Howard Overseas Development Administration, UK

Iamo Ila Department of the Environment and Conservation, Boroko, PNG

Dr Mikhail bin Kavanagh WWF–Malaysia

Dr Kam Suan Peng Penang Branch Malayan Nature Society, Malaysia

M. Kashio FAO, Bangkok, Thailand

G. Kent Lao/Swedish Forestry Co-operation Programme, Vientiane, Laos

Dr Alia Keto Rainforest Conservation Society of Queensland, Australia

Mr Daniel K. S. Khiong FAO, Bangkok, Thailand

M. Kishokumar Malayan Nature Society, Kuala Lumpur, Malaysia

Karol M. Kisokau Department of Environment and Conservation, Boroko, PNG

Professor B. Klankamsorn Royal Forest Department, Bangkok, Thailand

Dr D. Kretosastro Transmigration Department, Jakarta, Indonesia

Dr Ajith Kumar Wildlife Institute of India, Dehra Dun, India

Kanta Kumari WWF–Malaysia

J. B. Lal Forest Survey of India, Dehra Dun, India

Dr David Lamb University of Queensland

Lee Hua Seng Forest Department, Kuching, Sarawak

Dr Leong Yueh Kuong Malayan Nature Society, Kuala Lumpur, Malaysia

Dr Lim Meng Tsai Malayan Nature Society, Kuala Lumpur, Malaysia

Dr John MacKinnon Cambridge, UK

Dr John Makin National Resources Institute, UK

Dr Clive Marsh Sabah Foundation, Kotu Kinabalu, Sabah

Duleep Matthai Ministry of Environment and Forests, Delhi, India

Dr Steve McHugh BP International Ltd, London, UK

Jim McKay BP International Ltd, London, UK

Dr J. McNeely IUCN

Dr V. H. Meher-Homji Institut Français de Pondicherry, India

Adam Messer BIOTROP, Bogor, Indonesia

Dr Genevieve Michon BIOTROP, Bogor, Indonesia

Mok Sian Tuan ASEAN Institute of Forest Management

Franca Monti FAO, Rome, Italy

Dr Robert Nasi CTFT, Paris

François Nectoux South Bank Polytechnic, London, UK

Dr Francis Ng Forest Research Institute of Malaysia, Kuala Lumpur, Malaysia

Dr Csar Neuvo Institute of Forest Conservation, Laguna, Philippines

U Ohn Rangoon, Myanmar

James Paine WCMC

Dr Duncan Parish Asian Wetland Bureau, Kuala Lumpur, Malaysia

Reidar Persson SIDA, Stockholm, Sweden

Tho Yow Pong Malayan Nature Society, Kuala Lumpur, Malaysia

Dr Duncan Poore Oxford, UK

Mick Raga Wildlife Conservation, Department of Environment and Conservation, Boroko, PNG

Sinung Rahardjo Ministry of Forestry, Jakarta, Indonesia

Awang Hj Abd. Rahman Forestry Department, Brunei Darussalam

Abdullah Abdul Rahim WWF–Malaysia

M. S. Ranatunga IUCN, Sri Lanka

Hans Rasch Swedish Space Corporation

K. Ravindran Kerala Forest Research Institute, India

A. M. Ravuvu Ministry of Forests, Fiji

Alan Rodgers Wildlife Institute of India, Dehra Dun, India

Celso Roque DENR, Quezon City, Philippines

Alan E. H. Ross Department of Forests, Boroko, PNG

Philip Round Centre for Conservation Biology, Mahidol University, Bangkok, Thailand

Haji Mohd Yassin Bin Ampuan Salleh Director of Forestry, Brunei Darussalam

Guy Salmon The Maruia Society, Auckland

Dr Richard E. Salter Lao/Swedish Forestry Co-operation Programme, Vientiane, Laos

Dr Charles Santiapillai WWF-Indonesia

Dr Caroline Sargent ILED, London, UK

Vicente Sarmiento, Jr. RP-German Dipterocarp Forest Management Project, Manila

Dr Cerla B. Sastry International Development and Research Centre, Singapore

Jacqueline Sawyer IUCN

Dr Jürgen G. Schade RP-German Dipterocarp Forest Management Project, Manila

G. M. Shea Department of Forestry, Queensland, Australia

Birandra Singh National Trust for Fiji

Shekhar Singh Indian Institute of Public Administration, Delhi, India

Suvat Singhapant Royal Forest Department, Bangkok, Thailand

Som Thep Royal Forestry Department, Thailand

Dr Prem Srivastana Department of Forests, Boroko, PNG

Peter R. Stevens FAO, Dhaka, Bangladesh

Dr Effendy A. Sumardja Forest Protection and Nature Conservation Department, Ministry of Forestry, Bogor, Indonesia

Dr Harold Sutter FAO, Rome

Phairote Suvannakorn Royal Forest Department, Bangkok, Thailand

Dr Bill Syratt BP International Ltd, London, UK

Tai-Neu Liao Department of Forestry, Taiwan

Charles Tawhiao Department of Forests, Boroko, PNG

Dr J. Terborgh Princeton University, USA

Thang Hooi Chiew Forestry Department, Kuala Lumpur, Malaysia

Professor Andrew Vaydon Rutger University, USA

Dr J. R. D. Wall Regional Physical Planning Programme for Transmigration (RePPProT), Jakarta, Indonesia

Kembi Watoka Department of Environment and Conservation, Boroko, PNG

Dr Anthony J. Whitten Cambridge, UK

Mr Tony Wood ODA London, UK

Wong Khoon Meng Forestry Department, Brunei Darussalam

Peter Wyse Jackson IUCN

Boonthong Xaisida Lao/Swedish Forest Co-operation Programme, Vientiane, Laos

In addition authors and reviewers are acknowledged at the end of each chapter.

THE CONSERVATION ATLAS
OF
TROPICAL FORESTS
ASIA
AND THE PACIFIC

Editors

N. Mark Collins
World Conservation Monitoring Centre, Cambridge, UK

Jeffrey A. Sayer
International Union for Conservation of Nature and Natural Resources, Gland, Switzerland

Timothy C. Whitmore
Geography Department,
Cambridge University, UK

The World Conservation Union

SIMON & SCHUSTER
A Paramount Communications Company

New York   London   Toronto   Sydney   Tokyo   Singapore

ACKNOWLEDGEMENTS

This atlas was produced under the Tropical Forest Conservation Programme of IUCN, The World Conservation Union. Much of the research, editing and map preparation was done at the World Conservation Monitoring Centre which is supported by IUCN, the World Wide Fund for Nature (WWF) and the United Nations Environment Programme (UNEP); the Centre is also part of UNEP's Global Environment Monitoring System (GEMS) towards which this atlas is a contribution.

IUCN's work in tropical forests receives financial support from the government of Sweden.

IUCN is especially indebted to The British Petroleum Company p.l.c. for the original idea for the atlas, and for the generous funding which has enabled research for the project to be undertaken.

Thanks also go to IBM, who provided a computer which was used for running the geographic information system (GIS) needed to compile the maps, and to the Environmental Systems Research Institute (ESRI) of California who donated the ARC/INFO software for the project. Petroconsultants Ltd of Cambridge kindly made available 'Mundocart', a world digital mapping database which proved invaluable in the preparation of this atlas.

Contributors to the atlas are listed below. A work of this nature, however, inevitably represents the labours of hundreds of people who have painstakingly documented the forests, researching their ecology and wildlife, and who have laboured over the production of the maps from field work to final printing. The editors would like to offer their heartfelt thanks to all these un-named people.

The editors would also like to thank all their colleagues at IUCN and the World Conservation Monitoring Centre, without whose dedicated work this project would not have been possible. Particular thanks go to Mike Adam, who was responsible for operating the GIS, Clare Billington, who assisted in all aspects of the project, Barbara Brown, Michael Green, Veronica Greenwood, Jeffrey McNeely, James Paine and Jacqueline Sawyer.

Finally a meeting of the IUCN Tropical Forest Advisory Group was held in October 1989 in the Bako National Park, Sarawak, at which IUCN staff and representatives of development agencies and conservation organisations reviewed the text of this atlas. The editors would like to offer their sincere thanks in appreciation of this valuable task.

First published 1991 by Macmillan Press Ltd, London and Basingstoke

and in the USA by

Academic Reference Division
Simon & Schuster
A Paramount Communications Company
15 Columbus Circle
New York, New York 10023

Library of Congress Cataloging-in-Publication Data

The Conservation atlas of tropical forests.

"First published in Great Britain by Macmillan Press Limited, London" – Verso t.p.
"Copyright IUCN" – Verso t.p.
Includes glossary and bibliographical references.
Contents: The issues – Country studies.
1. Rain forests – Asia – Maps.   2. Rain forests – Pacific
Area – Maps.   3. Man – Influence on nature – Asia – Maps.
4. Man – influence on nature – Pacific area – Maps.
5. Conservation of natural resources – Asia – Maps.
6. Conservation of natural resources – Pacific Area – Maps.
I. Collins, N. Mark.   II. International Union for Conservation
of Nature and Natural Resources.   III. Title: Asia and the Pacific,
the conservation atlas of tropical forests.

G2201.K3C6 1991   333.75′16′095022   90-675139
ISBN 0-13-179227-X

Acknowledgement of Sources
The sources of the country maps are given at the end of each chapter. The sources of the illustrations and maps are given in footnotes and captions.

Designed by Robert Updegraff · Map Production by Lovell Johns, Oxford
Typeset by Rowland Phototypesetting Ltd, Bury St Edmunds, Suffolk · Printed and bound in Singapore

Contents

Foreword

When IUCN was founded in 1948, the conservation of tropical forests was already perceived as an important issue. But it was not until the publication of the seminal work of Persson (1974) and Sommer (1976) that the scale and rate of tropical deforestation became more widely recognised. Slightly later, the publication (1981) of the findings of FAO/UNEP's *Tropical Forest Resources Assessment Projects* coincided with campaigns to conserve tropical forests, run by organisations such as IUCN and WWF. Through these, and subsequent, campaigns, people throughout the world have been made increasingly aware of tropical forest conservation as one of the major environmental issues of our time.

The debate is now firmly established in the public arena and tropical forests have become a significant political issue in countries as far apart as Australia, Brazil and Thailand. In both the developed and developing worlds the media have given extensive coverage to the plight of tropical forest people in places such as Sarawak, to species conservation in Madagascar, and to the possible impact on world climate of deforestation in Indonesia and Brazil.

However, in spite of this enormous public, political and scientific concern, agreement on the measures that should be taken remains elusive. Thus the Tropical Forestry Action Plan launched by FAO in 1985 to mobilise international resources to support the conservation and rational use of tropical forests, is now attacked by some environmental groups who see it as aggravating the problems. And while some conservationists lobby the World Bank to invest in tropical forest and biological diversity conservation, others condemn aid programmes for fuelling forest destruction and campaign for development agencies to keep out of the forests.

Not only is there no consensus on solutions, but also views on the extent of the problem conflict with one another. Seemingly credible authorities predict the total destruction of tropical forests in one or two decades. Others point to the vast forest areas remaining in Borneo, Irian Jaya and Papua New Guinea, insisting that the situation is less critical.

Through this atlas IUCN hopes to introduce more objective and carefully researched information to the debate. It is the first of a series of three volumes, covering all the main tropical regions. Our editors have travelled to every country in tropical Asia to collect the latest data on forest distribution and trends. They have consulted a broad spectrum of specialists ranging from academic forest ecologists through members of the timber industry, to forest dwelling peoples and government authorities in the countries concerned. Our authors represent much of the best available expertise on forest science and management. Our maps and text have been reviewed by specialists from throughout the region who met in the delightful forest setting of the Bako National Park as guests of the Sarawak Forest Department. We have enjoyed a constant dialogue with FAO and UNEP – international organisations with a mandate from the United Nations to monitor tropical forests and promote their wise use.

We are confident that this atlas presents the *best available* information on the tropical forest resources of Asia and the Pacific. But we are also well aware of its shortcomings. There are large areas, for instance in Indo-China, for which up-to-date information on forest distribution is simply not available. And even with the latest advances in remote sensing, it is not always possible to distinguish between undisturbed closed canopy tropical forest and forests regenerating after logging or shifting cultivation. Much of the land which our maps show to be forested in Borneo and Burma is in fact quite seriously disturbed. For these reasons we have accompanied the maps with text which interprets them from the point of view of conservationists.

The chapters on the critical issues confronting forest conservation attempt to present a balanced view of knowledge. But often they illustrate just how complex the issues are and how intractable the solutions appear to be. The chapter on natural rain forest management, for example, shows that sustained yield management is technically possible, while acknowledging the general failure to achieve this goal in practice.

We could have waited ten years and published a definitive work on tropical forest resources. But in ten years many of our options will have been foreclosed. Meanwhile decisions are being taken and considerable international finance is available to support conservation programmes. We believe that lack of information and poor understanding of the issues are resulting in misguided decisions, causing money to be wasted on irrelevant or even counter-productive actions. It is our sincere hope that the information and arguments presented in this atlas will bring some rationale and rigour to the tropical forest debate and help the countries that own these magnificent living systems, and the international community that is so deeply concerned for their future, to reach agreement on the long-term effective conservation they require.

MARTIN HOLDGATE
IUCN, Gland, Switzerland
November 1990

References
FAO/UNEP (1981) *Tropical Forest Resources Assessment Project.* 3 volumes. FAO, Rome.

Persson, R. (1974)   Review of the world's forest resources in the early 1970s. In: *World Forest Resources.* Royal College of Forestry, Stockholm.

Sommer, A. (1976)   Attempt at an assessment of the world's tropical forests. *Unasylva* 28.

PART I

1 Introduction

Economic growth and demand for land is increasing day by day in the Asia–Pacific region. As a result the national and global significance of the rain and monsoon forests is becoming more widely appreciated. Sustaining the many benefits from tropical forests is no longer a matter of interest only for conservation organisations, it is the stuff of newspaper editorials in New Delhi, Bangkok, Kuala Lumpur, Jakarta and Port Moresby. Citizens of tropical forest countries are increasingly aware that their natural forests protect soil fertility, prevent flooding, provide valuable timbers for national revenue and useful non-wood crops for local sale and consumption. In short, the forests produce goods and services that are the basis of everyday life in the region.

This atlas aims to give an up-to-date bird's eye view of the extent of the Asia–Pacific closed canopy tropical rain forests, and the monsoon forests that abut onto them (for forest definitions see box on page 11). The coming decade is crucial. Planning for the future of tropical forests requires ready sources of up-to-date information on their cultural, biological and ecological importance, the agricultural and silvicultural potential of their soils, the value of their natural timbers and other forest products, and the best possible maps of their extent and location. The first eleven chapters of this volume discuss regional issues, while chapters 12–29 give a detailed survey of each country. Accompanying the text are detailed maps which form the heart of the book, enabling the reader to obtain a clear overview of where the remaining forests are situated.

Forests of the Region

The tropical, closed canopy forests of the Asia–Pacific region are centred on the Malay archipelago, the great festoon of islands which lie between the south-eastern tip of Asia and Australia, the region botanists call Malesia. These islands were once mostly clothed in rain forests, with a fringe of monsoon (seasonal) forests along their southern margin. To the north and west rain forests extend up into continental Asia, where they occur in the wetter and less seasonal parts of Burma,[1] Thailand and Indo-China (Cambodia, Laos, Vietnam), just extending into southernmost China, Bangladesh, Assam, and north-east India. There are also detached fragments of rain forest in peninsular India along the Western Ghats which fringe the Arabian Sea shoreline of the subcontinent, in south-west Sri Lanka and on the Andaman and Nicobar Islands.

[1] During the preparation of this atlas, Burma changed its name to Myanmar. The country chapters are arranged alphabetically and the editors have used the former, more commonly known, name in order to avoid major restructuring.

Geographical Boundaries

To the east rain forests extend beyond Malesia into the Pacific, along the tropical parts of the archipelagoes of Melanesia. Further out still there are tiny fragments on the specks of land which constitute the islands of Micronesia and Polynesia. Reaching south, rain forests run as a fringe down the eastern coastline of Australia.

At the northern and southern limits of the region, in areas of aseasonal climate, tropical rain forests gradually alter in floristic composition and become simpler in structure (in a manner not well defined). These are known as subtropical rain forests, and further still from the equator they turn into temperate rain forests. These changes are accentuated by increases in elevation. Thus, no sharp boundary can be drawn in upper Burma and in Assam between tropical rain forests in the lowlands and temperate rain forests in the high mountains of the southern Himalayas, which have a flora with a strongly north-temperate character. These forests are therefore included in the atlas. However, at the limit, the northern boundary becomes arbitrary, and we have excluded the forests of mid-elevations which stretch along the south flank of the Himalayas in India, Nepal and Pakistan and occur also in western China (including Tibet). These are of north temperate affinity, albeit very similar to those of northern Burma and Assam.

To the south of the region, in Australia, the only forests mapped are the rain forests of north Queensland. These are separate from the subtropical rain forests of the Queensland/New South Wales border region further south, which themselves merge southwards with temperate rain forests that extend to Tasmania.

The larger islands of the tropical western Pacific are mapped, down to a lower national size limit of 15,000 sq. km. The tiny tropical rain forest areas of Micronesia and Polynesia are thus excluded, as are the subtropical/warm temperate forests of New Caledonia and northernmost New Zealand. As with the northern boundary we have had to draw an arbitrary southern limit, and have done so in the light of the purpose of the atlas, which is to demonstrate the distribution of *tropical* rain and monsoon forest formations.

Climatic Boundaries

Just as there is a gradation of forest-type with increasing latitude, so there is another one with decreasing rainfall and an increasingly seasonal climate. This second gradation is, fortunately, better defined. In climates where the rainfall is well distributed throughout the year, and where there is no regular dry season and no months with rainfall of less than 60 mm, or with a dry season of only one or a few months' duration, the natural climax vegetation is tropical rain forest. Where there is a regular and longer annual dry season, tropical

In Java, both rain and monsoon forests are to be found, but only in relict patches. The rich soils of Java were deforested long ago. WWF/Tom Moss

Forest Cover

Technically, forests are defined as 'woody vegetation with a closed tree canopy' and woodlands as 'woody vegetation with an open tree canopy'. The division, which we follow, is commonly drawn at 40 per cent canopy cover. The maps in this atlas do not show open canopy woodlands and do not include forest plantations or areas of shifting cultivation where these are shown in source material. However, shifting cultivation occurs as a mosaic of cultivated fields and bush fallow areas at various stages of recovery to high forest, which are indistinguishable on remotely sensed images when forest-recovery is advanced. It is very difficult to recognise moist forest that has been disturbed by cultivation or felling. Even a heavily logged forest quickly redevelops a closed canopy and a few decades after disturbance it is hard for anyone but an expert to distinguish between logged and unlogged forest. On aerial photographs logged forest becomes indistinguishable from unlogged forest after a few years, and on satellite images it may never be detectable. *The areas mapped as single units of forest are therefore mosaics of relatively undisturbed, plus disturbed, forest.* It is vital for the reader to appreciate that even though large belts of shifting cultivation and plantations have been excluded from the maps, the areas of forest still include enclaves, sometimes quite extensive, of disturbed and degraded vegetation.

For three countries (Burma, Laos and the Philippines) we have had access, however, to reports which do actually delimit degraded forests, and which describe how it was recognised and defined, and for these countries it is shown as a separate category on the map. Details are explained in the map legends.

Major Issues which Affect the Asia–Pacific Forests

The first part of the atlas, chapters 2–11, sets out issues which affect forests throughout the Asia–Pacific region. Chapter 2 provides general background on the fauna and flora of the region, its importance to mankind, and the impact of deforestation on species' diversity. Chapter 3 discusses peoples of the rain forest. Chapters 4 and 5 examine some causes of forest loss, namely shifting agriculture and settlement schemes. Chapters 6 and 7 examine systems of forest management for timber production and the timber trade (which today is a major factor bringing change to the forests of this region).

These chapters are followed by others which describe attempts to control and limit human impact. Chapter 8 describes land-use planning; chapter 9 the attempts to protect representative areas for conservation purposes; and chapter 10 covers current attempts to rationalise external aid resources to these ends for sustainable forest development. Finally, the outlook for the forests and for the success of these efforts are described in chapter 11.

The Situation in Individual Countries

The second half of the atlas examines every country in detail. Firstly, a set of basic statistics is provided. Land area is taken from FAO (1988); economic data from World Bank (1989) or Paxton (1989) and demographic data from Vu *et al.* (1989). Data presented under forest cover are from various sources listed in the main body of the text.[3] Forest product information is for 1987, reported in FAO (1989). Definitions for production data are presented in chapter 7.

Following a summary, each country chapter has a general geographical introduction and a detailed description of the closed

seasonal forests occur; in Asia these are commonly called monsoon forests (see box on page 11). At their boundary rain and monsoon forests often form a mosaic due to the influence of soil and the impact of humans. Tropical rain and tropical seasonal forests are sometimes grouped together as tropical moist forests, which is useful, for example, when discussing human impact.[2]

Seasonal forests include a considerable proportion of deciduous trees so are easy to recognise on the ground in the dry season, but in the wet season more careful inspection of structure, physiognomy and floristics is needed (including leaf size and texture, bole, buttresses, position of inflorescences). Unfortunately both seasonal and rain forests look similar in aerial photographs and satellite images for much of the year. Furthermore, the seasonal monsoon forests are not clearly distinguishable from the much drier tropical thorn forests on remotely sensed images, which is why rain, monsoon and thorn forests are sometimes combined into the single category of closed forests (or moist forests, where thorn forests are absent), as in the FAO/UNEP Tropical Forest Resources Assessment of 1981.

[2] In popular parlance, the term 'rain' forest is often applied where 'moist' forest would be technically more correct. In this book 'rain' and 'monsoon' forests will be clearly distinguished.

[3] FAO made the only full pantropical survey of tropical closed forests in 1980 (FAO/UNEP, 1981), the results of which were reissued with corrections in 1988 (FAO, 1988). FAO (1987) is also important for the Asia–Pacific region. The FAO survey is being repeated in 1990 and results are expected to be published in 1992. At present it remains unclear whether the survey will include publication of maps.

canopy forests, particularly rain forests, their extent and their management. Basic statistics include original and remaining forest area, where known. Discrepancies are common between different estimates of remaining forest area – and it must be borne in mind that in some countries forest area is changing very fast. Statistics rarely accord with estimates of area taken from the maps used in preparing this atlas, even where both these sources were official. It is seldom possible to resolve these discrepancies. They are drawn to the reader's attention and the reference of the original source is given.

Much has been written recently on mangrove forests. This formation is seldom extensive, but is common as a narrow coastal and estuarine fringe. Its ecological importance as a coastline stabiliser, and its economic importance as a source of fuelwood, building poles, tannin, cordage, and honey to rural communities, as well as an important provider of prawns, shrimps and fish, is now thoroughly documented. So too is the role of mangroves as the essential breeding ground and nursery which sustains shallow-water offshore fishery industries. The threats mangrove forests face vary from country to country, but fall everywhere into the same few categories of destruction – to make way for prawn or fish ponds, or for housing or factories; overexploitation for fuelwood and building poles; or, over the last few decades, uncontrolled clear felling for chipwood, exported (mainly to Japan) for paper pulp or the manufacture of rayon.

In each country study the diversity of its flora and fauna is described to varying degrees, depending upon its regional significance and the state of available knowledge. This is followed by a section on conservation areas in which the protection of the nation's ecological and biological diversity is assessed. Where there are serious shortcomings in the protected area systems, details of critical sites for conservation are presented. General commentary and data on critical sites are not presented country by country, but are compiled in chapter 9.

Of particular interest, of course, in each country study is an assessment of the coverage of moist forest ecosystems within conservation areas, but this is no simple matter. Many parks are only partially forested and at the working scale of this atlas it is not possible to assess the proportion of forested land accurately. In each country chapter we have chosen to tabulate those protected areas (existing and proposed) which are at least 50 sq. km in size and for which we have location data. The remaining smaller areas, and the few areas where we have no location information, are combined into a single estimate of total size under a sub-heading 'Other Areas', enabling calculation of the total area under protection. Marine conservation areas, 'virgin jungle reserves', and forest reserves are listed or included in the country totals. Those protected areas containing moist forest (rain or monsoon forest) are flagged, and their

KINDS OF FOREST

Since they were defined by Schimper (one of the founding fathers of plant geography) in 1903, it has been common to recognise two major kinds of tropical forest: *tropical rain forest* and *tropical monsoon (seasonal) forest*. The combination of these is often referred to as *tropical moist forest*. All moist forests have a closed canopy and the term *closed forests* is also often used to denote rain and monsoon forests. However, dry thorn forests also have a closed canopy and may sometimes be included in the term. Caution is therefore needed in interpreting 'closed forests' in countries, such as India, Sri Lanka and Burma, where thorn forests, as well as rain forests and monsoon forests, occur.

• Vegetation types with less than 40 per cent tree canopy cover are technically called *woodlands* or sometimes *open forests*.
• *Tropical rain forests* occur in perhumid climates where the rainfall is well distributed through the year, there is no regular dry season and no month with rainfall less than 60 mm, or with a dry season of only one or a few months' duration.
• *Tropical monsoon forests* occur where there is a regular and longer dry season, usually more than three months with less than 60 mm rainfall.
• In areas with long dry seasons, monsoon forests grade into open canopy deciduous woodlands, then into closed canopy thorn forests of low stature (India, Burma), and finally into scrub, grassland and desert formations. None of these are mapped in this atlas.
• Within rain and monsoon forests there are various *forest formations* dependent upon local conditions of soil, topography, climate and groundwater. They are generally defined on structure of the canopy and physiognomy of their component species. They vary floristically from place to place.

The main focus of this atlas is on true rain forests, and more detail is shown for this formation, ie lowland and montane rain forest, mangrove and freshwater swamp forests. The monsoon forests are shown in a more generalised way, distinguishing only between lowland and montane distribution. The broad categories used are suited to the general working scales of 1:3 and 1:4 million. This is

not the place in which to delimit in detail either the formations or floristic variation, which are very fully described elsewhere. The publications of FAO/UNEP (1981), Unesco (1974) and Whitmore (1984; 1989) give such descriptions, plus a full guide to the original literature.

This atlas attempts to achieve a synoptic view by combining the forest formations into major groups as shown in the list below. Formations are progressively grouped into larger classes. The forest types and formations shown on the maps are *italicised* in the table.

Tropical rain forests (aseasonal)

Dry land rain forests
lowland rain forests
   tropical evergreen rain forest
   tropical semi-evergreen rain forest
   heath forest
   rain forest over limestone
   rain forest over ultrabasic rocks
   beach forest
montane rain forests
   lower montane rain forest
   upper montane rain forest
   subalpine rain forest

Wetland rain forests
coastal swamp forests
   mangrove forest
   inland swamp forests
   peat swamp forest
   freshwater swamp forest
   periodic freshwater swamp forest

Tropical monsoon forests (seasonal)
lowland monsoon forests
montane monsoon forests

total areas are calculated and presented in chapter 9, where information on areas designated as Biosphere Reserves and World Heritage sites may also be found.

The length of the text about each country and about the different types of human impact on the forests therein, is roughly balanced to the size of the country and the gravity of the deforestation. Much is known, for example, about the small areas of rain forest in Singapore and Australia, but in a broad context these forests are less significant than those of huge nations such as Indonesia.

Maps

Finally in the country surveys, but most importantly, are the forest maps themselves. The literature on rain and monsoon forests, their floristics, biology, rate of decline and importance to mankind is burgeoning. Yet there are very few published maps readily available. Newspapers and magazines regularly report development projects in rain forest countries, but whether the road, dam or settlement area lies within existing areas of rain forest or monsoon forest is frequently impossible to judge. All too often, projects reported to be within the 'rain forest' are completely outside the forest zone!

Each map is accompanied by a comprehensive legend that not only gives the source, but also explains fully what steps have been taken to harmonise the original map with the working classification of forest types given in the box on page 11. Within these limits the maps are reproduced as originally published. Where maps seem unduly optimistic, are somewhat out of date, or have been amended slightly, the matter is drawn to the reader's attention.

In line with the protected area tables, proposed and existing protected areas whose size exceeds 50 sq. km are mapped. If maps showing the precise boundaries are unavailable, the protected areas are represented by circles of an approximate size. Other, smaller areas cannot be satisfactorily mapped at the scale used in this atlas. Many genetic reserves, for example, are only a few hectares in size, and even a small name and dot would soon overwhelm the general appearance of the maps.

Availability of Data

In the final reckoning, the data presented in the text and maps that make up this atlas are a selection based on editorial discretion and the limitations of scale and design. The maps have been compiled using the latest computer technology, a Geographic Information System (GIS). A GIS consists of combined computer hardware and software for collecting, storing, displaying, manipulating and analysing digital spatial data. Once the data have been stored in a computer-readable form they remain accessible for reproduction and re-use for other purposes. The files on which this atlas is based are held at the World Conservation Monitoring Centre in Cambridge, UK, and IUCN will be pleased to collaborate with organisations wishing to apply the data in the interests of natural resource conservation.

References

FAO (1987) *Special Study on Forest Management, Afforestation and Utilization of Forest Resources in the Developing Regions. Asia–Pacific Region. Assessment of Forest Resources in Six Countries.* FAO, Bangkok, Thailand. 104 pp.

FAO (1988) *An Interim Report on the State of Forest Resources in the Developing Countries.* FAO, Rome. 18 pp. + 5 tables.

FAO (1990) *FAO Yearbook of Forest Products 1977–88.* FAO, Forestry Series No. 23, FAO Statistics Series No. 90. FAO, Rome, Italy.

FAO/UNEP (1981) *Tropical Forest Resources Assessment Project. Forest Resources of Tropical Asia.* Vol. 3 of 3 vols. FAO, Rome, Italy. 475pp.

Paxton, J. (ed.) (1989) *The Statesman's Year-book 1989–90.* Macmillan, London, UK. 1691 pp.

Schimper, A. F. W. (1903) *Plant Geography upon a Physiological Basis.* University Press, Oxford, UK.

Unesco (1974) *Natural Resources of Humid Tropical Asia.* Unesco, Paris, France.

Vu, M. T., Bos, E. and Bulatao, R. A. (eds) (1988) *Asia Region Population Projections.* Population and Human Resource Department, World Bank, Washington, DC, USA.

Whitmore, T. C. (1984) *Tropical Rain Forests of the Far East.* (2nd ed.) Clarendon Press, Oxford, UK. 352 pp.

Whitmore, T. C. (1989) Southeast Asian tropical forests. In: *Tropical Rain Forest Ecosystems. Ecosystems of the World* Vol. 14B. Eds H. Leith and M. J. A. Werger. Elsevier, Amsterdam, The Netherlands. 713 pp.

World Bank (1989) *World Development Report.* Oxford University Press, Oxford, UK. 251 pp.

2 Forest Wildlife

Introduction

Humans have lived in tropical Asia for at least 500,000 years, judging from fossil sites in Java. For most of human history, they were hunters and gatherers, but even at this early stage they had some impact on the environment (Rambo, 1979). Once fire became an important tool (probably several hundred thousand years ago), human impact on the environment began to grow, particularly as settlements increased along coasts and rivers. The alluvial flatlands of Asia, once clothed in various kinds of freshwater swamp forest, have long ago been almost completely replaced by rice fields. The development of shifting cultivation (see chapter 4) accelerated the impact, at least in the hilly areas. Irrigation, cultivation of wet rice, and the spread of industrial export-driven agriculture and logging during the past few decades now gives human beings the potential to overwhelm virtually all forested habitats.

Civilisations have waxed and waned in the monsoon forests of the seasonal tropics, for example in Sri Lanka and Indo-China. Some authorities believe that in these formations no significant pristine forest remains, all has been cleared for shifting agriculture at one time or another (see chapter 4). Vast areas of former monsoon forest are now permanently used for intensive agriculture.

The perhumid tropics, however, have always been less healthy for people, and rain forests were much more difficult to use for permanent agriculture. The lack of a dry-season break in the climate makes clearing and burning more difficult, and permits the continual build-up of pests, weeds and diseases. High density civilisations did not develop in these zones and, over the centuries, traces of small settlements have disappeared. Very careful scrutiny is needed to see if mankind has ever disturbed such rain forests. The traces are charcoal in the soil, earth mounds, and plants growing away from their natural area. Detailed studies have not yet been made in most of the remaining Asia–Pacific rain forests to see how ubiquitous mankind's influence has been over the millennia, but any remaining effect is so slight that the forests may be regarded as pristine up until the advent of industrial logging.

Since European penetration of the Malay archipelago, and for longer on the Asian continent, the moist forests have been progressively cut down. There has been an acceleration, from the time of the introduction of plantation crops for export (mainly tea, coffee, rubber and oil palm) at the end of the last century until today. The rapid and accelerating increase in human population means that forests which could still be perceived as a limitless resource in the middle of this century, now increasingly occur as scattered, isolated fragments. This fragmentation and its implications for the loss of the species of plants and animals is one of the great issues of our time – indeed it is the subject of this atlas.

The natural habitats of the region have certainly had to adapt to changing conditions. Climates have fluctuated throughout the Pleistocene (the last two million years), between extensively perhumid as today, and more strongly seasonal as at the Glacial maxima. At these latter times sea level was as much as 180 m below today's level, and Java, Sumatra, and Borneo have been repeatedly attached by land bridges to mainland Asia, with the latest attachment less than 18,000 years ago. The Philippines and Indonesia are among the most geologically active parts of the world, with commonplace volcanic eruptions and earthquakes. Typhoons often sweep across the Philippines into Vietnam and southern China, or hammer the lands of the Bay of Bengal. Monsoon climates alternately inundate and desiccate many parts of the mainland.

As a consequence of this dynamic geological and climatic history, many species have been lost, created or redistributed. For example, Java had at least seven species of elephants in the early Pleistocene, and once had numerous species which still survive elsewhere, including orang utan *Pongo pygmaeus*, Malayan sun bear *Helarctos malayanus*, Malayan tapir *Tapirus indicus*, tiger *Panthera tigris*, and clouded leopard *Neofelis nebulosa*. Generally speaking, the wildlife that has survived into the modern era has adapted to be able to cope with the effect of human impact on the tropical forest ecosystem. Unfortunately, however, the current impacts of logging, shifting cultivation, plantations, and pesticides have presented a totally different challenge to the wildlife.

Biological Diversity and the Impact of Deforestation

The Asia–Pacific region is famous for its rich wildlife. Animals such as tigers, orang utans, rhinoceroses, elephants, pheasants, birds of paradise, cobras and crocodiles, and plants such as the massive dipterocarp trees, *Rafflesia*, the world's largest flower, orchids and the pitcher plants *Nepenthes*, are all part of the region's natural heritage. Yet current patterns of development are depleting wildlife and its habitats at an alarming pace. Given current trends in agriculture, degradation of these rich tropical forests seems set to continue.

In this brief chapter it is not possible to review thoroughly the impact of deforestation and forest degradation on wildlife. Instead, a brief overview of plant and animal diversity, especially of species of actual or potential value to mankind, is presented, followed by some comment on their ability to survive in forests managed for the production of timber and other products. More detail concerning the wildlife of individual countries is presented in chapters 12 to 29.

Actions to prevent or mitigate destructive effects of deforestation or forest management are presented in the chapters on land-use planning, protected areas and the general outlook for the future (chapters 8, 9 and 11). Most of these actions concern *in situ* conservation measures. To balance these, the efforts for *ex situ* conservation in zoos and botanic gardens are presented in case studies on pages 19 and 22.

Plants

1 The scale of exploitation of the forests in the last few decades has placed their future in jeopardy. Timber is the major product, but forests are also cleared to grow plantation crops such as rubber, oil palm, tea and coffee, which make a major contribution to the region's economy, and for shifting cultivation of various kinds. At current rates of exploitation or conversion for other uses, virtually all of the region's forests will be either degraded or cleared by the end of the century. Not only will the lucrative source of timber have disappeared but with it the vast array of other economically important forest products.

The dipterocarp forests of Southeast Asia are today the largest source of hardwoods in international trade (see Chapter 7), but they are likely to be logged over within a decade or two. Their productivity from then onwards will depend upon the success with which they are managed for sustainable use, but timber output from secondary forests will never equal that of the primary forests currently being exploited (see Chapters 6, 8). In Peninsular Malaysia, about four-fifths of total timber produced comes from dipterocarps. The leading species of the monsoon forests of Burma, India, and Thailand is teak (*Tectona grandis*), now extensively planted there as well as in Vietnam, Sri Lanka, Java and Papua New Guinea. Some timber species have now become extremely rare, for example calamander (*Diospyros quaesita*), which produces the finest variegated ebony in Sri Lanka.

2 Many world crops and other plants and animals of economic importance came originally from the Asia–Pacific region (Hawkes, 1989). For a general account of the floristics of the region, refer to page 23. Forest plants provide beverages, fibres, fruits, gums, oils, bamboos, rattans, spices and vegetables. Fruits such as banana *Musa* spp., citrus *Citrus* spp., mango *Mangifera* spp., mangosteen *Garcinia mangostana*; spices, such as betel nut *Areca catechu*, cardamom *Elettaria cardamomum*, cinnamon *Cinnamomum* spp., clove *Syzygium aromaticum*, ginger *Zingiber officinale*, nutmeg *Myristica fragrans*, pepper *Piper nigrum* and turmeric *Curcuma longa*; fibres such as ramie *Boehmeria nivea* and jute *Corchorus capsularis* and root crops such as taro *Colocasia esculenta*, all originate in the Asia–Pacific region. The forests are rich in traditional medicinal plants and ornamental species such as orchids and palms (Arora, 1985; Burkhill, 1935; Jain and Mehra, 1983; Westphal and Jansen, 1989). India, Burma and Southeast Asia are rich centres of genetic variation in cultivated fruit trees and their wild relatives only about 30 per cent of which have so far been cultivated.

The genus *Mangifera* occurs from India to the Solomons, concentrated in West Malesia (Hou, 1978; Mukherjee, 1985). Thirty-nine species are currently recognised, and occur mainly in tropical rain forests (see Figure 2.1). Wild mango, *M. indica*, of India and Burma is the source of the cultivated mango, one of the most important of all tropical fruits. Several other species are used locally, such as *M. caesia* of Sumatra and Malaya, which is cultivated and has dispersed and become naturalised widely throughout Malesia. Genetic depletion has been reported in wild populations of this species as well as in *M. foetida*, *M. longipes* and *M. similis*.

Southeast Asia is also the centre of diversity of the Aurantioid subfamily of the Rutaceae, which includes oranges and other citrus fruits. Seventy-six per cent of the 33 genera and 68 per cent of the 204 species of the subfamily are native to the region. *Citrus* is the most important genus economically, with 16 species in the region. There is considerable interest in the lesser known wild species and in other more or less related genera as a source of material for genetic improvement. Malaysia has 78 per cent of the total number of genera in Southeast Asia and 50 per cent of the species. Collecting missions for germplasm have been undertaken recently by Malaysian universities, WWF and IBPGR.

Other important fruit trees that have their origin in the forests

Pitcher plants such as Nepenthes gymnophora *are a feature of Asian forests. Deriving some of their nourishment from insects that drown inside the pitcher, they survive well where nutrients are in short supply.* WWF/Alain Compost

include: durian (*Durio zibethinus* and related species), rambutan (*Nephelium lappaceum*), longan (*Dimocarpus longan*), mangosteen, rose apple (*Syzygium jambos*, *S. malaccense*), illipe nut (*Shorea macrophylla*), carambola (*Averrhoa carambola*) and Ceylon gooseberry (*Dovyalis hebecarpa*).

The Malesia–Western Pacific region is the home of *Artocarpus*, of which several species have ancient domesticates now grown for their fruits, useful fibrous barks and latex which is used for bird lime. The principal species are *A. utilis*, breadfruit, and *A. heterophyllus*, jackfruit. Some wild species are used as food in Malaysia, New Guinea and western Micronesia.

Bananas are another fruit which originated in this region. Most cultivated bananas are derived from *Musa acuminata* and *M. balbisiana*, wild species from Southeast Asia. A wide array of cultivars and wild races are to be found here and material has been collected for future breeding.

Musa textilis is the source of Manila hemp, a commercial fibre. Other important fibres which are native to the region are ramie *Boehmeria nivea*, jute (originating in China), tossa jute (*Corchorus olitorius*, from India), bow-string hemp (*Sansevieria zeylanica* from Sri Lanka, *S. roxburghiana* from India), and sunn hemp *Crotalaria juncea*, grown on a large scale in India and not known from the wild.

3 Both bamboos and rattans are a mainstay of traditional technology in villages across the region. The monsoon regions of the mainland are particularly rich in bamboo resources. Thailand, with over 750 sq. km of bamboo (Lessard and Chouinard, 1980), has 41 indigenous species; Indonesia has 35 and Malaysia 25. The most important genera are *Bambusa* and *Gigantochloea*.

The greatest concentration of rattan species occurs in Peninsular Malaysia and Borneo (104 and 151 species respectively) (Jacobs, 1982; Whitmore, 1973). Over half the species are from the genus *Calamus*, which includes those most commonly sought after. Their export is worth some $1500 million per year to the region (Caldecott, 1988), most of this being natural cane collected in the wild. The industry is, therefore, particularly valuable. Unlike bamboos, rattans are difficult to grow outside forests because of their climbing nature. However, two of the smaller species, *Calamus caesius* and *C. trachycoleus*, have been planted on a substantial scale (see also chapter 6, section on Management for Secondary Forest Products). They now provide 10–20 per cent of Indonesia's total exports, and plantations have recently been established in Malaysia (de Beer and McDermott, 1989). Coordinated genetic improvement programmes exist throughout the region, for both bamboos and rattans (Dhanarajan *et al.*, undated). Rattans are being fast depleted in the forests as a result of over-exploitation, especially when timber operations give easy access. Forest clearance is also depleting the resource.

4 Plants are a vital source of drugs and medicines for a large percentage of the inhabitants of the Asia–Pacific region; for example 80 per cent of inhabitants in China and 75 per cent in India rely on herbal remedies. At least 6500 species of plants, mainly forest species, are used medicinally in Asia. Many are collected from the wild and an increasing number are becoming rare or are losing diversity as the result of over-collection and the loss of habitat. They represent a major, largely neglected, and little explored genetic resource and urgent action is needed for their conservation and rational exploitation.

Rafflesia, the world's largest flower, is confined to Southeast Asia. Parasitic on the roots of certain trees, the foul-smelling flower attracts flies as pollinators. This is Rafflesia micropylosa *in Perak, Peninsular Malaysia.* WWF.

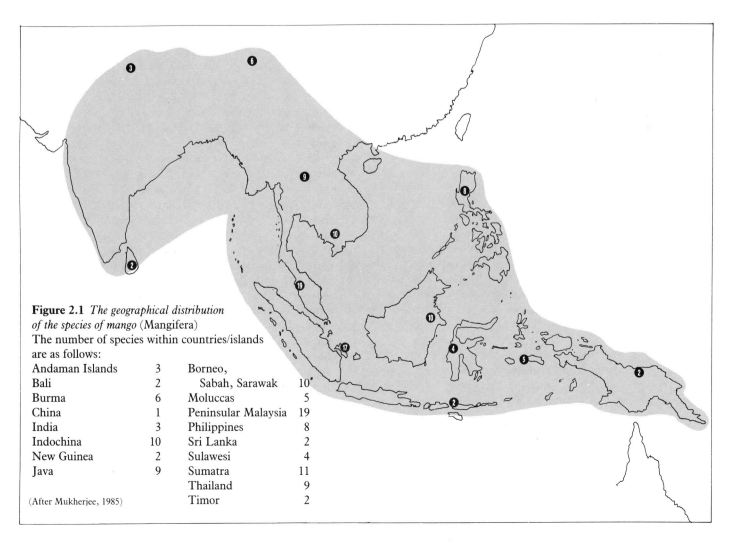

Figure 2.1 *The geographical distribution of the species of mango* (Mangifera)
The number of species within countries/islands are as follows:

Andaman Islands	3	Borneo,	
Bali	2	Sabah, Sarawak	10
Burma	6	Moluccas	5
China	1	Peninsular Malaysia	19
India	3	Philippines	8
Indochina	10	Sri Lanka	2
New Guinea	2	Sulawesi	4
Java	9	Sumatra	11
		Thailand	9
(After Mukherjee, 1985)		Timor	2

FOREST WILDLIFE

Animals

Zoogeographers recognise two principal assemblages of vertebrates in South and Southeast Asia, based on the Sunda and Sahul continental shelves of Asia and Australia respectively. Intervening between these is a transitional fauna on Sulawesi and associated islands. A rather special assemblage also exists on Mentawai and other islands to the west of Sumatra, separated from the Sunda shelf by a deep ocean trench. This heterogeneity embraces a wide range of animal life, much of it of direct benefit to mankind. Excellent general descriptions of the land and wildlife of tropical Asia have been presented by Ripley (1964) and Pfeffer (1968) (see also Table 2.1).

1 For many people throughout the region, wild animals provide a major proportion of dietary protein (see, for example, the case study on Hunting and Wildlife Management in Sarawak in chapter 6).

- A wide range of forest animals are hunted, but the chief targets are ungulates such as bearded pig (*Sus barbatus*), and several deer, including sambar (*Cervus unicolor*), muntjac, or barking deer (*Muntiacus* spp.), and mouse deer (*Tragulus* spp.).
- Primates, pangolins, bats, crocodiles, pythons and a variety of frogs are also hunted (Ahmad, 1981; de Beer and McDermott, 1989).
- Large birds, such as hornbills, pheasants, pigeons, birds of paradise and bower-birds are taken for personal decoration and ceremonies, as well as for the pot.
- Megapodes are exploited for their giant eggs.
- Cave swiftlets provide nests used by the Chinese for soup.
- Many invertebrates are also eaten, including Orthoptera (primarily grasshoppers and locusts), Isoptera (termites) and certain Coleoptera (beetles). Among the latter, the larva of the large palm weevil, *Rhynchophorus ferrugineus*, collected from wild sago stumps, is most commonly seen in the market place.

2 Forest animals are the basis of a flourishing local and international trade, often to the detriment of the species involved.

- Trade in birds from the Moluccas and New Guinea is notorious, particularly in live parrots and birds of paradise (Inskipp *et al.*, 1988), e.g. as many as 70,000 parrots may have been exported from the Moluccas in 1983, only 42,000 legally (Smiet, 1985).
- Reports from the Secretariat of the Convention on International Trade on Endangered Species of Wild Fauna and Flora (CITES) indicate an average annual export for 1980–5 of 23,000 crab-eating macaques (*Macaca fascicularis*) for bio-medical research from Indonesia, Malaysia and the Philippines. Most other primates from the region are prohibited in trade by the Convention, to which the majority of countries are party.
- Butterflies are traded both as deadstock and alive, for supply to specialist collectors, for use in curios, and for display in zoos and 'butterfly houses'. Although specimens are often brought dead from the wild, livestock is generally produced in smallholder butterfly farms, such as those that have developed to supply birdwing butterflies from Papua New Guinea (Collins and Morris, 1985). In 1986, exports of the New Guinea birdwing (*Ornithoptera priamus*) were estimated at over 7000 specimens (Luxmoore *et al.*, 1988).
- While most freshwater fish entering the aquarium trade are bred in captivity, one notable exception is the Asian bonytongue (*Scleropages formosus*). Despite being listed on CITES Appendix I, this is still actively traded, fetching up to US$2700 in Jakarta in 1986. It is reported that 7000 specimens were exported from Pontianak, in West Kalimantan in 1986 alone (Giesen, 1987).

3 The forests of the Asia–Pacific region are rich in wild relatives of domesticated animals, many of which are threatened by hunting and loss of suitable habitat. The most important domestic animals are the ungulates, including pigs, deer, antelopes and cattle.

- Pigs are generally common and able to adapt well to disturbance of natural forests. A comparative rarity, however, is the babirusa (*Babyrousa babyrussa*), which is confined to Sulawesi and vulnerable to loss of forest habitat. Also vulnerable in Indonesia is the Javan warty pig *Sus verrucosus*. Confined to Java and the small adjacent island of Bawean, very little of its forest habitat remains (see chapter 19).
- Several species of deer are threatened, including the Calamian deer (*Cervus calamianensis*) from the Calamian Islands of the Philippines, the rare Kuhl's deer (*C. kuhli*) from Bawean, the Visayan spotted deer (*C. alfredi*) from the Philippines, the Manipur and Thailand subspecies of the brow-antlered deer (*C. eldi eldi* and *C.e. siamensis*) and a number of Chinese deer (IUCN, 1978).
- Antelope and gazelle species are less numerous in Asia than in Africa. Worthy of particular note is the serow (*Capricornis sumatraensis*), endangered in Sumatra and with a vulnerable close relative in Taiwan (*C. crispus swinhoei*) (IUCN, 1988).
- Asia also has many wild relatives of cattle, most of which are vulnerable or endangered in their natural habitats. Gaur or seladang (*Bos gaurus*), banteng (*B. javanicus*), kouprey (*B. sauveli*) (see study on Zoos on page 19, and chapter 28), wild water buffalo (*Bubalus bubalis*), lowland and mountain anoas (*B. depressicornis* and *B. quarlesi* see chapter 19) and tamaraw (*B. mindorensis* see chapter 23), are all under threat despite having adapted to shifting cultivation in some cases (see chapter 4). Many are the subject of strategic plans for their continued survival, discussed in detail in the above chapters.

4 Of less immediate value to mankind and his domesticated species, but of very considerable concern in terms of Asia's natural heritage, are the carnivores, rhinoceroses, elephants and primates.

- The carnivores include a number of rather poorly known or threatened civets (Viverridae), e.g. the Javan small-toothed palm civet (*Arctogalidia trivirgata trilineata*), Owston's palm civet (*Chrotogale owstoni*) from Indo-China, the otter civet (*Cynogale bennettii*) from Southeast Asia, the Sulawesi palm civet (*Macrogalidia musschenbroekii*) and two civets from south and west India, Jerdon's palm civet (*Paradoxurus jerdoni*) and the Malabar large spotted civet (*Viverra megaspila civettina*) (Schreiber *et al.*, 1989).
- The Asia–Pacific region is rich in cats, Felidae. Most famous is the tiger, the subject of a successful conservation campaign in India (see chapter 9), but endangered in the Sundarbans, Sumatra and Malaya, and extinct in Java and Bali (IUCN/UNEP, 1986). The clouded leopard is believed to be in decline throughout its range, and the status of a number of less well-known species, such as the Bornean bay cat (*Felis badia*), the marbled cat (*F. marmorata*), the flat-headed cat (*F. planiceps*), the rusty-spotted cat (*F. rubiginosa*) and the Asiatic golden cat (*F. temmincki*), is cause for concern.
- All three species of Asian rhinoceros are on the brink of extinction (see case study on zoos). The Indian rhino (*Rhinoceros unicornis*) and the Javan rhino (*R. sondaicus*) are quite closely related to each other, but are distinct from the Sumatran (or hairy) rhino (*Dicerorhinus sumatrensis*). The Indian rhino inhabits open country and swamps, but the Javan and Sumatran species are denizens of rain forest. The status of these species is covered in detail in an action plan for conservation prepared by the Asian Rhino Specialist Group of the IUCN Species Survival Commission (Khan, 1989).
- The Asian elephant (*Elephas maximus*), which occurs throughout the region, from Pakistan and Sri Lanka to China, Indo-China, Sumatra and Malaya, has been the subject of extensive conservation effort, much of it directed towards avoidance of conflict with the agriculturalists who are breaking traditional migratory routes and leaving forest as isolated patches. WWF, through its Indonesian office, has carried out survey and strategic planning work in Sumatra for more than five years, and has studied elephants in Vietnam, Sri Lanka, Thailand, Bhutan, Malaysia, Burma, China, Cambodia and

Laos. While the Asian elephant is not threatened by ivory-hunters to the extent of the African species, its populations are declining rapidly through loss of habitat and culling of crop raiders. The IUCN/SSC Asian Elephant Specialist Group is preparing an action plan for continent-wide conservation activities and the present situation has been recently summarised by IUCN/UNEP (1986).

• Asian primates are the subject of a comprehensive action plan developed by the Primate Specialist Group of the IUCN Species Survival Commission (Eudey, 1987). Many of the actions needed concern basic survey work followed by consolidation of existing or proposed protected areas in the region. The pygmy loris (*Nycticebus pygmaeus*), tarsiers (*Tarsius* spp.) and a variety of macaques and leaf monkeys are subjects of conservation concern, many of them discussed in the country chapters. Of particular importance are the gibbons and the orang utan of Borneo and Sumatra.

5 The birds of the Asia–Pacific region have been extensively studied over the past century (see Table 2.1). In both the New Guinea part of the Sahul shelf and the countries of the Sunda shelf, most birds are forest adapted (Wells, 1985; Beehler, 1985; Diamond and Lovejoy, 1985). In the Sunda shelf countries over 78 per cent of the almost 500 resident species are dependent on closed canopy forest (Wells, 1985). Similarly, in New Guinea, which has the richest island avifauna in the world, 78 per cent of the 570 or so terrestrial species are adapted to closed forests (Beehler, 1985).

The countries of Sundaland have numerous threatened birds, most of them residents of the lowland rain and monsoon forests. Collar and Andrew (1988) gave details for every country; particularly notable are India (62 threatened species), Vietnam (34), Thailand (39), Malaysia (34), Indonesia (126) and Papua New Guinea (24). At present there is no indisputable evidence of recent extinctions. However, some species are now extremely rare, notably the white-eyed river martin (*Pseudochelidon sirintarae*) from Thailand (Round, 1988), Vo Quy's pheasant (*Lophura hatinhensis*), known from only two specimens in Vietnam, and Gurney's pitta (*Pitta gurneyi*), recently rediscovered in a 1.6 sq. km Thai forest after half a century (Round and Uthai Treesucon, 1986). With its forest habitat reduced to almost nothing, there seems little hope for the Caerulean paradise flycatcher (*Eutrichomyias rowleyi*) from Sangihe Island, not seen since 1978. Mystery surrounds the double-banded argus pheasant (*Argusianus bipunctatus*), described from feathers in the London Natural History Museum, believed collected in the 19th century from Java, where no such pheasant now exists (Wells, 1985).

Logging and Wildlife

In general, the effects of forest disturbance depend on a combination of the nature and extent of the change to the environment and the requirements and adaptability of each species. While most species are adapted to some level of disturbance, a few are dependent on mature forest to maintain breeding populations. Many other species on the other hand readily enter certain types of secondary forest and rarely venture deep into primary forest. Still other species enter secondary growth to feed on the abundance of young leaves and shoots, but always return to nearby primary forest to sleep or travel (Wilson and Wilson, 1975).

Modern advances in the theory of species extinction have used the theory of island biogeography of MacArthur and Wilson (1967). These models suggest that when only 10 per cent of a habitat is preserved as a single undivided area, about half of the species restricted to that habitat will eventually disappear from the reserve before a state of equilibrium is re-established. It is now realised that habitat fragmentation affects different types of organisms in different ways, but the principle that many species will be lost from fragmented habitats remains broadly correct. Smaller areas of habitat

Table 2.1 The wildlife of tropical Asia and the Pacific: sources of information

Country	Mammals	Birds
Asia–Pacific Region	Ellerman and Morrison-Scott, 1951; Chasen, 1940; Laurie and Hill, 1954; Wallace, 1869	Chasen, 1935; Delacour and Jabouille, 1940; King, et al., 1975; Mayr, 1945
Bangladesh	Pocock, 1939; 1941	Ali and Ripley, 1968–73
Brunei	Medway, 1965	Smythies, 1968
Burma	Peacock, 1933; U Tun Yin, 1967	Smythies, 1953
Cambodia		Delacour and Jabouille, 1940
China	Allen, 1938; 1940	
India	Pocock, 1939, 1941	Ali and Ripley, 1968–73
Indonesia	Medway, 1965	Smythies, 1968
Laos		Delacour and Jabouille, 1940
Malaysia	Medway, 1969	Delacour, 1947; Robinson and Chasen, 1927–39
Papua New Guinea	Laurie and Hill, 1954	Rand and Gilliard, 1968
Philippines	Alcasid, n.d.	Delacour and Mayr, 1946
Sri Lanka	Phillips, 1924	Henry, 1955
Thailand	Lekagul and McNeely, 1975	Lekagul, 1968
Vietnam	Van Peenan et al., 1969	Delacour and Jabouille, 1940

inevitably contain smaller populations of wildlife; and smaller populations are subject to a whole series of factors that can lead to their disappearance, including disease, random population fluctuations, and increased exposure to hunting.

One implication of the great diversity of species which characterises tropical rain forests is that each species tends to have relatively few individuals in any given part of a forest (Eisenberg, 1980; Elton, 1975). Therefore, in order to maintain sufficient individuals to comprise what biologists consider a viable breeding population, substantial areas may be required. Medway and Wells (1971) pointed out that areas in excess of 2000 sq. km need to be preserved to maintain populations of large frugivorous animals such as gibbons and hornbills, which occur at densities of less than five individuals per square kilometre.

While virtually all governments in the region have established protected areas, many of them to conserve their wildlife (see chapter 9), many of these may not be sufficiently large to maintain viable populations of all the species they were designed to conserve. While the protected areas need to be expanded and the effectiveness of their protection improved, it is also essential that mechanisms be discovered to enable timber exploitation and wildlife conservation to co-exist. As Johns (1985) put it, 'the long-term survival of many rain forest animals may be correlated realistically with their ability to persist in logging areas and in regenerating logged forest'.

There is no question that logging operations themselves disturb animals, as most mobile species are conspicuously absent from any active logging area. Species such as the Malayan sun bear, orang utan, proboscis monkey (*Nasalis larvatus*), and all four of the endemic Mentawaian primates are seriously affected by logging. All mammals which have been studied show a marked decrease in density in recently logged forest, as do the larger hornbill species and great argus pheasant (*Argusianus argus*) (Wilson and Johns, 1982). The arboreal primates seem to be better able to withstand pressures imposed by logging than the terrestrial mammals; this disparity may reflect the high dietary diversity of the arboreal primates.

When an area is cleared for agriculture, most invertebrates and amphibians and many reptiles are lost because they lack the mobility to escape. Moreover, most of the birds and primates which are displaced fail to re-establish themselves in adjacent forest because the population density there is usually already at full capacity.

Selective logging destroys far more trees than just the ones that are directly exploited. A typical example (Burgess, 1971) is that timber extraction even at the low level of 10 per cent of the trees destroys 65 per cent of the timber stand.

On the other hand, some moderate disturbance, such as that caused by natural tree falls or very carefully conducted selective logging at low density, may increase the available food through stimulating new growth and fruiting where gaps are formed in the canopy. Many native species are in fact adapted to this type of change, which is part of the natural dynamics of the forest (Whitmore, 1984).

Johns (1985) has pointed out that primary forest amphibians are seriously affected by logging. Species that are intolerant of the changed conditions rapidly disappear. Certain under-storey bird species may also be intolerant of altered micro-climatic conditions,

Within ten years of logging many species, such as this rhinoceros hornbill (Buceros rhinoceros) are able to return to the forest. WWF/M. Kavanagh

perhaps because of their sensitivity to temperature fluctuations or their unwillingness to cross sunlit patches. When the canopy is opened by logging operations, widespread drying and hardening of the soil may follow, leading to loss of soil organic matter and decline of many of the invertebrates such as termites, which feed upon it (Collins, 1980). This in turn severely affects terrestrial birds such as partridges and pittas, which feed to a large extent on litter arthropods. Hunting following logging operations can be a major problem, and the large reduction in the population of pigs certainly reflects high levels of hunting in logged forest (Wilson and Johns, 1982).

The species-rich avifaunas of tropical forests contain many birds with specialised diets, and habitat disturbance can lead to significant losses (see Table 2.2). Johns (1985) found that the most specialised feeders (notably insectivores) were most affected by logging, whereas birds with a varied diet were less affected.

Hornbills are of particular interest: their centre of diversity is Asian tropical forests, where some 24 species occur. Being large fruit-eaters, they forage over long distances as scattered figs and other favourite trees come into fruit. While primary forest is the most suitable habitat for hornbills, Wilson and Johns (1982) and Johns (1987) have found that regenerating logged-over forest can support the full complement of species (see chapter 22). It is encouraging to note that 10–13 years after logging, almost all species had recolonised the study area used by Johns.

Primates are invaluable indicators of forest condition, except where they are heavily hunted (Dittus, 1982; Wilson and Wilson, 1975; Johns, 1986; Marsh *et al.*, 1987). Some 62 species in five families occur in the Asia–Pacific region, 20 of them considered to be under threat and a further 17 in need of some conservation action (Eudey, 1987). Logging affects the community structure of primates. Those which survive quite well in logged forest tend to be the species that are relatively widespread and well able to adapt to change, including several of the macaques and a few of the leaf monkeys. In addition, the small nocturnal primates, the lorises and tarsiers, are largely insectivorous and can survive well in secondary forest and scrub. However, some threatened species are believed to be very badly affected even at low cutting densities; these include the orang utan, the proboscis monkey, and all four primates on the Mentawai Islands, namely Kloss's gibbon *Hylobates klossi*, pig-tailed langur *Simias concolor*, Mentawai leaf monkey *Presbytis potenziani* and Mentawai macaque *Macaca pagensis* (Marsh *et al.*, 1987). The prosperity of most of the remaining species, including the gibbons and most of the leaf monkeys, will depend on the intensity of logging and the security and management of the forest after logging.

Table 2.2 Trophic structure of primary and logged forest avifaunas in two areas of Southeast Asia

Trophic group	Bird species of Peninsular Malaysia		Bird species of Sabah	
	Primary	Logged	Primary	Logged
Frugivores	34	21	32	26
Insectivores/frugivores	43	28	30	29
Insectivores/ nectarivores	10	8	10	8
Insectivores	91	55	79	65
Carnivores	17	10	10	9
Totals	195	122	161	137

(*Source:* Johns, 1985)

ZOOS AND CONSERVATION

As the extent of the world's natural habitat declines, the importance of the modern zoo to conservation is increasing. International studbooks, breeding programmes and sophisticated techniques for genetic identification and management enable zoos to preserve species and sub-species such as the Bali starling *Leucopsar rothschildi* and the Formosan sika deer *Cervus nippon taiouanus*, which would otherwise disappear. A more recent but closely-related development is the use of zoo-bred animals to re-inforce or reintroduce populations into the wild, and thereby rehabilitate degraded ecosystems. Increasingly, such restoration programmes will require animals that are only available in zoos and other captive breeding institutions.

Zoos also contribute substantially to public education. As more and more people become detached from their natural heritage through urban existence, visiting the zoo is not only the closest they will ever come to a wild animal, it is also an effective way of conveying the variety and beauty of nature. This can be accomplished through the exhibition of a broad range of taxonomic groups or through specialist collections which concentrate on particular species or groups of species. Butterfly houses and insectaria, for example, are growing in number around the world, especially in Europe and North America, and now also in Australia, Japan and the Far East, where displays of butterflies are extremely popular.

Of growing importance is the zoo's role in the development of specialised techniques for the management of restricted populations. The constriction of the world's wild places into islands, parks and reserves isolated by human development and marginal lands means that the long-term viability of the animal populations may depend upon the same intensive management techniques already in use in zoos. The value of these techniques and expertise is only just beginning to be appreciated but they represent a major resource which will prove essential to the survival of many species.

Of course not all zoos contribute equally to conservation. The varying availability of technical and financial resources and varying popular attitudes to wildlife have resulted in a wide spectrum of institutions with vast differences in their standards of animal welfare, education and science. By and large, it has been the North American and European zoos which have developed keeping of exotic animals into the sophisticated science of the modern zoo. However, this pattern is changing with zoos in other regions such as those in Kuala Lumpur, Jakarta and Singapore, now becoming much more involved in local conservation and education.

A major international initiative has been in train over the last five years to save the highly endangered Sumatran rhinoceros. Isolated individuals, found in 'doomed' areas where the forest is being cleared, are being caught to establish breeding programmes both locally in Malaysia and Indonesia, and overseas in the United States and Great Britain. It is hoped that these animals will breed and thereby contribute to the long-term survival of their species. A similar joint initiative is being undertaken for the kouprey, which is also believed to be in imminent danger of extinction (see chapter 28). The Kouprey Trust, involving six zoos, aims to conduct field surveys to locate the remaining populations and then to establish a captive breeding centre in Vietnam to build up numbers as quickly as possible. The goal is quite simply to maintain a secure reserve stock of these animals as a safeguard against extinction.

Management techniques learnt in zoos have many applications. At the Sepilok Research Centre in Sabah, orang utans confiscated from pet dealers are rehabilitated for life in the wild. WWF/S. Sreedhara

Ultimately, the zoo's aim is to return animals to their natural environments and many zoos actively participate in such projects. The Taipei Zoo, for example, is providing Formosan sika deer for reintroduction into the Kengting National Park (see chapter 17) and the few remaining wild Bali starlings, are being augmented with captive-bred birds from American and European zoos, in cooperation with Jakarta Zoo. Opportunities for such reintroductions will undoubtedly increase if suitable habitat remains and if the causes of the species' original decline are controlled.

Unfortunately, it is often not possible to achieve these aims. Certain species of *Partula* snails, for instance, are extinct in the wild, and could, in theory, be reintroduced using captive-bred specimens. So far, this has not been feasible because introduced carnivorous snails, which originally eliminated the *Partula* snails, still abound on the Pacific island of Moorea. This sort of problem, where there are considerable stocks, even surplus, of a particular species in captivity, but no suitable wild habitat in which to release them, poses a difficult question for zoos – whether to let a species disappear completely or to maintain it only in captivity. So far, the decision has usually been taken in favour of preservation, but as the number of threatened species increases and the competition for the limited money and space available for captive breeding intensifies, choices will have to be made.

Nothing can replace an animal's natural environment and the ecosystem of which it is a part. Zoos can only preserve individual elements of an ecosystem and give visitors a glimpse of the variety of life; they are no substitute for the real thing.

Source: Alexandra Dixon

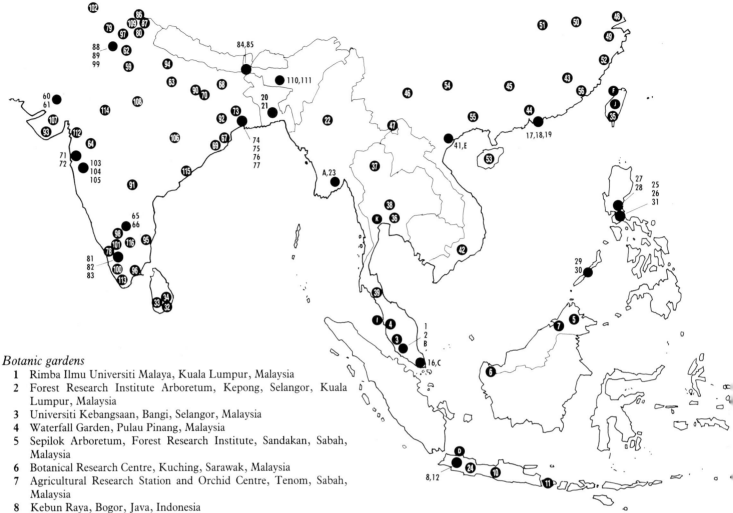

Botanic gardens
1 Rimba Ilmu Universiti Malaya, Kuala Lumpur, Malaysia
2 Forest Research Institute Arboretum, Kepong, Selangor, Kuala Lumpur, Malaysia
3 Universiti Kebangsaan, Bangi, Selangor, Malaysia
4 Waterfall Garden, Pulau Pinang, Malaysia
5 Sepilok Arboretum, Forest Research Institute, Sandakan, Sabah, Malaysia
6 Botanical Research Centre, Kuching, Sarawak, Malaysia
7 Agricultural Research Station and Orchid Centre, Tenom, Sabah, Malaysia
8 Kebun Raya, Bogor, Java, Indonesia
9 Lipizauga Botanical Sanctuary, Eastern Highlands Provincial Govt. Goroka, Papua New Guinea
10 Purwodadi Botanic Garden, Lawang, East Java, Indonesia
11 Cebang Balai Kebun Raya Eka Karya Bali, Denpasar, Bali, Indonesia
12 Arboretum and Experimental Gardens of Silviculture, Forest Research Institute, Bogor, Indonesia
13 National Botanic Garden, Office of Forests, Botany Branch, Lae, Papua New Guinea
14 Highland Orchid Collection, Laiagam, Enga Province, Papua New Guinea
15 Botanic Garden of the University, Port Moresby, Papua New Guinea
16 Singapore Botanic Garden, Cluny Road, Singapore
17 Agriculture and Fisheries Department, Canton Road Government Offices, 393 Canton Road, 12th floor, Kowloon, Hong Kong
18 Kadoorie Experimental & Extension Farm and Botanic Garden, Lam Kam Road, Tai Po, New Territories, Hong Kong
19 Hong Kong Zoological and Botanical Garden, Albany Road, Hong Kong
20 Baldah Garden, Wari, Dhaka, Bangladesh
21 Mirpur National Botanic Garden, Dhaka, Bangladesh
22 Government Botanic Garden, Maymo, Burma
23 The Agri-Horticultural Society of Burma, Rangoon, Burma
24 Cibodas Botanic Garden, Clanjur, West Java, Indonesia
25 The Hortorium, Museum of Natural History, Los Banos College, Laguna, Philippines
26 Makiling Botanic Gardens, University of the Philippines, Laguna, Philippines
27 Zoological and Botanical Gardens, Harrison Park, Malate, Manila, Philippines
28 Pharmaceutical Garden, University of Santo Tomas, Manila, Philippines
29 Philippine National Botanic Garden, University of the Philippines, Diliman, Quezon City, Philippines
30 Arboretum of the University of the Philippines, Diliman, Quezon City, Philippines
31 Philippine National Botanic Garden, Siniload, Laguna, Philippines
32 Hakgala Botanic Gardens, Hakgala, Sri Lanka
33 Gampaha Botanic Garden, Heneratgoda, Gampaha, Sri Lanka
34 Royal Botanic Garden, Peradeniya, Sri Lanka
35 Heng-chun Tropical Botanical Garden, Taiwan
36 Eastern (Khao Hin Son) Botanic Garden, Phanomsarakham, Chachoengsao, Thailand
37 Northern Mae Sa Botanic Garden, Mae Rim, Chiang Mai, Thailand
38 Central Phukae Botanic Garden, Mueng, Sara Buri, Thailand
39 Peninsular Khao Chong Botanic Garden, Trang, Thailand
40 Rove Botanic Garden, Forest Department, Honiara, Solomon Islands
41 Zoological-Botanical Garden, Hanoi, Vietnam
42 Zoological-Botanical Park, Ho Chi Minh City, Vietnam
43 Lushan Botanical Garden, Hanpokou, Lushan, Jiangxi, China
44 South China Botanical Garden, Longyandong, Guangzhou, Guangdong, China
45 Guilin Botanical Garden, Yanshan, Guilin, Guangxi, China
46 Kunming Botanical Garden, Helongtan, Kunming, Yunnan, China

Figure 2.2 Botanic and zoological gardens of the Asia–Pacific region
Out of a total of about 1500 botanic gardens in the world the Asia–Pacific region contains over 100 major ones with the majority in India and southern China. Several important and active botanic gardens exist also in Malaysia, Singapore and Indonesia. Few botanic gardens are presently active in Thailand, Laos, Cambodia and Vietnam, but there are encouraging new developments in Papua New Guinea and northern Australia.

47 Xishuangbanna Tropical Botanical Garden, Xishuangbanna, Yunnan, China
48 Shanghai Botanic Garden, Lunghua, Shanghai, China
49 Hangzhou Botanical Garden, Yuquan, Hangzhou, Zhejiang, China
50 Nanjing Botanical Garden, Mem. Sun Yat-sen Nanjing, Jiangsu, China
51 Wuhan Botanical Garden, Moshan, Wuchang, Hupeh, China
52 Zhejiang Institute of Subtropical Crops, Wenzhou, Zhejiang, China
53 Hainan Botanical Garden of Tropical Economic Plants, Academy of Tropical Crops of South China, Hainan, China
54 Guizhou Botanical Garden, Guiyang, Guizhou, China
55 Guangxi Botanical Garden of Medicinal Plants, Maoqiao, Nanning, Guangxi, China
56 Xiamen Botanical Garden of Ornamental Plants, Wanshishan, Xiamen, Fujian, China
57 Flecker Botanic Garden, Cairns, Queensland, Australia
58 Townsville Botanic Garden, Townsville, Queensland, Australia
59 Botanical Garden, Agra College, Agra, Uttar Pradesh, India
60 Sarabhai Foundation Botanic Gardens, Shahibag, Ahmedabad, Gujarat, India
61 Gujarat University Botanic Garden, Gujarat University, Ahmedabad, Gujarat, India
62 Aligarh Muslim University Botanic Garden, Aligarh, Uttar Pradesh, India
63 Experimental Garden, Botanical Survey of India (Central Circle), Allahabad, Uttar Pradesh, India
64 Marathwada University Botanic Garden, Marathwada University, Aurangabad, Maharashtra, India
65 Lalbagh Garden, Department of Horticulture, Bangalore, Karnataka, India

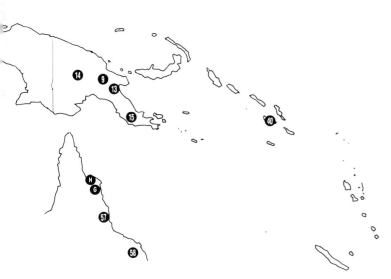

66 The Botanical Garden, Gandhi Krishi Vigyana Kendra, College of Basic Sciences and Humanities, University of Agricultural Sciences, Bangalore, Karnataka, India
67 State Botanic Garden, Barang, Cuttack, Orissa, India
68 Botanic Garden, Bihar Agricultural College, Sabour, Bhagalpur, Bihar, India
69 Utkal University Botanic Garden, Department of Botany, Utkal University, Vani Bihar, Bhubaneswar, Orissa, India
70 Magadh University Botanic Garden, Magadh University, Bodh Gaya, Bihar, India
71 Veermata Jijabai, Bhosle Udyan and Pranisangrahalaya, Byculla, Bombay, Maharashtra, India
72 Botanic Garden, Institute of Sciences, Bombay, Maharashtra, India
73 Burdwan University Botanic Garden, Burdwan, West Bengal, India
74 Eden Gardens, Calcutta, West Bengal, India
75 The Agri-Horticultural Society of India, Calcutta, West Bengal, India
76 Experimental cum Botanic Garden, Department of Botany, University of Calcutta, West Bengal, India
77 Indian Botanic Garden, Botanical Survey of India, Calcutta, India
78 Calicut University Botanical Garden, Calicut, Kerala, India
79 Panjab University Botanical Garden, Chandigarh, Union Territory of Chandigarh, India

80 Government Gardens, Chaubattia, Almora, Uttar Pradesh, India
81 Forest Research Centre, Coimbatore, Tamil Nadu, India
82 Botanical Survey of India (Southern Circle), Tamil Nadu Agricultural University, Lawley Road, Coimbatore, India
83 Sim's Park, Coonoor, Government Botanic Garden, the Nilgiris, Tamil Nadu, India
84 Lloyd Botanic Garden, Darjeeling, West Bengal, India
85 Botanic Garden of Darjeeling Government College, Darjeeling, West Bengal, India
86 Experimental Garden, Botanical Survey of India (Northern Circle), Garhwal, Uttar Pradesh, India
87 Botanic Garden, Forest Research Institute and College, Dehra Dun, Uttar Pradesh, India
88 Botanic Garden, National Bureau of Plant Genetic Resources, Issapur Village, Najafgarh Block, Delhi, India
89 Botanic Garden, Department of Botany, Delhi University, Delhi, India
90 Experimental Garden, Botanical Survey of India (Northern Circle), Pauri, Garhwa, Uttar Pradesh, India
91 Botanic Garden, Osmania University, Hyderabad, Andhra Pradesh, India
92 Jubilee Park, Jamshedpur, Singhbhum, Bihar, India
93 Botanic Garden, Gujarat Agricultural University, Junagadh, Gujarat, India
94 National Botanic Research Institute, Rana Pratap Marg, Lucknow, Uttar Pradesh, India
95 Agri-Horticultural Society, Madras, Tamil Nadu, India
96 Madurai Kamraj University Botanic Garden, Madurai, Tamil Nadu, India
97 Meerut University Botanic Garden, Meerut, Uttar Pradesh, India
98 Brindavan Gardens, Mysore, Mandya, Karnataka, India
99 Indian Agricultural Research Institute, New Delhi, India
100 Gurukula Botanical Sanctuary, East West University, North Wynad, Kerala, India
101 Government Botanic Garden, Ootacamund, the Nilgiris, Tamil Nadu, India
102 Panjabi University Botanic Garden, Patiala, Punjab, India
103 Experimental Botanical Garden, Botanical Survey of India (Western Circle), Pune, Maharashtra, India
104 Empress Botanic Garden, Pune, India
105 University of Poona Botanic Garden, Pune, Maharashtra, India
106 Ravi Sankar University Botanic Garden, Raipur, Madhya Pradesh, India
107 Saurashtra University Experimental Garden, Rajkot, Gujarat, India
108 Botanic Garden of the University of Sagar, Sagar, India
109 Horticultural Experiment and Training Centre, Saharanpur, Uttar Pradesh, India
110 Barapani Experimental Garden, Botanical Survey of India (Eastern Circle), Shillong, Meghalaya, India
111 National Orchidarium and Botanic Garden, Botanical Survey of India (Eastern Circle), Shillong, Meghalaya, India
112 South Gujarat University Botanical Garden, Surat, Gujarat, India
113 Tropical Botanic Garden and Research Institute, Karimancode, Pacha Palode, Trivandrum, Kerala, India
114 Botanic Garden, Vikram University, Ujjain, Madhya Pradesh, India
115 Andhra University Experimental Garden, Waltair, Visakhapatnam, Andhra Pradesh, India
116 National Orchidarium and Experimental Garden, Botanical Survey of India (Southern Circle), Yercaud, Salem, Tamil Nadu, India

Zoological gardens
A Rangoon Zoo, Burma
B Kuala Lumpur Zoo, Malaysia
C Singapore Zoo
D Jakarta Zoo, Indonesia
E Hanoi Zoo, Vietnam
F Taipei Zoo, Taiwan
G Australia Butterfly Sanctuary, Kuranda, Queensland, Australia
H Daintree Butterfly Farm, Queensland, Australia
I Penang Butterfly Farm, Malaysia
J Formosa Insect Farm, Taiwan
K Bangkok Zoo, Thailand

THE ROLE OF BOTANIC GARDENS

Tropical botanic gardens were mostly created by governments as instruments of colonial expansion and commercial development, playing a major part in establishing the patterns of agriculture in several parts of the world, most notably in Southeast Asia. Many crop plants were introduced by or through these gardens – often in association with European botanic gardens such as Amsterdam and Kew. They include cocoa, cinchona, tea, coffee, oil palm (*Elaeis guineensis*) and breadfruit. The emphasis was on economic development and several gardens were created specifically to act as nurseries or propagation centres for commercial crops. Notable amongst these were the Royal Botanic Garden at Peradeniya, Sri Lanka, founded in 1821, which wielded considerable influence on the development of agriculture in Ceylon, and the botanic garden of Singapore, founded in 1859, into which was first introduced Para rubber (*Hevea brasiliensis*), on which the prosperity of Malaya and later other parts of Southeast Asia was based.

Recently the importance of conservation has been recognised and botanic gardens have begun to act as centres for research on, and conservation of, plant genetic diversity. They recognise that new techniques must be developed to increase the ability to store germplasm of endangered species. This is important as many tropical species are difficult or impossible to maintain by conventional long-term storage in low-temperature seed banks. Germplasm in botanic garden collections may be maintained in cultivation, in nature reserves, as living plants, as *in vitro* cultures or as seedling collections. Some species can be preserved as seed or spores.

Botanic gardens have a particular role to play in the conservation of plant genetic resources. Thirty crops feed most of mankind and about a hundred play a dominant part in world trade. There is concern that the genetic base of the major crops in cultivation is very narrow, and that the wild populations of their ancestral species or relatives are rapidly disappearing due to loss of habitat.

The majority of wild, but potentially commercial, species has been neglected. Botanic gardens throughout the world are now beginning to mobilise their efforts to develop the potential of these species in a co-ordinated fashion. In 1987 the Botanic Gardens Conservation Secretariat was established by IUCN to help co-ordinate activities in conservation by maintaining a database of endangered species that are in garden collections, organising regional meetings, programmes for staff training and assistance for garden conservation and education programmes. Botanic gardens from nine countries in the Asia–Pacific region are already represented amongst the membership.

The work of botanic gardens may be illustrated by some examples of projects currently in progress.

Conservation of rain forest Citrus *species in Malaysia* The University of Malaya Rimba Ilmu botanic garden has established a living collection of *Citrus* and its wild relatives as part of the IBPGR network of conservation centres for crop gene pools. One species conserved is the 20m tree ketenggah (*Merrillia caloxylon*), the sole representative of the genus *Merrillia* and a close relative of the genus *Citrus*. It grows only in primary rain forest in Thailand, Peninsular Malaysia and Sumatra and is probably on the verge of extinction. The majority of known individuals exist in botanic gardens, where extensive propagation is now taking place to ensure its survival. Much of the natural range of ketenggah has been converted for agricultural development and, since 1981, efforts to locate wild populations in Peninsular Malaysia have failed.

Conserving highland rain forest species in Papua New Guinea Papua New Guinea has numerous endemic species, especially in the highlands. Situated in the Mount Gahavisuka Provincial Park in the mountains near Goroka is the Lipizauga Botanical Sanctuary. Maintained as a semi-natural area, the Sanctuary has been founded for conservation, research and recreation. Only plants native to Papua New Guinea are grown in this natural setting and species from all over the highlands are being added, especially rare and endangered ones. The Sanctuary occupies 10 ha of savannah grassland on the lower ridges with lower montane rain forest above. So far about 2000 accessions of about 500 taxa have been introduced. Well-represented genera include *Begonia*, *Impatiens*, *Rhododendron* and many orchids.

Preserving the ferns of Malaysia A new specialist fern garden, 12.8 ha in size, has recently been established at the Universiti Kebangsaan at Bangi, Selangor, Malaysia. To date about 150 species have been introduced. While the emphasis has been on rare and threatened species, the garden will also serve as an outdoor laboratory for morphological, cytological and phytochemical investigations.

Conserving medicinal plants of Sri Lanka Traditional medicines, especially those derived from wild plants, play an important part in everyday health care in Sri Lanka. The Royal Botanic Garden, Peradeniya, has recently carried out a programme to conserve over 200 medicinal plant species which occur in Kandy District. Sixty-four species were recognised as in danger of extinction, due to over-harvesting. The botanic garden has recommended large-scale cultivation in order to protect them.

Source: Peter Wyse-Jackson

Botanical gardens are important for the protection of plant germplasm. Illustrated here at Bogor, Java, the Nibong Oucosperma tigillarium *with its edible 'cabbage', is maintained. Steve Davis*

FLORISTIC REGIONS OF ASIA AND THE PACIFIC

The Asia–Pacific region includes five main floristic zones:

India The flora of the Indian region is estimated to be about 15,000 species. The whole area has suffered severe degradation due to human activity. Mani (1974) estimates that less than one per cent of India can be regarded as primary forest.

Indo-China The Indo-Chinese floristic region runs from Burma across to southern China, south through Thailand, Laos and Vietnam to Cambodia. The flora of Indo-China is not fully documented. Vidal (1960) listed only 1447 species in 754 genera for Laos, but the flora of Vietnam is estimated at about 12,000 species, of which 7000 have been described. The total flora of the region is probably about 15,000 species. At least one-third of these species are endemic. Endemism at generic level is rather less.

Malesia The northern limits of the Malesian floristic region are clearly marked by 'demarcation knots' at the Kra Isthmus and between the Philippines and Taiwan, which form the limits of many Indochinese and Malesian genera, and at Torres Strait between New Guinea and Australia. The Malesian flora is conservatively estimated to contain 25,000 species of flowering plants (van Steenis, 1971), about 10 per cent of the world's total. Peninsular Malaysia alone contains nearly 8000 species from 1500 genera (Whitmore, 1973). About 40 per cent of the genera found in Malesia, and even more of the species, are endemic.

Australasia Tropical rain forests constitute less than one per cent of Australia's tropical vegetation (Webb and Tracey, 1981). Important features include the similarity of their floristic composition with both Southeast Asia and Gondwanaland elements, and the stark contrast between the structure and floristics of the rain forest and the much more widespread forests and woodlands dominated by eucalypts. The rain forests of north-east Queensland rank with the south-west as one of the richest areas for plants in Australia, with an estimated 2500 species, including 800 species of tree. Australia's total flora is estimated at 18,000 vascular plants (IUCN, 1986).

Pacific The islands of the Western Pacific, such as the Solomons and Fiji, are relatively species-poor and low in endemism when compared with Malesia. The Solomons have c.2150 species of vascular plants, but only three endemic genera (IUCN, 1986).

References

Ahmad, A. M. (1981) Forest as a source of food: Malaysia. *Tigerpaper* 8: 9–16.

Alcasid, G. L. (n.d.) *Checklist of Philippine Mammals*. National Museum of the Philippines, Manila, 51 pp.

Ali, S. and Ripley, S. D. (1968–73) *Handbook of the Birds of India and Pakistan*. 10 vols. Oxford University Press, Bombay, India.

Allen, G. M. (1938 & 1940) *The Mammals of China and Mongolia, Parts 1 & 2*. American Museum of National History, New York.

Arora, R. K. (1985) *Genetic Resources of Less Known Cultivated Food Plants*. National Bureau for Plant Genetic Resources, New Delhi.

Beehler, B. (1985) Conservation of New Guinea rainforest birds. In: Diamond, A. W. and Lovejoy, T. E. (eds) (*loc. cit.*).

Beer, J. H. de and McDermott, M. J. (1989) *The Economic Value of Non-timber Forest Products in Southeast Asia*. IUCN Netherlands, Amsterdam. 175 pp.

Burgess, P. F. (1971) The effect of logging on hill dipterocarp forests. *Malay Nature Journal* 24: 231–7.

Burkill, I. H. (1935) (reprinted 1966) *A Dictionary of the Economic Products of the Malay Peninsula*. Crown Agents, London, UK.

Caldecott, J. (1988) Climbing towards extinction. *New Scientist* **9 June**: 62–6.

Chasen, F. N. (1935) A handlist of Malaysian birds: A systematic list of the birds of the Malay Peninsula, Sumatra, Borneo and Java, including the adjacent small islands. *Bulletin of the Raffles Museum, Singapore, Straits Settlements* No. 11.

Chasen, F. N. (1940) A handlist of Malaysian mammals. *Bulletin of the Raffles Museum* 15: 1–209.

Collar, N. J. and Andrew, P. (1988) *Birds to Watch. The ICBP World Checklist of Threatened Birds*. ICBP Technical Publication No. 8. ICBP, Cambridge, UK. 303 pp.

Collins, N. M. (1980) The effect of logging on termite (Isoptera) diversity and decomposition processes in lowland dipterocarp forests. In: *Tropical Ecology and Development*, Furtado, J. I. (ed.). International Society of Tropical Ecology, Kuala Lumpur.

Collins, N. M. and Morris, M. G. (1985) *Threatened Swallowtail Butterflies of the World. The IUCN Red Data Book*. IUCN, Cambridge, UK, and Gland, Switzerland. 401 pp.

Delacour, J. and Jabouille, P. (1940) Liste des Oiseaux de l'Indochine Francaise, complétée et mise a jour. *L'Oiseau* 10: 89–220.

Delacour, J. and Mayr, E. (1946 & 1947) *Birds of the Philippines* and *Birds of Malaysia*. Macmillan, New York, USA.

Dhanarajan, G., Rao, A. N. and Sastry, C. B. (n.d.) *The IDRC Bamboo and Rattan Research Network in Asia*. IDRC, Canada. 19 pp.

Diamond, A. W. and Lovejoy, T. E. (1985) *Conservation of Tropical Forest Birds*. ICBP Technical Publications No. 4. ICBP, Cambridge, UK. 318 pp.

Dittus, W. P. J. (1982) Population regulation: The effects of severe environmental changes on the demography and behaviour of wild toque macaques. *International Journal of Primatology* 3: 276.

Ellerman, J. R. and Morrison-Scott, T. C. S. (1951) *Checklist of Palearctic and Indian Mammals*. British Museum (Natural History), London, UK. 810 pp.

Eisenberg, J. F. (1980) The density and biomass of tropical mammals. In: *Conservation Biology*. Soulé, M. E. and Wilcox, B. A. (eds), Sinauer, Sunderland, Massachusetts, USA.

Elton, C. S. (1975) Conservation and the low population density of invertebrates inside Neotropical rain forest. *Biological Conservation* 7: 3–15.

Eudey, A. A. (1987) *IUCN/SSC Primate Specialist Group Action Plan for Primate Conservation: 1987–91*. IUCN Cambridge UK, and Switzerland. 65 pp.

Giesen, W. (1987) *Danau Sentarum Wildlife Reserves: Inventory, Ecology and Management Guidelines*. WWF, Bogor, Indonesia.

Hawkes, J. G. (1989) Our vanishing genetic resources. In: *Plants and Society*. Swaminathan, M. S. and Kochhar, S. L. (eds), Macmillan, London, UK.

Henry, G. M. (1955) *A Guide to the Birds of Ceylon*. Oxford University Press. London, UK.

Hou, Ding (1978) Anacardiaceae. *Flora Malesiana* Ser I. 8. 395–548.

Inskipp, T., Broad, S. and Luxmoore, R. (1988) *Significant Trade in Wildlife: A Review of Selected Species in CITES Appendix II. Vol. 3: Birds.* IUCN, Cambridge, UK, and Gland, Switzerland.

IUCN (1978) *Threatened Deer.* IUCN, Switzerland. 434 pp.

IUCN (1986) *Plants in Danger. What Do We Know?* IUCN, Cambridge, UK, and Gland, Switzerland. 461 pp.

IUCN (1988) *IUCN Red List of Threatened Animals.* IUCN, Cambridge, UK, and Gland, Switzerland. 154 pp.

IUCN/UNEP (1986) *Review of the Protected Areas System in The Indo–Malayan Realm.* Consultant authors J. and K. MacKinnon. IUCN, Cambridge, UK and Gland, Switzerland. 284 pp + maps.

Jacobs, M. (1982) The study of minor forest products. *Flora Malesiana Bulletin* 35: 3768–82.

Jain, S. K. and Mehra, K. L. (1983) *Conservation of Tropical Plant Resources.* Botanical Survey of India, Howrah.

Johns, A. D. (1985) Selective logging and wildlife conservation in tropical rain-forest: Problems and recommendations. *Biological Conservation* 31: 355–75.

Johns, A. D. (1986) Effects of selective logging on the behavioural ecology of West Malaysian primates. *Ecology* 67: 684–94.

Johns, A. D. (1987) The use of primary and selectively logged rainforest by Malaysian hornbills (Bucerotidae) and implications for their conservation. *Biological Conservation* 40: 179–90.

Khan, Mohd., bin Morin Khan (1989) *Asian Rhinos: An Action Plan for their Conservation.* IUCN, Switzerland. 23 pp.

King, Woodcock, and Dickinson, E. C. (1975) *A Field Guide to the Birds of Southeast Asia.* Collins, London, UK. 480 pp.

Laurie, E. M. O. and Hill, J. E. (1954) *List of Land Mammals of New Guinea, Celebes, and Adjacent Islands 1758–1762.* British Museum (Nat. Hist.) London, UK. 175 pp.

Lekagul, Boonsong (1968) *Bird Guide of Thailand.* Association for the Conservation of Wildlife, Bangkok, Thailand. 852 pp.

Lekagul, Boonsong, and McNeely, J. A. (1975) *Mammals of Thailand.* Association for the Conservation of Wildlife, Bangkok.

Lessard, G. and Chouinard, A. (eds) (1980) *Bamboo Research in Asia: Proc. Workshop Singapore 28–30 May, 1980.* IDRC: Canada.

Luxmoore, R., Groombridge, B. and Broad, S. (1988) *Significant Trade in Wildlife: A Review of Selected Species in CITES Appendix II: Vol. 2: Reptiles and Invertebrates.* IUCN, Switzerland. 306 pp.

MacArthur, R. H. and Wilson, E. O. (1967) *The Theory of Island Biogeography.* Princeton University Press, New Jersey, USA.

Mani, M. S. (ed.) (1974) *Ecology and Biogeography in India.* Junk, The Hague, The Netherlands.

Marsh, C. W., Johns, A. D. and Ayres, J. M. (1987) Effects of habitat disturbance on rain forest primates. In: *Primate Conservation in the Tropical Rain Forest*, Mittermeier, R. A. and Marsh, C. W. (eds) pp. 83–107. Alan R. Liss, New York, USA.

Mayr, E. (1945) *Birds of the Southwest Pacific: A Field Guide to the Birds of the Areas between Samoa, New Caledonia and Micronesia.* Macmillan, New York, USA.

Medway, Lord (1965) *Mammals of Borneo.* Royal Asiatic Society, Singapore. 193 pp.

Medway, Lord (1969) *The Wild Mammals of Malaya.* Oxford University Press, Kuala Lumpur, Malaysia. 127 pp.

Medway, Lord and Wells, D. (1971) Diversity and density of birds and mammals at Kuala Lumpur, Pahang. *Malayan Nature Journal* 24: 238–47.

Mukherjee, S. K. (1985) *Systematics and Ecogeographic Studies on Crop Genepools: I Mangifera L.* International Board for Plant Genetic Resources. FAO, Rome, Italy. 86 pp.

Peacock, E. H. (1933) *A Game-book for Burma and Adjoining Territories.* H. F. and G. Witherby, London, UK, 292 pp.

Pfeffer, P. (1968) *Asia: A Natural History.* Random House, New York, USA.

Phillips, C. J. (1924) A guide to the mammals of Ceylon. *Spolia Zeylanica* 13: 1–63.

Pocock, R. I. (1939 & 1941) *The Fauna of British India Mammalia I & II.* Taylor and Francis, London, UK.

Rambo, A. (1979) Primitive man's impact on genetic resources of the Malaysian tropical rain forest. *Malaysian Applied Biology* 8: 59–65.

Rand, A. L. and E. T. Gilliard (1968) *Handbook of New Guinea Birds.* Natural History Press, Garden City, New York, USA.

Ripley, S. D. (1964) *The Land and Wildlife of Tropical Asia.* Time-Life Books, New York, USA. 200 pp.

Robinson, H. C. and Chasen, F. N. (1927–39) *The Birds of the Malay Peninsula: A General Account of the Birds Inhabiting the Region from the Isthmus of Kra to Singapore with the Adjacent Islands.* Witherby, London, UK.

Round, P. D. (1988) *Resident Forest Birds in Thailand: Their Status and Conservation.* ICBP Monograph No. 2. ICBP, Cambridge.

Round, P. D. and Uthai Treesucon (1986) The rediscovery of Gurney's Pitta (*Pitta gurneyi*). *Forktail* 2: 53–66.

Schreiber, A., Wirth, R., Riffel, M. and Van Rompaey, H. (1989) *Weasels, Civets, Mongooses and their Relatives: An Action Plan for the Conservation of Mustelids and Viverrids.* IUCN, Cambridge, UK, and Gland, Switzerland. 99 pp.

Smiet, F. (1985) Notes on the field status and trade of Moluccan parrots. *Biological Conservation* 34: 181–94.

Smythies, B. E. (1953 & 1968) *The Birds of Burma* and *The Birds of Borneo.* (2nd eds) Oliver & Boyd, London, UK.

Steenis, C. G. G. J. van (1971) Plant conservation in Malaysia. *Bulletin Jardin Botanique Nationale Belgique* 41: 189–202.

U Tun Yin (1967) *Wild Animals of Burma.* Rangoon Gazette Ltd., Rangoon. 301 pp.

Van Peenen, P. F., Ryan, R. F., and Light R. H. (1969) *Preliminary Identification Manual for Mammals of South Vietnam.* Smithsonian Institution, Washington, DC, USA. 197 pp.

Vidal, J. (1960) *La Végétation du Laos.* (4 vols) Sonladowe, Toulouse.

Wallace, A. R. (1969) *The Malay Archipelago.* Macmillan, London, UK. 653 pp.

Webb, L. J. and Tracey J. (1981) Australian rainforests: patterns and change. In: *Ecological Biogeography of Australia.* A. Keast (ed.), pp. 605–94. Junk, The Hague, The Netherlands.

Wells, D. R. (1985) The forest avifauna of western Malesia and its conservation. In: Diamond, A. W. and Lovejoy, T. E. (*loc. cit.*).

Westphal, E. and Jansen, P. C. M. (eds) (1989) *Plant Resources of Southeast Asia.* Pudoc, Wageningen, The Netherlands.

Whitmore, T. C. (1973) *Palms of Malaya.* Oxford University Press, Kuala Lumpur, Malaysia.

Whitmore, T. C. (1984) *Tropical Rainforests of the Far East.* (2nd ed.) Clarendon Press, Oxford, UK. 352 pp.

Wilson, C. C. and Wilson, L. (1975) The influence of selective logging on primates and some other animals in East Kalimantan. *Folia Primatologica* 23: 243–74.

Wilson, W. L. and Johns, A. D. (1982) Diversity and abundance of selected animal species in undisturbed forest, selectively logged forest and plantations in East Kalimantan, Indonesia. *Biological Conservation* 24: 205–18.

Authorship

Jeff McNeely of IUCN, with contributions from Vernon Heywood of IUCN's Plants Conservation Programme; Peter Wyse Jackson of the Botanic Gardens Conservation Secretariat at the Royal Botanic Gardens, Kew, London; Mark Collins and Steve Davis of WCMC Cambridge; Alexandra Dixon of the Zoological Society of London.

3 People of the Tropical Forests

Introduction

The tropical rain forests of Asia and the Pacific islands are home to millions of tribal people, for whom the destruction or degradation of the forest means not just economic impoverishment but the end of their distinctive ways of life. Scattered thinly through the vast rain and monsoon forests of the region, their economies and cultures are as variable as the ecosystems they rely on, and their problems are as diverse as the policies and politics of the governments that now rule them.

Only a very small proportion of these peoples, most notably the Penan of Kalimantan and Sarawak, do not practise agriculture and rely entirely on hunted and gathered food for their subsistence. Other groups such as the Mrabri of Thailand, the Negrito peoples of the Philippines and Peninsular Malaysia, the Kubu of Sumatra, and a number of Melanesian groups in New Guinea still retain a way of life which is largely independent of agriculture. In coastal areas, especially in Indonesia and Melanesia, tribal groups relying on fishing and sago palm are also widespread. However, the majority complement the foods that they take directly from the forest with starch staples derived from trading, and crops grown in swidden[1] plots – mainly bananas, dry-land rice, sweet potatoes, tapioca, taro and yams. For some of these peoples, such as the Nu and Drung of the rugged, forested hills of China's Yunnan province, the transition to agriculture may have been quite recent, while for others swidden agriculture has long been central to their way of life (Xin Jiguang, 1987; China Reconstructs, 1984).

It is not just food that these peoples derive from their forests. Building materials, rattan for basketry, leaf wrappers, gums, resins, latex, drugs, poisons, medicines, perfumes, birds' nests, bone, horn and ivory have all become integral to their economies and have linked them over millennia to an extensive trade network that has encompassed the whole region and beyond. In India, for example, forest peoples of the Western Ghats, such as the Malaipantaram of Kerala, neither cultivate their own crops nor gain the major part of their diet from the forests but, instead, barter forest produce for food grown by other peoples in the lowlands (Morris, 1982). This dependence of tribal communities on products gathered in the forest is mirrored by the vast majority of the rural people of the Asian region who, whilst primarily dependent upon agriculture for their basic needs, still derive important medicines, foods and fibres from the natural forest (de Beer and McDermott, 1989).

[1] See chapter 4 for a description of swidden agriculture.

The intimate physical links between the forest peoples and their environment are echoed in religious belief, ritual, dance and song. Their subtle practical knowledge of the ways of the forest animals and plants is complemented by an equally complex familiarity with the ways of forest 'spirits'. The strong ties between the people and their lands are expressed as powerful links between ancestral spirits and the spirits of forest animals and plants, and link them to the needs of future generations; to 'our children who are still in the soil', as the Papuans refer to them. The forests are both the source of these peoples' livelihoods and the very foundation of their being (Colchester, 1986a).

Forest People under Threat

The inherently poor soils of much of upland tropical Asia, coupled with population growth, has meant that the swidden farmers are constantly in search of new lands (Geddes, 1976). In continental Asia these pressures, combined with pressure from their settled neighbours who have forced them off their lands, have resulted in long-term migrations of hill peoples (MacKinnon and Bhruksasri, 1986). As a result the Akha and the Hmong have been on the move for three or four millennia, from Tibet and eastern China respectively, and in the course of the last hundred years have pushed far south into what is now Thailand (Denslow and Padoch, 1988; Tapp, 1986).

At the same time there has been an expansion of areas of permanent (mainly wet-rice) cultivation in the lowlands. Though more labour-intensive than the extensive cultivations of the forest peoples, the sedentary and easily taxable incomes of wet-rice farmers have provided the basis for the growth of nation-states dating back over two millennia. And while some of these cultures, such as the Khmer in present-day Cambodia, have flourished and vanished again, others have endured and expanded, gradually pushing back the boundaries of wilderness as the lowlands have been progressively cleared for intensive and cash-crop farming (Dove, 1985).

The development of nation-states in the irrigable plains along the major rivers has in some cases resulted in the absorption of forest groups into the lowland peasant societies. In mainland Southeast Asia, however, the tribal groups of the hills have tended to remain independent of the lowlanders (Lewis and Lewis, 1984). Even these upland forests that have been their refuge are now approaching exhaustion and the upland peoples increasingly look out over a plain of settled cultivators, across a cultural divide of mutual mistrust and suspicion. For, whether newcomers or not, the tribal peoples'

Land laws provide little security to the Dani tribe of Irian Jaya. Development programmes generally override traditional tribal rights. WWF/Ron Petocz

relationship with their forests has not been readily intelligible to those from lowland civilisations. The forest peoples' apparent lack of ties to their lands, exemplified by their migratory hunting and gathering patterns, and their swidden agriculture, has led settled farming peoples to assume that they both underuse their lands and have no proprietary rights to them. The forest peoples dispute both conclusions. Their patterns of land-use have evolved over thousands of years to make an easy life from the forest with a minimum of effort; a way of life both rational and sustainable so long as their populations remained low and their territories extensive (Kunstadter *et al.*, 1978; and see chapter 4).

During the past century, the pressures on tropical forests have intensified massively. The progressive and slow expansion of sedentary farming has been overtaken as a pressure on rain forests by the accelerated expansion of industrialisation, rapid population increase, mass communications and transport, and the increasing linkage of the region with world markets. Logging, mining, plantations, agribusiness and colonisation schemes have brought the forest peoples into conflict with the outside world on an unprecedented scale.

Land Rights and Wrongs
For the forest peoples, the above-mentioned intrusion on their territories are seen as an invasion, and as something that derives from a lack of respect – both for their societies and their rights to their land. With the exception of the recently independent states of Melanesia – Papua New Guinea, the Solomon Islands and Vanuatu – national laws have seldom provided tribal peoples with secure tenure over the land that they have traditionally occupied (von Fuhrer-Haimendorf, 1982; Colchester, 1986a; b; 1989). In most of the Asia–Pacific countries populations in the forests now exceed the level where swidden agriculture can provide for their long-term livelihood (see chapter 4). Swidden agriculturalists have been joined by displaced and inexperienced agricultural smallholders whose shifting agriculture is damaging to forest and soil. The result has been conflict with government plans for land-use, which often do not recognise the need to find alternative means of meeting the legitimate requirements of the tribal minorities.

In many countries, forest areas have been placed under state control and the forest inhabitants are allowed to remain on sufferance – the long-term objective being to resettle these people in the lowlands. For example, in Thailand all land over 500 m elevation is defined as state land, and in October 1989 the Government announced its intention to relocate six million people residing in forest reserves, including 700,000 people from hill tribes (Bangkok Post, 1989). The Government's concern for the future of Thailand's forests is well founded since logging, encroachment by lowlanders and population growth amongst the hill tribes have led to unsustainable forest use and deforestation (see chapter 27). However, resettlement and development programmes in upland Thailand dating back to the 1950s have encountered many problems, and the difficulties involved in providing new lands and better standards of living for so many displaced people are awesome.

Similarly, a great many of the five million tribal people of the Philippines who occupy forest lands were effectively dispossessed by decree law PD 704 of 1975, by which all the lands steeper than 18 degrees in slope were defined as forest reserves (see chapter 23). The greater part of tribal lands in the Philippines are considered 'public domain'. As a result, tribal peoples have been unable to use legal means to prevent progressive takeover by loggers and business interests, and by dispossessed lowlanders (*kaingeros*). The latter themselves practise shifting cultivation and pose a major threat both to the original forest dwellers and to the little remaining catchment and watershed forest (Ganapin, 1987).

In Indonesia, land laws have provided little security to traditional owners and even where rights have been recognised this has not prevented the expropriation of land. Where Government development programmes are involved, such tribal rights as are recognised have been overridden by invoking the power of 'eminent domain'. For example, all development programmes in the Government's five-year plans, including the transmigration schemes, are considered to be in the 'national interest'. Very often, leases of tribal lands to foreign multinationals for mining and logging have been granted with minimal consideration of traditional land claims (Colchester, 1986a; b).

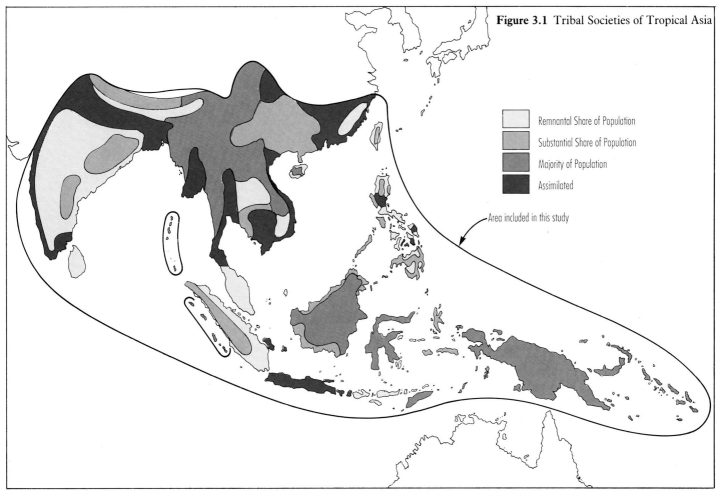

Figure 3.1 Tribal Societies of Tropical Asia

Remnantal Share of Population

Substantial Share of Population

Majority of Population

Assimilated

Area included in this study

(*Source:* Spencer, J. E. 1966)

Obstacles to Progress

Government policies towards the forest peoples in the Asian region (but not in the Pacific), while varying from country to country, are almost without exception directed towards the goal of integration – the gradual dismantling of cultural differences and the incorporation of the forest peoples into the society of the national majority. In some cases government institutions have been specifically created to carry out this role; as well as being charged with protecting the peoples' basic rights, a task they have accomplished rather less assiduously (Colchester, 1986c; Dove, 1989).

Resettlement has been central to many of these government-run programmes, whereby the people are moved out of their forest settlements and re-established as sedentary farmers or plantation workers (Carey, 1976). Although facilitating access to desired services – schools, clinics and markets – such moves, when too rapidly undertaken, have caused severe social and economic problems, sometimes with serious environmental consequences. They have also, often, been motivated by less charitable intentions, either to clear their lands for 'development' – dams, roads or mines – or to allow the takeover of the forests by other interested groups, settlers, agribusinesses or loggers. National security considerations also underlie many of these resettlement schemes, both for the classic purpose of counter-insurgency and also to promote government control over inaccessible regions (Budiardjo, 1986; Fay, 1987).

The rapid exploitation by outsiders of forests used by tribal people has not gone unprotested. Conflicts, often armed, have been widespread. For example, in northern Sarawak, their claims to traditional land rights denied, certain tribes have resorted to setting up barricades across the logging roads to defend the forests around their

In Mulu National Park, Sarawak, knowledgeable forest people like this Berawan guide make excellent caretakers of the forest. N. Mark Collins

villages and longhouses (Langub, 1988a; b; SAM, 1989). The Government has responded with arrests and by passing a new law making all interference with logging activity a criminal offence. Yet despite this, the blockades have been persistently re-erected, and timber extraction has been obstructed (Colchester, 1989).

The fundamental basis of this dispute is based on the way in which land rights have been conferred on people in Sarawak. Under the Land Code, tribal groups have claims to land if their rights were established prior to 1958. From this date it became illegal to clear virgin forests for shifting agriculture without permits, although they could still be used for collecting forest produce. Land rights were generally established through forest clearance and farming prior to 1955, and for almost 30 years there was little public concern. However, with the accelerated pace of logging in the 1980s, conflicts have arisen. Human rights organisations now claim that tribal peoples have 'Native Customary Rights' arising from non-commercial extraction of forest produce, i.e. beyond the areas of farmed and fallow land. This claim is supported by international law, including the International Convention on Civil and Political Rights, and Convention 107 of the International Labour Organisation. The Government of Sarawak, however, holds the view that many of the tribal people arrested at the blockades only moved into the hill forests recently, and they do not therefore have land rights, customary or otherwise (Hong, 1987).

Such cases of direct resistance to the exploitation of the resources of tribal peoples' lands come from all over the region, and have been exacerbated where internationally financed development schemes have accelerated the pace of change. A tragic example was the World Bank's support in the early 1980s for the Chico Dams project in the Philippines, which threatened to displace some 80,000 Bontoc and Kalinga people from their ancestral lands. When the local people protested against the project, the Marcos Government responded violently. Many tribals took to the hills and joined the New People's Army to defy the imposed development. The conflict endured long after the World Bank pulled out of the project (Fay, 1987).

Whether one's concern is for the survival of the region's tribal peoples or their forests, or both, the political reality of such armed conflict is an issue that cannot be ignored. Bitter conflicts between tribal peoples and government armed forces drag on, in India, Bangladesh, Burma, the Philippines, Irian Jaya and East Timor (Budiardjo and Liong, 1988; Anti-Slavery Society, 1984). The dense moist forests provide the perfect cover for such guerrilla warfare, tending to make governments perceive both forests and forest peoples as obstacles to national development.

Forest Peoples and Sustainable Development
Surprisingly perhaps, even well-intentioned conservation programmes have resulted in land conflicts, especially where the programme has been undertaken without due consideration of forest peoples' rights and needs. For example, evictions of forest peoples from protected areas have occurred in the forest reserves of Assam in north-east India, the Sundarbans National Park in West Bengal, the Thung Yai Wildlife Sanctuary in Thailand and the Siberut Biosphere Reserve in Indonesia (Malou-Nuzeman, 1984). Yet, imaginative conservation practices, linking close consultation with the affected forest peoples, and innovative legislation, have often obviated such conflicts. Legislation creating the Gunung Mulu National Park in Sarawak, for example, explicitly allows the resident Penan to continue hunting and gathering in traditional ways within the park's confines.

Conservation thinking has long advanced beyond a narrow concern with species or habitat protection towards a more comprehensive marriage of conservation and development goals, through the promotion of sustainable use of natural forest ecosystems. In support of this, important lessons can be learned from the way forest peoples use their environment sustainably to promote rational forest use.

The fundamental problem is that the forest-based economies themselves are under pressure. Economies that were once sustainable are now causing degradation of the land. As the population of hill peoples has increased and more and more of their land has been taken over for forestry and agriculture, the tribes have been obliged to adopt shorter and shorter fallow periods in the swidden cycle, while the loss of hunting and gathering lands has simultaneously exaggerated the importance of agriculture. The Aroman Manobo of Mindanao, for example, once a forest-dwelling group, used to move to new areas within their ancestral territory to prevent the ground becoming 'weak', as they put it. But the progressive takeover of their lands by settlers from the Visayas, themselves displaced by the expansion of agribusiness, has confined them to small pockets of their once extensive territories. For many tribal communities subsistence on inadequate plots is no longer possible and wage labouring or migration to the cities are their only options. Landlessness and debt have become the main scourges of the once carefree tribals of central Bangladesh, who now have less land per capita than the newly arrived Bengali settlers who have settled in their midst.

The integration of the economies of tribal peoples into world markets has exacerbated the problem, by encouraging more intensive and untenable forest use. The production of surplus crops to satisfy newly acquired needs – money to pay for taxes, medicine, school books, clothing, consumer goods, and new technological goods (outboard engines, rice mills, shotguns and chainsaws) – can only be achieved by intensified farming that the local forests may not be able to sustain. A sorry cycle is initiated by which the search for wealth leads to poverty.

Lack of land security is itself a major cause of extravagant forms of land use. Without assurances that the investments they make in land improvement will be of any benefit to them, many of the hill peoples of mainland Southeast Asia have been obliged to adopt crops and farming practices that are far from environmentally ideal. The opium poppy *Papaver somniferum*, for example, a major crop in the 'Golden Triangle' – the upland forests of Yunnan, Burma, northern Thailand, Laos and Vietnam – yields a quick and valuable harvest which can be readily exchanged for cash (Tapp, 1986). Yet the crop is very demanding both on labour and on the soils. Crop substitution therefore is only a realistic option for the tribal peoples if they have assured access to markets and secure title to their lands.

The Future of Tribal Peoples
Forest peoples are not just passive victims of outside forces, and this has been made clear by the way that they have actively resisted land invasion. Fortunately open conflict is somewhat exceptional, but everywhere that the tribal societies are under threat they are actively developing new strategies to cope with the social and economic pressures on their lands and ways of life. Some societies, such as the Akha (Hani) of Thailand, Burma and southern China, have developed what might be described as a culture of 'marginalisation', whereby their very identity is defined in terms of their opposition to, and exploitation by, lowlanders. Their involvement in wage-labouring, smuggling, drug trading, the accommodation of tourism, and even prostitution must all also be understood as responses to change; evidence both of the resilience of these societies and their critical situation.

On a more positive note, many forest peoples have begun to develop novel institutions especially formed to cope with their changed economic, legal and political circumstances. These include cultural associations, longhouse cooperatives, community development organisations, political fronts and human rights' networks, which have sprung up all over the region, at once joining together isolated and mutually suspicious communities in a common endeavour, and providing them with national and international links. Many of these novel institutions are, in fact, developments of traditional institutions, re-formed to meet new ends. For example, among the Igorot peoples of Luzon, in the Philippines, traditional peace treaties called 'bodong' have provided the basis for the linkage of some three hundred community associations into an effective alliance of nearly all the tribal peoples of the Central Cordillera. The so-created Cordillera People's Alliance has become internationally recognised

and has even sent representatives as far afield as the United Nations to campaign for changes favourable to its tribal constituency (Fay, 1987).

It is in the build-up of these novel institutions that the best hope for the future of the tribal peoples of the region resides. They also hold the key to the survival of the peoples' forests, for a truly sustainable development that respects the possibilities and constraints of the tropical moist forest environment can only develop with the active participation of the forest peoples themselves.

References

Anti-Slavery Society (1984) *The Chittagong Hill Tracts: Militarisation, Oppression and Hill Tribes*. Anti-Slavery Society, London, UK.

Bangkok Post (1989) *Bangkok Post*: 10 October.

Beer de, J. H. and McDermott, M. J. (1989) *The Economic Value of Non-Timber Forest Products in Southeast Asia*. IUCN, Amsterdam, The Netherlands.

Budiardjo, C. (1986) The politics of transmigration. *Ecologist* **16**: 111–18.

Budiardjo, C. and Liong, Liem Soei (1988) *West Papua: the Obliteration of a People*. 3rd edition. Tapol, London, UK.

Carey, I. (1976) *Orang Asli: the Aboriginal Tribes of Peninsular Malaysia*. Oxford University Press, UK.

China Reconstructs (1984) *China's Minority Nationalities*. Great Wall Books, Beijing, China.

Colchester, M. (1986a) The struggle for land: tribal people in the face of the transmigration programme. *Ecologist* **16**: 99–110.

Colchester, M. (1986b) Banking on disaster: international support for transmigration. *Ecologist* **16**: 61–70.

Colchester, M. (1986c) Unity and diversity: Indonesia's policy towards tribal peoples. *Ecologist* **16**: 89–98.

Colchester, M. (1989) *Pirates, Squatters and Poachers; the Political Ecology of Dispossession of the Native Peoples of Sarawak*. Survival International/INSAN, Kuala Lumpur, Malaysia.

Denslow, J. S. and Padoch, C. (eds) (1988) *People of the Rain Forest*. University of California Press, Berkeley, USA.

Dove, M. (1985) The agro-ecological mythology of the Javanese and the political economy of Indonesia. *Indonesia* **39**: 1–36.

Dove, M. (ed.) (1989) *The Real and Imagined Role of Culture in Development: Case Studies from Indonesia*. University Press of Hawaii, Honolulu.

Fay, C. (1987) *Counter-Insurgency and Tribal Peoples in the Philippines*. Survival International USA, Washington, DC, USA.

Geddes, W. (1976) *Migrants of the Mountains: the Cultural Ecology of the Blue Miao*. Clarendon Press, Oxford, UK.

Ganapin, D. (1987) Philippines ethnic minorities: the continuing struggle for survival and self-determination. In: Sahabat Alam Malaysia *Forest Resources Crisis in the Third World*: pp. 171–91, Penang, Malaysia.

Hong, E. (1987) *The Natives of Sarawak*. Institut Masyarakat, Penang, Malaysia.

Kunstadter, P., Chapman, E. C., Sabhasri, S. (eds) (1978) *Farmers in the Forest*. University Press of Hawaii, Honolulu.

Langub, J. (1988a) Some aspects of life of the Penan. Paper presented to the Orang Ulu Cultural Heritage Seminar, Miri, 21–23 June 1988.

Langub, J. (1988b) The Penan Strategy. In: *People of the Rain Forest*, Denslow, J. S. and Padoch, C. (eds) University of California Press, Berkeley, USA.

Lewis, P. and Lewis, E. (1984) *Peoples of the Golden Triangle*. Oxford University Press, Oxford, UK.

MacKinnon, J. and Bhruksasri, W. (eds) (1986) *Highlanders of Thailand*. Oxford University Press, Oxford, UK.

Malou-Nuzeman, H. (1984) 'Siberut Projekt Mislukt'. *Tribal* **14** (Mei): 16–20.

Morris, B. (1982) *Forest Traders: a Socio-economic Study of the Hill Pandaram*. Athlone Press, London, UK.

SAM (1989) *The Battle for Sarawak's Forests*. World Rainforest Movement and Sahabat Alam Malaysia, Penang.

Spencer, J. E. (1966) *Shifting Cultivation in Southeastern Asia*. University of California Press, Berkeley, USA.

Tapp, T. (1986) *The Hmong of Thailand: Opium People of the Golden Triangle*. Anti-Slavery Society, London, UK.

von Fuhrer-Haimendorf, C. (1982) *Tribes of India: the Struggle for Survival*. University of California Press, Berkeley, USA.

Xin Jiguang (1987) *Minority Peoples in China*. China Pictorial Publications, Beijing, China.

Authorship

Marcus Colchester of Survival International in London with contributions from Chin See Chung of the University of Malaya, Duleep Matthai of the Ministry of Environment and Forests in Delhi, M. S. Ranatunga of IUCN, Colombia, Lee Hua Seng of the Forest Department in Kuching, Mick Raga of the Department of Environment and Conservation, Boroko, Papua New Guinea, Prof. Andrew Vaydon of Rutger University, USA, and Caroline Sargent of the International Institute for Environment and Development in London.

4 Shifting Cultivation

Introduction

Late in the dry season, the skies of tropical Asia are heavy with smoke from thousands of small fires set by farmers following an age-old way of life: shifting cultivation.

Various systems of shifting cultivation, also called 'slash and burn' or 'swidden' (from the Old Norse word for 'singe'), are based on cutting living vegetation in the dry season (January–March for the south-west monsoon, June–August for the north-east monsoon), letting it dry, burning it late in the dry season, and then planting a crop in the ashes early in the wet season. In the most stable and productive systems, the fields are rotated on a 10 to 15 year cycle. Declining crop productivity, due to weed competition or soil nutrient depletion, leads to the field being abandoned after one or two years.

When the field is cleared, trees and shrubs are commonly cut at knee height and care is taken to leave certain deep-rooted species. These 'fallow' species regenerate rapidly after cultivation ceases. They tap the nutrients which have been leached deep into the soil, beyond the reach of annual crops, and some of them fix atmospheric nitrogen; these nutrients are accumulated in the living plants and released into the soil when the plant decomposes. Most nutrients in the generally infertile soils of the moist tropics are held in the organic matter in the topsoil. Traditional fallow systems allow these nutrients to build up to the point where another food crop is possible. The regrowing fallow continues to produce fruits, spices and other useful products, and provides excellent habitat for deer and other species which are hunted for food.

In traditional swiddens, the use of agricultural tools is minimal and ploughs are not used. The precious topsoil with its nutrient-rich organic matter is left intact and the cohesion and porosity of the soil retained, thus limiting water run-off and erosion. Although no draught animals are required, most villagers keep dogs, chickens and pigs. Much of their animal protein, however, comes from fish and wild game. Energy return for energy input in traditional swiddens is quite high, approaching 20:1 (Rappaport, 1972). Compare this with industrialised agriculture, which, from sowing to marketing, typically consumes more energy than it produces.

Yields from upland swiddens are variable. With favourable soils and climate they can be quite high, but average rice yields rarely exceed one ton per hectare. However, the yield per unit of effort is typically higher than in lowland systems, giving the upland farmer more time for hunting, social interactions, and ceremonial activities.

This general model of shifting cultivation greatly oversimplifies reality. In fact, shifting cultivation comprises a range of highly variable and localised systems that have developed in response to local environmental and cultural conditions (Phillips, 1964; Eden,

1987). The essentials are that fields are rotated rather than crops, and that a forest or bush fallow period restores nutrients to levels which permit a further crop cycle.

Fire is usually an important factor. Burning releases the phosphates and potassium from the plant-fibre and makes them available to the crop plants, but most of the volatile nitrogen compounds are lost to the system. In a few places, especially in wetter areas, fire is used only sparingly, or not at all. For example, on Siberut island, west of Sumatra, a simple form of dibble-stick agriculture is used. Small patches of forest (0.25–0.5 ha) are cleared, but not burned. Because of the shielding properties of the cut debris, the surface humus and soil are not leached of their nutrients, which remain available to the freshly planted crops of bananas, cassava *Manihot esculenta*, and taro. The leaves, twigs and wood decompose at different rates and new nutrients are released slowly from the debris to the soil. These nutrients are utilised by fruit and spice trees which are planted while the first crop is maturing. By the time the covering of debris has lost its protective properties, the surface soil is held together by a mat of grasses, shrubs, and low trees. Old traditional swiddens gradually become groves of mature fruit trees, which can take on a forest-like structure, with large durian and jack-fruit trees interspersed with guava *Psidium* spp., jambu *Eugenia* spp., langsat *Lansium domesticum*, lemons *Citrus limon*, and papaya *Carica papaya* (McNeely *et al.*, 1980).

History of Shifting Cultivation

For tens of thousands of years, people have used fire to modify the landscape. At the earliest hunting and gathering stage of human existence, people probably had little more impact on the ecosystem than any other medium-sized omnivore. As technology improved, however, the ecological niche of early man expanded. As people learned to control fire, they began to change their habitat to suit their needs, in particular by burning dry forests to create grasslands which supported more large mammals, which could then be hunted. Improved technology (axes, digging sticks, stone knives) also enabled a wider range of plant materials to be used.

Agriculture evolved from the increased use of plants, fire, and tools. The origins of shifting cultivation remain controversial, but stretch back into the very dawn of agriculture. In Thailand's Mae Hong Son Province, Gorman (1971) excavated a site called Spirit Cave, and discovered what may be some of the earliest evidence of shifting cultivation in Southeast Asia. Dating from about 10,000 years ago, just at the end of the Pleistocene epoch, the evidence from Spirit Cave, indicates that agriculture – generally thought to have originated in the Middle East – may have evolved first in Southeast Asia. Several authorities now question this interpretation of the

Spirit Cave excavations and claim that the deposits could have resulted from the activities of hunter-gatherer communities (Kunstadter, 1988). Nevertheless, according to anthropologist Wilhelm Solheim (1972), 'Some of the most technologically advanced cultures in the world in the period from about 13,000 BC to 4000 BC flourished not in the Middle East or the adjacent Mediterranean, but in the northern reaches of mainland Southeast Asia.'

The people at Spirit Cave had a varied menu that included several varieties of almond, beans, bottle gourds, cucumbers, peppers, and water chestnuts. The last items were served with numerous kinds of meat such as bat, deer, fish, monkey, pig, rat and squirrel. Gorman found that even the earliest shifting cultivators in Southeast Asia enjoyed a varied and balanced diet. Many of the ingredients used in those days are important components of the tastiest dishes in the finest Thai restaurants today.

Growing food plants and domesticating certain animals did not simply replace hunting and gathering, but rather supplemented it, allowing people to wrest more productivity from nature, and to occupy more diverse habitats. The human population could grow through more intensive use of the land – swiddens could support up to 20 people per square kilometre, while hunting could hardly support one person on the same amount of land.

Supporting more people in larger groups, the innovative upland technique of swidden agriculture spread quickly throughout all suitable areas in tropical Asia. Spencer (1966) came to the startling conclusion that virtually no pristine monsoon forest remains in all of Southeast Asia. All the drier forests have been cleared by people at one time or another, and many areas have been cleared repeatedly.

As long as the human population remained relatively low, traditional shifting cultivation permitted local self-sufficiency and resulted in great cultural diversity as groups adapted to the local resources which were available. Most shifting cultivation took place in the hills, where the soils and vegetation dried out more quickly and upward currents of wind helped fan the flames among the cut vegetation. The lowlands, many of which were seasonally flooded,

remained relatively intact and were used for hunting, fishing, and gathering of tubers and other plants. It was not until the recent advent of irrigated wet-rice agriculture that the lowlands became permanently inhabited. The clearance of vast areas of lowland forest for rice cultivation has mostly taken place within the last hundred years.

Today, the lowland irrigated rice-growing civilisations dominate the Asian landscape, and the shifting cultivators are spread thinly across the highlands. As marginal peoples living far from the centres of economic and political power, they have suffered from benign neglect, and have often formed buffers between more powerful political entities based in the more fertile, densely settled lowlands (Kunstadter, 1987). More recently, in some places, this neglect has ceased to be benign. The tribal peoples of the Indo-Chinese highlands, for example, suffered grievously during the wars that caused social upheaval from the 1950s to the 1980s. In areas where shifting cultivators occupy forests which contain rich timber resources, central governments have sold cutting rights to concessionaires from outside the region, thereby disrupting the traditional agroecosystems that had evolved over thousands of years (see chapter 3).

Shifting Cultivation, Wildlife and Biological Diversity

When shifting cultivation functions correctly, wildlife flourishes, with many herbivores feeding in the abandoned swiddens. Predators are in turn attracted by the herbivores. The older swiddens contain a high proportion of fruit trees, which are attractive to primates, squirrels, hornbills, and a wide range of other small animals. Mature tropical forests conceal most of their edible products high in the canopy beyond the reach of the terrestrial herbivores, while forest clearings bring the forest's productivity down to where it can be reached by hungry browsers; Wharton (1968) has provided convincing evidence that the distribution of the major large mammals of Southeast Asia is highly dependent on shifting cultivation (see case study on wild cattle). When the hill farmers have tenure over their land, the game is carefully cropped, with over-hunting prevented by religious and customary sanctions, as well as by primitive weapons.

Shifting cultivation can be very productive, and is sustainable when population pressure is low. More often nowadays, short fallow periods lead to soil degradation until only rank grasses survive. WWF/A. Compost

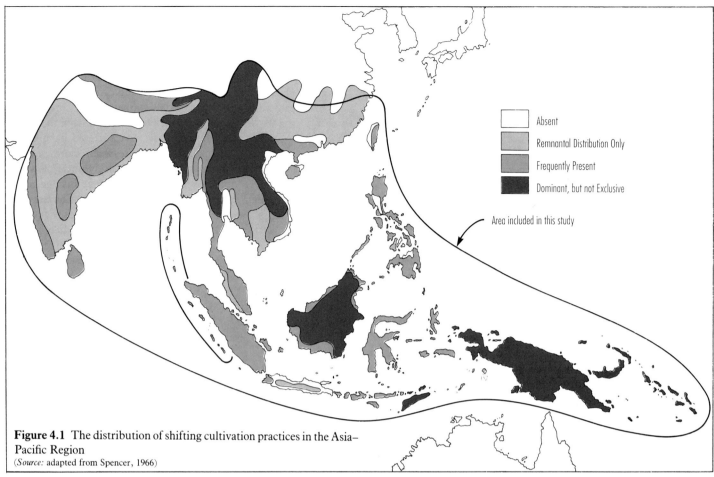

Figure 4.1 The distribution of shifting cultivation practices in the Asia–Pacific Region
(*Source:* adapted from Spencer, 1966)

Legend:
Absent
Remnantal Distribution Only
Frequently Present
Dominant, but not Exclusive

Area included in this study

This is not to say that wildlife is always welcome – far from it. Condaminas (1977), working among the Mnong Gar of Vietnam's Central Higlands, reported the excitement that surrounded the ripening grain crops:

'More time is given to guarding the fields against marauding wild animals. Most field huts are occupied every night, but for all the watchers' precautions, wild boar, deer, and bears manage to elude their vigilance. On two occasions, there have even been unwelcome visits from a herd of elephants that hitherto had been content to ravage other areas. During the day, clouds of predatory birds swoop down on the young grain and must be driven off; the sharp crackle of the scarecrows and the shouts of the watchers blend with the clear-toned music of the rustic xylophone.'

In New Guinea, an important part of the swidden process is the construction of sturdy fences to exclude the wild pigs, and to contain the domestic pigs when they are turned loose in the swidden after the main crops have been harvested. In their quest for tubers, these pigs soften and aerate the soil and thin the regenerating seedlings (Rappaport, 1972), thereby playing an important role in accelerating the regrowth of forest. Throughout tropical Asia and the Pacific, wild, feral and domestic pigs form an important part of almost all swidden systems.

A wide range of crops, often over 100 at one time, occur in swiddens and the regenerating fallow forest. Among the Lua (Lawa) of northern Thailand, about 120 crop species are planted, including 75 for food, 21 for medicine, 20 for ceremonial or decorative purposes, and seven for weaving or dyes. The fallow areas continue to be productive for grazing or collecting, with well over 300 species used (Kunstadter, 1970). The most important crop is upland rice. It is not unusual for 20 varieties of seed rice to be kept in a village, each with different characteristics and planted at different times in different places.

The Hanunoo of the Philippines may plant 150 species of crops at one time or another in the same swidden. At the sides and against the fences they grow low, climbing or sprawling legumes, such as asparagus beans *Vigna unguiculata*, and cowpeas, or hyacinth beans *Dolichos lablab*. Towards the centre, grain crops dominate, but numerous root crops, shrub legumes and trees are also found. Pole-climbing yam vines, heart-shaped taro leaves, ground-hugging sweet potato vines, and shrub-like cassava stems are the only visible signs of the large store of starch staples underground, while the grain crops flourish a metre or so above the swidden floor before giving way to the more widely spaced and less rapidly maturing tree crops. A new swidden produces a steady stream of harvestable food in the form of seed grains, pulses, tubers, spices, and fruits (Conklin, 1954).

Among the Tsembaga Mareng of Papua New Guinea, each field contains some 15 to 100 major crops, plus dozens of minor crops, spread seemingly at random through the field. 'This intermingling does more than make the best use of a limited area, it also discourages plant-specific insect pests, it allows advantage to be taken of slight variations in habitats, it is protective of the thin tropical soil and it achieves a high photosynthetic efficiency' (Rappaport, 1971).

This agricultural diversity far surpasses anything in the average western supermarket. Only 80 plant species are generally grown by market gardeners in the industrialised world, and 95 per cent of human nutrition is derived from just 30 species (Myers, 1985). The subsistence-level hill farmers of tropical Asia may enjoy a far more varied diet than the wealthiest industrialist.

Although shifting cultivation has, with growing human populations, become destructive of forests and watersheds, it is highly adaptive to a great variety of conditions. When properly carried out it is the only sustainable way of cultivating areas where poor soils, steep gradients, and heavy rainfall make conventional farming methods unproductive or impossible. As practised by stable groups, swidden agriculture is not particularly destructive of forest, land, or wildlife. Permanent villages are established, moving only if forced to do so by extremes of economic hardship, political disturbance, or population pressure, but not as a necessary consequence of the agricultural techniques of their inhabitants (Hinton, 1970).

Sedentary swidden agriculturalists have a strong interest in maintaining the fertility of the village territory, employing a number of long-term conservation measures which contribute to biological diversity. The following practices characterise many of the traditional systems:

1 Preservation of stands of primary forest in and around the swidden to serve as a seed reservoir for regrowth forest, a source of useful plants and as hunting grounds.

2 Fire breaks, fire-fighters, and coordination of burning to provide sophisticated fire control.

3 Early cutting of forest to retain soil moisture, reducing transpiration losses so that swidden soil is often more moist than adjacent forest soil.

4 Careful rotation of swiddens, using each one for only one year.

5 A sufficiently long bush-fallow period to allow a build-up of nutrients for the next cropping cycle.

6 Retention in the fallow of those plant species which provide useful products or enhance soil fertility.

7 Careful control of weeds.

8 Minimal disturbance of topsoil, thus reducing erosion.

Traditional swidden cultivation is highly diversified, which means that it is more stable and reliable for the farmer than many of the modern monocultural systems that now predominate in the tropics. Since traditional swidden farmers are concerned primarily with their immediate needs and those of the species sustaining them, they are not worried about external forces such as commodity prices, energy supplies, and environmental abuse. It is clear to all farmers living in such systems, says Rappaport (1972), 'that their survival is contingent upon the maintenance, rather than the mere exploitation, of the larger community of which they know themselves to be only part'.

In short, traditional shifting cultivation is a system which is well adapted to tropical moist forest environments. It maintains a higher level of biological diversity than many alternative uses of forest land, and provides significant benefits to wildlife populations. The maintenance of such systems is of considerable importance to modern forms of development. The wild relatives of a variety of important crop plants occur in the forests of Southeast Asia. These, and the primitive cultivars grown by the swidden cultivators, are potential sources of genetic material for modern plant breeders. Rice, for example, provides the main staple for all of Asia, and the traditional rice varieties grown in upland swiddens contain great genetic diversity.

Problems with Shifting Cultivation

The idyllic conclusion that shifting cultivation benefits both man and forest only applies if this cultivation is sustainable. Today this is becoming an extremely rare phenomenon. Swidden cultivation can become inappropriate in at least three main ways:

• By an increase in human population, which causes old plots to be recultivated too soon.

• By inept agricultural practices such as cultivating the land for so long that persistent weeds become established and soil fertility falls (Table 4.1).

• By extension into areas where soils are particularly erosion-prone or where the broader national interest requires that natural forest be retained, either to produce timber or to conserve biological diversity. Often the three factors work together, resulting in the destruction of extensive areas of tropical forest.

Table 4.1 Yields (kg per ha) for swidden agriculture under rainfed conditions from the same land over a period of three years in Nan Province, northern Thailand

	Cotton	Mung Bean	Rice	Maize
Year 1	1,094	956	2,538	2,675
Year 2	794	1,113	1,888	631
Year 3	600	431	1,388	344

(*Source:* adapted from Chapman, 1970)

The rapid growth of Asia's population in recent decades is the main reason why the age-old systems of agriculture are breaking down. When fallow periods are too short, or the soils are unsuitable for any form of farming, the cultivated land is invaded by weeds. Over wide areas of tropical Asia, tree cover has been replaced by bamboo scrub and *Imperata cylindrica* grasslands, which have very little diversity and very low productivity. The Lesser Sundas of Indonesia, parts of central Sulawesi, and the drier parts of India, Thailand, and Burma have all suffered from this form of ecological degradation, at the expense of both forests and people. A green or grassy desert has replaced one of the world's most diverse ecosystems.

Some of the higher elevation areas of mainland Southeast Asia are now being used for a very destructive type of shifting cultivation. Under this system, the same swidden is used for growing opium for five or six consecutive years (with other crops such as maize (*Zea mays*) grown during the 'off season'). This is continued until all residual soil fertility is lost, soil organisms destroyed, trees burned, and topsoil eroded. Upon abandonment, the land reverts to *Imperata* grassland. The villages are temporary, discouraging capital investment or long-term land conservation. The people are seldom able to feed themselves, and opium is used to purchase rice from lowland areas.

A variety of unstable shifting cultivation is also practised by smallholders who are forced to make agricultural settlements in the hills through competition for land in the lowlands. These people might be considered 'shifted cultivators' rather than 'shifting cultivators'. Lowland shifting cultivation is typically very destructive, and not based on the wealth of knowledge which the traditional swidden farmers of the uplands have accumulated. The villagers seldom have title to the land that they clear, and consequently little motivation to take long-term conservation measures. Cultivation is followed by fallow periods which are usually too short to restore soil fertility, leading eventually to permanent abandonment of the land.

As an example of poor agricultural practices, the Iban of Borneo have been described not so much as shifting cultivators as 'eaters of the forest' (Freeman, 1955). Occupying a primary forest area into which they have fairly recently expanded at the expense of less aggressive indigenous tribes, the Iban still over-cultivate, often using a single plot three years in a row or returning to a plot after just five years of fallow. As a result, wide areas of west and central Borneo have become deforested and replaced with *Imperata* grasslands (see maps in chapters 19 and 24). Geertz (1963) gives several reasons for this over-cultivation: 'An historically rooted conviction that there are always other forests to conquer, a warrior's view of natural resources as plunder to be exploited, a large village settlement pattern which makes shifting between plots a more than usually onerous task, and, perhaps, a superior indifference toward agricultural proficiency.' Using such profligate agriculture, one Iban group in central Borneo is known to have moved 300 km in just 50 years, devastating vast areas of forest in the process.

33

Solutions

Traditional swidden cultivation, is a highly diverse system which can be adapted to a variety of local environments. It aims to produce diversity and reliability of food supply and reduce the incidence of disease and insect problems. It uses labour efficiently, intensifying production with limited resources, and earns maximum returns with low levels of technology. By using many crop species and varieties, the swidden system is better able to cope with pathogens, pests and varying conditions of soil, rainfall, and sunlight. It provides sustainable yields by drawing on centuries of experience accumulated by farmers who do not depend on scientific information, external inputs, capital, credit, or markets. The traditional swidden farmers of tropical Asia have been truly independent and self-reliant.

The point has now been reached, however, where swidden cultivation is ceasing to be a viable option. The density of Asia's population is such that more and more agricultural settlers are adopting forms of shifting agriculture that almost invariably lead to long-term degradation of the agricultural and forestry potential of the land. Numerous attempts have been made to 'stabilise' shifting cultivators, but in most cases they have met with very limited success. The soils are intrinsically too poor to repay investments in more labour-intensive agriculture or to justify bringing in fertilisers. Where success has been achieved, it has occurred through the introduction of new cash crops, which place less demands upon the soil and enable the farmers to use their profits to purchase their food requirements elsewhere. Unfortunately, in most of Southeast Asia, markets for these products are too remote and few viable options exist for crop diversification.

Modern agricultural development in the uplands should take existing swidden systems as starting points and use modern agricultural science to improve on their productivity. Development should be based on the ability of swidden farmers to adapt to change, but should continue to draw on resource-conserving and yield-sustaining production technologies (Altieri and Merrick, 1987). The essential element is the design of self-sustaining agroecosystems which assure the maintenance of the local genetic diversity available to farmers, thereby enabling rural communities of swidden cultivators to maintain control over their production systems.

Solutions will also need to be based on cultural diversity, as local knowledge is essential to the success of the system. The social structure of most hill tribes is organised around the holding and control of swidden lands (Kunstadter, 1970), but since each tribe tends to have its own set of customary laws, seldom recognised by other tribes or by the dominant lowland government, land disputes are very common. Only if the tribe unequivocally controls its swidden land will long-term conservation measures be effective, not only for the land and vegetation but ultimately for the tribe itself. Establishing land title is often an essential element, not least to avoid conflicts with timber concessionaires (see chapter 3).

In addition, maintaining a stable and permanent relationship with forested land would enable some swidden farmers to invest time and effort in other permanent assets like fruit trees, fenced gardens, terraces, and irrigation canals. In the most suitable areas, the swiddens are supplemented by irrigated rice fields, thus allowing a considerably higher population density than if the swidden alone was relied upon for survival. Such mixed systems will often enable modern agricultural techniques to be wedded to the traditional ones, and lead to the establishment of more permanent villages.

Large areas of forest, protected against outside encroachment and assigned to specific ethnic groups for sustainable management, might be a means of ensuring the productivity of shifting cultivation systems. This should be coupled with a research effort aimed at improving the efficiency of shifting agriculture, for example by introducing new fallow trees and shrubs which are efficient at bringing nutrients and nitrogen into the above-ground biomass. In some places, also, community-level 'landrace custodians' might be given subsidies to maintain their traditional agricultural systems. This would promote the continuing evolution of genetic diversity, which is so important to agricultural development.

Even this will not be enough. Employment opportunities in forestry are needed, along with reforestation in the *Imperata*-covered uplands. Research on making the better upland soils more permanently productive is essential; the opium trade should be rationalised and regulated; and new cash crops should be introduced along with new systems of transport and marketing. Within its limits, swidden farming must continue to make a meaningful input into the total agricultural productivity of the region. But in the longer term most cereals will have to be produced intensively in the lowlands and the uplands will be used for perennial crops and forestry.

Rich forest soils in the Dumoga-Bone valleys of northern Sulawesi have been converted to permanent agriculture to support transmigrants from Java and Bali. Shifting cultivation is still a problem in the forested hills, but most are now protected. N. Mark Collins

WILD CATTLE AND SHIFTING CULTIVATION

Southeast Asia is the home of the wild cattle which are the closest relatives to domestic cattle, and therefore of particular importance for stock-breeders. There are three main species: gaur or seladang, found across the region from India and Nepal to Peninsular Malaysia; the banteng, found in Southeast Asia from Burma to Borneo, Java, and Bali, but found neither in Sumatra nor most of Peninsular Malaysia; and the kouprey, the rarest and most recently discovered species (first described in 1937), found only in Indo-China (see chapter 28).

Wharton (1968) found that each species has a close ecological relationship with shifting cultivation. The gaur prefers foothill tracts of forest adjacent to savanna woodland, glades or other open terrain affected by man and fire, and has followed shifting cultivation into Peninsular Malaysia. The banteng is confined to savanna woodland within the deciduous forest zones of the region; in the more humid areas, it occupies secondary forests. The best habitats for kouprey are rice fields abandoned by the ancient Khmer civilisation whose capital was Angkor Wat, these old fields are still burned annually by rural Khmer farmers, thus maintaining a savanna habitat which suits the kouprey and other wild cattle.

Wharton concludes that since fire definitely aids hunting and gathering in the savanna woodland areas such as northern Cambodia, it was probably equally useful during prehistoric times. It would thus appear that the dry forests of Southeast Asia may be

The banteng is the most likely ancestor of domestic cattle in Southeast Asia. WWF/Alain Compost

very ancient, having been created by human-caused fires and occupied by wild cattle and other large herbivores. The living wild cattle of Southeast Asia appear heavily dependent on an environment which, if not entirely created by man and fire, is certainly maintained by these agencies.

References

Altieri, M. A. and Merrick, Laura C. (1987) *In situ* conservation of crop genetic resources through maintenance of traditional farming systems. *Economic Botany* **41**: 86–96.

Chapman, E. C. (1970) Shifting cultivation and economic development in the lowlands of northern Thailand. *Proceedings of International Seminar on Shifting Cultivation and Economic Development in Northern Thailand*. Land Development Department, Bangkok, Thailand.

Condaminas, G. (1977) *We Have Eaten the Forest*. Hill and Wang, New York, USA.

Conklin, H. (1954) An ethnoecological approach to shifting cultivation. *Transactions of the New York Academy of Sciences* **17**: 133–42.

Eden, M. J. (1987) Traditional shifting cultivation and the tropical forest system. *Trends in Ecology and Evolution* **2**: 340–43.

FAO (1957) Shifting cultivation. *Unasylva* **11**: 23–8.

Freeman, J. D. (1955) *Iban Agriculture: A Report on the Shifting Cultivation of Hill Rice by the Iban of Sarawak*. Her Majesty's Printing Office, London, UK.

Geertz, C. (1963) *Agricultural Involution*. University of California Press, Berkeley, California, USA.

Gorman, C. (1971) The Hoabhinian and after: Subsistence patterns in Southeast Asia during the late Pleistocene and early Recent periods. *World Archeology* **2**: 300–21.

Hinton, P. (1970) Swidden cultivation among the Pwo Karen of Northern Thailand. *Proceedings of International Seminar on Shifting Cultivation and Economic Development in Northern Thailand*, Land Development Department, Bangkok, Thailand.

Kunstadter, P. (1970) Subsistence agricultural economics of Lua and Karen hill farmers of Mae Sariang District, Northern Thailand. *International Seminar on Shifting Cultivation and Economic Development in Northern Thailand*, Land Development Department, Bangkok, Thailand.

Kunstadter, P. (1987) *Social systems and upland management: Social ecology of shifting cultivation systems in mainland Southeast Asia*. Paper prepared for International Conference on Ecology in Vietnam, New Palz, New York, USA. 28–30 May.

Kunstadter, P. (1988) Hill people of northern Thailand. In: *People Of the Tropical Rain Forest*. Eds J. S. Denslow and C Padoch, pp 93–110. University of California Press, Berkeley. 232 pp.

McNeely, J. A., Whitten, A. J., Whitten, J. and House, S. (1980) *Saving Siberut: A Conservation Master Plan*. WWF, Bogor, Indonesia.

Myers, N. (ed.) (1985) *The Gaia Atlas of Planet Management*. Pan Books, London, UK.

Phillips, J. (1964) Shifting cultivation. In: Elliot, H. (ed.) *The Ecology of Man in the Tropical Environment*. IUCN (NS) **4**: 1–355.

Rappaport, R. A. (1971) The flow of energy in an agricultural society. *Scientific American* **225**: 116–32.

Rappaport, R. A. (1972) Forests and man. *Ecologist* **6**: 240–6.

Solheim, W. G. (1972) An earlier agricultural revolution. *Scientific American* **266**: 34–41.

Spencer, J. E. (1966) *Shifting Cultivation in Southeastern Asia*. University of California Press, Berkeley, California, USA.

Wharton, Charles H. (1968) Man, fire, and wild cattle in Southeast Asia. *Proceedings of the Annual Tall Timbers Fire Ecology Conference* **8**: pp. 107–67.

Authorship

Jeff McNeely and Jeff Sayer of IUCN, Gland, with contributions from Paul Anspach of IUCN Vientiane, Francis Ng of the Forest Research Institute of Malaysia, Suvat Singhapant of the Royal Forest Department in Bangkok, Cèsar Nuevo of the Institute of Forest Conservation, Laguna, Philippines, and Jan Van der Heide of the Institute of Soil Fertility, Gröningen, Netherlands.

5 Agricultural Settlement Schemes

Introduction

In Southeast Asia there has been much movement of people, sponsored or at least encouraged by their national government, to form new agricultural settlements away from their home area. The new area chosen and prepared by that government as a focus of development is always in an otherwise sparsely populated and relatively undeveloped region. Many such 'new' areas, almost by definition, are close or immediately adjacent to forests, and throughout the region loss of forests is one of the major environmental impacts of new settlement programmes.

The aims of the settlement schemes are to settle people in areas that have been rigorously selected, clearing the land using semi-mechanical methods, designing farm models that are capable of sustaining agricultural production, and planning for expansion caused by the population increase of the settlers (and any newcomers and indigenous people). This is in addition to providing communications and access to markets and employment (for example, in managed forests), particularly for second and subsequent generations.

It is likely, however, that in no sites can it be claimed that all these objectives have been achieved. Insufficient attention to the ideals results in barely sustainable agriculture, the creation of new groups of rural poor with all the social implications, and of wider areas of degraded lands, as well as the burden of large sums of borrowed money which the next generation will have to repay.

After several decades of settlement schemes in Southeast Asia and elsewhere, it is evident that the negative effects of poorly planned settlement can necessitate costly management interventions, or even abandonment of sites and a permanent reduction in the options for their future development. Recently, environmental guidelines for settlement projects in the humid tropics have been produced (Burbridge et al., 1988) in which a list is provided of 'Project Killers' which may severely limit the positive benefits of settlement projects. These include:

1 Selection of sites which are not capable of sustaining the planned economic activities and numbers of settlers.
2 Selection of economic activities which are inappropriate to the natural resources of the lands available for settlement.
3 Degradation of the resources by mechanical land clearance.
4 Lack of skills and relevant experience amongst settlers.
5 Failure to make provision for population expansion in the settlement area, caused both by the natural increase of the resident population and by spontaneous migrants.
6 Insidious degradation of the ecological qualities of settlement sites which reduce their economic viability.

The following account of new agricultural settlements in Indonesia, Malaysia and Vietnam illustrates these problems, and examines the effects and scale of settlement on forested lands.

Settlement Programmes in Indonesia

The term 'resettlement' is used in Indonesia to refer to the programmes of the Social Affairs Department in which isolated groups (frequently hunter-gatherers or swidden farmers) are brought into permanent settlements somewhere near their original home. Each project affects perhaps only a few hundred people. It does not have major environmental effects, and is not considered further here.

In Indonesia the programme for the movement of large numbers of people far from their homes is termed 'transmigration' (Whitten, 1988; World Bank, 1988). It is the world's largest programme for voluntary, assisted migration and has major environmental consequences. Nearly three million people have been moved from the crowded and environmentally degraded 'inner' islands of Java, Madura, Bali and Lombok, to new settlements in the less populated 'outer' islands (Figure 5.1 and Table 5.1). Although transmigration was started in 1905, 40 years before Independence, about half these people were moved during the Third Five-Year Plan (1979–84) when almost 366,000 fully-sponsored families (about 1.8 million people) were moved. Of the fully-sponsored families which have been moved, about 70 per cent have gone to Sumatra, 20 per cent to Kalimantan, 8 per cent to Sulawesi and 2 per cent to Irian Jaya. It has been estimated that the number of unassisted migrants is some two to three times greater than the number of government-sponsored migrants (Ross, 1985), although a ratio of 1:1 is often used. As a result of population growth and these additional unassisted migrants, the actual number of people in the outer islands who are there because of the transmigration programme must be several times higher.

Transmigration is said to be necessary because inappropriate land-use in the uplands of Java, resulting from dense human population, is endangering soil cover, dams, and human lives, as well as creating problems of sedimentation and flooding in the lower reaches of rivers. Transmigration is seen as just one of the means being used to tackle a massive problem; others include family planning, soil conservation, and agricultural intensification. The fully-sponsored transmigrants are selected (more apply than are accepted) primarily on the basis of two priorities: people are chosen mainly either from critically eroded areas or from ones which are densely-populated. There is, however, a certain amount of overlap between the two categories. It should be stressed, however, that although the Department of Transmigration (DoT) is responsible for the movement of all people displaced by development programmes or natural disasters, not everyone so affected chooses the transmigration option.

Transmigration costs an average of about US$10,000 per family (Gillis, 1988) and takes nine years from the allocation of areas to be surveyed and the planning of targets to the handing over of the settlement to the provincial governments (Whitten et al., 1987a).

Settlement occurs in the fifth year of the process, and by the time the settlement becomes a provincial village, and therefore eligible for village grants, the settlers should have received title to their land. In many cases, however, this process meets many problems, primarily due to insufficient manpower.

It seems reasonable to suppose that taking people from degraded areas should improve the environmental conditions that they leave behind. In fact, the problems of Java's hilly land are directly related to the amount of such land that is deforested, and thereby exposed to the rain, and are solved only by the introduction of strict soil conservation measures or by allowing permanent or semi-permanent vegetation to grow up on degraded soils. The vast majority of transmigrants own little, if any, land. The population of Java has been increasing throughout the programme faster than transmigration has taken place and the departure of transmigrants from Java does not in general seem to have had an obvious or documented positive impact on the environment of the most critically eroded, steep areas of the island.

Planning of Transmigration The land to which the transmigrants are moved has in many cases been manifestly inappropriate. By 1986, for political reasons if not others, these were increasingly being acknowledged and reported in the Indonesian and international press. Some of the sites were intrinsically unsuitable for agriculture, whereas others failed because of inadequate preparation or inappropriate land management. It was clear by the early 1980s that much of the land being used for new settlements was marginal for agricultural activities (Hanson, 1981), but such was the pressure to achieve targets that development continued despite appeals for moderation and for adherence to planning guidelines and manuals.

The most basic and crucial stage of site selection is the preparation of maps which are acceptable to the various agencies concerned with land matters. Although land-use maps have been available in Indonesia for some years, reliable maps for the whole country have only been available since 1988, as a result of a project called the Regional Physical Planning Programme for Transmigration (RePPProT). The primary aim of the project has been to produce a series of maps from

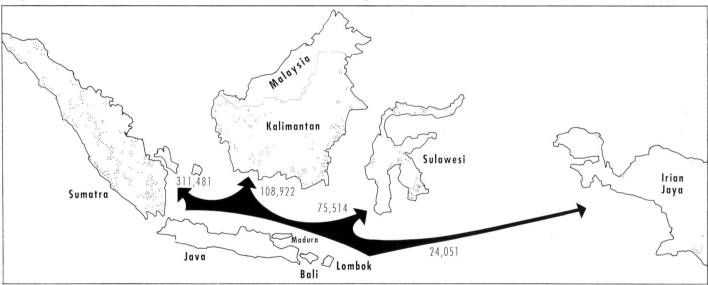

Figure 5.1 Transmigration in Indonesia

Dots represent settlement sites (not to scale) and arrows indicate movements of government sponsored transmigrants. The figures are for families (4 people on average) resettled from 1979–86. In addition to these sponsored migrants an estimated 104,544 families migrated without government assistance to Sumatra; 33,714 to Kalimantan; 8,478 to Sulawesi; 2,675 to Irian Jaya and 169,497 to unspecified locations.

Table 5.1 Transmigration to the less densely populated 'outer' islands of Indonesia

	Sumatra		Kalimantan		Sulawesi*		Irian Jaya		Totals
	sponsored	spontaneous	sponsored	spontaneous	sponsored	spontaneous	sponsored	spontaneous	
1950–4	20,400	—	1,400	—	500	—	—	—	22,300
1955–9	28,900	—	2,600	—	700	—	—	—	32,200
1960–4	21,000	—	4,500	—	1,000	—	—	—	26,500
1965–9	16,500	—	2,100	—	2,700	—	300	—	21,600
1970–4	22,000	—	6,000	—	11,400	—	100	—	39,500
1975–9	33,000	—	11,000	—	9,000	—	2,000	—	55,000
1979–80	16,384	—	565	—	3,854	—	290	—	21,093
1980–1	49,043	—	11,976	—	9,663	—	2,521	—	73,203
1981–2	48,520	—	17,378	—	15,890	—	2,688	—	84,476
1982–3	57,578	—	17,488	—	12,396	—	5,362	—	92,824
1983–4	55,540	—	23,207	—	9,879	—	5,755	—	94,381
April 1984– May 1986	84,416 (5,905)	104,544	38,308 (4,225)	33,714	23,832 (2,055)	8,478	7,435 (36)	2,675	303,402
Totals	453,281	104,544	136,522	33,714	100,814	8,478	26,451	2,675	866,479

(*Source of data:* Ministry of Transmigration Indonesia)

* Includes the Moluccas and other small eastern islands

1979–1984 total of 169,497 families migrated spontaneously but their movements were not known.

Figures in brackets indicate the number of partially assisted families. These are included under sponsored families.

A transmigration settlement in southern Irian Jaya. WWF/J. Ratcliffe

which the location of land most suited for possible future development as transmigration sites could be judged (these maps are the basis of the forest cover maps for Indonesia in chapter 19). A large proportion of the land so identified had in fact already been allocated for different purposes, but the decisions determining those allocations were usually based on inadequate or inappropriate information. These new maps therefore offer a chance for revised and more rational planning. This is particularly pertinent to forest use since it is possible now to recommend shifts in forest boundaries, the degazetting of some protected areas ('forests' that in reality are only scrub or even grass), the redefining and physical demarcation of new boundaries, and the gazetting of new areas. The Department of Forestry stands to gain at least as much land as it loses on most of the islands, and all its land would actually be forested.

Ensuring the integrity of protected areas is one of the highest priorities of the RePPProT project. What may seem such simple and sensible compromises are in fact, however, politically difficult. Nevertheless, it is of the highest priority that all sectors concerned with land and its allocation should revise the agreed land-status maps of each province based on the project. Fortunately this may be insisted upon because the National Development Planning Board (which allocates national budgets and decides development directions) has recognised the significance of the mapping and has commissioned a national overview of the results to illustrate the potential of land-use, as well as the accompanying conflicts and problems (RePPProT, 1990).

Transmigration and land-use planning need to be guided by ecological principles. Guidelines are now available on how to assemble a provincial land-use plan while also considering nature conservation (Davidson, 1987). These guidelines, using the province of South Kalimantan (Borneo) as a case study, were based on those produced by IUCN in 1976 and subsequently updated (Poore and Sayer, 1987). A draft was used in a workshop in Jakarta in 1986 that brought together planners from Transmigration and other departments to discuss issues in the context of natural resource conservation. As a result, an Indonesian language version of the guidelines will be published (Thohari *et al.*, in press).

Forest Loss in Indonesia It should be stressed that almost all areas of

Indonesia's forests have been designated for certain uses, ie grades of protection, production, or conversion (Whitten *et al.*, 1987b), although many areas are now known to have been given an inappropriate designation (RePPProt, 1990). The forest that has been lost to transmigration has in almost all cases been taken from areas that were scheduled as 'Conversion Forest', and virtually no protected area has been damaged directly by the migration.

While transmigration is blamed as a major cause of forest loss in Indonesia, the area cleared for sponsored settlements is actually small relative both to the total forest estate (Table 5.2) and to recently estimated figures of deforestation in Indonesia, which indicate that 5000 sq. km of forest is lost each year to smallholder activity. In almost all provinces the land allocated to sponsored transmigration is less than ten per cent of the Conversion Forest area and less than one per cent of the total forest. These are, of course, average figures, and certain forest types, such as forests on shallow peat, have suffered much more than others. It should be remembered that not all land allocated to transmigration is actually cleared, but that access roads and ribbon development along them are not included in the figures. In the latter case, it has been suggested that total land cleared as a result of the transmigration programme may be five times that originally planned for clearance (Ross, 1985).

Of more or less equal importance to the loss of forests in Indonesia is the plantation industry, for which large areas of forest have been converted. This is illustrated in Table 5.3, which shows the areas of land designated as Phase III transmigration sites (those which have already been cleared and settled, or for which official approval to clear and settle has already been given), tree crop plantations, and the land that is or should be gazetted as nature reserves or designated as protection forest based on the RePPProT study (RePPProT, 1990).

The area of forest lost to transmigration may be small relative to the size of the whole country – but Indonesia is a large country, and the forest loss is large in absolute terms. This might cause less concern if the many reserves gazetted, and due to be gazetted, were well-guarded, and genuinely protected the wildlife communities within them. At present, however, there are few signs that the integrity of most reserves is being maintained in the face of both grossly inadequate enforcement of regulations regarding illegal settlement and logging, and inadequate employment opportunities for

Table 5.2 Forest areas of Indonesia in sq. km by province (apart from Java) compared to land allocated for transmigration in the Third Five Year Plan

	Province area	Defined area	Conversion forest	Forest as a % of province land	Transmigration land		Allocated as a % of total forest land		Allocated as a % of converted forest land	
					Available	Allocated	30%	50%	30%	50%
Aceh	53,390	32,820	1,920	59	270	170	0.1	0.2	2.7	4.5
N. Sumatra	71,680	35,260	2,530	49	150	130	0.1	0.2	1.5	2.5
W. Sumatra	42,290	29,420	4,370	70	120	90	0.1	0.1	0.6	1.0
Riau	94,560	65,460	17,540	69	800	580	0.2	0.3	1.0	1.7
Jambi	51,000	26,140	10,130	51	530	380	0.3	0.5	1.1	1.9
S. Sumatra	102,760	40,280	11,860	39	1,740	1,710	1.0	1.6	4.3	7.2
Bengkulu	19,780	9,920	1,930	50	220	230	0.6	1.0	3.6	6.0
Lampung	32,000	12,440	0	39	1,020	1,000	2.4	4.0	—	—
Subtotals	469,490	251,740	50,280	54	4,890	4,290	0.4	0.7	2.6	4.3
W. Kalimantan	146,000	76,950	15,080	52	570	250	0.1	0.1	0.5	0.8
C. Kalimantan	153,000	109,970	30,000	72	510	480	0.1	0.2	0.5	0.8
S. Kalimantan	151,140	20,290	2,840	55	470	370	0.5	0.8	3.9	6.6
E. Kalimantan	37,000	159,510	35,000	75	300	260	0.0	0.1	0.1	0.4
Subtotals	548,240	366,720	82,920	67	1,870	1,360	0.1	0.2	0.5	0.8
N. Sulawesi	27,510	15,830	6,990	58	80	70	0.1	0.1	0.3	0.5
C. Sulawesi	68,030	41,650	3,350	61	380	300	0.2	0.3	2.7	4.5
S.E. Sulawesi	38,140	21,900	6,990	57	390	360	0.2	0.5	0.5	0.8
S. Sulawesi	62,920	33,510	2,590	53	120	120	0.1	0.2	4.2	7.0
Subtotals	196,600	112,890	19,920	57	970	850	0.2	0.3	1.3	2.1
Maluku	85,720	50,960	4,360	59	180	150	0.1	0.1	1.0	1.7
Irian Jaya	410,660	288,160	117,750	70	340	130	0.0	0.0	0.0	0.1
Subtotals	496,380	339,120	122,110	68	510	280	0.0	0.0	0.1	0.1
Totals	1,710,710	1,070,470	275,230	63	8,240	6,770	0.2	0.3	0.7	1.2

(*Source:* Based on FAO/World Bank, 1985)

There are two columns of figures for transmigration: allocated land as a percentage of total forest and of conversion forest. In both cases they have been calculated twice, once assuming 30 per cent of the cleared land was forested, and again assuming that 50 per cent was forested.

surrounding populations. In fact, some reserves have become so degraded by logging, smallholder intrusion and human-initiated fire that their conservation value has fallen dramatically. Examples are Gunung Nyiut and Kutai (both in Kalimantan), both of which were, until recently, of global significance.

Although transmigration settlers, sponsored and unsponsored, are an important factor in illegal forest loss, it should be remembered that far greater areas have been cleared by indigenous groups. These are not classic swidden cultivators but rather farmers whose practices are inappropriate or whose density is in excess of that which is appropriate for the land. Thus, large areas of deforested and now unproductive land throughout the archipelago, some of which has been blamed on transmigrants (the 'shifted cultivators'), in many cases pre-date the transmigration settlements.

There is an Indonesian proverb which asserts that 'Where there is sugar there are ants' (Anon., 1988a) and as mentioned above, the sponsored transmigrants are followed by twice as many unassisted or 'spontaneous' migrants moving in response to the encouraging news sent from friends and relatives who have already moved. These people can cause considerable damage if their inevitable influx is not

taken into account at the planning stage. The degradation of hillsides and previously forested lands in Lampung, Sumatra's southernmost province, which has received the most sponsored and unsponsored migrants because of its proximity to Java, attests to this. So critical is the situation in some areas that some of its migrant population has had to be moved to neighbouring provinces. Even so, it is believed that there are still about 39,000 spontaneous migrant families in

Table 5.3 Areas (in sq. km) of land designated as transmigration sites including proposed revisions to Nature Reserves and Protection forests

	Total area	Reserves	Protection Forest	Trans-migration areas	Tree crop areas
Sumatra	474,935	43,784	115,202	28,804	31,838
Kalimantan	529,639	65,164	65,360	14,872	16,168
Sulawesi	186,145	27,625	100,296	4,174	2,098
Irian Jaya	414,800	86,300	156,000	9,063	705

(*Source:* Data taken from RePPProT reports: RePPProT, 1990)

Lampung's prohibited areas such as reserves and protection forests (Anon., 1988a). The experience of Lampung is regrettably becoming the experience of other provinces.

The value and need for forest cover is not widely appreciated, and presents an enormous problem of education for the authorities. The settlers themselves are no lovers of the forest and have probably never actually seen any, except for remnants on Javan mountain tops, before they moved. Forest is perceived as being the home of spirits, ghosts and pests, and the settlers are quite happy to see it felled even though the resulting scrub is probably a more serious source of pests, such as pigs.

The most spectacular pest in Sumatra, and a protected one at that, is the elephant (see chapter 2). Elephants regularly raid transmigrants' fields (Anon., 1988e) and cause serious economic damage in plantations. One plantation in Riau (eastern Sumatra) recently reported damage of almost US$1 million (Anon., 1988b). Villagers are encouraged to scare off the animals before they reach the fields, but while the available habitat is so limited it is hard to see any prospect of amelioration of the problems. Some elephants are taken into training schools, but with little success so far. A more successful approach in Sri Lanka has involved the maintenance of forest corridors (see chapter 8).

The Current Economic Situation During the Fourth Five-Year Plan (1984–9), the price of oil, the mainstay of the Indonesian economy, plummeted. Government budgets were slashed, with that for transmigration being hit harder than most. As a consequence in 1987–8, the movement of families from Java virtually stopped and the thousand or so families who did move were destined for settlements relatively close to the island. Throughout the country in 1988, 30–50,000 houses remained officially empty. Although some may have been filled by local transmigrants and opportunists, and some repaired, many are certainly rotting in fields of encroaching bush. The 1989/1990 budget for transmigration was increased by 20 per cent to US$158 million, 52 per cent of which was in the form of foreign loans (Anon., 1989a).

The transmigration programme has attracted considerable criticism both from within and outside the country. The targets for the Third Five-Year Plan were enormous and it was relatively easy for the Indonesian press and others to reveal the shortcomings. The target had been 500,000 families, which was said to have been achieved and even exceeded by counting in unsponsored or partially-sponsored migrants. The target of the Fourth Five-Year Plan (1984–9) was even higher, 750,000 families, but, for many reasons, not least on the grounds of economics, the actual number of sponsored migrants has fallen far short of this, although the total is said to have just exceeded the target, again by counting unsponsored and partially-sponsored migrants.

The criticisms of the transmigration programme contain a great deal of truth. However, it remains that there are successful transmigration settlements occupied by satisfied transmigrants. Despite the pests and other problems, some transmigrants feel relatively fulfilled because their lives in Java were leading them nowhere, they had no space, no land, and only insuperable challenges.

The many failures, the severely restricted budgets, and the vociferous complaints from outside and within the country about the transmigration schemes, have caused a major rethink of policy. Most importantly, no new areas are being cleared for settlement and a period of consolidation has been agreed. This is referred to as 'second-stage development'. It comprises road and bridge building to ease communications, marketing of produce, modifying farm models, encouraging tree crops, providing alternative income sources (Anon., 1989b), and moving settlers from desperate situations to areas where the private sector is likely to sponsor settlements – these are most likely to occur near to tree crop plantations or other industrial projects (Anon., 1989c).

Taking account of this new trend, the World Bank has modified part of its current Fifth Transmigration Loan so that new settlement planning has been replaced with assessing second-stage development projects. It is also making studies, including environmental impact assessments, to appraise the possibility of a sixth loan specifically for second-stage development. Serious problems need to be faced, however, particularly breaking through the problem of issuing land titles. This is regarded as essential because a settler will not make any great effort to safeguard the long-term viability of his land and its surroundings until he is sure that the land he is tilling is his to keep. About 350,000 of 447,000 sponsored transmigrant families cannot yet be transferred to the authority of the provinces in which they live because of the absence of land titles (Anon., 1989c). In East Kalimantan alone there is a backlog of more than 34,000 titles to be processed (Anon., 1988d). Efforts are being made, however, and it was announced recently that even sponsored transmigrants whose land had accidentally been set in official Forestry Department land were to be given titles (Anon., 1988e).

Settlement Programmes in Malaysia

In 1956 the Malaysian Government began a large land development and settlement programme and established the Federal Land Development Authority (FELDA) as executing agency. By the end of 1984, 89,000 landless families (about 500,000 people) had been moved into 367 schemes covering over 6000 sq. km in Peninsular Malaysia, much of which had been forested before the schemes commenced (see Figure 5.2).

Jengka, Peninsular Malaysia The three Jengka Triangle projects were the first in a series of seven World Bank loans to Malaysia for the development of new lands that were to be planted with oil palm or rubber. The three projects, approved between 1968 and 1975, entailed the clearing of some 400 sq. km of forest and the settlement of about 9200 settler families. A retrospective evaluation made in 1985 found that FELDA was efficient, the economics and financial aspects of the project were satisfactory, but, although many of the detrimental environmental impacts such as soil erosion and quality of mill-effluent were not of major importance, insufficient attention had been paid to wildlife aspects during project preparation and implementation. The loss of forest was judged to have been the single most serious impact (World Bank, 1987).

The clearance of forest had a considerable effect in terms of reduction of the area of lowland forest and of wildlife populations (see chapter 22). The Jengka forest reserve would have been a valuable forest to retain, in fact, because a detailed study has already been made on part of it (Poore, 1968) and therefore it could have been monitored over a period of time to provide important perspectives in forest dynamics and management.

Forest unsuitable for agriculture or settlement within the Jengka project area was left as reserves. These have been logged and while their main function is perceived as being for watershed protection, their role as wildlife reserves is also relevant. Logged forests not subject to continual disturbance are able to support a considerable number of the smaller species found in undisturbed forests (see chapters 2 and 22). These forests are under no threat from the settlers since kerosene or bottled gas are the principal cooking fuels. In addition, strips of forest were left along the rivers, as required by the Department of Irrigation and Drainage, although these are less well protected near to the villages.

The cost of settlement is equivalent to approximately US$15,000 per family, half as much again as in Indonesia. In general the settlers are satisfied, particularly the oil palm growers. Social infrastructure, particularly education, has been an important factor in attracting and retaining settlers. The new migrants have a relatively high standard of living and are able to purchase a large range of consumer goods, but there are problems looming as few of their children are prepared to work in the plantations and it seems almost impossible for new job opportunities to be created within a rural environment. As in Indonesia, new plantations and crops suffer from the wildlife (pigs, deer and elephants) which they have displaced or next to which they have been established. FELDA, however, has been at the forefront of developing effective solar-powered electrical and other defences against elephants.

The 6000 sq. km of forested land lost to FELDA schemes is high, yet it represents only 20 per cent of the total land area of Peninsular Malaysia that is under oil palm and rubber, an area which has risen from 20,110 sq. km in 1970 to 23,000 sq. km in 1975, 26,039 sq. km in 1980, 29,628 sq. km in 1985, and over 31,000 sq. km expected by 1990. The FELDA developments must also be seen against national aspirations as detailed in development plans. Thus in the Fourth Malaysia Plan (1981–5) 6075 sq. km were to be opened for rubber and 8470 sq. km for oil palm – during the same period FELDA was to develop 1500 sq. km.

Throughout Malaysia the lowland forest has been largely lost and has given way to lucrative plantations of industrial crops, but the problem of landless people below the poverty level still exists. Few alternative opportunities exist to the traditional occupations of fishing, growing rice and farming coconuts.

Sahabat Project, Dent Peninsula, Sabah About ten years ago FELDA was invited by the Sabah State Government to implement large-scale land development schemes in its eastern regions around Tawau and Lahad Datu. The largest, and one of the more recent schemes, is located at the eastern extremity of the Dent Peninsula, east of Lahad Datu, and is known as the Sahabat Project. It entails conversion of approximately 1030 sq. km of unpopulated forest into oil palm and other plantations, together with a number of townships, a port, and several farming industries served by a resident population of about 90,000.

The area intended for clearance in this project might be described as tropical rain forest, but it had undergone a number of logging cycles producing timber of ever-decreasing value, and had become a mosaic of secondary forest. About 40 per cent of the area had already been cleared when the World Bank was asked for support, and an initial assessment of the environmental impacts highlighted the impacts on, among others, freshwater and coastal ecosystems, and the effects of man on the survival, migration, and isolation of the forest wildlife, particularly the larger species, including elephant and Sumatran rhinoceros.

The project is expected to be agreed soon by the parties concerned and the Wildlands Policy of the World Bank (Ledec and Goodland, 1988) has allowed and encouraged considerable attention to be paid to the Tabin Wildlife Reserve, which is immediately west of the project area. Thus, a technical aid package is likely to be arranged that would provide a manager for the Tabin Wildlife Reserve, a technical adviser to the Sabah Wildlife Department, and funding for a Conservation Strategy for Sabah as has been produced for most of the other Malaysian states by WWF–Malaysia.

Settlement in Vietnam

The other major new settlement project in the Asia–Pacific region is in Vietnam, although information is not abundant. The account here is based on the work of Hill (1984) and Le Trong Cuc (1988).

The programme in Vietnam is directed at the rehabilitation of previously cultivated and abandoned areas, particularly in the south, where deforestation is very serious (see chapter 28). The settlement

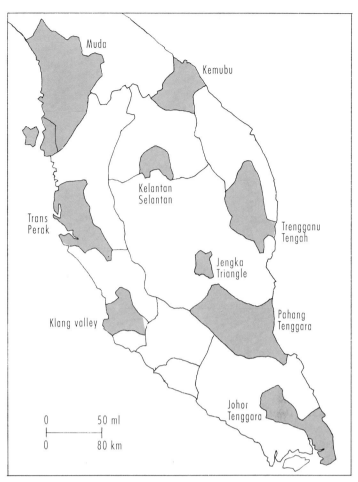

Figure 5.2 Regional development schemes in Peninsular Malaysia (*Source:* Ministry of Finance 1977 *in litt*)

areas or 'New Economic Zones' total about 7000 sq. km of cleared land and have been settled by some 1.47 million people between 1976 and 1980; this represents about 2.5 per cent of the population. The intention after 1980 was to maintain the rate of settlement. Indeed, the Five-Year Plan for 1981–7 planned the resettlement of 1–1.5 million people on a further 7000 sq. km of land by establishing about a hundred state farms for the cultivation of rice and other industrial crops.

Most of the settlers are ethnic Vietnamese (Kinh) from overpopulated areas in the Red River delta, coastal towns and crowded cities. They are given tax concessions and other advantages, and some are members of national minorities who have agreed to adopt settled agriculture instead of continuing damaging forms of shifting agriculture. The population density in the upland areas appears to be exceeding those previously experienced in those regions.

It seems that very little forest has been cleared, although there is a record of 40 sq. km of 'virgin land' being cleared in the Ha Tien district of Kien Gian Province and in An Giang, both near the southernmost border area with Cambodia, and of 530 sq. km in Binh Tri Thien near the south-east border with Laos. These areas have population densities of 100–200 people per sq. km (Le Trong Cuc, 1988). While it appears that the settlement has not led to large areas of forest being felled directly, there are indications that forest is being lost indirectly. For example, it seems that the emphasis on secondary food crops, notably cassava and maize has met urgent food needs, yet the harvest has deteriorated, the cleared land has been abandoned and neighbouring forest areas have been felled to compensate. It seems likely also that the presence of the settlers has exacerbated the problem of soil loss.

Conclusion

New agricultural settlement schemes have had an undeniably serious impact on the forests of several parts of Southeast Asia, and in many cases this could have been minimised if ecological principles had been applied at the planning stage. Nevertheless, the scale of deforestation caused by such schemes has often been exaggerated. Because the schemes are integrated across government sectors, and have a high profile, they receive more public attention than, for example, the expansion of the plantation industry. Unlike settlement schemes, plantations of oil palm and rubber continue to expand very rapidly and are likely to be major reasons for conversion of forest in Indonesia, in particular, in coming decades. Oil palm prices, while not stable, appear strong, and the world demand for rubber latex has increased of late.

With a growing population throughout the Asia–Pacific region, agricultural expansion is inevitable. Government-controlled schemes enable the processes to be regulated, but have at times been dogged by poor data on land-use potential and resulting inappropriate projects. Essential planning ingredients include rigorous application of ecological principles to minimise soil erosion and degradation, integration with protected area systems to ensure the conservation of biological resources, and attention to potential cultural conflicts. In this way the settlers will enjoy sustainable production from the land, and biological diversity will be maintained.

References

Anon. (1988a) Masalah sangat mendesak, mengatur transmigrasi swakarsa. *Kompas*, **9 May 1988**.

Anon. (1988) Riau forests proposed for elephant habitats. *Jakarta Post*, **26 November 1988**.

Anon. (1988) Sugiarto bolehkan transmigran Rumbia pindah. *Kompas*, **18 July 1988**.

Anon. (1988d) Penerbitan 34.376 sertifikat tanah transmigrasi di Kaltim tertunggak. *Suara Pembaruan*, **19 October 1988**.

Anon. (1988e) Presiden setujui pemutihan lahan transmigran. *Kompas*, **28 July 1988**.

Anon. (1989a) Transmigration budget up 20%. *Jakarta Post*, **13 January 1989**.

Anon. (1989b) Usaha sekunder akan dikembangkan di daerah transmigrasi. *Kompas*, **7 March 1989**.

Anon. (1989c) Pemerintah harapkan peran swasta untuk bantu program transmigrasi. *Kompas*, **15 March 1989**.

Burbridge, P. R., Norgaard, R. B. and Hartshorn, G. S. (1988) *Environmental Guidelines for Resettlement Projects in the Humid Tropics*. FAO Environment and Energy Paper 9, Rome, Italy.

Davidson, J. (1987) *Conservation planning in Indonesia's Transmigration Program: Case Studies from Kalimantan*. IUCN, Gland, Switzerland, and Cambridge, UK.

FAO/World Bank (1985) Working Paper No. 1. Indonesia Forestry Project, FAO/World Bank Cooperative Programme, Jakarta, Indonesia.

Gillis, M. (1988) Indonesia: public policies, resource management, and the tropical forest. In: *Public Policies and the Misuse of Forest Resources*. (eds) R. Repetto and M. Gillis. Cambridge University Press, Cambridge, UK. 432 pp.

Hanson, A. J. (1981) Transmigration and marginal land development. In: *Agricultural and Rural Development in Indonesia* Hansen, G. E. (ed.). Westview Press, Boulder, Colorado, USA.

Hill, R. D. (1984) Aspects of land development in Vietnam. *Contemporary Southeast Asia* 4: 389–402.

Ledec, G. and Goodland, R. (1988) *Wildlands: Their Protection and Management in Economic Development*. World Bank, Washington, DC, USA.

Le Trong Cuc (1988) *Agroforestry practices in Vietnam*. Working Paper No. 9, Environment and Policy Institute, East-West Center, Honolulu.

Poore, M. E. D. (1968) Studies in Malaysian rain forest. I. The forest on Triassic sediments in Jengka Forest Reserve. *Journal of Ecology* 56: 143–96.

Poore, D. and Sayer, J. (1987) *The Management of Tropical Moist Forest Lands: Ecological Guidelines*. IUCN, Gland, Switzerland. 63 pp.

RePPProT (1990) *National Overview of the Regional Physical Planning Programme for Transmigration*. Overseas Development Natural Resources Institute (ODA), Chatham, UK.

Ross, M. S. (1985) *A Review of Policies Affecting the Sustainable Development of Forest Lands in Indonesia*. International Institute for Environment and Development, London, UK.

Thohari, M., Haeruman, H., Alikodra, H., Whitten, A. J. and Kartikasari, S. N. (in press) *Pedoman Pembukaan Lahan Hutan Berwawasan Lingkungan*. Gadjah Mada University Press, Yogyakarta, Indonesia.

Whitten, A. J. (1988) Indonesia's Transmigration Program and its role in the loss of tropical rain forests. *Conservation Biology* 1: 239–46.

Whitten, A. J., Mustafa, M. and Henderson, G. S. (1987a) *The Ecology of Sulawesi*. Gadjah Mada University Press, Yogyakarta.

Whitten, A. J., Haeruman, H., Alikodra, H. and Thohari, M. (1987b) *Transmigration and the Environment in Indonesia: The Past, Present and Future*. IUCN, Cambridge, UK.

World Bank (1987) *The Jengka Triangle Projects in Malaysia: Impact Evaluation Report*. Operations Evaluation Department, World Bank, Washington, DC, USA.

World Bank (1988) *Indonesia: The Transmigration Program in Perspective*. World Bank, Washington, DC, USA.

Authorship

Anthony J. Whitten in Cambridge with contributions from Dinh Hiep of the Forest Department in Hanoi and Effendy Sumardja of the Forest Protection and Nature Conservation Department, Ministry of Forestry, Bogor, Indonesia.

6 Natural Rain Forest Management

Introduction

Southeast Asia[1] includes the tallest tropical rain forests of the world with the greatest timber volume, especially in western Malesia, where Dipterocarpaceae dominate. The number of dipterocarp genera and species decrease with distance from Borneo, but the commercial timber stocking is highest where comparatively few species dominate, as they do in the more seasonal climates towards the periphery of the region.

The very durable heavy construction timbers of certain types of *Shorea* (balau, selangan batu), together with *Neobalanocarpus heimii* (chengal) and some species of *Hopea* (giam), have always been in demand for local use within the region and in Hong Kong, but it is the light hardwoods of other species of *Shorea*, *Parashorea*, and *Pentacme* (meranti, lauan, seraya) which have been the basis of the lucrative export trade in logs, sawn timber and plywood from the region. The medium hardwoods of *Dipterocarpus* (keruing, apitong) and *Dryobalanops* (kapor) occupy an intermediate position. They are in demand for railway sleepers and for some constructional purposes but are too dense and sometimes too oily to make first-class sawmill and peeler logs (for planks or mouldings and veneers respectively).

Though current fellings in primary forest in Borneo may, over limited areas, yield more than 100 cu. m per ha, the regional average is about 45 cu. m per ha. There were stands in Negros Province in the Philippines which yielded, over limited areas, 450 cu. m per ha in the 1920s and 1930s, and on rich volcanic soils in Mindanao, Philippines, and in the Darvel Bay area of Sabah yields of over 270 cu. m per ha, mostly of *Parashorea*, were achieved in the 1950s and 1960s. East of Wallace's Line, which runs between Borneo and Sulawesi, very few dipterocarp species occur, but the timber stand may be almost entirely composed of a few species of *Anisoptera*, *Hopea*, and *Shorea*, and thus yield a very high volume of commercially valuable species.

Many of the forests of Irian Jaya and Papua New Guinea are almost entirely lacking dipterocarps, the timber stand varying widely from mixtures of *Dracontomelon*, *Intsia*, *Pometia* and *Vitex* to almost pure *Araucaria* in the hills and *Terminalia brassii* in the valley-bottom swamps of the Bismarck and Solomon Islands.

The forests of the region have developed over millennia, and unlogged forest may include trees which are several hundred years old. In this balanced ecosystem all the ecological niches have been filled by species through a long process of competition and adjustment. Much of the fertility is held within the mantle of forest rather than in the soil on which it grows, particularly in hill areas. It is not, therefore, to be expected that the forest, managed on a felling cycle of

35 years or so, will yield a harvest in each cycle as large as that produced by the initial felling of the unlogged forest. Conversely sites of low productivity may, in unlogged forest, show a stand with a relatively high timber volume, since that volume represents the accumulation of a very long period of growth, far longer than that envisaged in the felling cycles and rotations of a managed forest. In fact, the volume of the stand may have more to do with the longevity of the major species than with the productivity of the site. For all these reasons it is important to realise that sustained yield management of natural forests does not mean the harvesting of stands equivalent to those in the unlogged forest over an indefinite number of felling cycles, but rather the periodic harvesting of timber equal to the annual productive capacity of the site multiplied by the number of years in the cycle.

This annual productive capacity, based on the native species of the rain forest, is unlikely to exceed 1–2 cu. m per ha per year, compared with perhaps 30 cu. m per ha per year for closely spaced monocultures of fast-growing species. It may well be argued that under these circumstances it would be better to abandon the management of natural forest after the initial harvest of the virgin stand and replace it with plantations of fast-growing species. The arguments against such a policy are, of course, numerous, including the following:

1 Replacement of the natural forest with plantations of a few species destroys the genetic diversity of the forests.

2 Many forest sites are too steep to permit clear-fell-and-plant forest management on short rotations without severe damage.

3 The costs of clearing and planting are very high indeed compared with natural forest management.

4 There are great risks of pests and diseases in monocultures.

5 No really satisfactory fast-growing plantation species has yet been found for sites of low to moderate fertility in the region.

6 The sclerotic leaves of plantation species such as *Eucalyptus* and *Acacia mangium* decay slowly and can cause soil degradation.

7 A plantation crop is more market-specific and the time of harvest less flexible.

8 If it were decided to plant the better sites within the region and abandon the remaining forest after harvesting the virgin stand, the forest would undoubtedly be destroyed by illegal felling and cultivation, and its protective function as well as the habitat of vast numbers of animals and plants would be lost.

Management of Timber

The regeneration and management of tropical rain forest is based in most of the region on the light hardwood species of *Parashorea*, *Pentacme* and *Shorea* with low-density, pale reddish-brown timber (Burgess, 1975; Wyatt-Smith, 1963). These species are all fast

---

[1] The main focus of this chapter is on the dipterocarp-rich forests of Southeast Asia. Details of forest management in the rain forests of Australia and the monsoon forests of Burma are given in chapters 12 and 15 respectively.

growing when exposed to strong sunlight; they have winged fruits with a dispersal range of about 80 m from the parent tree with over 90 per cent of the seed falling within 60 m. The species fruit at the same time at intervals of up to five to seven years in the less seasonal parts of the region, but where there is a marked dry season, fruiting may take place every second year. Scattered fruiting of individuals may take place more frequently than this, but when it does the seed tends to be attacked by weevils on the tree and by foraging ants when it reaches the ground. Unless 'released' by undergrowth cutting or by tree-fellings, many of the seedlings die within the first two years and relatively few survive beyond three years. This means that if fruiting is long delayed the stock of seedlings may become very low in primary forest. Seedlings of these species respond very rapidly indeed to release and will survive for many years when they have reached half a metre tall without further release; when they have reached three metres or so in height they are very vulnerable to damage from felling operations.

The heavy hardwood species are all slow-growing shade bearers and will survive for many years in unopened forest. Some of them, e.g. *Neobalanocarpus heimii*, have wingless fruits, but one of the commonest, *Shorea laevis*, has winged fruits with a similar range of dispersal to the soft-wooded *Shorea* species mentioned above.

Successful sustained yield management of the forests will only be achieved if effective control is exercised over the following matters:
- Protection of the forest.
- Realistic assessment of annual cut.
- Orderly arrangement and demarcation of annual coupes (felling zones).
- Pre-felling inventory and allocation of silvicultural system.
- Marking of trees for retention or for felling.
- Exploitation of coupe to acceptable damage limits.
- Post-felling inventory.
- Check of harvest by species to prevent creaming (i.e. selection of only the most valuable timber).
- Silvicultural treatment of relic stand if necessary.
- Continuous forest inventory.
- Maintenance of main roads, control of erosion on spur roads and skid trails.

Different countries have adopted various management systems to achieve these objectives; some have been successful, others less so. The following review of each of the above points suggests where the major weaknesses lie.

Protection of the forest Protection of the forest is the basic requirement; it is useless to control logging operations if the worked coupes are then destroyed by shifting cultivators. The customary right to practise shifting cultivation and to take timber for domestic use is admitted in all the countries of the region, but in some, notably Peninsular Malaysia and Sabah, these activities have been controlled at an acceptable level. In all the Malaysian states the legal constitution of forest reserves by preliminary gazette notification, public enquiry, and final notification, carried out by the legislature, has been an essential step in the protection of the forests. India and Indonesia are similar in having a policy of reservation of forests for both productive and protective purposes, but in Indonesia the system lacks a strong legal base. Where forest lands are defined simply as the residual land left after alienation for other uses, as is the case in Thailand, Indonesia and the Philippines, both the public and the Government tend to take the protection of the forest lightly. The recent allocation of land by consensus at provincial level in Indonesia is a step in the right direction, but it seems doubtful whether forest so allocated will have the status of a definite forest reserve constituted by government. A public enquiry where rights within the forest may be claimed, and where they are then, if admitted, defined, is an essential

part of the reservation process, and after final notification the forest reserve is demarcated by a two-metre-wide cut line, notice plates and boundary stones at corners. As far as possible, of course, natural features such as rivers and ridges are used as boundaries.

It is essential when forest reserves are being established that enough forest land is left unreserved for the local people to practise their customary rights. In Sabah the practice has been to permit shifting cultivation outside forest reserves but to confine it to secondary forest by making it illegal to fell trees above a certain diameter limit. After forest reserves have been constituted and demarcated the boundaries must be patrolled and any encroachment firmly dealt with. In some countries, notably Indonesia and the Philippines, it is at this stage that forest protection becomes exceedingly difficult to enforce, partly because government has been unwilling to antagonise local communities by restricting shifting cultivation, partly because guerillas have taken the side of shifting cultivators against government, and partly because forestry departments have insufficient staff and resources to protect the forest and have tried to place the onus on concessionaires. It is clear that unless governments are prepared to give an unequivocal lead in the protection of forests, and forestry departments are given the resources and support to enable them to enforce protection by patrolling the areas, the future of sustained yield management is very bleak. While it is reasonable to expect concessionaires to assist in the patrol and protection of the forests it is utterly unrealistic to expect them to be solely responsible for it. The opportunities for exploiting concessions provides shifting cultivators and illegal timber workers with easy access to forests which in many cases they have never previously entered. It is essential, therefore, that concessionaires and the forest departments be given the legal authority to limit access along extraction roads.

The practice of making close-spaced plantations of industrial tree species in a band about one km wide along main logging roads within concessions has much to recommend it. The land so planted is the most valuable in the concession, due to its accessibility, and the existence of a barrier of cultivated trees has a deterrent effect on shifting cultivators. In addition, the making of such plantations provides an occupation and source of livelihood to many potential shifting cultivators.

Realistic assessment of the annual cut The control of the annual cut by both volume and area, and in some cases by volume alone, has been tried in some countries in the region. Volume control is desirable from the concessionaires' point of view since it means that in theory his volume output can remain constant; in practice, however, market conditions, weather, labour availability, plant breakdown and many other factors have an over-riding effect on the output of concessions. From government's point of view volume control has the great drawback that once logs have passed through scaling control there is no way of checking that they have been produced by a given coupe. In addition, there may be strong incentives to under-scale logs for export.

If the permitted annual cut in concessions is limited on an area basis alone, however, the cut-over area remains available for check by survey at any time, overcuts are immediately apparent by inspection of control maps, and there is no added temptation to under-scale logs for royalty assessment. Before the annual cut can be based on area it is essential that unproductive forest be mapped and scaled out of the total area of the concession. To do this, a topographical and vegetation map at a scale of at least 1:50,000 is necessary, and this can be made by air survey. In general dipterocarps run out at about 500 m above sea level, so all land above the 500 m contour should be disregarded as unproductive; any productive land above that limit will help to balance voids below it. Land steeper than 30°, or perhaps 35°, where work can be very carefully controlled, should also be regarded as unproductive if the forest is to be worked by tractor skidding. If cable yarding is possible and desirable (see page 46) the limit may be higher, perhaps 45°. Swamp and forest on poor soils should also be scaled out as permanently unproductive. Any areas of shifting cultivation and regrowth associated with it should also be deducted from the productive area, unless it proves possible to replant them. The annual coupe should then be defined as the productive area divided by the felling cycle, less a safety factor which should not be less than 20 per cent. The coupe will have to be revised each year to take account of forest where stand structure necessitates working on the Uniform System (see box on page 46).

Orderly arrangement and demarcation of annual coupes In most concession agreements the concessionaire selects his coupe each year and this is then approved (or not) by the Forestry Department. There is a tendency under these circumstances for blocks of desirable forest to be picked out for inclusion in coupes, leaving a matrix of unallocated forest. Unless operations have to be transformed for a good reason the Forestry Department should make sure that each year's coupe application is the same as the previous year's, the principle being that high profits from working good forest should be balanced by lower profits from poorer forest. If forest is found which is so poor as to be unworkable it should be bypassed only if it is deducted from the productive area of the concession and the coupe adjusted accordingly. Coupe boundaries must be demarcated with a 2 m wide cut line and paint marks, and surveyed so that the coupe becomes the permanent compartment for future management and is plotted on the control map.

Pre-felling inventory and allocation of silvicultural system With the exception of Sabah all countries in the region have now adopted Selection Fellings as general practice (Anon., 1980; Siapno, 1970; Thang, 1987; von der Heyde *et al.*, 1987; Weidelt and Banaag, 1982). Selection working is designed to conserve the trees of commercial species which are below the exploitation limit (Table 6.1) and, because of the increment which these trees represent, to reduce the felling cycle to approximately one-half of the rotation. If selection fellings are to proceed to perpetuity on short felling cycles, and the yield truly sustained, it is essential that the putative residual stand before each felling contains sufficient stems of commercial species between 20 cm dbh[1] and the minimum exploitable diameter, of good form, free from serious defects and with healthy crowns to provide a commercial felling at the end of the next cycle. The minimum number of such stems required is 25 per ha, and they must be well distributed. In Indonesia a simple minimum of 25 stems is prescribed (Anon., 1980), but in the Philippines percentages of groups of girth classes in the total stands are prescribed (Siapno, 1970). In Peninsular Malaysia a differential in size between dipterocarps and non-dipterocarps is prescribed in order to favour the former, and a procedure based on known growth rates is laid down to relate the residual stand to the length of the felling cycle, and to make up deficiencies between diameter classes (Thang, 1987). If the pre-felling inventory of the coupe reveals that insufficient potential residuals are present, then the coupe must be worked on the Uniform System with regeneration from seedlings and saplings, and the felling cycle extended to a full rotation. It is by no means certain that the majority of coupes will prove to be workable under the Selection System, so the pre-felling inventory is vital, and substantial reduction in the coupe may be necessary as a result. There has been a tendency in all countries where the Selection System has been adopted to double the coupe without ensuring that intermediate fellings will be sustainable, and firm action is required to correct the resultant overcutting.

[1] Centimetres of diameter at breast height. The standard measure of a timber tree.

Table 6.1 Cutting limits and felling cycles in the Asian region

	Silvicultural system	Cutting cycle (years)	Diameter limit (cm)[1]
Malaysia			
Peninsular	uniform	55–60	45
	selection	30	50 dipterocarps (45 non-dipterocarps)
Sabah	uniform	60	58
	selection	35	50
Sarawak	selection	25	48
Philippines	selection	30–45	retain: 70% of 15–65 cm class (40% of 65–75 cm class)
Papua New Guinea	selection	?	50
Indonesia	selection	35	50 but *Dyera* 60, *Agathis* 65

(*Source:* Burgess, in Poore *et al.*, 1989)

[1] Tree diameter at breast height, beneath which the tree may not be felled.

Marking of trees for retention or for felling Trees for retention should be marked with a continuous band of paint so that they can be seen from all directions, and be serially numbered. If reliable fallers are available it may not be necessary also to mark trees for felling, but if they are so marked they must be numbered above and below the felling line and hammer marked at least on the stump with all marks directly behind the prescribed line of fall, so that they are not covered by the fallen butt. Unless the stump carries all the felling marks it is impossible to check the fellings. Felling blocks should be small and only one gang of fallers should work in each block.

Exploitation of coupe to acceptable damage limits Directional felling will reduce damage to residuals, but not eliminate it. If the stand is of average stocking and the trees evenly distributed, about 25 per cent of the marked residuals must inevitably be damaged in fellings, but damage in excess of this should attract penalties. Trees should be felled as far as possible at acute angles to the skid trails to minimise damage to regeneration when pulling them out, and be skidded in tree lengths to reduce the number of passes along the skid trail. If selective felling is practised it will be necessary to skid by tractor or wheeled skidder unless exceptionally skilled operators under close supervision are continuously available, when high lead yarding may be permitted. These levels of skill are unlikely to be available outside the Philippines and Sabah. Under the Uniform System the use of high-lead yarding should generally be permitted, especially in steep country with heavy stands. Skyline working will reduce the amount of road building and the amount of damage to the environment.

Post-felling inventory This is essential in order to control the amount of logging damage and to check that an adequate residual stand has survived. The inventory should also record whether any of the marked residuals will require release by girdling or liberation fellings, and a sub-sample may also usefully record whether there is adequate young regenerative growth. In practice post-felling inventories, though prescribed, are frequently not carried out and much closer control over them is necessary throughout the region.

SILVICULTURAL SYSTEMS, MANAGEMENT SYSTEMS AND LOGGING METHODS

Two main silvicultural systems have been used in the Asia–Pacific region for the regeneration of rain forests rich in Dipterocarpaceae; the monocyclic Uniform System and the polycyclic Selection System. Under the Uniform System there is a uniform opening of the canopy over whole compartments at a time (compartments are units of forest which vary in size from 80 ha or less up to 1000–2000 ha), and there may be one or several openings to induce, release, and finally harvest the regenerated stand. By contrast, under the ideal Selection System as originally practised in Europe, single trees or small groups of trees scattered throughout the forest were felled and removed. In the extensive tropical forests of Southeast Asia selection fellings take place in compartments, which are opened up at intervals corresponding to the felling cycle; this is referred to by Troup (1952) as the Periodic Selection Systems.

The Uniform System with its uniform canopy opening clearly favours species which grow quickly when exposed to strong sunlight (fast-growing light demanders), of the light hardwood meranti group, while tending to shade out the heavy hardwoods such as bangkirai (*Shorea*) and merbau (*Intsia*). The Malayan Uniform System (MUS), developed in the 1960s and 1970s and described in detail by Wyatt-Smith (1963) and Nicholson (1979), proved extremely successful for the regeneration of the meranti forest. Unfortunately the MUS requires the establishment of young regeneration before fellings begin, and also relies on seedling regeneration – this means that a rotation cycle of some 60 to 70 years is necessary. The development of large-scale mechanical logging, however, with heavy capital investment, has meant that it is no longer practicable to wait for the infrequent and unpredictable seed years and established regeneration before fellings are opened; considerations other than silviculture have dominated the opening of forests to exploitation so that in recent decades the forestry departments have lost control over the timing of fellings.

The Selection System of felling, on the other hand, has been seen by almost all countries in the region as the ideal solution. In this system regeneration is derived not from an ephemeral crop of seedlings entirely dependent on the incidence of one or at most two seed years, but from a mixture of advanced growth derived from many such seed years and varying in size from saplings, to poles, to trees just below exploitable size. This system is best suited to solving the problem of regenerating mixed dipterocarp forest under large-scale mechanical logging, where the timing of fellings cannot be left to the silviculturist alone. In addition it soon became clear that since most of the regeneration was to be from trees of pole size and larger, rather than from seedlings, it would be possible to reduce the felling cycle from that of a rotation (of say

60 to 70 years) to about 30 years and thus double the area which could be opened to fellings each year. There is one proviso, however – if this ambition is to be realised, it is essential that the forest contains an adequate stock of pole-sized and larger trees, of commercial species, healthy and of good form before selection fellings are opened, and that those trees will survive the fellings undamaged and put on adequate increment after release by the felling. There is increasing doubt whether the majority of forests in fact carry an adequate stock of such trees before felling; where they do not, and selection fellings are permitted, there will be a progressive deterioration in the forest, and it will prove to have been heavily overcut.

Some confusion has arisen from the title of the Selective Management System used in Peninsular Malaysia. This use of the word 'selective' has nothing to do with selection fellings, but means that a silvicultural system is selected based on a pre-felling inventory in each compartment, and the system so chosen may be the Malayan Uniform System, the Selection System, or clear felling and planting.

Logging terminology In the Asia–Pacific region many logging terms are used which originated on the west coast of America and came via American logging companies operating in the Philippines (Nicholson, 1970). Thus, the extraction of logs from stump to a 'landing' or log dump where they are loaded on to road or rail, is known as 'yarding'. In theory yarding should be applied only where cable logging systems are used, and hauling by tractor should be called 'skidding'. Cable logging systems, where either a spar tree or a portable steel spar is used, consist first of 'high-lead yarding', where the logs are hauled to the base of the spar by a donkey engine or yarder with a wire cable passing over a block at the top of the spar so that the forward end of the log is raised to clear obstructions. In very rough country where road building is expensive, two or more spars are connected by a sky-line on which a carriage runs so that logs may be swung from one spar to the next, each spar also functioning as a high-lead unit. Tractor yarding causes more disturbance to the ground surface than does cable yarding, since skid trails have to be bulldozed to connect the tree stump to the landing. On the other hand tractor yarding generally causes less damage to the residual stand than does cable yarding. It follows that in general cable yarding is preferable where the Uniform System of silviculture is in use, and tractor yarding is better where Selection fellings are practised. In the Philippines, where very skilled cable yarding crews exist, Selection fellings with cable yarding are satisfactory, so long as the horse-power of the yarder is limited to about 150.

Check of coupe harvest by species The 'creaming' of coupes by removal of only the most profitable species and log grades is widespread, particularly where timber is removed by rafting down rivers – the species that are too dense to float ('sinkers') are left unfelled. In Borneo, and some other parts of the region, sinker species tend to occur together, often on ridge crests; *Shorea laevis* (bangkirai, and balaukuus) is an example. Where this is the case and exploitation involves rafting it may well be uneconomic to remove all the sinkers and in such cases there can be little objection from the conservation point of view to the by-passing of the whole area of sinkers so long as scattered logging within it for floaters is not permitted and the coupe is controlled by area and reduced accordingly to allow for the fact that

sinker forest has been allowed to remain unproductive. The by-passed forest provides a valuable haven for wildlife, particularly gibbons, and many plant species are conserved.

Creaming may also occur where sinkers and other less valuable species are scattered throughout the forest, and wherever unsound and poorly formed trees occur. To allow such trees to remain unworked results in a progressive deterioration of the stand at each logging and also in enhanced consumption of coupe area. The principle that the high profits from exploiting valuable species should offset the lower profits from logging less valuable species must be accepted. There must also be a list of obligatory species and grades which should include at least *Shorea* spp. (red, white, and yellow meranti, lauan, seraya, melapi), *Pentacme* spp. (lauan), *Parashorea* spp. (white seraya, bagtikan), *Anisoptera* spp., *Shorea laevis* (where scattered), *Dipterocarpus* spp., *Dryobalanops* spp., *Intsia palembanica*, *Agathis* spp. and *Podocarpus* spp., and perhaps *Dyera costulata* (also useful for jelutong, see below), and the coupe harvest must be checked periodically to see that the ratio between species is roughly the same as was recorded in the pre-felling inventory. The necessity for pre-felling inventories to be checked by the Forest Department in the field will be self-evident.

Silvicultural treatment of relic stand The post-felling inventory will show whether any of the marked residuals require release. If they do, the competing trees should be girdled with an appropriate arboricide (so-called 'liberation thinning'). In order to preserve the gene pool and to reduce costs it is most important that girdling be only carried out where it is really necessary; in many cases under present conditions the exploitation operation provides all the opening that is necessary or desirable. Where fellings are under the Uniform System the seedling regeneration may require release by improvement fellings or girdlings more than once during the rotation. Techniques for linear sampling to determine regeneration stocking and the necessity for its release have been well developed in Malaysia.

Continuous forest inventory (CFI) It is essential that the development of the residual stand be monitored by continuous forest inventory plots. In spite of the 80 years or so during which forest research has been conducted in the dipterocarp forests of the region, we have surprisingly little data on the growth of regenerated stands, and a rough figure of one centimetre diameter growth per year has been adopted in several countries as a basis for selection management. More information is required by different species, for varying degrees of dominance, for different soils and climatic types, for stages in the rotation, and for volume as opposed to diameter growth. Plots should be rectangular, one hectare in extent and there should be about 100 in each major forest type. The plots should be laid down by random means in the forest before exploitation, and be then treated exactly the same as the rest of the coupe, but with the yield of the plot being recorded separately. All trees of 5 cm dbh (not just dipterocarps) must be measured, and measurements should take place every five years. All measured trees must be properly identified to species and herbarium collections should support the identifications. A large number of CFI plots were established in the Philippines in the 1970s, but re-measurement was suspended in 1981. This was largely because the programme was too ambitious for the resources available, and it is necessary that due regard be given to this before any new programme is initiated.

Maintenance of main roads, erosion control on subsidiary roads Main roads are required for management and silvicultural purposes, and must be maintained so as to be passable by a four-wheel drive vehicle. Deep erosion gullies can form very rapidly on abandoned spurs and skid trails, and they must be plugged and drainage corrected before they become serious. Gullies are particularly liable to develop on granitic rocks. The possibility of seeding abandoned roads with grass or ground cover plants in a bitumen emulsion should be considered. (See also box on page 48, Table 6.1 and Figure 6.1).

Management of Secondary Forest Products

Secondary (i.e. non-timber, or minor) forest products are of great importance to the people who live in or near the forest, and rattan in particular has become increasingly important in world trade. The secondary products of tropical rain forest are legion and include gums and resins, bush meat, rattan, tanbark, illipe nuts, oleo-resin, edible birds' nests, bamboo, roofing materials, incense wood, pan-

Table 6.2 Suspended sediment load of some major rivers in Peninsular Malaysia

River	Drainage area sq. km	Suspended load cu. m/sq. km/year	Data source
KEDAH:			
Sg Muda at Titi Syed Omar	2,069	74	A
PERAK:			
Sg Ijok at Kg Titi	215	107	A
Sg Parit at Ipoh	272	3,767	A
Sg Kinta at Ipoh	313	260	A
Sg Bidor at m/s 18	344	428	A
Sg Perak at Iskander Bridge	7,770	40	A
Sg Perak at Temenggor	34,000	88	B
Sg Perak at Bersia	3,600	88	B
Sg Perak at Kenering	5,500	144	B
SELANGOR:			
Sg Klang at Puchong	712	3,810	A
Sg Langat at Dengkil	1,238	811	A
Sg Selangor at Rantau Panjang	1,450	1,332	A
KUALA LUMPUR:			
Sg Gombak	140	67	B
JOHOR:			
Sg Muar at Buloh Kasap	3,134	49	A
Sg Lenggor at m/s 42	207	791	A
PAHANG:			
Sg Kuantan at Bt Kerau	583	214	A
Sg Kial, Cameron Highlands	21	111	B
Sg Bertam, Cameron Highlands	73	103	B
Sg Telom, Cameron Highlands	77	21	B
TERENGGANU:			
Sg Cherul at Ban Ho	505	31	A

Sources of data:
A Soong (1980) suspended sediment load converted from ton/sq. km/year to cu. m/sq. km/year, assuming a bulk density of 1.33 g/sq. cm.
B Douglas (1970)
Abbreviations:
Sg = Sungei, river
Kg = Kampong, village
Bt = Bukit, hill
m/s = milestone

golin scales, honey, beeswax, palm wood, and many other products. Only the first three of these are generally of major importance, though the periodic harvest of illipe nuts in Borneo is very important indeed in restricted areas.

Gums and resins The most important gum is the latex of *Dyera costulata* and *D. lowii*, locally called jelutong and exported for the manufacture of chewing gum. *D. costulata* is a very large tree occurring in the lowland rain forest, while. *D. lowii* is confined to peat swamp and is much smaller. In many timber concessions in Indonesia jelutong is a prohibited species, but in Malaysia its felling is permitted when it occurs in felling coupes. The timber is used for making pencils and for foundry patterns. It is often unlikely that isolated jelutong trees left in a matrix of logged-over forest will ever be located and tapped, but their retention adds to the diversity of the forest. Their cutting adds little to the timber output and may occasionally remove one more item of potential income from the people who live near the forest. On balance, therefore, there appears to be a reasonable case for prohibiting the felling of jelutong, and this is strengthened where the forest is worked on a selection system; the trees can always be cut in the next cycle if they are not being tapped. If jelutong trees are to be tapped on any but a very short-term basis constant supervision by the Forestry Department is required to prevent the tapping panel being damaged by careless and over-deep tapping, which leads to termite attack and the death of the tree.

The resin known as 'copal' (almaciga in the Philippines, damar Pontianak in Indonesia) is produced by the coniferous trees *Agathis* spp., which occur throughout the region (Tongacan and Ordinario, 1974). The resin is used in the manufacture of paints and varnish and exports from the Philippines amount to about 800,000 kg per year with a value of about US$0.50 per kg. *Agathis* timber is in great demand in both local and export markets, but its felling is prohibited in the Philippines; in Malaysia and Indonesia it may be cut when it occurs in coupes. Unless tapping of *Agathis* is strictly controlled the tree is so damaged that rot develops and it dies or breaks off at the tapping panel; studies in the Philippines have shown that it is rarely possible to control tapping sufficiently well to prevent this happening. *Agathis* is not an easy tree to regenerate, and intermediate sized trees are usually conspicuously lacking; the trees are scattered but may be concentrated in groves in heath forest (kerangas) on white sand, limestone, ultrabasic or volcanic soil. There seems to be little point in sacrificing the timber value of *Agathis* if the trees are then destroyed by tapping, but a reasonable compromise would be to enforce a strict minimum tapping limit, perhaps restricting tapping to trees of 45 cm dbh, and permit felling of *Agathis* over perhaps 75 cm dbh in coupes. Forest Department inspection of tapping is essential if the trees are to remain productive. Dipterocarp resins are confined to the produce of *Shorea* spp., the fallen damar being dug up from below big trees. No special measures are needed to control the work. However, recent research has demonstrated the potential for tapping dipterocarp trees for damar production (see case study opposite).

Bush meat In Southeast Asia, bush meat is normally derived from wild boar *Sus scrofa*, bearded pig, sambar deer, barking deer, mouse deer, and wild cattle (gaur and banteng). Both species of pig are common in logged-over forest, though the bearded pig occurs commonly also in primary forest, where it migrates locally to follow the fruiting of dipterocarps, oaks and chestnuts. The sambar deer is also found in logged-over forest, but its main habitat is the margins of primary forest especially where there are salt licks. Both the barking deer and the mouse deer are common in logged-over forest, where they are frequently hunted with a spotlight at night. Banteng, and the Malayan gaur (known as seladang), are associated with secondary forest from shifting cultivation and move into logged-over forest to browse on the lush regrowth along tractor paths; they also migrate towards salt licks. In general, logging appears to improve the habitat of pig, deer, and wild cattle (see also the effect of shifting cultivation, chapter 4), but it also makes it very much easier to hunt them. Control over access to forest roads is an essential pre-requisite to game preservation (see Hunting in Sarawak on page 50).

Rattan The current fashion for rattan furniture, not only in the region but in the rest of the developed world, has led to a vast increase in the trade in these canes. In the Philippines, for example, no rattan, or almost none, was exported up to 1972, but from 1973 exports averaged some 2.2 million kg per year, which fell sharply in 1977 to 154,000 kg and since 1989 has been almost nil. The fall in rattan exports was caused partly by exhaustion of accessible supplies, but also by the great expansion of the local manufacture of knock-down (i.e. self-assembly) furniture for export.

Indonesia has imposed increasingly strict regulations on the export of unmanufactured rattan and from 1989 exports were entirely forbidden except as finished products. Most countries had made up their shortfall in rattan by imports from Indonesia, so the ban will result in increasing pressure on the rest of the forests in the region.

The principal canes in demand are from *Calamus manan*, the best source being the large-diameter rotan manau, and *C. subinermis* from Sabah, also used for furniture. *C. caesius* (rotan sega) and *C. trachycoleus* (rotan irit) are smaller rattans used for tying, and are frequently split. These smaller rattans have been successfully cultivated in both Sabah and Kalimantan, and it takes about ten years to produce an acceptable yield. The rotation for growing rotan manau is not yet known. All rattans, after an initial rosette stage, produce a stem of full diameter which thereafter grows only in length. In

DEGRADATION OF SOIL AND WATER RESOURCES FOLLOWING LOGGING IN PENINSULAR MALAYSIA

The worst environmental impacts of logging and deforestation are the degradation of soil and water resources. The impacts of logging are particularly severe in steep terrain, such as in the hill dipterocarp forests of Peninsular Malaysia, where the most damaging activities are road building and extraction by skidding using crawler tractors. Logging is helped in this terrain by easy log transportation using the *san tai wong*, which is an all-purpose winch lorry that can engage steep gradients. Burgess (1973) estimates that 6.6 km of road are constructed to exploit every sq. km of forest, giving an actual road surface of 6.25 ha per sq. km or 6.25 per cent of the land area. The damaged land area is increased further to 12 per cent by spoil from earth cuttings which erodes land along the roadside and destroys vegetation.

Logging roads are neglected after logging is completed. Erosion, however, will persist for some time. Burgess (1971) reported erosion gullies alongside logging roads which were deeper than a man's height. In Kelantan, he had noticed an erosion gully over four metres deep. Erosional hazards are even greater when deforestation occurs. The erosion map produced by Morgan (1974) for Peninsular Malaysia based on rainfall characteristics shows that the eastern and central highland areas have high erosion risk (Figure 6.1). Most of the major land development schemes, such as the Jengka Triangle, Pahang Tenggara and Johor Tenggara, are located in areas of high erosion risk.

The impact of forest clearing is reflected in the suspended sediment load of rivers draining areas which have different land cover or land use types (Table 6.2). High sediment loads occur in rivers draining mining areas (Sungei Parit, Sungei Klang, Sungei Langat, Sungei Selangor). In the Cameron Highlands, the sus-Highlands, the suspended sediment loads recorded in predominantly agricultural river basins (Kial and Bertam) were five times greater than that of the Sungei Telom, 94 per cent of whose catchment was covered by natural forest. Erosion in the upper reaches of a river basin results in increased silting and flooding in the lower reaches. A state-by-state compilation of flood events by the Malaysian Drainage and Irrigation Department from 1925 to 1979 showed relatively fewer flood events in the earlier years (before 1950s), before the pace of development had quickened.

RESEARCH ON DAMAR PRODUCTION IN SUMATRA

Some 20 different dipterocarp species are known to have potentially valuable resins, but only one is currently being systematically exploited. In the southern Sumatra province of Lampung, villagers tap cultivated stands of *Shorea javanica* for damar. This resin is used as an excellent varnish for fine art. Durable, clear and strong, yet easily removable, damar is considered superior to synthetic alternatives. As a result, there is a steady market for the substance in overseas markets, particularly Europe.

Villagers in some parts of Lampung earn about US$1000 per ha each year from tapping damar. This is about one-quarter of the potential value of the trees if exploited for timber. The timber value, however, is essentially one-off, whereas it is estimated that the damar can be tapped for 15–20 years. Other dipterocarp trees may prove to have even more valuable resins. Some, for example, have insecticidal properties that could possibly be exploited commercially.

(*Source:* Adam Messer (pers. comm.) and Goldstein, 1989)

Collecting damar, the resin of dipterocarp trees, in Kalimantan. A. Messer

primary forests rattans 100 metres long are not uncommon, but *C. trachycoleus* grows only about three to four metres per year.

The prospects for management of rattan are undoubtedly better under Selection Management than they would be under the Uniform System, since they require a forest matrix in which to climb. If rattan is to be harvested this must be done before logging commences, and combined with climber cutting this will also reduce damage to the residual stand by falling trees. Planting of rattan along skid trails, where the canopy opening will encourage them to climb, should provide a good harvest before the end of the next felling cycle.

Prospects for the Future

Burgess (in Poore *et al.*, 1989) carried out a survey of the logging practices in Asian members of the International Tropical Timber Organisation (Indonesia, Malaysia, Papua New Guinea, the Philippines and Thailand). He found that planning and controls towards sustained yield management were in place in all but Papua New Guinea (where the land tenure system makes this impossible), but the management tended to be inadequate. The most serious shortcomings were:

- Failure to protect the production forests before and after working (Sarawak, Thailand, Philippines, parts of Indonesia).
- Poor control of erosion damage to roads (except in Thailand, where elephants are used and rainfall is light).
- Post-felling silviculture is taken seriously only in Peninsular Malaysia.
- Re-logging between cycles has taken place in Peninsular Malaysia and the Philippines, and there is pressure to do so in Sabah.

A number of states and countries are taking action to improve these matters, but there is little doubt that in many cases political influences make it difficult (or impossible) for forestry departments to enforce concession agreements and raise the standard of management. Funding of most forest departments in the region is adequate, but all too often forest staff in the field depend on concessionaires for housing and transport, and senior forest department officials are outmanoeuvred by politicians in positions of influence in logging companies. Obviously it is essential that such political influences be removed, and the independence of the forest department strengthened, if forest management is to improve. Peninsular Malaysia has taken the important step of forming a National Forestry Council, chaired by the Deputy Prime Minister, to coordinate forestry policy and practice.

Figure 6.1 Risk of erosion in Peninsular Malaysia (from Morgan, 1974), showing the location of three Regional Development Schemes from unpublished data of the Ministry of Finance, 1977.

(The full range of Regional Development Schemes is shown in chapter 5, Figure 5.2).

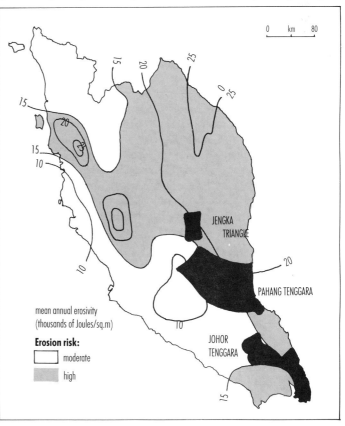

HUNTING AND WILDLIFE MANAGEMENT IN SARAWAK

Hunting is of great economic, nutritional, cultural and recreational significance in Sarawak, as a project funded by WWF–Malaysia recently showed. Rural people, in particular, benefit from the game-rich forests. In the interior of Sarawak there is one shotgun per two families, one blowpipe among four, and two hunting dogs and spears for every family. There are 60,000 legal shotguns in Sarawak and virtually any vertebrate is liable to be shot and eaten. Between 60 per cent and 90 per cent of kills are ungulates – either deer or wild pigs, with the latter being more important.

Caldecott (1988) estimates that between 9400 and 26,500 tonnes, perhaps 18,000 tonnes, of wild meat are harvested annually in Sarawak, amounting to 12 kg per person per year or 0.2 kg per sq. km of forest per year; the value of hunting to forest people throughout the region is thus very considerable.

Caldecott made proposals for improved management of hunting in Sarawak, and these are relevant to the rest of the region. They include, amongst many other matters, the gazettement and protection of wildlife reserves, the protection of salt licks, the appointment of paid wildlife protection staff from rural communities, the overall control of shotgun cartridge supply, regulation of trade in wild meat, and protection of trees which provide food for wildlife in logging areas.

The extension of logging throughout Sarawak has brought great pressure on some forms of wildlife, through habitat destruction and over-hunting by loggers and outsiders coming in along logged roads. The net effect for local residents in logged-over areas is a sharp decline in annual wild meat harvests, from 54 kg per person before logging to only 28 kg within ten years. Oil pollution and siltation of rivers result in declining fish stocks, compounding the problem.

Source: Caldecott, 1988

Past timber production has resulted largely from the alienation of conversion forests destined for agriculture. Such extraction is not sustainable, and is not intended to be so. Log exports will continue their present decline as alienable land becomes converted (the peak was 39.1 million cu. m in 1973) and should then, in theory, level out to a sustained yield from the region's permanent production forests.

Burgess (in Poore *et al.*, 1989) estimated what these sustainable yields might be for Malaysia, the Philippines and Indonesia, and compared them with recent productivity. Malaysian production is still high, as high-yield primary forests continue to be exploited in Borneo and conversion forests are alienated; Philippine production is low, possibly because the forest estate is largely degraded; and Indonesian production is low either because of over-estimation of the extent of productive forest or because there is scope for expansion of logging.

The techniques of regenerating and managing tropical moist forests in the region on a sustained-yield basis are now well enough understood for continuous production from permanent forest estates. Governments create conditions in which this knowledge may be applied by preventing illegal clearing (the main problem in Thailand, the Philippines, Sarawak and Indonesia); illegal logging (common in Thailand and the Philippines); exploitation of forest in excess of sustainable cut (Selection System) or when regenerative potential is weak (Uniform System); and over-riding of professional forestry advice for political or pecuniary advantage.

These actions require great government resolve and their introduction will require public support based on education programmes, and international assistance to improve the standards of living of rural people and to relieve the burden of international debts.

References

Anon. (1980) *Pedoman Tebang Pileh Indonesia. (A Guide to the Indonesian Selective System.)* Directorate General of Forestry, Jakarta, Indonesia.

Burgess, P. F. (1971) The effect of logging on hill dipterocarp forests. *Malay Nature Journal* **24**: 231–7.

Burgess, P. F. (1973) The impact of commercial forestry on hill forests of Malay Peninsula. *Proceedings of a Symposium on Biological Research and National Development*, pp. 131–6.

Burgess, P. F. (1975) *Silviculture in the Hill Forests of the Malay Peninsula.* Forestry Department, Kuala Lumpur, Malaysia.

Caldecott, J. O. (1988) *Hunting and Wildlife Management in Sarawak.* IUCN, Switzerland, and Cambridge, UK. 172 pp.

Douglas, I. (1970) Measurements of river erosion in West Malaysia. *Malay Nature Journal* **23**: 78–83.

Goldstein, C. (1989) The planters are back. *Far Eastern Economic Review* **13 April**: 51.

Morgan, R. P. C. (1974) Estimating regional variations in soil erosion hazard in Pen. Malaysia. *Malay Nature Journal* **28**: 94–106.

Nicholson, D. I. (1970) *Demonstration and Training in Forest, Forest Range, and Watershed Management: the Philippines.* F.O.: S.F./PHI 16 Technical Report 3, FAO, Rome, Italy.

Nicholson, D. I. (1979) *The Effects of Logging and Treatment on the Mixed Dipterocarp Forests of South-east Asia.* F.O. Misc/79/8. FAO, Rome, Italy.

Poore, D., Burgess, P., Palmer, J., Rietbergen, S. and Synott, T. (1989) *No Timber without Trees: Sustainability in the Tropical Forest.* Earthscan, London, UK.

Siapno, I. B. (1970) *Handbook of Selective Logging.* Bureau of Forest Development, Manila, The Philippines.

Soong, N. K., Haridass, G., Yeoh, C. S. and Tan, P. H. (1980) *Soil Erosion and Conservation in Malaysia.* FRIM. 64 pp.

Thang, H. C. (1987) *Selective Management System: Concept and Practice (Peninsular Malaysia).* Forestry Dept, Kuala Lumpur.

Tongacan, A. L. and Ordinario, F. F. (1974) Tapping of Almaciga resin. *Philippine Lumberman* **December 1974**: 18–22.

Troup, R. S. (1952) *Silvicultural Systems.* The Clarendon Press, Oxford, UK.

von der Heyde, B. *et al.* (1987) *T.S.I. (Timber Stand Improvement) Field Manual.* Bureau of Forest Development, Manila/German Agency for Technical Co-operation, Eschborn, West Germany.

Weidelt, H. J. and Banaag, V. S. (1982) *Aspects of Management and Silviculture of Philippine Dipterocarp Forests.* German Agency for Technical Co-operation, Eschborn, West Germany.

Wyatt-Smith, J. (1963) *Manual of Malayan Silviculture for Inland Forests.* Malayan Forest Record No. 23. Forest Department, Malaya, Kuala Lumpur, Malaysia.

Authorship

Peter Burgess in Laxfield, England, with contributions from Mok Sian Tuan of the ASEAN Institute of Forest Management, Reidar Persson of the Swedish International Development Agency in Stockholm, Eberhardt Bruenig of the World Forestry Institute in Hamburg and Lee Hua Seng of the Forest Department in Kuching.

7 Tropical Timber Trade

Introduction

The Asia–Pacific timber trade was analysed recently in a detailed report by Nectoux and Kuroda (1989), on which this chapter is based. Standard definitions of commodities described are given in the box on page 55.

Since the early 1970s the Southeast Asia–Pacific region has been the main source of the tropical timber trade – taking over from Africa, which supplied considerable quantities of logs to Western Europe during the 1950s and early 1960s (Nectoux and Dudley, 1987). In the mid-1980s, 83 per cent of tropical timber traded on the world market originated in the Southeast Asia–Pacific region. Three factors account for this:

1 The existence of dense forests throughout the region, comprising tree species with homogeneous characteristics, particularly the Dipterocarpaceae found in west Malesian lowland evergreen rain forests. These trees provide high-quality timber – traditionally, the best were traded as mahoganies in the USA, although they are unrelated to the true mahoganies (Meliaceae) of the Americas. Most are now used for utility grade lumber or plywood.

2 The development of a considerable market for tropical logs during the late 1950s and early 1960s. With the adoption and promotion of plywood as a basic construction material, firstly on the west coast of the USA and later in Japan, more and more cheap, tropical timber was required. During the 1950s, plywood production, largely for export to the USA, became especially important in Japan (Handa, 1988). Japan's domestic tropical plywood market grew at such a rate that the volume of Southeast Asian log imports increased sevenfold, reaching 23 million cu. m per annum.

3 Various Southeast Asian countries have promoted large-scale logging and exports of unprocessed timber. Local governments have permitted these actions for more than two decades now, imposing few restrictions.

Recent Developments

There has been a long tradition of timber exports from the Philippines, Thailand, Burma, Peninsular Malaysia and India to distant markets, as far apart as China, the Arabic countries, and Western Europe (the 'precious woods' of the Middle Ages, for instance). At a later stage trade in finished products – such as the ships built in Southeast Asia for Europe – developed. These were restricted to high-quality timber and a very narrow range of species (principally teak) from Burma and Thailand.

In the 1950s, foreign trading companies started organising large-scale exports of hardwood logs. The so-called 'logging booms' began with the onset of heavily mechanised extractive operations, largely financed by multinational companies. Some of these companies were based in the USA (most notably those which already had forestry and timber processing interests, such as Weyerhauser and Georgia Pacific). Others were based in Europe and included a large number of old colonial companies, originally involved in general trade and plantations, such as the UK-based Harrison and Crosfield, and Inchcape. Family-controlled interests such as Meyer and Mallison were also present. More recently, Japanese companies have occupied the market. Japanese timber operations tend to be organised through a general trading company (known as a *sogo shosha*). Sumitomo, Mitsui, and C. Itoh are some of the best-known (Nectoux and Dudley, 1987; Nectoux and Kuroda, 1989).

Logging booms occurred first in the Philippines in the 1950s, then in Peninsular Malaysia, and in Sabah in the 1960s. In the early 1970s the level of Indonesian exports increased rapidly. These were followed in the late 1970s by exports from Sarawak and Papua New Guinea, when old suppliers faded away due to declining timber resources. Exports from the Philippines to Japan, for example, reached a peak of 8 million cu. m in 1969, then fell to around 1 million cu. m in the early 1980s.

In most cases, sudden increases in logging and export activities resulted from a combination of incentives (tax concession licensing, low royalties, low export duties, favourable taxation systems, etc) provided by a sympathetic local government, and large-scale capital investments made by foreign companies. Thus in the Philippines, in the early 1950s, US army surplus lorries were used to shift logs out of the forests, especially those of Mindanao and other islands in the south of the archipelago. (The northern islands, such as Luzon, were exploited later.) In 1966, the new government of Indonesia invited foreign companies to log its forests and encouraged capital investment, especially from the USA. Prior to this, a Japanese report in 1961 had promoted the joint planning of the exploitation of Kalimantan's forests by Japanese trading companies and the Japanese and Indonesian governments, with funding made available partly by Japanese aid. Accordingly, Mitsui started logging in 1963, with many other companies following suit. At one stage, Sumitomo controlled 20 timber concerns. The Japanese government assisted Japanese corporations by channelling aid funds for surveys and road building to them, and by providing cheap official aid loans.

South Korea and Taiwan, and to a lesser extent Singapore, soon joined Japan as major processors of Southeast Asian rain forest logs. In the late 1960s South Korea supplanted Japan as the major supplier of tropical plywood to the USA, and was then itself replaced by Indonesia in the early 1980s.

Changes in the way in which the tropical timber trade operates started to occur in several countries in the late 1970s. The economic slump which followed the 1973 oil crisis meant that a number of countries modified their policies on commodity exports and foreign investment. In Sabah, the authorities attempted to extract a higher proportion of the considerable profits made by the timber trade, by greatly increasing the level of payments made by the concessionaires to the Government.

In Indonesia, government policies in the late 1970s sought to reduce the preponderance of foreign interests in the export process. Foreign firms were criticised for disregarding original agreements concerning local processing and also for engaging in transfer pricing and illegal exporting. Stricter regulations came into force requiring domestic processing of logs and the participation of local capital in joint ventures. A number of logging licences held by foreign interests were revoked. Many US and Japanese firms simply sold their share in local companies to their Indonesian partners. Then in 1986 a total ban on log exports was introduced and a large-scale plywood trade with North America and Europe established instead. Countries such as South Korea and Taiwan lost their dominant plywood exporting positions as a result. All concessions in Indonesia are now held by nationals (although joint ventures can use the logs extracted by the local partner). More recently, the Indonesian authorities decreed a ban on exports of low-value sawn timber (Gillis, 1988; Repetto and Gillis, 1988).

In the Philippines, the change of government in 1986 led to an effective ban on all log exports, something that the previous administration had been unable to implement. Also in Peninsular Malaysia, log exports are now so severely restricted that they are in effect non-existent. However, in Sabah and Sarawak, as well as in Papua New Guinea (where a White Paper in 1979 gave a new impetus to log exports), the majority of forest products exported still consists of unprocessed timber.

Asia–Pacific Region and the World Tropical Timber Trade

In the more densely populated, drier areas of the tropics, most of the wood extracted from forests is used as fuelwood. Industrial roundwood amounts to only 20 per cent of all wood extracted. There is, however, a geographical displacement between the two uses. In Asia, fuelwood comes mainly from tropical seasonal forests, whereas industrial wood is extracted mostly from the rain forests of Malesia (teak being a major exception). The majority of timbers extracted for industrial use are hardwoods, in direct contrast to the industrial wood of temperate and cold regions, which is mostly softwood from conifers (FAO, 1988; ECE, 1988).

Tropical hardwood products exported by tropical countries in 1986 represented only 3 per cent of total wood removals in roundwood equivalent, in the developing world. However, most of these exports originated from the rain forests of a small number of tropical countries, where they constituted a very large proportion of all wood removals. This was especially the case in the eastern tropics. According to FAO, nearly 68 per cent of all wood removals in Malaysia (the leading world trader) are exported (FAO, 1988).

Of a total of 25 million cu. m of tropical hardwood logs traded at world level in 1986, 21.4 million cu. m originated from Southeast Asia and the Pacific region (Figure 7.1). Sabah and Sarawak were the main sources. Together the two states exported 19 million cu. m of logs in 1986, and 22.8 million cu. m in 1987. Other major exporters included Papua New Guinea (1.44 million cu. m of exported logs in 1987) and the Solomon Islands (around 0.3 million cu. m).

Sawn hardwood is another important tropical timber export. A total of 6.7 million cu. m was exported from Southeast Asia in 1986, representing approximately 70 per cent of the world's tropical sawnwood trade (Figure 7.2).

Indonesia is now the world's major tropical plywood producer and exporter, with 5.48 million cu. m sold abroad in 1987, for which some 12 million cu. m of logs were required (Figure 7.3). Both Indonesia and Peninsular Malaysia are also exporters of veneers (FAO, 1989).

The main markets are similarly specialised. Most of the exported tropical logs are sold to Japan, which in 1986 imported 12.8 million cu. m mostly from Sarawak, Sabah and Papua New Guinea, and 14 million cu. m in 1987 (Figure 7.4). Other Far East markets (Hong Kong, South Korea, Taiwan and mainland China) are also important. Processed timber is mostly exported to Europe (sawnwood and plywood) and the USA (especially plywood), but Japan is also beginning to import plywood.

Environmental and Economic Problems

During the past 30 years, the commercial extraction of roundwood in Southeast Asia has proved to be singularly destructive. Silvicultural systems designed to ensure sustained yields have rarely been implemented (see chapter 6). According to a recent study for the ITTO, less than one per cent of natural forests in Southeast Asia undergo silvicultural management (IIED, 1988; Poore et al., 1989).

Numerous surveys have shown that in Southeast Asia up to 60 per cent of the vegetation not immediately affected by logging suffers either total destruction or severe damage (Wyatt-Smith, 1987). A preoccupation with speed is much to blame. Logging is carried out with the maximum possible speed to ensure a profitable return on capital investment, particularly in heavy machinery (Repetto and Gillis, 1988). Very little forest road maintenance is undertaken and commercial species regeneration is rarely practised. Bad felling practices and irresponsible management are widespread. The lack of directional felling, the failure to pre-cut climbers, badly designed skidding tracks, unnecessarily large roads and cleared storage areas, and insufficient care in the use of heavy tracked vehicles and overhead cables, all contribute to serious erosion (see chapter 6). The situation is exacerbated by the lack of plantations, because as well as rehabilitating degraded lands, they could relieve the pressure on natural forests by augmenting fuelwood and lumber production.

Nevertheless, the direct effects of logging, however destructive, are far less important than their indirect effects. Logging operations are one of the most significant causes of the opening up of closed tropical forests to other destructive land uses (Plumwood and Routley, 1982). The most common of these is shifting cultivation, as practised by settlers, who usually do not possess sufficient experience to minimise the impact of their farming on impoverished tropical forest soils. Current logging practices lead to the invasion of logged-over areas and post-logging protection has proved ineffective. The development of multi-purpose forestry, which can include the participation of the local population in the economic management of the forest – thereby making it a custodian of the resource base – could be an alternative (HIID, 1988).

There are also problems linked to industrialisation. A number of tropical countries hope to develop timber processing and wood manufacturing industries, in order to obtain more of the revenue accruing from the exploitation of their natural resources. But according to many analysts, this ambition is often thwarted by what can be termed the 'public income trap'. This can be explained as follows: when unprocessed logs form the basis of tropical timber exports, a government can earn a sizeable amount through taxes, royalties and duties (around one-third in Sarawak for instance). When logs are processed before export, however, the finished goods are far less heavily taxed and government revenue declines accordingly (Repetto and Gillis, 1988). There is therefore little incentive to encourage export-orientated sawmills, especially since there is strong competition from far cheaper temperate coniferous sawnwood in export

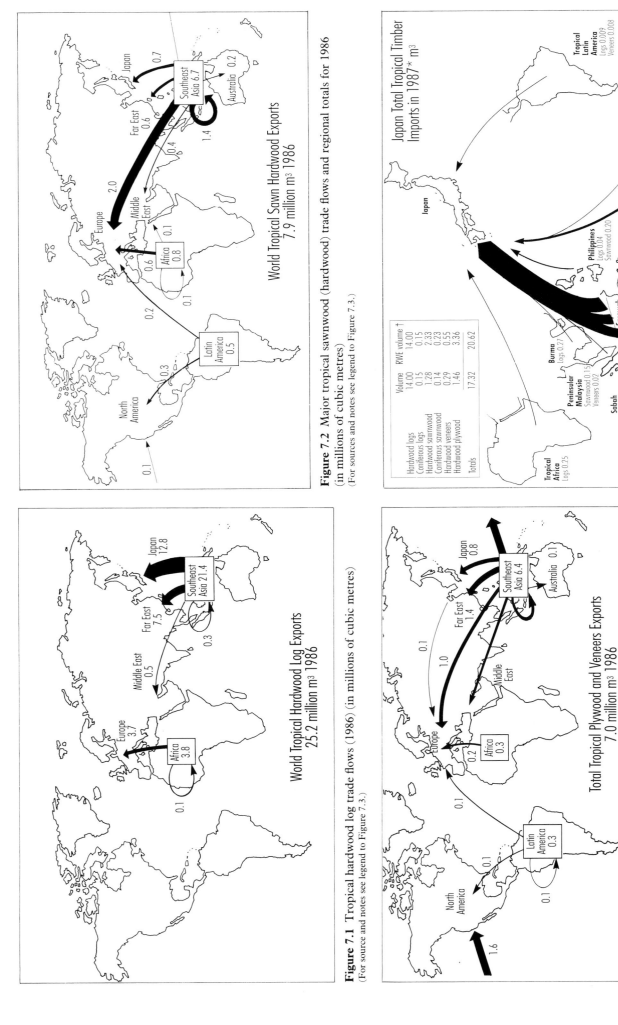

Figure 7.1 Tropical hardwood log trade flows (1986) (in millions of cubic metres)
(For source and notes see legend to Figure 7.3.)

World Tropical Hardwood Log Exports
25.2 million m³ 1986

Japan 12.8
Southeast Asia 21.4
Far East 7.5
Middle East 0.5
Europe 3.7
Africa 3.8
0.3
0.1

Figure 7.2 Major tropical sawnwood (hardwood) trade flows and regional totals for 1986
(in millions of cubic metres)
(For sources and notes see legend to Figure 7.3.)

World Tropical Sawn Hardwood Exports
7.9 million m³ 1986

Japan 0.7
Southeast Asia 6.7
Far East 0.6
Australia 0.2
1.4
0.4
2.0
Europe
Middle East 0.6
Africa 0.8
0.1
0.1
Latin America 0.5
0.2
0.3
North America
0.1

Figure 7.3 Major tropical plywood and veneer trade flows and regional totals for 1986
(in millions of cubic metres)

(*Sources*: FAO (1988); ECE (1988); Nectoux and Kuroda, 1989)

Notes: These maps present a simplified view of tropical timber trade flows. Some flows are not shown, particularly intra-regional ones. This explains occasional inconsistencies between world and regional totals. The Far East region here includes South Korea, China, Hong Kong, Taiwan and Macau. Southeast Asia statistics include Singapore, Papua New Guinea and the Solomon Islands. Central America is included in Latin America, which however excludes Paraguay, Chile and Argentina.

Total Tropical Plywood and Veneers Exports
7.0 million m³ 1986

Japan 0.8
Southeast Asia 6.4
Far East 1.4
Australia 0.1
1.0
0.1
Europe
Middle East 0.2
Africa 0.3
0.1
Latin America 0.3
0.1
North America
1.6

Figure 7.4 Main suppliers of tropical timber to Japan in 1987 (after Nectonx and Kuroda 1989)

* Pulpwood not included. All volumes are given in million m³.
†RWE = roundwood equivalent (see box on page 55).

Japan Total Tropical Timber
Imports in 1987* m³

Tropical Latin America
Logs 0.009
Veneers 0.008

Japan

Solomon Islands
Logs 0.17

Papua New Guinea
Logs 0.95

Philippines
Logs 0.04
Sawnwood 0.20

Burma
Logs 0.27

Peninsular Malaysia
Sawnwood 0.15
Veneers 0.02

Sabah
Logs 7.00
Sawnwood 0.15
Veneers 0.15

Sarawak
Logs 5.58

Indonesia
Sawnwood 0.67
Plywood 1.37

Tropical Africa
Logs 0.25

	Volume	RWE volume †
Hardwood logs	14.00	14.00
Coniferous logs	0.15	0.15
Hardwood sawnwood	1.28	2.33
Coniferous sawnwood	0.14	0.23
Hardwood veneers	0.29	0.55
Hardwood plywood	1.46	3.36
Totals	17.32	20.62

Men 'scaling', or measuring, the logs hauled from the forest to the dumping ground. Kimanis, Sabah, Malaysia. WWF/Sylvia Yorath

markets such as those to Japan. Only Indonesia has really managed to escape this trap. This is because it had considerable income and local capital at its disposal when it started to develop its plywood industry. Despite this success though, the Indonesian plywood industry is still criticised for its inefficient marketing, even to Japan, where since 1987 it has gained a respectable share of the market. (Japan has now supplanted the USA as Indonesia's major plywood client.)

In a number of Southeast Asian and Pacific countries, the reliance on raw commodity exports, compounded by a lack of market information, has opened the way to abuses and corruption. These have occurred at all levels, ranging from the failure to abide by logging rules, to the false grading of timber, to bribing officials in relation to export documentation, illegal exports and large-scale transfer pricing. In the Philippines these all came to light with the change of government in 1986. It has been shown that in the early 1980s around 40 per cent of logs exported from the Philippines to Japan went unrecorded and were in fact illegal (Nectoux and Kuroda, 1989). A recent official enquiry into commercial forestry in Papua New Guinea also unearthed similar practices on a considerable scale (see chapter 21).

In the long term there will be less and less commercially valuable timber available. Total deforestation is not likely to occur in the Asia–Pacific region, but in those countries where natural forests have been overlogged, and regeneration management is inadequate, it is unlikely that forests can remain productive. Thailand, once a significant timber exporter, has experienced a deficit in its timber requirement balance since the 1970s. Deforestation is so extensive that catastrophic flooding occurred in 1988. All commercial logging is now forbidden – officially at least (see chapter 27). In addition, agricultural settlement in some regions is destroying any remaining degraded forest remnants.

In the Philippines, the extensive high-density dipterocarp stands are now mostly logged out. Total roundwood production has halved over the last decade, falling from 11.6 million cu. m in 1976 to 5.7 million cu. m in 1986. However, the rate of logging still continues to an excessive degree in some regions, for example on Palawan (for details of a plan to avoid this see case study in chapter 8). Elsewhere, the quality of logs extracted is falling steadily. Girths and lengths are smaller than those of logs traded 20 years ago and come from either regrowth or lesser known species.

A Role for the ITTO?

The International Tropical Timber Organisation (ITTO) originated from the Integrated Programme for Commodities of the United Nations' Conference on Trade and Development (UNCTAD). It bears little resemblance to other attempts aimed at regulating world commodity markets. It does not include classic management tools such as a buffer stock, or price intervention mechanism, or a system of production or export quotas.

Mangrove chips ready to be shipped to Japan for manufacture of rayon and paper. Sandakan, Sabah, Malaysia. WWF/Sylvia Yorath

DEFINITIONS OF COMMODITIES

Roundwood (wood in the rough) Wood in its natural state as felled, or otherwise harvested, with or without bark. It may also be impregnated (e.g. telegraph poles) or roughly shaped or It comprises all wood obtained from removals during the period – calendar year or forest year. Commodities included are sawlogs and veneer logs, pulpwood, other industrial roundwood (including pitprops) and fuelwood. Statistics for trade include, as well as roundwood from removals, the estimated roundwood equivalent of chips and particles, wood residues and charcoal.

Fuelwood and charcoal The commodities included are fuelwood, coniferous and non-coniferous, and the trade statistics include the roundwood equivalent of charcoal, using a factor of 6.0 to convert from weight (metric tons) to solid volume units (cubic metres). Wood in the rough (from trunks and branches of trees) to be used as fuel for purposes such as cooking, heating or power production. Wood for charcoal, pit kilns and portable ovens is included.

Sawlogs and veneer logs Logs whether or not roughly squared, to be sawn (or chipped) lengthwise for the manufacture of sawnwood or railway sleepers (ties). Logs for production of veneer, mainly by peeling or slicing.

(*Source:* Simplified from FAO, 1990).

ITTO was created by the 1983 International Tropical Timber Agreement, signed between 18 'producer' tropical countries and 22 'consumer' (mostly industrialised) countries. This agreement is largely concerned with improving market conditions; but its importance lies in another of its stated objectives, namely encouraging the development of national policies aimed at 'maintaining the ecological balance in the regions concerned', a rare component for a trade agreement (United Nations, 1984).

ITTO is still a fragile organisation. It experienced serious difficulties in taking decisions early on in its operation, for example concerning the location of its headquarters (currently in Yokohama). The reluctance of some members to pay their dues on time has also been a problem. A further difficulty derives from the fact that the actions of the Secretariat and Council are not sustained by specific powers. Major policy decisions can only be reached by consensus. This is why piecemeal decision-making concerning project funding has occurred. The decision of a number of countries to fund specific ITTO projects has, however, helped to launch the first initiatives.

The most interesting ITTO projects, and the most important in the long term, are those agreed within the Reforestation and Forest Management Committee of the organisation. They mostly concern assessments or experiments in multiple-use forestry practices, natural forest management programmes and plantation development.

The Future: How Will the Timber Trade Survive?

The main features of the tropical timber trade in Southeast Asia and the Pacific are changing rapidly. There are considerable uncertainties concerning its future. On the one hand, the resource base is threatened by over-exploitation, which is leading to forest destruction and degradation. On the other, competition from temperate timber production, based on intensively managed coniferous forests, and increasingly on hardwoods from eastern USA and parts of Europe, is proving to be very strong. The inroads that Southeast Asian tropical timber exports have made in the international timber trade since the early 1960s may not last. The lack of proper long-term natural forest management and the negligible extent of plantations (the latter could meet local requirements) make it likely that rain forests outside parks and reserves will either disappear or become thoroughly degraded. In which case, the Southeast Asian timber trade will suffer heavily.

Other aspects of this trade will doubtless change too. Until recently, Japan was primarily a log importer. But increasingly it is beginning to import processed tropical timber, particularly plywood and joinery products. New clients of Southeast Asian timber producers are also emerging and competing with Japan, for example, Continental China and the Middle East. More countries will probably cease being mass exporters, becoming timber importers instead. The Philippines may soon follow Thailand in this respect.

References

ECE (1988) *Forest Products Trade Flow Data – 1986–87.* Timber Bulletin, XVI(7). UN Economic Commission for Europe and Food and Agriculture Organization, Geneva, Switzerland.

FAO (1988) *FAO Yearbook of Forestry Products, 1975–1986.* Food and Agriculture Organization, Rome, Italy.

FAO (1990) *FAO Yearbook of Forest Products 1977–78,* FAO Forestry Series No. 33, FAO Statistics Series No. 90. FAO, Rome, Italy.

Gillis, M. (1988) The Logging Industry in Tropical Asia. In: *People of the Tropical Rain Forest.* Denshaw, J. S. and Padock, C. (eds). University of California Press, Berkeley, USA.

Handa, R. (ed.) (1988) *Forestry Policy in Japan.* Association for Research and Publishing in Japanese Forestry, Tokyo, Japan.

HIID (1988) *The Case for Multiple-Use Management of Tropical Hardwood Forest.* Harvard Institute for International Development, Pre-project Report for the ITTO, Cambridge, Mass., USA.

IIED (1988) *Natural Forest Management for Sustainable Timber Production,* 2 volumes. Pre-project report for the ITTO, International Institute for Environment and Development, London, UK.

Nectoux, F. and Dudley, N. (1987) *A Hard Wood Story. Europe's Involvement in The Tropical Timber Trade.* Friends of the Earth, London, UK.

Nectoux, F. and Kuroda, Y. (1989) *Timber from the South Seas.* WWF–International, Gland, Switzerland.

Plumwood, V. and Routley, R. (1982) World rain forest destruction – the social factors. *The Ecologist* 10(1).

Poore, D., Burgess, P., Palmer, J., Rietbergen, S. and Synott, T. (1989) *No Timber Without Trees: Sustainability in the Tropical Forest.* Earthscan, London, UK. 252 pp.

Repetto, R. and Gillis, M. (1988) *Public Policies and the Misuse of Forest Resources.* Cambridge University Press, Cambridge, UK.

United Nations (1984) *International Tropical Timber Agreement 1983.* TD/TIMBER/11/Rev. 2, Geneva, Switzerland.

Wyatt-Smith, J. (1987) *The Management of Tropical Moist Forest for the Sustained Production of Timber.* IUCN/IIED Tropical Forest Policy Paper 4. International Institute for Environment and Development, London, UK.

Authorship

François Nectoux in London, with contributions from M. Kashio of the FAO Regional Office in Bangkok, Christopher Elliott of WWF International and Jacqueline Sawyer of IUCN, both in Gland.

8 Government Policies and Land Use Planning

Introduction

It must be clear to any dispassionate observer of the forest scene anywhere in the tropics, not least in Asia, that governments in general are failing to stem the tide of destruction and degradation which is sweeping through their forests. Indeed some, alarmed by the rate at which it is occurring and by unprecedented events like the fires which swept across large areas in Kalimantan and Sabah during 1982 and 1983 (Leighton and Nengah Wirawan, 1986), are taking emergency, even panic, action, such as the banning by the Philippines of sawn timber exports and the halt to all logging in Thailand. It is clear from the rapid destruction, however, that something is wrong with either present government policies or with their implementation.

No country can afford losses of forest on such a scale. There is little land to spare in the region, and as Table 11.4 in Chapter 11 shows, populations will continue to rise throughout the next century regardless of the success of national population policies. It is therefore vital that the most effective use is made of all resources of land and water. Much of the land degradation that we see today is, for all practical purposes, irreversible. At the very least, it is vastly expensive to restore forest cover, as is evident from the valiant efforts to reverse the deterioration of the mountain catchments in Java made over the years by the Indonesian Government and supported by FAO and others. Prevention, however, is preferable to a cure, and it is unfortunate that so much investment of time and money must still be devoted to rehabilitate degraded land rather than to prevent degradation in the first place.

Use of Tropical Forest Lands

There are at least three forms of rural land use which particularly require long-term planning, because they depend upon long periods of stability. These are irrigated agriculture; the maintenance of forest for the protection of soil, water and biological diversity; and the management of forest for the sustainable production of timber and other products.

The need for social and political stability is generally understood by governments in relation to irrigated farming, where it is recognised by guaranteed possession of land and rights of access to water supplies. But government policies, both in principle and in practice, fail to live up to the challenge of providing stability and security in either the protection of forest resources or in their sustainable use. There are also many unresolved questions of equity in relation to those native peoples who live in forested regions, for example in Indonesia and in Sarawak (Hong, 1987).

In the past, when there were large unbroken areas of natural vegetation, the conservation of nature and of biological diversity could look after itself. But now that the forest is being dissected into ever smaller blocks, the flora and fauna can only be saved by protecting and managing areas which have been carefully selected for their special biological value. The preservation of the diversity of species depends upon consistent care. The smaller and more isolated these areas of forest are, the more intensive must be the management required to maintain their richness; and the more important it is to link them by corridors and to surround them with forms of land use which are not totally alien – the 'buffer' concept. Thus it is better that reserves of natural forest should be surrounded by areas of managed forest than by farmland; and typical areas of untouched forest should, wherever possible, be left within forests which are managed for production. These will at the same time make a general contribution to the conservation of biological diversity and will provide populations from which the surrounding managed forest may be restocked. Existing examples of this policy can be seen in the Virgin Jungle Reserves of Malaysia (Anon., n.d.).

Ensuring migration corridors may also be important, particularly with large mammals such as elephants, in reducing potential conflict with new agricultural settlements. Where their range has been disrupted, elephants can cause considerable damage, as they do in Lampung province of south Sumatra (see chapter 5). But carefully planned corridors have successfully countered this problem in parts of the Mahaweli Development Scheme in Sri Lanka (Olivier, 1980; and see chapter 26).

Forest which is to be managed for the sustainable production of timber also requires continuity and stability of government policies. The life of a timber tree between the germination of the seed and the felling of the mature tree is likely to be at least 70 years, so consistent management is required at least for this period, and preferably for many rotations (see chapter 6 for management details). Production forests should, like conservation forests, be chosen for their intrinsic characteristics, in this case their capacity to grow valuable timber, and once these have been properly selected it is a serious waste of resources not to manage them for this purpose in perpetuity (Poore and Sayer, 1987).

Much of the forest land in the region has been used by people for centuries. Use or ownership of land was once regulated by custom, some of which became enshrined in law. However, in most countries customary law has been overlain by legislation which enables the allocation of land, in the national interest, for forest reserves, national parks, roads, agriculture and for many other purposes. Moreover, in some countries such as the Philippines, many large areas have been acquired by private individuals. The countries of the region greatly differ from one another in the extent to which customary law has been respected in modern developments. Parts of Melanesia are exceptional in that it is recognised that all land claimed by local communities belongs to them (see chapters 21 and 29). In most countries questions of land tenure now have a high priority for political action.

One feature of early land-use planning is that it was based on a hierarchy of uses, based essentially on the suitability of the land for agriculture. The best land was reserved for irrigated agriculture, the next best for dry land agriculture (both of these often used to raise cash crops), then pasture, with forestry and finally wildlife conservation coming at the end of the line. Forestry was considered to be a second or third best option – the land that was left after every other interest had taken its pick. This is clearly not satisfactory and is gradually being replaced by a comparative 'land evaluation', in which the land is assessed for its suitability of various kinds of use and the relative merits of these are set against each other (Poore and Sayer, 1987). This gives a better measure of the broader national interest and a better possibility that those uses which require long-term stability will receive it. But there is no guarantee that this will take place. In fact, many countries have been disillusioned by their experience of land-use planning. Plans have often not been implemented and, when they have, they have frequently not been supported by appropriate policies. The experience of Peninsular Malaysia on the other hand demonstrates the value of sound land-use plans (chapter 22), and it is hoped that the new evaluation of land-use potential in Indonesia will have a similar stabilising effect (see chapters 5 and 19 for details of the Regional Physical Planning Programme for Transmigration).

Planning for the Future
During the past few years there have been changes of public opinion which are rapidly leading to new emphases in the planning and management of forest lands. In countries where the density of population is high, more stress is being placed on growing food and, where energy is short, on supplying wood for fuel. Moreover, there is increasing public and political pressure over issues such as the customary rights of local people, land tenure, the environmental importance of the forest and the preservation of biological diversity. After a long period in the shadows, climatic warming, too, has reached the political limelight and the importance of maintaining on the land the highest amount of woody biomass is at last receiving the attention it deserves. Non-governmental organisations are beginning to play a significant part in these processes.

If one looks at the various ways in which tropical forest lands may be used (excluding from consideration their conversion to engineering works or towns), there are a number of possibilities, each of which is workable given proper management.
- Forests can be retained in their original state, either uninhabited, or lived in by hunter-gatherer peoples (while these live as though they were part of the natural ecosystem).
- Forests can be managed to produce a sustained yield of timber and/or other forest produce such as rattan or illipe nuts.
- Cyclical cultivation in forest land is possible, in which a period of cultivation alternates with a period of recovery to secondary forest.
- Stable agro-forestry systems can be implemented, in which trees and herbaceous crops are mixed in various proportions.
- Forests can be converted to tree crops for timber, fruit, fodder or industrial use.
- Forests can be used for dryland farming of, for example, hill rice, or as grazing land.

- Forests can be converted to irrigated land.

Each of these options, under the right conditions, is sustainable. On good soils and with careful management, high yields can be obtained on a continuous basis. All of the above, except the first two, can, if managed badly, mean that the forest degrades progressively to waste land. This degradation can become very rapid if forest turns into grassland or scrub which burns easily. Fire is becoming an increasingly serious problem.

Government policies adopted hitherto towards use of forests have not generally led to stability in land-use nor to practices which have encouraged sustainable management. What is now required is a new balance of use and new measures to promote and maintain that balance in ways which the older development strategies have failed to do. These new policies should depend upon an analysis of why the earlier ones have failed and try to correct these basic deficiencies. Otherwise they too will fail.

There is now reasonable agreement about why existing government policies have failed to provide security for the forest resource (Burns, 1986; HIID, 1988; Poore et al., 1989). The most basic reason is the undervaluation of forest by those responsible for national economic planning. This happens for two main reasons. The first is a serious underestimation of the non-market benefits of forests – in catchment protection, soil conservation, the preservation of biological diversity and moderation of climate. Consequently it is difficult to argue the political case in favour of the forests. The second is an equally serious overestimate of the benefits to be gained from converting forest capital into other forms of national capital. A further reason is the financial benefits that can be derived by some individuals from forest exploitation. There is, therefore, a great need to produce and deploy convincing arguments about the values of forest land which can be used in national economic planning, and to introduce control of logging and conversion to agriculture.

Lack of understanding means that a country's forest resources are not in themselves seen as a sufficiently important focus for national policy and they are thus affected in various, often harmful, ways by other national policies. They are caught in a cross-fire. In some countries the damaging conversion of areas which should remain forest is actually promoted by policies for agriculture and resettlement, or is encouraged by the building of new roads without adequate consideration of the environmental effects or control of later development (Repetto and Gillis, 1988). Pricing policies for forest products and fiscal incentives for wood-using industries have sometimes encouraged the excessive and wasteful use of forests rather than the opposite. Another consequence of the low political rating of forest management and conservation is the failure of many governments to provide sufficient resources for the necessary supervision and control of management.

There are many other examples of such conflicts of policy which seriously damage the forest, and there is a need to look comprehensively at all the policies which affect the future management of forest lands and to plan accordingly.

Reservation policies for national parks and for production forests have therefore had mixed success. Sometimes, of course, they have been the victims of political interest, but often they have failed because they have been established without sufficient sensitivity to the interests of local people. Control proves very difficult when those who live around the forest have no interest in seeing it remain as forest, or when those who are responsible for harvesting it can see no long-term advantage in managing it well.

Conclusions
From this analysis can be derived criteria for new policies to help ensure the future security of the forest. Among the most important of these are:

Land-use must take account of ecological characteristics. Farmers in the hills of Laos use a variety of tree crops and plantation species. J. A. Sayer

1 Government policies for land-use planning, economic development, employment, fiscal incentives and many other sectors should focus upon the sustainable and equitable use of forest lands.

2 Land evaluation should examine each of the productive and protective uses of the land separately and assess them against each other in order to obtain the best balance of use.

3 Land-use planning should take full account of the ecological characteristics of each piece of land and its social setting.

4 Conditions of land tenure and ownership of resources, by individuals, communities or industries, should give all a social and financial incentive to manage the land sustainably.

5 Government staff should be in tune with local people, and be in a position to control in a sensitive manner the management of government-owned lands.

The concept of the 'biosphere reserve' or of the 'protected landscape' are ideals towards which one should strive in the management of the whole forest landscape. The concept in both is one of graded control. At one end of the spectrum are areas which are totally protected, at the other end are those which are allowed to respond rapidly to any economic opportunity. In between are areas in which the natural resource may be used with discretion. The aim is to identify the limits within which land-use may be allowed to change, and to produce, by a combination of incentives and planning controls, the conditions under which it is profitable for people to manage the land in this way. The policies should be holistic, profitable to all partners and sensitive to the views and ideals of the local people. An example of this is the concept of the Environmentally Critical Areas Network, which has been prepared for the island of Palawan in the Philippines (see case study opposite).

In much of Asia the management of forest lands has tended to be the prerogative of governments, but this need not be so. It is essential, as has been explained above, that governments provide the framework of law and order that is needed for the security and stability of forest lands. The actual management or ownership of forest lands, however, may often be better in the hands of communities, private individuals or enterprises.

An important part can be played by government in creating the right financial environment (by encouraging markets and local industries, by providing selected incentives and subsidies, legal controls, etc) under which the sustainable management and utilisation of

forest can thrive. The management of non-timber products of the forest (meat, rattan, oil seeds, resins, medicinal plants, etc) could be classed as a significant example of this. At present, most of these, with the notable exception of rattan, are either harvested by local people for their own use or are traded in the informal market. If demand rises, they tend to be brought into cultivation, effectively destroying the market for produce collected in the wild. There is a case here for the sensitive manipulation of domestic markets by governments to favour sustainable management of the products of natural forests.

Finally, national perceptions of what constitutes a 'forest policy' need to be re-examined. At present such policies tend only to address the production of timber and fuelwood from the national forest estate, and this is proving unsatisfactory. Forest policies need to be viewed from two completely different perspectives, both making their proper contributions to a unified policy for the use of a nation's natural resources. One policy should be concerned with meeting the nation's requirements for wood (both for industry and for energy; for domestic use or for export) from whatever source – natural forest, plantations, trees in agricultural land, etc. The other should concentrate on sustainable management and conservation of the nation's forest lands, in which the production of wood would only be one of a number of objectives. These two policies combined should, ideally, ensure a sustainable supply of wood and the wise management of forest lands. Present policies often fail to accomplish either.

References

Anon. (n.d.) *Forestry in Malaysia.* Ministry of Primary Industries, Malaysia.

Burns, D. (1986) *Runway and Treadmill Deforestation.* IUCN/IIED Tropical Forestry Paper No. 2. London, UK.

Castanedo, P. and Poore, D. (unpublished report) *Environmentally Critical Areas Network.* (11 pp + 2 maps.)

HIID (1988) *The Case for Multiple Use Management of Tropical Hardwood Forests.* Study prepared for the International Tropical Timber Organization (ITTO) by the Harvard Institute for International Development, Cambridge, Massachusetts, USA.

Hong, E. (1987) *Natives of Sarawak: Survival in Borneo's Vanishing Forests.* Institut Masyarakakat, Malaysia.

Leighton, M. and Nengah Wirawan (1986) Catastrophic drought and fire in Borneo tropical rain forest associated with the 1982–83 El Nino Southern Oscillation Event. In: *Tropical Rain Forests and the World Atmosphere,* American Association for the Advancement of Science Symposium 101. Boulder, Colorado, USA.

Olivier, R. C. D. (1980) Reconciling elephant conservation and development in Asia: Ecological bases and possible approaches. In: *Tropical Ecology and Development* Furtado, J. I. (ed.). Proceedings of the 5th International Symposium of Tropical Ecology, 16–21 April 1979, Kuala Lumpur, Malaysia.

Poore, D., Burgess P., Palmer J., Rietbergen, S. and Synott, T. (1989) *No Timber Without Trees: Sustainability in the Tropical Forest.* Earthscan, London, UK.

Poore, D. and Sayer, J. A. (1987) *The Management of Tropical Moist Forest Lands: Ecological Guidelines.* IUCN, Gland, Switzerland. 63 pp.

Repetto, R. and Gillis, M. (1988) *Public Policies and the Misuse of Forest Resources.* Cambridge University Press, UK.

Authorship

Duncan Poore in Oxford, with contributions from Steve Bass at the Rockefeller Foundation, New York, and Jeff McNeely of IUCN, Gland.

ENVIRONMENTALLY CRITICAL AREAS NETWORK IN PALAWAN, PHILIPPINES

Palawan, located in the south-western portion of the Philippine islands, is 425 km long and only 6–40 km wide. The central spine is mountainous and forested, with narrow coastal plains fringed by mangroves and coral reefs. These forests, although largely intact, are steadily giving way to logging, mining and uncontrolled agricultural expansion. The island is ecologically fragile and without careful planning there will be severe environmental degradation and impoverishment of the people living there.

A recent survey of Palawan, designed to produce a Strategic Environmental Plan, concluded that a network of protected areas would not be sufficient to prevent environmental deterioration, mainly because it would not receive the support of local communities. Instead, it was proposed to create a Network of Environmentally Critical Areas, a graded system of protective management from strict control in certain areas to very light control elsewhere, spread over the whole of Palawan (see Figure 8.2). This will help ensure that no developments take place that will cause irreversible harm or loss of productive capacity to the natural resources of the island. This includes maintenance of the island's rich biological diversity (see chapter 23). The network would achieve the following:

- Protection of watersheds.
- Preservation of biological diversity.
- Protection of tribal people and their cultures.
- Maintenance of maximum sustainable yield.
- Protection of rare and endangered species and their habitats.
- Provision of areas for environmental and ecological research, education and training.
- Provision of areas for tourism and recreation.

The network will be divided between four land-use zones (see Figure 8.1).

1 Core area – a wilderness area strictly protected and free of human disruption. In general these are montane forests at altitudes above 1000 m.

2 Buffer zone – an area where regulated use is permitted. This may be divided into three sub-zones:

- Restricted Use Area, surrounding the core area; soft impact uses only.
- Controlled Use Area, encircling the core and Restricted Use Area, available for extraction of minor forest products.
- Traditional Use Area, where traditional land use is already stabilised.

3 Multiple Use Area – landscape modified for intensive timber extraction, grazing, agriculture and infrastructure development.

4 Marine Area – the coastal/marine boundary is where human communities are concentrated and management for extractive activities and tourism should be undertaken by communities at the 'grass-root' level. The general pattern is to have core areas of mangrove, seagrass and coral reefs within a larger area where compatible land use and other activities are undertaken.

Further, more detailed, land-use surveys are necessary to delineate these management zones more precisely. Given good legislation and public support developed through careful programmes of education and dialogue, the Ecologically Critical Areas Network offers Palawan the prospect of sustainable development and conservation of natural resources into the foreseeable future.

(*Source:* Castenedo and Poore, unpublished)

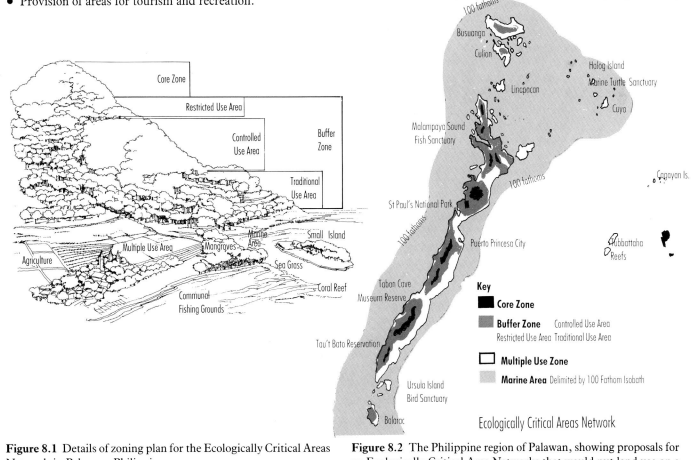

Figure 8.1 Details of zoning plan for the Ecologically Critical Areas Network in Palawan, Philippines

Figure 8.2 The Philippine region of Palawan, showing proposals for an Ecologically Critical Area Networks that would put land use on a sustainable basis

59

9 The Protected Areas System

Introduction

As the exploitation of tropical moist forests has accelerated in the Asia–Pacific region, governments have realised that conservation of samples of relatively intact forest is a necessary part of balanced land use. National parks and other forms of protected area have been one of the most universally adopted mechanisms for nature conservation. This is not to claim universal success; the great majority of protected areas are under some degree of threat from encroachment or poaching, resulting from a conflict between the conservation of nationally or internationally important sites and the needs of local communities traditionally dependent on the resources of such areas. The level of conflict is intensified in many tropical countries where the population is increasing, and will continue to do so in decades to come.

More effective means are required to ensure that conservationists and local people can work together as partners rather than antagonists. This chapter discusses why protected areas are necessary, what contributions they make to human society, and how they can be managed better to ensure that their contributions continue to meet the needs of society in the future.

How Protected Areas Contribute to Conservation of Tropical Moist Forests

Tropical moist forests are by far the richest of the earth's habitats in terms of their biological species diversity. This great diversity of plants and animals is associated with a low population density of many individual species, rendering them particularly vulnerable to local extirpation. Protection of extensive tracts of tropical moist forest, therefore, is of paramount importance to maintain global biological diversity.

Protected areas can be defined as predominantly natural areas managed in perpetuity through legal or customary regimes primarily for conservation. They provide the most effective means of conserving the range of biological diversity found in moist forests. Some examples may serve to illustrate their importance:

- In Taman Negara, Peninsular Malaysia's largest protected area, 142 of its 198 endemic mammal species are dependent on rain forest for their existence (Medway, 1971).
- Thailand's existing protected areas system provides refuge for all but 40 of its 595 resident, and mostly forest bird species (Round, 1988).
- Doi Suthep-Pui, a mountain protected area of 261 sq. km, which forms part of Thailand's system, supports 250 orchid species (25 per cent of the national total) and is the type locality for over 200 taxa of plants and animals (Bänziger, 1988).
- In India, a network of 16 reserves, covering 26,000 sq. km of forest, has been created to protect the tiger. This initiative, heralded as one of the greatest conservation successes in the whole of Asia (Panwar, 1984), has assured the future survival not only of the tiger

but also of its habitat, including large tracts of tropical moist forest and mangrove.

Tropical moist forests can be conserved and managed in a variety of ways. These can be classified according to management objectives using a system of management categories developed by IUCN's Commission on National Parks and Protected Areas (box on page 61). Strict nature reserves (category I) and national parks (category II) are by definition protected from exploitation, but they are complemented by other categories of protected areas in which sustainable forms of land use are accommodated. Multiple-use areas (category VIII), for example, may provide for the sustained production of timber, as in the case of some forest reserves.

The contribution of protected areas to the conservation of living resources and to sustainable development has been well documented (MacKinnon et al., 1986; McNeely, 1988; McNeely et al., 1989). The main direct and indirect benefits of conserving tropical moist forests are summarised and exemplified in the boxes on page 66. Most of these can be quantified in economic terms; indirect values, however, often overlooked in cost-benefit analyses, may far outweigh direct values. Less tangible, also, is the 'existence value' of protected areas, which reflects the empathy, responsibility and concern that some people feel towards the existence of ecosystems such as tropical rain forests, even though they have no intention of ever visiting or directly using them. Measures of this value include the numbers of people who enjoy wildlife films or television programmes, the donations that are made to conservation organisations such as WWF, and the concern expressed in the mass media about tropical forest destruction.

Protecting tropical moist forests also involves costs – particularly for those people living in the vicinity of protected areas who may be prevented from exploiting resources as freely as they might wish. Moreover, protected areas may well be perceived as harbouring 'pests', such as predators which kill domestic livestock or herbivores which damage crops. Retaining natural vegetation also denies immediate benefits from logging and conversion to other forms of use, although these may be less significant when compared to the value of conserving such a resource within a region as a whole. In short, the distribution of costs and benefits of both exploitation and conservation should be more equitable, if protected areas are to continue making their necessary contribution to human welfare.

The importance of conserving tropical rain and monsoon forests has received increasing public support as its values have become better understood. In a number of cases, intense lobbying by the public, often spearheaded by non-governmental organisations, has halted some large development projects that would have destroyed important tropical forest areas, for example:

1 A scheme to dam Silent Valley, considered to be one of the last

representative stands of mature tropical evergreen rain forest in India, became the focus of one of the fiercest and most widely publicised environmental debates in the region. After much debate the project was finally shelved in 1983 in deference to the sentiments of the Prime Minister of the day, Mrs Indira Gandhi, and the site has since been designated a national park.

2 Plans to build a dam on the Upper Kwae Yai in Thailand have been intensely and repeatedly debated over a ten-year period. A substantial area of mature forest would have been flooded, bisecting Thung Yai Naresuan, Thailand's largest wildlife sanctuary. Following an enquiry, the scheme was finally dropped in 1988, and the site, together with the adjacent Huay Kha Khaeng Wildlife Sanctuary, is in the process of being nominated for inscription on the World Heritage List.

3 There is an on-going controversy over the proposal made in 1972 to establish Endau-Rompin as a national park to protect one of the last extensive tracts of tropical rain forest in Peninsular Malaysia. Logging of part of the proposed core area in 1977 led to widespread public protest and the emergence of a campaign, led by the Malayan Nature Society, to save Endau-Rompin. The issue is politically sensitive because of the different powers, responsibilities and interests of federal and state authorities, but there are grounds for optimism now that the Pahang and Johor State Governments (whose borders bisect the area) have agreed to designate the area as a state park (see chapter 22).

On the other hand, some development projects have actually contributed to the establishment of protected areas. For example, Dumoga-Bone National Park in northern Sulawesi was established with funding from the World Bank to protect the watershed of an irrigation project downstream. The Mahaweli Project in Sri Lanka included a $6 million component to establish a new system of national parks as part of the water resources development effort.

Finally, an extensive system of protected areas was planned as part of the international efforts to develop the water resources of the Mekong River (McNeely, 1987).

History of Protected Areas in the Asia–Pacific Region

Protection of wildlife has a long tradition in the Indian subcontinent. The concept of protected areas dates back at least to the 4th century BC in India, with the establishment of Abhayaranyas, or forest reserves, advocated in the *Arthasashtra*, the well-known manual of state-craft (Singh, 1985). Similarly, in Sri Lanka, one of the world's first wildlife sanctuaries was created in the 3rd century BC by King Devenampiya Tissa (Dikshit, 1986), at the same time that Buddhism was being introduced to the island. Sacred groves are an even older institution, thought to date back to the pre-agrarian period of hunter-gatherer societies. These patches of forest were afforded special protection, with limited use of resources sanctioned only during times of calamity. In some countries, such as Thailand, areas surrounding temples and other religious sites have been protected due to the Buddhist prohibition on hunting.

In the Pacific region conservation practices have been closely linked with customary tenure systems, whereby a large degree of communal control is exercised over land use and natural resource exploitation. The imposition of taboo (or *tapu*) was one of the principal means by which wildlife and habitats were conserved. The existing protected areas network in the Pacific island of Niue, for example, is limited to a number of *tapu* forests, notably Huvalu Tapu Forest, which contains a significant proportion of the island's remaining tropical rain forest.

Much later in history, some areas rich in wildlife were preserved specifically for hunting by the privileged classes. These form the basis of a number of existing protected areas in India and Sri Lanka. The colonial era also involved the establishment of nature reserves by both colonial and indigenous governments. In Indonesia, for example, Java had a network of 55 nature reserves totalling 1300 sq. km by 1929, following the enactment of the Nature Monuments Ordinance in 1916; and reserves in Borneo and Sumatra, totalling well over 5000 sq. km, were established in areas under the 'indirect rule' of traditional Sultans (Westermann, 1945).

Many more protected areas were originally forest reserves established over the past hundred years or so to safeguard timber, soil and

---

CATEGORIES AND MANAGEMENT OBJECTIVES OF PROTECTED AREAS

I Scientific Reserve/Strict Nature Reserve

To protect nature and maintain natural processes in an undisturbed state in order to have ecologically representative examples of the natural environment available for scientific study, environmental monitoring, education, and for the maintenance of genetic resources in a dynamic and evolutionary state.

II National Park

To protect natural and scenic areas of national or international significance for scientific, educational and recreational use.

III Natural Monument/Natural Landmark

To protect and preserve nationally significant natural features because of their special interest or unique characteristics.

IV Managed Nature Reserve/Wildlife Sanctuary

To assure the natural conditions necessary to protect nationally significant species, groups of species, biotic communities, or physical features of the environment where these require specific human manipulation for their perpetuation.

V Protected Landscape

To maintain nationally significant natural landscapes which are characteristic of the harmonious interaction of man and land while providing opportunities for public enjoyment through recreation and tourism within the normal life style and economic activity of these areas.

VI Resource Reserve

To protect the natural resources of the area for future use and prevent or contain development activities that could affect the resource pending the establishment of objectives which are based upon appropriate knowledge and planning.

VII Natural Biotic Area/Anthropological Reserve

To allow the way of life of societies living in harmony with the environment to continue undisturbed by modern technology.

VIII Multiple-Use Management Area/Managed Resource Area

To provide for the sustained production of water, timber, wildlife, pasture, and outdoor recreation, with the conservation of nature primarily oriented to the support of the economic activities (although specific zones may also be designated within these areas to achieve specific conservation objectives).

Source: adapted from IUCN/CNPPA (1984a)

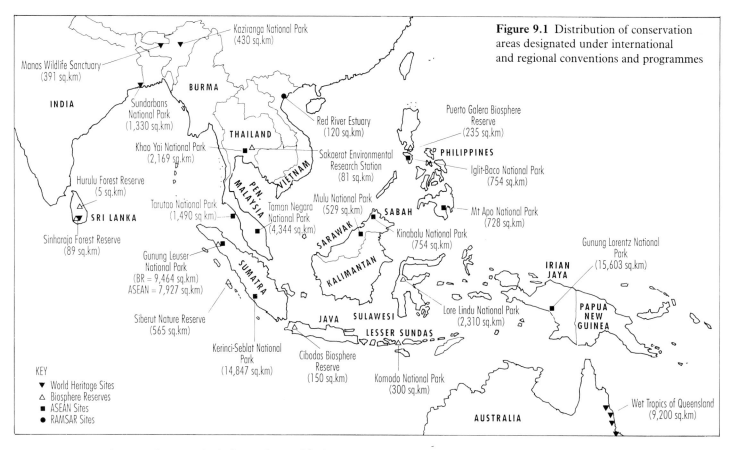

Figure 9.1 Distribution of conservation areas designated under international and regional conventions and programmes

water resources and were subsequently designated as national parks or sanctuaries. Many of the existing protected areas of India, Indonesia, Thailand and Malaysia, for example, have evolved from forestry traditions. While the primary role of forest reserves has usually been to provide for controlled commercial exploitation, their conservation importance is increasingly being recognised. Thailand, for example, had 1218 forest reserves covering 45 per cent of its total land area in 1989. Though some of them actually have few trees, they are classified as production or conservation forests; the latter category includes watershed areas, as well as national parks, wildlife sanctuaries, non-hunting areas and forest parks. Similarly, in Taiwan, some 23 per cent of the national forest estate, which covers approximately half of the country, has been reclassified as protection forest in ecologically sensitive areas such as watersheds. Commercial logging operations are being brought under increasingly strict control, to the extent that felling is prohibited above certain altitudes or gradients in countries such as India and Taiwan, or totally banned as in the case of Thailand and several provinces of the Philippines (though the effectiveness of such bans remains to be demonstrated).

Protected areas were often established on an *ad hoc* basis during the earlier part of this century, with little regard to ecological or other criteria. This is reflected in the existing networks of Bangladesh (Olivier, 1979) and Fiji (Watling, 1988), in which important biological resources are not adequately represented. More systematic approaches have been adopted in Indonesia (FAO, 1982; Petocz, 1984) and most recently in India (Rogers and Panwar, 1988) and the Philippines (Anon., 1988), while in Laos a national review is currently under way. In Malaysia such approaches are integral to the development of state conservation strategies, that for Sarawak being a notable example (see chapter 24).

International and Regional Initiatives

A number of countries in the Asia–Pacific region participate in the various international and regional conventions or programmes concerned with promoting the conservation of regionally or interna-

tionally important natural sites. Details are summarised in Table 9.1 (opposite). These conventions and programmes provide powerful forces for conserving some of the region's most important sites by strengthening the position of the responsible national authorities and gaining financial support from international sources. Opportunities to augment national resources available for managing the sites and their environs, however, are seldom exploited fully.

1 The Convention concerning the Protection of the World Cultural and Natural Heritage boasts the greatest number of member countries (ten) from the region. Tropical moist forest sites included on the list by 1989 include Manas Wildlife Sanctuary (India), Kaziranga National Park (India), Sundarbans National Park (India), Sinharaja Natural Heritage Wilderness Area (Sri Lanka), and Wet Tropics of Queensland (the latter is particularly significant, as it covers virtually all of Australia's remaining tropical rain forest). The Convention provides for the designation of natural and cultural areas of 'outstanding universal value' as World Heritage sites, in order to promote their significance at local, national and international levels. It imposes a legal duty on contracting parties to do their utmost to protect their natural and cultural heritage; this obligation extends beyond sites inscribed in the World Heritage List. The Convention also has provision for aid and technical cooperation to be offered to contracting parties for the protection of their World Heritage sites.

2 The Unesco Man and Biosphere Programme (MAB) provides for the establishment of a worldwide system of 'Biosphere Reserves', which are intended to be representative of natural ecosystems, to conserve genetic diversity and to promote monitoring, research and training. Particular emphasis is placed on the restoration of degraded ecosystems to more natural conditions, harmoniously integrating traditional patterns of land use within a conservation framework and involving local people in decision-making processes. A network of biosphere reserves, distributed among a number of countries, has been set up in the region, but only eight, in three countries, contain tropical moist forest, namely Hurulu and Sinharaja Forest Reserves in Sri Lanka, Mae Sa-Kog Ma Reserve in Thailand and Cibodas

Biosphere Reserve, Lore Lindu, Tanjung Puting and Gunung Leuser National Parks, and Siberut Nature Reserve in Indonesia. The MAB Programme is based on very sound principles, and the general approach is being adopted in many areas which are not formally designated as biosphere reserves. The main weakness of the programme is that, unlike conventions, it is not legally binding: implementation of the programme is the responsibility of National MAB committees, which lack legal powers.

3 Three countries within the region have also signed the Convention on Wetlands of International Importance especially as Waterfowl Habitat, otherwise known as the Ramsar Convention. This provides the framework for international cooperation to conserve wetlands. Contracting parties accept an undertaking to promote the wise use of all wetlands and to designate one or more wetlands for inclusion in a 'List of Wetlands of International Importance'. Red River Estuary in Vietnam is the only designated site in the region, but numerous freshwater and mangrove swamp forest areas would qualify for inclusion in this list.

4 The six countries constituting the Association of Southeast Asian Nations (ASEAN) participate in the ASEAN Environment Programme, which has been in existence since December 1978. One of the main goals of this programme is to develop and promote a regional network of protected areas of outstanding importance for their wilderness quality and biological diversity. Known as 'ASEAN Heritage Parks and Reserves', eleven such sites have been declared to date, all but one of which still contain tropical moist forest. Under an agreement reached in 1985, member countries are obliged *inter alia* to conserve the habitats of rare and threatened species through the establishment and maintenance of protected areas.

5 Of the South Pacific countries considered in this atlas, only Papua New Guinea has signed, but not ratified, the 1976 Convention on the Conservation of Nature in the South Pacific. Known as the Apia Convention, it requires four more countries to deposit instruments of ratification to enter into force. The Convention is coordinated by the South Pacific Commission and represents the first attempt within the South Pacific to cooperate on environmental matters. Among other measures, it encourages the creation of protected areas to preserve indigenous flora and fauna.

6 Papua New Guinea, Australia, Solomon Islands, Vanuatu and Fiji are party to the South Pacific Regional Environment Programme (SPREP) 1986 but only Australia and Vanuatu have ratified the 1986 SPREP Convention for the Protection of the Natural Resources and Environment of the South Pacific Region. The main objectives of the Convention are to combat pollution, although one article covers protected areas and protection of wild flora and fauna. Parties are required to protect and preserve rare and fragile ecosystems and depleted, threatened or endangered flora, fauna and their habitats. To date, however, insufficient countries have ratified the Convention for it to enter into force.

7 A new global Convention on the Conservation of Biological Diversity is in the process of being drawn up by IUCN and UNEP. The convention would extend across all species and habitats; moreover, it would provide for a global approach to financing the conservation of biological diversity.

The Coverage of Tropical Moist Forests by Protected Areas

Compared with other habitats, the world's tropical rain and monsoon forests are among the least well protected. Not only do new sites need to be protected, but also protected areas must be larger than at present if their biological diversity is to be maintained.

The protected areas systems of the Indo-Malayan and Oceanian realms have been reviewed by IUCN/UNEP (1986a) and IUCN/UNEP (1986b), respectively. These reports conclude that, as elsewhere in the world, protection of tropical moist forests is inadequate for most countries (Australia being a notable exception). Even where coverage appears to be sufficient, as in Thailand, effective on-the-ground protection is often lacking. Recommendations for developing national protected areas systems are outlined in these reviews and also in action strategies prepared by field managers in the respective realms (IUCN/CNPPA, 1985; SPREP, 1985).

Table 9.1 State parties to international and regional conventions or programmes concerned with the conservation of natural areas

	International			Regional		
	World Heritage Convention	*Biosphere Reserves*	*Ramsar Convention*	*ASEAN Convention*	*Apia Convention*	*SPREP Convention*
India	14 Nov 77 (3[1])		1 Oct 81			
Sri Lanka	6 Jun 80 (1)	(2)				
Bangladesh	3 Aug 83					
Burma						
Thailand	17 Sep 87	(1)		1967 (2)		
Vietnam	19 Oct 87		20 Sep 88 (1)			
Cambodia						
Laos	20 Mar 87					
China	12 Dec 85	(0)				
Malaysia	7 Dec 88			1967 (3)		
Singapore				1967 (0)		
Indonesia		(5)		1967 (3)		
Brunei				1984 (1)		
Philippines	19 Sep 85	(0)		1967 (2[a])		
Papua New Guinea						
Australia	22 Aug 74 (1)	(0)	8 May 74			24 Nov 87
Vanuatu						Aug 89
Solomons						
Fiji						

[1] Where applicable, the number of tropical moist forest sites recognised under respective conventions is given in brackets.

[a] Includes Mounts Iglit–Baco, which is deforested.

One of the central purposes of this atlas is to map the distribution of protected areas larger than 50 sq. km in relation to remaining rain and monsoon forests. To date the published statistical information on this subject has been difficult to interpret. While it is possible to calculate the total extent of protected areas within a country, or within a biogeographical realm or vegetation type, this does not necessarily reflect the extent of forest remaining in them. The maps in chapters 12–29 enable the reader to see at a glance which are the key areas in which the moist forests of the Asia–Pacific region are protected.

It would be immensely valuable to determine exactly how much tropical moist forest is distributed within the boundaries of protected areas, but to do this from the forest maps in this atlas would be unrealistic because of their small scale. Instead, all sites containing tropical moist forest have been identified in the tables of protected areas accompanying each country chapter. Data related to these properties are summarised in Table 9.2.

Extreme caution needs to be exercised in drawing overly general conclusions from Table 9.2 because circumstances differ considerably between countries. Of the three nations with over 300,000 sq. km of tropical moist forest, Burma and Papua New Guinea have very small existing and proposed protected areas systems, while Indonesia's is extensive. Cambodia, India, Laos, Malaysia and Thailand each has between 100,000 and 200,000 sq. km of tropical moist forest

and in all of these the extent of the existing and proposed protected areas systems is over 10 per cent of remaining tropical moist forests. It should not be overlooked, however, that these percentages will rise as the forests outside protected areas systems are progressively destroyed. In the nations with less than 100,000 sq. km of tropical moist forest, Australia, Brunei, Sri Lanka and Vietnam are well endowed with existing and proposed protected areas, but on the other hand existing protection in Bangladesh, China and the Philippines is critically low. In countries such as Burma, Laos and Malaysia there is a large backlog of proposed gazettements to implement.

Apart from inadequate representation of tropical moist forest within existing protected area systems, conservation efforts are limited by weaknesses in legislation and ineffective management. A recent survey of Indian protected areas, for example, shows that legal procedures have been completed in just 40 per cent of its national parks and 8 per cent of its sanctuaries (Kothari et al., 1989). The status of Indonesia's national parks is even less secure; despite their being officially declared, there is no legal basis for their existence.

The effectiveness with which protected areas are managed varies from country to country, often a reflection of relative economic prosperity. They also vary from site to site, depending on local conditions and other factors. India's prestigious Tiger Reserves, supported with Central Government assistance, tend to be well managed compared to many of its sanctuaries, which are often

Table 9.2 Protected area coverage of tropical moist forest (for definition see box, page 11)

	Land area ('000 sq. km)	Approximate original extent of closed canopy tropical moist forests (adapted from IUCN/UNEP, 1986a) ('000 sq. km)	Remaining area of tropical moist forest (sq. km)[1]	Total area of protected areas with tropical moist forest[2]			Existing tropical moist forest protected areas as a percentage of:			Existing and proposed tropical moist forest protected areas as a percentage of:		
				Existing (sq. km)	Proposed (sq. km)	Totals[6] (sq. km)	Land area	Original moist forest	Remaining moist forest	Land area	Original moist forest	Remaining moist forest
Australia	7,618	11	10,516[3]	7,605[3]	—	7,605[3]	0.09	69.1	72.3	0.09	69.1	72.3
Bangladesh	134	130	9,730	744	—	744	0.6	0.5	7.6	0.6	0.5	7.6
Brunei	5.8	5	4,692	1,078	104	1,182	18.5	21.5	22.9	20.3	23.6	25.1
Burma	658	600	311,850	5,641	7,399	13,040	0.9	0.9	1.8	2.0	2.2	4.2
Cambodia	177	160	113,250[4]	20,351	4,675	25,026	11.5	12.7	18.0	14.1	15.6	22.1
China and Taiwan	9,363	340	25,860	3,865	290	4,155	0.04	1.1	14.9	0.04	1.2	16.1
India	2,973	910	228,330[5]	22,658[5]	18,892[5]	41,500[5]	0.8	2.1	9.9	1.3	4.5	18.1
Indonesia	1,812	1,700	1,179,140	137,875	128,108	265,983	7.6	8.1	11.7	14.6	15.6	22.5
Laos	231	225	124,600	—	47,211	47,211	0	0	0	20.4	21.0	37.9
Federal Malaysia	329	320	200,450	13,263	14,388	27,651	4.0	4.1	6.6	8.4	8.6	13.8
Peninsular Malaysia	(132)	(130)	(69,780)	(6,181)	(6,519)	(12,700)	(4.7)	(4.8)	(8.9)	(9.6)	(9.8)	(18.2)
Sabah and Sarawak	(198)	(190)	(130,670)	(7,082)	(7,869)	(14,951)	(3.6)	(3.7)	(5.4)	(7.6)	(7.9)	(11.4)
Papua New Guinea	452	450	366,750	9,164	—	9,164	2.0	2.0	2.5	2.0	2.0	2.5
Philippines	298	295	66,020	1,775	620	2,395	0.6	0.6	2.6	0.8	0.8	3.6
Singapore	0.6	0.5	c.1	0.7	—	0.7	0.1	0.1	70.0	0.1	0.1	70.0
Sri Lanka	65	26	12,260	6,309	—	6,309	9.7	24.3	51.5	9.7	24.3	51.5
Thailand	512	250	106,900	44,790	11,855	56,645	8.7	17.9	41.9	11.1	22.7	53.0
Vietnam	325	280	56,680	6,252	—	6,252	1.9	2.2	11.0	1.9	2.2	11.0

[1] Figures given here are derived from the maps in chapters 12–29. As explained in these chapters some maps are based on more recent information than others.

[2] It must be emphasised that these totals are for protected areas greater than 50 sq. km in extent, which contain at least some tropical moist forest as determined in the maps in chapters 12–29. Since many of these protected areas are only partially forested the coverage will be over-optimistic but the numerous forested protected areas less than 50 sq. km in extent which have not been considered in this analysis will tend to redress the balance.

[3] Note that data for Australia refer only to tropical rain forests. Temperate rain forests and tropical monsoon forests are not mapped in chapter 12. Protected areas data refer only to national parks, not to the World Heritage site.

[4] Mapped data for Cambodia are out of date. FAO figures show closed forest extent in 1980 as 71,500 sq. km. See chapter 16 for details.

[5] Note that these data refer only to the Western Ghats, north-east India and the Andaman and Nicobar Islands, as mapped in detail in chapter 18. There are no tropical rain forests beyond these regions, but the monsoon forests are extensive. It has not been possible to estimate protected area coverage throughout the monsoon forests.

[6] Totals are derived from those protected areas mapped in chapters 12–29 which feature moist tropical forest within their boundaries.

inadequately staffed. By contrast, Taiwan boasts an extremely effectively managed protected areas system, doubtless a reflection of its economic prosperity. Second in the world only to Japan in terms of its foreign reserves, it invests up to US$110,000 per sq. km of protected area, which is an order of magnitude greater than in many European countries. At the other end of the scale, in countries such as Sri Lanka, Vietnam, and Cambodia, the repercussions of wars and civil unrest on protected areas have sometimes been disastrous.

Even in the absence of wars or natural hazards, such as fires and cyclones, legal protection does not necessarily guarantee the survival of tropical moist forest. Many of Indonesia's protected areas, for example, suffer from both legal and illicit logging. IUCN's Commission on National Parks and Protected Areas maintains a register of threatened protected areas in which several tropical moist forest sites in the Asia–Pacific region are currently listed. Most, such as Gunung Leuser, Kerinci Seblat and Kutai in Indonesia, are threatened by illegal logging and settlement, while, for example, Thaleban National Park in Thailand is becoming isolated as a result of clearance of adjacent forests in Malaysia. As the list is not yet compiled on a fully systematic basis, it does not represent a quantitative estimate of the total number of protected areas under threat, which is certainly much higher.

An Expanded Approach to Protecting Tropical Moist Forest

Traditional approaches to conservation, based on the preservationist concept of 'locking away' areas, are becoming increasingly inappropriate under ever mounting human pressures. They are being superseded by more modern strategic methods, that are based on the management of natural areas to support sustainable development (see McNeely and Miller, 1984; McNeely and Thorsell, 1985; McNeely et al., 1989).

This new conservation ethic forms the basis of the World Conservation Strategy, which was prepared by the world's leading conservation agencies and launched in 1980 (IUCN, 1980). In the Strategy, the conservation of living resources is shown to be vital for sustainable development. The essential contribution of protected areas to sustainable development is highlighted in the Bali Declaration prepared by participants at the Third World National Parks Congress (McNeely and Miller, 1984). Among the priorities identified, both in the Strategy and at the Bali Congress, is the need to ensure that tropical rain and monsoon forests are comprehensively represented within protected areas systems. The importance of developing national networks of protected areas to conserve tropical forests is endorsed by the Tropical Forestry Action Plan (FAO, 1985). This was formulated in recognition that failure to protect tropical forest ecosystems and their biological resources now will result in an inability to respond to future needs and challenges, as well as failure to take advantage of current opportunities for tourism, education, research and watershed protection (see chapter 10).

The need for a more strategic approach to conservation that anticipates and prevents the more destructive impacts of development policies is clearly identified in the final report of the World Commission on Environment and Development (WCED, 1987). A useful tool in promoting such an approach is the preparation and implementation of national conservation strategies whereby the processes of conservation and development are integrated. These are already completed or under way in Bangladesh, India, Sri Lanka, Thailand, Vietnam, Malaysia, the Philippines and Fiji.

Initiatives to link development and environmental protection are evident in a number of national and regional planning programmes. Palawan has been the subject of a strategic environmental plan based on a land capability assessment (see case study in chapter 8), and a recent assessment of land use in Indonesia has given due consideration to ecologically sensitive areas, including those represented within the country's protected areas system (see chapter 19). Another example is Siberut, off Sumatra, for which a plan was developed to zone the entire island and establish it as a biosphere reserve (McNeely et al., 1980).

At the local level, protected areas need to be linked with rural development projects rather than become increasingly isolated from surrounding land usage. This can be achieved through the establishment of buffer zones in which natural resources are managed sustainably for the benefit of the local people. The development of buffer zones, by which the protection of undisturbed core areas of biological richness is enhanced by surrounding multiple-use areas managed at least partly by the local people, is central to the biosphere concept. Buffer zone management in tropical moist forests is reviewed by Oldfield (1988), one example being a community-based forestry programme, which is being developed to stabilise the boundaries of Cyclops Mountains Nature Reserve in Irian Jaya. The reserve is surrounded by a buffer zone in which hunting and felling of timber for local use is permitted and controlled by the community.

In practice, the majority of protected areas tend to have uneasy relations with the people living around them. The reasons for this are apparent: the local people pay the costs of conservation through not being able to harvest resources as they might wish, while the bulk of the benefits go to the nation at large or even to the international community. Governments need to seek ways of redressing this imbalance to ensure that more of the benefits are delivered to the local community, because fostering local support for protected areas is essential for their ultimate survival. In Irian Jaya, where most protected areas are inhabited by traditional hunter-gatherers, farmers or fishermen, community involvement is central to their management. Arfak Mountains Nature Reserve, for example, is managed by a series of village committees, while in the surrounding buffer zone butterfly farming is being promoted. In neighbouring Papua New Guinea, where 97 per cent of the land is held under customary ownership, the protected areas system consists largely of wildlife management areas. These are reserved at the request of the land owners for the conservation and controlled utilisation of the wildlife and its habitat (Eaton, 1986).

The case for protecting tropical moist forest has been made. Yet, despite their value, all but the most remote protected areas are under threat, and only a small proportion are large enough to support ecological and evolutionary processes. There are no universal rules which address how areas should be protected, either in the short or long term. The concept of national parks as defensible treasure houses is becoming a thing of the past, but contemporary notions of buffering core areas with surrounding sustainable-use zones may also become outmoded as human values change. The concept of 'protected' areas is already being replaced by 'conservation' areas and in time may be replaced by harmoniously integrated land-use which satisfies the requirements of both people and wildlife.

Looking ahead 100 years or more, today's protected areas may be viewed as 'Holocene refugia', harbouring plants and animals in much the same way as 'Pleistocene refugia' accommodated species during the last ice age. These refugia can act as bridges from the relatively pristine past to a more environmentally secure future. We must hope that by the year 2100 human populations will stabilise, and resource exploitation will be based on sustainable principles. The diversity and abundance of biological resources that the present generation bequeaths to its descendants will define their range of options. Protected areas, in whatever form, will be keystones in that heritage (Hales, 1989; McNeely, 1989).

DIRECT BENEFITS OF PROTECTED AREAS

Direct benefits of protected areas are those which are tangible, immediate and measurable. They can include:

1 Protecting renewable harvestable resources

Protected areas act as refugia for crucial life stages or elements of wildlife populations that are harvested beyond their boundaries. The mangroves of the Sundarbans bordering the Bay of Bengal, for example, provide the main nursery for shrimps along the entire coast of eastern India, as well as spawning grounds for a wealth of fish and crustaceans.

2 Supporting nature-related recreation and tourism

The protected areas of the Asia–Pacific region receive an estimated 400 million visitors per year. Villagers from Ban Sap Tai, adjacent to Khao Yai, for example, Thailand's oldest protected area, act as guides and porters for trekking parties of 10–12 tourists to supplement their income. Profits average US $200 per trek (Praween *et al.*, 1988). Periyar, in the Western Ghats, is one of India's most popular protected areas. Visitors, mostly nationals (91 per cent), totalled nearly 200,000 in 1986, generating some Rs 400,000 (US $40,000) from entrance fees and further revenue from boat tours, treks and elephant rides (Bashir, 1988).

3 Protecting wild species

Some 15,000 species of plants and animals are known to be directly useful to mankind; some 100,000 have been used in the past, and many more may be of potential use. Protecting this biological diversity has immediate practical applications and also keeps options open for the future. Tropical forests support the greatest diversity of plants whose secondary compounds may be of potential pharmaceutical use. Villagers living around Gunung Leuser National Park in Sumatra, for example, rely almost entirely on 170 or more plants for all medical treatment (Brimacombe and Elliott, 1985).

INDIRECT BENEFITS OF PROTECTED AREAS

Protected areas provide a number of indirect benefits in the form of services which depend on intact ecosystems. These can include:

1 Stabilising hydrological regimes

The value of maintaining natural rather than plantation forest is evident from a Malaysian study, in which peak run-off from forested catchments was found to be half that from rubber and oil palm plantations, while minimum flows were approximately double (Daniel and Kulasingham, 1974). The costs of protecting catchment areas can often be justified as part of the hydrological investment, as in the case of the US $1.5 million budgeted annually for protecting the watershed of Nam Pong Reservoir in Thailand (Hufschmidt and Srivardhana, 1986).

2 Contributing to climatic stability

Current evidence indicates that undisturbed forest helps to maintain rainfall in its immediate vicinity and also keep down local ambient temperatures, benefiting agriculture and living conditions in surrounding areas. In Thailand, for example, Khao Yai's extensive tropical forest appears to ameliorate climatic conditions in the region, thereby benefiting agriculture (Royal Forest Department, 1987).

3 Protecting soils

In Malaysia, erosion from plantations is from 11 to 20 times higher than from primary rain forest, depending on the crop (Myers, 1988), while sediment loads increase by 70–97 per cent following logging. Apart from reducing erosion and sediment loads, protected areas also safeguard coastlines. A notable example is the Sundarbans, one of the world's most extensive mangrove forests, which helps to protect the plains of West Bengal (India) and Bangladesh from the ravages of cyclones.

4 Contribution to the natural balance of the surrounding environment

Protected areas afford sanctuary to breeding populations of birds, for example, which control insect and mammal pests in surrounding agricultural areas. In Sabah, high densities of birds that nest in natural forest limit the abundance of caterpillars that would otherwise defoliate *Albizia* plantations (Fitter, 1986).

5 Providing facilities for scientific research and education

Protected areas provide excellent living laboratories for applied and other research. For example, long-term ecological and socio-economic studies have been carried out at Sakaerat Environmental Research Station in Thailand in order to provide a scientific basis for the management of forest resources (IUCN/CMC, 1987).

References

Anon. (1988) *Development of an Integrated Protected Areas System (IPAS) for the Philippines.* WWF–USA/Department of Environment and Natural Resources/Haribon Foundation.

Bänziger, H. (1988) How wildlife is helping to save Doi Suthep: Buddhist Sanctuary and National Park of Thailand. *Symb. Bot. Ups.* 28: 255–67.

Bashir, S. (1988) *Problems in the Development of Wildlife Tourism in Periyar Tiger Reserve, India.* M.Phil. Dissertation, Department of Applied Biology, University of Cambridge, Cambridge, UK.

Brimacombe, J. and Elliott, S. (1985) *The Medicinal Plants of Gunung Leuser National Park, Indonesia.* WWF, Gland, Switzerland.

Daniel, J. G. and Kulasingham, A. (1974) Problems arising from large-scale forest clearing for agricultural use. *Malaysian Forester* 37: 152–60.

Dikshit, D. D. (1986) *Agriculture, Irrigation, and Horticulture in Ancient Sri Lanka.* Bharatiya Vidya Prakashan, Delhi and Varanasi, India.

Eaton, P. (1986) Grass roots conservation. Wildlife management areas in Papua New Guinea. *Land Studies Centre Report* 86/1. University of Papua New Guinea.

FAO (1982) *National Conservation Plan for Indonesia.* 8 Vols. FAO, Bogor, Indonesia.

FAO (1985) *Tropical Forestry Action Plan.* Committee on Forest Development in the Tropics. FAO, Rome, Italy.

Hales, D. (1989) Changing concepts of national parks. In: Western, D. and Pearl, M. C. (eds) *Conservation for the Twenty-first century.* pp. 139–44. Oxford University Press, New York.

Fitter, R. (1986) *Wildlife for Man: How and Why We Should Conserve Our Species.* Collins, London, UK.

Hufschmidt, M. M. and Ruangdej Srivardhana (1986) The Nam Pong water resources project in Thailand. In: *Economic Valuation Techniques for the Environment – A Case Study Workbook* Dixon, J. A. and Hufschmidt, F. (eds), pp. 141–62. Johns Hopkins University Press, Baltimore, MD, USA.

IUCN (1980) *World Conservation Strategy: Living Resource Conservation for Sustainable Development.* IUCN/UNEP/WWF, Gland, Switzerland.

IUCN/CMC (1987) *Directory of Indomalayan Protected Areas: Thailand, Draft.* IUCN Conservation Monitoring Centre, Cambridge, UK.

IUCN/CNPPA (1984a) Categories, objectives and criteria for Protected Areas. In: *National parks, Conservation and Development: the Role of Protected Areas in Sustaining Society* McNeely, J. A. and Miller, K. R. (eds), pp. 47–53. Smithsonian Institution Press, Washington, DC, USA.

IUCN/CNPPA (1985) *The Corbett Action Plan for Protected Areas of the Indomalayan Realm.* IUCN, Gland, Switzerland, and Cambridge, UK.

IUCN/UNEP (1986a) *Review of the Protected Areas System in the Indo-Malayan Realm.* IUCN, Gland, Switzerland, and Cambridge, UK.

IUCN/UNEP (1986b) *Review of the Protected Areas System in Oceania.* IUCN, Gland, Switzerland, and Cambridge, UK.

Kothari, A., Pande, P., Singh, S., and Variava, D. (1989) *Management of National Parks and Sanctuaries in India: A Status Report.* Indian Institute of Public Administration, New Delhi.

MacKinnon, J., MacKinnon, K., Child, G. and Thorsell, J. (1986) *Managing Protected Areas in the Tropics.* IUCN, Cambridge, UK, and Gland, Switzerland.

McNeely, J. A. (1987) How dams and wildlife can co-exist: natural habitats, agriculture, and major water resource development projects in tropical Asia. *Journal of Conservation Biology* 1: 228–38.

McNeely, J. A. (1988) *Economics and Biological Diversity: Developing and Using Economic Incentives to Conserve Biological Resources.* IUCN, Gland, Switzerland.

McNeely, J. A. (1989) Protected areas and human ecology: how National Parks can Contribute to Sustaining Societies of the Twenty-first Century. In: *Conservation for the Twenty-first Century* Western, D. and Pearl, M. C. (eds), pp. 150–7. Oxford University Press, New York, USA.

McNeely, J. A. and Miller, K. R. (eds) (1984) *National Parks, Conservation and Development: the Role of Protected Areas in Sustaining Society.* Smithsonian Institution Press, Washington, DC, USA.

McNeely, J. A., Miller, K. R., Reid, W. V. and Mittermeier, R. (1989) *Conserving the World's Biological Resources.* WRI/IUCN/World Bank/Conservation International/WWF, Washington, DC, USA.

McNeely, J. A. and Thorsell, J. W. (eds) (1985) *People and Protected Areas in the Hindu Kush-Himalaya.* King Mahendra Trust and ICIMOD, Kathmandu.

McNeely, J. A., Whitten, A. J., Whitten, J. and House, A. (1980) *Saving Siberut: A Conservation Master Plan.* WWF-Indonesia, Bogor.

Medway, Lord (1971) Importance of Taman Negara in the Conservation of Mammals. *Malayan Nature Journal* 24: 212–14.

Myers, N. (1988) Tropical forests: much more than stocks of wood. *Journal of Tropical Ecology* 4: 209–21.

Oldfield, S. (1988) *Buffer Zone Management in Tropical Moist Forests: Case Studies and Guidelines.* IUCN, Cambridge, UK, and Gland, Switzerland.

Olivier, R. C. D. (1979) *Wildlife Conservation and Management in Bangladesh.* 121 pp. UNDP/FAO Project No. BGD/72/005. Forest Research Institute, Chittagong.

Panwar, H. (1984) What to do when you've succeeded: Project Tiger, Ten Years Later, pp. 193–290. In: McNeely, J. A. and Miller, K. R. (eds) (1984) (*loc. cit.*).

Petocz, R. G. (1984) *Conservation and Development in Irian Jaya: A Strategy for Rational Resource Utilization.* Directorate General of Forest Protection and Nature Conservation, Bogor, Indonesia.

Praween Payapvipapong, Tavatchai Traitongyoo, and Dobias, R. J. (1988) *Using Economic Incentives to Integrate Park Conservation and Rural Development in Thailand.* Paper presented at Workshop on Economics, IUCN General Assembly, 4–5 February 1988, Costa Rica.

Rogers, W. A. and Panwar, H. S. (1988) *Planning a Wildlife Protected Area Network in India.* 2 Vols. FAO/Wildlife Institute of India, Dehra Dun.

Round, P. D. (1988) *Resident Forest Birds in Thailand: their Status and Conservation.* International Council for Bird Preservation Monograph No. 2. 211 pp.

Royal Forest Department (1987) *Khao Yai National Park Management Plan 1987–1991.* National Park Division, Royal Forest Department, Ministry of Agriculture and Cooperatives, Bangkok, Thailand.

Singh, Samar (1985) Protected areas in India. In: *Conserving Asia's Natural Heritage* Thorsell, J. W. (ed.), pp. 11–15. IUCN, Gland, Switzerland, and Cambridge, UK.

SPREP (1985) *Action Strategy for Protected Areas in the South Pacific Region.* South Pacific Commission, Noumea, New Caledonia.

Watling, D. (1988) The forestry sector development study. FIJ/86/004. Unpublished Report. Suva, Fiji.

Westermann, J. H. (1945) Wild life conservation in the Netherlands Empire, its national and international aspects. *Natur-wetenschappelijk Tijdschrift voor Nederlandsch Indië* 102 (Special Supplement): 417–24.

WCED (1987) *Our Common Future.* Oxford University Press, Oxford, UK.

Authorship

Michael Green and James Paine of WCMC, Cambridge, and Jeffrey McNeely at IUCN, Gland, Switzerland.

10 The Tropical Forestry Action Plan

Introduction

The World Conservation Strategy, published in 1980 by the major global conservation organisations, laid down new ground rules for natural resource conservation and management in the late 20th century (IUCN/UNEP/WWF, 1980). The basic thesis of the Strategy was that improvement of mankind's lot in the world, if it is to be sustained in the long-term, must satisfy the ecological and biological constraints of the planet on which we live. We must learn to regulate our consumption of living resources, whether it be fish, or any other wildlife, grazing lands or forest timber, at a rate that allows sustained renewal of stocks. Furthermore, exploitive actions must not disrupt essential ecological processes, nor destroy biological and genetic diversity.

These broad principles have come to be widely accepted, and in recent years organisations worldwide have begun to put them into practice. Many new initiatives owe their origin to the Strategy, including policy guidelines such as the report of the UN World Commission on Environment and Development (WCED, 1987), the strengthening of environment divisions in development banks and bilateral development assistance agencies, and the greatly increased public support for non-governmental organisations concerned with environment and development.

Nowhere has the impact resulting from contravention of the principles of the World Conservation Strategy been more strongly felt than in the world's tropical forests. Indeed, the Strategy recognised misuse of forest resources in the tropics as one of the major environmental issues. Deforestation across the spectrum of dry and moist, closed and open canopy forest has accelerated over the past 40 years to such an extent that soil erosion and flooding are widespread, and the renewable supply of fuelwood, building timber and other forest products from these ecosystems is in jeopardy (see chapters 2 and 11).

In 1981 the United Nations Food and Agriculture Organisation (FAO), which holds a mandate to monitor the world's forest resources and their management, published the first detailed, country-by-country assessment of the extent of tropical forests, to a 1980 dateline (FAO/UNEP, 1981; FAO, 1988). The results showed that in tropical Asia[1] there were some 2.9 million sq. km of closed canopy, broadleaved moist forests – about 25 per cent of the world total at that time. Every year throughout the early 1980s, however, FAO estimated that 17,410 sq. km were being logged over and a further 17,820 sq. km were being permanently cleared.

In many areas, forest clearance followed on from logging. Landless people, faced with the daily problem of feeding their families, were taking advantage of logging roads to give them access to new forest lands that, for a year or two at least, could grow enough crops to keep

hunger at bay. Definition of the real causes of the deforestation was emotive and hotly disputed. The poor settlers were not to blame, in the sense that they had no alternatives, but at the same time FAO declared that 'It is now generally recognised that the main cause of the destruction and degradation of tropical forests is the poverty of the people who live in and around the forests' (CDFT, 1985).[2] Logging companies, while bearing the onus of responsibility for mismanagement and degradation of many rain forests in the region, were not considered to be responsible for *permanent* deforestation to any great extent.

Had the deforested lands brought long-term improvement in the standards of living of forest peoples, their activities would have been more acceptable. But spontaneous agricultural settlement provides no more than the bare minimum needed for individual survival, while the impoverishment of soils and the loss of ecological services incur costs for the entire nation. The industrialised nations, recognising the dangers in this general pattern and spurred on by public concern, determined to focus development aid money on the tropical forests. They needed to coordinate their activities and their policies to achieve the best chance of reducing deforestation rates. The framework within which they chose to work is called the Tropical Forestry Action Plan (TFAP).

How the TFAP was Prepared

In 1983 the FAO Committee on Forest Development in the Tropics (CFDT), which brings together the Heads of Forest Departments from 45 tropical nations, representatives of the development agencies and observers from non-governmental organisations, noted with alarm that international funding for tropical forestry programmes, which had always been low in comparison with aid to agriculture, was decreasing still further. The Committee recommended that FAO should elaborate proposals for action programmes in priority areas, which it did, with the help of an informal meeting of experts in 1985. IUCN joined the World Resources Institute (WRI), the World Bank, the United Nations Development Programme (UNDP) and FAO in developing and promoting action programme proposals in five key areas of forestry (see Table 10.1) (WRI, 1985).

---

[1] The compiled data from the FAO assessment on Asia differed from the present work in including data for Bhutan (c. 14,900 sq. km of closed broadleaved forest) and Nepal (c. 16,100 sq. km), but not including data for Australia (10,510 sq. km) and the Western Pacific Islands (c. 34,700 sq. km). The net difference of 14,210 sq. km is less than half a per cent of the forest estate and the FAO data are therefore deemed broadly comparable with the data in this atlas.

[2] This conclusion is challenged by some non-governmental organisations, whose position is discussed on page 72 under 'NGO Involvement'.

The TFAP was formally adopted by the forestry authorities in most tropical and industrialised countries at the 9th World Forestry Congress in Mexico City in 1985. Subsequently the Plan was also endorsed by the International Conference on Trees and Forests ('Silva') held in France, by the FAO Committee on Forestry, and at the FAO Council and Conference and the 1987 Strategy Conference on Tropical Forestry at Bellagio in northern Italy. Since then, the multinational and bilateral development banks, and development assistance agencies, have all recognised tropical forest conservation as meriting priority attention under their loan, grant and technical assistance programmes.

The overall objective of the TFAP is to restore, conserve and manage forests and forest lands in such a way that they sustainably benefit rural people, agriculture and the general economy of the countries concerned. To do this, TFAP helps developing countries in deciding national priorities, in adapting their current policies to real needs, in preparing programmes and projects at the country level and in securing the financial support necessary to put those programmes and projects into action (FAO, 1990).

The essential tenet of the TFAP philosophy is that since poverty is the root cause of tropical deforestation, agencies should fund projects to alleviate that poverty and thus slow down deforestation. Many non-governmental organisations remain highly sceptical of the development agencies' ability to do this. They point out that the great majority of development aid projects are the direct cause of deforestation through alienation of forest lands for large-scale agricultural ventures, provision of roads, plantations of tree crops, mining and the building of hydroelectric dams. This much seems incontrovertible. But the development agencies rejoin that by learning from past errors, adding environmental expertise, and preparing a new breed of project, their growing investments in the forestry sector will indeed reduce deforestation. Whether they will succeed remains to be seen.

The World Resources Institute played a central role in the development of TFAP by convening a Task Force to examine what might realistically be done to control deforestation more effectively and support the sustainable use and improved management of tropical forests. In 1985 WRI published *Tropical Forests: A Call for Action*, which included an estimate of the cost of implementing measures to counter deforestation in 56 developing countries at US$5320 million for the period 1987–91 (Table 10.2[2]). Half of this amount was estimated to be overseas development assistance, the other half representing the contribution of national governments and the private sector. The WRI Task Force also estimated that the investment requirements for all tropical developing countries would add another 50 per cent to those for the 56 countries. In other words, investment needs in development aid for all tropical developing countries for the period 1987–91 could be estimated at about US$4050 million, or US$810 million per year, on average.

Table 10.1 The five priority areas of the TFAP[1]

1 Forestry in land use
Action in this area is at the interface between forestry and agriculture, and aims to conserve the resource base for agriculture, integrate forestry into agricultural systems and, in general, use the land more rationally.

2 Forest-based industrial development
Action in this area aims at promoting appropriate forest-based industries by intensifying resource management and development, promoting appropriate raw material harvesting, establishing and managing appropriate forest industries, reducing waste, and developing the marketing of forest industry products.

3 Fuelwood and energy
The aims are to restore fuelwood supplies in the countries affected by shortages, through global assistance and support for national fuelwood and wood energy programmes, development of wood-based energy systems for rural and industrial development, regional training and demonstration, and intensification of research and development.

4 Conservation of tropical forest ecosystems
The aims are to conserve, manage and utilise tropical plant and wild animal genetic resources through the development of national networks of protected areas; plan, manage and develop individual protected areas, and conduct research into the management of tropical forests for sustainable production.

5 Institutions
The aims are to remove the institutional constraints impeding conservation and wise use of tropical forest resources by strengthening public forest administrations and related government agencies, integrating forestry concerns into development planning, providing institutional support for private and local organisations, developing professional, technical and vocational training, and improving extension and research.

[1] Whilst designed to be comprehensive in their coverage, they do not preclude other projects and activities since development priorities must be established at country level (FAO, 1987; 1990).

Implementation of TFAP
Activities taking place under the TFAP banner are expedited and monitored by a small Coordination Unit based at FAO, Rome, where five staff respond to requests for information and for forest sector reviews, monitor progress and coordinate the activities of donors. To facilitate coordination, twice yearly, four-day meetings of the TFAP Forestry Advisers are held which bring together representatives (usually foresters) from the bilateral development agencies and

Table 10.2 Estimated costs of the Tropical Forestry Action Plan, 1987–91

Activity	Africa	% of total	Asia	% of total	Latin America	% of total	5-year totals	% of total
Forestry in land use	139	3	682	13	95	2	916	17
Forest-based industrial development	167	3	565	11	584	11	1,316	25
Fuelwood and energy	439	8	747	14	390	7	1,576	30
Conservation of forest ecosystems	105	2	148	3	195	4	448	8
Institutions	188	4	557	10	319	6	1,064	20
Totals	1,038	20	2,699	51	1,583	30	5,320	100

(*Source*: WRI, 1985)

banks, United Nations agencies (FAO, UNDP, UNEP and others), a number of NGOs, including ELC, IIED, IUCN, IUFRO, WRI and WWF, and representatives from countries with TFAP activities.

Implementation of TFAP is described in general terms in Table 10.3. It is essential to recognise, however, that the TFAP is a *proposed* framework for action by governments. It is for them to decide the most appropriate way to adopt the concepts of TFAP for more effective conservation and utilisation of their forest resources. They also decide on their own needs and priorities.

Participants in the process vary widely from one country to another. Some nations request technical assistance for the forestry sector review, while others (such as Malaysia and Indonesia) are carrying out the review as part of their national planning cycle, using local expertise. Participation by NGOs is explicitly encouraged by the TFAP guidelines and requested by some donors (see page 72).

Implementation of the TFAP began in early 1986. By September 1987 some 30 countries had initiated the planning process and by October 1989 67 countries had formally announced their decision to use TFAP to launch national forestry activities (Table 10.4). By October 1989 20 countries had completed forestry sector reviews, including Fiji, Papua New Guinea and Nepal, within the Asia–Pacific region. A further 38 reviews were on-going, including six within the region, while 15 countries had shown interest, including two in the region (see box on page 75 and country chapters).

The 67 countries involved with TFAP at the end of 1989 represent 52 per cent of the 129 potential participants and contain between them 87.4 per cent of the world's tropical closed broadleaved forests (FAO, 1988). By any standards this is a remarkable achievement, and a measure of the global determination to develop tropical forests in a rational and sustainable way.

Table 10.3 Elements in the implementation of the TFAP in a typical country exercise

1 Tropical forest country notifies the TFAP Secretariat in FAO of its intention to carry out a forestry sector review within the guidelines of TFAP.

2 Participation of donors is encouraged and, generally speaking, one donor country volunteers to act as the Lead Agency and to organise wide participation.

3 In-country review takes place of the role of the forestry sector in the national environmental, economic and social scene, in order to devise or update a national forestry development plan that integrates with other sectors, such as agriculture, and identifies the main causes of forest degradation and destruction.

4 Organisation of national seminars and round-table meetings to bring together concerned government sectors, non-governmental organisations, the private sector and the international voluntary community to raise awareness and discuss ways and means of addressing problems and priorities.

5 On the basis of the above, a long-term forestry sector plan is drawn up, with a strategy of targets for forest resources development.

6 A medium-term action plan is also prepared in the context of the long-term strategy and national development plan. This identifies priorities for immediate action, proposes precise programmes and projects, seeks legislative and institutional measures, if needed, and estimates costs and benefits.

7 Once the plan has been endorsed at the highest decision-making level in government, a donor round-table meeting is held to secure financing for the various programmes that have been identified.

8 With the necessary donor support assured, implementation of the TFAP programmes and projects begins.

9 FAO's TFAP Coordinating Unit monitors progress and promotes any complementary activities or follow-up that may be needed.

Harmonisation with Asian Development Bank Master Plans for Forestry Development

The Asian Development Bank (AsDB) Master Plans for Forestry Development are being, or have already been, prepared for a number of Asian countries. The broad objectives of these exercises are in line with the TFAP strategy, but tend to have longer-term objectives. In effect, Master Plans are TFAP exercises in which the Asian Development Bank takes the lead and thereby stamps its own particular pattern on the proceedings. Master Plans involve the formulation of long-term development programmes in the forestry sector broken down into five-year intervals. They take longer to prepare, mainly because fact-finding is lengthy, and they cost more than TFAP missions. The average cost of TFAP forest sector reviews is in the region of US$0.5 million, whereas Master Plans cost from US$0.75 million (Bhutan) to US$1.1 million (Nepal) and even US$1.37 million (Philippines) (Ganguli, 1988). They can take up to four years from initial contact to finalisation of reports and longer before projects to mitigate deforestation are in full swing.

Monitoring the Progress of TFAP

In recent meetings of the TFAP Forestry Advisers, there have been regular calls for a review of the achievements of TFAP. That so many countries wish to employ the strategy is to the credit of the Plan's authors, but *per se* it is no measure of success in reaching the main objective – a reduction in deforestation rates.

It is still too early to judge the long-term impact of TFAP on deforestation, but any contribution made so far has certainly been swamped by the general rising trend in deforestation rates. Recent statistics released by FAO show that deforestation in open and closed canopy tropical forests has gone up from 11.3 million ha per year in 1980 to 17.0 million ha per year in 1990. No precise data are available for closed forests alone, but the trend is similar.

TFAP aims to control deforestation by raising the standards of living of people inhabiting forest lands, and by conserving production forests in permanent forest estates, and by improved land use planning. Data are still too scattered and preliminary to make clear judgements on the effects of TFAP on rural development. Integration of TFAP into national development plans is only just beginning. However there is widespread concern that TFAP is not sufficiently influencing the agricultural sector, where many causes of deforestation have their origin.

What is possible is to examine some rather crude measures of success in raising investment levels in the tropical forest sector. Table 10.5 is a breakdown of international technical aid and investment in tropical forestry in 1984, before the TFAP was operational, and in 1988. Total technical aid and investment over the four-year period has increased by 80 per cent, and will probably double over a five-year period to 1989. However, as Table 10.7 shows, only US$576 million of the total aid for 1988 of US$1092 million was in investment (53 per cent), the remaining US$455.9 million being disbursed to pay for technical advisers. The TFAP called for an average US$810 million per year for 1987–91, so the 1988 level was still 29 per cent down (WRI, 1985). Bearing in mind that the Federal Republic of Germany was unable to disburse US$85 million of its allocation in 1988, the amount spent was in reality 39 per cent down.

This short-fall in spending is not easy to interpret. If the amounts derived by the World Bank/UNDP/WRI study are truly needed before any slowdown of deforestation might be expected, then clearly TFAP is not reaching its objectives. In reality, however, there are severe constraints on disbursement of such large sums. The expertise and infrastructures needed to handle the projects are simply not available in many parts of the tropical world (see section on constraints, page 73). A very detailed analysis of spending on a country by country basis, is beyond the scope of this volume, however.

Table 10.4 Status of the Tropical Forestry Action Plan implementation in 67 countries (as of 31 October, 1989), and of the Asian Development Bank's Master Plan for Forestry Development in 5 countries

1 Planning phase finalised (8 countries)

Country	Closed broadleaved forest area, sq. km (1980)
Argentina	427,400
Bolivia	440,100
Cameroon	179,200
Colombia	464,000
Honduras	18,550
Nepal[1]	16,100
Peru	693,100
Sudan	6,400
Sub total	2,244,850

2 Forestry sector review missions completed (12 countries)

Country	Closed forest area, sq. km (1980)
Belize	12,570
Dominican Republic	4,440
Fiji	840
Ghana	17,180
Guinea	20,500
Guyana	184,750
Panama	41,650
Papua New Guinea	337,100
Sierra Leone	7,400
Somalia	14,800
Tanzania	14,400
Zaire	1,056,500
Sub total	1,719,400

3 Ongoing forestry sector reviews (38 countries)

Country	Closed forest area, sq. km (1980)
Bhutan[1]	14,900
Burkina Faso	2,710
Congo	213,400
Costa Rica	16,380
Côte d'Ivoire	44,580
Cuba	12,550
Ecuador	142,300
Equatorial Guinea	12,950
Ethiopia	27,500
Gabon	205,000
Guatemala	37,850
Haiti	360
Indonesia	1,135,750
Jamaica	670
Laos[1]	75,600
Lesotho	—
Madagascar	103,000
Malaysia	209,960
Mali	5,000
Mauritania	290
Mexico	265,700
Nicaragua	41,700
Pakistan[1]	8,400
Philippines[1]	93,200
Senegal	2,200
Surinam	148,300
Togo	3,040
Venezuela	318,700
Vietnam	74,000
Sub total	3,216,190

CARICOM countries

Antigua and Barbuda	9
Barbados	—
St Christopher and Nevis	5
Dominica	41
Grenada	5
St Lucia	8
Montserrat	3
St Vincent and the Grenadines	12
Trinidad and Tobago	208
Sub total	2,910

4 Requests for TFAP implementation received (9 countries)

Angola	29,000
Burundi	—
Central African Republic	35,900
Kenya	6,900
Niger	1,000
Nigeria	59,500
Thailand	81,350
Zambia	30,100
Zimbabwe	2,000
Sub total	245,750

5 Inquiring (6 countries)

Brazil	3,562,800
Chad	5,000
Chile	71,800
Guinea Bissau	6,600
Rwanda	—
Solomon Islands	24,230
Sub total	3,670,430
Grand Total	11,099,530 (87.4% of world total)

[1] Exercises led by the Asian Development Bank under the Master Plan for Forestry Development programme. The Bank is also involved in Master Plans in Pakistan, China and Sri Lanka.

Table 10.5 International technical aid and investment for tropical forestry in 1984 and 1988 (millions of US dollars)

	1984	1988
Development banks		
African Development Bank	5	1
Asian Development Bank	30	75
Inter-American Development Bank	32	7
World Bank	106	130
Sub totals	173	213
International agencies		
FAO	8	11
ILO	n.d.	2
UNDP	28	25
UNEP	2	2
Unesco	n.d.	2
UNIDO	n.d.	3
UNSO	n.d.	12
WFP	110	131
Sub totals	148	188
National agencies		
Australia	3	5
Austria	1	<1
Belgium	3	1
Canada	15	75
Denmark	10	29
EEC	18	35
Finland	12	22
France	15	43
Germany, Federal Republic	25	147[1]
Ireland	1	<1
Italy	n.d.	11
Japan	13	86
Netherlands	10	32
New Zealand	3	4
Norway	5	13
Portugal	n.d.	<1
Spain	n.d.	1
Sweden	35	58
Switzerland	11	23
UK	5	23
USA	70	83
Sub totals	282	694
Grand Totals	603	1,095

(*Source:* adapted from FAO, 1989)

[1] US $85 million of this allocation was not disbursed during this year.

It is interesting to note the distribution of TFAP spending, as shown in Table 10.7. IUCN and many other observers of TFAP hold the view that the need to raise the *level* of investment in tropical forestry is secondary to the need to change the *way* in which the money is spent. Comparison between Tables 10.5 and 10.7 show that the proportions allocated to, and spent to date on, the five fields of action, are broadly similar. To date, fuelwood and energy have been under-funded, forestry in land use and forest-based industrial development have received a higher proportion than planned, while conservation and institutions are more or less on target.

On the face of it, this is good news for conservation, and certainly there has been a growing investment in the extension and management of protected area systems. However, it is implicit in the TFAP that the principles of the World Conservation Strategy should be applied in all five sectors of the plan, i.e. conservation applies as much to land use and industrial development sectors as to protection of biodiversity. It is in this regard that the implementation of TFAP still has a long way to go. There are too many traditional project proposals being developed that fail to integrate the conservation of ecological services and biological diversity into the plans. This is particularly worrying in the case of project proposals for industrial logging. It is generally agreed that TFAP reviews have not been sufficiently robust in requiring sustainable management systems to be in place *before* further investment in industrial logging can be considered. Sustainability in this context must mean conservation of ecosystems and their biodiversity, and integration with the needs of local people as well as the fundamental requirement for controlled harvesting rates.

NGO Involvement

Non-governmental organisations share the same aim with the development banks and aid agencies that devised TFAP. They recognise that tropical deforestation is a global crisis that threatens us all. Nevertheless, many NGOs disagree fundamentally with FAO's assessment of the *causes* of deforestation, and this means that they have a different set of priorities for action to prevent it progressing further.

For example, in 1987 the *Ecologist* magazine launched its own 'Tropical Forests: A Plan for Action' and petitioned worldwide for support (Ecologist, 1987). The editors gathered an astonishing 3 million signatures, from 23 countries, which were presented to the UN Secretary-General, Perez de Cuellar, in September 1989 in support of a call for an emergency session of the UN to consider ways to put an end to global deforestation (Hildyard, 1989). At the time of writing, there had been no response.

Table 10.6 The NGO perspective on TFAP

View of the TFAP promoters as seen by NGOs	*NGO community's view of TFAP*
1 Principal causes of deforestation:	
poverty	consumerism
population pressure	technological imperialism
shifting cultivation	development aid
2 Principal formulators of TFAP (national level):	
government	local communities
donors	traditional practices
expert missions	forest dwellers
planning from the top	consultations at local level
3 Principal aims of TFAP:	
more aid and investment	quality of aid and sustainable development
production	security
commodities	self reliance
generate wealth	improve welfare
4 Principal beneficiaries of TFAP:	
government bureaucracies	indigenous peoples
business	rural poor
developed countries' aid experts	landless

(*Source:* adapted from the TFAP Forestry Advisors, 1989)

Table 10.7 The distribution of technical assistance (TA) and investment (I) by TFAP fields of action in 1988 (US$ millions)

Fields of Action	Donor countries				Development Banks				UN Organisations				Grand Total			
	TA	I	Total	%	TA	I	Total	%	TA	I	Total	%	TA	I	Total	%
Forestry in land use	98.2	51.8	150.0	27.4	1.3	12.6	13.9	6.5	4.8	45.2	50.0	26.6	104.3	109.6	213.9	22.6
Forest-based industrial development	39.0	53.6	92.6	17.0	13.2	133.2	146.4	68.9	19.1	44.7	63.8	33.9	71.3	231.5	302.8	32.0
Fuelwood and energy	75.4	22.5	97.9	17.9	1.2	11.7	12.9	6.1	2.0	45.2	47.2	25.1	78.6	79.4	158.0	16.7
Conservation of tropical forest ecosystems	46.5	3.8	50.3	9.2	1.8	18.2	20.0	9.4	4.4	8.8	13.2	7.0	52.7	30.8	83.5	8.8
Institutions	133.9	21.6	155.5	28.5	1.7	17.7	19.4	9.1	13.4	0.4	13.8	7.4	149.0	39.7	188.7	19.9
Unallocated[2]			60.0												60.0	
Totals	393.0	238.7[1]	691.7[1]	100.0	19.2	193.4	212.6	100.0	43.7	144.3	188.0	100.0	455.9	576.4[1]	1,092.3[1]	100.0

[1] Includes undisbursed US$85.4, 13.5% of the total, from the Federal Republic of Germany.
[2] US$60m donated by Japan after the statistics were completed.
(*Source:* FAO (1989) *Review of International Cooperation in Tropical Forestry.* Unpublished)

Table 10.6 which was presented to the TFAP Advisors Group in Paris (May, 1989) by WRI summarises the main areas of conflict or differing perspectives. The contrasts are self-explanatory – for further details see Ecologist (1987), Muchiru (undated), Panos (1987) and Shiva (1987). In matters such as these, there is rarely one party which is entirely right or wrong. The most practical and achievable course of action generally lies somewhere between the two schools of thought.

In theory, partnerships between donor agencies and NGOs should be flourishing, and indeed there is a growing collaboration between donors and those NGOs that have an operational capability (WRI, 1988; 1989b). However, the majority of environmental NGOs are not operational in the sense that they do not carry out development and conservation projects in the field. They play a vital role in lobbying the public and spreading information about the problem of tropical deforestation. But if some of the more vociferous critics are to maintain their credibility they will have to show more willingness to work with others in tackling the practical difficulties. In too many cases the intransigent nature of NGOs does not now compare favourably with the fast-evolving attitude of the donor community.

At its Eighth Session in September 1989, the CFDT recommended that NGOs should be provided with more and better information, and more opportunities to participate in TFAP. The Committee also said that fuller use should be made of the capabilities of NGOs (CFDT, 1989). There is no doubt that many national forestry action plans would benefit from the experience and advice of local NGOs, which have sensitivity and contacts at the local level. The NGOs must sieze the opportunities that the TFAP is presenting (see Table 10.8) and find common ground with their counterparts in government. Arguably, the future of the forests depends on this partnership.

Constraints on Progress

The TFAP procedures are regularly scrutinised and refined by the participants at the Forestry Advisors' Meetings. Indeed, as this chapter is being prepared, the TFAP Coordination Unit is awaiting the conclusions of an independent review of achievements so far, for presentation to CFDT. Many NGOs are taking the opportunity to present their views to the review team. Constraints on progress are identified through the national forest sector reviews, which have been acknowledged as rather variable in their success, and through the feedback from the meetings between donors, national govern-

ments and NGOs. The main bottlenecks that limit the TFAP in reaching its objective of reducing deforestation may be characterised as follows:

1 Industrial Forestry – Plantations
Sector reviews and project proposals tend to adopt traditional attitudes to industrial forestry, both in natural forests and plantations. The development of plantations for pulp, for ecological services and for protection of natural forests is crucial to slowing deforestation, but too many plantations still *replace* natural forests rather than rehabilitate degraded lands.

2 Industrial Forestry – Natural Forest Management
Natural forests under careful management secure from encroachment are vital for maintaining biodiversity. They are particularly valuable when they link or surround protected areas. There is a need for projects with multiple-use management objectives, combining

Table 10.8 How the TFAP process is forging links with NGOs

1 Three NGO workshops organised by WRI and ELC took place in Africa (Nairobi, November 1986), Latin America (Panama City, February 1987) and Asia (Bangkok, February 1987). Their reports were particularly influential in the redrafting of the TFAP from its original form (CFDT, 1985) to its revised edition (FAO, 1987). The new edition put a greater emphasis on the need for grassroots participation and the role of NGOs in arresting and reversing deforestation.

2 In 1987 'Guidelines for Implementation of the Tropical Forestry Action Plan at Country Level' were prepared, explicitly requiring the involvement of NGOs in the consultative process and in project preparation and implementation.

3 From 1988 WRI began regular monitoring of the participation of NGOs in TFAP forest sector reviews, enabling donors to judge whether the 'guidelines' were being implemented.

4 From 1988 the meetings of the Forestry Advisors reserved a half day for public participation and dialogue (NGOs have observer status and can attend the meeting).

5 In April 1989 WRI convened an NGO consultation on TFAP to review critically its implementation at national level (WRI, 1989a). Various constructive recommendations emerged and continue to receive attention.

conservation of nature *and* sustainable utilisation of the natural resources (such as timber) which are of value to mankind. There are few examples of such systems in operation at present, yet the future of protected areas in rain forests may depend upon them. Projects combining timber extraction with harvesting of rattans, bamboos, fruits, nuts and other forest products are also needed.

3 Protected Areas

Rain forests in particular remain poorly protected in most countries of the tropics. Massive expansion of protected areas seems unlikely in most countries, and may not be desirable if resources to manage the reserves are scarce. The inclusion of most tropical forest species in protected area systems is a practical objective, but depends upon early identification of critical sites for conservation through analysis of the distribution of wildlife and ecosystems. Novel systems of conservation are needed in Melanesia, where forest lands are mainly in private hands.

4 Leadership of National Planning/Finance Ministries

Too often TFAP forest sector reviews have been carried out within the forestry sector alone, and in isolation from other natural resource related sectors and the national planning/financing authorities. The cross-sectoral nature of TFAP is central to its success, and applications for forest sector reviews must have the support of the highest government officials, preferably the heads of state. Bellagio, Italy, was the venue for a high-level meeting in 1987 to try to overcome such communication barriers, but it had little lasting effect. In many countries forests and Forestry Departments continue to suffer from agricultural and financial imperatives. Forests provide the short-term solution to the problem of feeding the nation and servicing debts, but the resulting deforestation has serious long-term consequences.

5 Facilitation of NGO Participation

The role of national and international NGOs in TFAP is growing. NGOs should be provided with more information and more opportunities to participate in TFAP, in order to make full use of their capabilities. Ways must be found to involve rural populations that are directly involved in the use of tropical forest resources, and the guidelines on addressing indigenous people issues should be respected and adhered to.

6 Facilitation of Private Sector Participation

Participation by the private sector has not been achieved in many TFAP activities and the CFDT has called for improvements in this regard (CFDT, 1989). IUCN believes that alienation of timber-bearing land to the private sector, including attribution of land tenure, could favour the maintenance of near-natural forest in the tropics, provided that retention of forest cover is mandatory.

7 Time Lag for Project Implementation

Few TFAP programmes are being completely implemented. The long interval between formulation of the plan and actual implementation is a severe constraint, and threatens to undermine political and financial support. TFAP must produce high-quality results quickly.

8 Project Preparation

One reason for slow implementation of TFAP is the shortage of national institutions and personnel capable of preparing projects for funding. Ways of strengthening project preparation capabilities must be considered, including the possibility of twinning forestry institutes in the developing and industrial worlds (CFDT, 1989).

9 Data Monitoring

With over 60 tropical countries now involved, the TFAP Coordinating Unit is already stretched. It is widely agreed that a computerised database would assist in monitoring the implementation and achievements of TFAP, and steps are being taken to achieve this.

10 A Wider View in Project Analysis

Conservation objectives should be built into all projects. To demonstrate the value of conservation, a better system of accounting for externalities should be applied in project analyses. The development of sound and practical methodologies for project analysis, including coverage of social and environmental impacts, will ease the introduction of new types of project. Analyses should be innovative and include environmental criteria such as conservation of genetic variety, carbon dioxide absorption, and social criteria such as creation of jobs, redistribution of income and impacts on indigenous people.

11 Training

A serious constraint on all aspects of TFAP is the global lack of expertise in tropical forestry, including economic, legal, administrative, analytical and field skills. An expansion in training is essential.

Conclusion

Ideally, the tropical forest lands of the 21st century will consist of a network of totally protected areas covering perhaps 5–20 per cent of forest land area within an extensive and secure permanent forest estate covering a further 30–60 per cent.

Outside these zones appropriate soils will be used for intensive agricultural and silvicultural production, as well as infrastructural development. This vision remains achievable, and the Tropical Forestry Action Plan is currently the best mechanism for focusing resources, intellectual as well as financial, on the problems along the way.

There is optimism that the goals for the protected area estate will be achieved so long as forest-dwelling people are involved in the process. The provision of a permanent forest estate in all countries, which is essential to the well-being of the protected areas, is less certain. Management of natural forests seems to be in decline. Over the past 40 years narrowly-based economic analyses have favoured the alienation of natural forest to plantations and traditional foresters' skills have been lost. Promotion of mechanised forestry has led to natural forest degradation and favoured homogeneous plantations.

Bureaucrats, and participants in forestry sector reviews, project preparation, and success analyses still tend to think of conservation as something that takes place only within protected areas. In reality, however, successful conservation and the continuing provision of ecological services and biological goods to the world depends upon management of forest lands outside protected areas. It will take time for institutional attitudes to evolve, but the winds of change are blowing and the Tropical Forestry Action Plan is at the centre of the storm.

STATUS OF TFAP MISSIONS IN THE ASIA–PACIFIC REGION

1 Bangladesh. TFAP/AsDB Master Plan exercise initiated June 1989. Draft project document prepared by AsDB, FAO and national participants includes the following core components: forest policy and institutions; forest management; resource economics; social and participatory forestry and environmental conservation. WRI is working separately on environment/natural resources assessment.

2 Bhutan. Government has agreed with AsDB to prepare a Master Plan. Donors met in July 1989, with wide participation (WB, AsDB, UNDP, FAO, WFP, DANIDA, SDC, HEL-VETAS, WWF). Government will set up a coordination unit.

3 Fiji. Field work began within the UNDP/FAO project 'Forestry Sector Development Study' in May 1988, including a national seminar seeking public opinion in November 1988. A national summit meeting was held in June 1989 to discuss the formulation of a national TFAP.

3 Indonesia. A mission in December 1987 led to a five-year forestry sector plan, developed by the Indonesian Government as the basis for a TFAP. Detailed documentation was prepared in February 1990, based on a national workshop. The major NGOs, WALHI and SKEPHI have been involved in these later stages.

4 Laos. Preparations began in September 1988, followed by a sector review one year later. A Symposium on 'Forestry and Environment' took place in October 1989. The draft plan is being reviewed at a series of regional seminars in 1990 and will be presented to a meeting of all donors.

5 Malaysia. TFAP-style forest sector review carried out in 1988 by the Government as part of the national planning cycle. A national workshop in July 1988 included NGO representation. Final draft submitted to Government in June 1989 (see also chapter 22).

6 Nepal. Master Plan finalised, identifying priority programmes and average annual investment requirements of US$79 million for the next 22 years. At a meeting in May 1988 the Master Plan was well received by donors. Following a further meeting in August 1989, 66 per cent of the external assistance was pledged. NGOs have not been involved, but the draft Master Plan was circulated.

7 Pakistan. Preparatory missions took place in 1987 and 1988. Harmonisation between the Master Plan approach and TFAP is proceeding through the efforts of UNDP, AsDB and FAO.

8 Papua New Guinea. Forest sector review took place in April–May 1989 with wide participation including NGOs. Draft report was circulated in October and is now finalised. Round table donors' meetings took place early in 1990.

9 Philippines. Terms of reference for a Master Plan project have been prepared by AsDB, co-financed by FINNIDA. Project work began in late 1988 and will be completed in 1990. Sectoral reports are already coming through (see chapter 23).

10 Solomon Islands. A request for information has been received by the TFAP Coordinating Unit (1989).

11 Sri Lanka was the subject of a Master Plan in 1986, before TFAP was fully operational. This was criticised by groups concerned at its emphasis on industrial timber production. Follow-up WB/FAO sector work has involved wide consultation with NGOs, including IUCN, and a WB loan will support implementation of the plan, now modified to address conservation issues.

12 Thailand. The government has agreed with UNDP and FINNIDA to prepare a Master Plan. Project implementation will begin in late 1990.

13 Vietnam. TFAP initiated in November 1988. Issue papers have been prepared and the sector review will take place in the course of 1990.

References

CFDT (1985) *Tropical Forestry Action Plan*. Committee on Forest Development in the Tropics. FAO, Rome, Italy.

CFDT (1989) *Report of the Ninth Session of the Committee on Forest Development in the Tropics*. FAO, Rome, Italy; v + 20 pp.

Ecologist (1987) Tropical Forests: A Plan for Action (Editorial). *Ecologist* 17: 129–33.

FAO (1987) *The Tropical Forestry Action Plan*. FAO, Rome.

FAO (1988) *An Interim Report on the State of Forest Resources in the Developing Countries*. FAO, Rome, Italy.

FAO (1989) Committee on Forest Development in the Tropics. Ninth Session. Papers supporting the Agenda.

FAO (1990) *The Tropical Forestry Action Plan. What it is and what it is doing*. FAO, Rome, Italy.

FAO/UNEP (1981) *Tropical Forest Resources Assessment Project. Forest Resources of Tropial Asia*. Vol. 3 of 3 vols. FAO, Rome.

Ganguli, B. N. (1988) *Tropical Forestry Action Plan and the Master Plan for Forestry Development: Need for Harmonization*. Report to the Sixth TFAP Meeting, FAO, Rome, Italy. 6 pp.

Hildyard, N. (1989) Three million signatures presented to UN. *Ecologist* **19**: 210.

IUCN, UNEP and WWF (1980) *World Conservation Strategy: Living Resource Conservation for Sustainable Development*. IUCN, Cambridge, UK, and Gland, Switzerland.

Muchiru, S. (undated) *The Tropical Forestry Action Plan. NGO's Concern*. Environment Liaison Centre, Nairobi. 5 pp. + 2 annexes.

Panos (1987) Focus on tropical forests. *Panoscope* **3**: 2–11.

Shiva, V. (1987) *Forestry Crisis and Forestry Myths. A critical review of Tropical Forests: A Call for Action*. World Rainforest Movement, Penang, Malaysia.

TFAP Forestry Advisers (1989) *Summary Report on the Eighth Meeting of the TFAP Forestry Advisors on Harmonizing International Forestry Development Cooperation*. FAO, Rome, Italy.

WCED (1987) *Our Common Future*. Oxford University Press, Oxford, UK.

WRI (1985) *Tropical Forests: A Call for Action*. World Resources Institute, Washington, DC, USA.

WRI (1988) *Status Report on NGO Participation in Country-level TFAP Activities. Number 1*. WRI, Washington, DC, USA.

WRI (1989a) *NGO Consultation on the Implementation of the Tropical Forestry Action Plan*. WRI Forestry Program, Washington, DC, USA.

WRI (1989b) *Status Report on NGO Participation in Country-level TFAP Activities. Number 2*. WRI, Washington, DC, USA.

Authorship

Mark Collins at WCMC with contributions from Effendy Sumardja of the Department of Forest Protection and Nature Conservation in Bogor, Oscar Gendrano from the Asian Development Bank in Manila, and Robert Winterbottom at WRI, Washington, DC.

11 A Future for Tropical Forests

Introduction

This atlas is the first attempt to compile all available maps showing the remaining extent of tropical rain and monsoon forests in the Asia–Pacific region. These maps are a unique assemblage of data from published and unpublished sources, and represent the best information available at the end of 1989. We have consulted specialists from relevant governments and international agencies, as well as numerous individuals with expertise in, and concern for, forest conservation (see 'Contributors' and 'Authorships' sections).

The use of a Geographic Information System (GIS) in the preparation of the maps has allowed an important advance over earlier reports. In the past there have been maps without statistics and statistics without maps, but combined maps and statistics have been available for only a few isolated countries. Once the coverages were filed using a GIS it was a simple matter to estimate the area of different forest types. The maps for every country have, therefore, been backed up by a table of statistics (Table 11.1).

This approach is not without its difficulties, as more data have become available, more anomalies and difficulties have arisen. FAO has, over the past decade, made enormous advances in estimating the extent and productivity of the world's forests. Tables 11.2 and 11.3 are summaries of FAO statistics relating to the Asia–Pacific and gathered from the Forest Departments of the region. These statistics will be referred to repeatedly in the following chapters, but it is not always easy to make cross-comparisons since the dates of available statistics and maps rarely match, and the forest categories employed are usually different.

Most of the maps are based on data from the late 1980s (Table 11.1), the exceptions being Cambodia (1971), China (1979), Papua New Guinea (1975) and Sarawak (1979). While Papua New Guinea remains little changed to this day, the forests of Cambodia, China and Sarawak have been depleted, and new coverage is urgently needed.

Overview of Forest in the Region

Table 11.1 gives the original and remaining extent of tropical moist forests in the region, as judged from map coverages presented here, and FAO data. The message that emerges is gloomy. Throughout most of the region, the once abundant and majestic moist forests have been reduced to half of their original extent. In many countries they remain only as isolated fragments set in a landscape dominated by agriculture or, even worse, in vast areas of degraded scrub, bamboo and grassland.

Even those forests that do remain have almost all suffered from human disturbance. Most have either at some time in their history been cleared by shifting agriculturalists, or suffer from poaching, exploitation for other non-timber products, and logging. The media

in the countries of the region and the industrialised north are replete with accounts of the effects of deforestation on their rural economies. The true impact, however, of tropical deforestation is only now beginning to be appreciated. The plight of these forests is of global concern.

The leaders of Asian nations have been joined by those of the super-powers in committing their governments to halt deforestation. The world's major financial institutions have announced policies to safeguard forests and allocate funds to conservation programmes. All this, however, does not seem to slow the inexorable process of destruction. With all the wealth and technology available to us, and an almost unanimous political and popular demand for action, we seem to be powerless in the face of one of the most serious environmental problems confronting mankind.

Why this powerlessness? Are the problems really insurmountable? Or is it that we are dissipating our efforts fighting the symptoms of deforestation, when we should be applying our resources to the root cause of the problem?

There is little question over what the root cause is. Forests are destroyed because people need land to grow food. Most Asian lowland forests were cleared long ago and the land now produces the crops that support a dense human population. But this population is still growing explosively and many people in the region are desperately poor. To meet their subsistence needs, or to earn the cash that they need to improve the quality of their lives, they are forced to clear even more forests. The cleared land is often on steep hillsides and its soil poor. After one or two harvests these farmers are therefore compelled to move on, leaving degraded scrub and grassland behind them.

The world's population is approaching 6 billion and will probably reach 10 billion in 2035. As many as 80 per cent of these people will live in the tropics and sub-tropics. The Asia–Pacific countries covered in this atlas already have a population over 2.5 billion (Table 11.4), about half of the world's total. It is predicted that their populations will stabilise at 4.75 billion by 2150, yet their forests are already under intense threat.

Population growth is not the sole problem, however. The region's economies are among the fastest growing in the world. Consumption is fuelled by the media which are creating expectations of a lifestyle similar to that of Japan, Western Europe, or North America. Thailand's economy, for instance, is growing at 9 per cent per year. Since land is needed to produce export crops to fuel the economy, and domestic consumption of paper and other forest products is accelerating, pressures on the remaining forests can only increase.

In the face of these pressures it is futile for the conservation

Table 11.1 Original extent of closed canopy moist forests (including tropical coniferous forests) in the Asia–Pacific region, compared with remaining extent as judged from most recently available maps and FAO statistics for 1980.

	Approximate original extent of closed canopy tropical moist forests (sq. km)[3]	From atlas maps; rain monsoon forests	Publication date of maps	FAO (1988) data for 1980, closed broadleaved plus coniferous forests	From map data	From FAO (1988) data
		Remaining extent of moist forests (sq. km)			% moist forest remaining	
Australia	11,000	10,516	1988	10,516[1]	96	—
Bangladesh	130,000	9,730	1981–6	9,270	7	7
Brunei	5,000	4,692	1988	3,230	94	65
Burma	600,000	311,850	1987	313,090	52	52
Cambodia	160,000	113,250	1971	71,680	71	45
Southern China and Taiwan	340,000	25,860	1979	25,860[1]	8	—
Fiji	18,000	6,970	(1980s)	8,110	39	45
India	910,000	228,330	1986	504,010[2]	25	55[2]
Indonesia	1,700,000	1,179,140	1985–9	1,138,950	69	67
Laos	225,000	124,600	1987	78,100	55	35
Malaysia	320,000	200,450	—	209,960	63	66
Peninsular	(130,000)	(69,780)	1986	—	(54)	—
Sabah	(70,000)	(36,000)	1984	—	(51)	—
Sarawak	(120,000)	(94,670)	1979	—	(79)	—
Papua New Guinea	450,000	366,750	1975	342,300	82	76
Philippines	295,000	66,020	1988	95,100	22	32
Singapore	500	20	(1980s)	—	4	—
Solomon Islands	28,500	25,590	(1980s)	24,230	90	90
Sri Lanka	26,000	12,760	1988	16,590	47	64
Thailand	250,000	106,900	1985	83,350	43	33
Vietnam	280,000	56,680	1987	75,700	20	27
Totals	5,749,000	2,849,608[1]		3,010,040[1]	50	52

[1] In the absence of comparable data for Australia and southern China, the figures from the maps have been used in calculating the FAO total.

[2] Note that for India the FAO figures are not directly comparable with our maps. FAO included India's extensive thorn forests in their forest assessment.

[3] Data for Asian countries are adapted from IUCN, 1986; Sources for other countries are given in the relevant chapters.

Table 11.2 FAO Rome statistics for remaining cover of tropical closed and open broadleaved, tropical coniferous, and bamboo forests in 1980

	Broadleaved closed canopy	Broadleaved open canopy	Natural coniferous	Bamboo	Total natural forest (sq. km)
Bangladesh	9,270	—	—	—	9,270
Brunei	3,230	—	—	—	3,230
Burma	311,930	—	1,160	6,320	319,410
Cambodia	71,500	51,000	180	3,800	126,480
China and Taiwan[1]	(476,740)	(172,000)	(469,730)	(32,000)	(1,150,470)
Fiji	8,110	—	—	—	8,110
India	460,440	53,930	43,570	14,400	572,340
Indonesia	1,135,750	30,000	3,200	—	1,168,950
Laos	75,600	52,150	2,500	6,000	136,250
Malaysia	209,960	—	—	—	209,960
Papua New Guinea	337,100	39,450	5,200	—	381,750
Philippines	93,200	—	1,900	—	95,100
Singapore	—	—	—	—	—
Solomon Islands	24,230	170	—	—	24,400
Sri Lanka	16,590	—	—	—	16,590
Thailand	81,350	64,400	2,000	9,000	156,750
Vietnam	74,000	13,400	1,700	12,000	101,100

(*Source:* from FAO, 1988)

[1] Tropical and temperate forests were not distinguished in China.

Table 11.3 FAO Bangkok statistics for remaining cover of tropical closed and open canopy broadleaved, tropical coniferous, and bamboo forests in 1980 and 1985, with extrapolations to 1990

Forest type (sq. km)

		Broadleaved closed canopy	Broadleaved open canopy	Natural coniferous	Bamboo	Total natural forest
Indonesia	1980	1,133,150	40,400	1,820	100	1,175,470
	1985	1,132,910	40,400	1,820	100	1,175,230
	1990	1,130,770	40,400	1,820	100	1,173,090
Malaysia	1980	186,590	—	—	—	186,590
	1985	176,890	—	—	—	176,890
	1990	165,830	—	—	—	165,830
Peninsular Malaysia	1980	66,220	—	—	—	66,220
	1985	61,870	—	—	—	61,870
	1990	57,090	—	—	—	57,090
Sabah	1980	36,370	—	—	—	36,370
	1985	33,130	—	—	—	33,130
	1990	29,110	—	—	—	29,110
Sarawak	1980	84,000	—	—	—	84,000
	1985	81,890	—	—	—	81,890
	1990	79,630	—	—	—	79,630
Papua New Guinea	1980	357,310	—	5,200	—	362,510
	1985	356,230	—	5,200	—	361,430
	1990	355,630	—	6,200	—	360,830
Philippines	1980	94,510	—	1,940	80	96,530
	1985	72,360	—	1,870	80	74,310
	1990	65,550	—	1,790	80	67,420
Thailand	1980	86,160	79,540	2,000	8,900	176,600
	1985	61,490	77,340	1,720	8,500	149,050
	1990	50,200	75,300	1,500	8,000	135,000
Vietnam	1980	59,350	4,120	2,300	14,000	79,770
	1985	47,020	3,120	1,600	15,000	66,740
	1990	32,760	2,520	1,300	14,020	50,600

(*Source:* FAO, 1987)

community to call for a halt to deforestation. We must know exactly what it is we wish to conserve and why. We must develop strategies which pay full attention to the inevitable changes which will take place in the societies and economies of the countries of the region. Above all, we must seek a realistic and optimum compromise over the allocation of land to different uses.

Most of the countries of the region have laws which allocate their forest lands to various categories of use. Most recognise the need to designate significant areas of their forests to nature conservation in *totally protected parks or reserves*. Many have adopted a target of total protection for 10 per cent of their forests. An important but variable proportion of the forests is allocated as *protection forest* to protect water catchments and prevent erosion. Other forests are identified as situated on land with agricultural potential and classed as *conversion forests*; to be cleared for farms or tree crops.

Very large forest areas have been allocated to *production forest*. In most cases, the policy of the governments of the region is selectively to log these forests and then to protect and manage them in such a way that it will be possible to obtain further timber crops on a 25–70-year cycle.

Totally Protected Forests

The first of these four categories of forest – totally protected forest – is the most secure. With the exception of Burma, Laos and Cambodia, protected areas covering many of the region's most biologically rich sites have been gazetted. These areas are not without their problems though. In many cases, even national parks are subject to poaching, logging and agricultural encroachment (see chapter 9). The good intentions of governments have often run far ahead of their capacity to undertake sound conservation management. Areas have been gazetted but no funds allocated to ensure their protection. Protected areas have also been established in situations where conflict with the interests of local people was inevitable.

Thailand has gazetted 59 national parks and plans a further 50. Yet few of these areas are adequately protected. Some people believe that Thailand would be better off with a small number of well-managed areas. Pragmatists, however, take the view that one should gazette as many areas as possible while it is still possible to do so, and worry later about managing them.

Across the board, the area of parks and reserves is increasing, as chapter 9 shows, and the government agencies responsible for their management are receiving more funding and employing better qualified staff. Even more significantly, in many countries a new generation of educated concerned citizens has emerged, constituting a powerful force for the support of protected areas. Conservation organisations are forming and the news media of India, Indonesia, Malaysia, the Philippines and Thailand are quick to seize upon abuses of national park and wildlife conservation laws.

The battle to allocate 10 per cent of land area to nature conservation is eminently winnable. The completion and consolidation of these protected area systems must be the first priority of the conservation community.

Protection Forests

The security of forests officially allocated to environmental protection varies greatly from country to country. In a few localities, strict measures are applied to protect the catchments of irrigation and hydro-power schemes. In these situations, protection forests are as secure as national parks. But this is the exception rather than the rule. In most countries, protection forests suffer from benign neglect. They are delimited on maps, but few resources are available to maintain them. Vast areas of protection forest in India, Indonesia, Laos, Thailand, and elsewhere, have already been seriously degraded by shifting agriculture and fire.

In most cases, it would be better if those protection forests which have features of special biological value were reallocated to park or reserve status. Those which do not should be reallocated to some form of production. In steeply sloping, highly erodible areas this should not be timber production. There is, however, a wealth of non-wood products which can be obtained from forests without detriment to their environmental protection role. Management systems must be developed whereby the communities living in or around forests can derive more benefits from the maintenance of forests for these non-timber products than from non-forest use of the land. Often, it is not difficult to achieve this. Attribution of land ownership, or at least

Parks need production forests to buffer them from deforestation, as here on the boundary of Gunung Leuser National Park, Sumatra. A. J. Whitten

Table 11.4 Population statistics for countries in the Asia–Pacific region (millions of people)

	1989	Population stabilises at (millions)	In year	% of world total at stabilisation
Australia	16.8	20.4	2025	0.03
Bangladesh	114.7	341.5	2150	3.16
Brunei	0.3	0.6	2075	—
Burma	40.8	102.1	2150	0.95
Cambodia	6.8	20.1	2150	0.19
China	1,103.9	1,694.8	2100	16.05
India	835.0	1,697.1	2150	15.72
Indonesia	184.6	354.9	2150	3.29
Laos	3.9	15.3	2150	0.14
Malaysia	17.4	32.3	2100	0.31
Papua New Guinea	3.9	9.9	2150	0.09
Philippines	64.9	137.0	2150	1.27
Singapore	2.7	3.0	2050	0.03
Sri Lanka	16.9	29.8	2125	0.28
Taiwan	20.0	30.6	2150	0.92
Thailand	55.6	98.9	2150	0.92
Vietnam	66.8	167.8	2125	1.57
Western Pacific Islands[1]	2.1	—	—	—

(*Source:* after Vu *et al.*, 1989)

[1] Data for the Western Pacific Islands are incomplete.

secure rights to the forest's resources, are the prerequisites of success (see chapter 3).

The harvesting of non-wood forest products does not usually require major investments. It is therefore a suitable enterprise for people in small rural communities. It may be easier to ensure sustainability of this sort of forest management than for timber harvesting, where expensive infrastructure requires heavy investments from powerful corporations (see chapter 7).

Production Forests

The conservation battle which is being fought most fiercely is for the future of production forests. Logging is inevitably noisy, dramatic and conspicuous. It arouses people's emotions and is widely perceived as one of the principal causes of forest destruction. Its immediate visible impact is often devastating. Yet most Asian rain forests will regenerate following the selective logging to which they are normally subject. Regenerating forests generally retain most of the animal and plant species of the original forest (see chapter 2), and, except in the immediate post-logging period, provide adequate protection of watersheds and soils. They may not be such rich sources of timber as the original forest, but a variety of silvicultural treatments can be applied to ensure good subsequent crops of valuable species (see chapter 6).

Most countries have strict laws governing timber harvesting and post-logging management. The conventional argument decrees that applying these rules results in a regenerating forest of such high value that it is in the interest of the country to protect the timber resource until the next harvest cycle. The dilemma is that this value does not accrue to the people living in and around the forest, nor to the timber concessionaires. The regulations are therefore widely abused and little is done to prevent farmers encroaching along logging roads and clearing the forest to plant their crops. This pattern is repeated throughout the Asian tropics. In a few situations, where pressure from landless farmers is not high – as in the remote parts of Indonesia and Papua New Guinea – or where post-logging protection rules are vigorously applied – as in parts of Burma, India and Malaysia – logged forests are left to regenerate naturally, and in fact do so very well. But such areas are exceptions, and throughout the majority of the region, logging is inevitably followed by slash-and-burn farming and degradation of the forest to scrub and grassland. Such degradation has almost invariably followed logging on the island of Borneo, in the Philippines and in Thailand. A study carried out by the International Institute for Environment and Development (IIED) on behalf of the International Tropical Timber Organisation (ITTO) has shown that intensive silvicultural management is applied to less than 0.1 per cent of the tropical forests of ITTO member countries (Poore *et al.*, 1989). In our region, it is only in parts of Australia, Burma, India and Peninsular Malaysia that management of production forests has even come close to sustainability.

Notwithstanding the present failure to manage production forests effectively, most foresters and many conservationists still view a healthy timber industry, dependent on an extensive natural forest, as the only hope for the long-term survival of extensive areas of moist forest. They believe that ethical and environmental arguments alone will never justify protecting more than 10 per cent of the region's forests in parks and reserves. They consider that the isolated forest fragments within these totally protected areas will neither protect all forest species, nor provide all the environmental services needed from forests. The only viable option is for the pristine parks and reserves to be buffered by extensive areas of near-natural forest which are put to productive, but sustainable, use. Timber production is held to be the only use of sufficient economic value to justify the maintenance of really large tracts of forest.

The ITTO is a major forum for debating the issue of natural forest management. The International Tropical Timber Agreement is a commodity agreement whose mandate calls for it to work with industry, governments and the conservation community in order to bring about the sustainability of the tropical timber trade. The bi-annual meetings of ITTO have become a meeting point for non-governmental organisations campaigning to save forests, the timber industry and the forest departments of tropical countries.

Most specialists agree that sustained yield management of tropical forests is technically feasible. It requires highly-skilled supervision and a disciplined workforce and, forest departments must be given political and material support by their governments. The techniques are relatively easy in the forests of the seasonal, monsoon tropics; the sal (*Shorea robusta*) forests of India are good examples. In the very humid tropics, however, the higher diversity of species, the greater erodibility and nutrient poverty of soils, and the proliferation of climbers and shrubs that grow when the canopy is opened by logging make management more difficult. Nevertheless, aseasonal rain forests in Malaysia and Australia have been successfully managed, and, in parts of Indonesia, rain forests that have escaped the attentions of shifting cultivators have regenerated satisfactorily after logging.

The stated policy of some countries with proportionally large forest areas – Burma, India, Indonesia, Laos, Malaysia, Papua New Guinea and Sri Lanka – is to allocate a major proportion of the permanent forest estate to sustained yield timber production. It is only Thailand, with its recent logging ban, and Australia who have decided that all remaining natural forests should be totally protected and that timber should either be imported or produced on plantations.

However, not a single country is making the investments needed to ensure that sustained forest management policies work. Forest departments responsible for forest management are almost always under-staffed and under-funded. Taxes imposed on the timber industry, ostensibly to pay for forest regeneration and management, are rarely used for this purpose. The Indonesian Reforestation Guarantee Fund, intended for reimbursing concessionaires who apply the Indonesian Selection System, is now used exclusively to establish plantations.

The policies and regulations which exist should ensure the sustainability of production from natural forests. But they are not applied and it appears that neither the governments concerned nor the tropical timber industry have a sincere commitment to selective harvesting from natural forests as a basis for the timber industry of the future. Throughout the region, the really big investments in both the private and public sector are in plantations of fast-growing species.

Plantations

The Asian Development Bank is investing heavily in plantations of *Acacia mangium* is Indonesia, Peninsular Malaysia and Sabah. These will feed Japanese pulp mills. There are numerous private sector initiatives to plant *Albizia*, *Acacia mangium* and *Eucalyptus* in India, Indonesia, Sabah and Thailand. Multinationals such as Mitsubishi and Shell are investing in plantations and a private sector consortium is embarking upon a massive *Eucalyptus* planting programme in Irian Jaya in response to the world's insatiable appetite for tissue paper.

These plantations can also produce utility grade lumber which can serve as a substitute for the bulk of natural forest timber. The high-grade timbers for joinery and decorative veneers will continue to be obtained largely from natural forests. But even for these uses, the teak plantations of India, Java and Thailand, and the mahogany (*Swietenia macrophylla*) plantations of Sri Lanka, Fiji, and elsewhere, could meet demand.

Fashions and technologies evolve rapidly. At present there is a strong demand for plywood faced with the dark colours of some tropical hardwoods. This is true of the red merantis (Dipterocarpaceae) from Indonesian and Malaysian forests and the rosewoods and pallisander (*Pterocarpus* spp.; *Dalbergia* spp.) from mainland Asia. These timbers can fetch very high prices, but in terms of volume they represent only a tiny proportion of the production of tropical forests. The vast majority of tropical timber is used to produce utility-grade plywood or in construction. There are huge timber reserves in the temperate forests of North America, Europe and parts of Asia that could satisfy this sector of the market. If tropical timber becomes scarce or excessively expensive, these temperate zone timbers will take its place.

Enormous progress has been made in recent years in developing new wood-based products. Products such as 'medium-density fibre board' and 'scrimber' can be made from a variety of low-grade timber by adding synthetic glue and filler. These timber substitutes can be made to whatever dimensions and specifications the market requires.

Natural forests under sustained yield management commonly produce 1–2 cu. m of timber per ha per year, whereas plantations in the tropics can produce 20–70 cu. m per ha per year. The World Bank has estimated that the world's industrial timber requirements for the year 2000 could be met if a mere five per cent of the tropical forests that existed in 1980 were converted to plantations of fast-growing species. All the world's predicted pulp and paper requirements could be met if plantations of fast-growing species were established on 10,000 sq. km of plantations in the wet tropics. This would be achieved using known tree varieties and existing plantation management techniques. New varieties and techniques are producing higher yields all the time.

Many countries in the tropics are turning to the private sector for the economic activity needed to fuel their development. Private industry favours clear commercial targets and is happiest with uniform products and intensive management systems. We may therefore, have to look to a future when most wood and wood-products will come from plantations. The conservation community must recognise that vast areas of natural forest managed for selective logging may be an illusory goal.

International Support

The rich nations of the industrialised world can influence events in the forested countries of the tropics through trade and aid. Many developed countries have pledged increased support for tropical forest conservation programmes. It is now broadly recognised that aid has often caused more harm than good. The Tropical Forestry Action Plan was born out of the desire to change aid, to improve the way in which it is coordinated and to focus it on the needs of tropical forest conservation. The plan calls not only for vastly increased aid to forestry in the tropics, but also advocates that aid should recognise the full social and environmental values of forests and the need to invest in maintaining the resource base. The TFAP includes a commitment from all the major aid donors to support totally protected parks and reserves in tropical forest areas (see chapter 10).

Conclusion

It is now unfashionable for conservationists to advocate a protectionist approach. The current approach is to support buffer zones, extractive reserves, sustained yield management. These all have their part to play. But our conclusion is that the highest priority must be to ensure that the remaining rain forests are managed to conserve the fabulous wealth of animal and plant species they contain. This will mean a major increase of investment in totally protected areas, parks and reserves. We must not only establish new ones, but ensure the protection of those already existing. It is inevitable, however, that extensive areas will be cleared so that food crops and forest products to fuel the region's development can be produced. Wealth must be generated and employment created to meet the needs of the rural poor who are at present destroying the forests.

Protected areas must be complemented by natural forests managed for timber and non-wood products, but this will only succeed if governments recognise that the main objective of these forests is environmental conservation. Awarding long-term logging concessions will probably be incompatible with the sound management of these forests. A better approach might be to sell the rights to stated timber volumes or timber products, with very strict control maintained by a forest department. This would be similar to the system applied to communally-owned forests in Switzerland, where the forests are considered to be far more than timber sources.

The fate of much of Asia's remaining forest will be determined in the next decade. We doubt if there is time for international diplomacy, debt swaps, action plans, conventions and other agreements to follow their tortuous paths to the point where they result in practical conservation on the ground. The scale of the problem is such that only a massive popular movement within the region's countries can bring about the necessary change. In Australia, the result of the 1989 general election was swayed by popular concern for the Queensland rain forests. Similarly, public concern at the floods and landslides in southern Thailand in late 1988 led to a logging ban. In India, deforestation is becoming an increasingly important political issue. The question is whether this wave of public sentiment will come in time to avert the frightening consequences of the loss of forests elsewhere in the region.

References

FAO (1987) *Special Study on Forest Management, Afforestation and Utilization of Forest Resources in the Developing Regions. Asia–Pacific Region. Assessment of Forest Resources in Six Countries.* FAO, Bangkok.

FAO (1988) *An Interim Report on the State of Forest Resources in the Developing Countries.* FAO, Rome. 18 pp. + tables.

Poore, D., Burgess, P., Palmer, J., Rietbergen, S. and Synott, J. (1989) *No Timber Without Trees: Sustainability in the Tropical Forest.* Earthscan, London, UK.

Vu, M. T., Bos, E. and Bulatao, R. A. (1989) *Asia Region Population Projections.* Population and Human Resource Department, World Bank.

Authorship

Jeffrey Sayer at IUCN, Switzerland and Mark Collins at WCMC, Cambridge, UK.

PART II

Map Compilation and Conservation Areas

The maps were compiled on computer using a Geographic Information System at the World Conservation Monitoring Centre in Cambridge. The sources of each map are given at the end of the appropriate chapter. For ease of comparison the editors used a uniform scale wherever possible and most have been produced at 1:3 million. All scales, however, are clearly given in the keyboxes. The editors have generally followed the placename style of *The Times Atlas of the World*, but where appropriate local names or anglicised names have been used.

It has only been possible to map conservation areas of 50 square kilometres and over. However in each chapter there is a list of all conservation areas, existing and proposed, including those of less than 50 sq. km. In some instances maps showing the exact boundaries of a protected area were unavailable, in which case the protected area is shown by a circle of an appropriate size.

Proposed and existing protected areas have been denoted by superimposing two shades of red over the different categories of forest. This produces a gradation of tone in the conservation colour. On each map there is a key to the conservation areas whereby each category of forest is shown combined with the conservation tint as it appears on the map.

12 Australia

Land area	7,617,930 sq. km
Population (1989)	16.8 million
Population growth rate (1987–2000)	1.4 per cent
Maximum expected population (2025)	20 million
Gross national product (1987)	US$11,100 per capita
Tropical rain forest	10,516 sq. km
Roundwood production*	20,677,000 cu. m
Roundwood exports*	8,497,000 cu. m
Fuelwood and charcoal production*	2,886,000 cu. m
Sawlogs and veneer logs production*	8,816,000 cu. m
Sawlogs and veneer logs exports*	26,000 cu. m

* 1988 data from FAO (1990)

A small area of the great Malesian tropical rain forests extends into Australia. The flora and fauna have some Malesian affinities, but include many unique species. The forests occur as small patches mainly close to the coast of Queensland. Despite their limited extent much of the original area has survived. Disturbance of the forest, including selective felling for high-quality timber, has been stopped by federal government decree and the forests have been listed as a World Heritage area.

INTRODUCTION

The huge continent of Australia extends between approximately 10°–50°S latitude and 110°–155°E longitude. The climate, soils, topography and vegetation are, necessarily, very varied over this large land mass. The tropical rain forests occur in Queensland, in the north-east of the continent, where they take up only a little over 0.1 per cent of the country. They are found along the coastal plains at sea level, over the undulating tablelands and reach to almost the top of the highest mountain in the area (Mount Bartle Frere, 1612 m). Much of the topography in the region is rugged, with numerous fast-flowing rivers, gorges and waterfalls. The rain forests are fringed and dissected by other vegetation types including sclerophyll forest and woodland, mangroves and swamps. This varied array of habitats supports a rich and diverse flora and fauna.

Rainfall is higher in the region of tropical rain forest than anywhere else in Australia. In some areas as much as 4000 mm can fall in a year, most of it in the summer months (December to April). At times, tropical low pressure systems cause continuous heavy rain and high winds for up to a week. Cyclones affect the rain forest region about once a year, damaging tens or even hundreds of square kilometres of trees. Mean maximum temperatures are as high as 29.5°C, though summer temperatures are influenced more by elevation than latitude. Mean minimum temperatures are around 20°C near sea level but, above 700 m, it can be cold enough in winter for frost damage to be significant.

Australia's population is concentrated along the damper, eastern coasts. Sugar cane has replaced some lowland tropical rain forest and the areas of higher population densities (between 3 and 25 people per sq. km), found between Cairns and Mackay, are associated with the sugar industry. The increasing popularity of the region for tourism implies substantial future population growth in urban and coastal areas.

The Forests

Australia has only a small area of tropical rain forest composed of what is believed to be residual fragments of the forests that covered Antarctica and Australia until about 15 million years ago. However, the forests are of particular interest because of their high southern latitude and the high degree of endemism of their plant and animal species. They are also a point of concentration of tropical Asian plants and animals that have migrated into Australia from Malesia.

Tropical moist forests occur in both north and north-eastern Australia. However, the monsoon forests that are scattered along the north coast are not mapped in this volume. Rain forests are found in a comparatively narrow strip along the north-east Pacific coast and are replaced inland in drier more seasonal climates by sclerophyll forests and woodlands. Temperate rain forests, not considered here, reach southwards to Tasmania (43°S).

A complex physiognomic classification of Australian rain forests was introduced by Webb (1959) and modified on several occasions since (e.g. Tracey and Webb, 1975). It is widely used in Australia, but has never been taken up by the rest of the world.

Forest Resources and Management

Australia's tropical rain forests cover about 10,516 sq. km (Bell *et al.*, 1987) and lie along the north-eastern coastline from 11°S to 22°S. They form two broad groups, the largest of which (7900 sq. km) lies between Townsville and Cooktown and covers part of the coastal plain as well as the mountain ranges lying parallel to the coast. These ranges reach to 900 m in many areas; the highest peak is Mount Bartle Frere (1612 m). Rain forest is found where the rainfall exceeds about 1500 mm per year, or where other conditions are favourable for the retention of moisture. West of the ranges, rainfall declines rapidly in the rain shadow and rain forest is replaced, often abruptly, by dry sclerophyll forest where the canopy is more open. This forest contains numerous eucalypts (Figgis, 1985).

The second major group of rain forests, 2600 sq. km in extent, lies further north and is separated from the Townsville forests by an area of open eucalypt forest. It consists of scattered patches of rain forest on the Cape York Peninsula. The largest is in the area between the McIlwraith Ranges and the Iron Range, just north of Coen. Smaller patches are found in the headwaters of the Jardine River and on the northern tip of Cape York at Lockerbie.

In both groups of forest, small-scale maps tend to exaggerate discontinuities of rain forest distribution. Except for the corridors of drier open eucalypt forest, the larger patches of forest are linked by frequent outlying clumps of rain forest occurring on suitable moist sites in gullies, along streams and on hill and mountain tops. South of latitude 19°S where frosts sometimes occur, fire-adapted rain forest species are sometimes present in open eucalypt woodlands on favourable soils. In addition there are some smaller patches of rain forest near Mackay at about 21°S. These are poorly documented but are believed to have southern subtropical floristic affinities.

Until recently most forests in the Townsville to Cooktown area have been administered as state forests or national parks by the State of Queensland. Historically this prevented indiscriminate felling for agriculture in the heyday of the dairy industry, and is the reason why so much forest cover has survived until today.

Part of the forest estate was production forest, felled on a selection system with a 30–40 year cutting cycle (Frawley, 1985; Queensland Department of Forestry, 1983). The Forest Department was able to show that tree species diversity at compartment scale was increased by this practice. It was claimed that there was no long-term ecosystem decline. Problems arose, however, because Department of Forestry management prescriptions were not strictly adhered to; in particular there was the problem of re-logging of forests at short intervals as markets developed for species which had not been commercially valuable at the time of former logging cycles.

The primary objective of forest managers has been to provide a sustained yield of rain forest timber. In the late 1940s the estimated sustainable yield was 75,000 cu. m per year. This rose to 600,000 cu. m per year in the late 1960s, but was then tightened to less than 80,000 cu. m per year in more recent years (Cassels et al., 1988). These adjustments, while based on professional silvicultural practice and rigorously enforced, fuelled public unease that management for timber did not necessarily ensure the future of other forest values and, coupled with concern that the national park system was inadequate, led to moves by the Federal Government to have the bulk of the Townsville and Cooktown rain forests included on the Unesco World Heritage List and to ban logging completely. The listing procedure was formally completed in 1988 amidst considerable controversy and opposition from the Queensland Government of the day. In late 1989, however, the newly formed Queensland Government stated that it was supportive of the nomination.

The northern rain forests of Cape York Peninsula are not included in the 'Wet Tropics' World Heritage site. Some of these are national parks, but the remainder are not and are unmanaged because of their isolation. Feral animals such as pigs and cattle are a particular problem in some areas, as is fire (Lavarack and Godwin, 1987).

Deforestation

Estimates of the proportion of existing original rain forest cover vary widely, and have been as low as only 50 per cent. Recently, detailed studies by Winter et al. (1987), however, suggest some of these earlier estimates included vegetation that was probably not originally rain forest. These researchers estimate 81 per cent of the southern group of rain forests (Townsville to Cooktown) and 99.5 per cent of the northern group (Cape York Peninsula) have remained uncleared.

Clearing has not been carried out uniformly and as a consequence of this, certain types of rain forest have been severely reduced in area while others have been hardly affected. Thus, in the Townsville to Cooktown region some 57 per cent of lowland rain forest below 80 m elevation has been cleared but only 14 per cent of that lying above 300 m. About 5 per cent of rain forest in the lowland foothills between 80 m and 300 m elevation has been cleared. Most of the forest clearing in the Cape York region has been carried out in the forests near Lockerbie.

Much of the deforestation in lowland areas has been to make way for agriculture, especially sugar-cane farms, and it first began in the late 1870s. In the uplands, clearing was mostly carried out to develop cattle pastures, especially on the Atherton Tableland. This too began many years ago and was mostly completed in the 1920s. In both cases rain forest on basalt soils was favoured for clearing.

Fire affects the Australian tropical rain forests, especially at its margins. Fires escaping from sugar-cane fields destroy the rain forest, and wet sclerophyll forest grows in its place. Aborigines who formerly lived in part of the area used fire to manipulate their environment and caused replacement of rain forest by scattered eucalypts (especially Eucalyptus grandis) growing in grassland. Now areas can be found where old relic eucalypts occur over a dense rain forest, the rain forest margin having advanced by several kilometres in places.

Small areas of deforestation have occurred as a consequence of road building. These roads have mostly been located in the more accessible areas below 1200 m. Two recent and environmentally damaging roads have been those constructed through the Cape Tribulation National Park between Daintree and Cooktown and the 'Quaid' road (named after a real estate agent). This latter road was important because it passed through the Black Mountain corridor, a narrow band of rain forest which links the Mount Carbine tableland and the Lamb Range rain forests.

Mangroves

Patches of mangroves occur round the Australian coast; they are most extensive in the north and north-east. There has been no heavy commercial exploitation. At their southern limit the mangrove forests are stunted and consist solely of Avicennia. In some places, especially Queensland, conversion to urban development is a threat. There is a copious recent literature (Clough, 1982; Davie, 1987; Galloway, 1982; Semeniuk, 1987 and Wells, 1982).

Biodiversity

Australia's tropical rain forests lie at the fringe of the great Malesian rain forest massif and have a strongly Malesian flora, which, due to its peripheral location, is rather less rich in species than much of the Malesian heartland. The flora and fauna also contain a Gondwanic element, which is shared to some extent with New Caledonia to the east and has dispersed into Malesia to the north, especially New Guinea.

A number of estimates have been made of floristic composition of the rain forests. A recent study (Rainforest Conservation Society of Queensland, 1986) estimated there were 1161 species of higher plants in the Townsville to Cooktown rain forests. These were represented in 516 genera and 119 families. Of the 516 genera, 68 are endemic to Australia and 36 are restricted to the region. With respect to the species, 710 are Australian endemics. Some 43 genera are monotypic, of which 37 genera are endemic to Australia. Another estimate (Barlow and Hyland, 1988) considered northern and southern blocks together and found 1328 species and 534 genera.

The forest fauna in Australia is also not particularly rich by Malesian standards. However, it also is strongly Australian in affinity, has numerous endemics and for several groups, such as butterflies, includes a high proportion of all Australia's species. About 95 bird species are associated with rain forests or with the land at their perimeters. Ten of these species are restricted to the lowlands, 25 are known only from the tablelands, and the remainder are widespread (Kikkawa, 1982).

Deforestation has had indirect effects on wildlife by increasing the degree of habitat fragmentation. This has caused the loss of certain vulnerable species. In the Atherton Tablelands, for example, Lawrence (1987) believed fragmentation had probably contributed to the local losses of spotted-tailed quoll Dasyurus maculatus, cassowary Casuarius casuarius and lemuroid ring-tail possum Hemibelideus

The identity of critical sites and areas of special ecological sensitivity is a subject over which there was considerable debate during the years prior to the decision to include much of the rain forests of the southern area on the World Heritage List. There has been general agreement, however, that some of the most important areas are the higher elevations and mountain tops of the Great Dividing Range as well as wet gullies and deep moist gorges of the coastal lowlands. These are some of the sites that are likely to have acted as refugia during periods of climatic stress in the Quaternary, when conditions were drier and cooler than at present (Webb and Tracey, 1981; Winter, 1985). Faunal and floral communities within these refugia have persisted as assemblages representative of a previously more widely-distributed rain forest, making these sites of special interest to rain forest conservationists. In recent times optimal conditions for rain forest growth were achieved between 7000 and 5000 years ago, and biota have expanded beyond the bounds of these refugia. Webb and Tracey (1981) estimate the total area of highland refugia to be about 1800 sq. km, while the refugia on the very wet lowlands total somewhere less than 4000 sq. km. Other probable refugia sites on Cape York include small areas on Mount Tozer, Mount Webb and the McIlwraith Range (Webb and Tracey, 1981).

Figure 12.1
The World Heritage Boundary in North-East Queensland.
(*Source:* Adapted from Queensland Government, 1987)

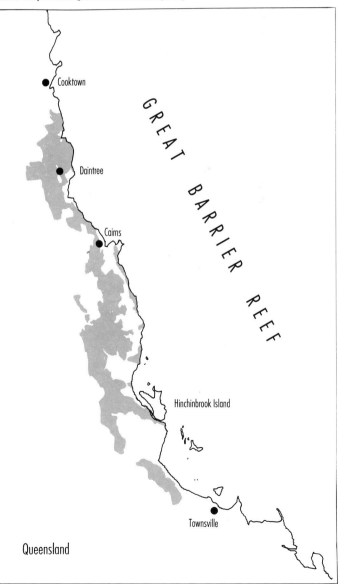

The spotted tailed quoll (Dasyurus maculatus), *a marsupial carnivore of the Australian rain forest, has suffered from forest fragmentation and from the skin toxins of the introduced cane toad.* WWF/G. D. Baker

lemuroides. Amongst plants, however, it is not at all clear what exact effect forest clearance and fragmentation has had on species loss over the years. Individuals are scattered, most species are uncommon or rare, and no information for documenting changes has been recorded.

The exotic cane toad *Bufo marinus* has spread into many deforested areas and its lethal skin toxin has had a devastating effect on many animals. Carnivores such as quolls seem to be sensitive to the toad's poison and the spotted-tailed quoll is now thought to have suffered a major population reduction as a result. Its conservation prognosis is poor (Winter, 1985). Feral pigs also cause severe wildlife management problems by upsetting the balance of indigenous species.

Conservation Areas

Most of the rain forest in the Townsville to Cooktown region was included in the World Heritage list in 1988 (IUCN, 1988; Government of Australia, 1988). Figure 12.1 shows the boundary of the World Heritage site. Under Australian commonwealth government legislation linked to the World Heritage Convention, all further disturbance of rain forests has been prohibited. World Heritage listing supersedes earlier conservation measures, summarised in Table 12.1. This decision was challenged by the Queensland Government in 1989, but the elections later that year brought in a new government and the challenge to World Heritage status has been dropped.

Not all forest types or areas of particular biological interest were included in the original reserves. Webb (1966) identified a number of areas having high conservation interest and Queensland Department of Forestry (1983) has provided an analysis of subsequent changes. Webb (1987) noted other omissions from the protected area system. Further details are given by the Rainforest Conservation Society of Queensland (1986).

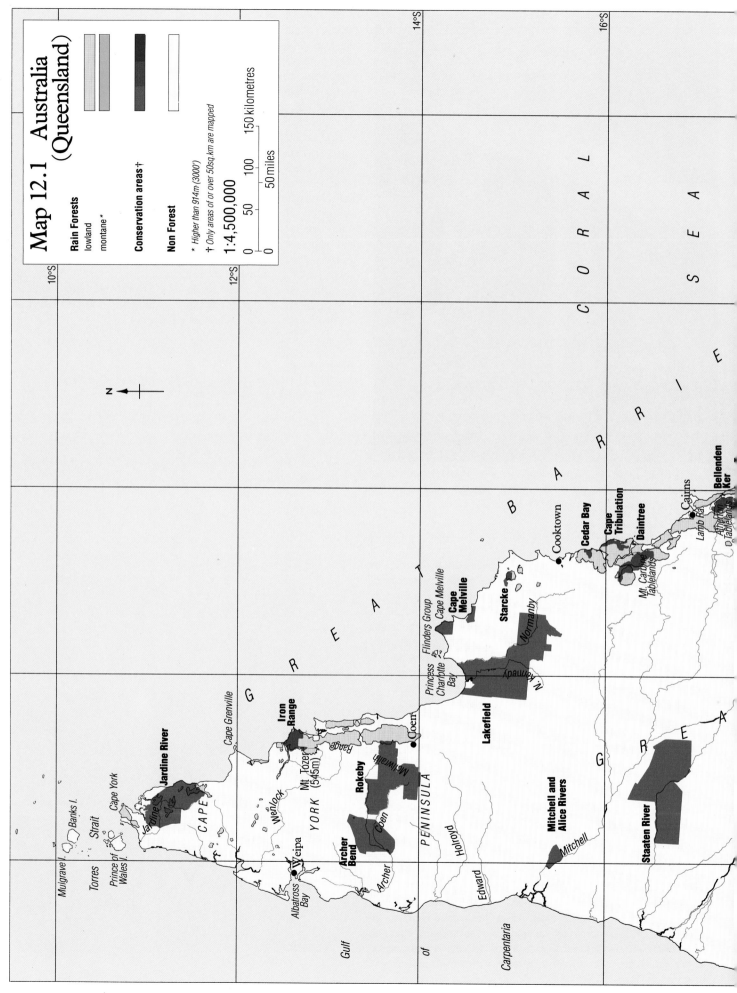

Map 12.1 Australia
(Queensland)

Rain Forests
lowland
montane *

Conservation areas †

Non Forest

* Higher than 914m (3000')
† Only areas of or over 50sq.km are mapped

1:4,500,000

0   50   100   150 kilometres

0   50 miles

N

10°S
12°S
14°S
16°S

Mulgrave I.
Banks I.
Prince of Wales I.
Torres   Strait
Cape York
CAPE
Albatross Bay
Weipa
Jardine
Jardine River
Wenlock
YORK
Mt. Tozer (545m)
Iron Range
Archer
Archer Bend
Coen
Coen
Rokeby
Range
Cape Grenville
GREAT
McIlwraith
PENINSULA
Holroyd
Edward
Mitchell
Mitchell and Alice Rivers
Mitchell
Staaten River
GREA
G R E A T
Gulf   of   Carpentaria
Princess Charlotte Bay
Flinders Group
Cape Melville
Cape Melville
Starcke
Normanby
N. Kennedy
Lakefield
Cooktown
Cedar Bay
Cape Tribulation
Daintree
Mt. Carbine Tablelands
Lamb Ra.
Cairns
Atherton Tablelands
Bellenden Ker
C O R A L   S E A
B A R R I E R   R E E F

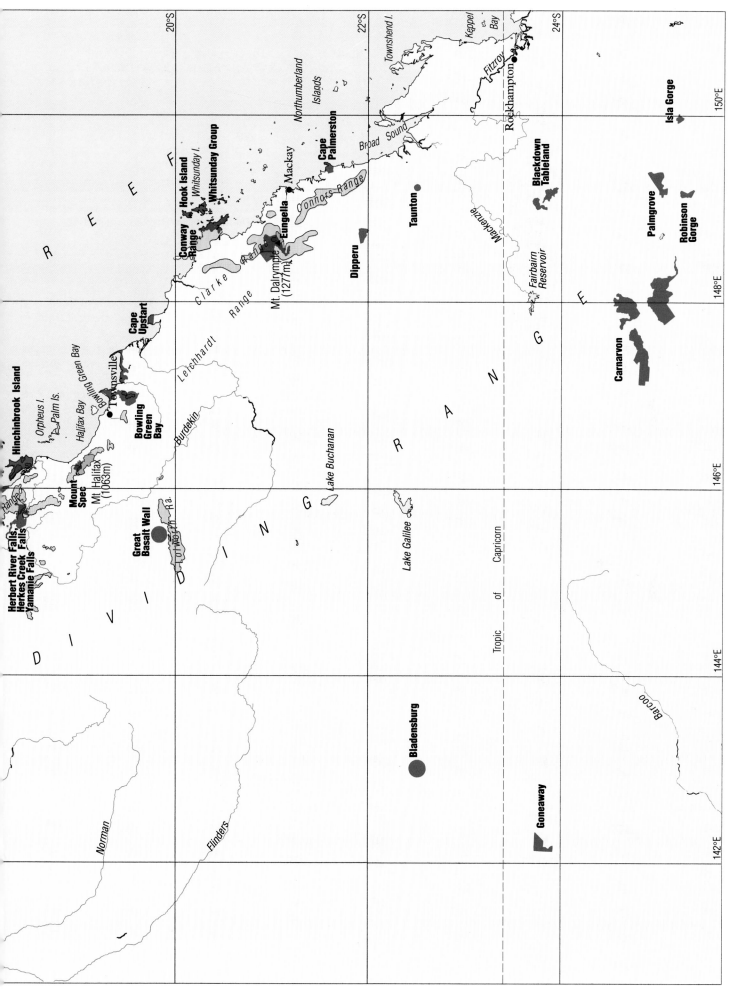

Table 12.2 Conservation areas of Australia (Queensland)

Existing areas, 50 sq. km and over, are listed below. The remaining areas are combined in a total under Other Areas. Forest reserves are not included. For data on World Heritage sites see chapter 9.

	Existing area (sq. km)
National Parks	
Archer Bend	1,660
Bellenden Ker★	310
Bladensburg	337
Blackdown Tableland	238
Bowling Green Bay★	553
Cape Melville	360
Cape Palmerston	72
Cape Tribulation★	170
Cape Upstart	56
Carnarvon	2,170
Cedar Bay★	57
Conway Range★	238
Daintree★	565
Dipperu	111
Edmund Kennedy	62
Eungella★	508
Great Basalt Wall★	524
Herbert River Falls, Herkes Creek Falls and Yamanie Falls★	1,238
Hinchinbrook Island, Nypa Palms and Hinchinbrook Channel★	452
Hook Island	52
Iron Range★	346
Isla Gorge	78
Jardine River★	2,350
Lakefield	5,370
Mitchell and Alice Rivers	371
Mount Spec★	72
Palmerston★	142
Robinson Gorge	773
Rokeby	2,910
Staaten River	4,700
Starcke★	80
Whitsunday Group	244
Environmental Parks	
Goneaway	248
Fauna Reserves	
Palmgrove	256
Fauna Refuges	
Taunton	53
Sub total	27,726
Other Areas	4,223
TOTAL	31,949

(*Source:* IUCN, 1990; Mobbs, 1988)
★ Area with moist forest within its boundary.

Table 12.1 The status of rain forests in north-east Australia

Region	Area (sq. km)	State Forest	Timber Reserve	% of land as Private Leasehold or Freehold	National Park
Townsville–Cooktown	7,913	51.6	9.8	23.3	15.3★
Cape York	2,603	0	17.4	58.9	23.7
Total	10,516	38.9	11.7	32.1	17.3

(*Source:* Bell *et al.*, 1987)

★ In the Townsville–Cooktown region 13.6 per cent of the land below 300 m elevation, and 14 per cent of the land above 300 m, is in the national park.

References

Barlow, B. A. and Hyland, P. (1988) The origins of the flora of Australia's wet tropics. *Proceedings Ecological Society of Australia* **15**: 1–17.

Bell, F. C., Winter, J. W., Pahl, L. and Atherton, R. (1987) Distribution, area and tenure of rainforest in north-eastern Australia. *Proceedings Royal Society of Queensland* **98**: 41–7.

Cassels, D. S., Bonell, M., Gilmour, D. A. and Valentine, P. S. (1988) Conservation and management of Australia's tropical rainforests: local realities and global responsibilities. *Proceedings Ecological Society of Australia* **15**: 313–26.

Clough, B. F. (ed.) (1982) *Mangrove Ecosystems in Australia.* ANU Press, Canberra, Australia.

Davie, J. D. S. (1987) Mangrove Ecosystems in Australia. In: Field, C. D. and Dartnell, A. J. (eds) (*op. cit.*) pp. 3–23.

FAO (1990) *FAO Yearbook of Forest Products 1977–1988.* FAO Forestry Series No. 23, FAO Statistics Series No. 90. FAO, Rome, Italy.

Field, C. D. and Dartnell, A. J. (1987) *Mangrove Ecosystems of Asia and the Pacific: Status, Exploitation and Management.* Australian Institute of Marine Science, Townsville.

Figgis, P. (ed.) (1985) *Rainforests of Australia.* Sydney: Weldons Pty. Ltd. 264 pp.

Frawley, K. (1985) Rainforest Management in Queensland after 1900. *Habitat* **13**: 4–7.

Galloway, R. W. (1982) Distribution and physiographic patterns of Australian Mangroves. In: B. F. Clough (ed.) (*op. cit.*): pp. 16–26.

Government of Australia (1988) Nomination of Wet Tropical Rain Forests of North Queensland. By the Government of the Commonwealth of Australia for inclusion in the World Heritage List.

IUCN (1988) Technical Evaluation of the Old Wet Tropics World Heritage Nomination. Report to the World Heritage Committee. December 1988.

IUCN (1990) *1989 United Nations List of National Parks and Protected Areas.* IUCN Gland, Switzerland and Cambridge, UK.

Kikkawa, J. (1982) Ecological association of birds and vegetation structure in wet tropical forests of Australia. *Australian Journal of Ecology* **7**: 325–45.

Lavarack, P. S. and Godwin, M. (1987) Rainforests of northern Cape York Peninsula. In: *The Rainforest Legacy.* National Rainforest Study Volume 1. Special Australian Heritage Publications Series No. 7(1). Australian Government Publishing Service, Canberra: pp. 201–22.

Lawrence, W. (1987) The rainforest fragmentation project. *Liane* **25**: 9–12.

DOWNEY CREEK CATCHMENT

Downey Creek lies 30 km south-west of Innisfail and covers an area of 70 sq. km. The valley floor lies at an elevation of about 300 m while the surrounding ridges reach up to 900 m. Rainfall is about 3750 mm per year. The floor of the valley is mostly basalt but other soil parent materials include granites and metamorphics.

The forests of Downey Creek are important because:

• Most of the forest cover is considered to represent the optimum development of rain forest in Australia under the most favourable conditions of climate and soil in the tropical humid lowlands.

• Very little of this forest type remains, making this an important conservation site.

• Furthermore the area contains at least two primitive plants, *Austrobaileya scandens* and *Galbulimima belgraveana*.

Some selective logging has been carried out in parts of the area since most of the land lies within several state forests. However, a part of the catchment has been designated a scientific area (960 ha) and six smaller areas (each 40 ha) have been set aside as benchmark reserves. The scientific areas cover much, though not all, of the most important forest type. Much of the area is now also within the World Heritage site. This system of setting aside part of the site for scientific purposes seems well designed to meet conservation interests, as well as allowing for timber production.

Mobbs, C. J. (ed.) (1988) *Nature Conservation Reserves in Australia*. Occasional Paper No. 19, pp. 32–9. Australian Parks and Wildlife Service.

Queensland Department of Forestry (1983) *Rain Forest Research in North Queensland*. Queensland Department of Forestry, Australia.

Rainforest Conservation Society of Queensland (1986) *Tropical Rainforests of North Queensland: Their Conservation Significance*. Special Australian Heritage Publication No. 3. Australian Government Publishing Service, Canberra.

Semeniuk, V. (1987) Threats to, and exploitation and destruction of, mangroves in Western Australia. In: Field, C. D. and Dartnell, A. J. (eds) (*op. cit.*): pp. 228–41.

Tracey, J. and Webb, L. (1975) *Vegetation of the Humid Tropical Region of North Queensland*. Fifteen maps at 1:100,000 scale and key. CSIRO Division of Plant Industry, Queensland, Australia.

Webb, L. (1966) The identification and conservation of habitat types in the wet tropical lowlands of north Queensland. *Proceedings of Royal Society of Queensland* 78: 59–86.

Webb, L. (1987) Conservation status of the rainforests of North Queensland. In: *The Rainforest Legacy*. National Rainforest Study Volume 1. Special Australian Heritage Publications Series No. 7: pp. 153–8. Australian Government Publishing Service, Canberra.

Webb, L. and Tracey, J. (1981) Australian rainforests: patterns and change. In: *Ecological Biogeography of Australia*, pp. 605–94. A. Keast (ed.), The Hague, The Netherlands.

Webb, L. J. (1959) A physiognomic classification of Australian Rainforests. *Journal of Ecology* 47: 551-70.

Wells, G. (1982) Mangrove vegetation of northern Australia. In: Clough, B. F. (ed.) (*op. cit.*): 57–8.

Winter, J. (1985) Problems of wildlife management peculiar to the tropical forests. In: *Wildlife Management in the Forests and Forestry Controlled Lands in the Tropics and the Southern Hemisphere*. J. Kikkawa (ed.). Proceedings of a workshop held at the University of Queensland 1984 IUFRO. Group S1.08: 7–14.

Winter, J., Bell, F., Pahl, L. and Atherton, R. (1987) Rainforest clearing in north-eastern Australia. *Proceedings Royal Society of Queensland* 98: 41-57.

Authorship

David Lamb at the University of Queensland, with contributions from Alia Keto of the Queensland Rainforest Conservation Society and G. M. Shea of the Queensland Forestry Department.

Map 12.1 Forest cover in Queensland

Rain forests and protected areas shown in this map are taken from two published maps at 1:500,000 scale: Department of Forestry Edition 1 *Far North Queensland* (1988) and Department of Forestry Edition 4 *North Queensland* (1987). These two maps are very detailed and it has been necessary to generalise the data and show only the main blocks of forest.

The recent listing under the Unesco World Heritage Convention has put most of the forests between Townsville and Cooktown within the World Heritage Site listing. Forests in Cape York are not, however, included on the World Heritage listing. The limits of the World Heritage Site shown in Figure 12.1 are from the *Nomination of Wet Tropical Rainforests of North-East Australia for Inclusion in the World Heritage List Map 2: Wet Tropical Rainforests of North-East Australia* at 1:500,000 scale (1987). This unpublished report of 31pp and lengthy annexes was reprinted in 1988 with corrections made by the Queensland Government, but only minor changes in boundaries have been made since the site was inscribed in 1988.

13 Bangladesh

Land area 133,910 sq. km	
Population (1989) 114.7 million	
Population growth rate (1987–2000) 2.4 per cent	
Maximum expected population (2150) 342 million	
Gross national product (1987) US$160 per capita	
Rain forest (see map) 964 sq. km	
Monsoon forest (see map) 90 sq. km	
Closed broadleaved/coniferous forest (1980)† 9270 sq. km	
Annual deforestation rate (1981–85)† 80 sq. km	
Roundwood production* 29,368,000 cu. m	
Fuelwood and charcoal production* 28,504,000 cu. m	
Sawlogs and veneer logs production* 467,000 cu. m.	

* 1988 data from FAO (1990)
† FAO/UNEP (1981)

Bangladesh, once forested with mangroves, rain forests and monsoon forests from the delta up into the hills, is now almost completely deforested. Less than five per cent of the original cover remains. Patches of rain forest only survive in the Chittagong Region in the south-east, where four hill ranges run parallel to the coast.

Bangladesh is one of the poorest countries in the world and the main reason for forest loss is demand for agricultural land. The already dense population, almost 800 per sq. km, is still growing rapidly.

The country's principal remaining forest heritage is the Sundarbans, a massive area of mangrove forest, 75 per cent of which lies in Bangladesh and 25 per cent in India. The mangroves are managed for timber production and wildlife conservation.

The mangrove forests of the Sundarbans serve many purposes, including providing substantial quantities of fuelwood and building timber. They also act as a refuge for the Bengal tiger. Species protection is especially important as, with the demise of its forests, Bangladesh has already lost most of its larger mammal species, including the rhinoceros, banteng, nilgai and swamp deer, while the elephant survives in only small pockets.

The country's system of protected areas is not extensive, and the future for forest habitat conservation must lie in improved management, both in totally protected areas and in forest reserves for timber production.

INTRODUCTION

Bangladesh has the largest area of river delta in the world, with three main rivers, the Ganges, the Brahmaputra and the Meghna.

Three geographical zones can be distinguished:
1 Hills occupy 10 per cent of the country. The Chittagong Hill Tracts in the south-east consist of a series of parallel ridges reaching 1000 m. Other hilly terrain occurs in the north-east.
2 The delta at the Bay of Bengal occupies the south and south-west.
3 The plains, generally composed of level alluvium, occupy most of the country and are the most fertile and heavily populated region. Vast areas of these plains are seasonally flooded.
In addition, the coastal area is broken into islands and tidal marshes, and the entire country is divided by the myriad tributaries and distributaries of the three main rivers.

With the highest population density in the world outside city-states, Bangladesh is also one of the poorest countries. Over 90 per cent of the population lives in rural areas and the mainstay of the economy is agriculture; rice and jute are the most important crops. About 60,000 families in the Chittagong Hill Tracts practise shifting cultivation, and there are extensive plantations of bananas and sugarcane in coastal regions and tea in the hills. Inland fishery is the second most important economic activity (UNEP, 1986).

The climate is tropical and wet to extremely wet, with annual rainfall ranging from 1200 to 6500 mm. Rainfall distribution patterns are uneven and erratic. A large part falls during the monsoon season, while the period from November to February is usually dry and relatively cool. Cyclones, coming from the Bay of Bengal, bring torrential rains, frequently followed by tidal waves that cause severe destruction in the coastal regions (UNEP, 1986).

The Forests

Most of Bangladesh was originally forested, with coastal mangroves backed by swamp forests and a broad plain of tropical moist deciduous forest (IUCN, 1986a). However, most of the original vegetation has been cleared.

There used to be three main forest formations (Ahman, 1987; FAO/UNEP, 1981):
1 The hills were once covered by tropical evergreen and semi-evergreen rain forest. Remnants of these forests are found in the eastern part of the country in the Chittagong Hill Tracts, Chittagong, Cox's Bazar and the Sylhet Forest Division. The merchantable species growing in the forests include *Dipterocarpus* spp., *Sterculia alata*, *Swintonia floribunda* and *Tetrameles nudiflora*. Bamboos, mainly *Melocanna bambusoides*, are abundant.
2 Tropical monsoon forests in Bangladesh, as in India, are known as sal forests after the main timber tree, *Shorea robusta*. At one time they covered relatively small areas of the inland plains of the Madhupur Tract. Relicts and may still be found in the Dhaka, Tangail and Mymensingh Forest Divisions and some badly managed patches survive in the north.
3 Tidal forests (mostly mangroves) are located in the Sundarbans (which continue into India) (see case study page 95), with small areas in the Chittagong district.

Forest Resources and Management

Scientific forest management in Bangladesh is more than fifty years old (FAO, 1987). Before independence (1971) it focused on teak production from plantations. The adoption of a National Forestry Policy in 1979 is indicative of the Government's desire to safeguard and manage scientifically the forest wealth, but its implementation has been slow (BARC, 1987). In view of the depleted forest reserves, the objectives of the Government's third Five-Year Plan (1985–90) are:

- To increase production of timber and non-timber crops through afforestation, reforestation and social forestry programmes.
- To accelerate the development of plantations of fast-growing trees.
- To exploit the forest resources to best advantage to meet the demand for timber, fuelwood, fodder, rubber and raw materials for paper and other industries, without disturbing the ecological balance.

Apart from a few privately owned forests, there are two main legal forest categories:

1 Reserved Forests and Protected Forests, managed by the Department of Forestry, which recognises some local rights.
2 Unclassed State Forests, mainly situated in the hill regions and managed by the District Administration.

The tropical rain forests are subject to working plans that involve either clear felling, followed by artificial regeneration or plantations; or selective logging based on short (30–40 years) or long (60–80 years) cycles (FAO/UNEP, 1981). The timber extracted is used for construction, pulping, packaging and plywood. In the Chittagong Hill Tracts large areas of bamboo are managed on a 3–4 year rotation. The sal forests, in former days managed under regimes of clear felling with coppice regeneration, are now excluded from production to recover from damage incurred during the War of Independence (FAO/UNEP, 1981).

The mangroves are covered by working plans based on forest inventories of 1960 and 1983, and a 20 year rotation operates that depends on natural regeneration (FAO/UNEP, 1981). However, overexploitation for firewood and timber has resulted in the erosion of this important barrier against cyclones and tidal waves. Reforestation is now being undertaken in a systematic manner and mangrove species are planted extensively under coastal afforestation projects (UNEP, 1986; see also case study on Sundarbans).

The most important forest products are construction timber, fuelwood and raw material for the wood-based industry. Fuelwood consumption, however, has fallen since the 1960s and crop residues, animal manure and bamboo tops are also important as an alternative source of energy. Bamboo is also used for paper pulp (FAO, 1987). Other forest products include golpata (leaves of *Nypa fruticans*), honey, wax, sungrass and cane (FAO/UNEP, 1981). The contribution of the forestry sector to GDP was 2.4 per cent in 1981–2 and 3.4 per cent in 1985–6 (BARC, 1987).

Plantation forests are now a major part of the country's timber resources, with about 2000 sq. km planted by 1985 (FAO/UNEP, 1981; BARC, 1987). About 70 per cent of this is teak, the remainder mainly being eucalypts and pines (Siddiqi, 1986).

Deforestation

A principal cause of deforestation in the hill regions is heavy encroachment by shifting cultivation (*jhum*) (BARC, 1987). In forest reserves, demand for timber is resulting in shorter rotations and greater forest degradation, including serious erosion.

Official forest figures for Bangladesh indicate that about 16.5 per cent of the country remains under forest cover: some 22,052 sq. km. Other estimates, including the accompanying Map 13.1, put the figure at well under half this amount (see Table 13.2), and much of what remains is certainly heavily degraded.

There are a number of forest cover estimates available, often conflicting and difficult to compare, but they all indicate forest cover of less than 14 per cent of land area and most recent figures given are around 7 per cent. As far back as 1976 and 1978 Unesco/MAB and the

Table 13.1 Estimates of forest extent in Bangladesh, based on analysis of Map 13.1

	Area (sq. km)	% of land area
Rain forests		
Lowland	5,310	4.0
Mangrove	4,330	3.2
Sub totals	9,640	7.2
Monsoon forests		
Lowland	90	0.1
Totals	9,730	7.3

(See Map Legend on p. 97 for details of sources)

Asian Development Bank respectively estimated forest cover at 14,000 sq. km (10.5 per cent) and 12,000 sq. km (9 per cent) (DS/DT, 1980). Gittins and Akonda (1982) put the figure at almost 16,000 sq. km (Table 13.2), but classed over half of this as degraded scrub forest. Further estimates were given by Khan (1985b), Olivier (1979) and Sarker and Fazlul Huq (1985).

FAO estimated that in 1980, 4700 sq. km of hill forest, 520 sq. km of monsoon forest and 4050 sq. km of mangrove forest remained, giving a total forest area of 9270 sq. km or 6.9 per cent of land area. Map 13.1 is in broad agreement as Table 13.1 shows, although the division between forest types is at variance. Both the FAO statistics and Map 13.1 are based on late 1970s data, and the situation now is certainly even more serious. The data in Table 13.2 are instructive in indicating the state of degradation of the forests. The estimated rate of deforestation for the years 1981–5 was 80 sq. km per year (FAO/UNEP, 1981). If we are to assume that this rate has prevailed throughout the 1980s, forest cover will now be reduced to little more than 6 per cent of land area.

Mangroves

The main area of mangrove, the Sundarbans, is described in a separate case study (see page 95).

Biodiversity

Bangladesh, an important transition zone between Indo-China, the Himalaya and the rest of the Indian subcontinent was once rich in wildlife species. These tropical moist forests were botanically amongst the richest in the Indian subcontinent, and they also supported the greatest diversity of mammals and a high diversity of birds.

In 1982, Khan published a complete fauna list of Bangladesh, updated by Rahman and Akonda (1987). The country has 113 species of mammals (out of 500 species in the Indian subcontinent), 574 species of birds (out of 1200), 123 species of reptiles, 19 species of amphibians, 107 species of freshwater fish and 120 species of estuarine fish, but only the turtle *Trionyx nigricans* is known to be endemic (DS/DT, 1980).

Although the species richness is relatively large for the small area of Bangladesh, endemism is low and the population size of most of the species has declined drastically (Khan, 1984, 1985; Sarker and Sarker, 1983). Eighteen species of wildlife are now extinct from Bangladesh (Rahman and Akonda, 1987). Among them are several internationally threatened species such as the three species of Asian rhinoceros, and also the gaur, banteng, nilgai *Boselaphus tragocamelus*, swamp deer *Cervus duvauceli*, pink-headed duck *Rhodonessa Caryophyllacea*, Bengal florican *Houbaropsis bengalensis* and mugger

Table 13.2 Estimated forest cover of Bangladesh (sq. km)

	Natural Forest	% of land area	Scrub forest (degraded)	% of land area	Total forest	% of land area
Rain forest	2,321	1.7	7,269	5.4	9,590	7.1
Monsoon forest	187	0.1	458	0.3	645	0.48
Mangrove forest	2,274	1.7	1,533	1.1	3,807	2.8
Totals	4,782	3.5	9,260	6.8	14,042	10.42

(Adjusted from Gittins and Akonda, 1982)

crocodile *Crocodylus palustris*. Except for the rhinoceroses, wild buffalo and pink-headed duck, all other locally extinct species disappeared from the country within the last two decades (WCMC, 1989).

There are several initiatives underway to conserve wildlife. For elephants (of which there are between 150 and 350) (IUCN/SSC, n.d.), primates (IUCN/SSC, 1987), and turtles and tortoises (IUCN/SSC, 1988), international action plans are proposed which include conservation activities in Bangladesh. A plan for artificial breeding of the endangered white-winged wood duck (*Cairina scutulata*) is under consideration (Rahman and Akonda, 1987). The tiger is nowadays confined to the Wildlife Sanctuaries of the Sundarbans, where there are estimated to be between 350 and 600 individuals (see case study opposite).

About 5000 species of higher plants are known from Bangladesh, a third of the number on the whole Indian subcontinent, where the main floristic affinities lie. The Chittagong area, however, has many Indo-chinese plant species.

Conservation Areas

The responsibility for wildlife conservation, as well as forest management for timber and other products, lies with the Forest Department. Divisional forest officers are able to deploy staff to protect national parks and wildlife sanctuaries, but in reality a large proportion of wildlife depends upon forest reserves. Management of these reserves is generally not adequate to ensure wildlife conservation (Blower, 1985; Olivier, 1979; Sarker and Fazlul Huq, 1985).

Major conservation efforts started in the 1960s, when, as a result of the recommendations of two surveys supported by WWF, the Government was urged to appoint its own Wildlife Inquiry Committee. Initial progress in the protected areas system, however, broke down during the War of Liberation (1971).

Existing and officially approved protected areas currently cover 1102 sq. km or 0.82 per cent of the total land area (Table 13.3) (WCMC, 1989). Protected areas comprise four national parks, ten wildlife sanctuaries (including three proposed sites) and one game reserve. This network is neither adequate nor representative of the country's range of habitats (IUCN, 1986b). It falls well below the target of 5 per cent of total land area recommended by the Ministry of Agriculture and Forestry task force (Rahman and Akonda, 1987). Small fragments of the main forest types, however, are represented in the protected areas network, as the accompanying map demonstrates.

The main areas of protected forest are as follows:
• Bhawal National Park, once almost completely deforested, is now 90 per cent covered in regenerating *sal* forest.

• Himchari National Park, a steep area in the Chittagong Hill Tracts, contains semi-evergreen rain forest.
• Madhupur National Park has the best *sal* forest in the country.
• Pablakhali Wildlife Sanctuary, important for its elephants, has a small area of forest which suffers from encroachment. This is an important wetland with perennial rivers, lakes and forest pools.
• Rema–Kalenga Wildlife Sanctuary has the last rain forests in Sylhet District.
• Teknaf Game Reserve is the most important area of rain forest in south-east Bangladesh, with one-third of the nation's elephants.
• The Proposed Wildlife Sanctuaries of Hazarikhil and Rampahar-Sitaphar include rain forest within their boundaries.

The existing system of protected areas is not comprehensive. Some effort has been made to include representative samples of the major habitats, but marine and freshwater areas have been largely neglected. Some areas have not been clearly defined or officially gazetted and few, if any, are effectively managed and protected. Lack of personnel trained in wildlife conservation is a further handicap (Olivier, 1979; Gittins and Akonda, 1982; Khan, 1985a).

The following actions have been recommended by Olivier (1979) and IUCN (1986b):
• Gazette proposed wildlife sanctuaries.
• Establish Rajkandi as a protected area.
• Discontinue forestry operations in protected areas.
• Develop and extend Madhupur National Park as the main conservation area for *sal* forest.
• Establish an independent Wildlife and Protected Areas Department.
• Improve levels of staffing and training in all protected areas.
• Improve conservation awareness at all levels within the country.

Further recommendations specific to Bangladesh are made in the Corbett Action Plan for protected areas in the Indomalayan Realm (IUCN, 1985). These include the establishment of St Martin's Island as a national park, the establishment of Teknaf Game Reserve and the Sundarbans wildlife sanctuaries as 'demonstration protected areas', the development of conservation policies which are socially acceptable and integrated into national development, and the strengthening of cooperation in the development of conservation activities in the region. As an example of the latter, the establishment of both the Sundarbans and the Kassalong reserved forests of India as an 'international peace park' is proposed.

Initiatives for Conservation

In September 1986, consensus was reached to move ahead with the National Conservation Strategy, at a seminar held in Dhaka (Rahman and Akonda, 1987). Bangladesh acceded to the World Heritage Convention on 3 August 1983, but no sites have been inscribed to date. Bangladesh has signed and ratified CITES. The country has a national committee for the Unesco–MAB programme, although no biosphere reserves have been established. Furthermore Bangladesh is a member of IUCN and of SACEP (South Asia Cooperative Environmental Programme) and an active partner of UNEP and ESCAP. Bangladesh is not yet a party to the Ramsar Convention.

The Bangladesh Government is considering a request for a forest sector review within the context of the Tropical Forestry Action Plan (de Montalembert, 1988). Having completed the forest inventories, management plans are being drawn up for the Sundarbans and the forests of Chittagong, Cox's Bazar and the Chittagong Hill Tracts. Research and training will receive new support. However, wildlife, an essential component of the forests and the national heritage, receives only passing mention in these plans (BARC, 1987).

Table 13.3 Conservation areas of Bangladesh

Existing areas, 50 sq. km and over, are listed below. The remaining areas are combined in a total under Other Areas. Forest reserves are not included.

	Existing area (sq. km)	Proposed area (sq. km)
National Parks		
Bhawal	50	
Madhupur	84	
Wildlife Sanctuaries		
Chunati	78	
Pablakhali★	420	
Sundarbans East★	54	
Sundarbans South★	179	
Sundarbans West★	91	
Game Reserves		
Teknaf	116	
Sub total	1,072	
Other Areas	30	73
Totals	1,102	73

(*Sources:* IUCN, 1990; WCMC data *in litt.*)
★ Area with moist forest within its boundary.

The Sundarbans are the most extensive mangroves in the world. A haven for wildlife, such as the Bengal tiger, they also provide the day to day needs of thousands of people. WWF/X. Lecoultre

SUNDARBANS

The Sundarbans of Bangladesh consist of over 4000 sq. km of mangrove forest. It extends westwards into India and is the largest mangrove forest in the world, followed by the mangroves of Irian Jaya (Scott, 1989).

Protected as Reserved Forest since 1875, the greater part is covered with tidal swamp consisting of a mosaic of mangrove forest types differing considerably in species composition. The main type is dominated by *sundri* (*Heritiera fomes*), which grades into low-stature stands with mixed *sundri*, *gewa* (*Excoecaria agallocha*) and *goran* (*Ceriops decandra*). A forest inventory was carried out by ODA in 1983. It is only to the west, where it borders with the similarly forested Indian Sundarbans, that any significant movement of terrestrial wildlife into or out of the area is possible (Blower, 1985). The whole area is intersected by an intricate network of interconnecting waterways, of which the large channels run in a generally north-south direction.

The major recent change in the physical environment of the Sundarbans is a reduction in the amount of fresh water flowing into the area. This is due to natural changes, river diversions and withdrawals of fresh water for irrigation. It is believed to be the cause of unusual mortality in some areas of the main commercial species *sundri*, especially since 1970 (Christensen, 1984). It seems unlikely that the trend of decreasing freshwater discharge can be reversed, indeed the problem is likely to be aggravated by a rise in sea level caused by global warming.

The Sundarbans provides ideal habitats for a variety of mammals (32 species are recorded), waders and seabirds and also suitable nesting sites for both marine turtles and the endangered estuarine terrapin *Batagur baska* (Blower, 1985). But above all the Sundarbans are well known as the home of the royal Bengal tiger *Panthera tigris tigris*, whose population is estimated at 350 to 600, one of the largest surviving populations in the world.

There has long been a problem of man-eating tigers in the Sundarbans, and this has attracted various studies. Siddiqi and Choudhury (1987) found that about 20 persons were killed annually between 1956 and 1983. The reasons why tigers become man-eaters are still not fully understood.

The Sundarbans are heavily utilised (Ahmad, 1984; Khan and Karim, 1982). One-third of the local population depends in one way or another on the mangroves for a livelihood. *Sundri* and *gewa* are harvested on a 20 year felling cycle. Other species, used mainly for timber and firewood, are harvested largely at the same time. Fishing takes place along the waterways throughout the year (Salter, 1984).

In 1966 the Forest Department programme to plant mangroves for protection and to encourage land accretion outside the coastal embankments was initiated. After ten years, 300 sq. km had been planted and cut in rotation. The project is now supported by the World Bank.

In 1977 three wildlife sanctuaries were declared. These are the 91 sq. km Sundarbans West Wildlife Sanctuary, the 179 sq. km. Sundarbans South Wildlife Sanctuary and the 54 sq. km Sundarbans East Wildlife Sanctuary. In 1978, under the joint WWF/IUCN Project Tiger, a management plan (Seidensticker and Hai, 1983) was prepared for the tigers in these sanctuaries, but it has not yet been implemented (Rahman and Akonda, 1987).

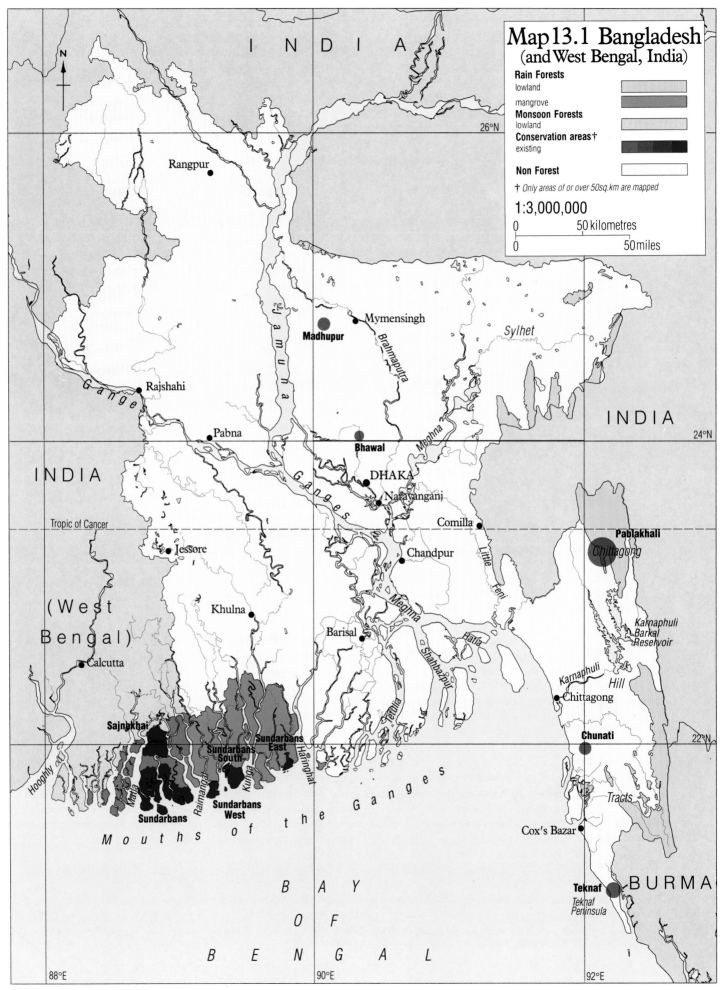

Map 13.1 Bangladesh
(and West Bengal, India)

Rain Forests
lowland
mangrove
Monsoon Forests
lowland
Conservation areas†
existing

Non Forest

† Only areas of or over 50sq.km are mapped

1:3,000,000

0   50 kilometres
0   50 miles

References

Ahmad, N. (1984) Some aspects of economic resources of Sundarban mangrove forest of Bangladesh. In: Soepadmo *et al.* (eds) (*op. cit.*) pp. 644–51.

Ahman, M. (1987) Bangladesh: How forest exploitation is leading to disaster. *Ecologist* **17**: 168–9.

BARC (1987) *National Conservation Strategy for Bangladesh. Draft prospectus (Phase I).* Bangladesh Agricultural Research Council/ IUCN, Gland, Switzerland. 154 pp.

Blower, J. H. (1985) *Sundarbans Forest Inventory Project, Bangladesh: Wildlife Conservation in the Sundarbans.* Project Report 151. ODA Land Resources Development Centre, Surbiton, UK. 39 pp.

Christensen, B. (1984) *Integrated Development of the Sundarbans, Ecological Aspects of the Sundarbans.* TCP/BGD/2309 (Mf) FAO, Rome, Italy.

DS/DT (1980) *(Draft) Environmental Profile on Bangladesh.* Science and Technology Division, Library of Congress, Washington DC, USA. 98 pp.

FAO (1987) *Forestry Project Profile Bangladesh.* FAO, Rome, Italy.

FAO (1990), *Yearbook of Forest Products 1977–88.* FAO Forestry Series No. 23, FAO Statistics Series No. 90. FAO, Rome, Italy.

FAO/UNEP (1981) *Tropical Forest Resources Assessment Project. Forest Resources of Tropical Asia.* Vol 3 of 3 volumes. FAO, Rome. 475 pp.

Gittins, S. P. and Akonda, A. W. (1982) What survives in Bangladesh? *Oryx* **16**: 275–81.

IUCN (1985) *Corbett Action Plan for Protected Areas of the Indomalayan Realm.* Prepared during the 25th Working Session of IUCN's Commission on National Parks and Protected Areas, 4–8th February 1985 Corbett National Park, India. IUCN, Cambridge, UK, and Gland, Switzerland. 23 pp.

IUCN (1986a). *Plants in Danger. What Do We Know?* IUCN, Gland, Switzerland, and Cambridge, UK. 461 pp.

IUCN (1986b) *Review of the Protected Areas System in the Indo-Malayan Realm.* Consultants: MacKinnon, J. and K. IUCN, Gland, Switzerland, and Cambridge, UK. 284 pp.

IUCN (1990) *1989 United Nations List of National Parks and Protected Areas.* IUCN, Gland, Switzerland, and Cambridge, UK.

IUCN/SSC (n.d.) *(Draft) Action plan for Asian Elephant Conservation.* WWF, Gland, Switzerland.

IUCN/SSC (1987) *Action Plan for Asian Primate Conservation.* IUCN/UNEP/WWF, Gland, Switzerland.

IUCN/SSC (1988) *Tortoise and Freshwater Turtle Specialist Group: Conservation Action Plan.* IUCN, Gland, Switzerland.

Khan, M. A. R. (1984) Endangered mammals of Bangladesh. *Oryx* **18**: 152–6.

Khan, M. A. R. (1985) Future conservation directions for Bangladesh. In: *Conserving Asia's Natural Heritage.* Thorsell, J. W. (ed.) pp. 114–22. IUCN, Gland, Switzerland.

Khan, M. S. and Karim, A. (1982) Study of the growth of plants in relation to edaphic factors in coastal afforestation plantation in Chittagong. In: Soepadmo E., Rao, A. N. and McIntosh, D. J. (eds) (1984) *Proceedings of the Asian Symposium on Mangrove Environment Research and Management.* University of Malaya and Unesco Kuala Lumpur pp. 195–9.

Montalembert, M. R. de (1988) TFAP-Update. *Tigerpaper* **19**: 10.

Olivier, R. C. D. (1979) *Wildlife Conservation and Management in Bangladesh.* UNDP/FAO Project No. BGD/72/005. Forest Research Institute, Chittagong, Bangladesh.

Queensland Government (1987) *Wet Tropical Rainforests of Northeast Australia.*

Rahman, S. A. and Akonda, A. Q. (1987) *Bangladesh National Conservation Strategy: Wildlife and Protected Areas.* Department of Forestry, Dhaka, Bangladesh. Unpublished report. 33 pp.

Salter, R. E. (1984) *Integrated Development of the Sundarbans, Bangladesh: Status and Utilization of wildlife.* TCP/BGO/2309 (MF) FAO, Rome, Italy.

Sarker, S. U. and Sarker, N. J. (1983) Endangered wildlife of Bangladesh. *Tigerpaper* **10**: 26–8.

Sarker, N. M. and Fazlul Huq, A. K. M. (1985) Protected Areas of Bangladesh. In: *Conserving Asia's Natural Heritage*, Thornsell, J. W. (ed.) pp. 36–8. IUCN, Gland, Switzerland.

Scott, A. D. (ed.) (1989) *A Directory of Asian Wetlands.* IUCN, Gland, Switzerland, and Cambridge, UK.

Seidensticker, J. and Hai, M. A. (1983) *The Sundarbans Wildlife Management Plan: Conservation in the Bangladesh Coastal Zone.* IUCN, Gland, Switzerland. 120 pp.

Siddiqi, N. A. (1986) Impact of forest management practices in Bangladesh on wildlife and the environment. *Tigerpaper* **13**: 8–9.

Siddiqi, N. A. and Choudhury, J. H. (1987) Maneating behaviour of tigers of the Sundarbans. *Tigerpaper* **14**: 26–32.

UNEP (1986) *Environmental Problems of the Marine and Coastal Area of Bangladesh: National Report.* UNEP Regional Seas Reports and Studies No. 75.

WCMC (1989) *Bangladesh, an Overview of its Protected Areas System.* WCMC, Cambridge, UK.

World Bank (1981) *Bangladesh-General Vegetation* Sheet No. G8 at 1:500,000. Prepared by the Resources Planning Unit, Agriculture and Rural Development Department, World Bank, Washington, USA.

Authorship

Guido Broekhaven at IUCN, Gland, with contributions from Franca Monti at FAO in Rome and Peter Stevens at FAO, Dhaka.

Map 13.1 Forest cover in Bangladesh

Forest cover in Bangladesh has been derived from *Bangladesh-General Vegetation* (1981) Sheet No. G8 at 1:500,000 scale, prepared by the Resource Planning Unit, Agriculture and Rural Development Department, World Bank, Washington. This is derived from updated and ground-truthed 1977 Landsat satellite imagery. (Categories used for the map in this atlas were numbers 25 and 26, main land use *Forest* and *Forest or Forest Reserve*.)

A useful additional map is *Bangladesh 1984 Landsat Satellite Digital Mosaic Sheet 4, Forest Areas*, published at a scale of 1:1 million by FAO (1986). The map theoretically accompanies Field Document No. 12 *Ecological Zones and Forestry in Bangladesh* by J. Davidson, of the UNDP/FAO Project BGD/79/017 *Assistance to the Forestry Sector*, but the editors have not been able to obtain the report. This map is overlaid by legal forest reserve boundaries, and shows that some of the reserves are no longer forested. Data for this map were obtained from 1984 satellite imagery; however, according to the literature some regeneration of forest has occurred in some protected areas occurring within the forest reserves; e.g. sal forest in Madhupur National Park.

Protected areas information has been largely derived from unpublished data on file at the World Conservation Monitoring Centre.

14 Brunei

Land area 5765 sq. km
Population (**1989**) 300,000
Population growth rate 2.7 per cent
Maximum expected population (**2075**) 600,000
Gross national product (**1987**) US$15.390 per capita
Rain forest (see map) 4692 sq. km
Closed broadleaved/coniferous forest (**1980**)† 3230 sq. km
Annual deforestation rate (**1981–5**)† 50 sq. km
Roundwood production* 294,000 cu. m (1988)
Fuelwood and charcoal production* 79,000 cu. m (1987)
Sawlogs and veneer logs production* 206,000 cu. m (1987)

1988 data from FAO (1990)
† FAO/UNEP (1981)

The small Sultanate of Brunei Darussalam is wealthy, its population is mostly urban and well-educated, and the Government has been careful in planning its land-use policies. This, combined with high oil revenue, has meant that to date the country has had little need for revenue from timber, and forest exploitation has been limited. No timber is exported, so large-scale forest destruction has not occurred. Timber extraction for local consumption is allowed, but only under strict control by the Forest Department, and clear felling is prohibited. Thus, Brunei is one of the few countries in the region, or, indeed, in the whole of the tropics, where widespread felling of the forests for shifting cultivation or the timber industry has not occurred to date. This explains why about 81 per cent of the land is still under forest cover, and about 59 per cent under primary forest.

INTRODUCTION

Brunei Darussalam is a small Sultanate in the north-west region of Borneo which became independent from Britain in 1984. It is inset into the Malaysian state of Sarawak, and comprises two sections which are separated by the Sarawak district of Limbang, which is about 6 km wide at the coast. Lying between 4°02′N and 5°03′N, and 114°04′E and 115°22′E, Brunei has a coastline of about 161 km facing the South China Sea.

Annual rainfall varies between 2310 mm on the coast to more than 5080 mm in the mountains. The north-east monsoon (December to mid-March) brings drier weather from January through to March. During the south-west monsoon period (mid-May to the end of October) it rains more frequently. November and December can often be rainy months also.

In western Brunei (the Districts of Brunei-Muara, Tutong and Belait), an alluvial and often swampy coastal plain is backed by low hills, with further swamps inland along the valleys of the Belait and Tutong rivers. Most of the interior in this part of the country lies below 90 m altitude, but rises to almost 400 m in the Labi Hills to the extreme west. Temburong District, the eastern part of Brunei, comprises a swampy coastal plain, rising to hilly and mountainous terrain inland. The main mountains are along the border with Sarawak, and rise to a peak of 1850 m above sea level at Gunung Pagon Priok.

The population is principally urban, with more than 85 per cent living in the capital, Bandar Seri Begawan, and in the oil-producing areas along the western coast. Malays comprise about 68 per cent of the population, followed by Chinese (18 per cent). Both groups live almost exclusively in Bandar Seri Begawan and the other coastal areas. A further 5 per cent of the population comprises a variety of races indigenous to Borneo such as Ibans, Dusuns, Muruts and Penans living in scattered rural communities.

The economy of Brunei depends almost entirely on the exploitation of its rich reserves of oil and natural gas. Between them, these account for more than 88 per cent of Government revenue. The abundant reserves of hydrocarbons and a relatively small population means that the country has one of the highest standards of living in eastern Asia. Brunei is now starting to plan diversification of its economy so that it will remain viable when oil supplies start to decline in the next century.

The Forests

The natural vegetation of Brunei includes various rain forest formations (Table 14.1).

● Most of the country is under lowland evergreen rain forest, rich in dipterocarps.

● From about 1000 m above sea level upwards, this gives way to montane forest, where dipterocarps are gradually replaced by Fagaceae and Lauraceae.

● Upper montane forest is only found above 1500 m, principally on Gunung Pagon Priok in the Temburong area.

● There are small areas of heath forest near the coast.

Mangroves (see below) and peat swamp forests, although representing only a small proportion of the total forest cover, are especially important because both have been disturbed excessively in other parts of northern Borneo (see chapter 24) and Brunei has probably the largest remaining intact patches. The main areas of peat swamp forest are in the Belait River basin in western Brunei, where characteristic raised peat swamp forests exist in a pristine state. All six characteristic peat swamp forest types occur here (Scott, 1989).

Forest Resources

Most of the population in Brunei live along the coast, and most of the country's development and economy has been centred around oil and gas. This means that the forest has not been widely exploited—almost 81 per cent of the land area is still under forest cover (Table 14.1; Map 14.1) and 59 per cent of the country is still under primary forest (Anderson and Marsden, 1988). Just over half of this is lowland evergreen rain forest rich in dipterocarps, and a further

Table 14.1 Estimates of forest extent in Brunei

	Area (sq. km)	% of land area
Rain forests		
Lowland	2,670	46.3
Montane	70	1.2
Inland swamp	1,750	30.4
Mangrove	200	3.5
Totals	4,690[1]	81.4

This is based on analysis of Map 14.1 (see map legend for details). The totals accord very closely with those of the authors of the source map, Anderson and Marsden (1988).

[1] Anderson and Marsden (1988) estimated that secondary forest covered 1279 sq km.

quarter is peat swamp forest. The rest comprises freshwater swamp forests, heath and montane forests (Table 14.1 and Map 14.1). Estimates of closed forest cover made during the FAO survey (3230 sq. km) are considered to be underestimates (FAO/UNEP, 1981).

Forest Management

The country has an extensive permanent forest estate, consisting of eleven legally constituted forest reserves totalling 2277 sq. km which are managed by the Forest Department. Forest reserves cover 39 per cent of Brunei's total land area. Almost 86 per cent of the whole reserve area is still under primary forest, three-quarters of it dipterocarp-rich rain forest. Swamp forest covers only 7.3 per cent of the primary reserved forest and 6.5 per cent of the total reserve area. This is a poor representation of the forest type, which covers over 30 per cent of Brunei's land area. Within forest reserves, a total of 151 sq. km has been exploited, almost entirely dipterocarp and peat swamp forests.

About 52 per cent of all forested land in Brunei, and 43 per cent of all primary forest, lie on state land outside the permanent forest estate. A portion of this state land forest is scheduled for conversion to other purposes.

There are no plans to export timber from Brunei, but internal demand for wood is expected to increase as the standard of living goes up. Brunei is aiming to increase its permanent forest estate with the aim that it can be self-sufficient in timber in perpetuity. Proposals to implement this ideal have been written as part of an overall strategic planning study on Brunei's forest resources (Anderson and Marsden, 1988) which suggests that a large new forest reserve, the Belait Peat Swamp Forest Reserve, should be created. In addition, the Forestry Department proposes to incorporate more lowland dipterocarp forest into the permanent forest estate. This proposal would include creating a second new reserve, the Bukit Biang Forest Reserve (27 sq. km), as well as extending several existing forest reserves, including an area contiguous with Gunung Mulu National Park in Sarawak (see chapter 24). If all these proposals go ahead as planned, the total area of permanent forest estate in Brunei would increase by 937 sq. km, an increase of 41 per cent in the area of reserved forest.

In 1989, the Forest Department began formulating proposals for forest development and conservation in a 'Forestry Strategic Plan' for Brunei. It stated that its four main priorities are:
- Adequate timber production.
- Development of the timber industry.
- Environmental conservation.
- Development of non-forest resources such as bamboo and rattan.

These objectives would be met by rehabilitating natural forest after logging and reducing timber wastage, coordinating the development of rattan and bamboo with that of the local furniture industry, and launching a tree plantation programme. The aim would be to have an annual yield of plantation timber of 100,000 cu. m by the year 2015.

Deforestation

The deforestation rate in Brunei was estimated at 50 sq. km per year by FAO (FAO/UNEP, 1981). No new statistics are available, but the rate is generally believed still to be very low indeed. The deforestation which has taken place has been largely associated with towns, roads, and the development of the oil and gas industry in coastal areas. The latter is a major factor that will continue to affect the conservation of coastal heath forests all along the west Bornean coast, including the Brunei coastal heath forests which are acknowledged as some of the finest in Borneo. Agriculture, however, is not a major cause of forest loss. Shifting agriculture is relatively rare, and is mainly practised by a small number of Ibans.

Plans to diversify the economy could result in further forest clearance, especially in the coastal areas, and indeed the Forestry Plan proposes increases in the amount of forest to be selectively logged. If carefully planned and tied in with an appropriate system of conservation areas, however, this should not result in further major forest loss. The only habitat which could be overexploited if plans go ahead are the peat swamp forests, specifically the zones rich in *Shorea albida*. Although the combined area of existing and proposed peat swamp conservation areas (Anduki and Badas Forest Reserves, the Ulu Mendaram Conservation Area, and the Belait Peat Swamp Forest Research Area) cover some 80 sq. km, these forest formations are under-protected at present.

Mangroves

Brunei Bay contains some of the most extensive and best-preserved mangroves in Southeast Asia. They cover a total area of 184 sq. km or 3.2 per cent of Brunei's total land area, and extend into Sarawak and Sabah, both of which also fringe the Bay. The mangrove forests of Brunei are used to a limited extent for fuelwood and poles. There have also been proposals for clearance to make way for fish and prawn ponds.

The Penan are nomadic hunter-gatherers of the rain forests of Brunei and elsewhere in Borneo. Families follow traditional trails, gathering the sago palm and hunting wild pig and other animals. N. M. Collins

Around the capital the mangrove forests are reported to have been damaged by effluent from Kampung Air, the old part of the town built out over the water, and by oil spills and industry at the mouth of Brunei River. The Brunei Bay mangroves in addition are under threat from clearance (mostly illegal) within Limbang, Sarawak, and from pollution by silt and debris from forests being logged inland (Scott, 1989). There is also a pollution threat from a paper pulp mill at Sipitang, Sabah, which discharges effluent into the heart of the bay, where it can remain for up to a month (Anon., 1985).

There are proposals to create mangrove conservation areas on Pulau Berambang (7 sq. km) and Pulau Siarau (5 sq. km) and to prohibit all timber exploitation in the Brunei mangrove forests (Farmer, 1986). The Forestry Department is examining plans to allocate more mangrove areas for conservation within the Labu and Selirong Forest Reserves.

Biodiversity

For two main reasons the diversity of flora and fauna in Brunei is at a particularly high level for a country of its size.

1 It lies within a zone where the floristic diversity is amongst the highest in the world and which has large stretches of primary forest of several different formations.

2 Animal diversity has been maintained – largely because a hunting lifestyle is not prevalent in Brunei. Guns have been prohibited since 1962, and the only hunting allowed is on a small scale in the interior, using strictly traditional methods (Mittermeier, 1981). Indeed compared to Sarawak and Sabah, hunting is likely to have a negligible effect on wildlife abundance.

Large tracts of primary forest and lack of hunting mean that many species and habitats which are declining rapidly in other parts of northern Borneo are still well preserved over significant areas of Brunei. All of northern Borneo's major species are likely to occur here, the only notable exceptions being the orang utan and Sumatran rhinoceros, which, for reasons unknown, have never been found.

A fair abundance of Brunei's species currently suffer little disturbance because of the inaccessibility of much of the interior of the country. Species which are close to the Sarawak borders, however, are subject to hunting by outsiders. Proboscis monkeys in the Bay migrate across from Brunei into Sarawak, where they are hunted, and this is depleting the population of the whole area. Similarly, flying foxes are often hunted when they fly into Sarawak. More seriously, there are reports that illegal poachers from across the border enter to shoot them at their roosts.

Wildlife in Brunei has been given added protection by the 1978 Wild Life Protection Enactment. This protects 34 species from being hunted, kept or exported without a special licence. They include the proboscis monkey, clouded leopard, dugong Dugong dugon, great argus pheasant Argusianus argus, all eight of Borneo's hornbill species and all three of its marine turtles (Mittermeier, 1981). In addition, the Forestry Enactment (1934) and Forest Rules (1956, 1960) regulate the taking of forest produce, whether mineral, plant or animal.

Conservation Areas

There is no special legislation allowing for the establishment of national parks in Brunei, although the 1978 Wild Life Protection Enactment provides for the establishment of wildlife sanctuaries by decree of the Sultan. The concept of wildlife sanctuaries in this Enactment is not narrowly defined and in current terms should cover a range of protected areas, including national parks.

Prior to this enactment, at least one wildlife sanctuary was established in the mangroves of the northern Temburong District: Labu-Selirong Wildlife Sanctuary (25 sq. km), which was gazetted in 1948 and extended in 1954 (to 90 sq. km) (Scott, 1989). It is included within the Labu and Selirong Forest Reserves.

All existing protected areas are within Forest Reserves, and are classified for the purposes of protection, conservation or research by the Forestry Department (Table 14.2). The Primary Conservation Areas at Ulu Temburong/Batu Apoi Forest Reserve, Sungei Ingei (in Labi Hills Forest Reserve) and the Ulu Mendaram are the most significant because of their large size, but no less value is accorded to Secondary Conservation Areas and other protected sites, which, although smaller, contain important samples of Brunei's varied forest and vegetation types.

Secondary Conservation Areas consist of small reserves or compartments within forest reserves, containing samples of various forest types. They occur in Andulau Forest Reserve (13 sq. km), Badas Forest Reserve (less than one sq. km), Anduki Forest Reserve (9 sq. km) and Bukit Biang (27 sq. km). Additional proposed areas include Tasek Merimbun (77 sq. km), Pulau Berambang (7 sq. km) and Pulau Siarau (5 sq. km), and the Belait Peat Swamp Forest Research Area (15 sq. km) (see below).

Four 'Recreation Areas' have been established by the Forestry Department within Forest Reserves. These do not have any legal protection above that of Forest Reserve, but they have been set aside for education and recreation, with visitor facilities. These are: Sungai Liang Arboretum Reserve (less than one sq. km); Luagan Lalak (3 sq. km); Berakas Forest Forest (2 sq. km) and Peradayan Forest Reserve (10 sq. km). A fifth area, at Bukit Shahbandar (c. 2 sq. km), is being developed.

Five Protection Forests play an important environmental role, as well as conserving wildlife. The two main areas, Bukit Teraja (68 sq. km) and Bukit Bedawan (76 sq. km), are shown on Map 14.1. Smaller areas are Bukit Batu Patam (9 sq. km), Bukit Ulu Tutong (3 sq. km) and the Benutan Catchment (29 sq. km).

Table 14.2 Conservation areas of Brunei

Existing and proposed areas, 50 sq. km and over, are listed below. The remaining areas are combined in a total under each designation. Only areas 50 sq. km or above are mapped.

	Existing area (sq. km)	Proposed area (sq. km)
Wildlife Sanctuaries		
Labu-Selirong*	90	
Primary Conservation Areas		
Ulu Temburong/Batu Apoi*	488	
Sungei Ingei*	185	
Ulu Mendaram*	62	
Secondary Conservation Areas		
Four sites (see text)*	50	
Additional Areas		
Tasek Merimbun*		77
Three sites (see text)*		27
Protection Forests		
Bukit Teraja*	68	
Bukit Bedawan*	76	
Three sites (see text)*	41	
Recreation Areas (within forest reserves)		
Five sites (see text)*	18	
Totals	1,078	104

(*Source:* 1989 data from the Forestry Department, Brunei Darussalam *in litt*)
* Area with moist forest within its boundary.

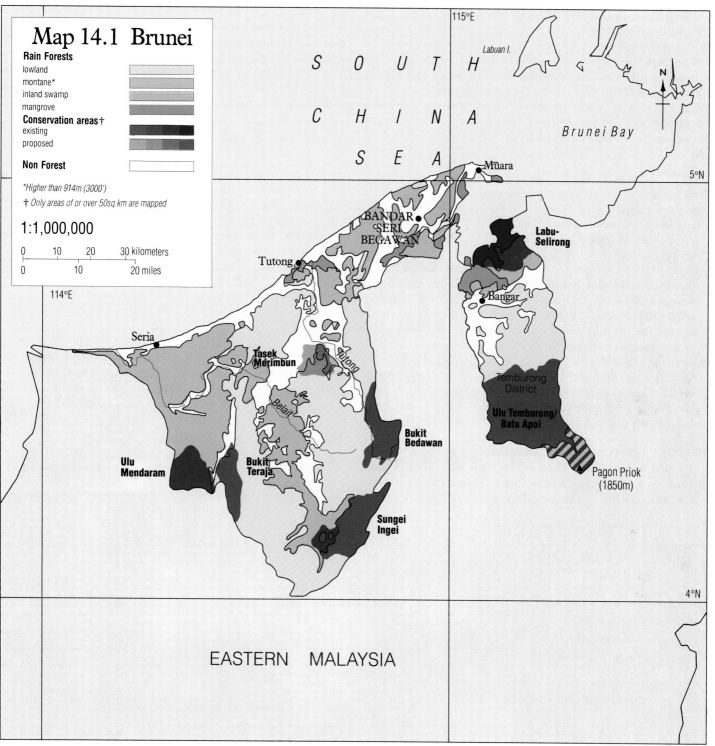

Map 14.1 Brunei

Rain Forests

lowland

montane*

inland swamp

mangrove

Conservation areas†

existing

proposed

Non Forest

*Higher than 914m (3000')

† Only areas of or over 50sq.km are mapped

1:1,000,000

0   10   20   30 kilometers

0   10   20 miles

114°E

SOUTH CHINA SEA

115°E

Labuan I.

Brunei Bay

5°N

Muara

BANDAR SERI BEGAWAN

Labu-Selirong

Tutong

Bangar

Seria

Tasek Merimbun

Temburong District

Ulu Temburong/Batu Apoi

Belait

Tutong

Bukit Bedawan

Ulu Mendaram

Bukit Teraja

Sungei Ingei

Pagon Priok (1850m)

4°N

EASTERN MALAYSIA

Six key critical sites merit priority attention and continued protection:

1 The primary inland forests of Ulu Temburong. These include the only montane forests of Brunei and the catchment zones of the important rivers Temburong, Temawai and Belalong. During a single three-week survey in the inland forests of the Upper Temburong, 48 species of mammals and 105 species of birds were recorded. Two species of leaf-monkey recorded were found at higher densities than at other sites surveyed in Borneo (Bennett *et al.*, 1984).

2 The peat swamp forests of the Belait. These should be given greater attention than proposed at present since they will soon be the region's only peat swamp forests that have not been highly disturbed. Present proposals suggest protecting only non-commercial forest types, but larger areas of the *Shorea albida* forest should also be protected. The commercial peat swamp forests are more diverse floristically than other types, and are likely to have a greater diversity of fauna.

3 The mangroves of Brunei Bay harbour important populations of the proboscis monkey, which is endangered in Sarawak and Sabah and greatly under-protected throughout its range. Within those mangroves lies the island of Pulau Siarau, which has a large colony of flying foxes. They can be seen leaving the island in thousands every evening to forage for fruit in the forests far inland. The mangroves also contain significant populations of silvered leaf-monkeys, which are endangered in Sarawak, and a variety of coastal birds.

4 Tasek Merimbun, a unique area of freshwater and peat swamps.

5 The Batu Patam-Sungei Ingei area, important mainly because it is contiguous with Sarawak's Gunung Mulu National Park. Its protection would contribute to an extremely spacious conservation area, which would offer effective protection even to the larger species of mammals and birds.

6 The coastal belt, where settlement and development will have an increasingly significant influence on Brunei's coastal heath forests. This also includes the Arboretum Forest Reserve and compartments seven and eight of Andulau Forest Reserve (coastal mixed dipterocarp forests) and the Anduki Forest Reserve, which contains Brunei's only sizeable tract of actively regenerating, dense *Dryobalanops rappa* swamp forest.

Initiatives for Conservation

The Strategic Forestry Plan for Brunei, mentioned in Forest Resources and Management above, will be the main vehicle for consolidating the nation's protected area system and maintaining sustained use of production forests. The main features of the plan already exist in an unpublished form, following extensive consultations with a range of NGOs in recent years.

References

Anderson, J. A. R. and Marsden, D. (1988) *Brunei Forest Resources and Strategic Planning Study*. Unpublished report to the Government of His Majesty the Sultan and Yang Di-Pertuan of Negara Brunei Darussalam.

Anon. (1985) Environmental impact assessment of the Sabah Timber, Pulp and Paper Project, Sipitang, Sabah. In: *Reports and Recommendations to the Dewan Undangan Negeri Select Committee on Flora and Fauna in Sarawak, Appendix B, Ad-hoc Subcommittee on Fisheries, Reptiles and Amphibians*. Pp. 158–60. Dewan Undangan Negeri, Kuching, Sarawak, Malaysia.

Bennett, E. L., Caldecott, J. D. and Davison, G. W. H. (1984) *A Wildlife Study of Ulu Temburong, Brunei*. Forest Department, Kuching and Universiti Kebangsaan, Malaysia. 61 pp.

FAO (1990) *FAO Yearbook of Forest Products 1977–1988*. FAO Forestry Series No. 23, FAO Statistics Series 90. FAO, Rome, Italy.

FAO/UNEP (1981). *Tropical Forest Resources Assessment Project. Forest Resources of Tropical Asia*. Vol 3 of 3 vols. FAO, Rome. 475 pp.

Farmer, A. S. D. (1986) *Negara Brunei Darussalam Master Plan*. Background Paper: Fisheries and Aquaculture. Huszar Brammah and Associates and Department of Town and Country Planning, Bandar Seri Begawan.

Mittermeier, R. A. (1981) Brunei Protects Its Wildlife. *Oryx* **16**: 67–70.

Scott, D. A. (ed.) (1989) *A Directory of Asian Wetlands*. IUCN, Gland, Switzerland, and Cambridge, UK. 1181 pp.

Authorship

Elizabeth Bennett in Kuching, with contributions from Wong Khoon Meng, Haji Mohd Yassin Bin Ampuan Salleh and Awang Haji Abd. Rahman of the Forestry Department and Peter Eaton of the University in Brunei Darussalam.

Map 14.1 Forest cover in Brunei

The distribution and areas of forest types were obtained from the *Brunei Forest Resources and Strategic Planning Study* prepared by Anderson and Marsden (1988), consultants to the Brunei Forest Department. Data on protected areas follow the existing classification of the Forestry Department, Brunei Darussalam.

15 Burma (Myanmar)

Land area[1] 657,740 sq. km
Population (1989) 40.8 million
Population growth rate (1987–2000) 2.2 per cent per year
Projected maximum population (2150) 102 million
Gross national product US$200 per capita
Rain forest (see map) 223,390 sq. km
Monsoon forest (see map) 88,460 sq. km
Closed broadleaved/coniferous forest (1980)† 313,090 sq. km
Annual deforestation rate: (1981–5)† 1015 sq. km[1]
Roundwood production* 21,033,000 cu. m
Roundwood exports* 206,000 cu. m
Fuelwood and charcoal production* 17,046,000 cu. m
Sawlogs and veneer logs production* 2,789,000 cu. m
Sawlogs and veneer logs export* 206,000 cu. m
[1] Also estimated at 6000 sq. km (Allen, 1984)
* 1988 data from FAO (1990)
† FAO/UNEP (1981)

The forests of Burma[1] are of enormous economic, social and environmental significance, but this wealth could be lost in just a few decades if the present rate of deforestation and degradation continues. Although Burma has a relatively low population density, population pressure is leading to land hunger in some areas, and unsustainable shifting cultivation is causing forest depletion on a huge scale. Timber poaching, especially to feed markets in neighbouring countries, and unsustainable felling rates in production forests, have also contributed to push Burma's rate of deforestation up to one of the highest in the world. The 1988 ban on logging in Thailand has exacerbated the situation; Thai logging entrepreneurs are shifting their attention to Burma as a source of material for the Thai timber mills.

Burma's potential for sustainable development will suffer an irreversible setback if present trends run their full course. Burma, an economically fragile nation, derives 25 per cent of its foreign earnings from timber exports, and most of this comes from teak. Burma once supplied 75 per cent of the world demand for teak, but timber from plantations in Java and elsewhere is now on the market.

Burma's wildlife populations, which are extremely diverse, with elements of central and Southeast Asian origin, are in decline, and becoming increasingly fragmented. Legally protected areas currently cover only 1 per cent of the country. Proposals to extend this to 4 per cent by the gazettement of new reserves and parks have stood neglected since 1984. Even these proposals fall far short of the minimum network of protected areas that would be required to include representative examples of all Burma's threatened ecosystems. Even the future of the elephant, a symbol of Burmese wildlife and industry, is far from assured and two species of rhinoceros, which occurred until well into this century, are now probably extinct.

INTRODUCTION

The Socialist Republic of the Union of Burma extends some 2093 km between 9°53′N and 28°25′N. An ecological spectrum of great variety is found between these extremes, ranging from tropical rain forests and coral reefs in the south to montane rain forests with a predominantly temperate flora of conifers, oaks and rhododendrons in the far north, where snow-capped peaks up to 5729 m mark the eastern extremity of the Himalayas. Mountain ranges, known in Burma as *yomas*, form a continuous barrier along the western border with India and Bangladesh, and extend southward parallel with the coast to the Irrawaddy Delta. In the north-east, the border with China follows the high crest of the Irrawaddy–Salween divide, then bulges out eastward to enclose the ruggedly mountainous Shan Plateau forming the border with Laos and Thailand.

Between these eastern and western mountain barriers lie the fertile, heavily populated plains of the Irrawaddy, with its largest tributary, the Chindwin, joining from the north-west. Burma's other great river, the Salween, lies further east. It enters Burma from neighbouring Yunnan and flows south, cutting through the Shan Plateau in deep gorges, once heavily forested, before running into the Gulf of Martaban. In the south lies Tenasserim, which extends south to the Kra Isthmus as a long hilly arm.

The Forests

Rain forests occur on the west-facing slopes of the mountains which run south to north along the western and eastern frontiers. Some tropical evergreen rain forests occur in the extreme south, but most of the rain forests are semi-evergreen. They have varied floras and in the far south there is a strong Malesian influence. To the north, temperate elements enter, and in the far north, on the south slopes of the Himalayas the montane rain forest has a completely temperate flora with various conifers and many rhododendrons. At the upper limit of the forest subalpine formations, with temperate floras, are found. Tiny patches of tropical montane rain forest occur further south, for example on Natma Taung (Mount Victoria, 3053 m).

The Irrawaddy plains, now almost entirely cleared for agriculture, lie in the rain shadow of the western ranges and, especially in the central area, have a very dry and seasonal climate. This area originally supported so-called *indaing*, a dry deciduous woodland dominated by species of *Dipterocarpus*, and, at its driest central part, a small area of tropical thorn forest. Around this dry core occur

---

[1] During the preparation of this atlas, Burma changed its name to Myanmar. The country chapters are arranged alphabetically and the editors have used the former, more commonly known, name in order to avoid major restructuring.

103

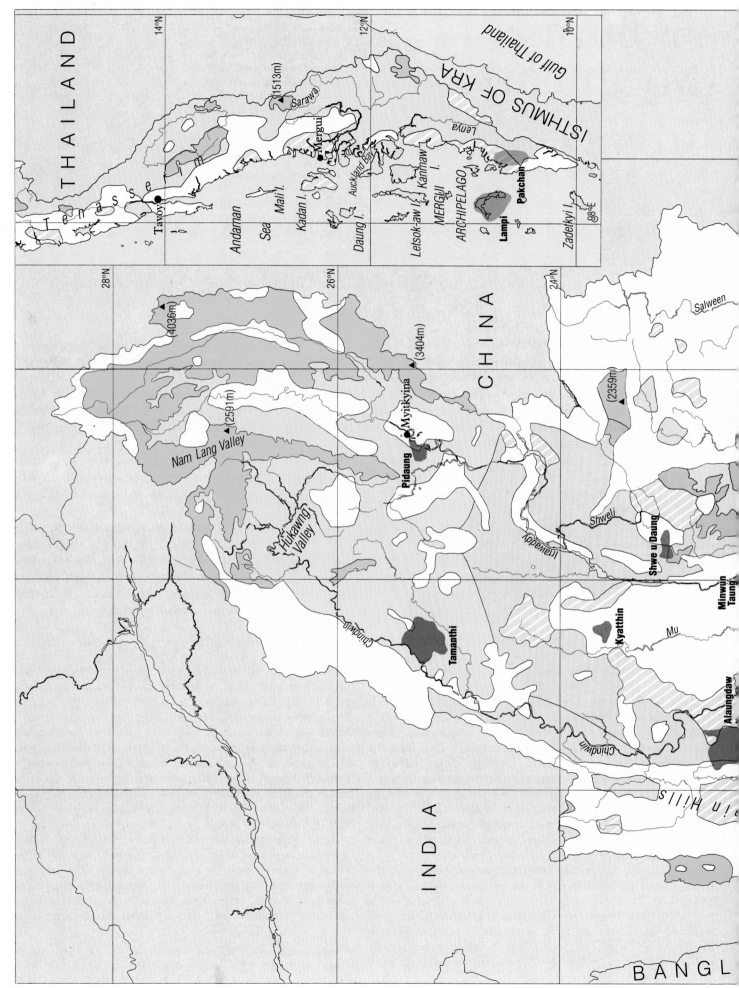

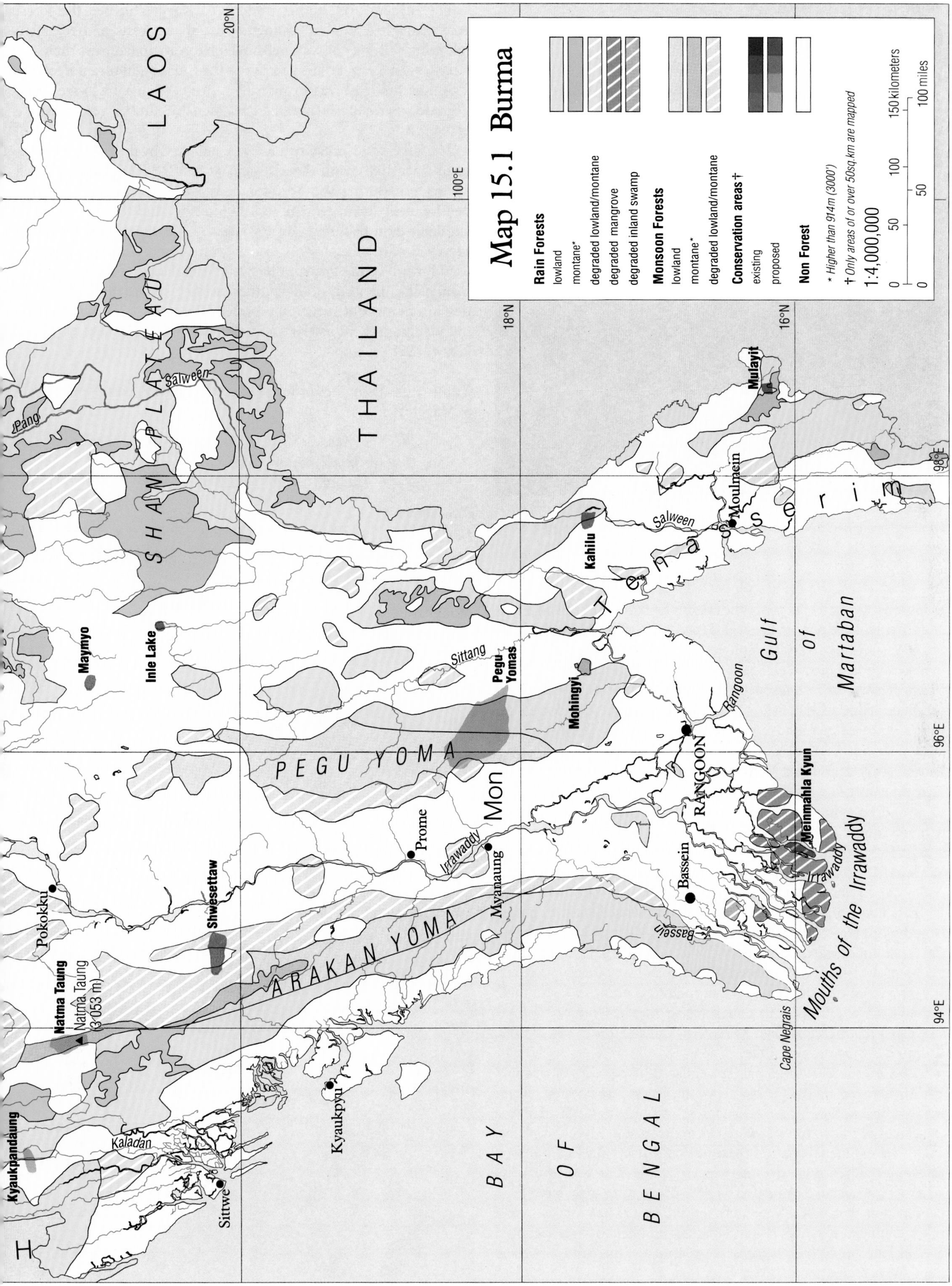

Map 15.1 Burma

Rain Forests
lowland
montane*
degraded lowland/montane
degraded mangrove
degraded inland swamp

Monsoon Forests
lowland
montane*
degraded lowland/montane

Conservation areas †
existing
proposed

Non Forest

1:4,000,000

* Higher than 914m (3000')

† Only areas of or over 50sq km are mapped

0   50   100   150 kilometers

0   50   100 miles

LAOS

THAILAND

SHAN PLATEAU

Salween

Pang

Maymyo

Inle Lake

Sittang

Pegu Yomas

Mohingyi

Kahilu

Moulmein

Salween

Tenasserim

Gulf of Martaban

PEGU YOMA

Mon

Prome

Irrawaddy

Myanaung

RANGOON

Rangoon

Bassein

Bassein

Meinmahla Kyun

Irrawaddy

Mouths of the Irrawaddy

Cape Negrais

ARAKAN YOMA

Shwesettaw

Pokokku

Natma Taung
Natma Taung
(3·053 m)

Kyaukpandaung

Kaladan

Kyaukpyu

Sittwe

BAY OF BENGAL

Mulayit

20°N

18°N

16°N

100°E

98°E

96°E

94°E

105

Elephants have been used for generations in the teak forest of the Pegu Yomas. Modern machines, increasingly in vogue, are far more damaging to the environment. J. A. McNeely

monsoon forests, which cover the eastern flanks of the Arakan Yoma and Chin Hills. Monsoon forests also occur east of the Salween on the Shan Plateau and to the south on the hills along the Thai border. The monsoon forests are rich in teak and are also important for pyinkado (*Xylia dolabriformis*). The once extensive inland swamp forests along the floodplains of the major rivers have been mostly cleared for agriculture (see case study, page 109).

Forest Resources and Management

Forest resource inventories in Burma date back to the 1850s, when D. Brandis inventoried the teak forests of the Pegu Yomas to obtain data for compiling working plans. In the late 1940s there remained almost 500,000 sq. km of forest. Aerial photographs taken between 1953 and 1962 showed an estimated 59 per cent of the country still under closed rain and monsoon forest (386,000 sq. km). The FAO/UNEP Tropical Forest Resources Assessment Project reported closed forest cover reduced to 47 per cent (311,090 sq. km), based on 1972–5 Landsat satellite imagery. New imagery for 1979–81, studied as part of the FAO-assisted National Forest Management and Inventory Project, showed a further reduction of intact forest to 42 per cent (276,250 sq. km) and a recent national report to FAO suggested that no more than 36 per cent remained in 1988 (245,000 sq. km) (U Shwe Kyaw, 1988).

Based on the 1979–81 imagery, updated by aerial photography, FAO produced in 1987 a map showing 'actual forest' and 'forest fallow' (Britto, 1987). The 'actual forest' was further subdivided into intact and degraded forests, which form the basis of Map 15.1. Table 15.1 gives estimated areas of these forests. Intact rain and monsoon forests cover 257,390 sq. km, which accords well with the FAO statistics given above. A further 54,460 sq. km were considered to be degraded at that time. Now, perhaps five years after the last aerial photographs were taken, it is certain that the extent of degradation is greater still, but as long as forest cover remains, there must be some hope for regeneration and recovery.

The earlier FAO studies undoubtedly overestimated the forest area through failing to distinguish bamboo forests and regrowth following shifting cultivation from high forest; nonetheless there has clearly been a rapid deterioration of the situation in recent decades. The now limited areas of monsoon forests (Table 15.1) are being degraded particularly rapidly, and valuable timber resources are being lost.

The large-scale forest inventories conducted by the Forest Department since 1982, with the assistance of UNDP/FAO, have focused on western Burma and are designed to provide a basis for forest development, management and monitoring, and to allow medium and long-term planning. By 1987 nearly 110,000 sq. km had been surveyed. The inventory data has been computerised, and can be used for projecting growth rates, the formulation of forest management plans, the study of silvicultural methods and to supply information to a number of agencies, especially the Ministry of Industry, for the planning of industrial and commercial development (U Shwe Kyaw, 1988)

Table 15.1 Estimates of forest extent in Burma, based on analysis of Map 15.1

	Areas intact (sq. km)	% of land area	Area degraded (sq. km)	% of land area	Totals	% of land area
Rain forests						
Lowland	147,340	22.4	16,460	2.5	163,800	24.9
Montane	56,520	8.6	—	—	56,520	8.6
Inland swamp	—	—	170	<0.1	170	<0.1
Mangrove	—	—	2,900	0.4	2,900	0.4
Sub totals	203,860	31.0	19,530	3.0	223,390	34.0
Monsoon forests						
Lowland	49,260	7.5	34,930	5.3	84,190	12.8
Montane	4,270	0.6	—	—	4,270	0.6
Sub totals	53,530	8.1	34,930	5.3	88,460	13.4
Totals	257,390	39.1	54,460	8.3	311,850	47.4

(See Map Legend for details of sources on page 110)

Burmese teak is a highly-prized timber, now much in demand by Thai timber companies frustrated by the logging ban in Thailand. J. A. McNeely

The Arakan Yomas have suffered extensive degradation.Their monsoon forests, now penetrated by extensive bamboo, have lost much of their value. J. A. Sayer

Forest-type maps are being prepared by the Burma Forest Department at 1:50,000 scale for the western part of the country, encompassing about 40 per cent of the closed forests. To 1987, 90 maps had been prepared, and half of them printed.

The monsoon forests in the hills and foothills are of supreme commercial importance for their stands of teak and this is one of the few areas where management for timber has proved sustainable over a long period. Twenty-five per cent of Burma's national revenue is still derived from the sale of teak, harvested under the 'Burma Selection System', a polycyclic silvicultural system in which low volumes of mature trees of stipulated minimum girth are harvested on a 25–40 year felling cycle. This system has been practised for longer than any other in the tropics and the forests of the Pegu Yomas, north of Rangoon, are now undergoing their third or fourth cycle of extraction. Traditionally, elephants are used to haul the logs to river banks from where they are floated to railways or ports. Post-logging silvicultural treatments include cutting of climbers and killing of uneconomic trees that are competing with desirable trees. This system has been in operation since the mid-19th century and has proved most successful in maintaining a sustained yield of top quality timber with minimum environmental disturbance.

The numerous external forestry aid projects during the 1980s, however, have favoured more intensive forest exploitation, with large investment in mechanised logging equipment. This trend has been exacerbated by Thailand's 1988 ban on timber exploitation, which has intensified the pressure to exploit Burma's forests. The replacement of elephants by machines has inevitably had serious environmental consequences. Not only will this cause degradation that could spell the end of economic logging but it will also diminish the value of the forests as wildlife habitat.

Even more seriously, the economies of scale associated with mechanisation will favour monocyclic clear-felling systems, or even the complete abandonment of natural forest management in favour of timber production from plantations. (For explanation of timber felling systems see chapter 6.)

The managed teak forests of the Pegu Yomas still retain most of the species of animals and plants found in natural forests, but if the present trends continue, and these are gradually converted to plantations or to more uniform systems, many species will be lost.

An associated problem has arisen, resulting from the amount of funds channelled into the State Timber Corporation for logging operations. This has diverted national personnel and funds away from the Forest Department, which has consequently been neglected, thereby greatly reducing its capacity for effective forest conservation and management.

There is great potential for plantation forestry on degraded and deforested lands in Burma, to relieve pressure on the remaining natural forests. However, by 1985 the total area of plantation forest in Burma was only about 2210 sq. km, less than one per cent of the country. In former times there was extensive planting of teak and other hardwoods, much of it by shifting cultivators using the taungya system (see below). More recently the trend has been towards fast-growing exotics, especially eucalypts, which are grown both for fuelwood and paper production. By 1985 175 sq. km of eucalypts had been planted, much of it in the central dry zone.

Deforestation

Prior to the second Anglo-Burmese war in 1852, large areas of the Irrawaddy delta and plains were still clothed in mangrove, monsoon and rain forests. At that time, the economic centre of Burma was in the dry zone around the ancient capital of Sagaing and cultivation in Lower Burma was limited to the Irrawaddy, Bassein and Sittang valleys. British officials however, regarded mangrove forest and lowland rain forest as impediments to economic development, and under the British colonial administration there was a great expansion of rice production in this area. In 1830 an estimated area of 2670 sq. km was under rice cultivation in Lower Burma, but this rose rapidly to 5397 sq. km in 1860, 34,610 sq. km in 1900 and 51,810 sq. km in 1940 (Golay et al., 1969; Bixler, 1971). The consequences for natural forest cover were devastating. Today, virtually the entire lowland area, apart from a few forest reserves in the delta, is used for growing rice. Crops are grown right up to the edges of river banks and only scattered trees remain. The estimated rate of deforestation is 6000 sq. km per year, equivalent to 0.88 per cent of the total land area, and is equal to over 2 per cent of the estimated remaining rain and monsoon forest cover (Allen, 1984). This is one of the highest deforestation rates in the world, representing a catastrophic rise from the previous, 1975, estimate of around 1250 sq. km per year (Allen, 1984).

The 1972–5 and 1979–81 satellite assessments estimate the areas of rain and monsoon forests affected by shifting cultivation as about 26 and 28 per cent of the country respectively (U Shwe Kyaw, 1988). The total remaining area of relatively undisturbed closed canopy rain and monsoon forest is probably less than 20 per cent of the total land area, much of it fragmented and in remote hill country. The proposed Pakchan Reserve with about 650 sq. km is the most viable site for protection, but even here the proportion of lowland forest is very low and considerable disturbance has already occurred (see case study).

Over a very long period of time the low-lying and densely populated Irrawaddy delta, Irrawaddy and Sittang plains, and the coastal regions of Arakan, Mon and Tenasserim have lost virtually all forest cover (Allen, 1984). Some coastal regions were settled by the Mons more than a thousand years ago. From the 9th century onwards, the Burmans settled in the Irrawaddy plains and forest destruction was probably underway many centuries ago, although some areas of swamp forest still existed along the Sittang valley until the Second World War (Smythies, 1953) in areas now totally devoted to agriculture.

In the uplands, shifting cultivation, known as taungya in Burma, is still the major agent of forest destruction, even in some areas which are theoretically protected as reserves. All forest types are affected as rising populations of itinerant farmers are steadily eating into the forest. Taungya farming has been practised for many years in the uplands by non-Burman Karen, Shan, Chin, Kachin and Chinese tribes. In the past, most forests were minimally affected by 'slash and burn', as a cultivation cycle of 20 years allowed fertility to be restored. However, increasing population pressure has led to a reduction in the number of years of the cycle and has forced farmers to penetrate further and further into the forest. The impact of shifting cultivation is most acute in the remote hill areas occupied by the ethnic minorities. Very large areas of forest have been cleared in eastern Shan State along the border with Laos and China; in Kayah State; in the north-east of Sagaing Division of upper Salween State, along the border with India; and in Chin State. In the Chin Hills, Arakan, and Pegu Yomas and on the Shan Plateau there are areas where the original forest is so degraded that it has been replaced by bamboo or by *Imperata* grasslands. Vast areas along the western flanks of the Arakan Yomas are now covered by virtually pure stands of the bamboo *Melocanna bambusoides*.

The precise impact of deforestation on Burma's environment is hard to gauge. Widespread clearance could lead to a cycle of droughts, floods and erosion as the protective forest cover is lost. However, it is worth noting that severe drought also occurred in the late 19th century, when forests were very much more extensive than today, and flooding in the Irrawaddy valley has underpinned rice production for centuries.

Mangroves

Mangrove forests occur along the coastline and their area has been variously estimated at 5000–8000 sq. km (FAO/UNEP, 1981; Saenger et al., 1983). Map 15.1 and Table 15.1 probably underestimate the total area remaining now, but it is certain that very little remains pristine. Exploitation by rural people is considerable.

The mouths of the Irrawaddy once had huge mangrove forests. Most remaining mangrove is in isolated blocks in the Irrawaddy Delta, on the Tenasserim and Arakan coasts and on offshore islands, notably Meinmahla Island.

Mangrove plantations have been established in Taikkyi, near Rangoon, at the rate of approximately 16 sq. km per annum, in an attempt to relieve exploitation pressure on natural forest. Areas for conservation have been suggested (FAO, 1985b; Scott, 1989), in-

cluding Meinmahla Kyun (Island), 129 sq. km, where exploitation is light (FAO, 1985b) and where an estuarine crocodile ranching operation is proposed.

Biodiversity

Approximately 7000 flowering plant species have been recorded in Burma (Hundley and Chit Ko Ko, 1961) and some 1071 vascular plant species have been identified as endemic (Chatterjee, 1939, cited in Legris, 1974). Burma is home to about 300 mammal species, and large mammals such as elephant, gaur, banteng, sambar, barking deer, tiger and leopard *Panthera pardus* are widely distributed in many of the less disturbed forested regions. The Javan rhinoceros and the Sumatran rhinoceros, however, are now almost certainly extinct in Burma (Blower, 1982). In the south, the lowland rain forests of Tenasserim support a quite distinct fauna with a Malesian character. Two species of mouse deer and the endangered tapir, which reaches its northerly limits in Tenasserim, add yet another element of diversity to Burma's forests.

About 1000 bird species have been recorded (Smythies, 1953). This enormously high diversity is due to the country straddling two zoogeographic regions, each with a different avifauna. The forests of Tenasserim in the south contain many Malesian species, whereas in the central and northern part of the country the birds have Indian and Chinese affinities. A large number of Himalayan species also occur in the montane forests of north and west Burma. Some 40 species throughout Burma are under world-wide threat (Collar and Andrew, 1988).

In general, Burma's wildlife is very diverse, but has few species which are native to the country. For example, 68 swallowtail butterflies are present, a total exceeded only by Indonesia, China, Brazil and India. This represents 12 per cent of all known swallowtail butterfly species in the world, but no endemic species have been found (Collins and Morris, 1985). Similarly, the avifauna includes about 12 per cent of all the birds in the world, but with unusually low endemism (Smythies, 1953). The forests of Burma can therefore be thought of as important reservoirs of biodiversity, supporting Indian and Chinese species in the north and Malesian types in the south.

Conservation Areas

The legal protection of natural resources in Burma rests on two laws, both dating from the colonial period. The 1902 Burma Forest Act (as amended) enables the Ministry of Agriculture and Forests to establish, manage and protect game sanctuaries and reserved forests on any government land. Reserved forests are production forests subject to exploitation for timber and other forest produce, but they are maintained under natural forest cover, and so have a valuable role to play in ecological conservation. A large number of reserved forests were established in the late nineteenth and early twentieth century, covering approximately 100,000 sq. km, or 15 per cent of land area. The distribution of these reserved forests, which almost exclusively fall between the 1000 mm and 2000 mm rainfall bands, indicates that the British colonial administration established them to provide a sustained output of hardwood timber, especially teak.

Wildlife in reserved forests in theory may not be hunted without a permit, but the conservation of biological resources *per se* was only addressed through the creation of game sanctuaries. These were primarily intended to protect hunting stock and the first was established in 1918. Local authorities were enabled to administer hunting in their areas but comprehensive game rules were not formulated until 1927 (Weatherbe, 1940).

The 1902 Forest Act was enhanced by the 1936 Burma Wildlife Protection Act (amended in 1954), which provides for the establishment of game sanctuaries on any government land or on private land where the owner's consent has been obtained. The Act prohibits hunting and fishing in game sanctuaries and requires a licence for these activities in reserved forests. One shortcoming, however, is that although the 1902 Forest Act and the 1936 Wildlife Protection Act theoretically provide protection for wildlife in both reserved forests and in game sanctuaries, neither act includes measures which specifically protect habitat.

Responsibility for managing forest resources, protecting wildlife and managing the 15 existing game sanctuaries rests with the Forest Department, which is one of the oldest in Asia. Its power is limited, however, because the State Timber Corporation, responsible for timber extraction, processing and sale (but which is not involved in forest management) is politically more influential (Blower, 1985). Due to the fact that the State Timber Corporation is a more powerful body, its interests have tended to predominate in decisions on the use of forest resources.

Between 1981 and 1984 UNDP and FAO carried out a Nature Conservation and National Parks Project to identify areas suitable for national parks and nature reserves. Surveys and feasibility studies were conducted over 24 areas, and several critical sites were identified in the rain forests, namely Nam Lang Valley, Packchan, Alaungdaw Kathapa, Lampi, Kyaukpandaung and the Moscos Islands. A proposal to follow up the work has not been pursued, at least partly because of political uncertainties.

The current, fully gazetted protected areas network comprises 15 game sanctuaries, two parks with primarily recreational functions, and a single national park. The legislative basis for the latter is not clearly defined. The 15 game sanctuaries have been badly neglected over the past 30 years and many of them have been encroached and have lost most of their conservation value. (See Table 15.2.)

The protected areas system covers 7080 sq. km, or one per cent of the national land area, an inadequate sample of the nation's natural resources (FAO, 1985a). If all proposed sites were to be gazetted, approximately 4 per cent of land would be protected, but even these areas do not provide adequate coverage of all major ecosystems, nor ensure the survival of even such significant species as elephant. In 1985 it was proposed that new legislation be passed which would not only strengthen conservation efforts but also make provision for the establishment of national parks and nature reserves (FAO, 1985b). However, these proposals have yet to be implemented.

Table 15.2 Conservation areas of Burma

Existing and proposed areas, 50 sq. km and over, are listed below. The remaining areas are combined in a total under Other Areas. Forest reserves are not included.

	Existing area (sq. km)	Proposed area (sq. km)
National Parks		
Alaungdaw Kathapa★	1,606	
Kyaukpandaung★		1,300
Lampi★		3,885
Natma Taung★		364
Pegu Yomas★		1,462
Game Sanctuaries		
Inle Lake	643	
Kahilu★	161	
Kyatthin	268	
Maymyo	103	
Minwun Taung	201	
Mulayit★	139	
Pidaung★	705	
Shwe u Daung★	327	
Shwesettaw★	552	
Tamanthi★	2,151	
Wildlife Sanctuaries		
Meinmahla Kyun★		129
Mohingyi		90
Nature Reserves		
Pakchan★		259
Sub total	6,856	7,489
Other Areas	224	12,201
Totals	7,080	19,690

(*Sources*: IUCN, 1990; WCMC data *in litt.*)
★ Area with moist forest within its boundary.

PROPOSED PAKCHAN NATURE RESERVE

The proposed Pakchan Nature Reserve (259 sq. km) lies between the Andaman Sea and the Thailand border in the far south of Burma. The reserve would be established in the Pakchan Reserved Forest (1453 sq. km), which was established in 1931. The land rises steeply from sea level to a north-south oriented watershed up to 900 m high. This constitutes part of the Isthmus of Kra, separating the Gulf of Thailand from the Andaman Sea. The climate is monsoonal, with a mean annual rainfall of about 4000 mm, and it is at a transition point between the distinct wet and dry seasons of most of Burma and the more even rainfall patterns of Peninsular Malaysia. The surrounding areas are sparsely populated, and there is thought to be no resident population in the reserved forest with the possible exception of a few resin tappers.

● Some of the little remaining mature rain forest in Burma is found here, although it is under threat by legally sanctioned timber extraction in the low-lying western areas and, more seriously, by extensive illegal logging in the east, allegedly by loggers from Thailand.

● The reserve is highly valued for its extensive and largely untouched evergreen dipterocarp rain forest.

● The forests support a diverse fauna and protect the watershed between the coast and the Pakchan Valley.

● The forest is characterised by a number of species restricted within the country to Tenasserim. Dipterocarpaceae are the dominant trees and the Burmese endemic palm *Calamus helferianus* is present.

● The coastal strip supports mangrove forests in excellent condition and these merge into small freshwater swamp forests. The latter, with an abundance of orchids and ferns, are now rare in Burma.

● Both typical Burmese species, such as elephant, tiger and leopard, and Malaysian species, such as clouded leopard, Malayan sun-bear and tapir, are found in the forest.

● Red jungle fowl (*Gallus gallus*), the rare great argus pheasant, Malay peacock-pheasant (*Polyplectron malacense*), crested fireback pheasant (*Lophura ignita rufa*), kalij pheasant (*L. leucomelana crawfurdii*), wreathed hornbill (*Rhyticeros undulatus*), and and possibly the endangered Gurney's pitta, are just a few of the birds to be found here.

The deficiencies of the protected areas system include the following:

• No significant rain forests are included in the present protected area system, although the proposed Pakchan Nature Reserve would to some extent rectify this.

• There are also no protected areas in the entire upper catchment of the Irrawaddy to the north of Myitkyina, where maintenance of forest cover is critical for watershed protection and where many rare and unusual plants and animals occur.

• No protected areas have been gazetted in North Kachin, the Chin Hills or the Arakan or Pegu Yomas (Blower, 1982; 1985).

• Monsoon forests are not widely represented but do occur in the proposed national park at Alaungdaw Kathapa and in the deciduous dipterocarp (indaing) woodlands of the game sanctuary at Kyatthin.

Initiatives for Conservation

Cooperative projects between the Government and international bodies are relatively rare, as the Burmese Government has for many years pursued an isolationist foreign policy. Individual researchers and international non-government organisations have had difficulty gaining access to the country. Consequently, efforts to mitigate or reduce deforestation through development assistance programmes have been quite limited. In addition to the UNDP/FAO activities described above, US-based organisations such as US–AID, US National Parks Service, and WWF–US, have made a limited contribution to the training of protected areas management staff in the Forest Department. Burma has not yet made any request for assistance under the Tropical Forestry Action Plan (see chapter 10).

An FAO/UNEP project provided technical advice and material support to nature conservation from 1981 to 1984. The project was then temporarily suspended. Negotiations for a resumption of activity were almost complete when the civil disturbance of 1988 intervened to cause further delays. In the meantime nature conservation activities are continuing at a modest level under a small division within the Forest Department. The Alaungdaw Kathapa National Park in the monsoon forests of the lower Chindwin and the Hlawga zoo and educational facility just outside Rangoon are the main focus of attention. No conservation programmes as such are being undertaken in rain forest areas and even the forest management work in these areas is suffering from neglect.

References

Allen, P. E. T. (1984) A quick new appraisal of the forest cover of Burma, using Landsat satellite imagery at 1:1,000,000 scale. *Technical Note* 11, FAO/UNEP National Forest Survey and Inventory. BUR/79/011. 6 pp.

Bixler, N. (1971) *Burma: a profile*. Preager Publishers, New York, USA. 244 pp.

Blower, J. (1982) Species conservation priorities in Burma. In: Species conservation priorities in the tropical forests of south-east Asia. *IUCN SSC Occasional Paper* No. 1. Mittermeier, R. A. and Konstant, W. R. (eds), pp. 53–8. IUCN, Gland, Switzerland.

Blower, J. (1985) Conservation priorities in Burma. *Oryx* 19: 79–85.

Britto, N. B. (1987) National forest management and inventory of Burma. Report on cartographic consultancy. Forest Department of Burma/FAO, Rangoon. 21 pp. and 3 appendices.

Champion, H. G. (1936) A preliminary survey of the forest types of India and Burma. *Indian Forest Record (n.s.) Silva* 1(1).

Chatterjee, D. (1939) Studies on the endemic flora of India and Burma. *Journal of the Royal Asiatic Society of Bengal Science* 5: 19–67.

Collar, N. J. and Andrew, P. (1988) Birds to watch. The ICBP World checklist of threatened birds. *Technical Publication* No. 8. International Council for Bird Preservation, Cambridge, UK.

Collins, N. M. and Morris, M. G. (1985) *Threatened Swallowtail Butterflies of the World. The IUCN Red Data Book*. IUCN, Gland, Switzerland, and Cambridge, UK. 401 pp.

FAO (1985a) *Burma: survey data and conservation priorities*. Nature conservation and national parks project FO:BUR/80/006. Technical Report No. 1. FAO, Rome, Italy. 102 pp.

FAO (1985b) *Burma: project findings and recommendations*. Nature conservation and national parks project FO:DP/BUR/80/006. Terminal Report. FAO, Rome, Italy. 69 pp.

FAO (1990) *FAO Yearbook of Forest Products, 1977–78*. FAO Forestry Series No. 23, FAO Statistics Series 1990. FAO, Rome.

FAO/UNEP (1981) *Tropical Forest Resources Assessment Project. Forest Resources of Tropical Asia*. Vol 3 of 3 vols. FAO, Rome. 475 pp.

Golay, F. H., Anspach, R., Pfanner, M. R. and Ayal, E. B. (1969) Burma. In: *Underdevelopment and Economic Nationalism in Southeast Asia*. Golay, F. H. (ed.), pp. 203–65. Cornell University Press.

Hundley, H. G. and Chit Ko Ko, U. (1961) *List of trees, shrubs, herbs and principal climbers etc. recorded from Burma with vernacular names*. Third edition. Government Printing Press, Rangoon. 532 pp.

IUCN (1990) *1989 United Nations List of National Parks and Protected Areas*. IUCN, Gland, Switzerland, and Cambridge, UK.

Legris, P. (1974) Vegetation and floristic composition of humid tropical continental Asia. In: *Natural Resources Research* 12: 217–38. Unesco, Paris, France.

Saenger, P., Hegerl, E. J. and Davie, J. D. S. (1983) Global status of mangrove systems. *Commission on Ecology Papers* No. 3. IUCN, Gland, Switzerland. 88 pp.

Salter, R. E. (1983) Summary of currently available information on international threatened species in Burma. FAO Nature Conservation and National Parks Project. Field Document 7/83. FAO, Rangoon, Burma. 76 pp.

Scott, D. A. (ed.) (1989) *A Directory of Asian Wetlands*. IUCN, Gland, Switzerland, and Cambridge, UK. 1,181 pp.

Smythies, B. E. (1953) *The Birds of Burma*. Oliver and Boyd, London, UK.

U Shwe Kyaw (1988) In: *National report: Burma. Ad Hoc FAO/ECE/FINNIDA Meeting of Experts on Forest Resource Assessment*. Bulletins of the Finnish Forest Research Institute 284, pp. 147–52. FINNIDA, Helsinki, Finland.

Weatherbe, D. A. (1940) Burma's decreasing wild life. *Journal of the Bombay Natural History Society* 42: 150–60.

Authorship

John Blower in Guernsey and James Paine at WCMC, Cambridge, with contributions from U Saw Hahn and U Ohn in Rangoon and Harold Sutter in FAO, Rome.

Map 15.1 Forest cover in Burma

Forest cover is taken from Britto (1987) Appendix III, an A4 sized coloured map, based on 1:1 million Landsat MSS and RBV imagery of 1979–81 carried out for the FAO/UNDP Tropical Forest Resources Assessment Project and updated using aerial photography. This map, essentially unpublished, is a product of the FAO Burma National Forest Management and Inventory Project, which included a report on cartography. 'Actual forest' category has been selected and 'Forest fallow' omitted on the grounds of low value for biological diversity and poor prognosis for the future. As in Britto's (1987) original map, forest cover is divided between intact and degraded forests. Forest types have been extrapolated from Champion (1936). Protected areas and proposed protected areas are taken from Salter (1983), an unpublished report of the FAO Nature Conservation and National Parks Project.

16 Cambodia

Land area	176,520 sq. km	
Population (1989)	6.8 million	
Expected maximum population (2150)	20 million	
Rain forest (see map)	65,500 sq. km	
Monsoon forest (see map)	47,750 sq. km	
Closed broadleaved/coniferous forest 1980†	71,680 sq. km	
Annual deforestation rate (1981–5)†	250 sq. km	
Roundwood production*	5,677,000 cu. m	
Roundwood exports*	No data	
Fuelwood and charcoal production*	5,110,000 cu. m	
Sawlog and veneer log production*	105,000 cu. m	
Sawlog and veneer log exports*	No data	

* 1988 data from FAO (1990)
† FAO/UNEP (1981)

Until the 1970s, Cambodia was a tranquil backwater in the heart of Indo-China. It had extensive forests whose valuable timber was largely unexploited, some of Southeast Asia's most important wetlands and the Khmer Ruins, a spectacular reminder of the turbulent history of the region. Then the Vietnam War spilled over into the country, and for 20 years every aspect of Cambodian life was totally disrupted. Data on the remaining extent and condition of Cambodia's forests are extremely poor. The only mapped information dates back to 1970 and statistical data to 1980.

INTRODUCTION

Cambodia is situated in tropical Indo-China, straddling the great Mekong River between Thailand and Vietnam, with Laos to the north-east. The greater part of Cambodia comprises the plain of the lower Mekong valley, with the western slopes of the Annamite chain in the east lying along the Vietnam frontier, and the isolated highlands of the Elephant and Cardamom mountains in the west, adjacent to south-east Thailand and the Gulf of Thailand. The country has a short coastline of only 435 km. The climate is dominated by the south-west and north-east monsoons; the south-west monsoon lasting from May to October and the north-east from November to March. The average annual rainfall is between 1200 mm and 1875 mm, with a pronounced dry season between November and March, but rainfall up to 3000–4000 mm may be experienced in the south-west (Legris and Blasco, 1972).

The Mekong river runs southward across the plains, its delta lying in Vietnam. Part of the western plains are occupied by the huge, shallow Tonlé Sap or Great Lake, which flows into the Mekong throughout most of the year, but which usually floods back from the main river during the rainy season, becoming a vast storage reservoir. During the dry season, the vast floodplains of the Mekong River and Tonlé Sap are extensively cultivated. The Cardamom mountain range dominates the south-west of the country, rising to an elevation of 1563 m. In the south and south-east are low plains bordering the Mekong River, extensive areas of which are seasonally flooded. North of Tonlé Sap, the area leading to the borders with Laos and Thailand consists of rolling savanna country with some open grassland and areas of deciduous forest.

The 1989 population was estimated at 6.8 million, more than 90 per cent of whom were Khmer, with small minorities of Vietnamese and Chinese. The southern part of the country is densely settled and largely given over to rice growing; indeed agriculture and fisheries are by far the most important sources of livelihood. Some 93 per cent of the cultivated land is dedicated to rice production, which accounts for 40 per cent of the gross domestic agricultural product. To the north the human population is generally low; for example, there are as few as four persons per sq. km in the Stung Treng and Mondulkiri Provinces.

The Forests

The Elephant and Cardamom mountains in the west, and the western slopes of the eastern Annamite chain, are open to the full force of the south-west monsoon. The tropical moist forests of these ranges and adjoining lowlands covered over half of Cambodia as recently as the 1960s. Evergreen rain forests were confined to the western slopes of the Elephant and Cardamom ranges, while semi-evergreen rain forests were extensive in the lowlands to the east of the Tonlé Sap and on the western slopes of the Annamite chain. The forests on the Annamite mountains have largely been cleared or severely damaged by shifting cultivation. They also suffered from defoliation and bombing during the Vietnam war.

By contrast, the forests of the Elephant and Cardamom mountains, particularly the rain forests on the western slopes, are said to be little disturbed, due to the very low human population of this region. Rollet (1972), and Legris and Blasco (1972) have described these rain forests. At lower elevations, *Palaquium obovatum* is common. Five species of Dipterocarpaceae – *Anisoptera costata*, *A. glabra*, *Dipterocarpus costatus*, *Hopea odorata* and *Shorea hypochra* – are widespread. Palms, particularly rattans, are especially abundant. Fagaceae are also present, notably *Castanopsis* and *Lithocarpus*. Curious patches of dwarf forest occur in poorly drained depressions. These are rich in palms, and also include the conifers *Dacrydium pierrei* and *Podocarpus neriifolius*. At elevations above 700 m, the forests are subject to frequent fog, high winds and low winter temperatures. Species of Fagaceae are more frequent and include an endemic oak, *Quercus cambodiensis*.

Freshwater permanent and seasonal swamp forest once occurred in the area surrounding the Tonlé Sap. The same formation, dominated by *Melaleuca*, also occurred in the Mekong delta on the south-east frontier adjacent to Vietnam. Mangroves were once extensive around Veal Renh and Kompong Som bays, and north of Kas Kong, up to the border with Thailand. Only discontinuous bands of mangrove now remain and production of firewood and charcoal has declined.

The rest of Cambodia has a drier, more seasonal climate and the climax vegetation normally consists of a variety of dense deciduous and semi-deciduous monsoon forest formations. Vast areas,

111

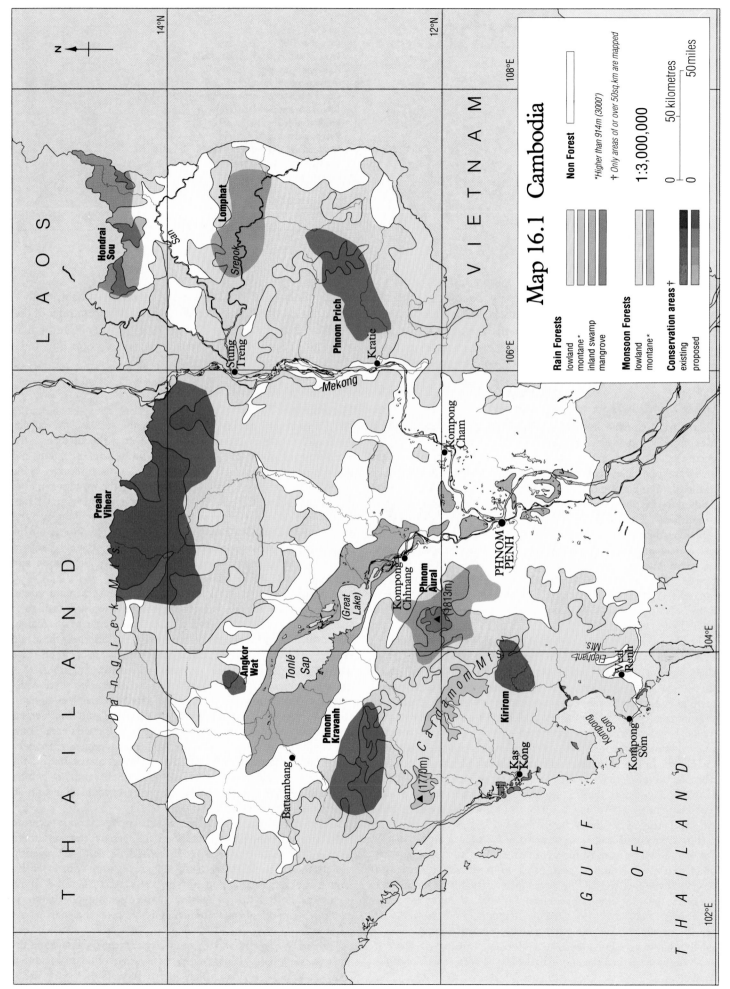

Map 16.1 Cambodia

Rain Forests

lowland
montane *
inland swamp
mangrove

Monsoon Forests

lowland
montane *

Conservation areas †

existing
proposed

Non Forest

Higher than 914m (3000')

† *Only areas of or over 50sq.km are mapped*

1:3,000,000

0   50 kilometres
0   50 miles

however, have been degraded by shifting agriculture and fire, and these areas are now covered with open savanna woodlands. It is this which is the predominant vegetation east of the Mekong River and in the area north of Tonlé Sap up to the borders with Thailand and Laos.

Forest Resources and Management

The most recent information on the forest resources of Cambodia derives from FAO/UNEP (1981), which was republished in FAO (1988). Closed broadleaved forests were estimated to cover an area of 71,500 sq. km in 1980, with open forest (woodlands) to cover a further 51,000 sq. km. The only available forest map of Cambodia, however, was published in 1971, based on late 1970 data (Legris and Blasco, 1971), and in the absence of anything more recent this forms the basis of Map 16.1. With 20 years intervening, it will come as no surprise that the forest areas indicated by this map are seriously at variance with current estimates. Table 16.1, derived from Map 16.1, for example, indicates closed forest cover of 113,250 sq. km up to 1970, over 50 per cent greater than the FAO/UNEP 1980 estimate of 71,500 sq. km and 70 per cent greater than a reasonable 1990 estimate of 66,500 sq. km. Estimates of closed forest cover of 131,735 sq. km in 1960–62 indicate a reduction of Cambodia's forests by half during the last 30 years (US Department of Energy, 1986). (See map legend on page 115 for further discussion.)

In 1970, 39,000 sq. km, 30 per cent of the national forest area, was given reserve status. Of this, 24,000 sq. km, or 62 per cent, was described as dense forest. The forest reserves were open to exploitation for timber and other products under Forest Department control. They were to be managed as permanent forest estate, but there were no plans to help forest regeneration (FAO/UNEP, 1981). Disruption caused by the war, however, has meant that the Forest Department has ceased virtually all activity in the past two decades. In recent years, some limited support has been obtained from Vietnam and FAO to rebuild an effective forest service, and FAO has begun work on an assessment of forest resources.

The forest reserves have an important part to play in the economy of Cambodia. The country produced 600,000 cu. m of sawlogs and peeler logs in 1969, which were mostly for domestic consumption. Nearly all forest exploitation was carried out by small-scale local enterprises. It has been tentatively estimated that production declined to about 100,000 cu. m per annum during the 1970s (FAO/ UNEP, 1981). Although 105,000 cu. m is quoted at the top of this chapter, in reality there is little information available on present production levels.

FAO/UNEP (1981) estimated the standing crop of timber in closed broadleaved forests in Cambodia in 1980 to be 1061 million cu. m. This is three times the volume (325 million cu. m) estimated for Thailand and double the volume estimated for Laos (644 million cu. m). This suggests that forestry could become a major contributor to the Cambodian economy. But it also points to the possibility that heavy commercial pressure from timber-starved Thailand, which banned logging in 1989, and from Vietnam, will force an acceleration of the logging of Cambodian forests. During 1989, reports appeared in the Thai press of Thai entrepreneurs negotiating contracts for large consignments of timber and rattan from Cambodia. Significant amounts of timber from northern Cambodia are already imported into Thailand through the Lao frontier post of Pakse.

Important yields of several non-timber products also have been obtained from Cambodia's forests in the past. These products were subject to government controls until 1970 and included honey, wood oil, resins from Dipterocarpaceae and *Pinus merkusii*, rattans, cardamom, bamboos and a variety of barks and tannins. Local exploitation of these products presumably continues, but no data are available and government control is presumably minimal.

Table 16.1 Estimates of forest extent in Cambodia

	Area remaining (sq. km)
Rain forests	
Lowland	55,500
Montane	2,250
Inland swamp	7,500
Mangrove	250
Sub total	65,500
Monsoon forests	
Lowland	47,750
Sub total	47,750
Total	113,250

Based on analysis of Map 16.1, which is derived from data published in 1971. (See Map Legend for details.)

Deforestation

Cambodia's great fertile plains, productive fisheries and valuable forests have been the home of several great kingdoms. The most powerful and influential of these was the Khmer empire of the 12th and 13th centuries. During this period most of the central forest lands of the country were cleared and farmed, and a formidable system of irrigation canals and reservoirs established. Tropical monsoon forests that now grow on these lands are sufficiently old to be indistinguishable from primary forest.

Ever since the collapse of the Khmer empire in the 15th century, Cambodia has suffered successive invasions by the Thais in the north of the country, and has also lost most of the Mekong delta regions to Vietnamese colonists in the south. Its population was small and the country itself remained a quiet backwater until colonisation by the French in the 19th century. At this time most of the moist forest types remained undisturbed. Some forest was cleared at this time for timber and more for industrial plantations, notably of rubber, but the pace of development did not noticeably quicken. The deciduous savanna forests were thinned by man-made fire, but this was used more as a hunting technique than an agricultural aid (Wharton, 1957). Semi-evergreen rain forests on the southern face of the Dangrek mountains were, however, destroyed by repeated burning.

The biggest incursions into the remaining forests were made during the Indochinese wars (starting in the 1960s) and during the brief regime of the Khmer Rouge in the 1970s under Pol Pot. Although officially outside the declared war zone, the eastern border of Cambodia was the scene of intense fighting. The various paths of the famous Ho Chi Minh trail, which provided a means of supplying the Vietcong forces fighting in South Vietnam, wound through the forests. The American airforce attempted to disrupt this supply line by repeated bombing, herbicide spraying, laying of mines and other military operations, and these forests are still littered with bomb craters and unexploded mines.

The Vietnam war was followed by civil war in Cambodia. The Khmer Rouge used the forest as a refuge and recruiting area until they were able to launch their successful attack on Phnom Penh in 1974. Immediately upon assuming power, the Khmer Rouge leaders ordered a redistribution of the population. Rural people were moved from one side of the country to the other and the entire population of Phnom Penh and of other towns was forced into the country to clear new lands for agriculture.

Apart from causing indescribable human misery and the deaths of perhaps as many as three million people, this policy had disastrous environmental consequences. Extensive areas of forest were cleared and the huge quantities of rat poison used in agriculture poisoned waterways, which in turn damaged the country's formerly prolific fisheries. Many of the originally well-organised irrigation and agricultural systems collapsed. Those who could escape the reign of terror fled the country or took refuge in the deep forests.

In 1978, Vietnam invaded Cambodia, ousted Pol Pot, and set up an alternative government under Hun Sen, restoring some sense of normality. But Vietnamese occupation resulted in condemnation world-wide, continuation of the civil war in several areas and an international embargo on aid and bank loans. In 1990 the situation remains uncertain. However, many of the northern forests are still littered with mines and these will remain a hazard to wildlife, forestry, and conservation efforts for many years to come.

FAO (1988) estimated that of the 71,500 sq. km of closed forests and 51,000 sq. km of open forests (woodlands) existing in 1980, 250 sq. km of closed forest and 50 sq. km of logged broadleaved forest were cleared for agriculture each year during 1981 to 1985.

Most forest loss was thought to be caused by shifting cultivation, known, in Cambodia, as *chancar leu*. In 1960, a study by the Mekong Committee estimated that 2.5 per cent of all Cambodia's forests were subject to clearance for swidden agriculture in any one year (cited in FAO/UNEP, 1981). A large proportion of the forest cleared for shifting cultivation will regenerate as secondary forest, but no figures are available.

The disruption caused by the events of the past 20 years will have had profound effects on the pattern of deforestation. In some depopulated areas, forest will have advanced into agricultural lands. In others, the arrival of displaced people will have intensified the pressures of shifting cultivation on the forest. The most recent attempt at assessing forest cover estimated that only about a quarter of the original forest cover remained, and that only a tenth was truly primary forest (IUCN, 1986).

Much lowland forest has been converted to agriculture and much has also been degraded to scrubland and *Imperata* grassland. The Tonlé Sap swamp forests have been greatly altered by the fishing communities living nearby. Misguided attempts to drain the swamps and cultivate the soil mean that the *Melaleuca* swamp forests have now been replaced by highly acidic treeless plains, covered extensively with reeds – useless for agriculture but a haven for waterfowl.

Opinions differ on the status of mangroves. FAO/UNEP (1981) states that they have been reduced to remnants, but IUCN (1986) indicate that they are still in a relatively good condition.

The authorities in Vietnam and Cambodia agree about one consequence of deforestation – that it has affected water-flow in the Mekong River system. The river now floods more frequently and violently in the wet seasons, and is very low during the dry seasons as a result of the loss of forest in its water catchments. The problem is compounded by similar deforestation in Laos, Thailand and southern China. To the many people living along the river this means fluctuating agricultural yields, and reduced fisheries. It also leads to premature siltation of reservoirs and hydropower projects. The most severe impact is felt outside Cambodia, in neighbouring Vietnam. Here the Mekong delta constitutes 50 per cent of the country's agricultural land and the erratic flow is causing increasing problems for local agriculture.

Biodiversity and Conservation Areas

Some nature reserves were proposed during the French period of rule, but were never adequately mapped or demarcated. Angkor Wat was declared a National Park in 1925 and was greatly extended in the 1960s. Reserves have been gazetted to protect the highly endangered kouprey, proclaimed the national animal by Prince Sihanouk. Three large reserves which fall within the habitat range of the kouprey are Phnom Prich, Prear Vihear (Koulen) and Lomphat. A number of faunal reserves were established in 1960 although there is no available information on them. Besides Angkor Wat National Park, in 1985 there were 172 production forest reserves covering 38,750 sq. km and six forest reserves for wildlife protection. In addition, a few new reserves have been proposed (Chan Suran, 1985), although most of these have never been subject to any conservation management. Some lie in military security zones, others in areas still controlled by the Khmer Rouge.

In total, 11.5 per cent of the country is legally protected, with new proposals adding a further 2.6 per cent. Table 16.2 gives a list of protected areas. This list may not be comprehensive as information is scanty.

There are no proposals to protect mangrove forest. This gap in the planned reserve system should be filled as soon as possible. The freshwater swamp forests around Tonlé Sap are amongst the most extensive in Southeast Asia, serving as a haven for wildlife and protecting the hydrological regime. The forests act as a huge sponge, absorbing the backflow of the Mekong River when it is in flood and releasing it slowly at drier times of the year. The forests thus perform an enormously important water regulatory function. In addition, the forests are also the breeding area for many of the fish in the Tonlé Sap, which is potentially one of the most productive freshwater fisheries in Southeast Asia. Protection of part of these forests has been proposed but, ideally, forest cover should be maintained over as much of the area as possible.

Although largely deforested, the *Melaleuca* swamp areas are critical sites for wetland bird conservation, being important feeding grounds for the eastern sarus crane *Grus antigone* and possibly the giant ibis *Pseudibis gigantea* and white-shouldered ibis *P. davisoni*.

Other important conservation sites in the country include the tropical forests of the north and east, which constitute important refuge and migration areas for large wildlife such as elephant, gaur and banteng. They are also still believed to shelter small populations of kouprey and Javan rhinoceros. Parts of this habitat may be gazetted as reserves for kouprey, but protection of the interconnecting forest is also important.

Initiatives for Conservation

Projects to conserve wildlife include:
- An international kouprey project co-ordinated by IUCN and WWF. Under this project, Cambodian personnel are being trained in reserve management and planning. Minor items of field equipment are being supplied, together with conservation awareness leaflets for local distribution.
- A joint project is underway with Vietnam to protect wetland birds in the Plain of Reeds area and Tonlé Sap forests.
- The Department of Forestry has plans for rational exploitation of its forest resources. In addition to the proposed and existing protected areas, sustainable logging of the 172 production forest reserves is planned. At present, some timber is harvested for domestic use and for export to Vietnam. Thailand has recently become an important market. However, until the threat of civil war is removed, and international relations become stable, little can be done in the way of scientific management. Indeed, most of the maps and documentation of forest blocks from the Lon Nol regime were destroyed during Pol Pot's regime, and many trained foresters were killed or fled the country.

Table 16.2 Conservation areas of Cambodia

Existing and proposed areas, 50 sq. km and over, are listed below. Forest reserves are not included. All areas include moist forest within their boundaries.

	Existing area (sq. km)	Proposed area (sq. km)
National Parks		
Angkor Wat	107	
Reserves		
Kirirom	817	
Lomphat		1,975
Phnom Aural		2,500
Phnom Prich	1,951	
Unclassified		
Phnom Kravanh	2,806	
Preah Vihear	14,670	
Hondrai Sou		200
Totals	20,351	4,675

(*Sources*: IUCN, 1990; WCMC *in litt.*)

Map 16.1 Forest cover in Cambodia

Forest distribution and formations are extracted from the 1:1 million full colour *Carte Internationale du Tapis Végétal et des Conditions Ecologiques, Cambodge* prepared by P. Legris and F. Blasco (1971). This is the most recent forest cover map for Cambodia.

Lowland rain forests were equated to Legris and Blasco's evergreen and semi-evergreen formations, monsoon forests to their deciduous dense forest, fresh-water swamp forest to their inundated forest, and mangrove swamps to their direct equivalent. Montane forests were delimited by a 3000 feet (*c.* 914 m) contour taken from the Jet Navigation Chart (JNC) 53, 1:2 million scale.

Because the basis of this map is 20 years old, some interpretation of the likely present scenario may be helpful. In their original form, the forests of Cambodia would probably have been evergreen over almost the entire area except in a south-east/north-west swathe from the delta along the line of the Tonlé Sap (Legris and Blasco, 1972). In Indochina, evergreen forests degrade first to semi-evergreen. As fire begins to play a dominant role, the forests become deciduous, and finally degrade to open woodland formations, bamboo and grasslands. The monsoon forests shown in the east of the country would not have been a climax vegetation even in the late 1960s, when the data were gathered, and now they are further degraded over large areas to open savanna woodlands. Similarly, many of the rain forests shown in the east will now certainly be more deciduous in character. In short, if it was possible to reassess the vegetation cover of Cambodia, we might find that much of the monsoon forest shown on the map has now been degraded to open woodland or grassland, and that the rain forest areas east of Tonlé Sap have been degraded to monsoon forest. It is probably no coincidence that the area of rain forest shown is 65,500 sq. km (Table 16.1), an area very close to current expectations of Cambodia's total forest cover area of all forest types.

Protected area data are taken from IUCN (1986).

References

Chan Suran (1985) Intervention de la delegation du Kampuchea. In: *Conserving Asia's Natural Heritage*, Thorsell, J. W. (ed.) pp. 23–5. IUCN, Gland, Switzerland and Cambridge, UK.

FAO (1988) *An Interim Report on the State of Forest Resources in the Developing Countries.* FAO, Rome. 18 pp. + 5 tables.

FAO (1990) *FAO Yearbook of Forest Products 1977–88.* FAO Forestry Series No. 23, FAO Statistics Series No. 90. FAO, Rome.

FAO/UNEP (1981) *Tropical Forest Resources Assessment Project. Forest Resources of Tropical Asia.* Vol. 3 of 3 volumes, FAO, Rome, Italy. 475 pp.

IUCN (1986) *Review of the Protected Area System in the Indomalayan Realm.* Consultants MacKinnon, J. and MacKinnon, K. IUCN, Gland, Switzerland, and Cambridge, UK.

IUCN (1990) *1989 United Nations List of National Parks and Protected Areas.* IUCN, Gland, Switzerland, and Cambridge, UK.

Legris, P. and Blasco, F. (1971) *Carte Internationale du Tapis Végétal et des Conditions Ecologiques, Cambodge.* Institut Français, Pondicherry. One sheet.

Legris, P. and Blasco, F. (1972) *Notice de la carte: Cambodge*, Carte International du Tapis Végétal. Extraits des travaux de la Section Scientifique et Technique de l'Institut Français de Pondichéry: hors série no 1, Toulouse, France.

Rollet, B. (1972) *La Végétation du Cambodge.* Bois et Forêts des Tropiques, Nos. 144, 145 & 146, Nogent-sur-Marne, France.

US Department of Energy (1986) *A Comparison of Tropical Forest Surveys.* US Department of Energy, Washington DC, USA. 66 pp.

Wharton, C. H. (1957) An ecological study of the Kouprey *Novibos sauveli*. Monographs of the Institute of Science and Technology, Manila, Philippines. 111 pp.

Authorship

Based on materials provided by John MacKinnon, with added data from James Paine at WCMC.

17 China and Taiwan

People's Republic of China	
Land area	9,326,410 sq. km
Population (1989)	1,103.9 million
Population growth rate (1987–2000)	1.3 per cent
Expected maximum population (2100)	1695 million
Gross national product (1987)	US$290 per capita
Rain forest (see map)	7150 sq. km
Monsoon forest (see map)	17,050 sq. km
Roundwood production*	276,060,001 cu. m
Roundwood exports*	10,000 cu. m
Fuelwood and charcoal production*	177,610,000 cu. m
Sawlog and veneer log production*	53,770,000 cu. m
Sawlog and veneer log exports*	10,000 cu. m

Taiwan	
Land area	36,179 sq. km
Population (1987)	19.7 million
Gross national product (1987)	US$5,075 per capita
Rain forest (see map)	1660 sq. km
Monsoon forest (see map)	

1988 data from FAO (1990)

A nationwide conference on forestry in China in 1979 warned that by the end of the century there will be no trees to harvest. Deforestation is contributing to desertification, erosion and air pollution. It is thought to have caused marked increases also in the frequency and extent of droughts and flooding.

Deforestation continues despite the great importance placed on protection of tropical forests through the establishment of institutions and regulations. This is largely due to overcutting; land clearance for growth of cereals, tropical crops and rubber trees; collection of firewood; and forest fires. Lack of an effective scientific approach to afforestation, lack of skilled manpower and funds, the absence of personal responsibility in a system of collective leadership, repeated policy reversals, combined with unrealistic goals and desperation of poor peasants, are all contributing to the problem (AsDB, 1987).

The Chinese have for centuries shown a love and respect for natural beauty, but there is a clear desire to tame and even to improve on nature rather than appreciate it *in situ*. There remains a need for public education to generate awareness and appreciation of natural habitats. The country's leaders have, nevertheless, recognised the need for conservation areas and for a more rational exploitation of natural resources. Legislation for wildlife protection, passed in November 1988, included harsh penalties for the killing of protected species. But these new approaches are not fully understood by the majority of people and conflict with traditional views and immediate economic needs.

High demand for timber for furniture, construction, paper and fuel, places an impossible strain on the remaining natural forests. The rate of cutting far exceeds the rate of regrowth. Large areas have been replanted, but almost entirely in the temperate zone and with monocultures. A new reafforestation programme is planned and may be assisted by loans from the World Bank. Despite these efforts, there will inevitably be a period of timber shortage when the natural forests have all been exploited but the newly planted forests are not yet mature for harvesting. Indeed timber imports have been steadily growing since the 1950s.

China, now has, on paper at least, a good system of nature reserves, covering most natural habitats, as well as laws to protect these areas and flora and fauna outside the reserve system. However, China has not yet developed adequate reserve management capability, or shown the determination to enforce the new laws.

INTRODUCTION

For convenience, the People's Republic of China, Hong Kong, Macau and Taiwan are considered together in this chapter; but virtually all of the remaining rain forests occur in the People's Republic of China and Taiwan. Despite its enormous total area of 9.3 million sq. km, greater China has only five tiny regions with moist forest in the far south. These are in Assam, south-west Yunnan, coastal southern China, Hainan and Taiwan. All of the rain forest areas in Assam claimed by China are within the disputed border areas with India and are currently controlled by India as part of Arunachal Pradesh (see chapter 18). They will not be considered further in this chapter.

China's attitudes to forests are overshadowed by population growth and lack of finance. Realising that overpopulation is crippling the country's attempts to modernise, China's leaders have introduced some of the most stringent family planning regulations in the world with only one child per family allowed for Han Chinese and only two per family for ethnic minorities. Even so the population continues to grow. Secondly, money for conservation activities is always short. The importance given to environmental protection in government policy is not always matched by the operational budgets eventually released. Despite this, compared to many other Asian countries, China has already put up large budgets for priority projects.

The Forests

As Map 17.1 shows:

- Lowland rain forest occupies a very small area in southern Hainan (Guangdong Province), southern Taiwan, southern China (Guangxi Province on the border with Vietnam) and southern Yunnan.
- Montane rain forests occur in Yunnan.
- Monsoon forest occurs on limestone in southern Guangxi and more extensive monsoon forest occurs in western and southern Hainan.

Small areas of rather stunted northern mangrove forests exist in southern China, Hainan, Hong Kong and Taiwan (FAO, 1982), but could not be mapped at the scale used here.

The lowland rain forests include some dipterocarp genera, such as *Dipterocarpus*, *Hopea*, *Shorea*, *Parashorea* and *Vatica*, but other tree families are also important, including Annonaceae, Lauraceae, Meliaceae, Moraceae, Myrtaceae and Sapindaceae (FAO, 1982). These rain and monsoon forests lie at the absolute limits of the moist tropics; some of them are situated further away from the equator than tropical rain forests anywhere else in the world. The climate of the region is barely warm and moist enough for some of the types of forest that occur, and rain forest can only persist in pockets in this climate because it creates its own microclimate. Delicate seedlings are protected from desiccation, wind and cold and other elements, by the humid air trapped within the forest canopy. Thus, evergreen forest is able to reproduce itself in a climate that is not truly perhumid. High humidity is maintained during the dry season by morning fog that often forms in the lower valleys. It is possible that these rain forests originally came into existence during a period of warmer climate and have been able to persist after the climate changed. As a result, the Chinese rain forests are a very fragile ecosystem. This means that when the canopy is opened up by removal of large trees, the exposed seedlings of the climax trees are unable to survive, and the forest changes its composition. These forests may be sensitive to further climatic change and close monitoring would be of great importance to detect any kind of change.

In larger clearings, the change in microclimate is so great after clearance that rain forest is unable to regrow. Instead the forest may be recolonised by species of subtropical forest, but only if there are suitable parent trees nearby. Although subtropical forest is the natural vegetation surrounding the tropical forests, and particularly to the north of the rain and monsoon forest patches, it has been extensively cleared. As a result subtropical forest seeds are usually unavailable near rain forest clearings. This means the rain forest clearings therefore become over-run by grass and shrubs.

Forest Resources and Management

The forest lands of China, including rain forest lands, are under the management of a national forest system for production and regeneration (FAO, 1982). Natural forests and plantations are used in the following ways:

- Nearly 80 per cent are designated for timber production.
- Seven per cent are allocated for tree crops (rubber, fruit, tung oil, medicines).
- Six per cent are kept as shelter.
- Three per cent are maintained for bamboo production.
- Four per cent are held for other uses such as fuelwood.

Natural forest cover in China is very limited in area and unevenly distributed. Most is in remote frontier regions of the temperate north-east and south-west regions, and consists of conifer forest. FAO (1982) gives data on the percentage forest cover in the 22 provinces and five autonomous regions of China, and also shows the distribution of the major forest types in China. However, there are no data on the remaining extent of natural forest types in each province, or in China as a whole. Since the 1960s, three nationwide inventories

Table 17.1 Estimates of the extent of rain and monsoon forests in China and Taiwan

	Area (sq. km)	% of land area
China		
Rain forests		
Lowland	6,600	0.07
Montane	550	<0.01
Sub total	7,150	0.08
Monsoon forests		
Lowland	14,600	0.16
Montane	2,450	0.03
Sub total	17,050	0.18
Totals	24,200	0.26
Taiwan		
Rain forests		
Lowland	1,660	4.58
Totals	1,660	4.58

(See Map Legend for details of sources.)

of forest resources have been conducted, the last one from 1977 to 1983 (Liu Longhui, 1987; Li Jinchang et al., 1988). This showed forest cover over 12 per cent of the nation (excluding Taiwan), i.e. 1.15 million sq. km. Three-quarters of this was natural forest, but again no indication is given regarding the extent of rain forests (Liu Longhui, 1987).

Table 17.1, which is an analysis of the forest cover on Map 17.1, shows that rain forest covers only 7150 sq. km in mainland China, and 1660 sq. km in Taiwan, while monsoon forests cover a further 17,050 sq. km in China. The remaining moist forests therefore cover no more than 0.26 per cent of China's land area and 4.58 per cent of Taiwan. Even these statistics, taken from rather generalised maps published in 1979, are certain to be optimistic.

In 1979 China adopted a new Forestry Act, which strictly forbade illegal felling of trees in state forests. Those convicted of violations are subject to heavy fines and also have to replant three new trees for every one cut (FAO, 1982). The reality, however, looks quite different since the provisions of the Act are largely unenforceable (Smil, 1983). The Policy Research Office of the Ministry of Forestry asserts that since 1979 forest destruction has actually spread, with 'hordes of people' illegally cutting and buying timber (Policy Research Office, 1981).

Another response to the shortage of forest products has been an increase in imports from 14,000 cu. m in the early 1950s to over 9.7 million cu. m in 1985 (Li Jinchang et al., 1988). Were it not for constraints on foreign exchange, especially in 1986 when imports declined as part of a nationwide effort to balance foreign trade accounts, import volumes would certainly be substantially higher (Li Jinchang et al., 1988).

Finally, although it is difficult to be specific about forest management in the humid zones, one observer stated that 'forest management is chaotic with overlapping, competing uncoordinated bureaucracies trying blindly to fulfil asserted plans' (Smil, 1983). 'One hoe making forests but several axes cutting them down', goes a new Chinese saying. Some of the statistics in the following section appear to bear this out.

Rain forest at Mengla in Yunnan, China. Mengla is part of the Xishuangbanna Nature Reserve. WWF/J. MacKinnon

Deforestation

The main reasons for the loss of Chinese rain forests are shifting and settled agriculture. Following logging, people migrate into new areas to collect fuelwood and to acquire new land for agriculture. Shifting cultivation is widespread among the ethnic minorities that inhabit these forest areas and whose population densities have greatly increased in recent years. Forests have been cleared to make way for crops and plantations and some sites have degraded to *Imperata* grassland or *Melastoma* shrublands.

In her long period of closed-door policy, China wished to be self-sufficient in many tropical commodities for which there was very little suitable land. The expansion of rubber plantations in Hainan and south-west Yunnan was particularly destructive of habitat because, here, rubber can only be grown below 800 m so its planting has involved the clearing of the best lowland rain forests.

There has also been extensive forest clearance to meet the fuelwood requirements of the dense population. Although China has applied strict birth control policies to its Han Chinese population, the same strict regulations are not applied to the minority groups that inhabit most rain forest regions. Their numbers have increased dramatically over recent decades, and so therefore has the amount of forest they need to fell for fuelwood and for agriculture.

Two historical events greatly accelerated the loss of forests. Firstly, in the Second World War massive cutting occurred to provide fuelwood for factories. In the 1950s, during the *Great Leap Forward*, the Chinese government ordered the establishment of thousands of village iron-smelting works. The policy was an economic and ecological failure, producing only small amounts of poor-quality iron, but at the expense of the forests.

In recent times, illegal logging, forest fires and shifting cultivation have destroyed about 330 sq. km per year of forest in Yunnan's southernmost region, Xishuangbanna, on the Burma/Laos border, which was formerly China's richest tropical rain forest. Rubber plantations are now extensive, and although the remaining rain forest is a protected conservation area, more than 7000 people have settled there in recent decades. They have established 40 villages and felled trees for building and firewood (Yang Yuguang, 1980). It has been

estimated that each rural household burns 10 cu. m of wood per year, more than is utilised for all other purposes. Natural forests in Xishuangbanna covered about 60 per cent of the area in the early 1950s, but only 32 per cent in 1981, a decrease of 2 per cent per year (Jiang Youxu, 1986).

In Xishuangbanna even the climate appears to have changed in recent times. Local weather is marginally warmer than it was 20 years ago, the dry season is longer, rainfall has become more erratic and, perhaps most serious of all, there is less dry-season fog. This loss of fog may cause not only the loss of the remaining rain forests but even of tropical crops such as rubber that are cultivated here at the limit of their climatic tolerances. Research has shown that Xishuangbanna is now also being subjected to acid rain caused by air pollution from heavy industries in distant parts of China.

The loss of rain forest and the increasingly large areas given over to shifting agriculture, unterraced dryland farming and plantations, have led to very high levels of soil loss in Xishuangbanna and elsewhere. Many rivers are now permanently polluted with red topsoil. This constitutes a waste of a precious resource, and renders large areas of the region agriculturally useless. It also causes siltation downstream, kills fish and reduces the quality of water for drinking and bathing (Dowdle, 1987).

China's other large area of tropical moist forest, on Hainan Island in the South China Sea, has suffered even greater ravages. In 1949 8630 sq. km (25.7 per cent of the island's area) was covered by tropical forests. Despite similar high levels of forest cover indicated by Map 17.1, recent reports suggest that the figure has now dropped to about 2420 sq. km. Timber resources have been reduced from 64 million cu. m in 1949 to 29 million cu. m by 1980 (Zhang Tianxiong, 1980). The Policy Research Office of the Ministry of Forestry estimates that between 1978 and 1980 nearly 4700 sq. km of forest, containing more than 9 million cu. m of wood, were destroyed in the whole province (Policy Research Office, 1981). Much of this was the result of shifting cultivation (Lu Junpei and Zen Qingbo, 1986).

Like Hainan, Taiwan once had a small area of rain forest along the southern and eastern coastal areas (Map 17.1). The forests were exposed to typhoons and generally stunted in appearance. Data on the rate of deforestation on Taiwan are lacking, but it is believed that Map 17.1 is very optimistic and that only relict stands remain, in Kenting National Park and on Orchid Island.

Mangroves

Chinese mangroves are stunted northern examples, and limited in extent. They have been heavily degraded or changed and many have been completely destroyed (Lin Peng, 1984, 1987, 1988; Lu Chang and Lin Peng, 1987; Wang Bao-Can, 1984; Yang Hanxi, 1985). No remaining areas are large enough to be shown on Map 17.1. Isolated examples of mangroves are as follows:

1 In Hong Kong the Mai Po marshes constitute a small but very well-managed mangrove reserve which includes some managed fish-ponds.

2 Much of the coast of Hainan was originally fronted with mangrove, but most has been destroyed. However, fairly extensive and well-formed mangrove forests are still protected in the Xin Ying Gang, Hua Chang, Dong Zhai Gang and Qing Lan Gang reserves.

3 A number of small mangrove forests are protected on Taiwan, including the Chang-Yun-Chia reserve.

Biodiversity

China is biologically very rich, with approximately 30,000 species of higher plants, including about 7000 tree species (IUCN, 1986b). 15,000 species occur in tropical and subtropical regions, of which 7000 are in Yunnan (NCC, 1982). Of 2980 higher plant genera, 214 are endemic.

The rain forests contain many species which are not found anywhere else in the country. The Xishuangbanna area alone contains 4000–5000 species of higher plants and over 500 species of vertebrates (Zhao Songqiao, 1986). However, many formerly widespread birds and mammals are now restricted to Mengla in the extreme south-east of Xishuangbanna. Some have already become extinct in China and many others are seriously threatened, for example:

• The brow-antlered deer (*Cervus eldi*) was formerly found in the swampy land along the Lancang River, but no longer occurs in China.

• The green peacock (*Pavo muticus*), which is the symbol of Xishuangbanna, may still occur in Mengkao and Mengyang reserves but appears to be extinct elsewhere.

• The sarus crane used to breed in swampy riverine habitat; no breeding birds remain, though the occasional crane still flies over the area.

• Tigers may number no more than 20 animals.

• Black gibbons (*Hylobates concolor*) are almost extinct.

Hainan island has a high rate of endemism with four endemic vertebrate species and 24 endemic subspecies, many of them endangered forest-dwellers. The black gibbon is reduced to 25 individuals in the Bawangling reserve. Other endemics are the Hainan moonrat (*Neohylomys hainanensis*) and the Hainan flying squirrel (*Petinomys electilis*) (IUCN, 1986a). The endemic Hainan partridge (*Arborophila ardens*) is not uncommon in Bawangling reserve, nor is the endangered silver pheasant (*Lophura nycthemera*), although they are very scarce elsewhere.

Species losses among plants and invertebrates are probably occurring at an even faster rate, and many southern Chinese species are presumed to have become extinct in the last 30 years.

Species are being lost as a result of over-exploitation, habitat loss or habitat fragmentation. Over-exploitation in Xishuangbanna includes excessive hunting of animals and overcollecting and cutting of medicinal and other useful plants (see case study). The Chinese depend heavily on their traditional medicines, many of which contain parts of animals and plants. Habitat fragmentation is a major problem; the total area of forest may still be extensive but it is fragmented into small, isolated blocks each too small to sustain populations of some species.

Serious loss of fish species is due partly to overfishing and the use of poisons and nets to catch fish, but is also due to the high levels of sediment in the rivers caused by soil erosion resulting from loss of tree cover. Higher temperatures in rivers, resulting from climate change, result in too many fish being the same sex (sex in many river fish is determined by temperature). The net result has been a drastic reduction of this important source of protein and this in turn has prompted an increase in hunting of other wildlife (J. Mackinnon, *in litt.*)

Some of the recent economic reforms in China have also had adverse side-effects on wildlife. People are now encouraged to develop private businesses in an attempt to generate greater wealth in the country. Economically this may be a good thing, but the exploitation of wild animals and plants has increased dramatically as a result. In particular, plants are sought after for medicinal purposes and mammals for their skins.

Conservation Areas

The concept of allocating wild areas for conservation was realised late in the People's Republic of China. The first nature reserves were established in 1956 amid a surge of interest that followed the establishment of the Republic. Both research and conservation activity slowed to a standstill during the Cultural Revolution of the late 1960s and early 1970s. This was a bleak period for nature conservation as well as many other academic and cultural aspects of life in China (Wang Yuqing, 1987). In the mid-1970s the bamboo in the Min Mountains of Sichuan flowered and died. Many pandas died

Rivers running through Xishuangbanna, China's most important rain forest reserve, an important resource for people in the region. J. A. McNeely

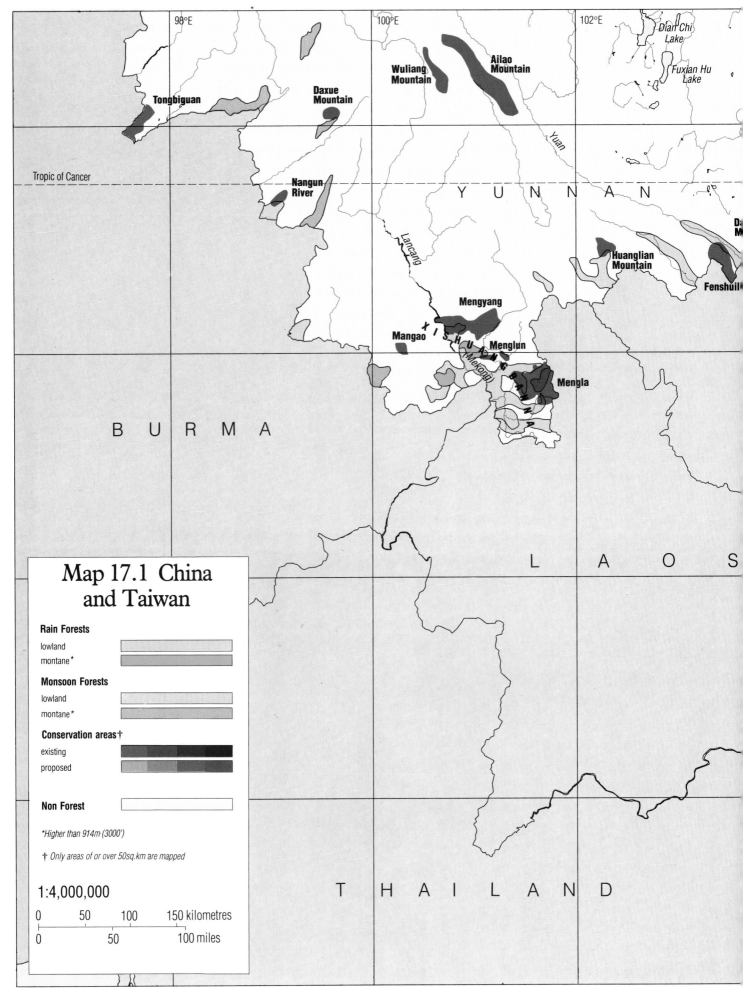

Map 17.1 China and Taiwan

Rain Forests

lowland

montane*

Monsoon Forests

lowland

montane*

Conservation areas†

existing

proposed

Non Forest

Higher than 914m (3000')

† Only areas of or over 50sq.km are mapped

1:4,000,000

0   50   100   150 kilometres

0   50   100 miles

of starvation. The crisis which ensued caused great concern; a huge programme of panda conservation was initiated, and a number of new panda reserves were established (Campbell, 1986). Following the panda crisis there has been a nationwide resurgence of interest in conservation and new reserves are being declared so fast it is difficult to keep up-to-date lists. In 1983 China had more than 120 nature reserves, but by 1988 the figure had topped 400. New areas are still regularly being established.

These reserves have been designed to include: representative examples of many typical natural landscapes and their ecosystems in different biogeographical zones; the habitats of threatened and endangered species of plants and animals; and places with outstanding geological or physical features. Established by several authorities, the reserves protect natural and scenic sites of national and international importance, and other places of special scientific, educational, or recreational interest. Over 300 reserves are in forested areas and were established by the Ministry of Forestry; thirty of these are national reserves administered directly from Beijing, but the remainder are established and managed at provincial level. The Environmental Protection Agency is also involved in establishing reserves in less forested parts of the country, including the Arjin Mountain reserve, which is the biggest in China.

Local government at town and county level can also establish reserves and natural park areas. Three reserves – Changbai, Wolong and Dinghu – are International Biosphere Reserves as part of the Man and Biosphere Programme of Unesco.

Finally, on Hainan Island there are a number of protected areas, including at least two with moist forest remnants: Bawangling Natural Protected Area and Jianfengling NPA in central/west Hainan. Wuzhishan NPA, established to protect the threatened black gibbon, is also presumed to contain some forest.

It is to China's credit to have allocated areas for conservation at a time when the country is facing so many other pressing priorities for social reform and modernisation. However, it must be recognised that the level of protection afforded to these reserves is generally low.

Hong Kong, on the other hand, despite its high human density and small size, has established some important and well-managed parks. Almost 40 per cent of the territory is what is called 'country park', each park having a protected wilderness zone. These parks are gradually reforesting after being almost totally cut for firewood during the period of Japanese occupation in the Second World War. In addition the energetic WWF–Hong Kong has established a valuable mangrove and wetland reserve at the Mai Po marshes, which is an excellent place for viewing wetland and shore birds and is equipped with a fascinating visitor centre (Hong Kong is not mapped in this atlas).

Lastly, Taiwan has four national parks accounting for 6 per cent of its land surface, and a number of small coastal reserves protecting mangroves and other habitats. Yushan is the largest and most remote of Taiwan's parks and here the rare Taiwan serow (*Capricornis crispus swinhoei*) and black bear (*Selenarctos thibetanus*) can be found, together with the vulnerable Taiwan macaque (*Macaca cyclopis*) and the endemic emperor pheasant (*Lophura imperialis*). True rain forests are confined to the south of the island and they are protected in Kenting National Park and on Orchid Island.

See Tables 17.2a and b overleaf for details of all reserves described above.

Initiatives for Conservation
During recent years, China has taken great strides in the conservation of wildlife and natural resources, and this is reflected in official government policies and actions. In 1980 China joined IUCN, became a party to CITES, and formulated a new Wildlife Policy Act, stressing the rational use and conservation of wildlife (FAO, 1982).

Xishuangbanna forest in Yunnan Province has been selected to partner Kinabalu National Park, Sabah, in a joint research programme within Unesco's Man and Biosphere Programme (see chapter 9). The two sites, representing extremes of the Southeast Asian fauna and flora, will be used for the study of the ecology of the forest canopy. Research will be multidisciplinary and multinational and will address species diversity and dispersal patterns, growth rates and reproduction strategies. Extensive walkways will be constructed in the canopy. Linked with the canopy research will be a series of conservation efforts that take account of human needs and economic realities as well as genetic richness and biological potential. This integrated approach in both Malaysia and China could serve as illustrative examples for other tropical forest areas, in Asia and elsewhere. The ultimate objective is to conserve remaining tropical rain forests through their management as a renewable resource. (Source: M. Hadley and K. Schreckenberg *in litt.*, February, 1989.)

KENTING NATIONAL PARK – TAIWAN

In Taiwan, tropical moist forest is confined largely to the south, where stands are protected within Kenting National Park and Orchid Island.

Kenting National Park is situated on the southern tip of Taiwan, bordered by the Taiwan Straits to the west, the Bashi Channel to the south, the Pacific to the east, and the north side of Nanjenshan to the north. On 1 January 1984 the park was officially established, and the Government of the Republic of China designated the Kenting area as Taiwan's first national park, covering an area of 326 sq. km (land and sea areas included).

The climate is sub-tropical, with hot, wet summers and dry winters, and variable weather between October and March due to the north-eastern monsoon, the 'Lo-shan-fong'. The geology and topography of the park is varied and can be roughly divided into a western and an eastern part, separated by the Hengchun valley plain. The western part is mainly composed of the Hengchun plateau, with coastal cliffs and fringing coral reefs. The eastern part mainly comprises sandstone peaks, limestone caves, uplifted cliffs, low-lying coral reefs, estuaries and lakes. Consequently an extraordinary variety of plant species thrive here. The shore, for example, maintains a complex of coastal coral reef plants and tropical coastal forests.

Two major belts of forest vegetation occur within the park, evergreen rain forest in the north-east and semi-deciduous monsoon forest in the south-west. The rain forests receive enough moisture from north-east winds to support evergreen trees, whereas in the leeward south-west district thorn scrub and deciduous woodlands predominate due to the drier climate (Horng-jye Su and Chung-yuan Su, 1988). More than 1000 species of vascular plants (one-quarter of the total for Taiwan) grow in the rain forests, including such rare and endemic species as *Schizea digitata* and *Actinostachys digitata*. There were once vast stretches of tropical coastal forest from South Bay to Oluampi, but only a remnant is left, at Banana Bay.

This great variety of topography and vegetation ensures a high faunal diversity. Although large mammals have become extinct in Taiwan, small mammals such as the squirrel can be found in the upland region (CPA, n.d.). The butterfly fauna includes the rare endemic Taiwan birdwing *Troides aeacus kaguya*. Bird life is rich, with more than 60 resident species. The Hengchun Peninsula is an important staging area for winter migratory birds, including brown shrikes (*Lanius cristatus*), grey-faced buzzards (*Butastur indicus*) and Chinese goshawks (*Accipiter soloensis*).

In 1969 the endemic Formosan sika deer (*Cervus nippon tiouanus*) became extinct in the wild. Twenty-two animals held in Taipei zoo were bred up to a herd of 42, and six have recently been released into a large fenced area around the Research Centre in Kenting.

MEDICINAL PLANTS OF XISHUANGBANNA

Approximately 60 per cent of the world's population are dependent on traditional medicines as their principal source of treatment for illness. In some countries, such as India and China, 80–90 per cent of traditional medicines are based on plant material.

In China these medicinal plants are especially abundant in the tropical forests of Xishuangbanna, where there are over four thousand species of higher plants, including three hundred or more of medicinal plants, over two hundred species of edible plants, over a hundred species of timber trees, over a hundred species of oil producers, and over fifty species of bamboo (Li Wenhua and Zhao Xianying, 1989). However, overcollection and loss of habitat have in some cases caused a serious decline in their abundance.

Even serious diseases have traditional remedies.
- Cancer is treated with a medicine made from the Hooker mayten *Maytenus hookeri*.
- Many-leaf paris *Paris polyphylla* and the chaulmoogra tree *Hydnocarpus anthelminthicus* form the basis of the product 'Yunnan white medicine', which is used as a cure for leprosy.
- The Yunnan devil pepper *Rauvolfia yunnanensis* is used to combat hypertension.
- Other medicinal plants include the cocaine tree *Erythroxylum coca*, cassia-bark tree *Cinnamomum cassia*, Japanese snowbell *Styrax japonica*, cablin potchouli *Pogostemon cablin* and cutch *Acacia catechu*.

In Nanyang Village, Xishuangbanna, a traditional doctor treats a patient. The backdrop to his surgery is a sacred grove, revered for the bounty of the forest. WWF/P. Wachtel

Table 17.2a Conservation areas in Southern China

Existing areas, 50 sq. km and over and for which we have location data, are listed below. The remaining areas are combined in a total under Other Areas. Forest reserves are not included.

	Existing area (sq. km)
GUANGDONG (including Hainan)	
Nature Reserve	
Wuzhi Mountain*	187
Other Areas	771
Province Total	958
GUANGXI	
Nature Reserves	
Buliu River	453
Chengbi River	162
Chongzuo	350
Chuangdon River	116
DaYao Mountain	135
Daming Mountain	582
Daping Mountain	204
Dawingling	192
Daxin*	299
Dehou*	122
Fusui	100
Huagon	157
Longgang*	80
Nongxin	105
Shiwandashan	267
Sub total	3,324
Other Areas	808
Province Total	4,132
YUNNAN	
Nature Reserves	
Ailao Mountain	504
Dawei Mountain	154
Daxue Mountain	158
Fenshuiling*	108
Huanglian Mountain*	138
Xishuangbanna:	
Mangao	
Mengla*	2,000
Menglun*	
Mengyang*	
Nangun River*	70
Tongbiguan	342
Wuliang Mountain	234
Sub total	3,708
Other Areas	6,739
Province Total	10,447

(*Sources:* Guangdong, Guangxi and Yunnan, adapted from Li Wenhua and Zhao Xianying, 1989)

★ Area containing moist forest within its boundaries.

Table 17.2b Conservation areas of Taiwan

Existing and proposed areas, 50 sq. km and over and for which we have location data, are listed below. The remaining areas are combined in a total under Other Areas. Forest reserves are not included.

	Existing area (sq. km)	Proposed area (sq. km)
National Parks		
Taroko	920	
Yushan	1,055	
Kenting*	326	
Yangmingshan	115	
Orchid Island*		290
Nature Preserves		
Ta-Wu Mountain	470	
Other Protected Areas		
Chang-Yu-Chia Coast	993	
Hua-Tung Coast*	535	
Northeast Coast	137	
Sue-Hua Coast	71	
Sub totals	4,622	290
Other Areas	244	1,002
Totals	4,866	1,292

(*Sources:* IUCN 1990, WCMC *in litt.*)

★ Area containing moist forest within its boundaries.

References

AsDB (1987) *People's Republic of China, Environmental and Natural Resources Briefing Profile.* Environment Unit, Asian Development Bank, Manila, Philippines. 11 pp. + 4 annexes.

Campbell, J. J. N. (1986) Giant panda conservation and bamboo forest destruction. *INTECOL Bulletin* 13: 121–5.

CPA (n.d.) *A Journey Through the National Parks of the Republic of China.* Construction and Planning Administration, Ministry of Interior, China. 80 pp.

Dowdle, S. (1987) Seeking higher yields from fewer fields. *Far Eastern Economic Review* 135: 78–80.

FAO (1982) *Forestry in China.* FAO, Rome, Italy. 305 pp.

FAO (1990) *FAO Yearbook of Forest Products 1977–88.* FAO Forestry Series No. 23. FAO Statistics Series No. 90. FAO, Rome.

Hou, H. Y. (ed.) (1979) *Vegetation Map of China: Scale 1:4,000,000* (In Chinese but with separate 12-page legend in English.) Chinese Academy of Sciences, Beijing, China.

Horng-jye Su and Chung-yuan Su (1988) Multivariate analysis on the vegetation of Kenting National Park. *Quarterly Journal of Chinese Forestry* 21: 17–32.

IUCN (1986a) *Review of the Protected Areas System in the Indo-Malayan Realm.* Consultants J. and K. Mackinnon, IUCN, Gland, Switzerland. 284 pp.

IUCN (1986b) *Plants in Danger. What do we know?* IUCN, Gland, Switzerland, and Cambridge, UK. 461 pp.

IUCN (1990) *1989 United Nations List of National Parks and Protected Areas.* IUCN, Gland, Switzerland, and Cambridge, UK.

Jiang Youxu (1986) Ecological exploitation of tropical plant resources in China. *INTECOL Bulletin* 13: 13–75.

Li Jinchang, Kang Fanwen, He Naihui and Lester Ross (1988) Price and policy: the keys to re-vamping China's forestry resources. In: *Public Policies and the Misuse of Forest Resources.* Repetto, R. and Gillis, M. (eds). Cambridge University Press, UK. 432 pp.

Lin Peng (1984) Ecological notes on mangroves in southeast coast of China including Taiwan Province and Hainan Island. In: *Proceedings of the Asian Symposium on Mangrove Environment Research and Management.* Soepadmo, E., Rao, A. N. and McIntosh, D. J. (eds) pp. 118–20. Kuala Lumpur: University of Malaya and Unesco.

Lin Peng (1987) The mangroves of China. In: *Mangrove Ecosystems of Asia and the Pacific: Status, Exploitation and Management.* Field, C. D. and Dartnell, A. J. (eds). Australian Institute of Marine Science, Townsville.

Lin Peng (1988) *Mangrove Vegetation.* Beijing: China Ocean Press.

Li Wenhua and Zhao Xianying (1989) *China's Nature Reserves.* Foreign Languages Press, Beijing, China. 191 pp.

Liu Longhui (1987) National report – China. In: *Ad Hoc FAO/ECE/FINNIDA Meeting of Experts on Forest Resources Assessment.* Bulletins of the Finnish Forest Research Institute No. 284. Finnida, Helsinki, Finland. 433 pp.

Lu Chang and Lin Peng (1987) Economic value of mangroves communities in China. In: *Mangrove Ecosystems of Asia and the Pacific: Status, Exploitation and Management.* Field, C. D. and Dartnell, A. J. (eds), pp. 143–50. Australian Institute of Marine Science, Townsville.

Lu Junpei and Zeng Qingbo (1986) Ecological consequences of shifting cultivation and tropical forest cutting on Jianfeng Mountains, Hainan Island, China. *INTECOL Bulletin* 13: 57–60.

NCC (1982) *Nature Conservation Delegation to China, 4–24 April 1982.* Nature Conservancy Council, London, UK. 44 pp.

Policy Research Office (1981) Run forestry work according to the law. *Hongqi (Red Flag)* 5: 27. (1 March).

Smil, V. (1983) Deforestation in China. *Ambio* 12: 226–31.

Wang Bao-Can (1984) Utilisation and development prospects of mangrove in China. In: *Proceedings of the Asian Symposium on Mangrove Environment Research and Management.* Soepadmo, E., Rao, A. N. and McIntosh, D. J. (eds), pp. 684–95. Kuala Lumpur: University of Malaya and Unesco.

Wang Yuqing (1987) Natural conservation regions in China. *Ambio* 16: 326–31.

Yang Hanxi (1985) The Mangroves of China. In: *Man's impact on Coastal and Estuarine Ecosystems.* Saeki, T., Hino, A., Hirose, T., Sakamoto, M. and Ruddle, K. (eds), pp. 41–6. Proceedings MAB/COMAR Regional Seminar, Tokyo, 23–26 November, 1984.

Yang Yuguang (1980) Protecting wildlife reserves of Xishuangbanna. *Guangming Ribao* January 18: 2.

Zhang Tianxiong (1980) Vigorously protect Hainan Island's forest resources. *Guangming Ribao* July 2: 2.

Zhao Songqiao (1986) *Physical Geography of China.* Science Press, Beijing, and John Wiley and Sons, New York, USA.

Authorship

John MacKinnon in Cambridge and Mark Collins at WCMC, with assistance from Michael Green, also at WCMC.

Map 17.1 Forest cover in China and Taiwan

A detailed *Vegetation Map of China* was published by the Institute of Botany of the Chinese Academy of Sciences in 1979 (edited by H. Y. Hou) at a scale of 1:4 million. This shows both the remaining natural vegetation and the main croplands and is accompanied by a legend in English (Hou, 1979). This is the most recent and authoritative map of the vegetation of China and has been used to delimit tropical rain and monsoon forests of China in this atlas. It must be acknowledged, however, that deforestation has been extensive in the intervening decade. In Taiwan, for example, there is reported to be little or no remaining rain forest outside Kenting National Park and Orchid Island (M. J. B. Green, pers. comm.), and deforestation has also been heavy on Hainan.

Two vegetation types have been selected from the *Vegetation Map of China* for portrayal here. Rain forests have been delimited using categories 33 a–d 'Tropical broadleaf evergreen rain forest'. Monsoon forests have been delimited using categories 31 'Seasonal forest on limestone soil' and 32 'Seasonal forest on acid lateritic soil'. The limestone forest occurs mostly in southern Guangzi Province, while the seasonal forest on acid soil is mostly on Hainan Island. Forests in montane areas have been delimited using a 3000 ft (914 m) contour.

The system of protected areas depicted in this atlas is very selective. As indicated in the text, the protected areas system is changing rapidly and it has proved impossible to prepare definitive tables and maps. Instead, only those protected areas in or near the remaining forest areas are shown, based on location data supplied by John MacKinnon, currently working on a WWF project in China. Data on the protected areas of Taiwan were obtained from various documents held at the World Conservation Monitoring Centre.

18 India

Land area	2,973,190 sq. km
Population (1989)	835 million
Population growth rate (1987–2000)	1.8 per cent
Expected maximum population (2150)	1697 million
Gross national product (1987)	US$300 per capita
Rain forest (see maps and Figure 18.1)	158,950 sq. km
Monsoon forest (see maps)	162,170 sq. km
Closed broadleaved/coniferous forest (1980)†	504,010 sq. km
Annual deforestation rate (1981–5)†	1320 sq. km
Roundwood production*	264,412,000 cu. m
Roundwood exports*	76,000 cu. m
Fuelwood and charcoal production*	240,184 cu. m
Sawlog and veneer log production*	18,350,000 cu. m
Sawlog and veneer log exports*	61,000 cu. m

* 1988 data from FAO (1990)
† FAO/UNEP (1981)

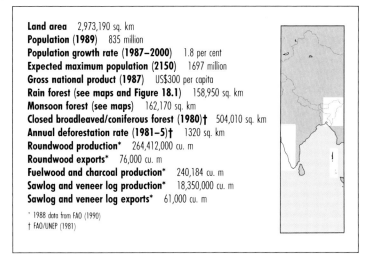

Fifty years ago, India had extensive natural forests with a rich diversity of animal and plant life. Now, the rapid growth in human population and in cattle herds in recent decades has put these forests under more pressure than they can bear. The resource is dwindling and the country as a whole has much less forest cover than is required to maintain environmental stability. The extent of pressures on the forests can be judged from the fact that with less than two per cent of the total forest area of the world, the country supports over 15 per cent of global population and nearly 15 per cent of the cattle. Many of the people and cattle are totally dependent on the forest resources.

During the three decades from 1950 to 1980, India lost large areas of its tropical forests. Fortunately, in the 1980s a strong political will developed to conserve and protect them. New laws have been enacted, new policies have been formulated, and steps have been taken to reduce human pressures. These efforts to conserve and protect forests are continuing but the socio-economic pressures are great, and it will take great political determination and social effort to save the remaining tropical forests from destruction.

INTRODUCTION

India, home for about 15 per cent of the world's population, is the seventh largest country in the world and Asia's second largest nation after China. For administrative purposes India is divided into 24 states and seven union territories. Physically, the massive country is divided into four relatively well-defined regions – the Himalayan mountains, the Gangetic river plains, the southern (Deccan) plateau, and the islands of Lakshadweep, Andaman and Nicobar. The Himalayas in the far north include some of the highest peaks in the world. The highest in India is Khangchenjunga (8586 m). The northern plains are crossed by the great rivers Ganga (Ganges), Ghaghara, Brahmaputra and Yamuna. Topographically homogenous, the variation in relief does not exceed 300 m, but the soils vary widely in fertility. The Deccan plateau constitutes peninsular India, generally sloping eastwards from the Western Ghats, drained by large rivers such as the Mahanadi, Krishna and Godavari. The Western Ghats rise to 2450 m and the smaller Eastern Ghats to 600 m.

The climate of India is dominated by the monsoons, most importantly by rains from the south-west between June and October, and drier winds from the north between December and February. From March to May the climate is dry and hot.

Half the population of India lives on less than one-quarter of the available land; one-third is concentrated on less than 6 per cent of the land (Sukhwal, 1987). The peoples of India are extremely varied, best described in terms of communities that are primarily separated by religion, but with an overlay of race, language, geography and culture. Most Indians are Hindus (83 per cent in 1981), but Muslims,

Buddhists, Sikhs, Christians, Parsis and Jews are also present. There are also more than 400 ethnic groups (c. 44 million people) who are collectively referred to as the 'Scheduled Tribes'. These communities are distinct from one another in terms of language, religion, social structure and economic condition. Most inhabit the less accessible, often forested areas of India and, with the exception of a few hunter-gatherers, depend primarily on permanent or shifting agriculture.

The Forests

India possesses a distinct identity, not only because of its geography, history and culture, but also because of the great diversity of its natural ecosystems. The panorama of Indian forests ranges from evergreen tropical rain forests in the Andaman and Nicobar Islands, the Western Ghats, and the north-eastern states, to dry alpine scrub high in the Himalaya to the north. Between the two extremes, the country has semi-evergreen rain forests, deciduous monsoon forests, thorn forests, subtropical broadleaved and subtropical pine forests in the lower montane zone and temperate montane forests (Lal, 1989).

One of the most important tropical forest classifications was developed for Greater India (Champion, 1936) and later republished for present-day India (Champion and Seth, 1968). This approach has proved to have wide application outside India. In it 16 major forest types are recognised, subdivided into 221 minor types. Structure, physiognomy and floristics are all used as characters to define the types. Here we are concerned mainly with the tropical types.

The main areas of tropical rain forest are found in the Andaman and Nicobar Islands; the Western Ghats, which fringe the Arabian Sea coastline of peninsular India; and the greater Assam region in the north-east. Small remnants of rain forest are found in Orissa State (see Figure 18.1). Semi-evergreen rain forest is more extensive than the evergreen formation partly because evergreen forests tend to degrade to semi-evergreen with human interference. There are substantial differences in both the flora and fauna between the three major rain forest regions (IUCN, 1986; Rodgers and Panwar, 1988). For example, the Western Ghats have 13 species of the important tree family Dipterocarpaceae, and the north-east has nine species, but they have none in common, and all but two of the eight species of the Andaman and Nicobar Islands are endemic. In the Western Ghats different floristic associations have been recognised and related to the length of the dry season (Singh *et al.*, 1983; Pascal, 1988), which varies from three to seven or eight months between the south and Maharashtra further north.

The Western Ghats Monsoon forests occur both on the western (coastal) margins of the Ghats and on the eastern side where there is less rainfall. They include several tree species of great commercial significance (e.g. Indian rosewood *Dalbergia latifolia*, Malabar kino *Pterocarpus marsupium*, teak, and *Terminalia crenulata*), but these have now been cleared from many areas.

In the rain forests there is an enormous number of tree species – indeed at least 60 per cent of the trees of the upper canopy are of species which individually contribute not more than one per cent of the total number (Champion and Seth, 1968). Giant trees with buttressed bases and boles that are unbranched for over 30 m are common; typical components include species of *Calophyllum*, *Dipterocarpus*, *Hopea* and *Mesua* (Pascal, 1988.)

The montane rain forests of the Western Ghats include an evergreen formation commonly referred to as *shola* forest, which contains both tropical and temperate floristic elements. This forest is associated with rolling grasslands (*sholas*) and is found in patches on the higher hills of Tamil Nadu, Karnataka and Kerala above 1500 m where the rainfall may vary from 1500 to 6250 mm or more.

Clumps of bamboo occur along streams or in poorly drained hollows throughout the evergreen and semi-evergreen forests of south-west India, probably in areas once cleared for shifting agriculture.

North-east India The tropical vegetation of north-east India (which includes the states of Assam, Nagaland, Manipur, Mizoram, Tripura and Meghalaya as well as the plains region of Arunachal Pradesh) typically covers elevations up to 900 m. It embraces evergreen and semi-evergreen rain forests, moist deciduous monsoon forests, riparian forests, swamps and grasslands. Evergreen rain forests are found in the Assam Valley, the foothills of the eastern Himalayas and the lower parts of the Naga Hills, Meghalaya, Mizoram and Manipur, where the rainfall exceeds 2300 mm per annum. In the Assam Valley the giant dipterocarps *Dipterocarpus macrocarpus* and *Shorea assamica* occur singly, occasionally attaining a girth of up to 7 m and a height of up to 50 m. They tower over a closed evergreen canopy at about 30 m, often with *Mesua* and *Vatica* predominant and many palms and orchids (Rao, 1974).

The monsoon forests are mainly moist *sal* (*Shorea robusta*) forests. They occur widely in this region (see Map 18.2). Some subtropical hill forests have developed on the upper slopes of the Khasi and other adjacent hills below an altitude of 1500 m, but in many parts repeated shifting cultivation with felling and burning have cleared and greatly altered the original forest cover.

Tropical rain forest in the lowlands alters in character with increasing elevation developing strong temperate floristic affinities in montane areas. The different formations are variously described as

subtropical and temperate montane evergreen forests. Such forests extend westwards along the south-facing slopes of the ranges of the Himalayas, where they have been highly disturbed and over large areas replaced by *Pinus roxburghii*, *P. k. hasiana* and *P. wallichiana* woodland over grass, or by treeless land. Singh and Singh (1987) give a good account. This western extension is not mapped here. Much less extensive stands of temperate rain forests also occur east of India in upper Burma and in China, where they have been included in our maps because, as in Assam, there is no sharp boundary or distinction between them and tropical formations.

Andaman and Nicobar Islands are a group of about 350 islands situated in the Bay of Bengal, with a combined area of 8249 sq. km (Saldanha, 1989). Since 1960 the human population of the Andamans has grown from 50,000 to 180,000 (Whitaker, 1985) and forestry exploitation has disturbed much of the natural vegetation. The interior regions remain relatively undeveloped (IUCN, 1986). The Andamans have tropical evergreen rain forest and tropical semi-evergreen rain forest as well as tropical moist monsoon forests (IUCN, 1986). The tropical evergreen rain forest is only slightly less grand in stature and rich in species than on the mainland. The dominant species is *Dipterocarpus grandiflorus* in hilly areas, while *Dipterocarpus kerrii* is prominent on some islands in the southern part of the archipelago. The monsoon forests of the Andamans are dominated by *Pterocarpus dalbergioides* and *Terminalia* spp.

The flora of the Nicobar Islands (which are located approximately 300 km south of the Andamans) is allied to that of Sumatra and

Tropical moist forests in the Blue Mountains of Nilgiri Tamil Nadu; habitat of the threatened Nilgiri woodpigeon, the Nilgiri tahr and many other endemic species. WWF/M. Rautkari

Malaysia (IUCN, 1986). These 22 islands have rain forest which includes species of *Calophyllum*, *Garcinia*, *Mangifera* and *Terminalia* but no dipterocarps. The remaining forested areas are under some pressure from agricultural activities. Scrub forest occurs on the low, flat islands at the northern end of the archipelago (IUCN, 1986). The coastal margins of both the Andamans and Nicobars support mangrove forests, beach forests and various other littoral formations.

Forest Resources and Management

The majority of India's forest lands (97 per cent) are under public ownership and most of these (85 per cent) are managed by the forest departments of the different state governments. Others are owned by corporate bodies (eg municipalities, village communities) and by private individuals (FAO/UNEP, 1981).

Three main legal classes of forest are recognised:

1 Reserve forests: these are primarily for conservation or scientific management for various forest products or for watershed protection. They attract the highest degree of state control and local villagers are excluded from entering them.

2 Protected forests: these are similar to reserve forests but the government exercises a lower degree of control. Local villagers can exercise certain, defined rights.

3 Unclassed forests: these are all the other publicly owned forests, where the state government exercises the lowest degree of control.

India has about 751,000 sq. km of 'legally classified forests', but only 640,134 sq. km has been officially recognised as 'effective forest zone'. Of this area, only 378,470 sq. km is 'adequately stocked forest land', ie with greater than 40 per cent crown cover (Table 18.1). On the basis of visual interpretation of 1985–7 Landsat imagery, the Forest Survey of India has estimated further coverage of woodland (257,409 sq. km) and mangrove (4255 sq. km) (Table 18.1), a total which is less than a quarter of the geographical area of the nation (FSI, 1989). These figures, covering the whole of India, include woodlands as well as temperate tropical forests making up about 40 per cent of the total. In the 1987 assessment based on 1981–3 satellite imagery, tropical rain forests were said to occupy about 77,700 sq. km (FSI, 1987). Our maps, based on 1986 imagery, indicate a total of 69,380 sq. km including mangroves (Table 18.2).

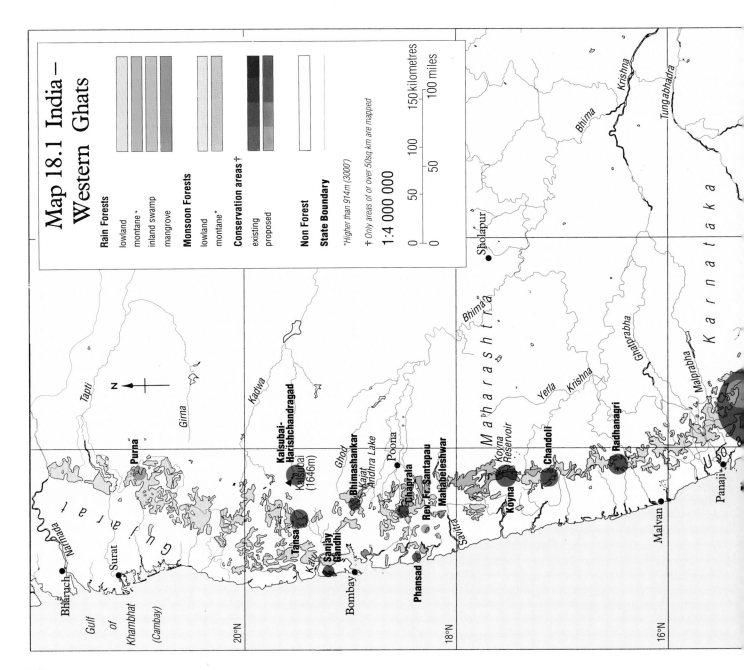

Map 18.1 India – Western Ghats

Table 18.1 Estimate of forest and woodland cover in India

	Area (sq. km)	% of land area
Forest (crown density 40% and over)	378,470	11.51
Woodland (crown density 10–40%)	257,409	7.83
Mangrove forest	4,255	0.13
Total	640,134	19.47

(Adapted from FSI, 1989)

Table 18.2 (shown on page 130) is a breakdown of the areas of rain and monsoon forest shown in a generalised form in Figure 18.1, with details of the Western Ghats and north-east India shown in Maps 18.1 and 18.2. The total area of rain forest is 69,380 sq. km, or 2.3 per cent of India's land area. In Maps 18.1 and 18.2, there are an additional 64,030 sq. km of monsoon forest, or 2.2 per cent of India's land area, but this is incomplete as monsoon forests are extensive in central India. Figure 18.1 (overleaf) is a sketch map showing the approximate extent of monsoon forests throughout India. This indicates a total area of monsoon forest of 158,950 sq. km (5 per cent of land area).

The National Forest Policy of India (1952) suggested that the nation as a whole should aim to maintain one-third of its total land area under forests and this remains part of the 1988 policy (see Initiatives for Conservation on page 138). In the hills, the proportion of forests should be 60 per cent and in the plains 20 per cent.

A new national forest policy was adopted in 1988 which specifically laid down that environmental stability is to be the primary consideration in forest management. Efforts are now directed towards ensuring that ecological considerations are not subordinated to immediate material needs. Moreover, the country has launched a large-scale programme of wasteland afforestation in order to develop new fodder and firewood reserves to reduce the two main pressures on natural forests (see Initiatives for Conservation).

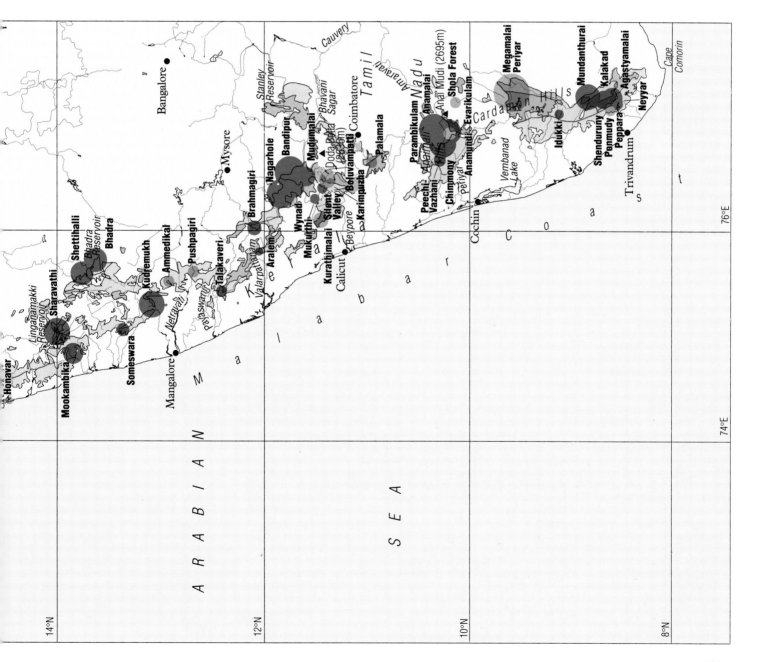

Table 18.2 Estimates of the extent of rain forests and monsoon forests in India with emphasis on the Western Ghats, north-east India and the Andaman and Nicobar Islands

	Area (sq. km)	% of land area		Area (sq. km)	% of land area
Western Ghats			**Andaman and Nicobar Is**		
Rain forests			*Rain forests*		
Lowland	15,010	0.5	Lowland	2,650	0.1
Montane	4,950	0.2	Mangrove	570	—
Inland swamp	110	—			
Mangrove	130	—	*Sub totals*	3,220	0.7
Sub totals	20,200	0.7	*Monsoon forests*		
			Lowland	3,620	0.1
Monsoon forests					
Lowland	15,850	0.5			
Montane	2,560	0.1	**Other regions**		
			Rain forests		
Sub totals	18,410	0.6	Lowland (Orissa)	915	0.03
North-east India			Mangrove[2]	1,235	0.04
Rain forests					
Lowland	18,860	0.6	*Sub totals*	2,250	0.07
Montane	22,530	0.8			
Mangrove[1]	2,320	—			
Sub totals	43,710	1.5			
Monsoon forests			*Monsoon forests*		
Lowland	25,340	0.9	Lowland	98,140	3.3
Montane	13,440	0.4			
			Total rain forests	69,380	2.3
Sub totals	38,780	1.3	Total monsoon forests	158,950	5.0

Statistics are based on analyses of Maps 18.1 and 18.2 (see Map Legends for details of sources)

[1] This area refers to the Sundarbans in India, which are portrayed on the western border of Bangladesh on Map 13.1.

[2] This figure is deduced from the State of the Forest Report 1989 (FSI, 1989), in which an analysis of the same imagery used here gave an estimated total of 4255 sq. km of mangrove in all India (see Table 18.1).

A major drawback in forest resource management is that it has not been sufficiently integrated with general land use planning, and overall has been notably isolated from agriculture, fisheries and grassland management. The management of grasslands has a significant effect on the maintenance of forests because if they are not sufficiently productive, domestic animals are forced to move into the forests to graze.

Deforestation

Mainland India has suffered rapid deforestation in the past few decades. As much as 1500 sq. km of forest lands have been officially diverted per year to non-forest use. In addition, some 7000 sq. km of forest lands have been illegally occupied for settled cultivation and 43,500 sq. km have been used for shifting cultivation. The remaining forest lands have suffered extensive degradation because of the enormous demands for firewood (FSI, 1987).

Much of this forest conversion was not inevitable, and if the state governments had considered the situation from the national perspective, it would not have been allowed, as the environmental costs resulting from forest depletion have often exceeded the economic gains.

To check indiscriminate conversion of forests, the Central Government enacted the Forest (Conservation) Act in 1980 whereby state governments were required to obtain prior Central Government agreement. Permission for conversion of forests is only given after all possible alternatives have been examined and when the project will give more economic benefits than the environmental loss entailed. The Act is reported to have produced the anticipated results: official forest land conversion has been reduced from 1500 to 65 sq. km per annum.

Ecological considerations in forest management have only started gaining precedence over socio-economic factors in the late 1980s with the issue of a circular by Central Government to state governments that replacement of natural forests by monoculture plantations must be stopped, and that ecologically sensitive areas should not be disturbed in any way.

Agriculture Shifting agriculture is one of the most important factors in the conversion of the country's forest vegetation (see chapter 4). It is widely practised in the north-eastern states of India (i.e. Arunachal Pradesh, Nagaland, Manipur, Meghalaya, Mizoram and Tripura, see Table 18.3) where it is legally recognised as an acceptable form of land use. Practised on a small scale by a very small population using clearing cycles of 15–20 years, shifting agriculture has little lasting impact on the environment and the forest eventually recovers. In many parts of India, however, the rapid shortening of the cycle, due to increased population pressure and decreased land availability, has resulted either in the colonisation of vast areas of forest land by exotic weeds or in extensive 'desertification' of the landscape; this has occurred even in high rainfall areas. In Meghalaya the reduced cycle combined with the steepness of the terrain and the high rainfall of the region (which averages 2–3000 mm per annum) has caused particularly severe erosion.

Large areas of reserve forest have been released for permanent agricultural expansion since the Second World War. Between 1951 and 1976 agricultural land increased by 430,000 sq. km (15 per cent of the land area), much of this through conversion of non-reserve forests which were originally intended to meet rural fodder, fuel and small timber supplies. This policy was followed in order to meet the food needs of the human population and to cash in on timber assets before nationalisation, but has now been reversed because forest products are in short supply, and the ecological changes associated with forest clearance are causing human suffering (Shyamsunder and Parameswarappa, 1987).

Logging Logging operations, originally entrusted to private contractors but now increasingly coming under the control of public forest corporations, have also contributed to the overall decline in the country's moist forest resources. In theory contractors are expected to follow ecologically sensitive 'working plans', but in practice poor management and slack supervision of timber harvesting operations

Table 18.3 Shifting cultivation details by state/union territories

Shifting cultivation takes place on almost 10,000 sq. km in any one year, with almost 68,000 sq. km being affected during the cultivation cycle (mid-1980s data). Over 40 per cent of this activity takes place in the forest lands of the north-east, while more than 50 per cent occurs in the now largely deforested state of Orissa.

	Area under cultivation in a year (sq. km)	Shifting cultivation cycle (years)	Estimated total area under shifting cultivation (sq. km)
Arunachal Pradesh	703	4	2,812
Assam	700	7	4,900
Manipur	500	6	3,000
Mizoram	600	8	4,800
Meghalaya	760	6	4,560
Nagaland	730	9	6,570
Tripura	170	8	1,360
Total North Eastern States	4,163	–	28,002
Andhra Pradesh	173	6	1,038
Bihar	162	6	972
Kerala	19	6	114
Madhya Pradesh	81	6	486
Orissa	5,298	7	37,086
Total Southern States	5,733	–	39,696
Total India	9,896	–	67,698

(Adapted from Report of Task Force on Shifting Cultivation, *in litt.*)

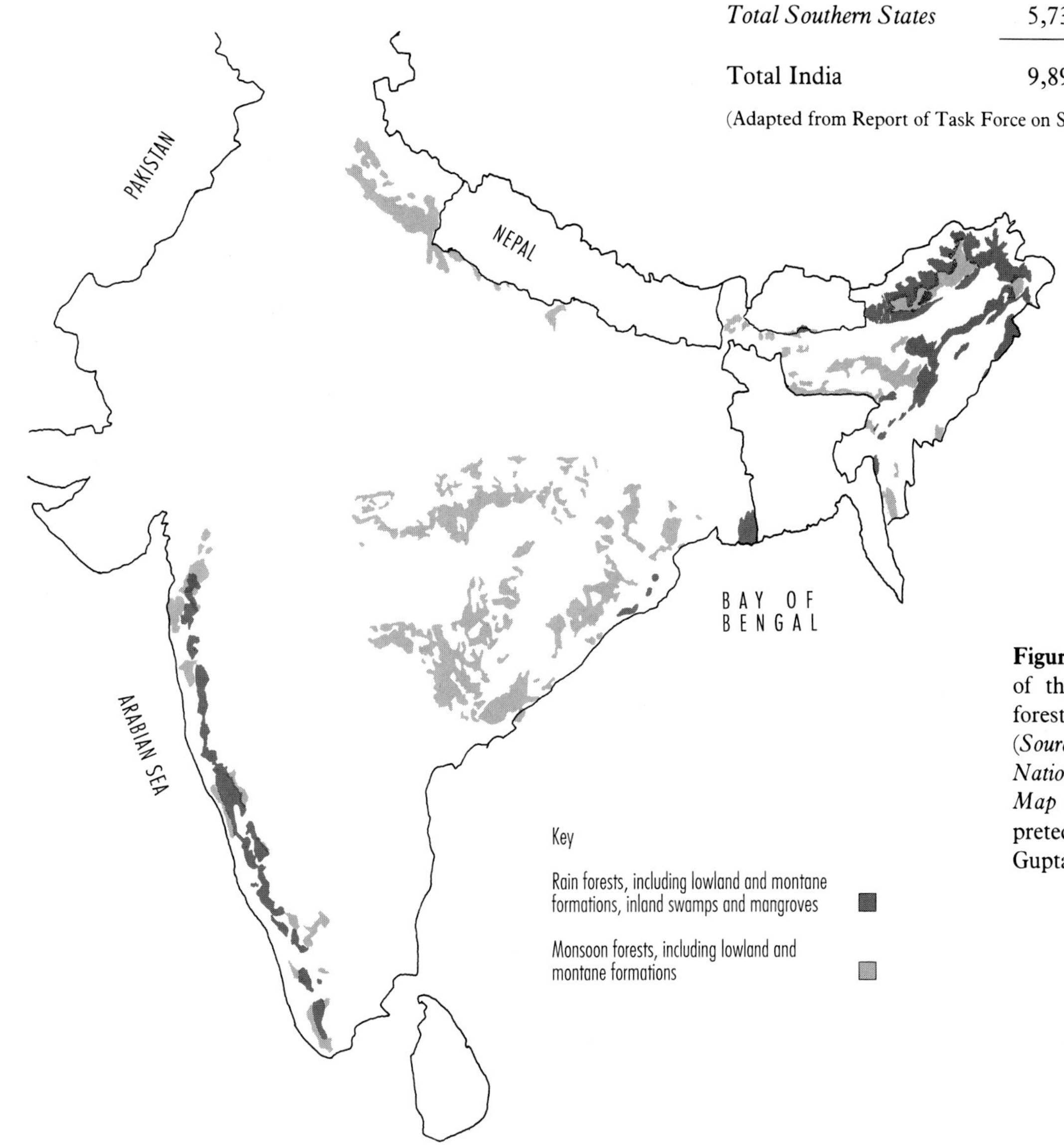

Figure 18.1 Sketch map of the remaining moist forests of all India. (*Source*: Data from the *National Forest Vegetation Map* (FSI, 1986), interpreted through Das Gupta, 1976.)

Key

Rain forests, including lowland and montane formations, inland swamps and mangroves ▪

Monsoon forests, including lowland and montane formations ▫

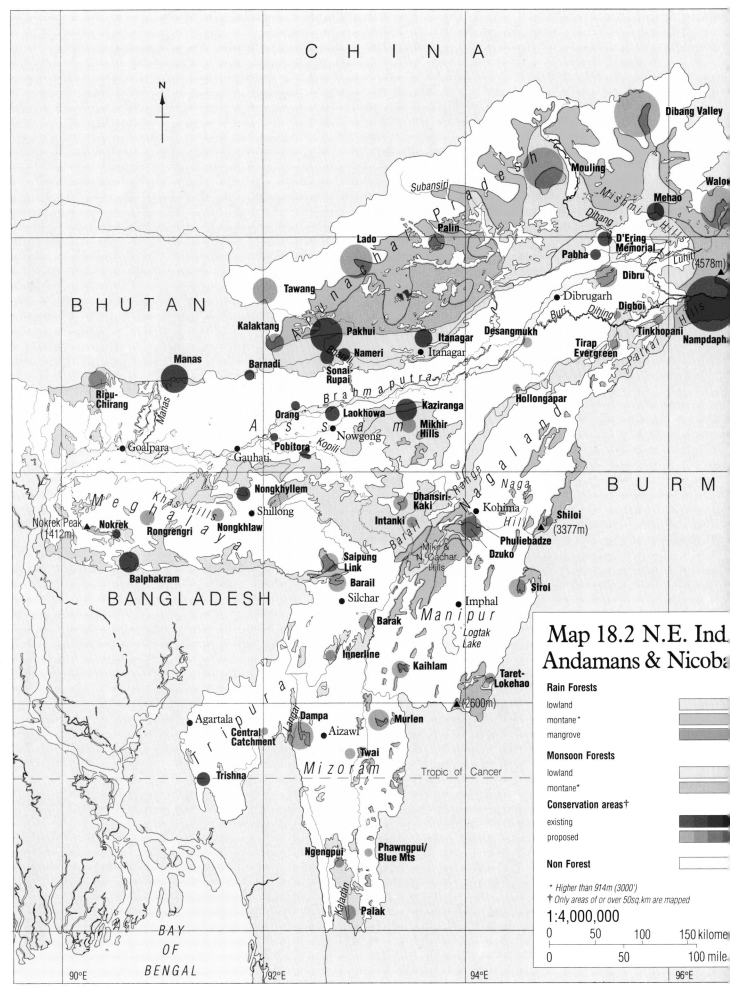

C H I N A

Dibang Valley

Mouling

Walo

Mehao

Subansiri

Arunachal Pradesh

Lado

Palin

D'Ering
Memorial

Pabha

Luhit

(4578m)

Dibru

BHUTAN

Tawang

Dibrugarh

Digboi

Kalaktang

Pakhui

Itanagar

Desangmukh

Tinkhopani

Nampdapha

Nameri

Itanagar

Tirap
Evergreen

Patkai Hills

Manas

Barnadi

Sonai-
Rupai

Brahmaputra

Kaziranga

Hollongapar

Ripu-
Chirang

Manas

Orang

Laokhowa

Mikhir
Hills

Goalpara

A   s   s   a   m

Pobitora

Nowgong

Kopili

Gauhati

Nongkhyllem

Nagaland

Naga

BURM

Meghalaya

Khasi Hills

Shillong

Dhansiri-
Kaki

Range

Kohima

Shiloi
(3377m)

Nokrek Peak
(1412m)

Nokrek

Rongrengri

Nongkhlaw

Intanki

Barail

Phuliebadze

Dzuko

Saipung
Link

Mikir &
N. Cachar
Hills

Balphakram

Barail

Siroi

Silchar

BANGLADESH

Imphal

Manipur

Barak

Logtak
Lake

Innerline

Kaihlam

Taret-
Lokehao

(2600m)

Agartala

Dampa

Murlen

Tripura

Central
Catchment

Aizawl

Langai

Twai

Trishna

Mizoram

Tropic of Cancer

Ngengpui

Phawngpui/
Blue Mts

Kaladan

Palak

BAY
OF
BENGAL

90°E

92°E

94°E

96°E

Map 18.2 N.E. Ind.
Andamans & Nicoba

Rain Forests

lowland

montane*

mangrove

Monsoon Forests

lowland

montane*

Conservation areas†

existing

proposed

Non Forest

* Higher than 914m (3000')
† Only areas of or over 50sq.km are mapped

1:4,000,000

0   50   100   150 kilome

0   50   100 mile.

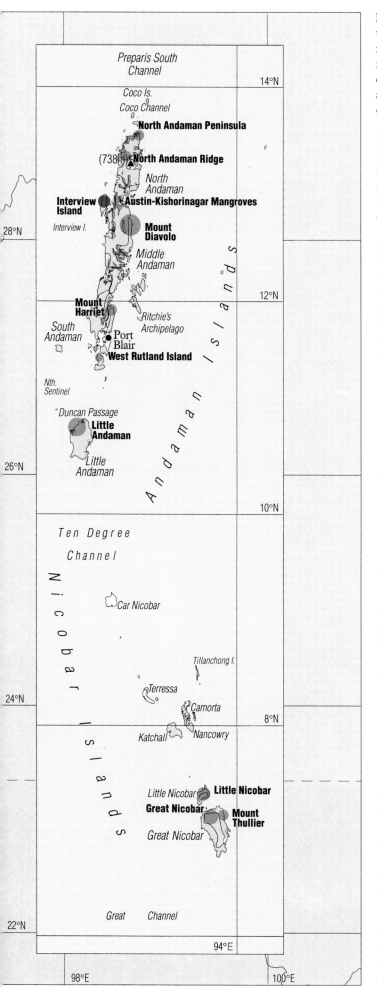

Preparis South Channel

14°N

Coco Is.
Coco Channel
North Andaman Peninsula

(738m)▲**North Andaman Ridge**

North Andaman

Interview●**Austin-Kishorinagar Mangroves**
Island

Interview I.

28°N

Mount Diavolo

Middle Andaman

12°N

Mount Harriet

Ritchie's Archipelago

South Andaman

●**Port Blair**

West Rutland Island

Nth. Sentinel

Duncan Passage
Little Andaman

26°N

Little Andaman

10°N

Ten Degree Channel

Car Nicobar

Tillanchong I.

24°N

Terressa

Camorta

8°N

Katchall *Nancowry*

Little Nicobar **Little Nicobar**
Great Nicobar **Mount Thullier**

Great Nicobar

22°N

Great Channel

94°E

98°E

100°E

Andaman Islands

Nicobar Islands

have caused a widespread decline in forest quality. The environmental advantages of enforcing non-destructive timber extraction techniques and maintaining a substantial forest resource base are recognised by the Indian authorities, but in many cases inadequate control and short-term economic considerations have superseded the application of sound ecological principles. This insensitive forest destruction has caused a reduction in species diversity.

Harvesting of fuelwood is an important factor in deforestation. India produces thirteen times as much fuelwood as sawlogs (FAO, 1990) and fuelwood is an important source of energy for Indian rural households, which make up 75 per cent of the population. Although some villagers have been granted the right to take fallen material from certain forests for their domestic requirements, a far larger quantity is illegally removed by way of lopping and cutting of small trees. With growing population pressure, there is an increasing gap between supply and demand, and there can be no doubt of the serious impact this demand is making on forests. In 1975–6, 183 million cu. m of firewood were consumed in mainland India, while the sustainable level of production was estimated to be less than 41 million cu. m per annum (FSI 1987). Over the last few years the firewood cut has far exceeded the prescribed silvicultural limit. Current requirement for fuelwood is running at about 240 million cu. m per year, i.e. 199 million cu. m above the sustainable yield. The situation is aggravated by industrial wood requirements that are over twice as high as the silvicultural productivity. India has the potential to meet these demands from the nation's forest lands, but plantation forestry will need to be extended and natural forests managed more carefully.

Grazing on forest land Since the time when India's forests were first reserved, India's human population has more than trebled and the cattle population has grown by a factor of 2.5 (Shyamsunder and Parameswarappa, 1987). In 1975 India had about 15 per cent of the world's cattle, 46 per cent of its buffaloes, 17 per cent of its goats and 4 per cent of its sheep (Centre for Science and Environment, 1982). With the rapid increase in the size of irrigated and cultivated lands in recent years, many livestock owners have been forced to rely on forest areas as grazing land for their herds. Of over 400 million cattle, about 90 million graze in the forests, where the carrying capacity is estimated at only 31 million (FSI, 1987). In Karnataka, one of the leading forestry states, cattle-grazing was formerly restricted and regulated, but today it has become uncontrollable because of the huge numbers involved. This is leading to heavy trampling, fodder lopping and fire-setting, which significantly diminish opportunities for forest regeneration.

Hydroelectric projects Dams are very often built on rivers running through the most fertile forest lands, which means that dam construction has become part of the destructive process. Between 1947 and 1957 about half a million hectares of forest were lost due to major river-valley projects (Centre for Science and Environment, 1982). By the late 1980s it is expected that several million hectares of reserve-forest land will be lost through submergence and clearance for irrigated agriculture (Shyamsunder and Parameswarappa, 1987). The intensive utilisation of water resources in the Western Ghats gives particular cause for concern. This escarpment is the major watershed in peninsular India and the steep western slopes of the Ghats are ideal for generating hydroelectric power. Eleven dams have already been constructed along the course of the Periyar River (one of the largest waterways in the state of Kerala) and their creation has submerged large stands of valley forest. The activities associated with their construction (e.g. improved or new access roads) have also led to increased human encroachment and to the irreversible fragmentation of more than 60 per cent of the remaining vegetation in the river's catchment area (Nair, 1985). In the headwaters of the Chalakudi River construction of four dams has not only resulted in the submergence of large areas of forest (Sebastine and Ramamurthy, 1966), but the increased human use of the area associated with the operation of the dams has had an adverse impact on the integrity of habitats, and on populations of certain animal species (Vijayan, 1978).

Deforestation in the catchment areas of India's dams and reservoirs is a major problem because it has led to widespread siltation and correspondingly reduced storage capacity. By 1980 India's investment in reservoirs was of the order of US $12 billion (Government of India, 1980), but most major reservoirs are silting up at rates several times faster than those projected at the time of their construction. The capacity of the Nizamsagar Reservoir has been more than halved from almost 900 million cu. m to less than 340 million cu. m. There is now not enough water in this dam to irrigate the 1100 sq. km of sugar cane and rice for which it was built, and therefore there is insufficient sugar cane to supply local sugar factories (Das, 1977).

The ecological damage which may result from the construction of artificial reservoirs is beginning to cause much concern in India. For example, public opposition to the loss of habitat, and species extinctions which would result from inundation of 540 ha of tropical rain forest along the Kunthipuzha River, was instrumental in halting the Silent Valley Hydroproject in January 1980 (Goodland, 1985).

Deforestation in the Andaman and Nicobar Islands The forests of the Andaman and Nicobar Islands, though widely logged-over, have remained relatively intact. Nevertheless they are under threat from a growing population and from unsustainable industrial logging practices. The north and middle Andamans have suffered severe degradation, and forests in the south Andamans are over-exploited, the only pristine stretch being the Jarawa reserve (Centre for Science and Environment, 1985). Parts of Great Nicobar also support pristine forests.

Mangroves

There is a very extensive block of mangrove forests on the east coast of India 2000–5000 sq. km (Scott, 1989), part of, and contiguous with another block of mangrove in Bangladesh. This is the Sundarbans mangrove forest, the largest in the world, infamous for man-eating tigers (see chapter 13). Apart from the Sundarbans, mangroves are not extensive in India (Blasco, 1975). In the north-west they are near their northern limits of occurrence and are poor in species and low in stature.

Biodiversity

The rich and diverse flora and fauna of India are a reflection of the country's wide range of climates, latitudes, elevations and biogeographical history. The rain forests hold a high concentration of the nation's total plant and animal diversity and include many species which are endemic.

The Indian mainland flora has been largely derived from Indochina via the Assam corridor, but 35 per cent of species have Southeast Asian affinities. The Andaman Islands have floristic affinity with Burma, the more southerly Nicobars with Malesia. Taken together these two archipelagos have 2200 higher plant species with 10 per cent endemism.

There are estimated to be possibly 45,000 species of plants in India (Lal, 1989). Of these, 15,000 are higher plants, over 4000 species being found in the Western Ghats, just 5 per cent of the land area. Of the 4000, 1800 species are endemic to the Ghats, most of them found in the evergreen forests.

Several distinct centres of endemism exist (Ahmedullah and Nayar, 1987; Nair and Daniel, 1986). The Agastyamalai Hills in the southern part of the Western Ghats are home for at least 150 localised endemics. The Silent Valley–New Amarambalan Reserve basin, also in the Ghats, contains some of the least disturbed rain forest in India, and many rare species. Periyar National Park in Kerala contains no less than 60 per cent rain and monsoon forest and has a rich diversity of plant life.

Threats to plant diversity A workshop held in 1982 indicated that as many as 3–4000 higher plants may be under a degree of threat in India. Since then, the Project on Study, Survey and Conservation of Endangered Species of Flora (POSSCEP) has partially documented the problem, and published its findings in Red Data Books (Nayar and Sastry, 1987).

Certain groups of plants are particularly at risk, notably medicinal plants. A wide variety of these are harvested from the wild in India, and have been over-exploited as local pharmaceutical industries have developed (Husain, 1983). The market continues to grow; demand is estimated to have risen by 7 per cent over the last two decades (Gupta and Sethi, 1983). In the forests, food plants are also widely collected. India, a centre of diversity of wild relatives of domestic food crops, has about 250 such species identified of which 60 are either rare or threatened (Arora *et al.*, 1983).

CONSERVING THE LION-TAILED MACAQUE (*Macaca silenus*)

The lion-tailed macaque is one of the very few mammals that are truely endemic to the south Indian rain forest. Slow to reproduce, it is threatened by loss of habitat, and the long-term stability of the rain forest is vital to its survival.

Its habitat is now confined to the Western Ghats mountain ranges in the states of Kerala, Karnataka and Tamil Nadu. About 60 per cent of the existing 5000 sq. km of habitat has been fragmented into small patches ranging in area from 20 ha to 20 sq. km, and only 20 per cent occurs as patches of more than 100 sq. km. The present population of the lion-tailed macaque is about 3–4000, and about 60 per cent of them are scattered between isolated populations confined to small patches of rain forest, some as small as 30 ha. Many of the patches support only one group, and many more only two or three groups. Patches with more than ten groups are very few.

More than 90 per cent of the existing habitat has been selectively logged in the recent past, but logging activities have now ceased. Nevertheless the smaller forest patches, in particular, are under great pressure from demand for firewood, timber and other forest produce. Hunting in some areas has caused severe population depression or even local extinction of the macaque. Many of the small patches are privately owned and have been underplanted with cardamom or coffee.

Although clear felling and selective logging in rain forest have been stopped, a major threat still facing the lion-tailed macaque comes from proposed hydroelectric projects, especially in the region of Kerala.

More areas of rain forest need to be given the better protection status of a sanctuary or national park if further loss and fragmentation of habitat are to be prevented, and hunting is to be controlled. In addition, more intensive management measures have to be planned in order to ensure the continued survival of macaque populations in small forest patches.

Source: Ajith Kumar

The reserves in the Nilgiri area of Tamil Nadu are treated as a national biosphere reserve with multiple-use objectives. Here a stream runs through the summer resort, used for relaxation by locals and tourists alike. WWF/M. Rautkari

Animal species All vertebrate groups are abundant in India, which has 365 species of mammals, about 1250 species of birds (14 per cent of the world total), over 180 amphibians and over 60,000 described invertebrates (Zoological Survey of India, 1980; WCMC, 1989).

Six endemic mammals are found in the Western Ghats: lion-tailed macaque (*Macaca silenus*) (see case study), Nilgiri leaf monkey (*Trachypithecus johnii*), palm civet (*Macrogalidea musschenbroeki*) Malabar civet (*Viverra megaspila*), spiny-tailed mouse (*Mus* spp.) , and Nilgiri tahr (*Hemitragus hylocrius*). These and many other vertebrates and invertebrates, are protected under the Wildlife (Protection) Act 1972 (as modified), but the legislation does little or nothing to prevent the main cause of threat – loss of habitat.

The rain forest ecosystems of India are very important also for bird diversity. At least 20 threatened species are found there (Collar and Andrew, 1988; WCMC, 1989), most of them in north-east India and on the Andaman and Nicobar Islands. In the Western Ghats the Nilgiri woodpigeon is threatened.

Finally the Western Ghats are renowned for their extraordinary richness of amphibians. Of India's 112 endemic amphibians, 84 are found there (Inger and Dutta, 1987).

Conservation Areas

Protection of wildlife has a long tradition in India, with the establishment of forest reserves and sanctuaries for wildlife advocated as far back as the fourth century BC. Uniform federal legislation for conservation areas came in after Independence in 1947, but well before this a number of national parks and sanctuaries were designated by respective states under a variety of laws. One of the oldest of the sanctuaries is Orang in Assam, established in 1915, while Corbett in the *sal* forests of northern Uttar Pradesh became the country's first national park in 1936.

An extensive system of protected areas was not developed until the 1970s, however, following the enactment of the Wildlife Protection Act in 1972. By 1988 there were 66 national parks and 434 wildlife sanctuaries, covering an area of approximately 141,000 sq. km (4.7 per cent of land area).

In 1988, the Wildlife Institute of India published a comprehensive review of the protected areas system, as part of the National Wildlife Action Plan (see Initiatives for Conservation below) (Rodgers and Panwar, 1988). Based on a biogeographical analysis, the report recommends increasing coverage to 148 national parks and 503 sanctuaries, making a total area of 151,342 sq. km (5.1 per cent of India's land area). A number of these recommendations have already been accepted and the network in December 1989 totalled 65 national parks and 407 sanctuaries, covering 131,787 sq. km. In fact, however, only in about 40 per cent of national parks and 5 per cent of sanctuaries have legal procedures of establishment been completed. This is among a number of significant findings emanating from a recent assessment of national efforts to safeguard and manage India's biological diversity through its protected areas network (Kothari *et al.*, 1989).

The Western Ghats cover an estimated 159,000 sq. km in which there are currently eight national parks with a total area of 2848 sq. km (1.8 per cent) and 39 wildlife sanctuaries covering 13,862 sq. km (8.7 per cent). The management status of the wildlife sanctuaries in this part of India varies enormously. Tamil Nadu's Nilgiri Wildlife Sanctuary (also known as Mukurthi Sanctuary) for example, has no human inhabitants and only small abandoned plantations, while the Parambikulam Wildlife Sanctuary in Kerala includes considerable areas of commercial plantations with heavy resource exploitation. Proposals contained in the Wildlife Institute of India Report increase the number of parks from 7 to 18 and the number of sanctuaries from 37 to 50. The overall extent of protected area coverage would decrease, however, from 15,935 sq. km or just over 10 per cent of the zone to 15,528 sq. km or 9.7 per cent of the zone. This is the result of actions that have already been taken to degazette much of the large Dandeli Wildlife Sanctuary in Karnataka from 5730 sq. km to two smaller areas (Rodgers and Panwar, 1988). Proposed and existing parks in the forest zones are listed in Table 18.4.

North-east India is one of the most crucial areas in the sub-continent for attempts to develop a comprehensive conservation network. It includes a rich diversity of habitats, and significant levels of endemism are present in all animal and plant groups. The states of Assam, Manipur, Meghalaya, Mizoram, Nagaland and Tripura cover 171,423

Table 18.4 Conservation areas of India

Existing and proposed areas, 50 sq. km and over, are listed below. The remaining areas are combined in a total under Other Areas. Forest reserves are not included. For data on World Heritage sites, see chapter 9.

	Existing area (sq. km)	Proposed area (sq. km)		Existing area (sq. km)	Proposed area (sq. km)
WESTERN GHATS – Gujarat			Chimmony★	105	40 (ext)
Sanctuaries			Idukki★	70	
Purna★		160	Kurathimalai★		200
			Neyyar★	128	
WESTERN GHATS – Maharashtra			Palamala★		100
National Parks			Parambikulam★	285	405
Sanjay Gandhi★	87	30 (ext)	Peechi-Vazhani★	125	
			Periyar★	427	427
Sanctuaries			Peppara★	53	
Bhimashankar★	131		Ponmudy★		100
Chandoli★	309		Shenduruny★	100	
Chaprala★	135		Shola Forest		100
Kalsubai-Harishchandragad	362		Wynad★	344	
Koyna★	424†				
Mahabeleshwar★		50	**WESTERN GHATS – Tamil Nadu**		
Phansad★	70		*Sanctuaries*		
Radhanagri	372†		Anamalai	850†	
Rev. Fr. Santapau★		70	Boluvampatti		107
Tansa★	305		Kalakad★	224†	50 (ext)
			Megamalai★		400
WESTERN GHATS – Goa			Mudumalai★	322†	
National Parks			Mundanthurai★	567†	
Bhagwan Mahavir★	107		Mukurthi	78†	
Sanctuaries			*Sub totals*	16,597	5,546
Bhagwan Mahavir★	133				
Cotigao★	105		*Other Areas*	338	*c.* 88
WESTERN GHATS – Karnataka			**WESTERN GHATS Grand Totals**	16,935	5,634
National Parks					
Bandipur★	874		**NORTH-EAST INDIA – Assam**		
Kudremukh★	600		*National Parks*		
Nagarhole★	643	78 (ext)	Dhansiri-Kaki★		100
			Kaziranga★	430	
Sanctuaries			Manas★		317
Ammedikal★		100	Tinkhopani★		100
Bhadra★	492†				
Brahmagiri★	181†		*Sanctuaries*		
Dandeli★	5,730	995	Barail★		300
Gunjawatti/Anjni★		350	Barak★		190
Honavar★		50	Barnadi	26	74 (ext)
Mookambika★	247	120 (ext)	Desangmukh		90
Pushpagiri★		108	Dhansiri-Kaki★		100
Sharavathi★	431	210 (ext)	Dibru★		425
Shettihalli★	396	80	Digboi★		50
Someswara★	88	53 (ext)	Hollongapar★		50
Talakaveri★	105		Innerline★		100
			Laokhowa	70	125 (ext)
WESTERN GHATS – Kerala			Manas	391†	
National Parks			Mikhir Hills★		200
Agastyamalai★		200	Nameri★	137	
Anamudi★		300	Orang	73	
Evarikulam★	97		Pabha	49	41 (ext)
Karimpuzha★		225	Pobitora	16	44 (ext)
Periyar★	350	50 (ext)	Ripu-Chirang★		300
Silent Valley★	90		Sonai-Rupai★	175	
Sanctuaries			**NORTH-EAST INDIA – Meghalaya**		
Agastyamalai★		181	*National Parks*		
Anamudi★		207	Balphakram★	220	150 (ext)
Aralem★	55				

Nokrek★	68	
Nongkhlaw		150
Sanctuaries		
Nongkhyllem★	24	156 (ext)
Rongrengri		200
Saipung Link★		300

NORTH-EAST INDIA – Tripura
Sanctuaries

Central Catchment		50
Trishna	171†	

NORTH-EAST INDIA – Nagaland
Sanctuaries

Intanki★	56†	46 (ext)
Shiloi★		100
Phuliebadze★		70

NORTH-EAST INDIA – Manipur
National Parks

Dzuko★		300
Siroi★		200

Sanctuaries

Dzuko★		100
Kaihlam★		260
Siroi★		100
Taret-Lokehao★		100

NORTH-EAST INDIA – Mizoram
National Parks

Phawngpui/Blue Mts		60
Murlen★		200

Sanctuaries

Dampa★	681†	
Murlen★		200
Ngengpui★		100
Palak★		200
Twai		104
Sub totals	2,587	5,752
Other Areas	343	237
NORTH-EAST INDIA Grand Totals	2,930	5,989

EASTERN HIMALAYA – Arunachal Pradesh
National Parks

Nampdapha★	1,985	515 (ext)
Mouling★	483	317 (ext)
Dibang Valley★		1,000
Lado★		500
Walong★		800
Tirap Evergreen★		100
Tawang		300

Sanctuaries

Itanagar★	140	150 (ext)
Mehao★	282	
D'Ering Memorial	190†	
Pakhui★	862†	138 (ext)
Tawang		300
Kalaktang★		300
Dibang Valley★		1,000
Palin★		250
Lado★		500
Namdapha★		200
Mouling★		700
Walong★		700
Sub totals	3,942	7,770
Other Areas	—	65

ARUNACHAL PRADESH

Grand Totals	3,942	7,835

EAST COAST (West Bengal)
National Parks

Sundarbans★	1,330	

Sanctuaries

Sajnakhali★	362	—
EAST COAST Grand Totals	1,692	

ANDAMAN ISLANDS
National Parks

Little Andaman★		300
Mount Diavolo★		200
Mount Harriet★		110
West Rutland Island★		50

Sanctuaries

Austin-Kishorinagar Mangroves★		50
Interview Island★	134	
Mount Diavolo★		200
North Andaman Peninsula★		100
North Andaman Ridge★		100
Sub totals	134	1,110
Other Areas	386	30
ANDAMAN ISLANDS Grand Totals	520	1,140

NICOBAR ISLANDS
National Parks

Little Nicobar★		159
Mount Thullier★		100

Sanctuaries

Great Nicobar★		200
Sub totals		459
Other Areas	—	10
NICOBAR ISLANDS Grand Totals	—	469

(Adapted from Rodgers and Panwar, 1988; IUCN, 1990 and WCMC *in litt.*)

NB   Only conservation areas in the following biogeographical zones are listed: East Himalaya, Malabar Coast, Western Ghat Mountains, Brahmaputra Valley, Assam Hills, Andaman Islands, Nicobar Islands, West Coast, East Coast (West Bengal only); (Rodgers and Panwar, 1988).
* Area containing moist forest within its boundaries.
† Part or all of sanctuary proposed for designation as national park.
(ext) = extension

sq. km, and yet by December 1989 only four national parks and three wildlife sanctuaries with a total area of 1880 sq. km (1.1 per cent) had been established. Rodgers and Panwar (1988) put forward recommendations for 17 new parks and 50 new sanctuaries which would create a protected area estate of 9381 sq. km (5.5 per cent of the zone's total land area). Protected areas are listed in Table 18.4.

Andaman and Nicobar Islands Six parks and 94 wildlife sanctuaries covering 708 sq. km have already been created on the Andaman and Nicobar Islands. Of the existing protected area system 500 sq. km is terrestrial. This represents six per cent of the islands' combined land area of 8327 sq. km. However, the vast majority of protected areas are small islet reserves (57 have an area of less than one sq. km, only eight cover more than 10 sq. km).

Furthermore, the larger and biologically more significant islands of the Andaman archipelago (North, South, Middle, Little, Baratang and Rutland) have only three small national parks and one tiny wildlife sanctuary. The biggest island, Middle Andaman, has no protected area except the Jarawa Tribal Reserve, which is not designed specifically to protect flora and fauna, although it may play a role in this regard. Proposals published by Rodgers and Panwar (1988), however, would redress this imbalance (see Table 18.4).

Initiatives for Conservation

National Forest Policy The serious depletion of India's forest resources has made it necessary for the Ministry of Environment and Forests to revise the National Forest Policy of 1952. In December 1988 the Ministry announced the new National Forest Policy, the main objectives of which include the following:

- Maintenance of environmental stability through preservation and restoration.
- Conservation of the country's national heritage by preserving the remaining natural forests.
- Checking soil erosion and denudation of water-catchment areas.
- Preventing sand-dunes increasing in desert areas and coastal tracts.
- Initiation of afforestation and social forestry programmes to increase tree cover.
- Ensuring that rural and tribal peoples have adequate supplies of fuelwood, fodder, minor forest products and timber, and increasing the productivity of forests to meet essential needs.
- Encouragement of efficient utilisation of forest produce and maximising the substitution of wood with other products.
- Creation of a people's mass movement, with the involvement of women, to achieve the policy's objectives and to minimise pressure on existing forests.

The Government aims to have at least one-third of the total land area under forest or tree cover. Moreover, in the hilly and mountainous regions, two-thirds of the area should be maintained under such cover to prevent erosion and land degradation. Forest management must also provide 'corridors' of forest to link protected areas and enable separated populations of migrant animals to interbreed. The National Forest Policy makes allowances for tribal and poor people whose livelihoods revolve around forests, by stating that their rights and concessions should be fully protected (Government of India, 1988).

National Wildlife Action Plan At the 15th meeting of the Indian Board for Wildlife in October 1982, Prime Minister Indira Gandhi outlined the basis for a strategy to protect the nation's wildlife resources. A National Wildlife Action Plan was subsequently formulated and presented to the Government of India in November 1983. It was accepted as an official prospectus of actions for wildlife conservation. The main objectives of the National Wildlife Action Plan are:

1 Establishment of a representative network of protected areas. This would cover all significant biogeographic sub-divisions within the country. In 1984 the Government of India commissioned the Wildlife Institute of India to review the existing system and to formulate plans for a revised network of national parks, sanctuaries and biosphere reserves. This review has been completed and many of its conclusions described above (see Rodgers and Panwar, 1988).

2 Management of protected areas and habitat restoration. In order to improve the management of protected areas this would:

- Develop appropriate management systems for protected areas, giving due consideration to the needs of the local population.
- Develop a professional cadre of personnel fully trained in all aspects of wildlife management.
- Restore degraded habitats to their natural state.

3 Wildlife protection in multiple-use areas. The aim is to provide adequate protection for wildlife in multiple-use areas so as to form corridors linking protected areas, and providing for genetic continuity of flora and fauna between them. Specifically the aims are to:

- Evolve guidelines for the management of multiple-use areas which provide for wildlife habitat needs and protection alongside the production of timber, fuelwood and other forest products.
- Develop courses for India Forestry Service probationers and officers in the management of multiple-use areas which include catering for wildlife needs and requirements.

4 Rehabilitation of threatened species. The objective is to rehabilitate indigenous, threatened species of Indian flora and fauna and restore them to protected portions of their former habitats in a manner which reflects their distribution in recent historic times (100–150 years ago). Action required includes:

- The development of guidelines for the assessment of degrees of threat, as a prelude to drawing up a list of threatened species.
- The Government of India should set up a Central Wildlife Translocation Unit in order to assist translocation and re-introduction projects.

5 Captive breeding programmes. This would introduce captive propagation and breeding programmes for selected plants and animals, reintroduce threatened species to the wild, and commercially exploit those species which are plentiful. Specifically the aims are to:

- Identify candidate species for Government-sponsored captive propagation and breeding, and design specific projects for each species.
- Provide training in the propagation of plants and breeding of animals in captivity.

6 Wildlife education and interpretation. The Government is specifically encouraged to promote the concept of wildlife education by:

- Addressing wildlife education to a broader range of target groups, particularly politicians, decision-makers and administrators; school and college students at all levels; and communities living in and around wildlife areas.
- Improving training of government personnel in wildlife education.
- Increasing support for non-governmental organisations.

7 Research and monitoring. The Government aims to develop a better scientific understanding of wildlife populations and habitats to provide for their proper management and, where appropriate, utilisation. This initiative would include collation of data on ecosystems, communities and species, according to priorities determined by a national committee on wildlife research.

8 Domestic legislation and international conventions. Under the Action Plan the Government will review and update statutory provisions which provide protection to wildlife and will regulate all forms of trade. The specific aims are:

- Production of comprehensive legislation, including provision for wildlife and habitat protection; improvement of protected area management; compulsory assessment of environmental impact for all development projects impinging on wildlife areas; and assessment of trade in wildlife.

• Implementation of international conventions, e.g. CITES in India.

9 National Conservation Strategy. A National Conservation Strategy for all living natural resources is already being formulated along the lines of the World Conservation Strategy launched in 1980 by the IUCN, with the collaboration of WWF and UNEP.

10 Collaboration with voluntary bodies. The aim is to enlist support from and collaborate with voluntary non-governmental agencies in achieving the objectives identified by the Action Plan. There is an urgent need to define the role of such organisations and identify particular ways in which they can be of assistance. The Ministry of Environment and Forests has taken a number of initiatives in this respect, including the establishment of ten Environmental Information System (ENVIS) centres, some of which are based with NGOs. It is also supporting the establishment of the Indira Gandhi Conservation Monitoring Centre, in New Delhi, recently created to serve as a central repository for information on India's biological diversity.

References

Ahmedullah, M. and Nayar, M. P. (1987) *Endemic Plants of the Indian Region. Vol. 1. Peninsular India.* Botanical Survey of India, Howrah.

Arora, R. K., Mehra, K. L. and Nayar, E. Roshini (1983) *Conservation of Wild Relatives of Crop Plants in India.* National Bureau of Plant Genetic Resources, Science Monograph no. 6. 14 pp.

Blasco, F. (1975) Les Mangroves de L'Inde. *Institut Français de Pondicherry, Travaux de la Section Scientifique et Technique* **14**: 175

Centre for Science and Environment (1982) *The State of India's Environment 1982: A Second Citizens' Report*, pp. 343–51. Centre for Science and Environment, New Delhi, India.

Centre for Science and Environment (1985) *The State Of India's Environment 1984–5. A Second Citizen's Report.* Centre for Science and the Environment, New Delhi, India.

Champion, H. G. (1936) A preliminary survey of the forest types of India and Burma. *Indian Forest Record (New Series)* **1**: 1–286.

Champion, H. G. and Seth, S. K. (1968) *A Revised Survey of the Forest Types of India.* Manager of Publications, New Delhi.

Collar, N. J. and Andrew, P. (1988) *Birds to Watch. The ICBP World Checklist of Threatened Birds.* ICBP Technical Publication No. 8. Smithsonian Institution Press, Washington, DC, 303 pp.

Das, D. C. (1977) Soil conservation practices and erosion control in India: a case study. In: *Soil Conservation and Management in Developing Countries.* FAO report of an expert consultation, 22–26 November 1976. FAO, Rome, Italy.

Das Gupta, S. P. (1976) (ed.) *Atlas of Forest Resources of India.* National Atlas Organisation, Department of Science and Technology, Government of India, Calcutta. 36 maps.

Department of Forests, Government of West Bengal (1973) *Management plan of Tiger Reserve in Sundarbans, West Bengal, India.* (Map III – District 24 Parganas.) Unpublished. 101 pp.

FAO (1990) *FAO Yearbook of Forest Products 1977–88.* FAO Forestry Series No. 23. FAO Statistics Series No. 90. FAO, Rome.

FAO/UNEP (1981) *Tropical Forest Resources Assessment Project. Forest Resources Of Tropical Asia.* Vol. 3 of 3 vols. FAO, Rome.

FSI (Forest Survey of India) (1986) *National Forest Vegetation Map.* Forest Survey of India. 26 map sheets at 1:1 million scale.

FSI (Forest Survey of India) (1987) *The State of Forest Report.* Government of India, Ministry of Environment and Forests.

FSI (Forest Survey of India) (1989) *The State of Forest Report.* Government of India, Ministry of Environment and Forests.

Goodland, R. (1985) *Environmental Aspects of Hydroelectric Power and Water Storage Projects (with special reference to India).* Paper presented at an International Seminar on the Environmental Impact Assessment of Water Resources Projects, University of Roorkee, Uttar Pradesh, December 12–14, 1985. 30 pp.

Government of India (1980) *Sixth Five Year Plan.* Government of India, New Delhi.

Government of India (1988) *National Forest Policy 1988.* Government of India, Ministry of Environment and Forests, New Delhi.

Gupta, R. and Sethi, K. L. (1983) Conservation of medicinal plant resources in the Himalayan region. In: Jain, S. K. and Mehra, K. L. (eds), *Conservation of Tropical Plant Resources*, pp. 101–9. Botanical Survey of India, Howrah.

Husain, A. (1983) Conservation of genetic resources of medicinal plants in India. In: Jain, S. K. and Mehra, K. L. (eds), *Conservation of Tropical Plant Resources*, pp. 110–17. Botanical Survey of India, Howrah.

Inger, R. F. and Dutta, S. K. (1987) An overview of the amphibian fauna of India. *Journal of the Bombay Natural History Society*, 1886–1986, Centenary Supplement, 135–46.

IUCN (1986) *Review of the Protected Areas System in the Indo-Malayan Realm.* Consultants J. and K. MacKinnon. IUCN, Gland, Switzerland. 284 pp.

IUCN (1990) *1989 United Nation List of National Parks and Protected Areas.* IUCN, Gland, Switzerland, and Cambridge, UK.

Kothari, A., Pande, P., Singh, S. and Variava, D. (1989) *Management of National Parks and Sanctuaries in India.* Indian Institute of Public Administration, New Delhi. 298 pp.

Lal, J. B. (1989) *India's Forests: Myth and Reality.* Natraj Publishers, New Delhi, India.

Mani, M. S. (ed.) (1974) *Ecology and Biogeography in India.* Junk, The Hague, The Netherlands.

Nair, S. C. (1985) Wasting wealth of Western Ghats. In: Bandyopadhyay, J., Jayal, N. D., Schoettli, U. and Chhatrapati Singh (eds), *India's Environment*, pp. 41–51. Natraj, Dehra Dun.

Nair, N. C. and Daniel, P. (1986) The floristic diversity of the Western Ghats and its conservation: a review. *Proceedings of the Indian Academy of Sciences (Suppl.).* Nov. 1986, pp. 127–63.

Nayar, M. P. and Sastry, A. R. K. (eds) (1987) *Red Data Book of Indian Plants*, Vol. 1. Botanical Survey of India, Calcutta. 367 pp.

Pascal, J. P. (1986) *Explanatory Booklet on the Forest Map of South India.* Travaux Français de Pondicherry, India. 87 pp. + 3 map sheets.

Pascal, J. P. (1988) *Wet Evergreen Forests of the Western Ghats of India. Ecology, Structure, Floristic Composition and Succession.* Institut Français de Pondicherry. Tome 20.

Rao, A. S. (1974) The vegetation and phytogeography of Assam-Burma. In: Mani, M. S. (ed.) *Ecology and Biogeography in India*, pp. 204–44. Junk, The Hague, The Netherlands.

Rodgers, W. A. and Panwar, H. S. (1988) *Planning a Wildlife Protected Area Network in India.* Wildlife Institute of India, Dehra Dun. 2 vols.

Saldanha, C. J. (1989) *Andaman, Nicobar and Lakshadweep – An Environmental Impact Assessment.* Oxford and IBH Publishing, New Delhi, India.

Scott, D. A. (1989) *A Directory of Asian Wetlands.* IUCN, Gland, Switzerland, and Cambridge, UK. 1181 pp.

Sebastine, K. M. and Ramamurthy, K. (1966) Studies on the flora of Perambikulam and Aliyar submergible areas. *Bulletin Botanical Survey India* **8**: 169–82.

Shyamsunder, S. and Parameswarappa, S. (1987) Forestry in India – the forester's view. *Ambio* **16**: 332–7.

Singh, J. S., Singh, S. P., Saxena, A. K. and Raivat, Y. S. (1983) The forest vegetation of Silent Valley, India. In: Chadwick, A. C. and Sutton, S. L. (eds), *Tropical Rain Forest: Ecology and Management*. Supplementary Volume. Leeds Philosophical and Literary Society.

Singh, J. S. and Singh, S. P. (1987) Forest vegetation of the Himalaya. *Botanical Review* **53**: 80–192.

Sukhwal, B. L. (1987) *India. Economic Resource Base and Contemporary Political Patterns*. Oriental University Press, London, UK.

Vijayan, V. S. (1978) Parambikulam Wildlife Sanctuary and its adjacent areas. *Journal of the Bombay Natural History Society* **75**: 888–900.

WCMC (1989) *India. Conservation of Biological Diversity*. 58 pp. + 12 appendices. Unpublished.

Whitaker, R. (1985) *Endangered Andamans*. Managing Tropical Moist Forests. Environmental Services Group, WWF–India, MAB India and Dept. of Environment. 52 pp.

Zoological Survey of India (1980) *State of Art Report: Zoology*. Zoological Survey of India, Calcutta. 302 pp.

Authorship

J. B. Lal of the Forest Survey of India with Alan Rodgers and Ajith Kumar of Dehra Dun, with contributions from Duleep Matthai of the Ministry of Environment and Forests in Delhi, V. H. Meher-Homji in Pondicherry, K. Ravindran at the Kerala Forest Research Institute, Shekhar Singh and Pallava Bagla at the Indian Institute of Public Administration in Delhi and Sultana Bashir of Cambridge University, UK.

Maps 18.1 and 18.2 Forest cover in India

In preparing map coverage of India, the editors have been guided by the central purpose of this atlas, which is to portray the remaining rain forests of the region. Where monsoon forests abut onto the rain forests, these have been mapped, but in India, where monsoon forests are very widespread, we have not given complete coverage on the colour maps. There are extensive monsoon forests in central and eastern India, in northern India along the foothills of the Himalaya, and to the west of Bangladesh, as well as in the western and north-eastern areas shown here. These are shown in a generalised way in Figure 18.1.

Forest cover data were digitised from the *National Forest Vegetation Map* (FSI, 1986) published by the Forest Survey of India in 26 sheets at 1:1 million scale. Map sheets used in this analysis were 2. *Arunachal Pradesh*, 3. *Assam*, 5. *Gujarat*, 9. *Karnataka*, 10. *Kerala*, 12. *Maharashtra*, 13. *Manipur*, 14. *Meghalaya*, 15. *Mizoram*, 16. *Nagaland*, 21. *Tamil Nadu*, 22. *Tripura*, 24. *West Bengal*, 25. *Andaman and Nicobar Islands*, and 26. *Union Territories* (Goa only). In addition the following maps were used in preparing figure 18.1: 1. *Andhra Pradesh*, 4. *Bihar*, 11. *Madhya Pradesh*, 11B. *Madhya Pradesh*, 12. *Maharashtra*, 17. *Orissa*, 23. *Uttar Pradesh*, 24. *West Bengal*. For each map, the two categories dense forest (crown density above 40 per cent) and mangrove forest were extracted.

Monsoon and rain forests were further delimited using Champion (1936), Champion and Seth (1968) and, in particular, the *Atlas of Forest Resources of India* (Das Gupta, 1976). Map sheets 16–20 from the atlas, showing forest types of India, were digitised, harmonising forest categories as follows: 'tropical wet evergreen', 'tropical semi-evergreen', 'subtropical broadleaved hill' and 'montane wet temperate' forests were combined into rain forests. The categories 'tropical moist deciduous' and 'tropical dry evergreen' forests were used to delimit monsoon forest. Montane sectors were delimited using a 3000 ft (914 m) contour taken from JNC (Jet Navigation Charts) 36, 37 and 53. Further information on the mangrove forest of the Sundarbans was taken from Department of Forests, Government of West Bengal (1973). *Forest Map of South India* (Pascal, 1986), published by the Karnataka and Kerala Forest Departments and the French Institute, Pondicherry, in three sheets at 1:250,000 scale with an explanatory booklet by J. P. Pascal, was a valuable reference, but was not used in the preparation of our maps. The islands of Lakshadweep (Laccadive) have not been mapped as FSI (1986) and Das Gupta (1976) indicate no tropical forests exist there.

Protected area locations are based on Rodgers and Panwar (1988). Maps showing precise boundaries are unfortunately unavailable to us, and protected areas are represented by circles of an appropriate size.

19
Indonesia

Land area	1,811,570 sq. km†, 1,918,663 sq. km (official)
Population (1989)	184.6 million
Population growth rate (1987–2000)	1.7 per cent
Expected maximum population (2150)	355 million
Gross national product (1987)	US$450 per capita
Rain forest (see maps)	1,148,400 sq. km
Monsoon forest (see maps)	30,740 sq. km
Closed broadleaved/coniferous forest (1980)†	1,138,950 sq. km
Annual deforestation rate (1981–5)†	6000 sq. km
Annual deforestation rate (late 1980s)	up to 12,000 sq. km
Roundwood production*	173,598,000 cu. m
Roundwood exports*	1,131,000 cu. m
Fuelwood and charcoal production*	133,989,000 cu. m
Sawlog and veneer log production*	36,690,000 cu. m
Sawlog and veneer log exports*	3000 cu. m

* 1988 data from FAO (1990)
† FAO/UNEP (1981); FAO (1988)

Indonesia is a huge archipelago extending for 4500 km between the Asian and Australian continents. Once more or less completely covered in tropical rain and monsoon forests, Indonesia still retains well over one million square kilometres of such forests, more than any other nation in the region. Worldwide, only Brazil has more rain forest than Indonesia. There are major biogeographical differences between the different parts of Indonesia, of which the most important are between the western and the eastern ends. This difference is most clearly seen in the animals, which form two groups, divided by Wallace's Line, which lies east of Borneo at the edge of the Sunda continental shelf and is one of the sharpest zoogeographical frontiers in the world. The single most important family of tropical timber trees, the Dipterocarpaceae, is found almost entirely in the lowland rain forests west of Wallace's Line, but in general this frontier is much less important for plants than for animals.

Major exploitation of the Indonesian rain forests for timber began in the 1960s and is continuing today. The lowland rain forests of Sumatra and Kalimantan have been particularly heavily logged and now, although very large areas of forest cover remain, very little is pristine. Exploitation has often been destructive because Forest Department rules have been widely ignored. Moreover, once roads have given access to formerly inaccessible areas, farmers have often moved in after the timber companies and then cleared the relict, regenerating forest for either permanent or shifting cultivation. An exceptionally long and severe drought in 1982–3 was followed in Kalimantan by forest fires, mostly started inadvertently by these farmers. Over thirty thousand sq. km were burned, mostly comprising logged forest containing a lot of dry debris, but there are reports of widespread regeneration. Forests have also been lost through conversion of land to plantation agriculture and to transmigration schemes (see chapter 5).

In recent years the government has progressively tightened enforcement of regulations concerning forest exploitation and timber processing. Indonesia prohibited log exports in 1980; all exported timber is now either sawn or converted to plywood, of which Indonesia is a major world supplier. Export of raw rattan was banned in 1986.

Indonesian forests are fabulously diverse and rich in species. Serious damage, however, has been done over the past quarter century by the rampant timber industry, especially to the west Indonesian dipterocarp rain forests. Some wildlife is known to have been seriously affected, for example clouded leopard, Sumatran rhinoceros and elephant in Sumatra. Exploitation is now starting to focus on the east Indonesian forests. In the late 1970s, FAO and IUCN collaborated on a major review of the requirements for adequate conservation. Reserves which exist, or were proposed following this review, cover 10 per cent of the land area and if effectively implemented should conserve most of the nation's heritage of species. In Indonesia there is now a need to implement existing conservation plans and this will necessitate the strengthening of conservation institutions and a greater conservation awareness amongst decision makers and the public.

INTRODUCTION

Indonesia comprises a 4500 km long chain of islands stretching from Sumatra in the west to Irian Jaya, the western half of the island of New Guinea, in the east. This archipelago of 13,667 islands, of which about 1300 are habitable, forms the greater part of the phytogeographic region technically termed Malesia.

The three islands of Sumatra, Borneo and Java, together with intervening smaller ones, lie on the Sunda continental shelf and formed part of mainland Southeast Asia until geologically recent times. To the west of Sumatra, however, lie the Mentawai Islands separated from it by a deep ocean trench. New Guinea lies on the Sahul continental shelf and has had a land connection with Australia.

In contrast Sulawesi and many of the Moluccan islands appear to have had no recent connection with either continent and to have been islands for a very long time.

The long arc of Sumatra, Java and the Lesser Sundas has a spine of high mountains which in Sumatra runs close to the western coast and which contains many extinct and a few active volcanoes. The island of Borneo is mountainous in the centre and to the north, and has a main range separating Kalimantan from Sarawak and Sabah. Sulawesi is mountainous virtually throughout. New Guinea contains some of the highest country in the southern hemisphere, with most of its mountain ranges lying just to the north of the island's north-west/

south-east axis. Much of this high country exceeds 4000 m and it culminates in Irian Jaya, in the 5039 m Gunung Jaya (Mount Carstenz). In contrast the eastern half of Sumatra, southern and eastern Borneo, and south-western New Guinea are low-lying and in parts swampy.

The peoples of Indonesia are diverse in racial origin, and the nation contains a rich mixture of languages, cultures, religions and customs. There is a central government based in Jakarta (which as Batavia was capital of the former Dutch East Indies), but the country is divided for many administrative purposes into provinces.

The Forests

Indonesia was once clothed in tropical rain forests except for the southern islands of eastern Java, Madura, Bali and the lesser Sunda islands which had tropical monsoon forests. This belt of seasonally dry climate and forests extends into southern Irian Jaya, and northwards into parts of southern Sulawesi.

Indonesia contains more tropical rain forest than any other nation in the Asia–Pacific region. All the different tropical rain forest formations found in Malesia occur in Indonesia, and in fact form their greatest extent here, as is described in the next section.

There are major regional differences in the floristics of the forests. The most important is that lowland rain forests of the Sunda shelf islands, Sumatra and Borneo, have an abundance of Dipterocarpaceae. Animals show even stronger regional differences between western and eastern Indonesia, bounded by Wallace's line. Some key features of the original forest cover may be summarised by islands and island groups as follows:

Sumatra (Sumatera)

• Lowland evergreen rain forest, dominated by dipterocarps, once occurred throughout the lowlands.
• Peat swamp forest and mangroves are extensive along the eastern coast.
• The major mountain spine has extensive montane rain forest, much of it still intact.
• In parts of the slightly dry central intermontane valley and in the far north occur the only natural pine (*Pinus merkusii*) forests in Indonesia (FAO, 1982; Whitten *et al.*, 1984).

Java

• Rain forests were probably originally found in south-western Java and in montane areas, but are now restricted to isolated montane patches.
• Teak, probably introduced by man, is extensively planted in the seasonal lowlands in the centre and east.
• Natural monsoon forests, formerly extensive in northern and eastern Java, are now all heavily disturbed.
• Where fire is excluded the forest begins to change to lower montane forest, subalpine forests and, on the highest mountains, temperate herbaceous formations. Extensive montane grasslands have resulted from forest destruction by fire.
• Limestone karst occurs on the southern and north-eastern coasts, most of which are now planted with teak.
• Freshwater swamp forests and mangroves occur in a few small patches.

Lesser Sunda Islands (Nusa Tenggara)

• Savanna woodland with *Casuarina* and *Eucalyptus* now covers most of these islands.
• Evergreen rain forest was never extensive and only survives in isolated patches in steep valleys on south-facing sides of mountain ranges; elsewhere, there are monsoon forests and extensive grasslands.
• Timor once had extensive natural sandalwood (*Santalum album*) forests (FAO, 1982).
• The montane rain forests are not luxuriant and are characterised by an absence of swathing bryophytes, although some have beards of the lichen *Usnea*.

Kalimantan

• Lowland evergreen rain forests occur up to about 1000 m; above them occur montane forests which, as is the case everywhere in the region, have abundant Fagaceae, Lauraceae and Myrtaceae.
• Kalimantan has massive areas of lowland rain forest as well as extensive mangroves, peat and freshwater swamp forests, and the largest heath forests (kerangas) in Southeast Asia.
• Degradation is extensive, and there are now large areas of secondary forest, and *Imperata cylindrica* grasslands on land degraded by shifting cultivation and excessive forest exploitation.

The Toraut River in Dumoga-Bone National Park, Sulawesi, provides water for irrigation schemes in the valley below. N. M. Collins

Sulawesi
- Extensive tracts of montane rain forests still occur.
- Tracts of lowland rain forests, except in the southwest peninsula, also occur extensively.
- There are few dipterocarps; the main timber species include *Agathis dammara* and ebony *Diospyros* spp. and the flora is less rich than on islands to the west.
- Sulawesi has the biggest tracts of forest over ultrabasic rocks in the tropics (at the head of the Gulf of Bone) with their distinctive forest formation, and also has large areas of karst limestone (especially in the south-west).
- There are only small areas of inland swamp forests.
- Mangroves occur in isolated patches in the south.
- Seasonal climates which once supported monsoon forests occur, mainly in the south (Whitten *et al.*, 1987a).

Moluccas (Maluku)
- The Moluccan archipelago is partly perhumid and partly seasonal so has both rain and monsoon forests, both lowland and montane.
- Other formations include small areas of mangroves and freshwater swamps with extensive stands of sago (*Metroxylon sagu*).

Irian Jaya
- Apart from a belt of monsoon forest and savanna woodland in the far south, the vegetation is one of the largest expanses of pristine tropical rain forest in Southeast Asia.
- Timber trees include *Calophyllum* and *Intsia* in the lowlands and *Agathis* and *Araucaria* in the hills, where they occur as dense stands.
- Lower montane rain forests are found at 1400–3000 m, upper montane forests up to 3400–3600 m, above which subalpine forest and alpine heathland are found.
- Freshwater swamp forests with sago palm and extensive mangrove forests are present, as well as huge tracts of peatswamp forest on the west coast, only discovered in the 1980s.
- In the south is monsoon forest, savanna woodland with much *Eucalyptus*, and grassland.
- The Fak Fak Mountains have limestone forest and large areas of anthropogenic grassland.
- Beach forests have a typical Indo-Pacific strand flora and are better preserved than elsewhere in Malesia.

Forest Resources and Management

Land-use planning in Indonesia depends upon a process of land-use classification at provincial level. This process resulted in the publication of an account of Indonesian forest resources in 1985 (Table 19.1). The *Consensus Forest Land Use Plan* reveals that about 1.13 million sq. km of permanent forest has been identified, and that a further 0.3 million sq. km of forest land is suitable for conversion to non-forest use. This is in addition to 0.49 million sq. km already alienated. Since this assessment was undertaken, there have been improvements in the availability of data on slope, soil, climate and vegetation coverage that have enabled some fine-tuning. The Regional Physical Planning Programme for Transmigration (RePPProT), funded by a loan from the World Bank and bilateral aid from the UK, has undertaken a complete reclassification of Indonesia, based on available satellite imagery, aerial photography and local information. At the time of writing, the data are being drawn together and cannot be presented in detail (RePPProT, 1990), but the general conclusions are clear. There has been considerable agricultural encroachment into forest reserved for conservation or timber production purposes, and there is an urgent need for enforcement of conservation laws. At the same time, the new review of land use potential is likely to recommend that substantial areas of land previously classified as production forest is in fact suitable

Table 19.1 Indonesian forest resources

	Area (sq. km)	% of land area
Permanent forest		
Protection forest	303,160	16
Nature conservation forest	175,213	9*
Production forests		
Permanent	338,660	18
Limited	305,250	16
Sub totals	1,122,283	58
Other land		
Forests for alienation	305,370	16
Alienated	491,010	26
Sub totals	796,380	42
Total	1,918,663	

(Adapted from Departamen Kehutanan (1985), Burgess (1988) and RePPProT (1990))

* This figure includes gazetted terrestrial reserves (see Table 19.3), but not marine reserves. It differs slightly from the figure of 187,250 sq. km given by Burgess (1988), which cannot be reconciled with data available for this atlas.

for alienation (i.e. conversion to other uses), particularly to agricultural tree-crops.

The official statistics resulting from the RePPProT study are as yet unpublished, but the RePPProT team has generously released a set of 1:2.5 million scale forest cover maps for use in the preparation of this atlas (see Map Legend). Using GIS techniques it has been possible to estimate forest cover statistics, detailed in Table 19.2. It must be emphasised that these data are for use only until the official RePPProT report is available, but the data on these maps are expected to be accurate within fairly narrow limits.

Table 19.2 indicates 1,179,140 sq. km of tropical moist forest in Indonesia, of which 1,148,400 sq. km are rain forest. Rain forests occur throughout the archipelago but the greatest extents are in Kalimantan and Irian Jaya, each with over a third of a million sq. km, and Sumatra with almost a quarter of a million. Monsoon forests are much less extensive, only found in the Lesser Sundas, Sulawesi and the Moluccas, with a total of just 30,740 sq. km.

FAO/UNEP (1981) estimated the closed broadleaved and coniferous forest cover of Indonesia in 1980 at 1,138,950 sq. km. In 1987 FAO in Bangkok published a slightly adjusted figure of 1,134,970 sq. km for 1980, a figure of 1,134,730 sq. km for 1985 and a projected figure of 1,132,590 sq. km for 1990 (FAO, 1987).

As so often is the case, the mapped information is slightly more generous in terms of forest cover than data from FAO would suggest. Nevertheless, the difference between the two sets of figures is small, only 4 per cent. It is encouraging to know that the RePPProT project has been able to produce a set of reliable forest maps for one of the largest and most important rain forest areas of the world.

The present extent of unlogged productive forest remains in doubt. Large-scale logging began in 1967 and production figures show that some 435 million cu. m of timber were removed over the following 20 years. Burgess (1988) estimated that this represents the produce from about 120,000 sq. km of production forest and that 524,000 sq. km of unlogged production forest remains as operable production forest and forest for alienation (Table 19.1). This figure does not include the 305,000 sq. km of limited production forest which is at present inaccessible and assumed to be unlogged, although some will have been affected by shifting cultivation.

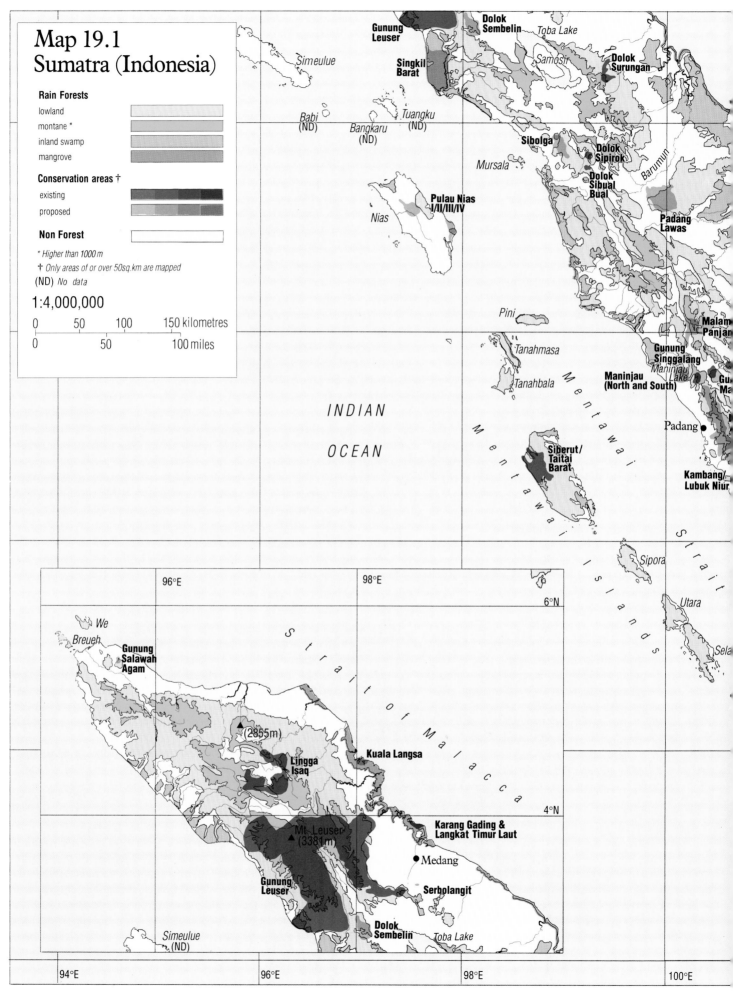

Map 19.1
Sumatra (Indonesia)

Rain Forests

lowland

montane *

inland swamp

mangrove

Conservation areas †

existing

proposed

Non Forest

* Higher than 1000 m

† Only areas of or over 50 sq.km are mapped

(ND) No data

1:4,000,000

| 0 | 50 | 100 | 150 kilometres |
| 0 | | 50 | 100 miles |

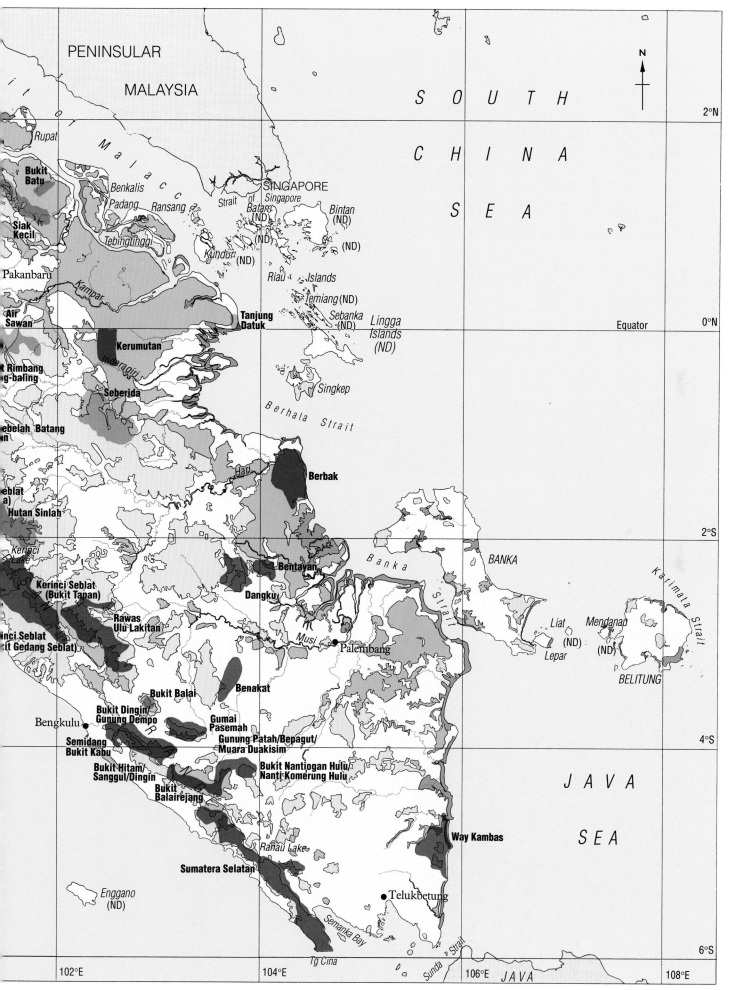

PENINSULAR

MALAYSIA

S O U T H

N

C H I N A

S E A

2°N

Rupat

**Bukit
Batu**

Benkalis

SINGAPORE

Padang   *Ransang*

Strait   of   Singapore

*Bintan
(ND)*

**Siak
Kecil**

Tebingtinggi

*Batam
(ND)*

(ND)

(ND)

*Kundur
(ND)*

**Air
Sawan**

Pakanbaru

Kampar

Riau   Islands

Temiang (ND)

**Tanjung
Datuk**

*Sebanka
(ND)*

*Lingga
Islands
(ND)*

Equator

0°N

Kerumutan

Inderagiri

**t Rimbang
g-baling**

Seberida

Singkep

Berhala   Strait

**ebelah Batang
n**

**eblat
a)**

Hutan Sinlah

Hari

Berbak

*Kerinci
Lake*

2°S

**Kerinci Seblat
(Bukit Tapan)**

Banka

Bentayan

BANKA

Dangku

Karimata Strait

**Rawas
Ulu Lakitan**

Musi

*Liat
(ND)*

*Mendanau
(ND)*

**nci Seblat
it Gedang Seblat)**

Palembang

Lepar

Benakat

BELITUNG

Bukit Balai

**Bukit Dingin/
Gunung Dempo**

**Gumai
Pasemah**

Bengkulu

**Semidang
Bukit Kabu**

**Gunung Patah/Bepagut/
Muara Duakisim**

4°S

**Bukit Hitam/
Sanggul/Dingin**

**Bukit Nantiogan Hulu/
Nanti Komerung Hulu**

**Bukit
Balairejang**

J A V A

Ranau Lake

Way Kambas

S E A

Sumatera Selatan

*Enggano
(ND)*

Telukbetung

6°S

Semanka Bay

Tg Cina

Sunda   Strait

J A V A

102°E

104°E

106°E

108°E

Table 19.2 Estimates of forest extent

	Area (sq. km)	% of land area
SUMATRA (472,610 sq. km)		
Rain forests		
Lowland	123,150	26.1
Montane	32,190	6.8
Inland swamp	65,310	13.8
Mangrove	10,010	2.1
Sub totals	230,660	48.8
JAVA and BALI (138,580 sq. km)		
Rain forests		
Lowland	7,370	5.3
Montane	5,450	3.9
Inland swamp	70	0.1
Mangrove	850	0.6
Sub totals	13,740	9.9
LESSER SUNDAS (89,770 sq. km)		
Rain forests		
Lowland	130	0.1
Montane	210	0.2
Inland swamp	70	0.1
Mangrove	490	0.5
Sub totals	900	1.0
Monsoon forests		
Lowland	12,590	14.0
Montane	1,100	1.2
Sub totals	13,690	15.2
KALIMANTAN (534,890 sq. km)		
Rain forests		
Lowland	298,070	55.7
Montane	25,540	4.8
Inland swamp	62,210	11.6
Mangrove	11,500	2.1
Sub totals	397,320	74.3
SULAWESI (184,840 sq. km)		
Rain forests		
Lowland	77,680	42.0
Montane	21,920	11.9
Inland swamp	2,510	1.4
Mangrove	2,170	1.2
Sub totals	104,280	56.4
Monsoon forests		
Lowland	8,120	4.4
Sub totals	8,120	4.4
MOLUCCAS (69,230 sq. km)		
Rain forests		
Lowland	44,160	63.8
Montane	1,310	1.9
Inland swamp	60	0.1
Mangrove	1,610	2.3
Sub totals	47,140	68.1
Monsoon forests		
Lowland	8,820	12.7
Montane	110	0.2
Sub totals	8,930	12.9
IRIAN JAYA (410,650 sq. km)		
Rain forests		
Lowland	232,610	56.6
Montane	54,660	13.3
Inland swamp	49,590	12.1
Mangrove	17,500	4.3
Sub totals	354,360	86.3
INDONESIA (1,918,663 sq. km)[1]		
Rain forests		
Lowland	783,170	40.8
Montane	141,280	7.4
Inland swamp	179,820	9.4
Mangrove	44,130	2.3
Sub totals	1,148,400	59.9
Monsoon forests		
Lowland	29,530	1.5
Montane	1,210	0.1
Sub totals	30,740	1.6
GRAND TOTALS[1]	1,179,140	61.5

Based on analyses of Maps 19.1 to 19.7. See Map Legend for details of sources.

[1] The areas of the regions are estimated from the maps and are not official statistics. The total area of the country by this method is 1,900,570 sq. km, but for calculating the percentage forest cover for the whole nation we have adopted the official figure for total land area, i.e. 1,918,663 sq. km.

Regional Resources
Sumatra
- The population density on Sumatra (59 people per sq. km in 1980) is relatively high and large areas of rain forest have been cleared for agriculture or industrial plantations (Whitten *et al.*, 1984). On the flat lowlands of southern Sumatra, for example, the great stands of ironwood *Eusideroxylon zwageri*, a species of great commercial importance producing an exceptionally durable timber, have been almost entirely destroyed.
- Relatively large areas of the shallower peat swamp forests along the Malacca Strait are being drained to provide farmland for new transmigrants (see chapter 5).
- About 230,660 sq. km, or 49 per cent, of the original forest cover remains (Table 19.2 and Map 19.1), but there is no doubt that large areas are degraded.
- In recent years there has been heavy logging in the lowlands east of the main mountain spine. Estimates from 1975 indicated that 42 per cent of Sumatra was covered with primary forest at that time (FAO/UNEP, 1981), but the figure is certainly much lower now.
- Figure 19.1 dramatically illustrates the rapid depletion of pristine lowland tropical rain forest in Sumatra (Map 19.1 shows logged as well as pristine forest).
- Sumatra probably continues to lose its natural vegetation faster than any other part of Indonesia.

Figure 19.1 Pristine forests in Sumatra

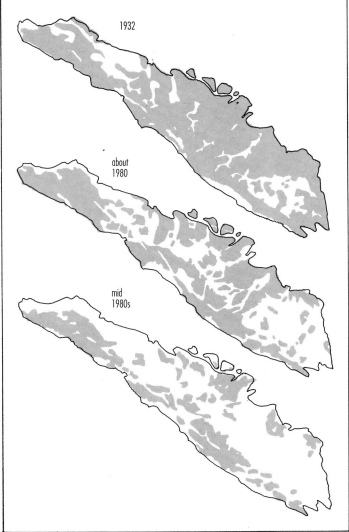

This is based on data from 1932 (Whitten *et al.*, 1984), about 1980 (Whitmore, 1984a) and the mid-1980s (Laumonier *et al.*, 1986). Note that logged forests are excluded from this overview, but are included in Map 19.1, which therefore shows more extensive cover.

Java and Bali
- Java, one of the most densely populated islands in the world, has lost more than 90 per cent of its natural vegetation.
- Primary forests remain only in mountainous regions at elevations above 1400 m.
- Virtually all lowland rain forests have been replaced by farms or plantation forests.
- At the end of 1980 closed broadleaved forest cover was estimated to be only 8 per cent, 11,800 sq. km (FAO/UNEP, 1981), although Map 19.2 indicates slightly more, 13,740 sq. km or 9.9 per cent.

Lesser Sunda Islands
- Tropical rain forests were never extensive and survive only in small isolated patches, usually in steep valleys. Map 19.3 indicates 900 sq. km remaining.
- Seasonal monsoon forests were more widespread, and still cover 13,690 sq. km (15 per cent of land area).
- Closed broadleaved forests were estimated by FAO to cover 25,250 sq. km (28 per cent) at the end of 1980 (FAO/UNEP, 1981), over 10,000 sq. km more than our maps suggest.
- Much of the original forest cover has been degraded by human activity to open savanna woodlands or converted to agriculture.

Kalimantan
- Kalimantan supports the largest expanse of tropical rain forest in Southeast Asia. It is less densely populated than other parts of the archipelago and our data indicate that almost three-quarters of the land surface was still under natural vegetation in the second half of the 1980s, an estimated 397,320 sq. km (Map 19.4 and Table 19.2).
- FAO estimated only 353,950 sq. km of closed forest in 1980, so there is some discrepancy between the data-sets (FAO/UNEP, 1981).
- The lowland forests have been heavily logged since the late 1960s.
- In 1983 a huge area (over 30,000 sq. km) of Kalimantan, including 8000 sq. km of primary forest, was destroyed by fire or drought (Malingreau *et al.*, 1985) (see case study).
- Much of the land officially classed as forest is seriously degraded and huge areas of *Imperata* grassland exist.

Sulawesi
- Sulawesi has extensive tracts of primary rain forest although large areas in the south and some parts of the centre and north of the island have been cleared for permanent and shifting cultivation. Table 19.2 and Map 19.5 indicate forest cover over about 60 per cent of the island, virtually all of this being rain forest.
- The forest cover per inhabitant is greater than in Sumatra, Java, Bali, or the Lesser Sundas. This is partly due to the high proportion of land on steep slopes which are unsuitable for agricultural development (Whitten *et al.*, 1987a).

Moluccas
- The Moluccas comprise an archipelago of hundreds of islands ranging in size from Seram and Halmahera, *c.* 18,000 sq. km each, to small, mostly uninhabited islets with an area of only a few ha.
- The largest tracts of tropical rain forest occur in Halmahera and Seram.
- The small areas of freshwater swamp forest have been partly replaced by stands of sago palm introduced from Irian and cultivated as an important source of starch.
- The Moluccas have an estimated 56,070 sq. km of moist forest, covering over 80 per cent of the land area.
- Although Map 19.6 indicates monsoon forest on Batjan Island and southern Halmahera, recent reports indicate that this may in fact be rain forest.

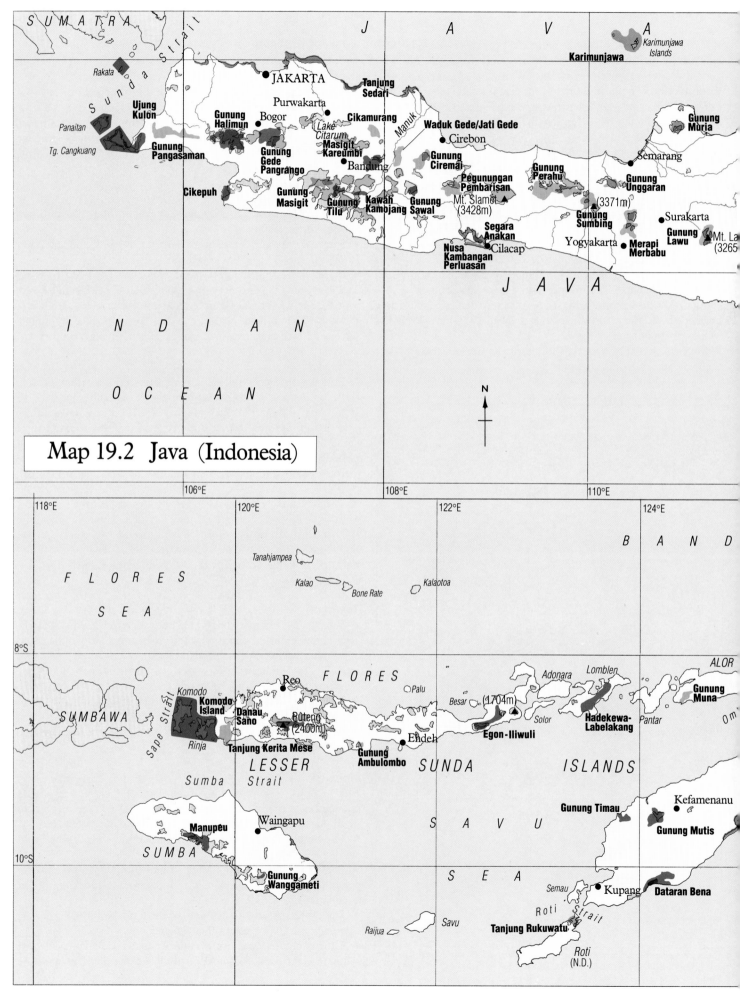

SUMATRA

J A V A

Rakata

Sunda Strait

Ujung Kulon

Panaitan

Tg. Cangkuang

JAKARTA

Purwakarta

Tanjung Sedari

Gunung Halimun

Bogor

Cikamurang

Lake Citarum

Waduk Gede/Jati Gede

Manuk

Cirebon

Gunung Pangasaman

Gunung Gede Pangrango

Masigit Kareumbi

Bandung

Gunung Ciremai

Pegunungan Pembarisan

Gunung Perahu

Karimunjawa Islands

Karimunjawa

Gunung Muria

Semarang

Gunung Unggaran

(3371m)

Cikepuh

Gunung Masigit

Gunung Tilu

Kawah Kamojang

Gunung Sawal

Mt. Slamet (3428m)

Gunung Sumbing

Surakarta

Yogyakarta

Merapi Merbabu

Gunung Lawu

Mt. La (3265

Segara Anakan

Nusa Kambangan Perluasan

Cilacap

J A V A

I N D I A N

O C E A N

N

Map 19.2 Java (Indonesia)

106°E

108°E

110°E

118°E

120°E

122°E

124°E

B A N D

Tanahjampea

F L O R E S

S E A

Kalao

Bone Rate

Kalaotoa

8°S

ALOR

F L O R E S

Adonara

Lomblen

Reo

Palu

Besar

(1704m)

Solor

Gunung Muna

Komodo

Komodo Island

Danau Sano

Ruteng (2400m)

Endeh

Egon-Iliwuli

Hadekewa-Labelakang

Pantar

O m

SUMBAWA

Sape Strait

Rinja

Tanjung Kerita Mese

Gunung Ambulombo

S U N D A

I S L A N D S

Sumba

LESSER

Strait

Manupeu

Waingapu

Gunung Timau

S A V U

Kefamenanu

Gunung Mutis

SUMBA

10°S

Gunung Wanggameti

S E A

Semau

Kupang

Dataran Bena

Raijua

Savu

Tanjung Rukuwatu

Roti Strait

Roti (N.D.)

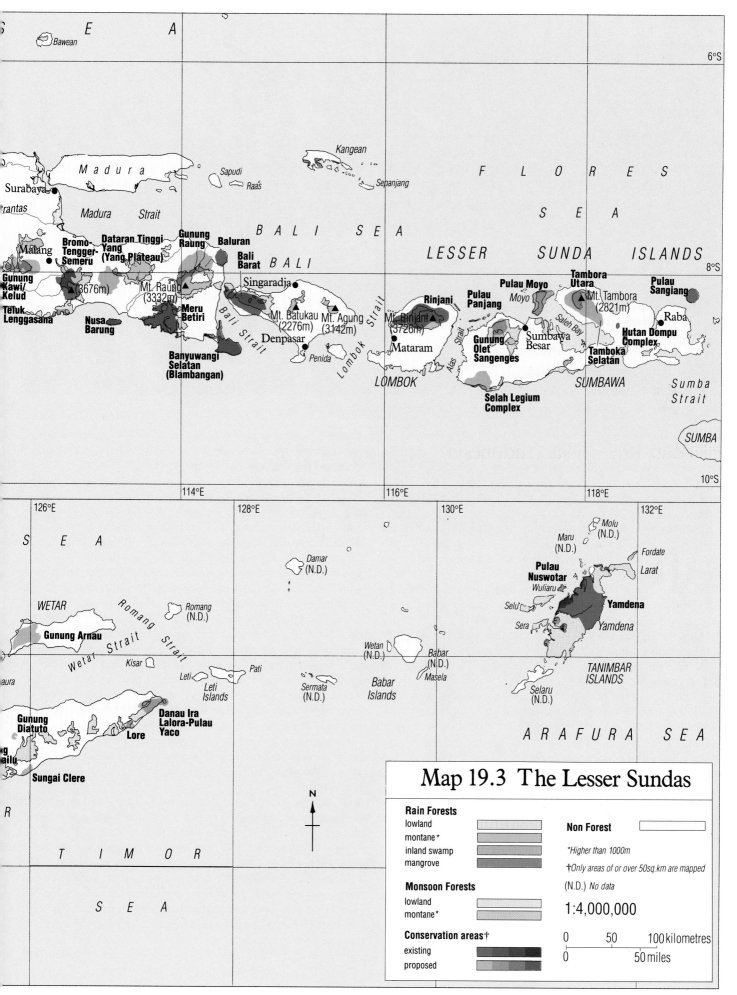

6°S

Bawean

E A

Madura

Sapudi

Kangean

F L O R E S

Surabaya

Raas

Sepanjang

S E A

rantas

Madura   Strait

B A L I   S E A

LESSER   SUNDA   ISLANDS

8°S

Bromo-
Tengger-
Semeru

Dataran Tinggi
Yang
(Yang Plateau)

Gunung
Raung

Baluran

Bali
Barat

B A L I

Tambora
Utara

Pulau
Sangiang

Malang

Gunung
Kawi/
Kelud

(3676m)

Mt. Raung
(3332m)

Meru
Betiri

Singaradja

Pulau Moyo

Moyo

Mt. Tambora
(2821m)

Raba

Teluk
Lenggasana

Mt. Batukau
(2276m)

Mt. Agung
(3142m)

Mt. Rinjani
(3726m)

Rinjani

Pulau
Panjang

Sumbawa
Besar

Hutan Dompu
Complex

Nusa
Barung

Denpasar

Mataram

Gunung
Olet
Sangenges

Saleh Bay

Tamboka
Selatan

Banyuwangi
Selatan
(Blambangan)

Penida

Bali Strait

Lombok Strait

Alas Strait

LOMBOK

Selah Legium
Complex

SUMBAWA

*Sumba
Strait*

SUMBA

10°S

114°E   116°E   118°E

126°E   128°E   130°E   132°E

S   E   A

Molu
(N.D.)

Maru
(N.D.)

Fordate

Larat

Damar
(N.D.)

Pulau
Nuswotar

WETAR

Romang
(N.D.)

Wuliaru

Selu

Yamdena

Gunung Arnau

Romang

Strait

Sera

Yamdena

Wetar   Strait

Kisar

Pati

Wetan
(N.D.)

Babar
(N.D.)

*TANIMBAR
ISLANDS*

aura

Leti

Leti
Islands

Sermata
(N.D.)

Masela

Babar
Islands

Selaru
(N.D.)

Gunung
Diatuto

Danau Ira
Lalora-Pulau
Yaco

Lore

A   R   A   F   U   R   A   S   E   A

ailu

Sungai Clere

R

N

T   I   M   O   R

S   E   A

149

Map 19.3 The Lesser Sundas

Rain Forests

lowland

montane*

inland swamp

mangrove

Non Forest

*Higher than 1000m

†Only areas of or over 50sq.km are mapped

(N.D.) No data

Monsoon Forests

lowland

montane*

1:4,000,000

Conservation areas†

existing

proposed

0   50   100 kilometres

0   50 miles

Logged-over and heavily degraded forest on Obi Island in the Lesser Sundas, Indonesia. D. Laurent

Irian Jaya

● Irian Jaya, the eastern-most province of Indonesia, shares a common 736 km long border with Papua New Guinea.

● The freshwater swamp forests include huge stands of native sago palm, managed and utilised as their staple food by the indigenous people.

● The mangrove forests are second in extent only to those of the Sundarbans forest of India and Bangladesh. They have recently come under threat of exploitation, and possible destruction, to provide wood chips (Petocz, 1985).

● About 86 per cent (354,360 sq. km) of Irian Jaya remains forested and relatively undisturbed, because the population is low and concentrated mainly in some parts of the mountains.

● Extensive logging concessions have now been granted and there are plans for substantial transmigration schemes.

Deforestation

The annual rate of deforestation in Indonesia was estimated at 5500 sq. km per year for the years 1976–80, and 6000 sq. km per year for 1981–5. More recently rates of 7000 sq. km per year have been quoted (Repetto, 1988), but 11,000 sq. km per year (Gillis, 1988) and even 12,000 sq. km per year (Myers, 1989) have been feared. Such deforestation rates place Indonesia second in the world only to Brazil. Despite the high rate of deforestation in the Indonesian archipelago, however, tropical rain forests still occur extensively on all the large islands. Nevertheless, the area of the original vegetation cover has been considerably reduced, and much of the remaining forest has been seriously disturbed by logging and shifting agriculture.

Agricultural settlement Traditional swidden agriculture within large expanses of rain forest is relatively harmless, in contrast to smallholder agricultural settlement, which gradually makes inroads at the forest margins. Where the latter is unplanned, it has become a major factor contributing to the degradation of Indonesia's forests. All too often spontaneous agricultural settlement (shifting cultivation) along

the forest margins employs crude and exploitative agricultural techniques which, combined with inappropriate soils, inevitably lead to forest and soil degradation (see chapter 4).

Shifting cultivation is far more extensive than traditional swidden and is now the dominant form of land-use in most of Kalimantan and Irian Jaya, and frequently in Sumatra, Sulawesi and the Lesser Sundas. Indonesian Forestry Department Statistics (1985–6) indicate that approximately one million families are practising shifting cultivation on 73,000 sq. km of land. However, the number of part-time shifting cultivators in Indonesia undoubtedly far exceeds this figure, and the national Land Resources Development Centre estimates the area under shifting cultivation in Kalimantan alone to be 112,000 sq. km. Furthermore, the area of forests affected by shifting agricultural activities in the Indonesian archipelago is increasing, possibly by as much as 5000 sq. km per year (chapter 5). There is some local resistance to suggestions that shifting cultivators are responsible for forest degradation, particularly from people who believe that the response will be attempts to relocate families from the forest without providing them with an alternative means of support. This is a valid concern because a number of such initiatives which were sponsored by Indonesian agencies in the past (e.g. village ment programmes), have failed because they involved forced relocation or because they provided insufficient land to maintain productivity.

In addition to the enormous spread of unplanned smallholder agricultural settlement, Indonesia has undertaken a substantial planned settlement programme within the rain forests. This 'Transmigration Programme', and its impact on the forests, is described in detail in chapter 5.

Substantial areas of Indonesia's lowland forests have been converted, or are scheduled to be converted, to industrial tree crop plantations such as oil palm and rubber. The recent reassessment of land use potential throughout the archipelago has indicated that many more areas currently under natural forest are suitable for such conversion (RePPProT, 1990). Deforestation to accommodate these crops is likely to accelerate rapidly in years to come.

Logging The logging industry has developed from almost nothing since about 1967, soon after President Suharto came to power, though the groundwork had been laid several years earlier. The new government awarded generous timber concessions to foreign companies eager to exploit the vast, untapped stands of valuable hardwoods. By 1988 concessions had been established over approximately 534,000 sq. km (Burgess, 1988), slightly in excess of Indonesia's potentially productive lowland forests (see Forest Resources and Management, page 143). There has been progressive replacement of foreign by local companies and an increase in local processing of the timber so that, instead of logs, sawn timber and plywood have been exported since 1980.

Timber concessions are granted by the Forestry Department for 20 years, which is substantially shorter than the harvest cycle of 35 years. This encourages some timber companies to take a short-term view because they believe it is not likely that they will be able to take advantage of a second harvest. Dipterocarp forests are exploited on a selection system with a minimum felling diameter of 50 cm dbh, but enforcement of concession terms has been difficult as there are insufficient staff to monitor harvesting in remote areas. Felling below the legal girth limit is apparently rarely practised, but the residual stand is very badly damaged because of poor techniques (Burgess, 1988). Concessions tend to be creamed for the best trees so that the whole forest is logged long before the expiry of the cycle; this is then followed by requests to relog before the cycle period has elapsed (Burgess, 1988). The Forest Department has progressively tightened enforcement of the regulations, but huge areas of forest have been destructively exploited and these degraded areas pose a serious future challenge. A completely unexpected hazard of logging is that the rain forest becomes vulnerable to fires (see case study below).

THE GREAT FOREST FIRE OF BORNEO, 1982–3

At the end of an uncommon (but not unprecedented) 18-month long drought in 1982–3 the largest forest fire in recorded history burned a huge area of East Kalimantan. The total area destroyed either by fire or by the drought itself was *c*. 33,000 sq. km, equal in size to the whole of Taiwan or the Netherlands (Figure 19.2), 17 to 20 times the area of the much publicised Australian bush fires of 1982, or about 1500 times the size of the area burned by forest fires which raged in France at the end of 1984. In East Kalimantan, the province which makes the greatest contribution to Indonesia's timber production, the area affected included approximately 8000 sq. km of unlogged dryland primary rain forest, 5500 sq. km of peat swamp forest, 12,000 sq. km of selectively logged forest and 7500 sq. km of shifting cultivation and settlements (Malingreau *et al.*, 1985). In the Malaysian state of Sabah a further 10,000 sq. km of forest lands were severely damaged.

The drought was associated with the 1982–3 El Niño Southern Oscillation Event. The fire started during the drought in the fields of farmers who had moved in after logging, in many cases illegally. It was able to spread quickly in logged forest where dead, dry remains of trees littered the forest floor and also in peat swamp forest, where the dry surface peat burned fiercely, destabilising trees which were then toppled by the wind. In the peat swamps near the Mahakam River coal seams at the surface also caught alight and assisted the fire's progress.

Besides damage to the forests, other consequences of the Great Forest Fire of Borneo included:
• Significant increases in erosion (with associated damage to fisheries and reduced navigability of rivers).
• Disruption of the traditional lifestyles of local inhabitants through loss of forest products.
• Destruction of wild animal populations.
The same drought also resulted in fires in Sumatra and Halmahera (Moluccas). Another lesser drought in 1987 was followed by fires in Sumatra and in south Kalimantan.

300 km

Figure 19.2 The location of forest areas killed by drought and fires in Borneo, 1982–3
(*Source:* after Malingreau *et al.*, 1985)

Logging in Indonesia leaves behind large quantities of debris that represent a serious fire risk during periods of drought. WWF/A. Compost

There is little or no published information about the regeneration of the drought-stricken and burnt forests; indeed there was little information made available at the time of the drought itself. There are now reports that over 600 sq. km of former natural forest land is being turned over to industrial timber plantations, mainly of *Albizia*, *Gmelina* and *Eucalyptus*. At the height of the drought vast areas of forest appeared to be dead. Only the biggest trees, such as *Koompassia excelsa*, remained in leaf. By 1989, however, P. Burgess, a forester working in the region, noted that many of the dipterocarps were turning green once more. The areas affected by drought and fire have not been excised from Map 19.4 partly because of a lack of detailed data, but also because regeneration appears to be quite possible if the forest is given an opportunity to recover.

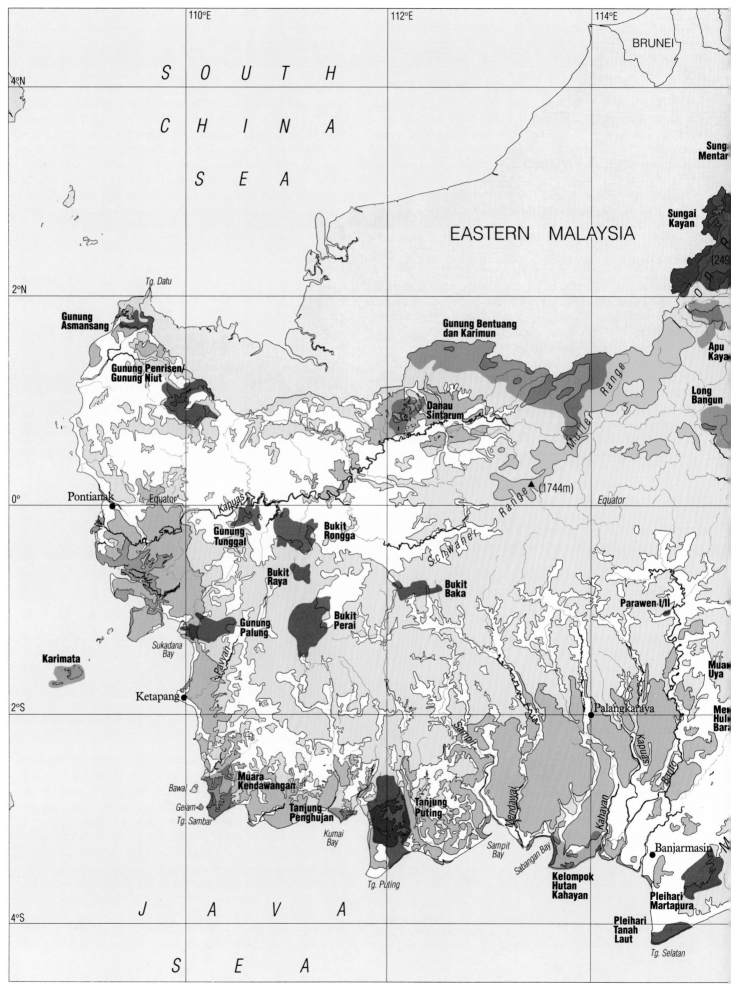

Map 19.4 Kalimantan (Indonesia)

Rain Forests

lowland

montane*

inland swamp

mangrove

Conservation areas†

existing

proposed

Non Forest

* *Higher than 1000m*

† *Only areas of or over 50sq.km are mapped*

(N.D.) *no data*

1:4,000,000

| 0 | 50 | 100 | 150 kilometres |

| 0 | 50 | 100 miles |

Consequences of deforestation Loss of Indonesia's tropical rain forests has had severe biological, social and physical consequences. In Indonesia, as elsewhere, careless forest exploitation with cynical disregard of the rules laid down for log extraction and road construction, has led to substantial soil erosion, with consequent silting of rivers and irregularity of river flow. In the uplands of Java dense populations, continually advancing into steeper upper watersheds and more marginal environments, have had significant and destructive effects on nutrient outflow, total water yield, peak stormflows and stream sedimentation (see also Bengkulu case study for Sumatra). On Java, particularly extensive erosion has occurred, notably in areas under annual cropping systems where the soil is disturbed and left exposed during critical periods (e.g. during the transition from the dry to the wet seasons). A variety of government projects and programmes seek to promote changes in farming systems and land use in order to limit environmental degradation, but in many upland communities soil and water conservation practices have been adopted only to the extent that they serve to improve yields in the short term.

Erosion can also make a serious and expensive impact on irrigation schemes. For example, in 1973 the Gumbara irrigation scheme was initiated in the Palu valley (Sulawesi) with the intention of supplying water for the development of 115 sq. km of rice fields. Twenty-three years later, however, only 50 sq. km were being irrigated and the irrigation canals now have to be dredged every year when about 30,000 cu. m of soil is removed. This excessive siltation results largely from the activities of a logging company which has been active since 1978 (Whitten *et al.*, 1987a).

HEAVY FLOODS FOLLOW FOREST DESTRUCTION IN BENGKULU PROVINCE, SUMATRA

The conversion of forest into agricultural holdings, some of which have proved ephemeral and been abandoned, is a particularly serious cause of conservation problems in Sumatra. It is estimated that between 65 and 80 per cent of the forests in the lowlands of Sumatra have already been lost (see Figure 19.1). The mountain areas have so far been less seriously affected, but the disruption of continuous cover is already substantial in some cases (see Kerinci-Seblat case study), and perhaps 15 per cent of their total area has already been removed.

The lowland forests that are so rich in both plants and animals are being destroyed indiscriminately in Bengkulu Province and this has led to serious environmental problems affecting thousands of villages. The loss of lowland forests is nowhere more serious than on either side of the main road running north from Bengkulu to Muko-Muko. The scale of deforestation of such rich wildlife habitat is enormous, and their destruction had been carried out with international involvement in replacing tropical rain forest by monocultures of oil palm and cocoa. These activities were directly responsible for floods which in 1988 in Bengkulu province destroyed the possessions of thousands of people. Deforestation was followed by soil erosion and massive landslides and floods when the rains finally arrived. In the absence of forests, flood control measures have proved both expensive and rather ineffective.

Source: Charles Santiapillai

Mangroves

Mangroves are estimated to cover 44,130 sq. km in Indonesia (Table 19.2), representing a major increase over an earlier estimate of 21,700 sq. km (IUCN, 1983). They are most extensive in Irian Jaya, particularly around Bintuni Bay in the north-west, but large tracts and many smaller formations occur scattered throughout the archipelago (Koesoebiono et al., 1982; Soegiarto and Polunin, 1982; Petocz, 1985 and Subagjo, 1987).

Indonesian mangroves were little affected by large-scale forest exploitation until 1975 (IUCN, 1983), but they are probably now the most threatened forests in the archipelago (Petocz, 1985). Some destruction of mangroves has occurred as a result of over-exploitation by traditional users, but most destruction results from conversion of the land for agriculture, brackish water fishponds, salt ponds, and human settlement (Hanson and Koesoebiono, 1987). Fishponds are particularly extensive in Sulawesi, Java and Sumatra, extending to about 1850 sq. km by 1982 (Soemodihardjo, 1984).

Since the mid-1970s mangrove forests in Indonesia have also been utilised for wood chips, exported to Japan for the production of cellulose or paper. There is no evidence that the care necessary to exploit the mangroves in a non-destructive manner is being taken, and in consequence forest regeneration is poor.

Biodiversity

No other country has responsibility for more diverse and unique species than does Indonesia. Although Indonesia occupies only 1.3 per cent of the land surface of the globe it contains an estimated 10 per cent of all plant species, 12 per cent of mammals, 16 per cent of reptiles and amphibians and 17 per cent of birds. This is partly because it is situated at the heartland of the Asia–Pacific humid tropics, but also spreads into large areas of seasonal climate, so that both rain forest and monsoon elements occur. Indonesia's wildlife is influenced by both the geological supercontinents of Gondwanaland and Laurasia, each of which has contributed a rich and distinctive biota, fairly sharply delimited (especially for animals) at Wallace's Line. The small geologically isolated islands west of Sumatra, particularly the Mentawai Islands, have developed a suite of endemic species, including four primates. New Guinea and Borneo are probably the individual islands with greatest richness and diversity. Information on the non-Indonesian parts of these great islands may be found in chapters 21 and 24 respectively.

Indonesia's flora is one of the richest in the world, encompassing most of the Malesian floristic region, which has over 25,000 species of flowering plants including about 10,000 trees (FAO, 1982). About 40 per cent of plants are endemic at the generic level. Western Malesia is the centre of diversity of dipterocarps, which form the basis of the logging industry. About 262 of 386 species of dipterocarps are found in Kalimantan, which is being heavily logged as a result. On small plots of about one hectare Bornean rain forests are uniquely rich in tree species, only equalled by parts of Amazonia (Whitmore, 1990).

About 430 of Indonesia's 1500 species of birds, almost 200 of its 500 mammals, and a large proportion of the 1000 reptiles and amphibians and unknown numbers of invertebrates are found nowhere else. Even within Indonesia many are very localised. The parts of Indonesia lying on the Sunda Shelf, i.e. Sumatra, Java, Bali and Kalimantan, include some of the large placental mammals, such as tiger, rhinoceros, elephant, orang utan, serow and banteng. In contrast, the mammalian fauna of Irian Jaya, on the Sahul Shelf, is

The consequences of total deforestation are disastrous for soils. Even on gentle slopes, gulley erosion can occur, as here in Sulawesi. N. M. Collins

characterised by marsupial cuscuses (*Phalanger* spp.), tree kangaroos (*Dendrolagus* spp.), and bandicoots (*Echymipera* spp.), and the monotreme long-nosed echidna (*Zaglossus bruijni*). Other than man, there are no primates in Australia and New Guinea. Between these Sunda and Sahul groups of islands lies Wallacea, a biogeographical zone that includes Sulawesi, the Lesser Sundas and the Moluccas, which contain a curious mixture of Asian and Australian fauna including bizarre forms such as the babirusa and the anoas (*Bubalus* spp.), as well as macaques, tarsiers, squirrels and cuscuses. Rodents and bats are numerous and include a wealth of endemic forms such as the true giant rats and water rats of Irian Jaya as well as smaller nectar-eating bats upon which many fruit trees are dependent for pollination.

The bird life is extraordinary in its richness and range of form and habitat. Among the endemics are the birds of paradise and bower birds, the flightless cassowaries, diverse families of honeyeaters, kingfishers, pigeons, and various parrots. The megapodes are large ground-nesting birds that incubate their eggs in soil warmed by hot springs or rotting organic matter. Other spectacular species include hornbills, many raptors and a wealth of forest specialists such as barbets, pittas, pheasants, flycatchers and whistlers.

Four species of crocodiles occur in swampy and coastal areas, some of which are bred in special ranches that bring revenue to rural people. The small islands off Flores are home to the world's largest lizard, the Komodo dragon *Varanus komodoensis*. Flying and frilled lizards, freshwater turtles, skinks, geckos and tree frogs form rich assemblages of species.

Insect life is spectacular, and includes the birdwings (*Troides* and *Ornithoptera* spp.), which are the largest butterflies in the world and some of the rarest (Collins & Morris, 1985). Several species are being reared in butterfly farms to supply zoos in Europe and North America.

There have already been extinctions, of which the Bali and Java subspecies of tiger (*Panthera tigris balica* and *P. tigris sondaica*) are probably best known. Unfortunately Indonesia has the world's longest list of vertebrates threatened with extinction, including 126 birds (Collar and Andrew, 1988), 63 mammals and 21 reptiles (IUCN, 1988). Most species are threatened because they cannot survive rain forest clearance. A few examples may be given here:

1 The most serious threat to the clouded leopard and other large mammals in Sumatra is clear felling of forests for conversion to agriculture or human settlements. At the turn of the century when much of Sumatra was principally covered with primary rain forest, the clouded leopard probably maintained continuous populations throughout the island. Today this species, although still found in the eight provinces of Sumatra, occurs only in a few isolated areas (Santiapillai, 1986).

2 Forest clearance has also adversely affected the status of some bird populations. The last recorded sighting of the Caerulean paradise-flycatcher took place in 1978 on the upper slopes of Mount Awu on Sangihe, an island located off the northern tip of north Sulawesi (White and Bruce, 1986). Virtually all of Sangihe has now been converted to coconut and nutmeg plantations or else is covered by patches of secondary forest. Some primary forest remains on Mount Sahendaruman in the south of Sangihe, but even if a few flycatchers remain in this small area it is unlikely to be large enough to ensure the survival of the species (Whitten *et al.*, 1987b). The Javan wattled lapwing (*Vanellus macropterus*) is already believed to be extinct (MacKinnon, 1988).

To those who appreciate Indonesia's incredible natural wealth, little more needs be said to warrant its preservation and protection. To the vast number of rural Indonesian citizens, whose lives are closely tied to the forests or depend upon the sea for their subsistence and livelihood, conservation of natural resources has become a growing imperative, so that the benefits they now enjoy can be sustained into the future. Those who seek to exploit the natural resources on an industrial scale remain to be persuaded that the long-term wealth of the archipelago, and perhaps the welfare of the world, is linked with sustainable utilisation of this biological diversity.

Conservation Areas and Initiatives for Conservation

Conserving the nation's biological heritage presents an exceptional challenge to Indonesia, but one that can be met. The Government has recognised the urgent need for conservation and, in view of the progressive loss of its natural vegetation, is planning to increase substantially the area of forest estate under protection by the end of the century. With the present rate of change, any areas left unprotected by that time are not likely to remain intact.

At present the archipelago has over 320 conservation reserves covering some 175,000 sq. km or 9.1 per cent of land area (Table 19.3). In addition to these gazetted areas, there are several major sources of proposals for new protected areas and extensions to existing areas.

1 A further 185 areas encompassing almost 30,000 sq. km have been recommended by PHPA, and await a decision by the Ministry of Forestry. Many of these areas have been chosen because of their water catchment functions as well as to protect areas of biological richness (FAO, 1982; IUCN/UNEP, 1986).

2 Additional proposals have been made in an eight-volume National Conservation Plan produced in 1982 by the government of Indonesia with FAO assistance (FAO, 1982). Objectivity to ensure conservation of all species and habitats was a major tenet of the Plan. However, practical considerations were also taken into account and the candidate sites were evaluated by quantifying the relationship between three factors: importance in preserving genetic diversity, socio-economic justification, and management viability.

3 Proposals in the Conservation Plan have been supplemented by the identification of key conservation sites in the Marine Conservation Plan (Salm and Halim, 1984), the Irian Jaya Conservation Development Strategy (Petocz and Raspado, 1984) and the Indonesian wetland inventory (Silvius *et al.*, 1987).

These proposals together recommend an additional 200 areas which have yet to be approved. They total 212,530 sq. km (11.1 per cent of land area).

The existing and proposed protected area system of the country offers excellent coverage of all habitat types. If the Government implements in addition most of the recommendations included in the National Conservation Plan it will have one of the finest and most comprehensive protected area networks in Southeast Asia (IUCN/ UNEP, 1986). There is no need for further surveys to identify more new protected areas; the priority must now be the implementation of existing proposals and management plans (IUCN/UNEP, 1986). These have recently been further refined by the identification of key reserves for priority action (RePPProT, 1990).

One of the major constraints to implementation, however, is a lack of trained and motivated personnel. Staff recruited from the forestry service are usually not trained in the theory or practice of protected area management, and forest guards and park wardens lack motivation and are poorly paid. There is therefore an urgent need for manpower development before conservation work can begin. Increased funding is also needed. The total budget and revenues provided by the Ministry of Forestry for conservation in Indonesia's fourth Five Year Plan (1984–9) were about US $12 million. Less than US $2 million were allocated for protected area management. This is not sufficient to ensure that the country's reserves are efficiently managed. Increased financial resources must be mobilised if Indonesia's network of parks is to provide any meaningful protection to a biological heritage that is of major global significance.

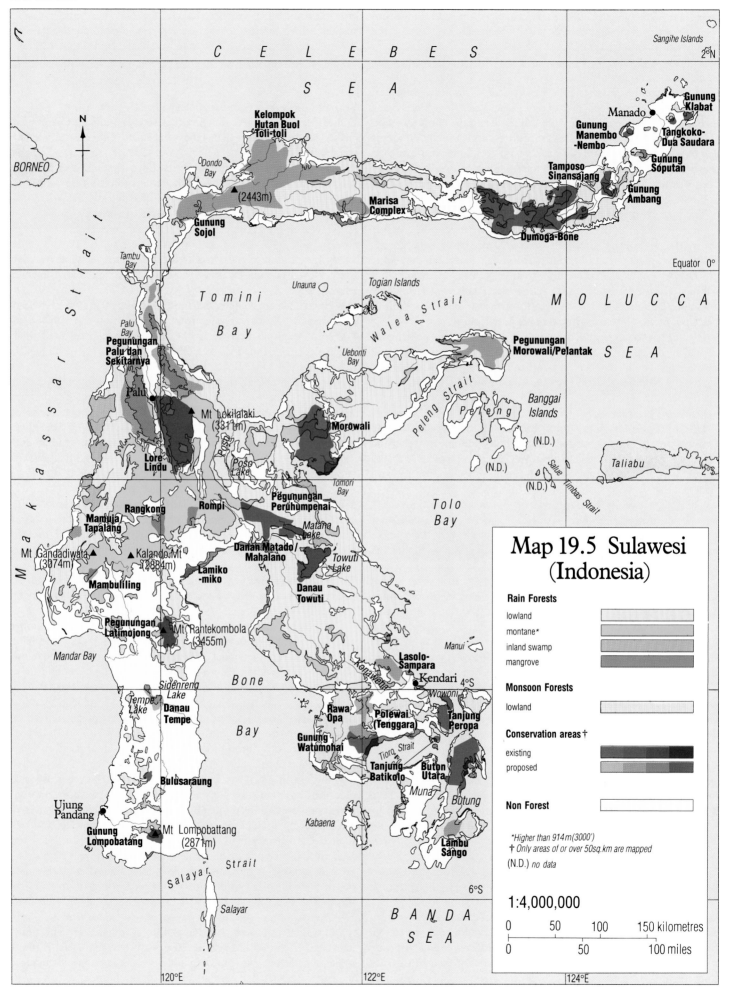

C E L E B E S

S E A

Sangihe Islands

2°N

Kelompok Hutan Buol Toli-toli

BORNEO

N

Dondo Bay

Manado

Gunung Klabat

Gunung Manembo-Nembo

Tangkoko-Dua Saudara

Gunung Soputan

Tamposo Sinansajang

Gunung Ambang

(2443m)

Gunung Sojol

Marisa Complex

Dumoga-Bone

Tambu Bay

Equator 0°

Togian Islands

M O L U C C A

T o m i n i

Unauna

Walea Strait

Pegunungan Morowali/Pelantak

Palu Bay

B a y

Uebonti Bay

S E A

Pegunungan Palu dan Sekitarnya

Peleng Strait

Banggai Islands

Palu

Pe l e n g

(N.D.)

Lore Lindu

Mt Lokilalaki (3311m)

Salue Timbas Strait

Taliabu

Poso Lake

Morowali

(N.D.)

Tomori Bay

(N.D.)

T o l o

M a k a s s a r   S t r a i t

Rangkong

Rompi

Pegunungan Peruhumpenai

B a y

Mamuja Tapalang

Matana Lake

Mt Gandadiwata (3074m)

Kalando Mt (2884m)

Danau Matado/ Mahalano

Towuti Lake

Lamiko-miko

Mambuliling

Danau Towuti

Map 19.5 Sulawesi (Indonesia)

Pegunungan Latimojong

Mt Rantekombola (3455m)

Manui

Rain Forests

lowland

Mandar Bay

montane*

inland swamp

Sidenreng Lake

Lasolo-Sampara

mangrove

B o n e

Kendari

4°S

Wowoni

Monsoon Forests

Tempe Lake

Danau Tempe

Konaweha

lowland

B a y

Rawa Opa

Polewai (Tenggara)

Tanjung Peropa

Conservation areas†

existing

Gunung Watumohai

proposed

Bulusaraung

Tiora Strait

Tanjung Batikolo

Buton Utara

Muna

Non Forest

Ujung Pandang

Butung

Kabaena

Higher than 914m(3000')

Gunung Lompobatang

Mt Lompobattang (2871m)

Lambu Sango

† *Only areas of or over 50sq.km are mapped*

(N.D.) *no data*

S a l a y a r   Strait

1:4,000,000

Salayar

B A N D A

0   50   100   150 kilometres

S E A

0   50   100 miles

120°E

122°E

124°E

6°S

126°E 128°E 130°E

P A C I F I C

Wayabula *Tg. Sopi*

Rau *Morotai*

Doi
(N.D.)

2°N

O C E A N

M O L U C C A

Mayu **Gunung
Gamkonora** **Lolobata**

S U L A W E S I *H a l m a h e r a*

Ternate *Buli
Bay*

*Ternate
Islands
(N.D.)* Soasiu **Ake Tajawi** *Sayafi*

S E A *Weda
Bay*

Equator 0°

Mauri **Saketa**

Latalata *Gebe*

Kasiruta H A L M A H E R A

Bacan S E A

Mandioli **(211m)** *Tg. Libobo*

**Gunung
Sibela** *Damar*

O b i *S t r a i t*

(N.D.) *Bisa*

Obilatu **Pulau
Obi** *Tubalai*
(N.D.)

Taliabu *Mangole* *Obi* *Misool*

Taliabu *Gomumu* 2°S

(N.D.) *(N.D.)*

Sula Islands *Sanana*

Tg. Waka S E R A M S E A

**Manusela
Wai Nua /
Wai Mual**

*Sawai
Bay* **Wae Bula**

Boano **Gunung
Sahuai** Bula

Melang *Manipa*

**Gunung
Kelapat
Muda** **(2114m)** *Piru
Bay* **(3019m)**

B *u* *r* *u* *Manipa
(N.D.)* *Elpaputih
Bay* *Teluti
Bay*

Ambon *Saparua*

Ambelau Ambon *Haruku*

Ambon 4°S

Map 19.6 Moluccas (Indonesia)

Rain Forests

lowland

montane*

mangrove

Non Forest areas

* Higher than 1000m

† Only areas of or over 50sq.km are mapped

(N.D.) no data

Monsoon Forests

lowland

montane*

1:4,000,000

Conservation areas†

existing

proposed

0   50   100   150
kilometres

0   50   100 miles

B A N D A   S E A

HUMAN ENCROACHMENT IN SUMATRA'S CONSERVATION AREAS

The Kerinci–Seblat National Park (Figure 19.3) is situated along the Barisan mountain range in the southern half of Sumatra. With a total area of 14,847 sq. km it is the largest conservation area in Sumatra. The importance of Kerinci–Seblat lies in the fact that the forests protect the watersheds of two of Sumatra's most important rivers, the Musi and Batang Hari. Its strength so far has been its sheer size, but, given the current rate of deforestation, as a result of human encroachment both from within and outside the park, it is one of the most seriously threatened parks in Indonesia. The main conservation problem is the conversion of forest to agriculture by shifting and shifted cultivators resident in the enclave, whose area is 1460 sq. km. This enclave is inhabited by a population of about 273,000 people that is growing at an annual rate of 3.6 per cent.

Given the richness of the volcanic soil, the principal activity of the human population in the enclave is agriculture. Paddy is cultivated extensively on the plateau and Kerinci Province is self-sufficient in rice. Recent immigrants into Kerinci have extended their activities beyond the border of the enclave well into the park, clear felling forests to cultivate paddy. When soil fertility decreases, other cash crops such as cinnamon, cloves and coffee are grown. Large areas of forests have so far been replaced by cinnamon plantations. Misuse of land is the most serious conservation problem in Kerinci and already the hills that border the enclave have been completely deforested.

The buffer-zone in Kerinci covers about 500 sq. km and consists of denuded hills and abandoned clearings. The most important conservation measure that needs to be adopted here is a complete ban on any further encroachment and the relocation of all illegal settlers to areas outside the park. Hand in hand with this must be the restoration of all the derelict lands through reforestation programmes using Indonesian species such as *Paraserianthes (Albizia) falcataria*, *Pinus merkusii* and surian (*Toona sureni*). The development of the buffer zone and the regulation of the land-use activities of the settlers is vital to such measures. The current trends are likely to result in the gradual but certain destruction of Sumatra's most important conservation area.

Source: Charles Santiapillai

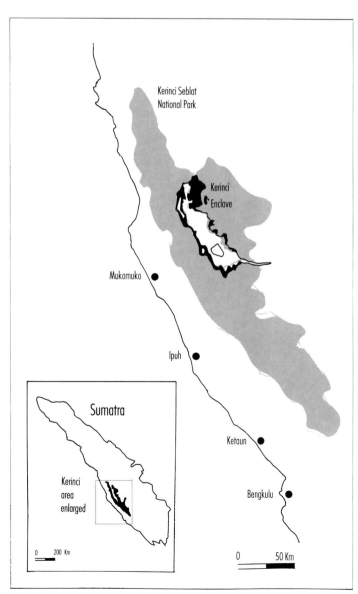

Figure 19.3 The Kerinci Seblat National Park, Sumatra
(*Source*: Charles Santiapillai)

On Obi Island in the Lesser Sundas, logging on 45° slopes has led to severe damage to the forest cover, resulting in erosion and loss of fertility. D. Laurent

Table 19.3 Conservation areas of Indonesia

Existing and proposed areas, 50 sq. km and over and for which we have location data, are listed below. The remaining areas are combined in a total under Other Areas. Protected forests are included, but Forest Reserves have been excluded. For data on ASEAN sites and Biosphere reserves see chapter 9.

	Existing area (sq. km)	Proposed area (sq. km)
INDONESIA – Sumatra		
National Parks		
Gunung Leuser	8,097	600 (ext)
Kerinci Seblat★	14,847	
Nature Reserves		
Bukit Balai★		136
Bukit Rimbang Baling-baling★		1,360
Bukit Sebelah Batang Pangean★		328
Bukit Tapan★ (Part of Kerinci Seblat)	665	
Dolok Sembelin★		339
Dolok Sibual Bual★	50	
Dolok Sipirok★	70	
Gian Duri★		400
Gunung Sago Malintang★		50
Gunung Salawah Agam★		120
Indrapura★ (Part of Kerinci Seblat)	2,367	
Kuala Langsa★		70
Lembah Anai★		960
Malampah Alahan Panjang★		369
Maninjau (North and South)★		221
Seberida★		340
Siak Kecil★		1,200
Siberut/Taitai Balti★	965	560 (ext)
Sibolga★		201
Singkil Barat★		650
Tanjung Datuk★		288
Game Reserves		
Air Sawan★		1,400
Bentayan★	193	
Berbak★	1,900	
Bukit Batu★		180
Bukit Gedang Seblat★ (Part of Kerinci Seblat)	488	
Bukit Kayu Embun★	1,060	
Dangku★	291	
Dolok Surungan★	238	
Gumai Pasemah★	459	
Karang Gading & Langkat Timur Laut★	158	
Kerumutan★	1,200	
Pulau Nias I/II/III/IV★		480
Rawas Ulu Lakitan★	2,134	
Sumatera Selatan★	3,568	
Way Kambas★	1,300	
Hunting Reserves		
Benakat	300	
Lingga Isaq★	800	
Padang Lawas★		687
Semidang Bukit Kabu★	153	
Recreation Parks		
Serbolangit		544
Protected Forests		
Bukit Balairejang★	167	
Bukit Dingin/Gunung Dempo★	381	
Bukit Hitam/Sanggul/Dingin★	694	
Bukit Nantiogan Hulu/Nanti Komerung Hulu★	362	
Gunung Merapi★	97	
Gunung Patah/Bepagut/Muara Duakisim★	917	
Gunung Singgalang★	97	
Hutan Sinlah★		810
Kambang/Lubuk Niur★	1,000	
Sub totals	45,018	12,293
Other Areas	c. 18,419	c. 26,730
INDONESIA – Java		
National Parks		
Baluran	250	
Bromo-Tengger-Semeru★	576	
Dataran Tinggi Yang (Yang Plateau)★		142
Gunung Gede Pangrango★	140	
Merapi Merbabu★		100
Meru Betiri★	495	
Ujung Kulon★	761	
Nature Reserves		
Gunung Halimun★	400	
Gunung Kawi/Kelud★		500
Gunung Lawu★		60
Gunung Masigit★		90
Gunung Muria★		120
Gunung Raung★		600
Gunung Sumbing★		100
Gunung Tilu★	80	
Gunung Unggaran★		55
Kawah Kamojang★	75	
Nusa Barung★	61	
Nusa Kambangan Perluasan★		221
Pegunungan Pembarisan★		130
Segara Anakan★		153
Tanjung Sedari		82
Teluk Lenggasana★		160
Waduk Gede/Jati Gede		105
Game Reserves		
Banyuwangi Selatan (Blambangan)★	620	
Cikepuh★	81	
Gunung Sawal★	54	
Cikamurang		55
Gunung Liman Wilis★		450
Gunung Perahu★		250
Karimunjawa		1,100
Hunting Reserves		
Gunung Pangasaman		340
Masigit Kareumbi★	124	
Recreation Parks		
Gunung Ciremai★		120
Sub totals	3,717	4,933
Other Areas	c. 1,729	c. 1,902

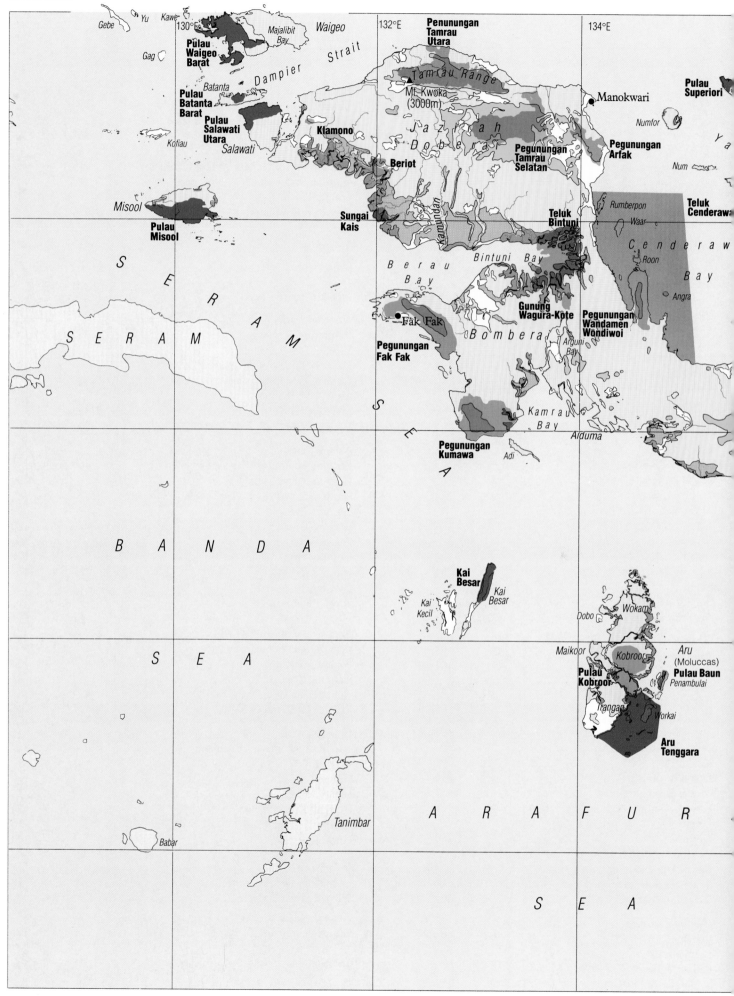

Gebe

Yu Kawe

Gag

130°E

Pulau
Waigeo
Barat

Majalibit
Bay

Waigeo

Strait

Dampier

Batanta

Pulau
Batanta
Barat

Pulau
Salawati
Utara

Kofiau

Salawati

Klamono

Beriot

Penunungan
Tamrau
Utara

132°E

Tamrau Range

Mt Kwoka
(3000m)

J a z i r a h

D o b e r a i

Pegunungan
Tamrau
Selatan

134°E

Manokwari

Pulau
Superiori

Numfor

Pegunungan
Arfak

Ya

Num

Misool

Pulau
Misool

Sungai
Kais

Teluk
Bintuni

Rumberpon

Waar

Teluk
Cenderawa

C e n d e r a w a

S
E
R
A
M

SERAM SEA

Berau
Bay

Bintuni Bay

B o m b e r a i

Roon

Bay

Angra

Fak Fak

Pegunungan
Fak Fak

Gunung
Wagura-Kote

Pegunungan
Wandamen
Wondiwoi

Arguni
Bay

Kamundan

Kamrau
Bay

Aiduma

Pegunungan
Kumawa

Adi

B A N D A

Kai
Besar

Kai
Besar

Kai
Kecil

Dobo

Wokam

S E A

Maikoor

Kobroor

Aru
(Moluccas)

Pulau
Kobroor

Pulau Baun

Penambulai

Trangan

Workai

A R A F U R

Tanimbar

Aru
Tenggara

Babar

S E A

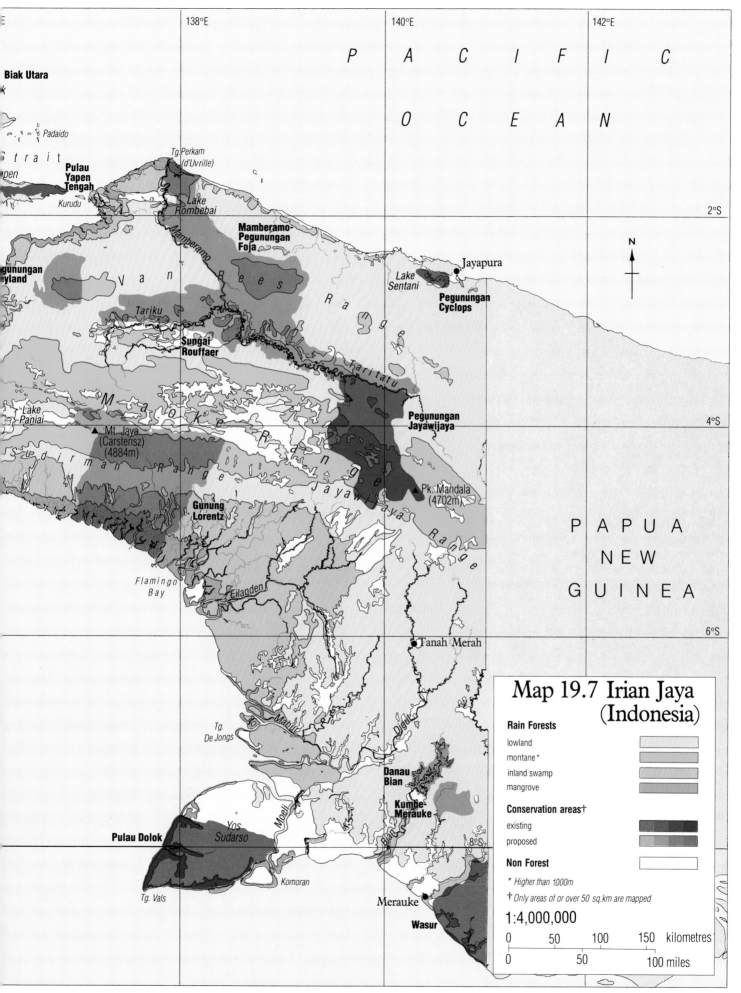

138°E 140°E 142°E

P A C I F I C

O C E A N

Biak Utara

Padaido

t r a i t

Pulau
Yapen
Tengah

pen

Kurudu

Tg. Perkam
(d'Urville)

Lake
Rombebai

2°S

Mamberamo-
Pegunungan
Foja

gunungan
yland

Jayapura

V a n

Lake
Sentani

Pegunungan
Cyclops

Tariku

R e e s

R a n g e

N

Sungai
Rouffaer

Taritatu

M a

Lake
Paniai

o k e

Pegunungan
Jayawijaya

4°S

▲ Mt. Jaya
(Carstensz)
(4884m)

S u d i r m a n

R a n g e

R a n g e

Pk. Mandala
(4702m) ▲

P A P U A

Gunung
Lorentz

J a y a w i j a y a

R a n g e

N E W

G U I N E A

Flamingo
Bay

Eilanden

6°S

Tanah Merah

Tg.
De Jongs

Jo

Mabu

Digul

Danau
Bian

Kumbe-
Merauke

Pulau Dolok

Yos
Sudarso

Moeli

Bia

8°S

Komoran

Tg. Vals

Merauke

Wasur

Map 19.7 Irian Jaya (Indonesia)

Rain Forests

lowland

montane *

inland swamp

mangrove

Conservation areas†

existing

proposed

Non Forest

* Higher than 1000m

† Only areas of or over 50 sq.km are mapped

1:4,000,000

| 0 | 50 | 100 | 150 | kilometres |

| 0 | 50 | | 100 miles |

INDONESIA

INDONESIA – Lesser Sunda Islands

National Parks

Bali Barat*	777	
Komodo Island	407	

Nature Reserves

Gunung Ambulombo*		50
Gunung Diatuto (East Timor)		150
Gunung Muna (Alor Is.)		150
Gunung Olet Sangenges (Sumbawa Is.)*		350
Ruteng (Flores Is.)*	300	

Game Reserves

Danau Ira Lalora-Pulau Yaco (East Timor)*		250
Gunung Talamailu (East Timor)		200
Gunung Wanggameti (Sumba Is.)*	60	
Hutan Dompu Complex (Sumbawa Is.)		100
Lore (East Timor)*		102
Pulau Moyo (Sumbawa Is.)*	188	
Pulau Panjang		100
Pulau Sangiang (Sumbawa Is.)		160
Rinjani (Lombok Is.)*	410	
Sungai Clere (East Timor)		300
Tambora Utara (Sumbawa Is.)*		800
Tanjung Kerita Mese		150
Tanjung Rukuwatu		60
Timolar (East Timor)		50

Hunting Reserves

Dataran Bena*	114	
Tamboka Selatan (Sumbawa Is.)	300	

Protected Forests

Egon-Iliwuli (East Flores)*	149	
Gunung Mutis (West Timor)*	100	
Gunung Timau (West Timor)	150	
Hadekewa-Labelakang (East Flores)	125	
Manupeu (Sumba Is.)*	120	
Selah Legium Complex (Sumbawa Is.)*	500	

Recreation Parks

Danau Sano		55

Sub totals	3,027	3,027
Other Areas	c. 2,925	c. 845

INDONESIA – Kalimantan

National Parks

Kutai*	2,000	
Tanjung Puting*	3,550	

Nature Reserves

Apar Besar*		900
Apu Kayan*		1,000
Bukit Baka*	705	
Bukit Raya*	1,100	
Gunung Bentuang dan Karimun*		6,000
Gunung Beratus*		1,300
Gunung Berau*		1,100
Gunung Lumut*		300
Gunung Palung*	300	
Hutan Kapur Sangkurilang*		2,000
Karimata*		1,500
Long Bangun*		3,500
Meratus Hulu Barabai*		2,000
Muara Kaman Sedulang*	625	
Muara Kayan*		800
Muara Kendawangan*		1,500
Muara Sebuku*		1,100
Muara Uya*		250
Pamukan*		100
Pantai Samarinda*		950
Pararawen I/II*	62	
Sungai Kayan Sungai Mentarang*	16,000	
Tanjung Dewa Barat*		163
Tanjung Penghujan*		400
Ulu Kayan*		8,000
Ulu Sembakung*		5,000

Game Reserves

Danau Sintarum*		800
Gunung Penrisen/Gunung Niut*	1,800	
Kelompok Hutan Kahayan*		1,500
Pleihari Martapura*	364	
Pleihari Tanah Laut	350	
Sungai Mahakam Danau Semayam Kutai (Perluasan)*		2,000

Protected Forests

Bukit Perai*	1,000	
Bukit Rongga*	1,100	
Gunung Asmansang*	280	
Gunung Tunggal*	508	

Sub totals	29,744	42,000
Other Areas	c. 21,008	c. 28,353

INDONESIA – Sulawesi

National Parks

Dumoga-Bone*	3,000	
Lore Lindu*	2,310	

Nature Reserves

Bulusaraung*	57	
Gunung Ambang*	86	
Gunung Soputan*		80
Kelompok Hutan Buol Toli-toli*		5,000
Lamiko-miko*		50
Lasolo-Sampara*		450
Morowali*	2,250	
Pegunungan Peruhumpenai*	900	
Tangkoko-Dua Saudara*	89	

Game Reserves

Buton Utara*	820	
Danau Tempe		94
Gunung Manembo-Nembo*	65	
Lambu Sango*		200
Mambuliling*		100
Mamuja/Tapalang*		125
Marisa Complex*		940
Pegunungan Morowali/Pelantak*		5,000
Pegunungan Palu dan Sekitarnya*		6,000
Polewai (Tenggara)*		80
Rangkong*		590
Rawa Opa*		1,500
Tanjung Batikolo*	55	
Tanjung Peropa*	380	

Hunting Reserves

Gunung Watumohai*	500	
Rompi*		150

Recreation Parks		
Danau Matado/Mahalano*	300	
Danau Towuti*	650	
Protected Forests		
Gunung Kelabat*	57	
Gunung Lompobatang*	200	
Gunung Sojol*		70
Pegunungan Latimojong*	580	
Tamposo-Sinansajang	150	
Sub totals	12,458	20,429
Other Areas	c. 11,110	c. 19,097

INDONESIA – Moluccas

National Parks		
Manusela Wai Nua/Wai Mual*	1,890	
Nature Reserves		
Ake Tajawi*		1,200
Aru Tenggara*		800
Gunung Arnau*		450
Gunung Sahuai*		300
Gunung Sibela*		400
Kai Besar*		370
Pulau Nuswotar*	75	
Pulau Obi*		450
Saketa*		1,040
Taliabu*		700
Waya Bula*		600
Yamdena*		600
Game Reserves		
Gunung Gamkonora*		320
Gunung Kelapat Muda*		1,450
Lolobata*		1,890
Pulau Baun*	130	
Pulau Kobroor*		1,700
Wayabula*		450
Sub totals	2,095	12,720
Other Areas	110	8,885

(*Sources:* IUCN, 1990 and WCMC *in litt.*)

★ Area with moist forest within its boundary.
(ext) = extension

INDONESIA – Irian Jaya

National Parks		
Gunung Lorentz*		1,675
Mamberamo-Pegunungan Foja*		14,425
Nature Reserves		
Gunung Wagura-Kote*		150
Kumbe-Merauke*		1,268
Lorentz*	21,500	
Pegunungan Arfak*		450
Pegunungan Cyclops*	225	
Pegunungan Fak Fak*		510
Pegunungan Kumawa*		1,180
Pegunungan Tamrau Selatan*		2,479
Pegunungan Tamrau Utara*		2,657
Pegunungan Wandamen Wondiwoi*		795
Pegunungan Weyland*		2,230
Pulau Batanta Barat*	100	
Pulau Biak Utara*	110	
Pulau Misool*	840	
Pulau Salawati Utara*	570	
Pulau Superiori*	420	
Pulau Waigeo Barat*	1,530	
Pulau Yapen Tengah*	590	
Sungai Kais*		1,220
Teluk Bintuni*		4,500
Game Reserves		
Pegunungan Jayawijaya*	8,000	
Pulau Dolok*	6,000	
Danau Bian*		500
Sungai Rouffaer*		819
Teluk Cenderawasih*		825
Wasur*	3,040	
Recreation Parks		
Beriot*		124
Klamono*		100
Sub totals	42,925	35,907
Other Areas	3,102	1,338
GRAND TOTALS	c. 198,060	c. 218,459

References

Burgess, P. F. (1988) *Natural Forest Management for Sustainable Timber Production in the Asia/Pacific region.* Report to ITTO. 97 pp. Unpublished.

Collar, N. J. and Andrew, P. (1988) *Birds to Watch.* The ICBP world checklist of threatened birds. *Technical Publication* No. 8. International Council for Bird Preservation, Cambridge, UK. 303 pp.

Collins, N. M. and Morris, M. G. (1985) *Threatened Swallowtail Butterflies of the World. The IUCN Red Data Book.* IUCN, Cambridge, UK, and Gland, Switzerland. vii + 401 pp. + 8 pls.

Departamen Kehutanan (1985) *Draft Long-term Forestry Plan.* Jakarta, Indonesia.

FAO (1982) *National Conservation Plan for Indonesia.* 8 vols. FAO, Bogor, Indonesia. (1–Introduction; 2–Sumatra; 3–Java and Bali; 4–Lesser Sundas; 5–Kalimantan; 6–Sulawesi; 7–Maluku and Irian; 8–General topics.)

FAO (1987) *Special Study on Forest Management, Afforestation and Utilization of Forest Resources in the Development Regions. Asia-Pacific Region. Assessment of Forest Resources in Six Countries.* FAO, Bangkok, Thailand. 104 pp.

FAO (1988) *An Interim Report on the State of Forest Resources in the Developing Countries.* FAO, Rome, Italy. 18 pp + 15 tables.

FAO (1990) *FAO Yearbook of Forest Products 1977–88.* FAO Forestry Series No. 23. FAO Statistics Series No. 90. FAO, Rome.

FAO/UNEP (1981) *Tropical Forest Resources Assessment Project.* Vol 3 of 3 vols. FAO, Rome, Italy. 475 pp.

Gillis, M. (1988) Indonesia: Public Policies, Resource Management, and the Tropical Forest. In: *Public Policies and the Misuse of Forest Resources.* Repetto, R. and Gillis, M. (eds). World Resources Institute/Cambridge University Press, UK. 432 pp.

Hanson, A. J. and Koesoebiono (1977) *Settling Coastal Swamplands in Sumatra: A Casestudy for Integrated Resource Management.* Research report No. 4. Center for Natural Resource Management and Environmental Studies. Bogor Agricultural University, Indonesia.

IUCN (1983) *Global Status of Mangrove Ecosystems.* Commission on Ecology Papers No. 3. IUCN, Gland, Switzerland. 88 pp.

IUCN (1986) *Plants in Danger. What do we Know?* IUCN, Gland, Switzerland, and Cambridge, UK. 461 pp.

IUCN (1988) *1988 IUCN Red List of Threatened Animals.* IUCN, Gland, Switzerland, and Cambridge, UK. 154 pp.

IUCN (1990) *1989 United Nations List of National Parks and Protected Areas.* IUCN, Gland, and Cambridge, UK.

IUCN/UNEP (1986) *Review of the Protected Areas System in the Indo-Malayan Realm.* MacKinnon, J. and Mackinnon, K., consultants. IUCN, Gland, Switzerland, and Cambridge, UK. 284 pp. + maps section.

Koesoebiono, Collier, W. L. and Burbridge, P. R. (1982) Indonesia: resource use and management in the coastal zone. In: Soysa *et al.* (eds) *Man, Land and Sea* (1982), Bangkok. pp. 115–34.

Laumonier, Y., Purnadjaja and Setiabudhi (1986) *Sumatra* (Map in 3 sheets). Institut de la Carte Internationale du Tapis Végétal/SEAMEO-BIOTROP.

MacKinnon, J. (1988) *Field Guide to the Birds of Java and Bali.* Gadjah Mada University Press, Yogyakarta. 390 pp.

Malingreau, J. P., Stephens, G. and Fellows, L. (1985) Remote Sensing of Forest Fires: Kalimantan and North Borneo in 1982–83. *Ambio* 14: 314–21.

Myers, N. (1989) *Deforestation Rates in Tropical Forests and their Climatic Implications.* Friends of the Earth, London, UK. 116 pp.

Petocz, R. G. and Raspado, G. (1984) *Conservation and Development in Irian Jaya: a Strategy for Rational Resources Utilisation.* WWF/IUCN Report. PHPA, Bogor, Indonesia.

Petocz, R. G. (1985) *Irian Jaya, the other side of New Guinea: Biological Resources and Rationale for a Comprehensive Protected Area Design.* Paper presented at the Third South Pacific National Parks and Reserves Conference and Ministerial Meeting. Apia, Western Samoa, 24 June–3 July, 1985. 11 pp + maps.

Repetto, R. (1988) *The Forest for the Trees? Government Policies and the Misuse of Forest Resources.* World Resources Institute, Washington, DC, USA.

RePPProT (1990) *National Overview of the Regional Physical Planning Programme for Transmigration.* Overseas Development Natural Resources Institute (ODNRI), Chatham, UK.

Salm, R. V. and Halim, M. (1984) *Marine and Coastal Protected Areas in Indonesia.* IUCN/WWF Report. WWF Indonesia Programme, Bogor, Indonesia.

Santiapillai, C. (1986) *The Status and Conservation of the Clouded Leopard* (Neofelis nebulosa diardi) *in Sumatra.* Report to WWF and IUCN. 13 pp.

Silvius, M. J., Steeman, A. P. J. M., Berczy, E. T., Djuharsa, E. and Taufik, A. W. (1987) *The Indonesian Wetland Inventory.* 2 vols. PHPA, AWB and EDWIN, Bogor, Indonesia.

Soemodihardjo, S. (1984) Impact of human activities on mangrove ecosystems in Indonesia: An overview. In: *Proceedings of the MAB/COMAR Regional Seminar*, November 13–16, 1984, Tokyo, Japan, pp. 15–19.

Soemodihardjo, S. (1987) Indonesia. In: Umali R., Zamora, P. M., Gotoera, R. R., Jara, R. R. and Camacho, A. S. *Mangroves of Asia and the Pacific.* Ministry of National Resources, Manila. pp. 89–130.

Soegiarto, A. and Polunin, N. (1982) *The Marine Environment in Indonesia.* Report for the Government of the Republic of Indonesia sponsored by IUCN and WWF. University of Cambridge: Department of Zoology, UK.

White, C. M. N. and Bruce, M. D. (1986) *The Birds of Wallacea (Sulawesi, The Moluccas and Lesser Sunda Islands, Indonesia).* British Ornithologists' Union, London, UK. 524 pp.

Whitten, A. J. (1987) Indonesia's transmigration program and its role in the loss of tropical rain forests. *Conservation Biology* 1: 239–46.

Whitten, A. J., Damanik, S. J., Anwar, J. and Hisyam, N. (1984) *The Ecology of Sumatra.* Gadjah Mada University Press, Yogyakarta, Indonesia.

Whitten, A. J., Muslimin Mustafa and Henderson, G. S. (1987a) *The Ecology of Sulawesi.* Gadjah Mada University Press, Yogyakarta, Indonesia. 777 pp.

Whitten, A. J., Bishop, K. D., Nash, S. V. and Clayton, L. (1987b) One or more extinctions from Sulawesi, Indonesia? *Conservation Biology* 1: 42–8.

Whitmore, T. C. (1984a) A vegetation map of Malesia at scale 1:5 million. *Journal of Biogeography* 11: 461–71.

Whitmore, T. C. (1990) *An Introduction to Tropical Rain Forests.* Clarendon Press, Oxford, UK.

Authorship

Roger Cox in London, Mark Collins at WCMC, with contributions from Tony Whitten in Cambridge, Adam Messer in Bogor, D. Kretosastro of the Transmigration Department in Jakarta, John Makin in Chatham, UK, J. R. D. Wall in Jakarta, Genevieve Michon of BIOTROP in Bogor, Russell Betts and Charles Santiapillai of WWF in Jakarta, Sinung Rahardjo and Effendy Sumardja of the Forest Protection and Nature Conservation Department, Ministry of Forestry in Jakarta.

Maps 19.1–7 Forest cover in Indonesia

The Regional Physical Planning Programme for Transmigration (RePPProT) began work in 1984 in association with the National Centre for Coordination of Surveys and Mapping (BAKOSURTANAL). The programme has now completed a rapid reconnaissance of Indonesia using existing reports, air photographs and satellite or radar imagery with selective field checking. Reviews for each of the eight regions have been published with complete map coverage at 1:250,000 scale in three map themes: land systems and land suitability, land use and land status. A total of 693 thematic maps have been prepared.

Remote sensing imagery for Indonesia used in preparing the maps included air photography, Landsats 2, 3, 4 and 5, SPOT, and radar, including SAR and SLAR. Dates, scales and areas covered varied greatly and full details are available from BAKOSURTANAL and RePPProT's regional reviews.

The RePPProT team is now preparing a *National Overview of Land Resources of Indonesia for Physical Land Use Planning*, which will summarise the results from the eight regions. This *Overview* will include 32 compiled maps at scales of 1:2 million or 1:4 million showing geology, agro-climatic zones, hydrological zones, landforms, soils, land cover, land status, environmental hazards, population distribution and areas of potential development.

Data used in the preparation of the maps of Indonesia's forest cover and protected areas in this atlas were generously provided by the RePPProT team in the form of hand-coloured draft maps at 1:2.5 million scale. The legend included eight forest and eight non-forest categories. The forest categories were harmonised with the scheme used in this atlas in the following way (category in brackets is RePPProT title): lowland rain forest (lowland moist forest), inland swamp forest (swamp forest), mangrove (mangrove and other tidal forests), montane rain forest (submontane and montane forest). RePPProT appear to have taken 1000 m as the upper limit of lowland rain forest, over most of the region. Seasonal (monsoon) forests have been delineated from data published in Whitmore (1984a).

In this atlas, forest logged but left to regenerate either with or without silvicultural treatment is not distinguished from pristine forest. Thus, in Indonesia the atlas does not distinguish separately the areas of recently logged forest which were identified by RePPProT. Areas which RePPProT showed as converted from forestry to other land uses are of course clearly identified.

Some notes on the origin and interpretation of Maps 19.1 to 19.7 are given below. In each case the date of origin of the bulk of the information is given in brackets (these being the publication dates of RePPProT's Regional Reviews), but since a wide variety of sources make up the whole series, it is important to refer to the original RePPProT regional reviews or BAKOSURTANAL itself if detailed information is needed.

Map 19.1: Sumatra (1988)

The RePPProT maps included no data for Singkil Barat or for the islands of Simeuluë, and Enggano, nor for the Riau and Lingga groups. Whitmore (1984a) shows some lowland rain forest on northern Simeuluë and central Singkilbaru, but none on Enggano, Riau and Lingga, which are believed to be largely deforested.

Map 19.2: Java and Lesser Sundas (1989)

The climate becomes increasingly seasonal from Java along the Lesser Sunda Islands. Remaining forests on Java are marked as rain forests since they are on mountain slopes and peaks, but much of the island was probably originally clothed in monsoon forest.

Map 19.3: Lesser Sundas (1989)

No data are available for the island of Roti. Whitmore (1984a) indicates some monsoon forest in the south-west of the island. No data are available for the Babar Islands between Tanimbar and Leti, nor for the southernmost island in the Tanimbar group. The latter is believed to be deforested, but Babar and Leti have some monsoon forest (Whitmore, 1984a).

Map 19.4: Kalimantan (Central, 1985; South, West and East, 1987)

The main point to note here is that substantial areas of forest in the southeast were killed or degraded by drought and fire in 1982–3. The area affected is indicated in Figure 19.2, but much is now believed to be regenerating. There are no data for the Anambas and Bunguran (Natuna) Islands in the South China Sea, but Whitmore (1984a) indicated small areas of lowland rain forest in the centres of the main islands.

Map 19.5: Sulawesi (1988)

The now deforested Talaud and Sangihe Islands have been omitted from this map to enable a larger scale to be used. No data are available for the southernmost Banggai Islands. Banggai itself is deforested, but Bangkulu and Labobo are believed to have small patches of lowland rain forest (Whitmore, 1984a).

Aopa swamp, in the southeast arm of Sulawesi, is the best known area of peatswamp forest on the island, forming part of a national park. It has been overlain onto the RePPProT data.

Map 19.6: Moluccas (1989)

See the note on Banggai Islands above. In Seram some areas marked by RePPProT as swamp forest are believed to be cultivated land and have been marked as such (after Whitmore 1984a). The island of Bacan is labelled as monsoon forest after Whitmore (1984a). Recent reports indicate that the island in fact bears rain forest (T. C. Whitmore, personal communication).

Map 19.7: Irian Jaya (1986)

Monsoon forest indicated in the southeastern corner of Irian Jaya by Whitmore (1984a) is adjudged by RePPProT to be open savanna woodland and is therefore labelled as non-forest on this map.

The editors are especially grateful to the Director General of Settlement Preparation, Ir. Djatijanto Kretosastro for use of data from the RePPProT project; to BAKOSURTANAL for their support; and to Dr David Wall, the RePPProT team leader, and his cartographers, for their cooperation in providing draft maps.

20 Laos

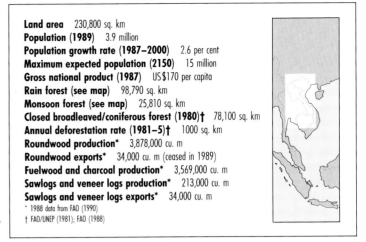

Land area 230,800 sq. km
Population (1989) 3.9 million
Population growth rate (1987–2000) 2.6 per cent
Maximum expected population (2150) 15 million
Gross national product (1987) US$170 per capita
Rain forest (see map) 98,790 sq. km
Monsoon forest (see map) 25,810 sq. km
Closed broadleaved/coniferous forest (1980)† 78,100 sq. km
Annual deforestation rate (1981–5)† 1000 sq. km
Roundwood production* 3,878,000 cu. m
Roundwood exports* 34,000 cu. m (ceased in 1989)
Fuelwood and charcoal production* 3,569,000 cu. m
Sawlogs and veneer logs production* 213,000 cu. m
Sawlogs and veneer logs exports* 34,000 cu. m
* 1988 data from FAO (1990)
† FAO/UNEP (1981); FAO (1988)

Data on forest cover and rates of forest loss in Laos are in short supply. There are few primary sources, and those that are available on a national level are somewhat generalised. The best map available, a 1:1 million scale map from 1987, indicates that there is 67,780 sq. km of closed forest, with a further 56,820 sq. km of degraded formations (roughly 29 and 25 per cent of land area, respectively).

Poor forest management practices and shifting cultivation together comprise the greatest threat to the forests, but at the moment it is impossible to determine the absolute importance of each. Management of the forest resource is severely constrained by lack of trained people and the poorly developed communication and transport system. These problems are recognised by Government and internationally, but will take some time to rectify. On the positive side, forest management problems and the need to institute conservation measures appear to be recognised at the highest levels. The policies put forward by the recent Nationwide Forestry Conference and the Tropical Forestry Action Plan exercise are also positive developments, but the success with which ensuing forest land-use policies can be implemented remains to be determined.

INTRODUCTION

Laos is a mountainous, land-locked country. The major topographic features are the southward-flowing Mekong River and its flat, low-lying plain, which lies mainly below 200 metres; steep, rugged hills throughout the north of the country and in the Annamite Mountains, the latter forming the border with Vietnam; and the Bolovens Plateau, an outlying massif in the south rising to over 1500 m. The highest point in the country is the 2820 m Phou Bia, located 130 km north-east of the capital city, Vientiane.

With an average population of 15 people per sq. km, Laos is sparsely settled by Southeast Asian standards. Approximately 75 per cent of its population lives in rural regions (FAO/UNEP, 1981; FAO, 1985), primarily in the rice-growing areas of the Mekong Plain.

The Forests

Laos experiences a seasonal monsoonal climate, with two to five cool and dry months between November and April. Nevertheless, there are large areas of more or less evergreen forests whose original extent was about 160,000 sq. km or approximately 70 per cent of the land area (Salter and Phanthavong, 1989). Lowland and montane rain forests occupied much of the mountainous northern part of the country, including the Annamite Mountains and the Bolovens Plateau, as well as the Mekong Plain. Monsoon forests occur on particular soils, and once occupied about 57,500 sq. km. They still occur in areas to the north and west of the Mekong, and contain valuable stands of teak. As is common, the evergreen and semi-evergreen rain forest formations are replaced by deciduous monsoon formations after human disturbance.

In the evergreen rain forests emergent trees reach 35–60 m tall, over a 10–30 m tall and dense lower storey. Characteristic trees are *Anisoptera cochinchinensis*, *Dalbergia* spp., *Dipterocarpus alatus*, *Hopea* spp., (Fidloczky 1986; Bochkovetal 1988) *Parashorea stellata* and *Pterocarpus macrocarpus*, depending on location.

Forest Resources and Management

Map 20.1 shows the most recent data on forest distribution in Laos. Intact rain forest is estimated to cover 41,970 sq. km (18 per cent of land area), monsoon forest 25,810 sq. km (11 per cent) and degraded rain forest a further 56,820 sq. km (25 per cent) (Table 20.1). The total area of intact closed forest, 67,780 sq. km, represents a 10 per cent reduction of the FAO statistics for 1980 (FAO/UNEP, 1981).

The best moist forests are now confined primarily to the central and southern parts of the country, the northern areas previously occupied by moist forest having been largely deforested. With the exception of the four to six per cent of land area under permanent agriculture (FAO/UNEP, 1981; FAO, 1985), most of the remainder of the country is under secondary grasslands, savannas, shrublands or bamboo forests.

The rate and extent of commercial logging in Laos has in the past been low, due primarily to constraints imposed by poor infrastructure, and lack of transport, equipment, maintenance and fuel. It has been concentrated in the most accessible areas of the Mekong Plain and adjacent areas. Roundwood timber production of 4.3 million cu. m in 1987 fell slightly to 3.6 million cu. m in 1988 (FAO, 1990). Felling has been selective (based on species and diameter guidelines), but there are no country-wide standards. In practice, felling has been poorly controlled, wastage high and many standing trees damaged by poor techniques. Silvicultural treatment of logged areas has been non-existent or at best minimal, and the level and rate of natural regeneration have not been documented. Over the past decade a number of state enterprises have been created, but virtually all lack trained personnel and equipment and are operating without adequate forest management plans (Young and Hyde, 1988; SIDA, 1988). The lack of sustained-yield management is seen as a major threat to the forest resource (IUCN, 1988a; SIDA, 1988).

Restrictions on the export of raw logs have been imposed at various times in the past, but this has been mainly to increase the availability of logs for domestic processing rather than designed as a forest conservation measure. The latest export ban has now effectively been superseded by a revised system of extraction and export taxes.

Deforestation

Shifting cultivation (see chapter 4) and attendant uncontrolled fires (the latter also to facilitate hunting and to improve livestock grazing), have long been the major cause of deforestation in Laos. Recently though, uncontrolled or poorly controlled logging have increasingly contributed to forest loss. Since the 1970s it has been a priority of government to try to stop shifting cultivation. The rate of forest loss is very poorly known, but figures developed by FAO/UNEP (1981) from earlier sources indicate a net annual deforestation rate of 1250 sq. km between 1976 and 1980, of which 50 sq. km a year was conifer forest. A reduced net annual deforestation rate of 1000 sq. km was assumed for the period 1981–5, based primarily on the assumption that shifting cultivation would be reduced as a result of government control programmes (see also the case studies, page 170). A recent ministerial pronouncement indicated that 2000 sq. km of forest are currently being destroyed per year, but the source of data is unknown (KPL, 24/5/89).

Table 20.1 Estimates of forest extent in Laos

	Areas intact (sq. km)	% of land area	Area degraded (sq. km)	% of land area	Totals	% of land area
Rain forests						
Lowland	31,130	13.5	56,820	24.6	87,950	38.1
Montane	10,840	4.7	—		10,840	4.7
Sub totals	41,970	18.2	56,820	24.6	98,790	42.8
Monsoon forests						
Lowland	22,220	9.6	—		22,220	9.6
Montane	3,590	1.6	—		3,590	1.6
Sub totals	25,810	11.2	—		25,810	11.2
Totals	67,780	29.4	56,820	24.6	124,600	54.0

(*Source:* based on analysis of Map 20.1; see Map Legend for details)

Other factors such as mining, dams and roads have so far had relatively minor effects on Laotian forests. However, the improvement of the national road network, due for completion in the 1990s, will provide access to areas hitherto untouched, which is likely to increase exploitation and lead to forest destruction by migrant agricultural settlers.

Laotian forests sustained bombing damage during the Indo-Chinese War, but the extent has not been documented (FAO/UNEP, 1981). An estimated two million tons of bombs were dropped over Laos during the 1960s and 1970s, primarily along the length of the Ho Chi Minh trail in the Annamite Mountains.

Semi-evergreen forest in the limestone mountains of central Laos, with rice paddy in the lowlands. J. A. Sayer

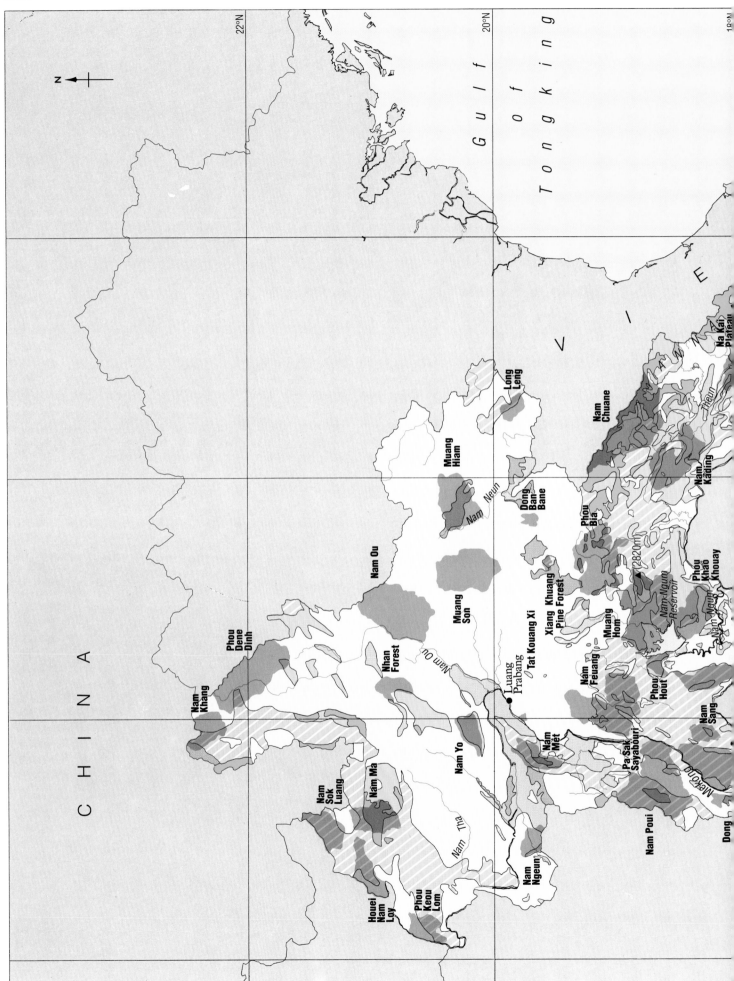

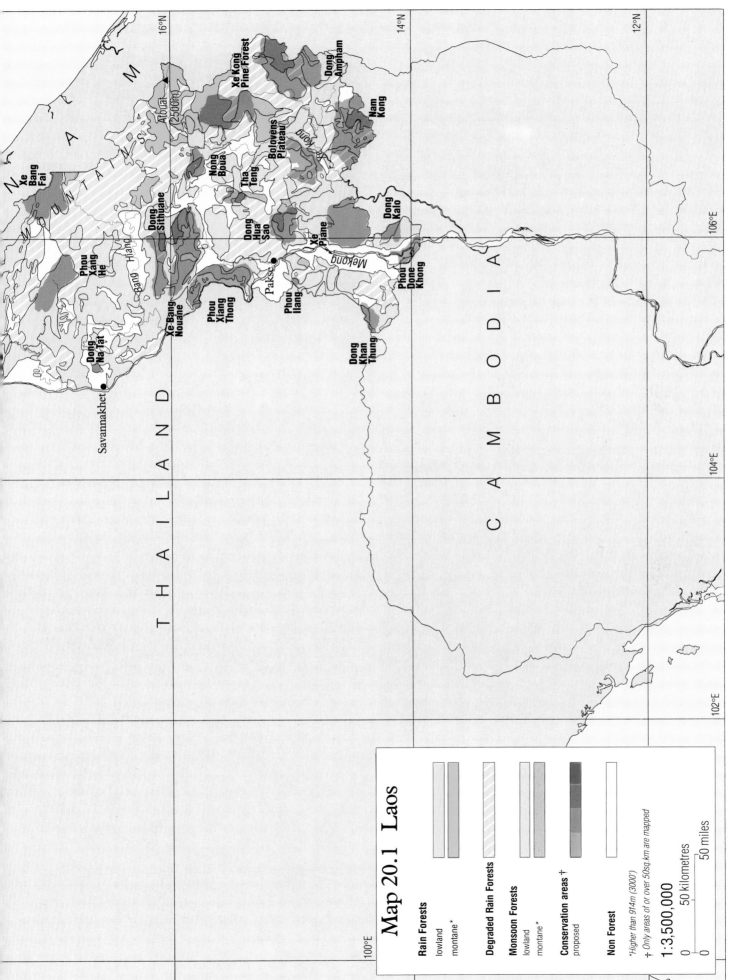

Map 20.1 Laos

Rain Forests
lowland
montane*

Degraded Rain Forests

Monsoon Forests
lowland
montane*

Conservation areas †
proposed

Non Forest

*Higher than 914m (3000')
† Only areas of or over 50sq.km are mapped

1:3,500,000

| 0 | 50 kilometres |
| 0 | 50 miles |

SHIFTING CULTIVATION IN LAOS

Although a variety of shifting cultivation systems are in use in Laos, a distinction can be made among those used by the three main ethnic groups:

Lao Loum The Lao Loum are lowland people whose traditional form of agriculture is rain-fed rice cultivation on terraces or flat valley bottoms. However, in response to recent population increases and a shortage of suitable lowland areas for cultivation, agriculture has expanded into the adjacent uplands. Plots are cleared completely and one crop of rain-fed rice is grown, followed by a fallow period of only three or four years, after which the plot is again cleared and the cycle repeated. Soil exhaustion (as a result of no secondary crops or fertiliser being ploughed back into the earth), complete clearing of fallow tree species, and the short rotational period, result in extremely low crop yields, declining productivity from cycle to cycle and problems with weeds. This is an unsustainable system, which has led to deterioration of the forests around the agricultural lowlands.

Shifting agriculture and permanent irrigated fields exist side by side in Laos. P. Anspach

Clearing, planting, cultivating and harvesting are the cycle of tasks for the swidden farmer in northern Laos. P. Anspach

Lao Theung The Lao Theung include a number of ethnic groups living in the hills. Fields are cropped for one or two years followed by a fallow period of five to fifteen years. During land clearing, tree stumps and some trees are left to promote regeneration after cropping, and care is taken with burning and weeding. Rice is the main crop although others such as maize, chillies and cassava are grown. This system of cyclical reoccupation of agricultural land is basically ecologically stable, although in some areas it has started to break down as a result of increasing demand for land.

Lao Soung On high slopes above about 1000 m in northern Laos, the Lao Soung people cultivate opium poppy as a cash crop, and rice, maize, tobacco and vegetables for subsistence. Primary forest sites are preferred for poppy cultivation. No trees are left standing, and the plots are used continuously for five to ten years, after which they are abandoned. As a result of soil impoverishment and weed invasion these plots regenerate to infertile grass savannas rather than forest. This system, which is accompanied by uncontrolled fires during the burning season, is the major cause of deforestation in upland areas.

Source: IUCN (1988a)

THE IMPACT OF DEFORESTATION ON RURAL PEOPLE

Loss of forest cover has a particularly severe impact on rural residents, of whom there are some 3,000,000 in Laos. For these people the forest is a source of building materials, fuelwood, food, medicinal plants and other products both for family use and for sale.

A recent study of eight villages and two forest enterprises in east-central Laos found that 141 different types of forest products were hunted or gathered, including 37 food items, 68 medicinal products and 18 types of animals. One village was critically affected by state enterprise logging activities that reportedly resulted in complete destruction of the area logged. Impacts included killing or scaring away of animals, increased hunting and explosives fishing by enterprise employees, blocking of forest pathways by felled timber, and drying up of streams and wetlands. The study concluded that villagers who experience logging of adjacent forests may respond by moving into more remote areas, where they will revert to shifting cultivation and forest gathering.

Source: Ireson (1989)

Biodiversity

The flora and fauna of Laos are incompletely known, there being no national herbarium or reference collections. Natural wildlife habitat in Laos includes dense moist forests, pine forests, dwarf forest and shrubland on limestone, subalpine formations and wetlands.

Floral lists and nomenclature currently in use are based on the work of Vidal (1960). Although there are no exact figures for the size of the flora or the number of endemics (IUCN, 1986), plant species richness is considered to be high, with a moderate level of endemism. Approximately 600 tree and shrub species (Bochkov *et al.*, 1988) and over 300 orchid species (IUCN, 1986) have been identified. The fauna of Laos includes 623 bird species, of which 28 are endemic to the Indo-Chinese region (King *et al.*, 1975; Interim Mekong Committee, 1978; King and Dickinson, n.d.). Of particular note are the sooty babbler *Stachyris herberti*, found only in central Laos, and the emperor pheasant *Lophura imperialis*, grey-faced tit-babbler *Macronous kelleyi* and white-cheeked laughing thrush *Garrulax vassali*, which occur only in Laos and adjacent parts of Vietnam. Some 186 mammal species are known to occur in Laos, 20 of these endemic to the Indo-Chinese region (Interim Mekong Committee, 1978; Lekagul and McNeely, 1988). There is a high degree of endemism among the forest-dwelling primates; the pygmy loris *Nycticebus pygmaeus*, Francois' langur *Presbytis francoisi*, douc langur *Pygathrix nemaeus* and black gibbon *Hylobates concolor* are all confined to Laos and other parts of the Indo-Chinese peninsula east of the Mekong.

Comprehensive listings of the reptiles, amphibians, fishes and invertebrates of Laos are not available.

Conservation Areas

Laos has never had an effective protected area system. A total of 17 forest reserves covering 1280 sq. km have been declared in the past,

but protective measures were never implemented (FAO/UNEP, 1981). Some provinces have now begun developing their own forest reserves but details are not available.

A recent analysis of the needs and priorities for a protected area system indicated that sufficient forest cover remains for all forest formations to be protected at or about 10 per cent of their original area, and that for most (including all evergreen types) 20 per cent can still be protected (Salter and Phanthavong, 1989). Based on considerations of size, completeness of original cover, representativeness, regional priorities and degree of threat, 11 forested areas and two wetland areas have been identified as important for field surveys and establishment of protected measures (see the case study on Xe Piane below). The field survey programme is currently in progress, but the current proposals are listed in Table 20.2 and mapped on Map 20.1.

Initiatives for Conservation

The Mekong Committee was set up by the governments of Thailand, Laos, Cambodia and Vietnam, in the early 1960s to develop (and conserve) the shared water resources of the Mekong River. The Committee has recently completed a project – Watershed Management: Fruit and Tree Propagation and Planting – focused on developing new methods for reforestation, for fruit tree propagation and for control of soil erosion after shifting cultivation.

The AsDB/UNDP-financed Southern Area Master Plan, completed in 1988, reviewed forestry and agriculture issues in the four southern provinces of Laos – including shifting cultivation, fire and logging – and gave a number of recommendations for future forest management.

Several projects in the Lao/Swedish Forestry Programme provide continuity by addressing forest land use issues. The Forest Inventory Project is assisting with formulation of plans and policies on land use, forest resource management and regional economic development. Specific activities to the end of 1990 include a reconnaissance survey

XE PIANE AND BUNG NONG NGOM

The Xe Piane and Bung Nong Ngom areas in extreme southern Laos have been identified as priority sites for conservation. Both of these areas have been surveyed in the past by Lao Government personnel, and were again visited during March 1989 to obtain up-to-date information on vegetation, wildlife and land use.

The Xe Piane area consists of 1438 sq. km of both hilly and low, rolling terrain on the Cambodian frontier. Most of the area is covered by dense evergreen and semi-evergreen monsoon forest, but there are also tracts of open deciduous monsoon forest and small wetlands on the flatter areas. Villagers reported wildlife to be varied and abundant, including a number of threatened species: black gibbon *Hylobates concolor*, wild dog *Cuon alpinus*, clouded leopard *Neofelis nebulosa*, leopard *Panthera pardus*, tiger *Panthera tigris*, Asian elephant *Elephas maximus*, brow-antlered deer *Cervus eldi*, gaur *Bos gaurus*, banteng *Bos javanicus*, kouprey *Bos sauveli*, crested argus *Rheinardia ocellata* and green peafowl *Pavo muticus*. There was one unconfirmed but recent (1985) report of a rhinoceros, presumably a Javan rhinoceros *Rhinoceros sundaicus*, and two reports of herds of wild water buffalo *Bubalus bubalis*. Irrawaddy dolphins *Orcaella brevirostris* reportedly formerly occurred in the Xe Khampho, which forms the proposed eastern boundary, and Siamese crocodiles *Crocodylus siamensis* were said still to occur in this river and in other rivers in the interior. The wetlands, although limited in extent, support a variety of waterbirds, including sarus cranes *Grus antigone*.

Three small villages, occupied by about 400 people in total, occur within the currently proposed boundaries, and several other

villages are situated on the periphery. The villagers collect a variety of forest products and cultivate a small area for wet rice, hunting, fishing and limited livestock grazing. One village mounts periodic elephant capture operations and has caught about 15 elephants, which are used as draught animals, in the past decade. It is likely that future management will need to recognise specified use rights of the forests for these local inhabitants.

The proposed Bung Nong Ngom protected area consists of about 800 ha of seasonally flooded grasslands and permanent wetlands. It is located less than 5 km north of Xe Piane, separated by a settled area given over primarily to wet rice cultivation. Although heavily used for livestock grazing and fishing, the wetland area supports an abundance and variety of waterbirds. Crocodiles are also reported to occur, mainly during the rainy season when flooding is widespread. Similar but smaller wetlands are located between Bung Nong Ngom and the proposed Xe Piane boundary, and support a similar variety of waterbird species.

Taken together, Xe Piane and Bung Nong Ngom constitute an area of major national significance for conservation, and probably of international importance for the conservation of a number of vulnerable or endangered animals. Management will for the foreseeable future be constrained by a lack of trained personnel and by the relative remoteness of the area. For these and other reasons cooperation with local residents is seen as critical to the success of any conservation initiatives. A preliminary management plan addressing these issues is now in preparation.

Sources: IUCN (1988b); Salter and Phanthavong (1989)

to provide country-wide data on land use and forest areas, distribution, and classification, plus mapping of selected areas (total 70,000 sq. km) at 1:50,000 scale; development of a national inventory methodology; and an evaluation of the rate of depletion of forest cover due to shifting cultivation and other factors. The Silviculture Project is providing assistance in reforestation and silviculture, specifically with regard to development of a research programme. Assistance to the Borikhamxai Logging and Wood Processing Company and to State Forest Enterprise Number 3 includes development of land use plans, and development of suitable harvesting and regeneration systems. The Borikhamxai Regional Development Project is providing assistance toward increasing productivity of wet rice cultivation as an alternative to shifting agriculture. The Forest Resources Conservation Project is surveying proposed protected areas and implementing pilot management programmes, and is assisting with staff training, public education and conservation policy. The Shifting Cultivation Project is working towards viable agricultural and socio-economic systems which will contribute to the stabilisation of shifting cultivation practices.

The Soviet Union, while not directly involved in projects dealing with deforestation, has assisted with aerial photography of the entire country (1980–1). This has been used for forest inventory, for preparation of the 1:1,000,000 scale forest cover map used as a basis for Map 20.1, and with preparation of topographic maps. A current project is engaged in a country-wide reconnaissance soil survey and in more detailed studies and mapping of soils, erosion, and land use in selected areas.

Integrated rural development projects, generally featuring measures to improve use of forest resources and limit shifting cultivation, are being supported in both northern and southern Laos by UNDP, the World Bank and the governments of Australia and the United States. For example, the UNDP-financed/FAO-executed Forest Development and Watershed Management Project (1982–9) had as its main aim the introduction of more efficient, productive and sustainable land uses to shifting cultivators; technological development focused primarily on terracing, agroforestry and reforestation.

A Tropical Forestry Action Plan, with support or participation from the Laotian Ministry of Agriculture and Forestry, UNDP, FAO, AsDB, the World Bank, SIDA and IUCN, was begun in September 1989 and is due for completion in mid-1990.

Government has also developed a number of policy initiatives without external assistance. During the 1970s and early 1980s efforts focused on settling shifting cultivators in permanent agricultural areas. A total of 6700 families were resettled prior to 1977; 10,760 families were resettled during the period 1977–80 (FAO/UNEP, 1981). This programme has now been scaled down but efforts are still under way to encourage fixed or rotational farming, in lieu of slash and burn cultivation. Methods favoured include clearing or rehabilitation of wet rice fields, intensification of agriculture on favourable land, and planting of fruit trees. The restriction and eventual elimination of slash and burn cultivation has recently been reiterated as one of the strategic programmes for the future socio-economic development of Laos (KPL, 23/5/89).

A recently completed study entitled 'Reduction of Shifting Cultivation and Protection of the Environment Programme' identifies targets of 50,000 sq. km to be managed as production forest, 95,000 sq. km to be managed as protection forest, and 25,000 sq. km to be managed as conservation forest. Implicit in these figures is an intention to reafforest cleared and degraded forests lands, and some efforts have already been made. Hundreds of thousands of tree seedlings are planted on National Arbor Day, which is symbolically important. Limited replanting of areas formerly under shifting cultivation has also been undertaken by logging enterprises. Establishment of plantations of industrial species is still at the experimental stage.

Table 20.2 Conservation areas of Laos

Proposed areas 50 sq. km and over are listed below. The remaining areas are combined in a total under Other Areas. Forest reserves are not included. All areas include moist forest within their boundaries.

Forest Areas	Proposed area (sq. km)
Bolovens Plateau	794
Dong Ampham	1,625
Dong Ban Bane	386
Dong Hua Sao	707
Dong Kalo	349
Dong Khan Thung	379
Dong Na Tat	84
Dong Sam Sak	294
Dong Sithuane	757
Houei Nam Loy	675
Long Leng	297
Muang Hiam	1,357
Muang Hom	2,495
Muang Khi	1,187
Muang Son	1,339
Na Kai Plateau	1,618
Nam Chuane	2,077
Nam Feuang	2,242
Nam Kading	1,294
Nam Khang	766
Nam Kong	1,220
Nam Ma	868
Nam Met	755
Nam Ngeun	462
Nam Ou	2,434
Nam Poui	1,478
Nam Sang	462
Nam Sok Luang	695
Nam Theun	1,627
Nam Yo	598
Nhan Forest	228
Nong Boua	413
Pa Sak Sayabouri	1,248
Phou Bia	1,605
Phou Dene Dinh	2,229
Phou Done Khong	110
Phou Hout	324
Phou Ilang	150
Phou Keou Lom	642
Phou Khao Khouay	1,307
Phou Pha Nang	696
Phou Xang He	753
Phou Xiang Thong	954
Tat Kouang Xi	200
Tha Teng	298
Xe Bang Fai	1,029
Xe Bang Nouane	1,263
Xe Kong Pine Forest	825
Xe Piane	1,438
Xiang Khuang Pine Forest	178
Sub total	47,211
Other Areas	108
Total	47,319

(*Source*: Salter and Phanthavong, 1989)

References

Bochkov, I. M., Korolev, I. A. and Filipchuk, A. N. (1988) Inventory of Tropical Forests (case-study of Laos). In: *International Training Seminar on Forestry Applications of Remote Sensing, Moscow, 1988*. United Nations Environment Programme, Nairobi, Kenya, pp. 277–95.

FAO (1985) *Agriculture in the Asia-Pacific Region – a Pictorial Profile*. FAO, Bangkokm, Thailand.

FAO (1988) *An Interim Report on the State of Forest Resources in the Developing Countries*. FAO, Rome, Italy. 18 pp + 5 tables.

FAO (1990) FAO *Yearbook of Forest Products 1977–88*. FAO Forestry Series No. 23, FAO Statistics Series No. 90. FAO, Rome.

FAO/UNEP (1981) *Tropical Forest Resources Assessment Project. Forest Resources of Tropical Asia*. Vol 3 of 3 vols. FAO, Rome.

Fidloczky, J. (1986) *Manual of Aerial Photo-interpretation in Laos*. Lao-Swedish Forestry Cooperation Programme, Vientiane, Lao PDR.

Interim Committee for Coordination of Investigations of the Lower Mekong Basin (1978) *Wild Life and National Parks in the Lower Mekong Basin*. Unpublished Report.

Ireson, C. J. (1989) *The Role of Women in Forestry in the Lao PDR*. Silvinova, Vientiane, Lao PDR.

IUCN (1986) *Plants in Danger. What do we Know?* IUCN, Gland, Switzerland, and Cambridge, UK.

IUCN (1988a) *Shifting Cultivation in Laos*. Technical report by IUCN for the Government of Lao PDR and the Swedish International Development Authority.

IUCN (1988b) *Review of the Protected Areas System in the Indo-Malayan Realm*. Consultants J.&K. MacKinnon. IUCN Gland, Switzerland, and Cambridge, UK. 284 pp + maps.

King, B. and Dickinson, E. C. (n.d.) A distribution table of the birds of S.E. Asia. Unpublished.

King, B. F., Dickinson, E. C. and Woodcock, M. W. (1975) *A Field Guide to the Birds of South-east Asia*. Collins, London, UK.

KPL (various dates) *Khao San Pathet Lao News Bulletin*. Vientiane, Lao PDR.

Lao PDR Forestry Department (1987) *Forest Management Map, Lao PDR*. Inventory Division, Forestry Department, Vientiane.

Lekagul, B. and McNeely, J. A. (1988) *Mammals of Thailand*. Second Edition. Association for the Conservation of Wildlife, Bangkok, Thailand.

Salter, R. E. and Phanthavong, Bouaphanh (1989) *Needs and Priorities for a Protected Area System in Lao PDR*. Forest Resources Conservation Project, Lao/Swedish Forestry Cooperation Programme, Vientiane, Lao PDR.

SIDA (1988) Swedish training support to the forestry and forest industries sectors in Lao PDR. Unpublished report by the Review Mission in February–March 1988. Swedish International Development Authority, Stockholm.

Vidal, J. (1960) *La Végétation du Laos*. 4 volumes. Souladoure, Toulouse, France.

Young, V. and Hyde, M. J. (1988) *Southern Area Development Master Plan*. Sectoral Report. Forestry. Prep. by Lavalin International Inc. and MPW Rural Development Pty for State Planning Committee, Lao PDR.

Authorship

Richard Salter and Boonthong Xaisida in Vientiane, with contribution from Paul Anspach in Vientiane and Geoff Kent, G. Hindsen, Joseph Fidloczky and J. Axelsson of the Lao Swedish Forestry Programme in Vientiane.

Map 20.1 Forest cover in Laos

Forest cover is taken from *Lao PDR Forestry Department* (1987), a 1:1,000,000 scale blueline hand-coloured map. The Forestry Department map is an update and extension based on 1980–1 black and white aerial photography, and an earlier 1:1,000,000 scale land use map prepared by the Mekong Secretariat from 1972–3 Landsat imagery. Forest types were harmonised as follows: rain forests – dense and mainly evergreen forests; monsoon forests – open and mainly deciduous forests, conifer forests and forests on limestone.

Proposed protected areas are from a 1:1,000,000 scale outline map (initially prepared as an overlay of the forest type map) used for planning purposes by the Lao/Swedish Forest Resources Conservation Project.

21 Papua New Guinea

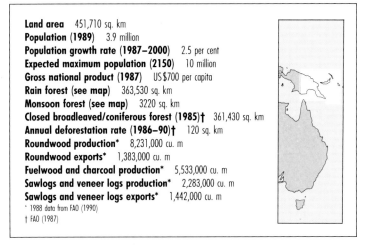

Land area	451,710 sq. km
Population (1989)	3.9 million
Population growth rate (1987–2000)	2.5 per cent
Expected maximum population (2150)	10 million
Gross national product (1987)	US$700 per capita
Rain forest (see map)	363,530 sq. km
Monsoon forest (see map)	3220 sq. km
Closed broadleaved/coniferous forest (1985)†	361,430 sq. km
Annual deforestation rate (1986–90)†	120 sq. km
Roundwood production*	8,231,000 cu. m
Roundwood exports*	1,383,000 cu. m
Fuelwood and charcoal production*	5,533,000 cu. m
Sawlogs and veneer logs production*	2,283,000 cu. m
Sawlogs and veneer logs exports*	1,442,000 cu. m

* 1988 data from FAO (1990)
† FAO (1987)

The rich and complex geology of Papua New Guinea is reflected in the diversity of its vegetation and fauna. It contains important ecosystems, including extensive wetlands and virtually pristine coral reefs; but what distinguishes Papua New Guinea from most other tropical regions is the relatively low rate at which its forests have been converted or destroyed – in 1985 forests covered 77 per cent of the country. A contributory factor to the slow deforestation rate is the low population density which, at eight people per sq. km, is among the lowest in the world. However, the situation is rapidly changing. Ninety per cent population live in rural areas, where the old system of shifting agriculture is now breaking down under growing population pressure. Establishment of plantations for cash crops, such as cocoa, coffee, oil palm, rubber and tea; logging of large tracts of lowland rain forest on the north coast of the mainland, New Britain and New Ireland; and damage by large-scale mining; are all helping to increase the rate of forest loss.

Papua New Guinea's forests are not yet managed in order to sustain regeneration as well as to provide forest products. Their extent, ecological characteristics, regenerative capacity and potential yields are all very poorly known. Only 150,000 sq. km, 40 per cent of the natural forest estate, are considered suitable for logging, but gradient and soils limit operations within logging concessions to an average of 30 per cent of the area. Exports of unprocessed logs are rising, to the concern of the Government, who wish to encourage local industry and to protect high-quality timber from rapid depletion – thus the export of raw logs of ten species has been banned.

Deforestation is proceeding at a rate of about 220 sq. km per year, while a further 600 sq. km of forest is disturbed in some way by logging (FAO, 1987; 1988). About 10,000 sq. km of former forest has now been converted to grassland as a result of over-intensive shifting agriculture.

Only two per cent of the land area is under conservation management, and the complex land tenure system militates against major extensions. The most practical option is a system of multiple-use management areas, based on the existing PNG concept of Wildlife Management Areas (see below), but on a much larger scale. The concept of World Heritage Sites, where conservation and sustained yield management of forest products could take place side by side, offers opportunities. However, substantial international assistance will be needed in order to bring this about. Conservation currently has a low political and economic priority in the country and the relevant government departments are limited by low budgets.

INTRODUCTION

Papua New Guinea consists of the eastern half of the large island of New Guinea, together with the Bismarck, Trobriand, D'Entrecasteaux and Louisiade archipelagos and the island of Bougainville, northernmost of the Solomon Islands archipelago.

A series of high mountain ranges rising to over 3000 m (highest point Mount Wilhelm), run east–west throughout the main island, separated by valleys dropping to c. 500 m above sea-level. In the east, these mountains rise close to the sea, but in the west there are extensive areas of low-lying country to both the north and south of the central ranges. To the north the lowlands comprise the Sepik and Ramu river valleys. In the west there is a coastal range, the Torricelli mountains, separating the lowlands from the sea. In the east there are two coastal cordilleras, the Adelbert and Finisterre Ranges. The low country to the south of the central range is more extensive, and mainly comprises the drainage systems of the Fly river and its tributary the Strickland, abutting up to the border with Irian Jaya.

Most of PNG experiences relatively high rainfall of 2500–3500 mm per annum with little or no dry season. A few lowland areas are drier, but rainfall of less than 1000 mm is unknown except around the national capital, Port Moresby. By contrast, the extensive uplands of the main central range experience over 4000 mm, and in some locations even 10,000 mm per annum (McAlpine et al., 1983).

Approximately 97 per cent of the land in Papua New Guinea is held by ethnic groups who occupy the land under customary ownership. The remaining 3 per cent of land (14,000 sq. km) had been alienated from the customary system at the time of self-government in 1973; of this 1600 sq. km was freehold, 3400 sq. km was leased to private interests, and the rest was held by the Government. The situation has remained basically unchanged since Independence. For most legal and administrative purposes there are two distinct systems of land tenure: an introduced western-style legal system applying to alienated lands, and a plethora of customary systems based on the

The 'singing' or 'killpig' ceremony remains a favourite activity amongst Papuans in the southern highlands of PNG. WWF/G. Favre/Spelefilm

traditions of the ethnic groups occupying the remaining land. Only the Government may acquire lands from customary landowners. If necessary, it may do so by compulsory means for specified public purposes, but this authority is rarely exercised. Instead, any acquisition generally involves protracted negotiations at the local level. Even then, perceptions of land-ownership in PNG mean that previous owners still expect to be involved in decisions on land-use.

By law, all minerals and the rights to use all natural water resources are vested in the state. Forests, on the other hand, are regarded as private property. The Government may authorise entry onto any forest land for mineral prospecting or water resource investigation, and it may also issue permits for timber exploitation, but it must first negotiate acquisition of the rights from local communities (Eaton, 1985).

The people of Papua New Guinea are Melanesians, but there are many different ethnic types and over 700 linguistic groups. A few predominantly hunting and gathering groups still exist but most of the population practise subsistence agriculture, tending and planting indigenous crops such as bananas, breadfruit, sago and sugarcane, exotic crops such as sweet potatoes, taro and yams as well as gathering plant products and hunting small animals.

About 89 per cent of the population live in rural areas. Population densities are generally very low (2–4 persons per sq. km) in coastal and lowland swamp areas, and in grassland and open woodland areas with marked seasonal rainfall, somewhat higher (8–16 persons per sq. km) in lowland and montane rain forest areas, and very high (occasionally up to 200 persons per sq. km) in the intermontane valleys and basins of the central cordillera. The population live in small communities, and there are a multitude of tribes, clans and smaller groups, often of widely differing ethnic origin and language. Almost all practise shifting cultivation and all are heavily dependent on wildlife for food. Certain animals, notably the birds of paradise, cassowaries, New Guinea harpy eagle, some phalangers, the tree-kangaroos and the echidnas, are much sought after for adornment or pets. Despite this, many local communities have a natural feeling for conservation and practise self-imposed restraints in their hunting so as not to exterminate the wildlife on which they depend.

Approximately 20 per cent of PNG is currently used for agriculture and 10 per cent, or 46,000 sq. km, is under intensive cultivation (Freyne and McAlpine, 1985). Soils with good agricultural potential, however, are estimated to total 4960 sq. km, or about one per cent of the total land area. They consist of alluvial and volcanic ash-covered plains and gently sloping land in parts of Madang, Northern Central and Milne Bay provinces, and along the north coast of New Britain. Land of moderate agricultural potential and suitable for grazing includes many coastal areas, valleys in the highlands, Markham and Ramu valleys, Sepik lowlands and much of Western Province, and comprises about 28 per cent of total land area. The remaining 71 per cent of land, much of which is mountainous or swampy, is unsuitable for large-scale agriculture although in many areas subsistence shifting agriculture occurs (UNEP, 1986).

The Forests

The forests of PNG are similar to those of neighbouring Irian Jaya (see chapter 19). The lowland evergreen and semi-evergreen rain forests suffer continual disturbance from cyclones, earthquakes, landslides, volcanoes, changing river courses, occasional fires and, in some places, from a long history of agricultural activity. These disturbances are reflected in the abundance of certain tree species, for example gregarious *Eucalyptus deglupta* or *Octomeles sumatrana*, which occur on fresh riverside alluvium. Dipterocarps are patchy, but there are a few areas where *Hopea* and *Vatica* frequently occur, and *Anisoptera thurifera* is an invasive gregarious species of certain ridge crests and disturbed sites. The following are features of forest cover in Papua New Guinea:

1 There are extensive lower and upper montane rain forests which have abundant Fagaceae including *Nothofagus*, which is often gregarious. The high peaks of the central cordillera have subalpine forest up to the, often fire-determined, tree-line, and alpine grassland, moss tundra and shrub heaths beyond.

2 There are huge freshwater swamp forests in the valleys of the big rivers. Some, especially the Fly River, have big swamps of sago palm *Metroxylon sagu* and of *Nypa*. Other important forested wetlands

PNG is over three-quarters covered by forest. Shifting cultivation is becoming a problem and logging activities are set to extend in the coming decade. WWF/ G. Favre/Spelefilm

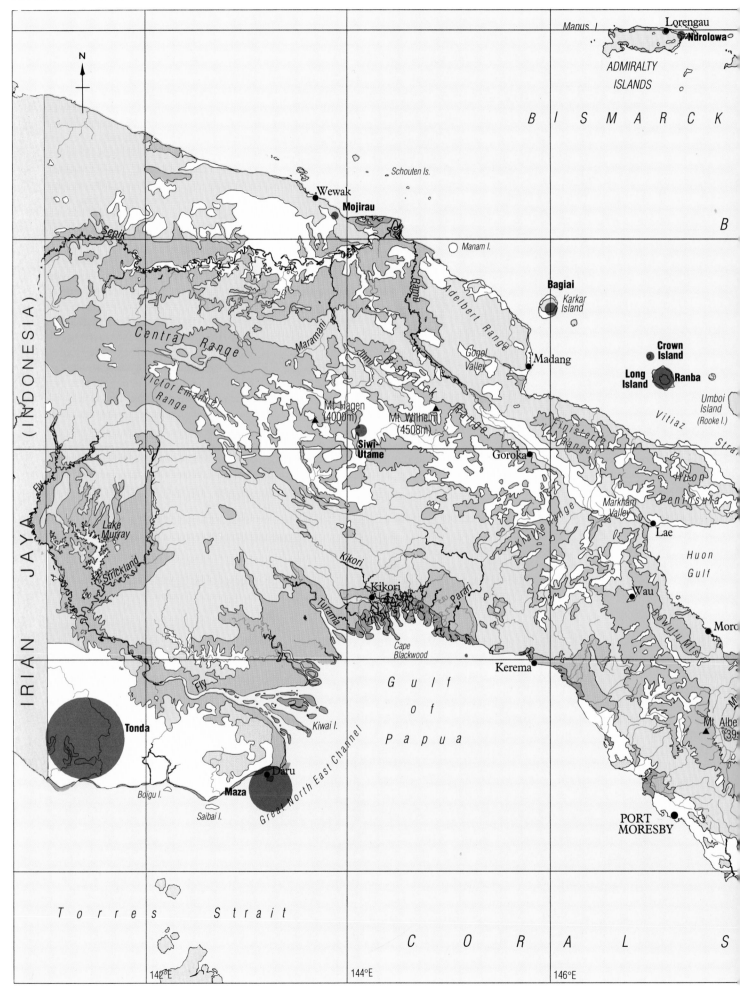

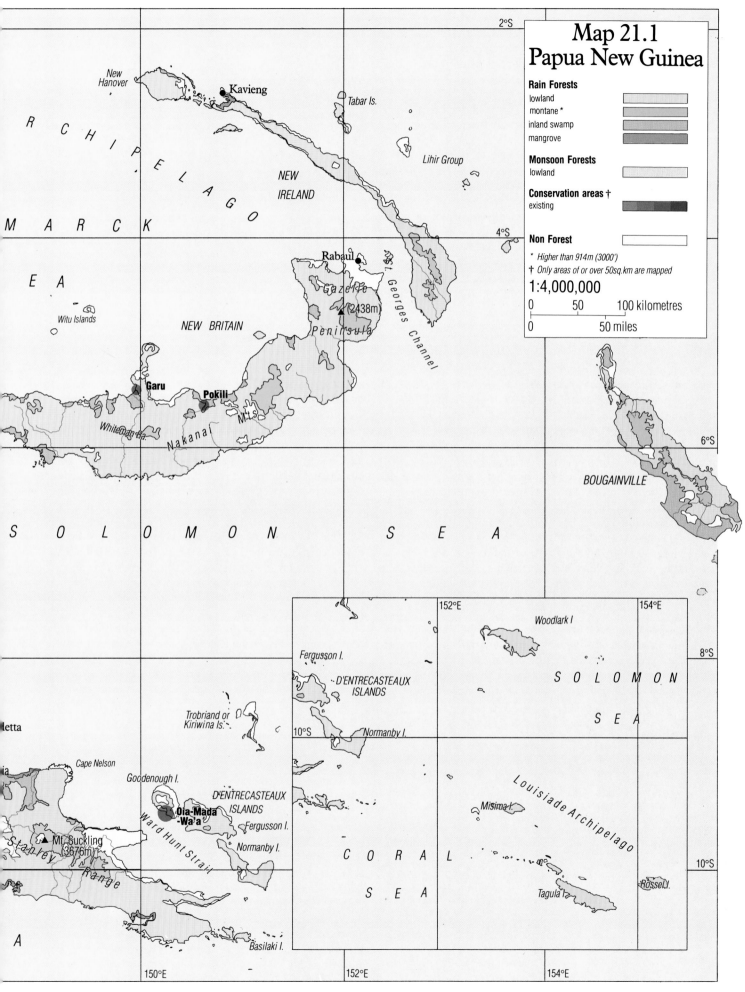

Map 21.1
Papua New Guinea

Rain Forests
lowland
montane *
inland swamp
mangrove

Monsoon Forests
lowland

Conservation areas †
existing

Non Forest

* Higher than 914m (3000')
† Only areas of or over 50sq.km are mapped

1:4,000,000

0   50   100 kilometres

0   50 miles

include the Sepik and Ramu rivers in the north and the Purari, Kikori and Turama rivers in the south (Scott, 1989).

3 There are extensive areas of limestone, including the spectacular needle karst. The distinctive forests of limestone hills are found on the karst, except where the limestone is blanketed with volcanic-derived soils.

4 Scattered outcrops of ultrabasic rocks, for example in a belt along the Sepik, carry distinctive forest in which *Agathis labillardierei* may be gregarious.

5 In the areas which have a seasonal climate, which are most extensive in south Papua, there are monsoon forests and savanna woodlands with a strong Australian floristic element; the latter are subject to annual flooding.

Paijmans (1975) classified and mapped the vegetation of Papua New Guinea. He wrote an account later which used slightly different vegetation types (Paijmans, 1976) and both accounts differed from a series of CSIRO land use surveys which preceded them and from a 1971 set of maps which Beehler (1985) has analysed. In this atlas and on Map 21.1 we follow Paijmans (1975), but have reconciled his categories with our own nomenclature.

Forest Resources and Management

In 1985 FAO estimated that 361,430 sq. km of Papua New Guinea (77 per cent) was covered in natural closed forest, 356,230 sq. km of which was broadleaved and 5200 sq. km coniferous (FAO, 1987). A further 300 sq. km of land was laid to plantations. Table 21.1 is an analysis of the forest cover shown on Map 21.1. It shows 366,750 sq. km (81 per cent of land area) under forest, most of it rain forest. As the Map Legend explains, the data presented here have their origin in the 1970s, and more recent statistics, such as those of FAO (1987), would be expected to show lower forest cover. However, the difference is rather slight and Map 21.1 is a close approximation to the state of the nation's forests today.

Sustainable natural forest management is implicit in the fourth goal of the national constitution. In 1986, however, an unpublished FAO review was in no doubt that the sustained yield objective was not being met in Papua New Guinea, in that the rate of timber cutting 'greatly exceeds the rate at which it is being replaced so that PNG's forest capital is being depleted. This clearly contravenes the fourth aim of the constitution . . .'.

In 1974, based on aerial photographs from 1944–5 and the early 1960s, FAO estimated that 150,000 sq. km were suitable for logging. A major problem in assessing potential sustained yield, however, is that little is known about rates of natural and man-made deforestation before and after logging, or about the proportion of concession

Table 21.1 Estimates of forest extent

	Area (sq. km)	% of land area
Rain forests		
Lowland	229,870	50.9
Montane	63,840	14.1
Inland swamp	64,420	14.3
Mangrove	5,400	1.2
Sub totals	363,530	80.5
Monsoon forests		
Lowland	3,220	0.7
Totals	366,750	81.2

The figures are based on an analysis of Map 21.1 (see Map Legend for details)

Table 21.2 Operable areas in logging concessions, to end of 1984, by province

Province	Total concessions area (sq. km)	Total operable area (sq. km)	% operable of total area
Central	2,250	1,618	71.9
E & W Sepik	5,798	2,530	43.6
W New Britain	4,988	3,563	71.4
Morobe	1,893	598	31.6
Western	28,449	2,040	7.2
Northern	2,983	1,573	52.7
W Highlands	1,270	870	68.5
Manus	920	380	41.3
Gulf	10,500	1,625	15.5
Madang	2,350	1,200	51.1
N Solomons	600	470	78.3
Totals	62,001	16,467	26.6

(*Source*: Unpublished data from Srivastava, 1985)

areas physically accessible. As is common in mountainous rain forest, less than 30 per cent of concession areas may be accessible, and therefore loggable (Table 21.2). On the basis of a generous 40 per cent of the utilisable estate being accessible, only 60,000 sq. km are truly productive (16 per cent of the forest estate).

Even less is known about the regenerative capacity of the forests, in terms of tree girth increments and species composition. Official estimates of the quantities of merchantable wood per hectare are 50–60 cu. m, but actual production is generally 20–30 cu. m. The 60,000 sq. km of productive forest has a total volume of 180 million cu. m, at 30 cu. m per ha. With a very conservative annual dbh increment of 0.75 cm (annual volume increment 0.6 cu. m per ha), and an estimated regeneration cycle of 50 years, the annual allowable cut for sustained production of sawlogs and veneer logs is 3–6 million cu. m.

The timber industry in PNG has developed rapidly over the past 30 years (see chapter 7). Total output of sawlogs and veneer logs has increased from 46,000 cu. m in 1952 to 910,000 cu. m in 1979 and almost 2.5 million cu. m in 1988; three-quarters of this is destined for the export market. Volumes of log exports rose significantly after 1979, when a new, more liberal, Forestry Act was promulgated. In 1988 PNG earned about US$111 million from forest products, of which US$94 million was for logs. Despite this enormous increase in output, however, the manpower in the Forestry Department has been halved since 1975.

PNG remains a relatively minor world supplier of export logs, but its share of the Asian market has increased dramatically due to the combination of rising exports from PNG and declining log exports from other major sources. Japan, Korea and Taiwan between them import more than 90 per cent of PNG log exports.

The Government, concerned at these rising exports of raw logs, had imposed a ban on ten species of unprocessed timber by June 1989. The intention is that by 1991 no more new log export permits will be issued and exporters will be charged higher fees. The bans are aimed at protecting high-quality timber from rapid depletion and at encouraging local processing and the export of sawn lumber.

In PNG at present there is no formal application of sustained yield management. Forests logged over for the more valuable species are simply left to recover naturally. Some environmental safeguards are included in the logging agreements, for example logging is not allowed within 20 m of streams, or 50 m of major rivers, nor on gradients above 25–30°, but the application of these rules is patchy.

The 1989 TFAP mission team detected lowering of tree species diversity, and poor regrowth of valuable species in logged forest. Their conclusion was that on a simplistic analysis the existing management system was resulting in a significant reduction of natural growing stock. The problem is compounded by a lack of long-term commitment to the land by the timber concessionaires.

The Forestry Act 1973 defines the overall responsibilities for the conservation and management of the nation's forest resources. It empowers the Minister for Forests, through the Department of Forests, to acquire the rights to harvest timber from willing customary landowners through a Timber Rights Purchase. The Government arranges for logging by private industrial companies.

The Forestry Private Dealings Act 1973 offers an alternative mechanism whereby private landowners deal directly with developers, subject only to the approval of the Minister, who declares a 'Local Forest Area' in order to safeguard the owner's and the nation's interests. It is likely that these two mechanisms will be replaced by Forest Management Agreements, which will require management plans and should improve consultation with landowners.

In PNG at present there is concern that these regulations are being abused. The Government has set up a Commission of Inquiry into Aspects of the Forestry Industry to investigate allegations of malfeasance. Through a combination of misdeclarations on species, grades and volumes, up to US $14 million per year is being lost to the nation, 10 per cent of this being lost government revenues.

Deforestation

The two major causes of deforestation are shifting cultivation and logging. Fuelwood collection (5.5 million cu. m in 1988) is also responsible for some deforestation, particularly in areas with high human density, such as the highland provinces, the Gazelle Peninsula of New Britain, and around Port Moresby and Lae. Some forest lands are also cleared for cash crops such as oil palm, rubber, cocoa and coffee. Estimates of the overall level of deforestation remain highly speculative. A rate of 220 sq. km per year was published for 1981–5 (FAO, 1988) and 120 sq. km per year for 1986–90 (FAO, 1987), mostly as a result of shifting cultivation. Degradation of forests as a result of commercial logging probably accounts for a further 600 sq. km per year (WEI, 1988).

Agriculture Traditional forms of agriculture have been practised in PNG for 9000 years, and extensive parts of the 200,000 sq. km lowland forests are secondary (Saulei, 1987). Shifting agriculture continues today and, where human population densities are low, it is probably sustainable. However, certain areas, particularly in the highlands, some coastal areas and the Gazelle Peninsula, have suffered permanent deforestation. In these regions the short fallow period has resulted in manmade grasslands about 10,000 sq. km in extent. K. J. White (in Saulei, 1987) has estimated that grasslands are extending by 100–200 sq. km per year.

Logging Saulei (1987) gives the area under logging concession in 1984 as 41,000 sq. km, with a further 6000 sq. km applied for. Unpublished data from P. B. L. Srivastava (1985), however, lists 62,000 sq. km by the end of the same year, 1984 (Table 21.2). Current figures have not been obtained. At the end of 1984 there were 16 major timber companies, logging up to 500–600 sq. km per year.

The first large-scale clear-felling operation in the lowland rain forests of PNG began in 1973 in the Gogol valley, Madang Province. Some 680 sq. km of rain forest in the area are destined for clearance, with most going for wood chips. By the end of 1983, 370 sq. km had been cleared. Only 48 sq. km had been developed for reforestation and there were serious fears about the economic viability and environmental impact of the project (Seddon, 1984).

Mangroves

Mangrove forests occupy large parts of the coast, notably in the Gulf of Papua with 1620–2000 sq. km, and in the Sepik estuary. There is interest in their commercial timber potential, which has not been developed significantly as yet, although a pilot project has been established. The extensive *Nypa* stands in the Gulf of Papua are viewed as a potential source of ethanol for fuel; a pilot project has been established to produce syrups and vinegar. Salt production has been investigated in the vicinity of Port Moresby, but commercial development has not proved feasible.

Most mangrove forests in PNG are sparsely populated and remain virtually intact. However, schemes for large-scale chipping in the region are being considered and could in time constitute a serious threat. The forests traditionally provide many forest products, particularly for medicine, firewood and building materials (Cragg, 1987).

Biodiversity

New Guinea, the largest and highest tropical island, has an extraordinary diversity of ecosystems, from mountain glaciers to tropical rain forests. This richness is reflected in some of the most remarkable wildlife on earth. The island is so large that it has some of the attributes of a small continent, including its own centres of endemism, montane, lowland and off-shore islands, each with its own complement of unique species. The faunistic and floristic affinities of New Guinea extend in all directions: the Philippines, Malaysia, the western Pacific and Australia (Gressitt, 1982).

There are believed to be 11,000 or so species of vascular plants in New Guinea, plus about 2000 ferns (Parris, 1985; IUCN, 1986). Over half are probably endemic but precise counts do not exist. The lowland forests are the richest, with over 1200 species of trees. Diversity declines with increasing altitude, but the higher mountain peaks, such as the Finisterres and Mounts Wilhelm (4508 m), Giluwe (4088 m), Amungwiwa (3277 m), Victoria (4073 m) and Albert-Edward (3993 m), have many unique species.

PNG has almost 200 species of mammals, some threatened, including Doria's and Goodfellow's tree-kangaroos (*Dendrolagus dorianus notatus* and *D. goodfellowi*) and the Woodlark Island cuscus (*Phalanger lullulae*). A number of other species of marsupial, including several cuscuses and the Papuan dorcopsis (*dorcopsis macleayi*) are rare. The Wildlife Division has a recording scheme based on a 10 km grid for the whole country. Record sheets are being compiled for mammals, birds and butterflies, but few are yet complete.

New Guinea and nearby islands together have one of the richest and most varied bird faunas in the world, with about 740 species recorded, 10 per cent of them endemic (Coates, 1985). Of the 570 species of non-marine breeding birds, 445 dwell in rain forest. None of these is considered to be in danger of extinction, but 24 species are now very rare, and possibly coming under threat. All species of birds of paradise are protected by law in Papua New Guinea.

The rich PNG reptile fauna includes 90 species of snake, 170 lizards, 13 turtles and two crocodiles (Allison, 1982; Whitaker *et al.*, 1982). Relatively little is known about their distribution, and there is little evidence of threat, with the exception of marine turtles and crocodiles. Crocodiles are farmed widely, with about 55,000 in captivity in 1988.

Nearly 200 species of frogs have been described from PNG (Zweifel and Tyler, 1982). The majority of these are endemic but little is known of their distribution or status. About 40 per cent are tree frogs, dependent largely upon the native forests. There is little evidence of threat. Other amphibian groups do not occur.

The New Guinea insect fauna is striking, with many large and beautiful forms, and high levels of endemism (Gressitt, 1958). Over 80 per cent of the 455 species of butterflies are endemic and perhaps best known are the birdwing butterflies (*Ornithoptera* and *Troides*). A number of these superbly beautiful species are under threat, including the world's largest and most endangered butterfly, Queen Alexandra's birdwing (*Ornithoptera alexandrae*), from Northern Province. An Insect Farming and Trading Agency based at Bulolo organises local farmers to breed selected species to supply to collectors, in an effort to take pressure off wild populations and at the same time provide a source of income for rural people (Collins and Morris, 1985).

Conservation Areas
Protected areas currently cover only 2 per cent (9427 sq. km) of Papua New Guinea (Table 21.3). They comprise four National Parks, two Provincial Parks, two Memorial/Historic parks and one Sanctuary established under the National Parks Act. A further 16 Wildlife Management Areas, three Sanctuaries and one 'Protected Area' are designated under the Fauna (Protection and Control) Act. In addition, Mt Wilhelm National Park, Horseshoe Reef Marine Park, Mt Gahavisuka Provincial Park, and Kokoda Trail National Walking Track have been approved but await final declaration (Eaton, 1985). Among recently established protected areas is the Jimi Valley National Park in the Western Highlands. It is a sparsely populated area which is especially rich in birds.

While traditional beliefs and customs have helped to protect the environment in the past, the integrity of the forests is under increasing threat from pressures associated with population growth, increased mobility and growth of the cash economy. The establishment of a protected areas system has proved to be extremely difficult because of the complex traditional land tenure system. New legislation and novel approaches to environmental management are proving necessary. The Wildlife Management Area approach, whereby areas are reserved for conservation and controlled utilisation purposes at the request of the land-owners, was designed to overcome this, but those WMAs that have been established so far have suffered from a lack of investment and trained staff.

Although concerned primarily with endangered species, the Fauna (Protection and Control) Act 1966 provides for the establishment of sanctuaries, 'protected areas' and wildlife management areas on land held under customary ownership. The National Parks Act (1982) provides for the preservation of the environment and of the national cultural heritage and contains provisions for reserving government land and for leasing land. The Conservation Areas Act 1978 has similar objectives to the National Parks Act but is more comprehensive and, to some extent, remedies deficiencies in the other legislation. Papua New Guinea is not yet party to the World Heritage Convention, Unesco Man and Biosphere Programme or the Convention on Wetlands of International Importance especially as Waterfowl Habitat (Ramsar Convention), all of which encourage habitat protection while allowing human use.

PNG is in the enviable position of still having most of its forested land intact. Pressures are building up from agriculture and logging, but the fauna and flora remain rich and in little danger of extinction. However, the protected area system is inadequate for a land of such outstanding biological diversity. Numerous attempts have been made to identify key conservation areas, based on analyses using birds, butterflies and ecosystem types (see case study below), but there are no practical means for gazetting such areas. None of them has had the two elements needed to establish a conservation programme: i.e. a dialogue between the inhabitants and the Government and financial support for management. Since so much of the land is in private hands, novel approaches to conservation will be needed, particularly in the forestry sector where pressure from logging companies for individuals to sell their timber rights is growing daily.

Initiatives for Conservation
Of paramount importance in Papua New Guinea is the need to develop a national conservation strategy. More protected areas are required on the mainland, and on outlying islands, notably New Britain, New Ireland, Manus, Goodenough, Fergusson and Bougainville. Smaller islands with significant levels of endemism, such as the Ninigo and Luf (Hermit) Islands, may require priority action, because they are thought to be under greater threat (Dahl, 1986).

South Pacific Regional Environment Programme (SPREP) An action strategy for protected areas in the south Pacific region has already been launched (SPREP, 1985a). Principal goals of the strategy cover conservation education, conservation policies, establishment of protected areas, effective protected areas management, and regional and international cooperation.

PROTECTED AREA PLANNING IN PAPUA NEW GUINEA

A number of reviews have drawn attention to critical sites for the conservation of the biological and ecological richness of PNG. The protected areas system review of Oceania prepared for IUCN (Dahl, 1986) assessed the conservation importance of individual islands and identified priorities for further action. However, gaps were not identified at national level. Further recommendations were made in the action strategy for protected areas in the south Pacific region adopted at the ministerial meeting of the Third South Pacific National Parks and Reserves Conference (SPREP, 1985a). Other major sources of information are the proceedings of the Third South Pacific National Parks and Reserves Conference (SPREP, 1985b), and the recent directories of coral reefs (UNEP/IUCN, 1988) and wetlands (Scott, 1989).

Diamond (1976) proposed a system that built on a scheme by Specht *et al.* (1974) in which 22 areas that would incorporate an almost complete range of biogeographical and ecological patterns were defined. Unfortunately, the majority of existing protected areas lie outside the areas that he identified, and most of his priority areas are not protected.

Less ambitious, and focused principally on conserving birds of paradise and their rain forest habitat throughout New Guinea, is a 4882 sq. km system of eight reserves proposed by Beehler (1985). Of the four proposed reserves that lie in mainland Papua New Guinea and cover a total area of 932 sq. km, only Giluwe and Finisterre lie within officially proposed protected areas. In addition to providing safe breeding habitat for populations of all 40 species of Papuan birds of paradise, the proposed system would benefit other birds, including the many endemic species. This system represents an initial compromise plan, dictated by politics and economics, that could be expanded later.

Similarly, Parsons (1983) has proposed the establishment of a network of 20 reserves to meet the conservation requirements of birdwing butterflies, which are Papua New Guinea's national insects. Many of these proposed sites coincide or overlap with those recommended under the schemes already discussed.

The Government has recently endorsed Regional Sanctuaries in four regions (islands, mainland, highlands and southern), but implementation has been delayed due to lack of finance.

Table 21.3 Conservation areas of Papua New Guinea

Existing areas, 50 sq. km and over and for which we have location data, are listed below. (Sizes of proposed conservation areas are not known and have therefore not been listed.) The remaining areas are combined in a total under Other Areas. Forest reserves are not included. All areas include moist forest within their boundaries.

Wildlife Management Areas	Existing area (sq. km)
Bagiai	138
Garu	87
Maza	1,842
Mojirau	51
Ndrolowa	59
Oia-Mada-Wa'a	228
Pokili	98
Ranba	419
Siwi-Utame	125
Tonda	5,900
Sanctuaries	
Crown Island	60
Long Island	157
Sub total	9,164
Other Areas	705
Total	9,869

(Taken from documentation provided by the Department of Environment and Conservation, PNG and IUCN, 1990)

Tropical Forestry Action Plan (TFAP) Papua New Guinea made an official request for assistance under the Tropical Forestry Action Plan in 1988, and an international team with local counterparts from the PNG Government carried out a month-long forestry sector review in April 1989 (see also chapter 10). Their main finding was that forest legislation, policy and management suffered from problems serious enough to warrant a completely new approach to forest administration. This should include new legislation, the establishment of a decentralised management system, and provision for environmental monitoring.

The mission proposed a series of forest conservation activities in tune with the practicalities of the land tenure system:

1 Development of a national conservation strategy based on a seminar prepared and organised by a competent local institute.

2 Rehabilitation of existing national parks, development and implementation of management plans.

3 Support for non-governmental organisations in the field of forestry and conservation.

4 National accession to the World Heritage Convention and the establishment of one or more major World Heritage sites linked with sustained yield forestry projects. This is similar to the Biosphere Reserve approach, where pristine core areas are surrounded by shells of forest under various forms of sustained yield management.

This last proposal would represent a great step forward, linking the concept of sustained yield forestry with biological conservation in an integrated and mutually dependent way. With large areas of logging concessions inaccessible, the scheme has the advantage of giving value to what are largely considered to be unloggable wastelands. The challenge is to achieve what would be a complex exercise in diplomacy and planning in one of the most complicated societies in the world.

References

Allison, A. (1982) Distribution and ecology of New Guinea lizards. In: Gressitt, J. L. (ed.) (*loc. cit.*), pp. 803–14..

Beehler, B. M. (1985) Conservation of New Guinea forest birds. In: *Conservation of Tropical Forest Birds*. Diamond, A. W. (ed.) ICBP Technical Publication No. 4, pp. 223–46. International Council for Bird Preservation, Cambridge, UK.

Coates, B. J. (1985) *The Birds of Papua New Guinea, Including the Bismarck Archipelago and Bougainville*. Volume 1. *Non-passerines*. Dove Publications, Alderley, Queensland, Australia. 464 pp.

Collins, N. M. and Morris, M. G. (1985) *Threatened Swallowtail Butterflies of the World. The IUCN Red Data Book*. IUCN, Cambridge, UK, and Gland, Switzerland. 401 pp.

Cragg, S. M. (1987) Papua New Guinea. In: *Mangroves of Asia and the Pacific: Status and Management*. Umali, R. M. *et al.* (eds), Natural Resources Management Center and National Mangrove Committee, Ministry of Natural Resources, Manila, pp. 299–309.

Dahl, A L. (1986) *Review of the Protected Areas System in Oceania*. IUCN, Gland, Switzerland, and Cambridge, UK. 239 pp.

Diamond, J. M. (1976) A proposed natural reserve system for Papua New Guinea. Unpublished report. 16 pp.

Eaton, P. (1985) Land tenure and conservation: protected areas in the South Pacific. *SPREP Topic Review* No. 17. South Pacific Commission, Noumea, New Caledonia. 103 pp.

FAO (1987) *Special Study on Forest Management, Afforestation and Utilization of Forest Resources in the Developing Regions. Asia-Pacific Region. Assessment of Forest Resources in Six Countries*. FAO, Bangkok, Thailand. 104 pp.

FAO (1988) *An Interim Report on the State of Forest Resources in the Developing Countries*. FAO, Rome, Italy. 18 pp. + 5 tables.

FAO (1990) *FAO Yearbook of Forest Products 1977–88*. FAO Forestry Series No. 23, FAO Statistics Series No. 90. FAO, Rome.

Freyne, D. F. and McAlpine, J. R. (1985) Land clearing and development in Papua New Guinea. In: *Tropical Land Clearing for Sustainable Agriculture*. IBSRAM, Jakarta, Indonesia.

Gressitt, J. L. (1958) New Guinea and insect distribution. *Proceedings of the Fourth International Congress of Entomology* 1: 767–74.

Gressitt, J. L. (ed.) (1982) *Biogeography and Ecology of New Guinea*. Monographiae Biologicae No. 42. Junk, The Hague. 983 pp.

IUCN (1986) *Plants in Danger: What do we Know?* IUCN, Gland, Switzerland, and Cambridge, UK. 461 pp.

IUCN (1990) *1989 United Nations List of National Parks and Protected Areas*. IUCN, Gland, Switzerland, and Cambridge, UK.

McAlpine, J. R., Keig, G. and Falls, R. (1983) *Climate of Papua New Guinea*. ANU Press, Canberra, Australia. 200 pp.

Paijmans, K. (1975) Vegetation map of Papua New Guinea (1:1,000,000) and explanatory notes to the vegetation map of Papua New Guinea. *CSIRO Land Research Series* 35: 1–25, and 4 map sheets.

Paijmans, K. (ed.) (1976) *New Guinea Vegetation*. Elsevier, Amsterdam, The Netherlands. 213 pp.

Parris, B. S. (1985) Ecological aspects of distribution and speciation in Old World tropical ferns. *Proceedings of the Royal Society of Edinburgh* 86: 341–6.

Parsons, M. J. (1983) *A Conservation Study of the Birdwing Butterflies* Ornithoptera *and* Troides *(Lepidoptera: Papilionidae) in Papua New Guinea*. Final Report to Department of Primary Industry, Papua New Guinea. 111 pp.

Saulei, S. M. (1987) The forest resource development crisis in Papua New Guinea. In: *Forest Resources Crisis in the Third World*. Sahabat Alam, Penang, Malaysia, pp. 81–92.

Scott, D. A. (ed.) (1989) *A Directory of Asian Wetlands*. IUCN, Gland, Switzerland, and Cambridge, UK. 1181 pp.

Seddon, G. (1984) Logging in the Gogol Valley, Papua New Guinea. *Ambio* **13**: 345–50.

Specht, R. L., Rae, E. M. and Boughton, V. H. (1974) *Conservation of Major Plant Communities in Australia and Papua New Guinea*. Australian Journal of Botany Supplementary Series **7**: 591–605.

SPREP (1985a) *Action Strategy for Protected Areas in the South Pacific Region*. South Pacific Commission, Noumea, New Caledonia. 21 pp.

SPREP (1985b) *Report of the Third South Pacific National Parks and Reserves Conference*. Volume 3. *Country reviews*. South Pacific Commission, Noumea, New Caledonia, pp. 175–94.

Srivastava, P. B. L. (1985) Environmental and socio-economic aspects of tropical deforestation in Asia and the Pacific – Papua New Guinea. Unpublished report. 149 pp.

UNEP (1986) *Environmental Management in Papua New Guinea*. 3 volumes. UNEP, Nairobi.

UNEP/IUCN (1988) *Coral Reefs of the World. Volume 3: Central and Western Pacific*. UNEP Regional Seas Directories and Bibliographies. IUCN, Gland, Switzerland, and Cambridge, UK/ UNEP, Nairobi, Kenya. 329 pp.

WEI (1988) *Protecting the Environment. A Call for Support*. Wau Ecology Institute, Wau, Papua New Guinea. 19 pp.

Whitaker, R., Whitaker, Z. and Mills, M. (1982) Reptiles of Papua New Guinea. *Wildlife in Papua New Guinea* No. 82/2. Division of Wildlife, Department of Lands and Environment, Konedobu. 53 pp.

Zweifel, R. G. and Tyler, M. J. (1982) Amphibia of New Guinea. In: Gressitt, J. L. (ed.) (*loc. cit.*), pp. 759–802.

Authorship

Mark Collins at WCMC, with contributions from Mick Raga in Port Moresby, Caroline Sargent of IIED, Iamo Ila, Karol Kisokau and Kembi Wotoka of the Department of Environment and Conservation in Boroko and Alan Ross, Prem Srivastava and Charlie Tawhiao of the Department of Forests, Boroko.

Map 21.1 Forest cover in Papua New Guinea

As described above (see *The Forests* section) there have been several accounts and maps of vegetation types and forest cover of Papua New Guinea. A set of 18 maps at 1:500,000 scale dating from 1971 is still available: *PNG Vegetation and Timber Resources Edition 2*. Compiled by the Australian Department of Defence from air photography and radar imagery, these maps show the distribution of major forest types. Given the relatively slow rate of change in PNG, they are still of value. However, K. Paijmans' (1975) set of four 1:1 million scale maps remains the most useful and recent set of data, and formed the basis for the map presented in this atlas. *Vegetation of Papua New Guinea* and the accompanying *Explanatory Notes* show 13 forest categories, mangrove and 10 other categories. In the forest categories, lowland rain forests mapped here have been compiled from Paijmans' categories large to medium crowned and small crowned forests on plains and farms (FPl, FPs), littoral forest (FB), medium, small and large crowned lowland hill forests (FHm, FHs, FHl) and dry evergreen forest (Fd). Freshwater swamp forest comprises Paijmans' open forest on plains (FPo), swamp forest (Fsw) and moist swamp woodland (Wsw). Montane forest comprises lower montane (FL), coniferous lower montane (FLc), very small-crowned lower montane (FLs) and montane (FM) forests, and begins at 1400 m altitude. Seasonal (monsoon) forest is Paijmans' woodland category W. Non-forest comprises Paijmans' categories of scrub (Sc), savanna (Sa), grassland (G, Gsw) mixed herbaceous vegetation (Hsw) and gardens (Ga). Areas of secondary forest, indicated by an overlay of dots onto the forest type by Paijmans, have not been distinguished on the map shown here. Pioneer vegetation (Pi) has been included with its neighbouring climax forest type.

The locations of protected areas have been extracted from a number of sources, but particularly maps made available by the Department of Environment and Conservation in Papua New Guinea. Unfortunately maps showing precise boundaries are unavailable, and protected areas are here represented by circles of an appropriate size.

22
Peninsular Malaysia

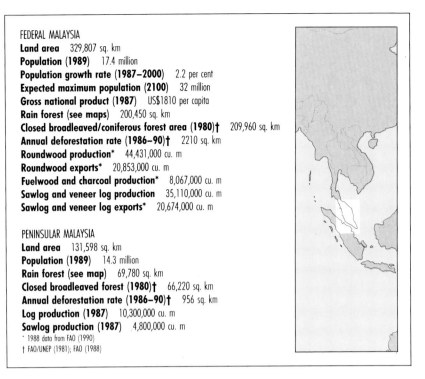

FEDERAL MALAYSIA
Land area 329,807 sq. km
Population (1989) 17.4 million
Population growth rate (1987–2000) 2.2 per cent
Expected maximum population (2100) 32 million
Gross national product (1987) US$1810 per capita
Rain forest (see maps) 200,450 sq. km
Closed broadleaved/coniferous forest area (1980)† 209,960 sq. km
Annual deforestation rate (1986–90)† 2210 sq. km
Roundwood production* 44,431,000 cu. m
Roundwood exports* 20,853,000 cu. m
Fuelwood and charcoal production* 8,067,000 cu. m
Sawlog and veneer log production 35,110,000 cu. m
Sawlog and veneer log exports* 20,674,000 cu. m

PENINSULAR MALAYSIA
Land area 131,598 sq. km
Population (1989) 14.3 million
Rain forest (see map) 69,780 sq. km
Closed broadleaved forest (1980)† 66,220 sq. km
Annual deforestation rate (1986–90)† 956 sq. km
Log production (1987) 10,300,000 cu. m
Sawlog production (1987) 4,800,000 cu. m
* 1988 data from FAO (1990)
† FAO/UNEP (1981); FAO (1988)

Peninsular Malaysia has a long history of careful forest management, and conservation of its extremely rich biological reserves is well developed. Rapid development of the land has occurred over recent decades, but this has now begun to stabilise. Under the 5th Malaysia Plan an area of only 1286 sq. km has been scheduled for deforestation, much less than in previous plans. However, it is envisaged that all stateland forests (approximately 8700 sq. km) not included either in the Permanent Forest Estate (currently 47,500 sq. km) or in the protected area network (c. 5700 sq. km) will eventually be deforested and converted to other land uses.

At the moment there is a good network of representative areas for the conservation of ecosystems, biological diversity and ecological services, but the time is ripe to examine their adequacy, and to set aside further conservation areas before later development diminishes the opportunity to do so. When considering the management of production forest within the Permanent Forest Estate, it is essential to balance conservation needs with timber production. It is vital to protect and maintain pristine areas of natural forest in order to recolonise the degraded forests' stock of flora and fauna. This is especially important now, because most of the production forests are located in hilly terrain, where environmental damage caused by logging is considerable.

The rationale for conservation of natural forests needs to be clearly communicated to all levels of Malaysian society. The essential ecological benefits that can accrue from having adequate cover of a matrix of both undisturbed and production forests needs to be emphasised in order that conservation matters can be viewed clearly. Ultimately it will be the Malaysian public that rallies political and economic forces in support of conservation of the Malaysian environment.

INTRODUCTION

Malaysia is a federation of 13 states, 11 in the Malay peninsula (West or Peninsular Malaysia), and Sarawak and Sabah[1] in Borneo (East Malaysia). Peninsular Malaysia accounts for 40 per cent of the land area and over three-quarters of the population. The principal highlands, set inland from the coastal plains, consist of several roughly parallel ranges that run down the centre of the country from the Thai border to the south of Negeri Sembilan. Peaks range up to c. 2000 m in height and divide the western states from Kelantan, Terengganu and Pahang to the east. There is a more dispersed mass of mountains to the east of the main ranges with an east-west watershed separating the northward flowing rivers of Kelantan and north Terengganu from the south flowing catchment of the Pahang river, on which lies Gunung Tahan (2189 m), the highest mountain. There are other lower mountains further south around the Pahang–Johor border.

[1] See Chapter 24 for Sarawak and Sabah

The population of Malaysia is racially mixed, with about 54 per cent Bumiputras (Malays and other indigenous races), 35 per cent Chinese and 10 per cent Indians. In the Peninsula the religion of the majority (Malays) is Muslim, and Islam is the official religion. In 1984 the Government announced a policy of encouraging population growth from the present 17 million to 70 million people. Tax incentives to encourage this were passed by Parliament in 1985.

The Forests

Lowland evergreen tropical rain forest is the principal forest formation on dry land at low altitudes in Peninsular Malaysia, as Map 22.1 shows. In the extreme north-west this is replaced by the semi-evergreen formation. The rain forest is rich in Dipterocarpaceae, notably *Anisoptera, Dipterocarpus, Dryobalanops, Hopea* and *Shorea*. It is subdivided into lowland (below 300 m) and hill (300–1300 m) forest, on floristic composition. Along the east coast there remain a

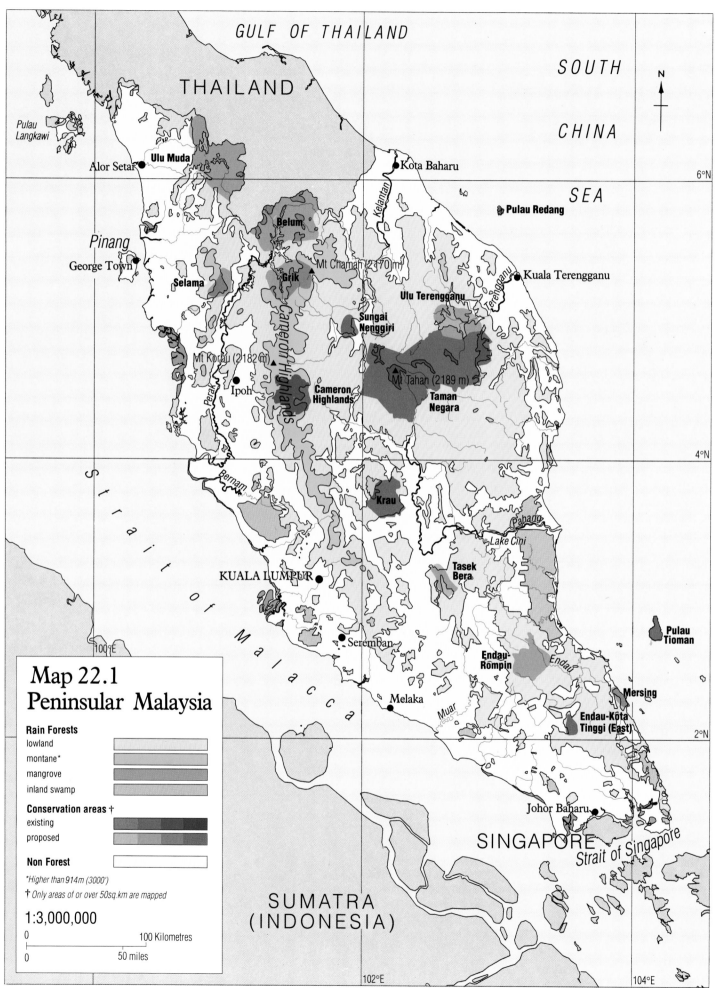

Map 22.1
Peninsular Malaysia

Rain Forests
lowland
montane*
mangrove
inland swamp

Conservation areas †
existing
proposed

Non Forest

*Higher than 914m (3000')
† Only areas of or over 50sq.km are mapped

1:3,000,000

0   100 Kilometres
0   50 miles

few patches of heath forest on recent, unconsolidated sands, but most have been degraded to open savanna. Tiny fragments of rain forest occur inland. Other forest formations are as follows:

1 There are extensive karst limestone hills from Kuala Lumpur northwards and these carry the limestone forest formation. Only one small area of ultrabasic rocks occurs.
2 Peat swamp and freshwater swamp forests were extensive on both the east and west coasts (see Map 22.1), but most of the latter and some of the former have been cleared for agriculture.
3 Montane rain forests occur extensively on all the main mountains; both lower and upper montane formations are found. The former have been logged to some extent and three hill stations have made inroads into both formations. Plans for a road linking these are currently being actively considered but will pose severe environmental difficulties if they are implemented (Anon., 1989).
4 Monsoon forests do not occur in Malaysia.

Forest Resources and Management

About 100 years ago, rain forests probably covered over 90 per cent (c. 120,000 sq. km) of the land area, much of it in the lowlands. In 1966 it was estimated that 68 per cent (c. 90,000 sq. km) of the land area was under natural forest cover (Lee, 1973). The National Forest Inventory of 1970–2 showed that this figure had dropped to c. 83,000 sq. km or 63 per cent (Mohd Darus, 1978). At the end of 1985 forest cover was reported reduced to 61,870 sq. km or 47 per cent (Ministry of Primary Industries, 1988) (see Table 22.1). FAO (1987) agreed with this figure and also taking the statistic for 1980, 66,220 sq. km, they extrapolated forward to reach a figure for 1990 of 57,090 sq. km.

Table 22.2 is a breakdown by major forest types of the areas of forest shown on Map 22.1 (refer to the Map Legend for details of the origin of the map). A comparison of Tables 22.1 and 22.2 shows a discrepancy in that the extent of the mapped forests exceeds the 1985 statistics by 7850 sq. km. It seems likely that the original map used to prepare Map 22.1 was little changed from the Forest Map of Peninsular Malaysia based on 1981–2 data and published in 1986 (see Map Legend).

Peninsular Malaysia has had a Forest Department since the early years of the century and thus has a long record of forest reservation and management. The Forest Departments of the Peninsula and the Eastern Malaysian states of Sarawak and Sabah are independent; the latter manage their own forest estates and are therefore considered separately (see chapter 24).

Silviculture has been one of the concerns of the Forest Department since its inception and has evolved as market conditions have changed. Major logging at high intensity began in the 1950s, under the famous monocyclic Malayan Uniform System (MUS). This has

Table 22.1: Status of forested land in Peninsular Malaysia (thousands of sq. km)

Reporting date	1977	1984	1985
Permanent Forest Estate:	51.7	46.8	47.5
Undisturbed	12.5	9.6	9.8
Logged-over	20.2	18.2	18.7
Protective & Amenity	19.0	19.0	19.0
Agri-conversion forest:	20.2	16.4	14.4
Undisturbed	5.7	1.8	1.6
Logged-over	14.5	14.6	12.8
Total forested land:	71.9	63.2	61.9
Percentage of land area:	54.6	48.0	47.0

(*Sources:* 1977 data from Arshad (1979), 1984 data from Thang (1984), 1985 data from Ministry of Primary Industries (1988))

Table 22.2: Estimates of forest extent

	Area (sq. km)	% of land area
Rain forests		
Lowland	57,610	43.8
Montane	6,880	5.2
Freshwater swamp	4,060	3.1
Mangrove	1,200	0.9
Totals	69,750	53.0

(Based on analysis of Map 22.1. See Map Legend for details of sources)

now been replaced by the Selection Management System (SMS), which includes polycyclic logging as one of its options. Chapter 6 on natural rain forest management describes these systems, including their strengths and weaknesses.

Stand improvement by poison-girdling has been abandoned as part of the silviculture system. This development plus adoption of a polycyclic system are more compatible with conservation of biological diversity and the retention of ecosystem functions. The polycyclic option is also more suitable than the MUS for the highly mixed hill forest areas. With flexible cutting limits, it nevertheless requires that logging must ensure that a residual stocking of 32 trees per hectare of 30 cm dbh and above are left behind (Mohd Darus, 1988). The MUS is still practised in the lowland dipterocarp forests to obtain a more even-aged forest with a higher proportion of commercial species.

By the late 1970s, it became accepted that the rates of logging and deforestation were not sustainable. Moreover a higher priority was placed on agricultural development, specifically cash cropping, evident from the Land Capability Classification scheme (Lee and Panton, 1971), whereby forested land with agricultural potential was categorised as having a higher capability than that without, which carries the implication that such land will ultimately be excised. To ensure that there would be sufficient forest land left and to provide guidelines for the management of the remaining forest resources, the National Forestry Policy was formulated in 1977 and accepted in 1978. The main feature of the policy is the establishment of a Permanent Forest Estate within the government-owned state lands, which in principle will not be converted to other forms of land use.

The Permanent Forest Estate is comprised of areas designated for productive, protective and amenity purposes. Productive forests will be managed for sustained timber production. Protective forests serve to prevent erosion, silting and flooding and to maintain water supplies, and therefore are mainly situated in water-catchment areas and mountain ranges. The amenity forests are meant for conservation, recreation, education and research purposes (Muhammad, 1980).

Forested lands outside the Permanent Forest Estate (apart from those already pronounced as conservation areas) are known as agri-conversion forests. These forests are designated to be logged, re-logged and eventually converted for agricultural use.

As shown in Table 22.1, there have been a number of revisions to the allocation for the Permanent Forest Estate, but 47,500 sq. km of forest are included in the latest statistics. Of this total 28,500 sq. km will be managed as production forest and another 19,000 sq. km is designated as protection forest. Although most of the protection forests will be located in the mountainous areas, they nevertheless represent very important areas for conservation and habitat protection. The production forests will be managed on a sustained yield basis whereby a designated annual coupe of c. 700–750 sq. km will be allowed.

Taman Negara National Park is one of the largest in Southeast Asia and is vital to the conservation of the nation's biodiversity. WWF/M. Kavanagh

With the gradual reduction of forest area there has been a gradual decline in the rate of logging of forest over the last 20 years (Thang, 1984). During the Second Malaysia Plan period (1971–5) logging occurred at 3660 sq. km per year. During the Third Malaysia Plan (1976–80) and Fourth Malaysia Plan (1981–5), the amounts of forest logged were 3184 sq. km and 2230 sq. km per year respectively. In the Fifth Malaysia Plan period (1986–90), the amount of forest logged was scaled down still further to 1521 sq. km per year (Mohd Darus, 1988). Although there appears to be a cumulative total of 53,000 sq. km of forest logged over a 20-year period from 1971–90, the actual amount of forest land logged was much lower, as some areas were relogged, especially those targeted for conversion to agricultural land. The relogging of forests is possible because the first logging usually leaves behind trees which may be worth extracting if market demand improves. Relogging sets back forest recovery by introducing another round of damage and soil erosion. Originally, relogging was only permitted in forests scheduled to be cleared for agriculture, but the increasing market for timber has led to relogging in the Permanent Forest Estate, without assessment of the effect on the next and future rotations. This practice is clearly against the principle of sustained yield (see chapter 6).

It has been estimated that by the early 1990s timber extraction from agri-conversion forests will be exhausted and that the timber industry will have to rely on the productive forest reserves within the Permanent Forest Estate for log supply (Mohd Darus, 1978). The Forest Department recognises that sustainable forest management will need to be implemented in these areas. In this respect, all future logging in already identified production forest within the Permanent Forest Estate will be regulated (712 sq. km per year for the Fifth

Malaysia Plan, 1986–90). It has also increased its efforts in reforestation and rehabilitation of logged forest through silvicultural treatment. However, the rate at which this has been undertaken has not kept up with the rate of logging. At the end of 1988, an accumulated total of 9366 sq. km of inland forest had been silviculturally treated, while enrichment planting in poorly stocked logged areas amounted to 172 sq. km (Thang, 1989). For the period 1988–90 there are plans to treat another 2502 sq. km of logged over forest, 36 sq. km of which is to be enriched with indigenous species (Mohd Darus, 1988). To complement as well as to relieve pressure of supply from natural forest, the Forest Department had already taken steps to establish plantations of fast growing trees with an expected rotation of 15–20 years, and by 1988 306 sq. km had been established. The compensatory plantation project was launched in 1982 and there are plans to establish by the year 2000 a total of 1882 sq. km (Thang, 1989).

Deforestation

FAO (1987) provided three estimates of closed forest cover for Peninsular Malaysia, for 1980, 1985 and an extrapolation to 1990. These figures suggest an expected average annual deforestation rate of 956 sq. km for the 1985–90 period. This is a considerable reduction from rates of over 2500 sq. km per year in the late 1970s.

The major cause of forest depletion in Peninsular Malaysia has been conversion of land from forest to agriculture. In comparison, the loss of forest land to other uses, such as shifting cultivation, mining and building of reservoirs, is relatively small.

Clearing of forests for agriculture on a large scale for cash crops began on the west coast, where private plantations were set up for rubber, coconut and subsequently oil palm. The more recent agro-conversion of forested land has been due to land development schemes carried out by various federal and state government agencies, to provide agricultural land and employment for settlers. The biggest agency is FELDA (Federal Land Development Authority), which began operations in 1956 (see chapter 5). By 1985 FELDA had developed 6600 sq. km of agricultural land throughout the peninsula. By the end of the Fifth Malaysia Plan in 1990, this total will have increased to 8355 sq. km. The most extensive land development schemes have been carried out in Pahang and Johor, the two biggest states of Peninsular Malaysia. In the 1971–80 period FELDA developed 2069 sq. km of land, 46 per cent of which was in Pahang, 22 per cent in Johor and 17 per cent in Negeri Sembilan. This does not include other large-scale agricultural schemes carried out by the state development agencies of Pahang and Johor.

After logging, any remaining vegetation is cleared and burnt before conversion of the land into oil palm or rubber plantations. The developed land is then managed by settlers brought in to live in new townships. These schemes are generally regarded as successful in terms of resettlement of landless populations, generating employment, and also in boosting palm oil and rubber production for the country. Malaysia is the top producer and exporter of these two agricultural commodities in the world.

The second cause of forest depletion is construction of dams for hydroelectric power and irrigation schemes, but total areas lost have so far been relatively small. Of the major hydroelectric dams in Peninsular Malaysia, six are located within the Main Range in Perak. The Temenggor Dam, for example, with 350 MW capacity, flooded about 140 sq. km of forest. The largest hydroelectric dam is the Kenyir Dam in Terengganu with 400 MW capacity. In Kedah, the Muda and Pedu Dams are used for irrigation. The most controversial hydroelectric project in the Peninsula was the proposed Tembeling Dam. In the early 1970s and again in the early 1980s, the Government proposed to construct the dam within and adjacent to the Taman Negara (national park). This would have flooded 97 sq. km of pristine lowland forest within the national park and another 110 sq. km outside the park area. After much public protest, the proposals were shelved.

The third important cause of deforestation is mining. The major mining activities occurred in the late 19th and early 20th centuries, the most extensive being exploitation of alluvial tin in Perak and Selangor. The result was retention ponds and mine spoils in the form of mud sludge and sand piles. Miners were not obliged to refill or rehabilitate the land and the scars remain until today. Natural revegetation of minespoils is very slow and is often set back by remining. The most extensive re-use of these lands is for re-working of old mines which are deemed commercially viable, and building houses and roads in areas close to towns.

The extent of shifting cultivation by indigenous people in Peninsular Malaysia is small. An extensive programme to resettle the indigenous people, or *orang asli*, was initiated after the Second World War for security reasons. Since then, as a result of resettlement and education of the younger generation, many of the indigenous groups have been incorporated into the mainstream of Malaysia's economic activities. Some of the resettlements are large and close to the main towns. An example of this is Gombak, close to Kuala Lumpur. Other settlements are smaller and located closer to the forest, thus allowing the indigenous people the opportunity to practise their traditional way of life.

The Government is still continuing to regroup *orang asli* into settlements. Under the Fifth Malaysia Plan there is a comprehensive programme to regroup 23,000 *orang asli* from the Main Range into five settlement schemes which are agriculture-based.

The groups of indigenous people who are not settled in government-created schemes are widely scattered through the remaining forested areas. Some are nomadic, and are predominantly hunter-gatherers, while others are shifting cultivators. The extent of forest clearing by the shifting cultivators is small because of the low population density of the groups practising it, but there is some evidence that logging companies moving into remote areas are affecting the livelihood of people living traditionally.

Although logging in natural forest does not constitute deforestation, nevertheless it can cause significant ecological damage and degradation of the forest environment. Exploitation has been documented by the National Forest Inventory 1981–2, which showed that, except for protected areas, most of the lowland and hill dipterocarp forests have now been logged. The remaining primary forests are mostly confined to the upland areas along the Main Range (where a new road is planned) and in the east coast states of Kelantan and Terengganu. It is important to bear this fact in mind when studying Map 22.1

Generally, the main watersheds are on high, steep land, and these have been left relatively unexploited and unaffected by deforestation. The Land Capability Classification (Lee and Panton, 1971) categorised these watersheds as Class V, i.e. areas best left in their natural state for soil and water conservation purposes. The National Forestry Policy (Muhammad, 1980) has recommended that these areas be designated as protection forests. There are, however, isolated cases where smaller catchments have been threatened with severe environmental problems due to the opening up of forest land on steep slopes. For example forest clearing in the upper Gombak catchment near Kuala Lumpur resulted in heavy silting of the Gombak River and reduced water supply; so much so that a thriving agricultural area downstream was turned into a wasteland (Soong *et al.*, 1980). Similarly the conversion of steep forested land to vegetable farms in the Cameron Highlands has resulted in increased run-off, severe soil erosion and the silting up of a hydroelectric dam.

Mangroves

Mangroves are to be found mainly along the sheltered west coast fronting the Straits of Malacca, where they form an almost continuous belt, about 20 km at its greatest width. The most extensive groups of mangroves occur along the estuaries of the larger rivers, and are managed by the State Forest Departments for timber production on a sustained yield basis. The most extensive area is the Matang Forest Reserve in the Perak area, which has been managed since last century. In recent years there has been severe pressure to use the mangrove lands for agriculture, urbanisation, ponds and fisheries. Forest Department records show that over a 20-year period from 1965 to 1985, the total area of mangroves declined from 1184 sq. km to 983 sq. km (Anon., 1986), a rate of alienation of about 5–6 sq. km per year. In Selangor alone, 86 sq. km were cut down in 1988–9 (Salleh and Chan, 1988).

Biodiversity

Peninsular Malaysia has a rich flora and fauna with an overwhelmingly Asian (Laurasian) affinity, and a small Australian (Gondwanic) component.

There are about 8000 species of plants, about 200 species of mammals, including 81 bats, 110 species of snakes, and thousands of insect species. About 60 per cent of the bird species and 78 per cent of the land mammals (excluding bats) live in the primary and tall secondary forests.

Various estimates of endemism have been made for flowering plants in Peninsular Malaysia; 30 per cent for tree species (Ng and Low, 1982), 90 per cent for the Begoniaceae, 80 per cent for the Gesneriaceae (Kiew, 1983), and 50 per cent for the orchids.

Deforestation and forest degradation have significantly affected wildlife populations, especially in the lowlands which have the richest wildlife and where deforestation and logging are most extensive. Stevens (1968) concluded from two years' study that 52 per cent of the mammals live at altitudes below 330 m, 81 per cent live below 660 m and only 10 per cent occur at higher elevations. Only 9 per cent can exist at all altitudes. He also found that 53 per cent of the mammals are confined to the primary forest, 25 per cent live in primary or tall secondary forest, 12 per cent live in primary or tall secondary forest or can subsist in cultivated areas, while only 10 per cent live in cultivated or urban areas. Clearly, therefore, forest degradation severely reduces species diversity.

Impacts of habitat loss and forest degradation are best documented for the larger mammals, which require large areas of land for foraging and breeding. The Javan rhinoceros, for example, had become extinct by 1932. The Malayan tiger, thought to number 3500 in the early 1950s, has dwindled to about 250 and is now confined to the areas of Perak, Kelantan and Terengganu (MNS, 1983). The elephant population is now estimated at 700.

However, there are many wildlife species which can adapt to forest degradation. These include a number of totally protected species such as the brush-tail porcupine and the giant squirrels, which mainly dwell in secondary forest (Cadigan and Lim, 1973). See also the case study on hornbills opposite.

Conservation Areas

Species conservation in Peninsular Malaysia dates back to early this century, when various game reserves were created. It was not until 1935, however, when the King George V National Park (now Taman Negara) was created, that large areas of natural ecosystems began to be set aside for conservation. The first comprehensive protected areas plan was contained in the Third Malaysian Plan (TMP) for 1976–80 (Government of Malaysia, 1976). In the TMP, Taman Negara, and 22 other wildlife reserves, game reserves and bird sanctuaries were recognised, and a further two national parks and 21 other reserves were proposed. The TMP was designed to include the representative ecosystems and the major biological communities suggested by the Malayan Nature Society in its Blueprint for Conservation (MNS, 1974).

The present record of conservation areas falls a little short of that proposed under the TMP. The total for new conservation areas proposed under TMP was 8985 sq. km; the total has now reached 8293 sq. km, including the 4344 sq. km Taman Negara (Table 22.3 and Map 22.1). A further 7086 sq. km have been proposed. (These areas do not include forest reserves or virgin jungle reserves.)

An important restraint on new initiatives is that conservation areas gazetted under different legislation come under the jurisdiction of different state and federal government departments. The National Parks Act of 1980 was unpopular with state governments, who were unwilling to transfer land to the Federal Government. Even after amendments to the Act in 1985, state governments were more inclined to establish state parks than national parks under the National Parks Act. So far there has been no national park constituted in Peninsular Malaysia under the National Parks Act.

Besides the conservation areas listed in Table 22.3, the Forest Department has set aside single compartments of forest reserves as virgin jungle reserves (VJRs), which are permanent nature reserves for the preservation of pristine representative forest types and their component species (Figure 22.1). However, these VJRs are small, some have been damaged by logging, and because they are part of forest reserves their viability depends on them being surrounded by managed forest. Some state forest departments have also set up various recreational forest areas.

The existing conservation area system in Peninsular Malaysia relies heavily on one large national park, Taman Negara. Taman Negara is not only the largest park in Malaysia but is also one of the

Table 22.3: Conservation areas of Peninsular Malaysia
Existing and proposed areas, 50 sq. km and over, are listed below. The remaining areas are combined in a total under Other Areas. Forest reserves are not included. For data on ASEAN sites see chapter 9. All areas include moist forest within their boundaries.

	Existing area (sq. km)	Proposed area (sq. km)
National Parks		
Taman Negara	4,344	
Parks		
Endau-Rompin	c. 500	c. 430
Pulau Redang (part marine)		250
Wildlife Reserves		
Belum		2,072
Endau-Kota Tinggi (East)	74	
Grik		518
Krau	531	
Mersing		74
Pulau Tioman	82	
Selaama		222
Sungai Nenggiri		370
Tasek Bera		265
Ulu Muda		1,153
Ulu Terengganu		1,165
Wildlife Sanctuaries		
Cameron Highlands	650	
Sub totals	6,181	6,519
Other Areas	2,135	567
Totals	8,293	7,086

(*Sources* IUCN, 1990 and WCMC *in litt.*)

largest in Southeast Asia, encompassing the largest area of pristine lowland dipterocarp forest left in the country, montane rain forests, and rain forests on limestone. The highest mountain in Peninsular Malaysia, Mt Tahan, is located within the Park. Although Taman Negara encompasses a wide range of vegetation types and supports a viable breeding population of large animals (MNS, 1971), the present network of protected areas in Peninsular Malaysia is by no means adequate, as it does not include some of the critical habitats that are under threat. These include wetland forests such as the peat swamp forest in Pahang and Johor, mangrove forests, and open lake ecosystems. Most importantly, the lowland dipterocarp rain forests are seriously under-represented.

While it is arguable that many of the above ecosystems are represented within forest reserves, the management of such areas is not designed for conservation of the natural forest communities (with the exception of the small virgin jungle reserves). Forestry activities result in drastic changes of the biological communities and their original habitats. This is especially so for forests managed under the MUS. Besides, it is very easy for forest reserves to be excised by state governments. Therefore forest reserves do not adequately conserve either biodiversity or habitats.

Major proposals for extension of conservation areas and concern for existing parks and reserves may be sub-divided by ecosystem.

Lowland rain forest This was once the most extensive forest formation in Peninsular Malaysia, yet there is relatively little left of it today. The few sites that remain more or less in their original condition include Pasoh Forest Reserve and Endau-Rompin.

Although Pasoh Forest Reserve covers an area of only 24 sq. km, it is one of the most intensely studied lowland dipterocarp forests in Southeast Asia. This is largely due to the International Biological Programme (IBP) of the 1960s and early 1970s, which funded a wide range of studies covering flora, fauna, soils and hydrology. It is now hemmed in by oil palm plantations, and because of its small size, disturbance at its edges is significant. It is therefore important that there is no more conversion of forest land. Pasoh is now managed by the Forest Research Institute of Malaysia (FRIM), with long term study plots, including a 50 ha plot where all trees 1 cm dbh and above have been tagged, identified and mapped.

The Endau-Rompin area constitutes the only sizeable undisturbed lowland evergreen rain forest in Peninsular Malaysia besides Taman Negara. It was proposed as a national park in the Third Malaysia Plan, but has still not attained that status to date (see overleaf).

Mangroves and other wetland forests Only about 20 per cent of wetland areas are gazetted as forest reserves and virgin jungle reserves; the rest do not have any legal protection. Mangroves and peat swamps forests are generally considered to be land of low value and are likely to be reclaimed for agriculture, etc. They are seriously under-represented in the conservation area system, yet some have international significance as rest stops or wintering grounds for at least 100 species of migratory birds from continental Asia. Tasek Bera and Tasek Cini together form the two largest freshwater swamp and natural lake complexes in Peninsular Malaysia. Both areas have been encroached by agricultural development. Although proposed for conservation in the Third Malaysia Plan, neither yet has any legal conservation status (Malaysian Wetland Working Group, 1987).

Limestone hills occur throughout the country from Kuala Lumpur northwards, and are generally covered in forest. Kelantan has the largest. Limestone is quarried for construction and road building, and this has caused rapid depletion of limestone hills in Perak and Selangor. Limestone areas with karst landscape are not only scenic but are also floristically rich. Chin (1977) listed 1216 species of vascular plants belonging to 582 genera and 124 families. Of these, 129 species are endemic and are confined to the limestone hills. There are also cave systems that contain a unique fauna (Bullock, 1965). The development of Malayan prehistoric archaeology has depended a great deal on investigations of limestone caves (Peacock, 1965). Several proposals have been made for the conservation of limestone hills (Aw, 1978; Ding, 1976). The Third Malaysia Plan included Mt Tempurong and Batu Caves, but no action has yet been taken.

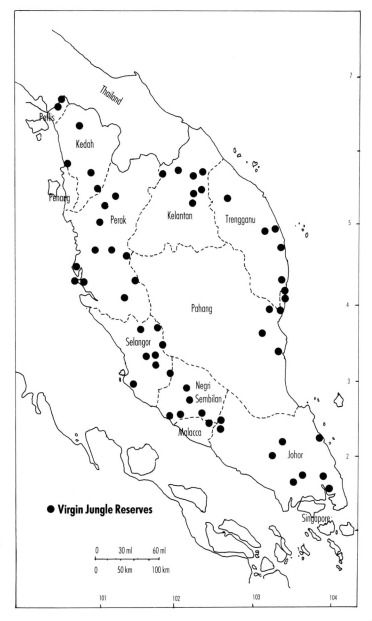

Figure 22.1 The states of Peninsular Malaysia, and the network of Virgin Jungle Reserves. There are 81 VJRs in Peninsular Malaysia, covering 910 sq. km.
(*Source*: Department of Forestry, Peninsular Malaysia)

HORNBILLS AND LOGGING IN MALAYSIA

Hornbills are amongst the noisiest and most conspicuous of rain forest birds. As many as eight species may occur together in the forests of Peninsular Malaysia. Being fruit-feeders, they forage very widely and there have been fears that, if they are unable to persist in areas that are being cleared and logged, they may become restricted to protected areas. Fortunately, it appears that hornbills survive in the regenerating forest remarkably well.

Logging operations have a severe impact on the fruit trees used by hornbills. Typically, logging reduces the number of all trees in a forest by 50 per cent, but up to three-quarters of some of the preferred fruit trees may be lost – notably figs. Recent studies in the Tekam Forest Reserve in central Peninsular Malaysia have demonstrated that, despite this destruction, hornbills can obtain all their needs from logged-over forest as little as 10 years after logging operations. Not only that, but they appear able to maintain their former numbers.

Why hornbills can survive so well remains unclear. There is no evidence of a shift in diet, and it appears that even the greatly reduced stocks of fruit trees are sufficient to maintain populations. In the pristine forest some other factor is clearly controlling the population, possibly the availability of large rot holes in which to breed. So long as silvicultural practices do not require eradication of fruit trees (which have no timber value), the future of hornbills seems assured in the production forests.

Source: Johns (1988)

THE PROPOSED ENDAU-ROMPIN NATIONAL PARK FOR PENINSULAR MALAYSIA

The story of Endau-Rompin serves to highlight the commitment and perseverance of Malaysians to establish a new national park for Peninsular Malaysia. Although there are 7460 sq. km of natural forested land in the country under conservation, there has only ever been one national park, Taman Negara, covering an area of 4343 sq. km. It was constituted in 1935 through the simultaneous gazetting of three separate state parks. Recognising the need for more such parks, the Federal Government under the Third Malaysia Plan identified the Endau-Rompin forest, which straddles the states of Johor and Pahang, an area chosen because it is one of the few remaining stretches of undisturbed forest in the southern part of the peninsula. It has also been known for many years to be an area rich in wildlife, so much so that a part of it on the Johor side had already been gazetted as a wildlife sanctuary as early as 1933, on the directive of the Sultan of Johor.

The original proposal was to include about 2023 sq. km. This was a forward looking plan, which aimed to set aside an inviolate core of 919 sq. km to conserve biological diversity and to protect the watershed of the many rivers that originate from the area. The remaining buffer area of 1105 sq. km would then be managed as a permanent forest reserve, where sustained yield forestry would be practised. Before much could be done, it was revealed in early 1977 that the Pahang State Government had approved plans to log 120 sq. km within the core area and that logging had already started. Shocked by this, Malaysians throughout the country registered their protest through meetings and in the media. The country had never experienced such a vociferous and sustained protest which was a clear indication of the level of environmental awareness already established. Although acknowledging that the area should not be logged, the Federal Government was reluctant to intervene as land matters are the concern of individual states. After continued protest, however, the State Government of Pahang finally yielded and declared that no more logging licences would be issued in the core area. When logging did cease in 1978, an estimated 52 sq. km in the core area had been logged. With the adoption of the National Parks Act in 1980, there was hope that Endau-Rompin would be the first park to be gazetted. However, despite negotiations, the state governments would not agree to handing over land to the Federal Government, as was required by the Act. No progress was made therefore to have the park established as a protected area. This stalemate goaded the Malayan Nature Society, a non-profit, non-governmental organisation, to organise the first ever Malaysian Scientific Expedition into the area, to revitalise and regenerate interest in the need for a park. MNS raised funds, coordinated the scientific personnel and brought in many volunteers, including students, lay public, the press and politicians, to work in the base camp. As public interest grew with the mass media providing extensive coverage of the expedition and its findings, Endau-Rompin became a household topic. The sustained publicity, which extended for over a year, pressed the Johor and Pahang Governments to respond. In 1988, yielding to demand, the two state governments announced their agreement to give Endau-Rompin park status. They decided that the park, which will cover an area of 930 sq. km and essentially be the core area of the original proposal, would be constituted by two separate state enactments that would guarantee its status as equivalent to a national park. A similar mechanism half a century earlier had led to the creation of Taman Negara, the first national park.

Large stretches of rain forest remain undisturbed at Endau-Rompin in the southern part of Peninsular Malaysia, providing critical habitat for rhinoceros and other wildlife. WWF/S. K. Yong

The Malayan Nature Society in response has provided comprehensive reports to the Johor State Government, including management guidelines for the proposed park. In addition, the Society provided assistance to the Johor state government by drafting and formulating their new National Parks (Johor) Act, which was to be adopted in 1989 and constitute the Johor part of Endau-Rompin area as a new national park. The Pahang Government is expected to do the same soon.

Thus Endau-Rompin is one national park that the Malaysian public has caused to come into being and one they can rightly be proud of.

Initiatives for Conservation

The Tropical Forestry Action Plan, a programme to encourage investment in tropical forestry by development agencies, was initiated in Malaysia in 1987. The Federal Government chose to carry out the forestry review using national expertise, without technical assistance from other nations or agencies. A first draft of the Malaysia TFAP was prepared in 1988 and submitted to Government for approval in 1989. The plan will be integrated into the national five-year planning cycle. Development agencies and bilateral donor organisations were invited to consider the plan in late 1989, with a view to investments in Malaysian forestry.

A key feature of the TFAP is the participation of national and international non-governmental organisations in the consultative process. In the case of Malaysia, a workshop was held in Kuala Lumpur in July 1988, with WWF–Malaysia and other interested organisations in attendance. At the time of writing, the TFAP report has not been released outside government circles. It remains to be seen to what extent conservation issues have been attended to.

References

Anon. (1986) *Annual Report of the Forestry Department, Peninsular Malaysia*. Forest Department Publication.

Anon. (1989) Mountain unease. *The Planter* 65: 36–8.

Arshad, A. (1979) National Agricultural Policy and its Implications on Forest Development in the Country. *Malaysian Forester* 42: 348–64.

Aw. P.C. (1978) Conservation of limestone hills – a geologist's view. *Malayan Nature Journal* 30: 449–59.

Bullock, J. A. (1965) The ecology of Malaysian caves. *Malayan Nature Journal* 19: 57–64.

Cadigan, F. C. and Lim, B. L. (1973) Protected habitats for protected animals. *Proceedings of a Symposium on Biological Resources and Natural Development*: pp. 153–7.

Chin, S. C. (1977) The limestone hill flora of Malaya I. *Gardens' Bulletin, Singapore* 30: 165–219.

Ding. C. H. (1976) Proposal for an integrated plan of a National Park in Perak. *Malayan Nature Journal* 29: 282–92.

FAO (1987) *Assessment of Forest Resources in Six Countries*. FAO, Bangkok, Thailand. 104 pp.

FAO (1990) *FAO Yearbook of Forest Products 1977–88*. FAO Forestry Series No. 23, FAO Statistics Series No. 90. FAO, Rome.

FAO/UNEP (1981) *Tropical Forest Resources Assessment Project. Forest Resource of Tropical Asia*. Vol 3 of 3 vols. FAO, Rome.

Government of Malaysia (1976) *Third Malaysia Plan, 1976–1980*. Government Press, Kuala Lumpur.

Government of Malaysia (1986) *Fifth Malaysia Plan, 1986–1990*. Government Press, Kuala Lumpur.

IUCN (1990) *1989 United Nations List of National Parks and Protected Areas*. IUCN Gland, Switzerland, and Cambridge, UK.

Johns, A. (1988) New observations on hornbills and logging in Malaysia. *Oriental Birdclub Bulletin* 8: 11–15.

Kiew, R. (1983) Conservation of Malaysian plant species. *Malayan Naturalist* 37: 2–5.

Lee, P. C. (1973). Multi-use management of West Malaysia's forest resources. *Proceedings of a Symposium on Biological Resources and Natural Development*: 93–101.

Lee, P. C. and Panton, W. P. (1971) *First Malaysia Plan Land Capability Classification Report for West Malaysia*. Economic Planning Unit, Prime Minister's Department, Kuala Lumpur.

Malaysian Wetland Working Group (1987) *Malaysian Wetland Directory, Vol. I. Introduction*. Department of Wildlife and National Parks, Peninsular Malaysia.

Ministry of Primary Industries (1988) *Forestry in Malaysia*.

MNS (1971) The need for the conservation of Taman Negara. *Malayan Nature Journal* 24: 196–205.

MNS (1974) A blueprint for conservation in Peninsular Malaysia. *Malayan Nature Journal* 27: 1–16.

MNS (1983) Species conservation priorities in the tropical rain forests of Peninsular Malaysia. *Malayan Naturalist* 36: 2–8.

Mohd Darus, H. M. (1978) Forest resources of Peninsular Malaysia. *Malaysian Forester* 41: 82–93.

Mohd Darus, H. M. (1988) Forest conservation, management and development in Malaysia. Forest Department Headquarters, Kuala Lumpur, Malaysia.

Muhammad, J. (1980) The National Forest Policy (Editorial). *Malaysian Forester* 43: 1–6.

Ng, F. S. P. and C. M. Low (1982) Check list of endemic trees of the Malay Peninsula. *Forest Research Inst. Research Pamphlet* 88.

Peacock, B. A. V. (1965) The prehistoric archaeology of Malayan caves. *Malayan Nature Journal* 19: 40–56.

Salleh, M. N. and Chan, H. T. (1988) Mangrove forests in Peninsular Malaysia, an unappreciated resource. Seminar on the Marine Environment: Challenges and Opportunities. Institute of Strategic and International Studies, Kuala Lumpur.

Soong, N. K., Haridass, G., Yeoh, C. S. and Tan, P. H. (1980) *Soil Erosion and Conservation in Malaysia*. FRIM.

Stevens, W. E. (1968) *The Conservation of Wildlife in West Malaysia*. Office of the Chief Game Warden, Federal Game Department, Ministry of Lands and Mines.

Thang, H. C. (1984) *Timber Supply and Domestic Demand in Peninsular Malaysia*. Forest Department, Kuala Lumpur.

Thang, H. C. (1989) *Current Status of Forestry Sector in Peninsular Malaysia*. Forest Department Headquarters, Kuala Lumpur.

Wyatt-Smith, J. (1964) A preliminary vegetation map of Malaya with descriptions of the vegetation types. *Journal of Tropical Geography* 18: 200–13.

Authorship

Officers of the Malayan Nature Society including M. Kishokumar, Kam Suan Peng, Henry Barlow and Tho Yow Pong with contributions from Thang Hooi Chiew of the Forestry Department, Mikhail bin Kavanaghm, Ishak bin Ariffin, Kanta Kumari and Abdullah Abdul Rahim of WWF, Duncan Parish of the Asian Wetlands Bureau, Chin See Chung of the University of Malaya, Francis Ng of the Forest Research Institute and Mok Sian Tuan of the Asian Institute of Forest Management.

Map 22.1 Forest cover in Peninsular Malaysia

Forest cover shown on Map 22.1 complies with *Peninsular Malaysia: The Forest Area*, at a scale of 1:1 million, a hand-coloured map obtained from the Forest Department in Kuala Lumpur in May 1989. Although undated, this unpublished map is the latest mapped information available. It is an amended version of the published *Peta Khazanah Hutan Semenanjung Malaysia* (Forest Map of Peninsular Malaysia), based on 1981–2 data and published in 1986 at 1:750,000 scale.

Peninsular Malaysia: The Forest Area shows hill, montane, swamp and mangrove forests. We have only used the mangrove category directly. The original hill and montane forests have been combined and separated again at a lower contour, 914 m (3,000 feet), to comply with the *Vegetation Map of Malaya, 1962* (Wyatt Smith, 1964), and the rest of mainland Southeast Asia shown in this atlas. The distribution of swamp forest in the south-east of the country has also been adjusted slightly to comply with that work. Protected areas were extracted from *Permanent Forest Estate Peninsular Malaysia*, an unpublished, hand-coloured map at scale 1:750,000, updated to April 1988 and obtained from the Forest Department in Kuala Lumpur, and from data on file at the WCMC.

As explained in the text, the forest area portrayed in this map exceeds the official statistics for 1985 by 7850 sq. km.

23 Philippines

Land area	298,170 sq. km
Population (1989)	64.9 million
Population growth rate (1987–2000)	1.9 per cent
Expected maximum population (2150)	137 million
Gross national product (1987)	US$590 per capita
Closed broadleaved/coniferous forest area (1988)[1]	64,606 sq. km
Rain forest (see map)	50,740 sq. km
Monsoon forest (see map)	15,280 sq. km
Closed broadleaved/coniferous forest (1985)†	74,230 sq. km
Annual deforestation rate (1986–90)†	1380 sq. km
Roundwood production*	38,214,000 cu. m
Roundwood exports*	603,000 cu. m
Fuelwood and charcoal production*	32,028,000 cu. m
Sawlogs and veneer logs production*	3,185,000 cu. m
Sawlogs and veneer logs exports*	176,000 cu. m

[1] GT2 estimate Forest Management Bureau (1988)
* 1988 data from FAO (1990)
† FAO (1987)

The Philippine archipelago has a rich flora and fauna, with high levels of endemism in both plants and animals, but its conservation programmes are generally weak. The existing protected area system includes only 1.3 per cent of the land and effective measures to prevent illegal logging and human encroachment are severely hampered by inadequate staffing and funds. At least two-thirds of Philippine national parks now contain human settlement and much of their original vegetation has been destroyed.

Most of the forest estate outside the protected area system is leased to private timber companies for logging, but the selective logging system, in operation since 1955, is not closely followed and the residual stand is often severely damaged by the use of poor log extraction techniques. Consequently, many critical catchments are severely eroded and siltation has affected water quality and hindered the operation of hydro-electric dams.

A recent survey and inventory conducted with German technical assistance has found that only 64,606 sq. km remain under forest, a mere 40 per cent of the 159,000 sq. km of so-called 'forest land'. Near-natural dipterocarp forest remains on 9880 sq. km, of which 7000 sq. km are accessible to logging and will have been logged by 1995. After roads have been built and timber extracted, often in a very damaging way, the final destruction of the forest is conducted by shifting cultivators who enter illegally.

If the present annual rate of forest destruction could be halved to 950 sq. km, then by 1995 a maximum of 34,000 sq. km of rain forest will remain in the Philippines, almost all of it logged-over forest. The survey referred to above found good regeneration in 20,000 sq. km of forest, and considered this to be suitable for silvicultural treatment to produce 2 cu. m per ha per year of timber growth. Even if this rather high output could be achieved, however, the current state of the forests in the Philippines is arguably the worst in tropical Asia. In less than 20 years the production of tropical timber has declined by 90 per cent. As a result of uncontrolled agricultural encroachment and an absence of forest management, the entire timber industry, from logging to furniture-making, is reduced to a shadow of its former status, and is increasingly dependent upon imports from other Asian nations.

The Government of the Philippines is now seeking external assistance to rehabilitate its forest resources and protect remaining fragments. A Master Plan for Forestry Development is in preparation, including a strategy for consolidation of the protected area system. Logging has already been banned in all provinces with less than 40 per cent forest cover; only nine of the nation's 73 provinces meet this criterion.

INTRODUCTION

The Republic of the Philippines is an archipelago of approximately 7100 islands, only 462 of which exceed 2.5 sq. km in area. Eleven have areas greater than 2500 sq. km and the two largest, Luzon (104,688 sq. km) and Mindanao (94,630 sq. km), constitute 68 per cent of the total land surface.

Nearly all the islands have rugged uplands in the interior, usually rising to between 1250 and 2500 m. The highest mountain is Mount Apo in Mindanao (2954 m), while Mount Pulog in Luzon reaches 2930 m. Short, violent, immature streams typify the drainage and consequently the upland areas are very susceptible to erosion. The lowlands are restricted, coastal plains rarely as much as 15 km wide, even on the larger islands.

The south-west monsoon brings rain from June to October while the north-east monsoon brings rain between November and February and provides the eastern Pacific coasts with a prolonged wet season. The western coasts of Luzon, Mindoro, Panay, Negros and Palawan receive little rainfall from the north-east monsoon, because of intervening mountain ranges, and these western parts have distinct wet and dry seasons. Typhoons bring 25–35 per cent of the annual rainfall and sweep north and west across the central and northern parts of the archipelago from July to November.

The Philippines is one of the most densely populated countries in Southeast Asia, with 173 people per sq. km. The majority of the population is of Malay descent with significant Chinese and Caucasian minorities. More than 80 per cent are Roman Catholics. However, a rich heritage of indigenous cultural diversity exists, with more than fifty tribal groups, almost all of whom live in areas designated as forest lands by the Government. Their land rights are enshrined in a pantheon of religious beliefs and traditional laws that pre-date the creation of the Philippine state. Furthermore, the socio-economic systems of many minority groups are closely linked to the forest through hunting and the collection of forest produce. As deforestation has progressed, minority tribal groups have increasingly come into conflict with central authorities who threaten to undermine their forest-based livelihood.

The Forests

The Philippines were originally clothed wholly in forest. The western side bore both lowland and montane monsoon forests; the eastern side, exposed to the onshore north-east monsoon, bore lowland and montane rain forests. The monsoon forests included areas of *Pinus kesiya* and *P. merkusii*. There were scattered areas of mangrove, none very extensive, and small areas of inland swamp forest on Mindanao.

Lowland evergreen rain forest occurs today on well-drained soils and on the lower slopes of mountains where the dry season is not pronounced. They are rich in Dipterocarpaceae and were subdivided early this century on the basis of the dominant species into four forest floristic sub-types which have been followed widely ever since.

1 Lauan (*Shorea*) forest occurs in lowland areas and foothills up to 400 m. It is dominated by red and white lauan (mainly *Shorea almon*, *S. contorta*, *S. negrosensis*, *S. palosapis* and *S. polysperma*).
2 Lauan-Apitong (*Dipterocarpus*) forests occur between lauan and lower montane forest wherever there is a pronounced dry season. The forest is not as tall, is more open and has denser scrub and layers of ground flora than the lauan forest. Many tree species are deciduous.
3 Lauan-Yakal (*Hopea*) forests occur on volcanic soils as narrow coastal bands immediately behind beach forest, but only on southern and eastern Luzon, Leyte and Mindanao in areas with a short dry season. Many of the tree species are either deciduous or semi-deciduous. Important species include *Hopea basilanica*, *H. cagayanensis*, *Shorea astylosa* and *S. gisok*. The area covered by this forest sub-type was never large and it has now largely been cleared for cultivation.
4 Finally, Lauan-Hagakhak (*Dipterocarpus warburghii*) forest was restricted to areas without a dry season and with a high water table. It was rich in timber species but it has now been cleared for rice production.

The rain forests of eastern Mindanao were amongst the grandest in the world. Nearly all the big trees were members of the Dipterocarpaceae, and reached 60 m tall, with clear boles of 40–50 m. These forests have been almost totally cleared. They were never fully described, and studies of their plants and animals were never completed.

Montane forests are widely distributed, particularly on windward slopes where there is plenty of moisture, and include *Agathis* on the lower parts.

Pine Forests. Two species of pine are indigenous to the Philippines. There are extensive stands of the Benguet pine *Pinus kesiya* in the mountains of northern and central Luzon between 450 and 2450 m. The Mindoro pine *P. merkusii* occurs at 600 m elevation and less, and occupies a much smaller area estimated at only 60 sq. km. This is divided into two separate areas, one on the Zambales and Carabello mountains in Luzon, and one in northern Mindoro.

Table 23.1 Estimates of natural forest resources of the Philippines (sq. km)

	1981 report (FAO/UNEP, 1981)		1985 report (FAO, 1987)			
	1980	1985	1980	1983	1985	1990
Natural forest						
Broadleaved closed	93,200	88,650	94,510	81,220	72,360	65,550
Bamboo	—	—	80	80	80	80
Coniferous	1,900	1,850	1,940	1,900	1,870	1,790
Totals	95,100	90,500	96,530	83,200	74,310	67,420

(After FAO/UNEP, 1981; FAO, 1987; FAO, 1988)

Molave forests are a form of monsoon forest which occurs in well-drained, limestone soils immediately behind beach forest or mangroves where conditions are too dry for rain forests. Molave *Vitex parviflora*, a member of the teak family, is dominant. The wood is highly prized for its great strength and hardness, but a combination of these commercially very desirable properties with the accessibility of the formation has now resulted in the complete disappearance of molave forests from most areas. A relatively well-preserved molave forest still occurs on the narrow coastal plain west of the Zambales mountains in Luzon.

Forest Resources and Management

Table 23.1 is a summary of data from FAO reports on the extent of the Philippines' natural forests. They show a decline from around 95,000 sq. km in 1980 to a projected 67,420 sq. km in 1990. It is of interest that the FAO/UNEP (1981) projection for 1985 of 90,500 sq. km proved to be optimistic. The FAO (1987) report recorded only 74,310 sq. km in 1985. The 1990 projection has proved to be relatively accurate. The GTZ–Philippine forest inventory project completed in 1988 recorded 64,606 sq. km of forest land, categorised as in Table 23.2.

The map of forest cover prepared by the GTZ–Philippine project was used in the preparation of Map 23.1 (see Map Legend). Table 23.3 is a breakdown of forest extent based on a computer analysis, and indicates a total forest area of 66,020 sq. km. The small discrepancy between this figure and the GTZ data is a consequence of scale. In this atlas, a compiled 1:2 million map was used as the source, whereas the GTZ team worked from the original 1:50,000 data. Map 23.1 shows very graphically how little forest remains, and how seriously degrated the remnants are.

Responsibility for the protection and management of Philippine forests is vested almost entirely in the Department of Environment

Table 23.2 Natural forest cover in the Philippines in 1985

Forest formation	Area (sq. km)
Dipterocarp old growth forest	9,883
Dipterocarp residual forest	34,128
Pine forest	2,388
Mossy forest	11,374
Submarginal forest	5,442
Mangroves	1,391
Total	64,606

(Adapted from Forest Management Bureau, 1988)

Table 23.3 Estimates of forest extent, based on analysis of Map 23.1

	Area intact	% of land area	Area degraded	% of land area	Totals	% of land area
Rain forests						
Lowland	13,870	4.6 ⎫	29,185	9.8	50,715	17.0
Montane	7,660	2.6 ⎭				
Mangrove	25	<0.1	—		25	<0.1
Sub totals	21,555	7.2	29,185	9.8	50,740	17.0
Monsoon forests						
Lowland	3,930	1.3 ⎫	6,530	2.2	15,280	5.1
Montane	4,820	1.6 ⎭				
Sub totals	8,750	2.9	6,530	2.2	15,280	5.1
Totals	30,305	10.1	35,715	12.0	66,020	22.1

(See Map Legend for details of sources)

and Natural Resources (DENR). In theory, one of the principal tasks of the DENR is to limit illegal *kaingin* (shifting cultivator) activities, but in practice staff and funding are very limited. In 1988 it was estimated that each forest guard employed by the Department had responsibility for approximately 45 sq. km of forest land and, although *barangay* (district) captains have been deputised by the DENR to assist as forest protection officers, they do not have the authority and training to be effective. The Philippine Government has recently introduced the Integrated Social Forestry Program (ISFP) to address the issue of shifting cultivation in forest lands, and families in selected regions have been given tenure to any land they have occupied for more than 25 years, as an incentive to adopt sustainable farming systems. The federal authorities supplied over 12 million seedlings to launch the programme in 1983, and there are now more than 4300 sq. km of deforested lands under ISFP projects in the Philippines with an estimated 175,000 families as beneficiaries (Myers, 1988). The full potential of the ISFP initiative has not been realised, however, because of financial and managerial constraints (Repetto, 1988).

The DENR also has responsibility for monitoring the activities of logging companies. It requires forest management plans to be submitted by all concessionaires. These would prescribe selective logging techniques, establish measures to protect concessions from encroachment by shifting cultivators, and allow for regeneration of those areas from which timber has been extracted. Although some companies honour these obligations most do not, apparently because of a reluctance to reduce profit margins. But the most important factor is that government funding and personnel have been extremely limited for many years and harvesters are easily able to avoid the regulations.

In early 1989 the Philippine House of Representatives approved a bill banning tree cutting in all provinces with less than 40 per cent tree cover. Only nine of the nation's 73 provinces contain forest resources in excess of this figure, but enforcing the ban in the remaining 64 provinces will undoubtedly prove difficult. Vested interests run into millions of dollars and logging companies are generally well-connected at political levels (*International Conservation News*, 1989).

194

Deforestation

Two complete maps of forest cover based on aerial photographs and Landsat satellite images exist for 1969 and 1979–83 (Forest Management Bureau, 1988; see also Map Legend). The picture they show is of horrific destruction. The Philippines were, in their natural state, essentially entirely forested, but by 1969 forest cover was already reduced to 105,000 sq. km, little more than one-third of the total national land surface area. The rest had already been converted to shrubland or agriculture. Of that area 80,000 sq. km were rain forests, of which 47,000 sq. km were still in a near-natural state.

By 1988 total forest cover had been reduced to 64,606 sq. km, only 22 per cent of the national land area. Of the 44,011 sq. km of dipterocarp forests only 9,883 sq. km were still intact. Forest loss during the 20 years between 1969 and 1988 was on average 2100 sq. km per year or 2 ha every five minutes, i.e. a rate of 2.5 per cent per year or three times the average for all tropical rain forests. The fastest loss was during the 1970s. By the late 1980s it had declined to 1300 sq. km per year. Another recent survey, using SPOT satellite imagery, as yet unpublished, will show an even worse situation. Deforestation can be attributed to the following causes:

Logging. Logging operations, entrusted entirely to private entrepreneurs through a system of licences and permits, have contributed substantially to the overall degradation of forests. Intensive logging took place in the Philippines from the end of the Second World War until the early 1970s, because successive governments viewed forest exploitation as a good way of raising revenues. By 1969 the annual export exceeded 11 million cu. m, nearly triple that of 1955. Annual outputs averaging 10 million cu. m were maintained until 1974, at which time forest depletion, world recession, competition from other log-producing countries, and heightened conservation awareness prompted an initiative to curb timber exports through a variety of forest protection ordinances. Logging was banned in parts of Luzon, Catanduanes, Masbate, Leyte and Negros as well as on all small islands with an area of less than 500 sq. km. Implementation of the law has been limited by short-term economic considerations, and timber smuggling continues. In 1986, for example, it was estimated that the volume of logs smuggled to Japan exceeded 1 million cu. m (MacKenzie, 1988). A log export ban was imposed in 1989, but is likely to be too late to be effective.

Shifting agriculture. Although logging has contributed substantially to forest degradation, logged forests do eventually recover and the principal cause of actual deforestation is shifting agriculture. Traditional, low-intensity shifting agriculture was once widely practised by indigenous tribal groups, but the population has increased dramatically in recent years and large numbers of unemployed people have migrated from the lowlands into the interior. Consequently, traditional methods of cultivation have been replaced by a more intensive and unsustainable form, which is extremely harmful to the environment. Forest is cleared and farmed until the soil is completely exhausted. The natural vegetation has little opportunity to become re-established, and soil erosion is common. It is estimated that between 800 and 1400 sq. km of forest, including previously logged forest, are destroyed annually by inappropriate shifting agricultural practices in the Philippines (Myers, 1980). Furthermore, there is the risk of forest destruction from uncontrolled fires originating in areas of shifting agriculture, and this may worsen if climatic disturbances, particularly abnormal dry spells, become more pronounced.

Soil erosion and watershed degradation. One of the most devastating effects of deforestation in the Philippines is soil erosion. Preliminary estimates suggest that more than 90,000 sq. km are already so badly degraded that they can no longer support agriculture (David, 1986).

THE AGNO RIVER BASIN DEVELOPMENT PROJECT

The first major hydro-electric power generating scheme to be initiated in the Philippines was the Agno River Basin Development Project which began in 1952. The Agno River basin lies in the Cordillera mountain range of northern Luzon and is a major centre of mining activity. Eighty-nine per cent of the Philippines' gold is produced in the province of Benguet and the mines have become major consumers of Agno electricity. The first phase of the project was completed in 1956 with the construction of the Ambuklao dam. This dam was originally planned to have an effective life-span of 75 years but is no longer fully operational. Extensive logging for pit-prop timbers within the watershed by mining companies has caused severe siltation and erosion. Large-scale dumping of mine waste into the rivers that feed the reservoirs has further compounded the problem. A recent analysis of the upper catchments of the Agno River has shown that at least 30 per cent are now subject to very severe erosion and the siltation rate into the Ambuklao dam is estimated at 2.7 million cu. m per annum. The valuable stabilising role of forest cover in critical watershed areas such as the Agno River basin is recognised by Presidential Declaration No. 705 (Forestry Reform Code), but effective resources management policies are difficult to implement and ecological values have often been ignored in favour of short-term economic considerations.

Source: Roger Cox

Soil erosion in the uplands is particularly severe and widespread, and it is likely to become worse as population pressure increases. By late 1986 the uplands population totalled more than 18 million people, or nearly one-third of all Filipinos (Myers, 1988). The Government has been unable to remedy this, in part because of land tenure problems, but also because of inadequate training of agricultural agents, and inadequate incentives to improve farming practices.

Many catchments have been indiscriminately logged and then converted to systems of permanent agriculture not suitable for sloping areas. It is estimated that some 16,000 sq. km of deforested Philippine uplands are located in critical watershed areas that are important for reliable water supplies to feed hydropower plants, irrigation projects and domestic needs in urban areas (David, 1986; Leong and Serna, 1987). The two largest cities, Manila and Cebu, now periodically experience water shortages due to the denuded condition of their catchments (Ganapin, 1987). Damage to the catchment areas of some of the country's biggest dams have also adversely affected several hydro-electric power generating schemes.

Deforestation and tribal Filipinos. The tribal peoples of the Philippines depend a great deal on the resources of the forest. For example the Itawe people of north-east Luzon, with a long cultural tradition, utilise at least 250 species of indigenous plants for nutritional, medicinal and religious purposes.

Deforestation has destroyed sources of minor forest products for many Filipino tribal people and siltation of creeks and rivers has eliminated inland fish stocks. There is often a conflict of interest between these people on the one hand, who expect to be able to live and share in the wealth of the forest, and the logging companies on the other. In a large number of cases tribal people's livelihoods have been put in jeopardy by logging operations. Many logging concessions encroach upon or completely engulf their ancestral lands (Anti-Slavery Society, 1983). In 1983 there were at least 33 logging and wood-processing companies based in Luzon whose activities affected national minorities in this way. Occasionally, excessive damage to the natural resource base and political pressure have compelled national minority peoples to abandon the territory on which their culture and economy depend, and relocate elsewhere. Under these conditions the social cohesiveness of the society is rapidly dissipated, traditional knowledge is eroded, and group members become squatters on land with which they have no historical association.

Mangroves

Mangrove forests declined in area from 4–5000 sq. km in 1920 (Brown and Fischer, 1920) to 1000 sq. km by the mid-1980s, with attrition continuing at 50 sq. km per year (Howes, 1987). This massive loss resulted from all the factors which variously affect mangroves in the region (see other country chapters).

As everywhere else the mangrove forests are an important source of many different products for rural societies (Arroya and Encendencia, 1985; Howes, 1987; Natmancom (Philippines), 1987; Zamora, 1984).

Important mangrove forests currently under threat include the following: the Bugney wetlands; Balayan Bay; Tayabas Bay; Ragay Gulf and Inabanga coast, amongst others (Scott, 1989).

Recently fishermen on Cebu have planted a new mangrove forest and begun to harvest the marine life which it has attracted.

Biological Diversity

The original rain forest flora of the Philippines has never been fully studied. The very substantial loss of forest, including complete deforestation of whole islands and other large areas of the country, makes it extremely likely that species have become extinct, though this is difficult to prove.

The forests of the Philippines support rich and diverse flora and fauna. Of the 12,000 or so species of plants and fungi, about 3500 are endemic, with 33 endemic genera (Madulid, 1982). The fauna of the archipelago is also characterised by a high degree of endemism – of approximately 96 species of non-flying land mammals occurring in the archipelago, at least 70 are found nowhere else. There is also a high degree of endemism in Philippine species of birds, amphibians and reptiles.

More than 950 terrestrial vertebrate species are known to occur in the Philippines and many of these are now threatened by forest degradation and loss. Endemic land mammals which are threatened include: tamaraw *Bubalus mindorensis*, tarsier *Tarsius syrichta*, Philippine spotted deer *Cervus alfredi*, Calamian deer *C. calamianensis*, Mindanao gymnure *Podogymnura truei*, Visayan wild pig *Sus barbatus cebifrons* and the forest rat *Batomys granti* (IUCN, 1988). On Cebu, where almost all of the natural forest cover has been removed, only one out of ten endemic bird species has managed to adapt to the new habitat (Rabor, 1977). Deforestation is also the main cause of breeding failure in the Philippine eagle *Pithecophaga jefferyi*, which is seriously endangered and may now number no more than 200 birds in the wild (Kennedy, 1987).

Conservation Areas

At least 59 national parks have been created in the Philippines since 1900, and two have been declared ASEAN Natural Heritage Sites. The legal basis for protected areas is outdated, fragmented and complex. Since 1900 there have been at least 262 enactments relating to the establishment or modification of protected areas. In a number

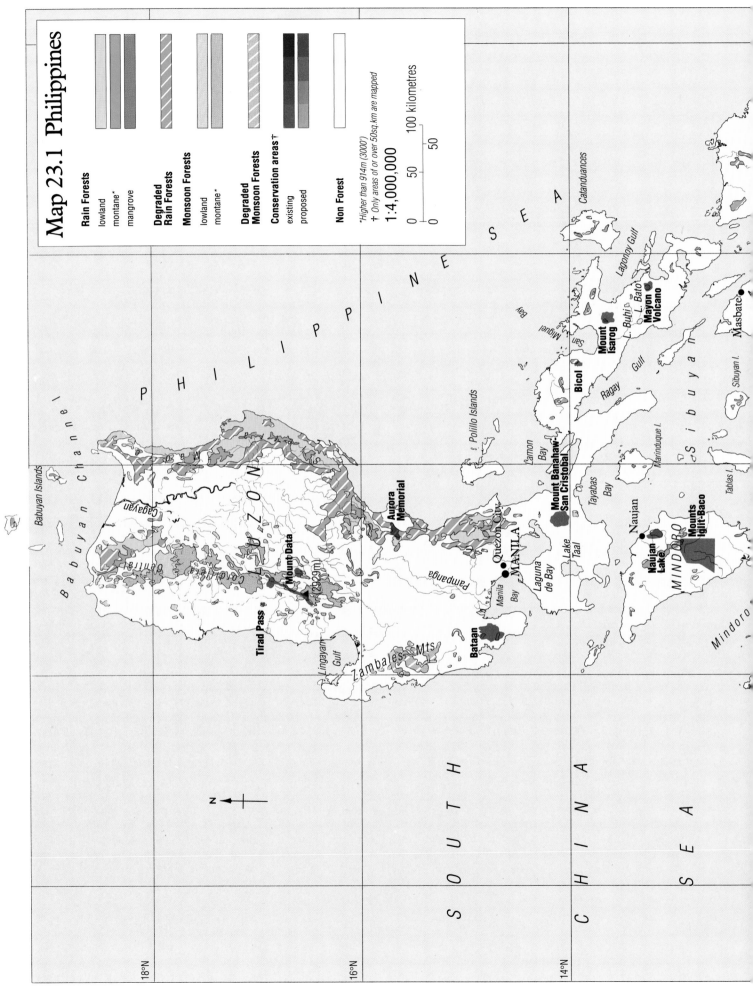

Map 23.1 Philippines

Rain Forests
lowland
montane*
mangrove

Degraded Rain Forests

Monsoon Forests
lowland
montane*

Degraded Monsoon Forests

Conservation areas†
existing
proposed

Non Forest

*Higher than 914m (3000')
† Only areas of or over 50sq.km are mapped

1:4,000,000

100 kilometres

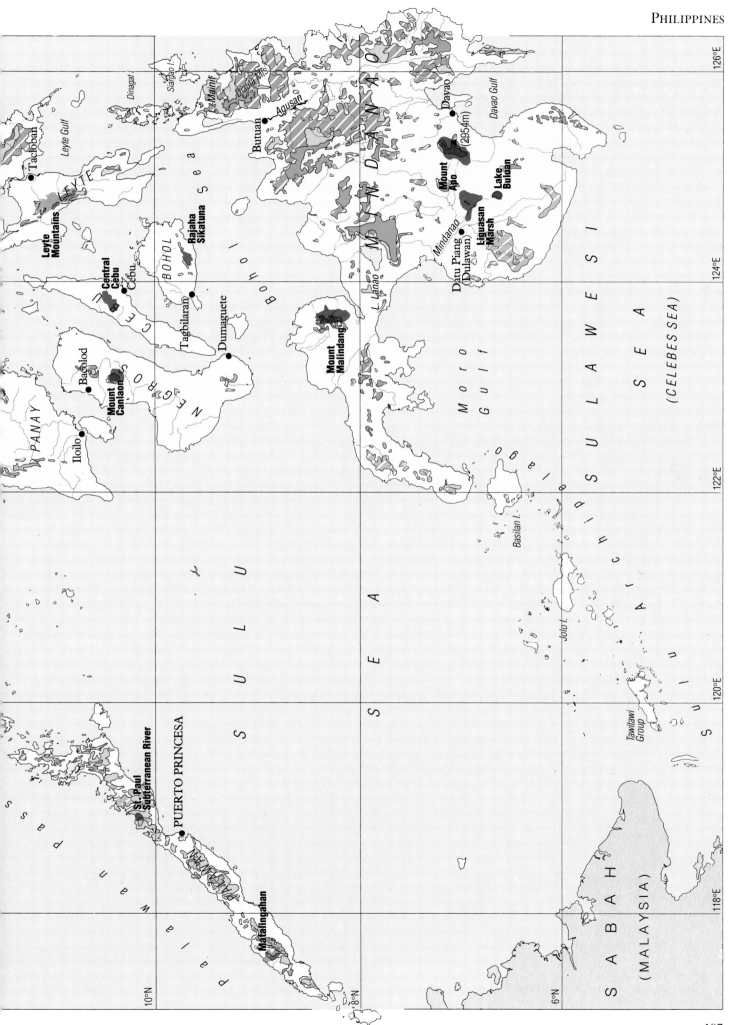

THE ENDANGERED TAMARAW

The tamaraw *Bubalus mindorensis* is a small buffalo endemic to Mindoro, where its preferred habitat is a mosaic of thick forest (for cover) and open grazing areas. An estimated 10,000 tamaraw occurred in 1900 but by 1949 numbers had dwindled to about 1000 and by 1953 to fewer than 250. In 1969 a field survey could only locate three small populations, totalling about 100 animals. The current population is not known but numbers have probably increased slightly in recent years. Small tamaraw populations occur in Mounts Iglit–Baco National Park (754 sq. km) but the Philippine Protected Areas and Wildlife Bureau has found it impossible to prevent illegal farming and ranching, and habitat destruction has occurred throughout the park. In July 1979 a 3 sq. km fenced enclosure was established at Cantoroy, Rizal in Occidental Mindoro to breed the tamaraw in captivity. This enclosure currently holds 13 animals and capture of additional stock is envisaged.

Source: Roger Cox

ASEAN NATURAL HERITAGE SITES IN THE PHILIPPINES

Mounts Iglit–Baco National Park (754 sq. km), situated in Mindoro, is one of the only two ASEAN Natural Heritage Sites in the Philippines and is important for its population of tamaraw. The park spans the central north-west/south-east divide of Mindoro and includes several distinct physiographic regions. The vegetation of much of this reserve is fire-maintained grassland with *Imperata cylindrica* and *Sacchareum spontaneum*. Some very small dipterocarp rain forest remnants persist in the north and patches of mossy montane forests occur above 1500 m. Mounts Iglit–Baco is inhabited by the Mangyan people who burn large parts of the park annually for cattle grazing. Ranching and uncontrolled hunting activities have contributed substantially to the decline of the tamaraw.

The other ASEAN Natural Heritage site, Mount Apo National Park (728 sq. km), on the slopes of Mount Apo, the highest peak in the Philippines (2954 m), is located on the south-east coast of Mindanao, close to the Davao Gulf. The park supports many species of plants, birds and mammals endemic to the archipelago. It is one of the last remaining localities inhabited by the endangered Philippine eagle *Pithecophaga jefferyi*. Some montane rain forests still remain but most of the areas originally covered by lowland rain forests have been logged, and then cleared by slash-and-burn cultivators. There is no effective management regime for the park and few protective regulations are adequately enforced. Consequently, human encroachment is an enormous problem and it is estimated that at least 20,000 people live within the park's boundaries.

Source: Roger Cox

of cases enactments have overlapped or been inconsistent, providing insufficient parameters for a protected area to be accurately delimited. Most protected areas have suffered from this confused legislative and administrative background. A lack of clear definition and of clear criteria for selecting areas has led to a proliferation of reserves – to the point where the total number of national parks created is itself subject to debate, with different authorities stating a total of 62 (NRMC, 1983), 59 (Haribon Foundation/DENR, 1988), or 72 (Petocz, 1988). However many parks there are, however, they provide little effective protection for the country's environment. Moreover, levels of management have been poor; indeed in 1986 the Haribon Foundation, an influential national non-governmental organisation, claimed that none would satisfy international standards established by IUCN, and a recent report for the Master Plan for Forestry Development described the situation as critical (DENR, 1989). (See Table 23.4 for listing of conservation areas.)

The conservation management of virtually all the existing reserves, which cover less than 1.3 per cent of the country, is weak. In 1978 it was reported that approximately 76,000 people were permanently settled in park-lands and that 540 sq. km of protected areas were under some form of cultivation (Haribon Foundation, unpublished). A further 40 sq. km were being actively logged. More recent information is not available, but it is likely that these figures now drastically underestimate the current problem. Most park boundaries are not demarcated, law enforcement is lacking, and current staffing and funds are such that the Bureau of Protected Areas and Wildlife is unable to deploy an effective corps of forest guards and park rangers.

The inadequacy of the Philippine national park system has been recognised by the Haribon Foundation, which, together with the Department of Environment and Natural Resources, and more recently with help from the World Bank, has put forward proposals for extensions of the system. By enlarging existing sites and demarcating critical sites for conservation and protection, an Integrated Protected Areas System (IPAS) will be developed. Preliminary proposals published by the Haribon Foundation/DENR (1988) were not entirely acceptable to Government and the World Bank has now stepped in with an environmental grant for 1990–5 to complete the plan and put it into effect. The two-stage programme will include preparation of draft legislation, provide training seminars and develop an operational framework for the planning and management of ten top priority protected areas. The second phase will implement management plans in these reserves and their buffer zones, and provide staff reorientation and training in protected areas management (Petocz, 1989).

Initiatives for Conservation

Decades of unchecked exploitation have recently encouraged the Government to seek external assistance for the reconstruction of the nation's forest resources, and a Master Plan for Forestry Development is currently being prepared by the DENR with the assistance of the Asian Development Bank, FINNIDA and other bilateral aid organisations, IUCN and other NGOs. The over-riding priority is to identify and develop projects which will form components of a 25-year strategy for the restoration of Philippine forests. Some of the issues being considered in the Forestry Master Plan include:
- Preparation of short, medium, and long-term projections for timber and fuelwood demand, based on estimated domestic consumption and estimated export demand for wood-based products.
- Participation of local communities in reforestation and other

Table 23.4 Conservation areas of the Philippines

Existing and proposed areas, 50 sq. km and over and for which we have location data, are listed below. The remaining areas are combined in a total under Other Areas. Forest reserves are not included. For data on Biosphere reserves and ASEAN sites, see chapter 9.

	Existing area (sq. km)	Proposed area (sq. km)
National Parks		
Aurora Memorial★	57	
Bataan	239	
Bicol	52	
Central Cebu	119	
Leyte Mountains★		420
Matalingahan★		200
Mayon Volcano	55	
Mount Apo★	728	
Mount Banahaw-San Cristobal	111	
Mount Canlaon★	246	
Mount Data	55	
Mount Isarog	101	
Mount Malindang★	533	
Mount Pulog	116	
Mounts Iglit–Baco†	754	
Naujan Lake	217	
Rajaha Sikatuna★	90	
St Paul Subterranean River★	58	
Tirad Pass★	63	
Wildlife Sanctuaries		
Liguasan Marsh	300	
Game Reserves		
Lake Buluan	63	
Sub totals	3,957	620
Other Areas	1,699	61
Totals	5,656	681

† Mounts Iglit–Baco National Park, which is mainly deforested, has a small remnant of moist forest in the northern section. The vegetation mostly consists of fire-maintained grassland.
(*Sources:* IUCN, 1990, WCMC *in litt.*)
Because data are sketchy in parts, the above list is restricted to national parks, wildlife sanctuaries and game reserves. The final total is therefore an estimate.
★ Area with moist forest within its boundary.

forest management schemes, including an assessment of the characteristics of the local communities now involved in traditional agriculture and their attitudes towards established livelihood patterns, forest management and logging.

- The role of the private sector in Philippine forestry, including the prospects for promoting commercial tree plantations on privately owned lands.
- The development of proposals for the establishment of new mangrove plantations.
- Formulation of a long-term strategy for the cultivation of minor forest products (e.g. medicinal plants) of known potential.
- Identification of critically degraded watershed areas for rehabilitation and protection.
- Re-evaluation and consolidation of the system of national parks, based on the considerations described above.

This last subject was the basis of a recent report on protected areas management and wildlife conservation (DENR, 1989). The report concluded that the immediate future would be the last opportunity for setting up an Integrated Protected Areas Scheme. Forests are dwindling so rapidly, and unspoilt habitat is now so rare, that within a decade or so there will be little left to protect. The report calls for legislative reform, institutional changes, international support for identification and protection of biologically rich sites, site-specific management and development plans, establishment of monitoring systems and a robust conservation education programme. In conclusion, the report acknowledges the formidable obstacles to the creation of a Philippine IPAS, but is optimistic that renewed commitment to conservation from the Philippine Government, backed by international investment can still be effective.

Implementation of the Master Plan for Forestry Development should contribute decisively to improved management, not only of protected areas, but also of the whole forest estate. National forest resources will be sustainably managed and used for the benefit of whole communities, creating employment and income and introducing new and improved social and health facilities for rural areas. However, successful implementation of the Plan will require a commitment on the part of Government to give it high national priority. Success will also depend on the support and involvement of small farmers and village communities, local and national NGOs, and on the ability to raise funds and improve the coordination of international aid.

A recent study to integrate land use planning and conservation on Palawan is described in chapter 8.

References

Anti-Slavery Society (1983) *The Philippines. Authoritarian Government, Multinationals and Ancestral Lands.* Anti-Slavery Society, London.

Arroya, C. A. and Encendencia, M. E. M. (1985) Status of mangrove ecosystems in the Philippines In: Coasts and *Tidal Wetlands of the Australian Monsoon Region.* Bardsley *et al* (eds). Australian National University Press, Canberra. pp. 327–44.

Brown, W. H. and Fischer, A. F. (1920) Philippine mangrove swamps. In: Brown, W. H. (ed.), *Minor Products of Philippine Forests.* Manila, Bureau of Printing. pp. 9–125.

David, W. P. (1986) *Soil erosion and soil conservation planning – issues and implications.* College of Engineering and Agro-Industrial Technology, University of the Philippines, Banos, Philippines.

DENR (1989) Master Plan for Forestry Development. Protected Areas Management and Wildlife Conservation. Unpublished report. Department of Environment and Natural Resources, Manila, Philippines. 82 pp. + annexes.

FAO (1987) *Special Study of Forest Management Afforestation and Utilization of Forest Resources in the Developing Region, Asia–Pacific Region. Assessment of Forest Resources in Six Countries.* FAO Field Document 17. 104 pp.

FAO (1990) *FAO Yearbook of Forest Products 1977–88.* FAO Forestry Series No. 23, FAO Statistics Series No. 90. FAO, Rome, Italy.

Forest Management Bureau (1988) *Natural Forest Resources of the Philippines.* Philippine-German Forest Resources Inventory Project. Forest Management Bureau, Department of Environment and Natural Resources, Manila, Philippines. 62 pp.

Ganapin, D. J. (1987) Forest resources and timber trade in the Philippines. In: *Proceedings of the Conference in Forest Resources Crisis in the Third World*, pp. 54–70. 6–8 September, 1986, Kuala Lumpur, Malaysia. Sahabat Alam Malaysia, Kuala Lumpur.

Haribon Foundation/DENR (1988) *Development of an Integrated Protected Areas System (IPAS) for the Philippines*. World Wildlife Fund – USA, Department of Environment and Natural Resources, Haribon Foundation, Manila, Philippines.

Howes, J. (1987) *Rapid Assessment of Coastal Wetlands in the Philippines*. IPT–Asian Wetland Bureau, Kuala Lumpur.

International Conservation News (1989) Philippines to ban logging. *Conservation Biology* **3**: 339.

IUCN (1988) *The Conservation Status of Biological Resources in the Philippines*. IUCN Conservation Monitoring Centre, Cambridge.

Kennedy, R. S. (1987) Threatened and little-known birds of the Philippines. Draft manuscript prepared for the International Council for Bird Preservation. 10 pp.

Leong, B. T. and Serna, C. B. (1987) *Status of Watersheds in the Philippines*. National Irrigation Administration, Quezon City.

MacKenzie, D. (1988) Uphill battle to save Filipino trees. *New Scientist* **118**: 42–3.

Madulid, D. A. (1982) Plants in peril. *The Filipino Journal of Science and Culture* **3**: 8–16.

Myers, N. (1980) *Conversion of Moist Tropical Forests*. National Academy of Sciences, Washington, DC, USA.

Myers, N. (1988) Environmental degradation and some economic consequences in the Philippines. *Environmental Conservation* **15**: 205–14.

Natmancom (Philippines) (1987) Philippines. In: *Mangroves of Asia and the Pacific*, pp. 175–20. Umali *et al.* (eds) Ministry of National Resources.

NRMC (1983) *An Analysis of Laws and Enactments Pertaining to National Parks*. Volume One. Natural Resources Management Centre, Quezon City, Philippines.

Petocz, R. (1988) *Philippines. Strategy for Environmental Conservation*. A draft plan report to WWF–US and Asian Wetland Bureau. 66 pp.

Petocz, R. (1989) The Philippines: establishment and management of an integrated protected areas system. Unpublished report to the World Bank. 130 pp.

Rabor, D. S. (1977) *Philippine Birds and Mammals*. University of the Philippines Press, Quezon City.

Repetto, R. (1988) *The Forest for the Trees? Government Policies and the Misuse of Forest Resources*. World Resources Institute, Washington, DC, USA.

Scott, D. A. (ed.) (1989) *A Directory of Asian Wetlands*. IUCN, Gland, Switzerland, and Cambridge, UK. 1181 pp.

Whitmore, T. C. (1984) A vegetation map of Malesia at scale 1:5 million. *Journal of Biogeography* **11**: 461–71.

Zamora, P. M. (1984) Philippine mangrove: assessment of status, environmental problems, conservation and management strategies. In: Soepadmo E., Rao, A. N. and McIntosh D. J. (eds) (1984) *Proceedings of the Asian Symposium on Mangrove Environmental Research and Management*. pp. 696–707. Kuala Lumpur: University of Malaya and Unesco.

Authorship

Roger Cox in London with contributions from Cesar Nuevo of the Institute of Forest Conservation in Laguna, Hans Rasch of the Swedish Space Corporation, Solna, Jürgen Schade and Vicente Sarmiento of the Dipterocarp Management Project in Manila, Jesus B. Alvarez in Quezon City, Oscar Gendrano of the Asian Development Bank, Manila, and Celso Roque of the Department of Environment and Natural Resources, Quezon City.

Map 23.1 Forest cover in the Philippines

Forest cover data were taken from the 1988 *Forest Cover Map of the Philippine Islands* published in a single, hand-coloured dyeline sheet at 1:2 million. The map, generalised from the original set at 1:50,000 scale, is accompanied by an extensive explanatory report published by the Forest Management Bureau (1988), and is the product of a collaboration between the Philippine Department of Environment and Natural Resources and GTZ, the technical aid agency of the Federal Republic of Germany. For technical reasons, preparation of the generalised GTZ forest cover map resulted in a slight over-reduction of the mapped forest areas. This has been allowed for in preparation of the statistics in Table 23.3, but could not be amended in Map 23.1.

Lowland rain forest has been taken as a combination of old growth, submarginal and residual forest in the GTZ report. Montane forests have been delineated using a 914 m (3000 ft) contour from Operational Navigation Charts ONC J–12, K–11 and L–12. Monsoon forests have been delineated from data in Whitmore (1984). Mangrove forests are not shown separately in the GTZ map, and have been extracted from the Swedish Space Corporation map (see below). They are, however, now very restricted.

A second forest mapping exercise was recently undertaken in the Philippines. The *Philippines Land Use Map* (1988) at 1:2 million, summarised from 43 *Land Cover Maps* at 1:250,000, was prepared from 1987–8 SPOT imagery for the World Bank by the Swedish Space Corporation in cooperation with the Department of Environment and Natural Resources. This map shows dipterocarp forest divided into two categories, ie less than 50 per cent and greater than 50 per cent canopy cover. Pine forest and mangrove vegetation are also shown. For the purpose of this atlas, the categories of dipterocarp forest cover were considered difficult to interpret and the map was not used. However, as mentioned above, the extent of mangrove forests was extracted from this source.

24 Sabah and Sarawak (Eastern Malaysia)

SABAH
Land area 73,710 sq. km
Population (1989) 1.4 million
Rain forest (see map) 36,000 sq. km
Closed broadleaved/coniferous forest (1980)† 36,370 sq. km
Annual deforestation rate (1985–90)† c. 800 sq. km
Sawlog and veneer log production (1984) 10.5 million cu. m
Sawlog and veneer log exports (1987) 10.1 million cu. m
SARAWAK
Land area 124,499 sq. km
Population (1989) 1.6 million
Rain forest (see map) 94,670 sq. km
Closed broadleaved forest (1980)† 84,000 sq. km
Annual deforestation rate (1985–90)† c. 450 sq. km
Sawlog and veneer log production (1987) 13.6 million cu. m
Sawlog and veneer log exports (1987) 12.8 million cu. m
† FAO (1987)

In Sabah and Sarawak rain forests cover 46 per cent and 70 per cent of the land respectively (1985 data; FAO, 1987). Predicted cover for 1990 based on these data were 39 per cent and 64 per cent respectively. In both states the control of forests is a state matter, although coming under an overall federal policy. About 45 per cent and 37 per cent of Sabah and Sarawak's land area are included in the Permanent Forest Estate (PFE). Outside the PFE, much of Sarawak's land consists of stateland forest, while much of Sabah's land has already been converted to other land use, mainly agriculture.

A major factor responsible for deforestation in Sarawak is shifting agriculture, often following provision of access to the land by the logging companies. By 1978, about 23 per cent of the state's land area had been used for shifting agriculture at some time, and the amount was growing by 0.5 to 1 per cent per year. However, all but 2.5 per cent of the PFE remains unaffected.

Much concern has been expressed that Sarawak's logging levels are unsustainable and damaging to the interests of rural people. In 1989/90 an ITTO mission visited Sarawak to investigate. The results were released as this atlas was going to press, and do recommend a reduction in logging levels.

In Sabah, shifting agriculture only affects about 15 per cent of the land area. A further 12 per cent is due to be converted to settled agriculture. There is little doubt that the main cause of forest degradation and deforestation here is logging. Furthermore, in 1983 an estimated 20 per cent of Sabah's forested land was burnt; 85 per cent of this was logged forest.

Mangrove forest receives little protection, and logging has been widespread, primarily for woodchip exports to Japan and Taiwan.

Both states have systems of totally protected areas. National parks cover 0.65 per cent and 1.9 per cent of Sarawak and Sabah respectively, and other protected areas cover a further 1.4 per cent and 7 per cent respectively. Several new areas have been proposed for protection and, if gazetted, will result in protection of 8.1 per cent and 8.9 per cent of Sarawak and Sabah respectively. These will cover most of East Malaysia's ecological and biological diversity, but increasing pressure on land and particularly timber resources means that few, if any, areas are totally secure. Proper management for both forest conservation and production will require a substantial increase in trained manpower.

INTRODUCTION

Sarawak and Sabah are the two states that comprise Eastern Malaysia. They lie on the north and north-western parts of the island of Borneo and between them occupy one-third of its area.

The climate is typically wet equatorial. Rainfall is heavy, especially during the north-east monsoon season between November and February, and to a lesser extent between May and June. Rain falls in most, if not all, months, with a minimum annual total of 1730 mm in the driest parts of central Sabah, while 5000 mm plus falls in the montane areas such as Mount Mulu, Sarawak. The annual average is about 2500 mm. Humidity as expected, is always high.

Borneo is the biggest exposed part of the Sunda Shelf, and consists mostly of young, uplifted sedimentary rocks. Sabah and Sarawak consist of alluvial and often swampy coastal plains with hilly rolling country inland intersected by large rivers and mountain ranges in the interior. In Sabah, the central mountain ranges rise abruptly from the west coast to the granodiorite peak of Mount Kinabalu (4094 m), the highest summit in Southeast Asia. The Trus Madi (2649 m) and

Crocker ranges extend south and south-west respectively. In central Sabah, Mount Lutong (1657 m) is a striking sandstone arc, while in eastern Sabah few areas rise above 500 m. Sabah also has some extinct volcanic peaks (Tawau Hills, 1303 m) and ultrabasic mountains (Silam, Tawai). The largest river, the Kinabatangan, drains eastwards, is navigable for long distances and waters an extensive plain.

Sarawak has mountains along two-thirds of its inland frontier. Mount Mulu in the north reaches 2371 m and has spectacular karst formations nearby, which include the largest underground cave in the world. The Kelabit Highlands reach 2438 m on Mount Murud. From the mountains of the border flow the great rivers Trusan, Limbang, Baram, Rajang and Lupar, which create coastal swamps covering 14 per cent of the State's land area, mainly in the coastal plains. The Rajang is the largest river.

The human population of both states is low: Sabah has 1.4 million and Sarawak 1.6 million. It is also ethnically diverse, particularly in Sarawak, which has some 28 tribal groups. The Malays, Chinese and other non-native groups are largely urban and coastal, while indigenous groups such as Iban (30 per cent of Sarawak's population), Bidayuh, Kelabit, Lun Bawang, Kayan, Kenyah, Berawan and many other *orang ulu* groups are largely inland farmers (Hong, 1987). Many of these still have a culture and livelihood which is linked, at least loosely, to the forest. The Penan are a people from the interior of Borneo who traditionally live a nomadic life of hunting and gathering. While the majority are now settled, several hundred still live entirely on the products of the natural forest (see chapter 3).

Both states have locally elected governments which sit in the capital cities Kota Kinabalu (Sabah) and Kuching (Sarawak) and send separate representatives to the Federal Assembly in Kuala Lumpur. Land management issues are in the hands of the state authorities.

The Forests

Both Sarawak and Sabah were originally entirely clothed in tropical rain forest. Existing forest formations include the following:

1 Lowland evergreen rain forest rich in dipterocarps (known in Sarawak as mixed dipterocarp forest) is the natural vegetation throughout the interior in the, sometimes rugged, lowlands. Dominated by Dipterocarpaceae, these multi-storeyed forests are of great commercial value for their timber species, particularly *Dipterocarpus*, *Dryobalanops* and *Shorea*. Individual trees may reach 60 m in height and exceed 80 cm in diameter. On a one hectare plot near Mount Mulu, 225 species over 10 cm in diameter were found (Proctor *et al.*, 1983). It has been estimated that there are at least 3000 species of trees in this formation, 890 of which reach exploitable sizes (Thang, 1987).

2 Peat swamp forest was originally extensive in Sarawak and also occurred in south-west Sabah. Consisting of domed peat bogs, *Shorea albida* is an important species, and *Gonystylus bancanus* (ramin) is the single most valuable species. Other genera of trees often found in Sarawak and Sabah include *Calophyllum*, *Dryobalanops* and *Melanorrhea*. In Sarawak, peat swamp forests were the first formations to be logged on a commercial scale and for many years were Sarawak's main source of timber. By 1972, they had all been licensed for timber extraction, and by the year 2000 all due to have been logged (Chan *et al.*, 1985).

3 Heath forest (or *kerangas*) mainly occurs in small patches inland on sandstones. The forests are characteristically low in stature, even-canopied with pole-like trees and rich in ant-plants (*Myrmecodia*) and pitcher plants (*Nepenthes*). The tree flora typically contains species of *Dipterocarpus*, *Shorea albida*, *Melanorrhea* and *Tristaniopsis*, with *Agathis* and *Gymnostoma* dominant in some forests.

4 Forest occurs on limestone in karst regions in Sarawak at low elevations and up to high elevations on Mount Api and other outcrops around Mount Mulu (Anderson, 1965; Collins *et al.*, 1984). In Sabah there are important karst hills, all with caves, on the east coast. In both Sabah and Sarawak, some of the caves are inhabited by the swiftlets which produce edible birds' nests (Sabah Forest Department, 1984; Chan *et al.*, 1985).

5 A floristically distinctive forest formation occurs on the ultrabasic rocks which form a mountainous arc extending from Mount Kinabulu to the east coast. This forest has little commercial timber and is sometimes of low stature.

6 Lower and upper montane rain forests are mainly restricted to the eastern frontier of Sarawak with Indonesia and Sabah. In Sabah montane forests are widespread on Trus Madi, the Crocker Range and Mount Kinabalu, which is rich in endemic flora. The families Fagaceae, Flacourtiaceae, Guttiferae, Myrtaceae, and Sapotaceae provide the principal dominant species at lower altitudes, while in the upper montane forests the conifers *Dacrydium* and *Phyllocladus* are common.

Spectacular fields of limestone pinnacles bar the ascent to Gunung Api (Fire Mountain), whose forests have burnt from lightning strikes in living memory. The area is part of the Gunung Mulu National Park. N. M. Collins

Forest Resources and Management

According to FAO (1987) the forest estate in Sarawak stood at 84,000 sq. km of broadleaved forest in 1980 (67.5 per cent of land area), 81,910 sq. km in 1985 (65.2 per cent) and a predicted 79,630 sq. km in 1990 (64 per cent). Table 24.1 is an analysis of maps published in 1979 by the Sarawak Forest Department (see legend to Map 24.1). The total forest area shown on the map is 94,670 sq. km, or 76 per cent of land area, i.e. 14 per cent larger than FAO's estimate of the extent of the forest estate in 1990 (FAO, 1987). This should be borne in mind when studying the map.

In Sabah in 1953 natural forests covered 63,275 sq. km (Fox, 1978), or 86 per cent of the land area. Thirty years later the rain forest was reduced to 46,646 sq. km (63 per cent) (Sabah Forest Department, 1984). According to an FAO assessment in 1985 the rain forest cover was 33,130 sq. km (45 per cent) and the prediction was that this would fall to 29,110 sq. km (39 per cent) by 1990 (FAO, 1987). Table 24.1 gives an analysis of maps made available by the Sabah Forest Department (see legend to Map 24.1). This shows about 36,000 sq. km of rain forest in the Forest Reserves and protected areas, or 49 per cent of land area, i.e. 10 per cent bigger than FAO's estimate of the extent of the forest estate in 1990 (FAO, 1987).

Throughout Malaysia, land, including forest, is defined by the constitution as a state matter. Each state is responsible for the management of its forests, but it does so under a forest policy that is common. The 1977 Malaysia National Forest Policy emphasises that each state should keep 47 per cent of its land as forest reserves for sustained yield production of timber and other products. (See also chapter 22.) At present, however, only about 37 per cent of Sarawak and 45 per cent of Sabah is under the gazetted Permanent Forest Estate.

Stateland forests are also available for conversion to non-forest use, such as agriculture and urban expansion. In Sarawak, stateland forests are still extensive, probably in the region of 35,000 sq. km, and there is room to gazette further areas under the Permanent Forest Estate. During the 1990s the Forest Department intends to increase the PFE to about 63,000 sq. km or 51 per cent of the total land area. In Sabah stateland forests outside the Permanent Forest Estate are believed to be virtually non-existent since the FAO projected total forest area for 1990 is already smaller than the PFE itself. The Sabah Forest Department has available a map *State of Sabah: Tree Crop Areas* (1988) that shows the stateland forests, but it does not indicate how much (if any) of this remains under natural forest.

For management purposes, the PFE is divided broadly between protection forests for control of watersheds, and production forests for timber production. In Sabah 28 protection forest reserves are gazetted, covering 9 per cent of the PFE. In Sarawak 'protected forests' cover about 30 per cent of the PFE (Forest Department, 1987), but they are set aside by local administrations and do not have the same legal status as the protection reserves in Sabah or in Peninsular Malaysia. A small number of communal forests have also been established for the use of local communities.

In Sarawak, where a uniform system was once used for logging, it is now policy to log lowland rain forests selectively on a cycle of 25–30 years; in peat swamp forest, a uniform system has operated on a 45-year cycle since the 1950s. Selective poisoning of unwanted trees was practised over 330 sq. km in Sarawak (liberation thinning), but has now been abandoned as impractical and undesirable.

Sabah still uses a modified uniform system, originally on a 70 to 80 year rotation, but this was changed in the mid-1970s when felling rates were increased to produce greater revenue for the state. As a result, the area of undisturbed forest in Sabah was halved between 1973 and 1983. By 1980, essentially all of Sabah's productive forests had either been logged or licensed for logging (FAO/UNEP, 1981). Timber production there peaked at 12 million cu. m in 1983 and is now declining. Commercial yields have been very high, up to 90 cu. m per ha, only exceeded in the Philippines. In Sabah the recent freeze by the government on all future concession applications is an indication of the high level of concern that the timber resources have been too quickly exploited.

In Sarawak, early logging concentrated on peat swamp forests, which were all licensed by 1970. By 1978, most timber was coming from lowland rain forests, and about 60 per cent of these forests have now been licensed for logging. Each year in Sarawak, about 2500 sq. km of dipterocarp and 350 sq. km of peat swamp forest are logged. About 30,000 sq. km have been logged so far, and each year 300 sq. km is being cut for the second time, usually after a very short cycle of ten years or so. Timber production stands at 13.6 million cu. m per year.

In both States, timber accounts for about half of the revenue and employs about a tenth of the workforce. Since royalty revenue from timber is retained entirely by the State, while 95 per cent of oil sales goes to the Federal Government, the importance of timber to the state is even greater than it appears in export statistics.

Tree plantations, mainly of exotic light hardwood species, have been widely introduced in Sabah. In Sarawak, the policy has been to manage natural forests rather than replace them with plantations, although there are plans to plant up degraded land within the PFE in future. In neither state have plantations reduced pressure on primary forests because the timbers produced are different and are sold in different markets. However, plantations should be encouraged in degraded forest outside the PFE, and as an alternative crop on agricultural land.

Deforestation

Sarawak. By the mid-1970s shifting cultivation was becoming an acute problem, not only from the point of view of forest loss, but also in terms of human nutrition (Anon., 1978; Hatch, 1982). Surveys by the Department of Medical and Health Services from 1974 revealed malnutrition among children of shifting cultivators, particularly in the western lowlands, where population pressure has caused a reduction in land availability and ever-shorter fallow periods. Shifting cultivation is the biggest agricultural land user, covering over 30,000 sq. km (one-quarter of the land area) in 1978 (Hatch, 1982). The area of non-forested land in Sarawak stands at 28 per cent (Sarawak Forest Department, 1987), and it would appear that much of this increase is the result of shifting cultivation, although plantation agriculture has also contributed. The area of land slashed and burned annually for hill padi was between 750 and 1500 sq. km in the late 1970s and may be even higher now (Hatch, 1982).

A report of a workshop in 1978 concluded that the net revenue loss to the State through destruction of timber by shifting cultivation in Sarawak was about M\$300 million per year (Anon., 1978). For every log exported at that time, the equivalent amount of timber was going up in smoke. The Forest Department recently carried out a further survey to map the main areas of encroachment into the Permanent Forest Estate, and found that 1160 sq. km (2.5 per cent) has been lost in this way. Often this encroachment occurs after logging roads have provided access to previously unreached forests.

Shifting cultivation has resulted in total deforestation of much of western Sarawak. Coupled with very heavy logging, it continues to threaten the forest estate. N. M. Collins

Table 24.1 Estimates of forest extent in Eastern Malaysia

	Area (sq. km)	% of land area of state
SABAH		
Rain forests		
Lowland	29,500	40.4
Montane	3,100	4.5
Mangrove	3,400	5.0
Sub totals	36,000	49.9
SARAWAK		
Rain forests		
Lowland	61,170	49.1
Montane	17,060	13.7
Inland swamp	14,800	11.9
Mangrove	1,640	1.3
Sub totals	94,670	76.0
Totals	130,670	66.0

(Based on analysis of Map 24.1. See Map Legend for details)

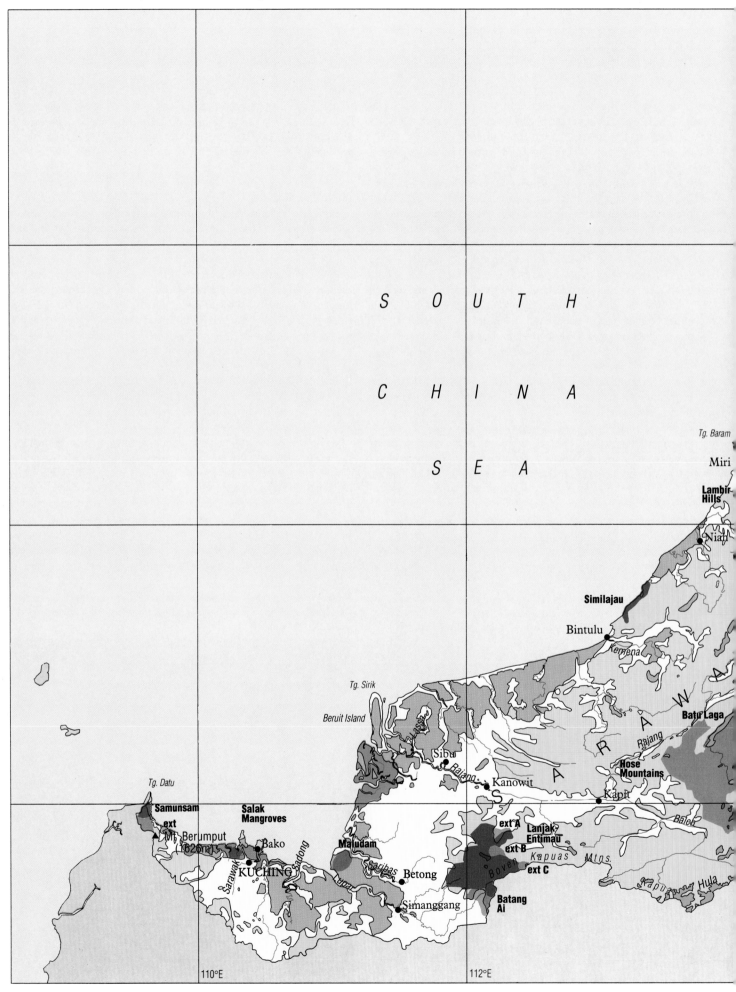

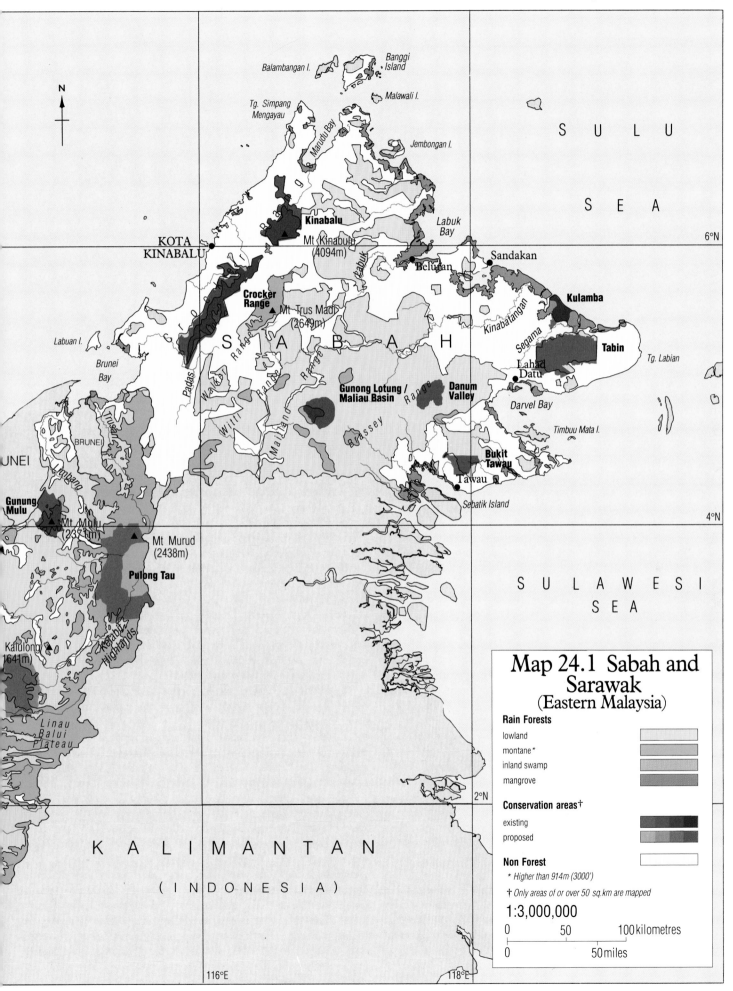

Balambangan I.
Banggi Island
Tg. Simpang Mengayau
Malawali I.
Marudu Bay
Jembongan I.

S U L U

S E A

Kinabalu
Labuk Bay
KOTA KINABALU
6°N
Beluran
Sandakan

Crocker Range
Mt Kinabalu (4094m)
Mt Trus Madi (2649m)
Kulamba

Labuan I.
Brunei Bay
S A B A H
Kinabatangan
Segama
Tabin
Tg. Labian

BRUNEI
Witti Range
Maitland Range
Crocker Range
Trusan
Timbang
Padas
Walk Range
Brassey Range
Gunong Lotung / Maliau Basin
Danum Valley
Lahad Datu
Darvel Bay
Timbuu Mata I.

UNEI
Gunung Mulu
Mt Mulu (2377m)
Mt Murud (2438m)
Pulong Tau
Kalulong (1641m)
Kelabit Highlands
Linau Balui Plateau

Bukit Tawau
Tawau
Sebatik Island
4°N

S U L A W E S I

S E A

K A L I M A N T A N

(I N D O N E S I A)

2°N

116°E
118°E

Map 24.1 Sabah and Sarawak
(Eastern Malaysia)

Rain Forests

lowland

montane *

inland swamp

mangrove

Conservation areas†

existing

proposed

Non Forest

* Higher than 914m (3000')

† Only areas of or over 50 sq.km are mapped

1:3,000,000

0   50   100 kilometres

0   50 miles

Tabin Wildlife Reserve in Sabah includes a mud volcano, which is rich in exposed mineral salts that attract large mammals. WWF/S. Yarath

Sarawak has a low population density, but the land is not free from human pressure. In fact, 80 per cent of the land is incapable of supporting any commercial agricultural crop, while yet more is of a very marginal nature. Of the 80 per cent of unsuitable land, 12 per cent is swamp and the remainder is mountainous with shallow infertile soils. Most of the marginal land is already under shifting agriculture; the extension is largely into unsuitable lands at present under forest which are scarcely able to support even shifting agriculture.

Timber extraction from inland forest does not cause deforestation unless followed by shifting agriculture. However, there is widespread concern that in Sarawak the current level of forest exploitation, mainly to supply the Japanese market (see chapter 7), is unsustainable in the long term and will cause degradation of forest resources. Given that the soils are generally not suitable for non-forest uses, this is a serious matter, economically, ecologically and, not least, sociologically. In Sarawak, logging has caused serious difficulties for the rural population, who live either settled in longhouses or, in the case of some of the Penan, as nomadic hunter gatherers subsisting on wild sago palm (*Eugeissona utilis*). The concerns of these people are discussed in chapter 3.

In 1989 and 1990 an international forestry team was commissioned by ITTO to study the present management of Sarawak's forests. This review, welcomed by the Forest Department, which is anxious to ensure sustainable use of the Permanent Forest Estate, was officially accepted by the ITTO Council in November 1990. Recommendations include substantial strengthening of the Forest Department and a reduction in timber production from current levels of over 13 million cu. m per year to a maximum of 9 million cu. m per year. Concerned NGOs are calling for a more substantial reduction, to 5 million cu. m per year.

Drought periods occasionally occur, and there is a danger that recently logged forest could burn in such periods. So far, however, there has been no serious forest fire to compare with those in Sabah and Kalimantan – the only fires recorded are those which result from a strike by lightning or which periodically destroy limestone hill forest after dry weather. A fire on Gunung Api in the Mulu area in 1929–30 was reputed to have burnt for several weeks.

Sabah. Development in general has, in fact, been slow in Sabah due to poor roads, labour shortage and poor prices for cocoa (1984 onwards) and palm oil (1984–6), but is planned eventually to cover much of eastern Sabah. Plantation agriculture is less extensive than in Peninsular Malaysia, but more extensive than in Sarawak.

By comparison with Sarawak, shifting cultivation is a lesser form of disturbance to forests in Sabah, affecting about 11,000 sq. km or 15 per cent of the land area, almost entirely in western and central districts. However, substantial areas in lowland eastern Sabah are in the process of conversion to settled agriculture. This is land that is still partly under forest but is not in the Permanent Forest Estate or national parks.

The Permanent Forest Estate in 1984 stood at 33,500 sq. km, or 45 per cent of land area. The Forest Department has a policy to increase this to 50 per cent (Sabah Forest Department, 1984), yet the 1984 figure represents a drop from the 1982 level of 35,700 sq. km, mainly due to conversion of land to agriculture.

The El Niño/Southern Oscillation phenomenon of 1982/3 resulted in perhaps the most extreme drought of this century in Sabah with severe consequences for the rain forests. At its height (February–April 1983), rainfall was only 15 per cent of normal. Prior to the fires, the forests were already under severe drought stress. Many evergreen trees had shed their leaves and the accumulation of dry litter on the forest floor was generally high. Logged forests fared worse because of the massive accumulations of organic debris that intensive logging leaves behind. Primary forests that burned were mostly those on steep slopes over thin, ultrabasic soils. Fires began in January and were at their greatest extent in March to May. Over 10,000 sq. km of forest were burnt, of which 85 per cent had been logged. This represents about one-third of Sabah's total forested land, and the economic and ecological losses were enormous. Extensive areas of plantation forests and agricultural crops also burned (Beaman *et al.*, 1985). Until this event, evergreen rain forests had been believed to be non-flammable. The fires were mainly triggered by agriculturists, who habitually set dry-season fires when clearing land, and there is evidence that shifting agriculturists tried to take advantage of the drought to extend their farms (Malingreau *et al.*, 1985).

Mangroves

There are about 1740 sq. km of mangrove forest in Sarawak, of which only 25 per cent is gazetted as Permanent Forest Reserve and almost none of which is totally protected.

Exploitation of mangroves to provide woodchip for Japan and cordwood for Taiwan began in Sarawak in 1969, and now utilises about 20 sq. km of mangrove forest annually. Trees over 23 cm diameter are felled, which is about 90 per cent of the forest. Rules prescribe that buffer strips along banks of rivers and coasts should be retained. Contravention of this rule and heavy felling leave few seed trees and regeneration is sometimes poor. The only sizeable unlogged area which remains is the Sarawak Mangroves Forest Reserve, and even this has been partially excised. In 1988 it was recommended that a national Mangrove Management Committee be established which should include the creation of a mangrove biosphere reserve.

In Sabah woodchipping concessions have been allowed over 40 per cent (1230 sq. km) of the mangrove forests. As in Sarawak, there is great concern that regeneration will be limited by an absence of propagules and by changes to the environment from drying and through the associated invasion of colonies of *Thallasina* lobsters and the weeds *Achrostichum* and *Acanthus*. Recent work includes Chai and Lai (1984) and Phillips (1984).

Biodiversity

Borneo, the heart of Sundaland, has an extremely rich flora and fauna. It is the headquarters of the Dipterocarpaceae and 265 of Southeast Asia's 390 species are found here, 155 of them endemic. During past glacial eras, when sea levels were as much as 180 m lower than today, the Sunda Islands of Sumatra, Java and Borneo were partially and intermittently joined to one another, and to the continent, allowing the movement of plants and animals. Consecutive sets of migrations, followed by periods of isolation, have contributed to the great diversity of plants and animals in the Sunda region, especially on Borneo.

Mountains are local centres of endemism, with Kinabalu the best-studied example. Of Borneo's 135 *Ficus* species, 75 have been collected on Kinabalu, 13 of them endemic. Kinabalu also has one of the highest species densities of the Magnoliaceae and 72 species of Fagaceae in its floristically rich lower montane rain forests.

The diverse flora supports an equally diverse fauna. The mammals have been best studied, with 196 species recorded – 40 of them

Unknown insects like this new species of stagbeetle, Odontolabis *from Sarawak, are abundant in the tropical forest canopy.* N. Mark Collins

The western tarsier (Tarsius banucanus) *is one of Borneo's most unusual primates. It is rarely seen, but apparently able to survive well in disturbed forests.* Royal Geographical Society/R. Hanbury-Tenison

endemic to Borneo. At least 167 mammals have been recorded in Sabah and 180 in Sarawak. The mountain ranges host 18 species (11 endemic) of vertebrates only occurring above about 1000 m. Coasts and rivers are home to a distinct community of primates (proboscis monkey (Bennett, 1988), silvered langur *Presbytis cristata*, and long-tailed macaque), birds and plants. Other species such as orang-utans have a very patchy distribution. Caves, such as those at Gomantong and Niah, house huge colonies of edible-nest swiftlets, upwards of 14 species of bats, and associated animals such as the bat hawk *Macheiramphus alcinus*. The rarest mammal is the Sumatran rhinoceros, which has been lost from most of its range, including Mulu, through hunting. A localised population of about 20 survives in the Dent Peninsula of eastern Sabah, some scattered individuals occur in other upland areas elsewhere in Sabah, and a population was recently located in northern Sarawak. In 1986 a captive breeding project was initiated in Sabah. Other large mammals occurring in small numbers include the banteng, elephant (eastern Sabah) and clouded leopard. Several of the smaller carnivores are also found rarely or are very localised (marbled cat *Felis marmorata* and ferret-badger *Melogale everetti*).

The avifauna is rich, with four alpine species, 14 endemic montane species, a further nine non-endemic montane species and over 470 species at lower elevations, including coastal birds and migrants. Rare birds tend to be the larger hunted species: Malay peacock pheasant (*Polyplectron malacense*), Bulwer's pheasant (*Lophura bulweri*), helmeted hornbill (*Rhinoplax vigil*). Megapodes in Sabah are threatened by egg collectors. Other rare species include the large green-pigeon (*Treron capellei*) (confined to lowland forests), Everett's ground thrush (*Zoothera everetti*) (mountains) and Storm's stork (*Ciconia stormi*) (riverine and wetlands) (Collar and Andrew, 1988).

The unique earless monitor lizard (*Lanthanotus borneensis*), which belongs to a monotypic genus and family, has been recorded only from lowlands in restricted areas of north and south Sarawak, where it is protected by law.

There is a very diverse insect fauna which is still poorly studied, but more than 290 species of butterfly and moth have been recorded on Kinabalu and more than 280 on Mulu. Three out of a total fauna of 43 species of swallowtail butterfly are rare or threatened: *Graphium*

Sabah and Sarawak (Eastern Malaysia)

Table 24.2 Conservation areas of East Malaysia

Existing and proposed areas, 50 sq. km and over, are listed below. The remaining areas are combined in a total under Other Areas. Forest reserves are not included. For data on ASEAN sites see chapter 9. All areas include moist forest within their boundaries.

	Existing area (sq. km)	Proposed area (sq. km)
SARAWAK		
National Parks		
Batang Ai		271
Gunung Mulu	529	
Hose Mountains		2,847
Lambir Hills	70	
Loagan Bunut		107
Pulong Tau		1,645
Similajau	71	
Salak Mangroves		103
Usun Apau		1,130
Wildlife Sanctuaries		
Batu Laga		1,000
Lanjak-Entimau	1,688	
Lanjak-Entimau – ext A		
Lanjak-Entimau – ext B		184
Lanjak-Entimau – ext C		
Maludam		434
Samunsam	61	
Samunsam – ext		148
Sub totals	2,419	7,869
Other Areas	174	89
Totals	2,593	7,958
SABAH		
National Parks		
Crocker Range	1,399	
Parks		
Kinabalu	754	
Bukit Tawau	280	
Wildlife Reserves		
Tabin	1,205	
Kulamba	207	
Sabah Foundation Conservation Areas		
Danum Valley	428	
Gunung Lotung/Maliau Basin	390	
Sub total	4,663	
*Other Areas**	1,023	200
Totals	5,686	200

Source of Sarawak figures: 1989 data from the Sarawak Forest Department.
Source of Sabah figures: WCMC *in litt.*

* Including 1000 sq. km of Protected Forest

procles, *Troides andromache* and *Papilio acheron*, all from lower montane forests in northern Borneo.

More than 100 species of indigenous fish have been recorded in Sarawak (59 species in the Rajang River) many of which are important foods, such as *Toranbrides*. Only incomplete surveys of Sabah and Sarawak's fish have been made, but there are already fears that some species are becoming rare due to over-fishing and siltation of rivers as a result of logging. Marine species are also declining, possibly due in part to the loss of mangroves.

Conservation Areas

The protected areas of Sarawak and Sabah are listed in Table 24.2 opposite. Existing national parks cover 0.67 per cent and 1.9 per cent of Sarawak and Sabah respectively. Other categories of existing reserves cover 1.4 per cent of Sarawak and 4.9 per cent of Sabah. Sarawak has a further 5 per cent in proposed national parks and 1.4 per cent in proposed wildlife sanctuaries. In addition, Sabah has 883 sq. km of virgin jungle reserves and about 1000 sq. km of protection reserve forests that play an important role. Including all categories, 8.3 per cent of Sarawak and 8.9 per cent of Sabah will be under protection for ecological and biological purposes if all the new reserves are gazetted.

The protected area systems in both Sarawak and Sabah contain a good representation of Eastern Malaysia's ecological and biological diversity. However, there is concern that few of these areas are under complete protection, and they could be subjected to disturbance as pressure for land and timber resources grows. The main shortcomings and priorities are as follows:

• In Sabah, some of the virgin jungle reserves, the Tabin Wildlife Reserve (formerly a commercial forest reserve) and the Tawau Hills have been partially or totally logged.

• Important parts of Kinabalu State Park have been excised to make way for a golf course, a dairy farm and a copper mine.

• The *Rafflesia* Virgin Jungle Reserve is threatened by shifting cultivators, who are already active in the lower slopes of the Crocker Range National Park.

• The Tabin Wildlife Reserve has suffered sporadic depredations of rhinoceros poachers.

• In Sabah, before 1984 the Head of State could mark any area of state park for degazettement, and in 1981 the Klias National Park reverted to forest reserve. In 1984, however, the State Government passed a bill requiring all dereservations to go to the floor of the State Assembly. This has not prevented reductions in the area of Kinabalu Park, Borneo's greatest centre of diversity.

• In Sarawak, great progress has been made in extending and managing the protected area system in recent years. The State Conservation Strategy, still a confidential document, identified various new areas for protection and good progress has been made, but until the proposed areas are gazetted, there are important gaps in the system.

• Wildlife sanctuaries in Sarawak still have dual status as part of the PFE, which gives less protection to biodiversity. Proposed amendments to the law will give them much greater protection.

Conservation Proposals – Sarawak

Sarawak has developed an extensive list of proposed wildlife sanctuaries and national parks, all due to be gazetted. Some features of these proposals may be mentioned.

• The Samunsam and Lanjak-Entimau Wildlife Sanctuaries are due to be extended to strengthen their capacity for conservation of proboscis monkey and orang utan respectively.

• The Batu Laga Wildlife Sanctuary (1000 sq. km) will complement the adjacent proposed Hose Mountains National Park (2847 sq. km) in central Sarawak.

• Several new wetland protected areas have been proposed as a result of a World Wide Fund for Nature (Malaysia) project on the conservation and management of wetland areas in Sarawak. These include the proposed Salak Mangroves National Park, the 434 sq. km peat swamp forests of the proposed Maludam Wildlife Sanctuary (which has populations of red-black-and-white banded langur *Presbytis melalophos* of global importance), and the proposed Limbang Mangroves National Park (Bennett, 1989).

• Two large national parks have been proposed for the eastern side of Sarawak: Pulong Tau National Park (1645 sq. km) and Usun Apau National Park (1130 sq. km). The former will protect Sarawak's major montane area, including Mount Murud, the State's highest peak. The latter is a plateau area near the Baram River.

Other proposals highlighted in the State Conservation Strategy for Sarawak include:

• An extension to Mount Mulu National Park in the region of the Medalam Protected Forest to the north. The benefits of the extension would be to include more lowland forest; facilitate tourism; enclose more traditional lands of the Penan; and include Gunung Buda, a limestone massif (Anderson *et al.*, 1982). The Mulu National Park deserves nomination as a World Heritage Site, following the recent ratification of the World Heritage Convention by Malaysia.

• A hornbill 'flyway' system linking totally protected areas should be developed within the Permanent Forest Estate.

• The Pedawan limestone areas in First Division should be considered for inclusion in the protected area system, being floristically distinct from other limestone areas to the north of the State.

• Gunung Pueh and Gunung Berumput in southern Sarawak have been recommended as Wildlife Sanctuaries for conservation of reptiles and amphibians by the Select Committee on Flora and Fauna. Part of the former would be included in Samunsam Wildlife Sanctuary if it is extended as proposed.

Conservation Proposals – Sabah

Mount Trus Madi, the second highest mountain in Borneo, stands in a Forest Reserve that was designated as watershed protection until 1984, when it was changed to a commercial forest reserve. Many of the lower slopes have since been logged, in some areas resulting in serious erosion. However, there is still scope for a new State Park in the upper and some lower reaches.

Danum Valley (428 sq. km) is the site of a research station and is the largest piece of intact lowland forest remaining in Sabah. It contains all of eastern Sabah's large mammals, including the Sumatran rhinoceros and overall densities of animals are high. It is currently maintained as a conservation area by the Sabah Foundation, which has land on long lease.

Maliau Basin, another Sabah Foundation conservation area, is montane and may well be the most pristine ecosystem in Borneo. Potential threats come from coal deposits and oil prospecting.

The Sabah Foundation includes conservation amongst its management objectives. However, these areas will come under increasing pressure as timber resources run out, and legal protection would be beneficial. Like Sarawak, Sabah suffers from a lack of adequate protection for mangroves in its protected area system.

The recently published *Directory of Asian Wetlands* draws attention to large areas of forested wetland in Sarawak and Sabah whose integrity is of concern for both ecological and biological reasons (Scott, 1989). Whilst too large to be totally protected, their development and use requires an integrated management approach that will ensure the future maintenance of downstream and offshore ecosystems.

Initiatives for Conservation

In November 1984, a Select Committee on Flora and Fauna was formed to advise the Sarawak State Assembly on the danger of depletion of its wildlife, and to make appropriate recommendations. The State already protects a number of bird, reptile, mammal and tree species by law and the Committee set up several expert sub-committees and public debates to gather data. A final report submitted to the State Assembly in 1988 included the following selected points:

• Over-hunting, logging and shifting agriculture are threatening a growing number of species and the protected species list requires review.

• Wildlife Sanctuaries and other conservation areas require extension, in particular to include peat swamp and mangrove forests.

• Hunters should require special licences, with conditions on numbers to be shot and seasons for shooting.

• Some captive breeding programmes are needed, notably for certain deer and pheasants.

• Crocodiles, snakes, lizards and amphibians require surveys and the setting up of new reserves for protection of key habitats.

• Thirteen tree species, five pitcher plants, three palms and eight orchids are of particular environmental significance or are threatened by over-exploitation, and should be protected.

In Malaysia development and conservation plans evolve at a state level and are harmonized into national programmes later. The National Conservation Strategy for Malaysia is no exception. So far, seven states have been covered, including Sarawak. Plans are in hand for preparation of such an exercise in Sabah. Only when all states are completed will the strategies be combined at the national level. This process, which has already been in train for almost ten years, is WWF-Malaysia's largest and longest-running project.

The Sarawak Conservation Strategy, completed in 1985, is a comprehensive report on all natural resources. The report contains numerous recommendations for action, many of which are being acted upon in advance of national initiatives. For example, surveys of coastal forests have been completed and have culminated in proposals to protect several new areas of mangrove and peat swamp. Studies on wildlife conservation in relation to shifting agriculture and logging are already under way, as are a management study of marine turtles and a conservation education programme. Proposed revisions of the Wild Life and National Parks Ordinances have included many recommendations of the Strategy. One additional major recommendation was a thorough revision of the Natural Resources Ordinance which would greatly facilitate cross-sectoral planning and management of resources. A draft new ordinance has been written, but political changes have stalled its gazettement.

References

Anderson, J. A. R. (1965) Limestone habitat in Sarawak. *Proceedings of the Symposium on Ecological Research into Humid Tropics Vegetation*, pp. 49–57. Unesco, Kuching, Sarawak.

Anderson, J. A. R., Jermy, A. C. and the Earl of Cranbrook (eds) (1982) *Gunung Mulu National Park: A Management and Development Plan*. Royal Geographical Society, London, UK. 345 pp.

Anon. (1978) Shifting cultivation in Sarawak. Unpublished report based upon the Workshop on Shifting Cultivation held in Kuching, 7–8 December 1978. 28 pp.

Beaman, R. S., Beaman, J. H., Marsh, C. W. and Woods, P. V. (1985) Drought and forest fires in Sabah in 1983. *Sabah Society Journal* 8: 10–30.

Bennett, E. L. (1988) Proboscis monkeys and their swamp forests in Sarawak. *Oryx* 22: 69–74.

Bennett, E. L. (1989) Conservation and management of wetland areas in Sarawak. Final project report WWF Project No. 3518 (MYS 92/86). 21 pp. Unpublished.

Chai, P. P. K. and Lai, K. K. (1984) Management and utilization of mangrove forests in Sarawak. In: Soepadmo *et al.* (eds) (*op. cit.*), pp. 211–18.

Chan, L., Kavanagh, M., Cranbrook, Earl of, Langub, J. and Wells, D. R. (1985) *Proposals for a Conservation Strategy for Sarawak*. WWF Malaysia, Kuala Lumpur/State Planning Unit of Sarawak, Kuching.

Collar, N. J. and Andrew, P. (1988) *Birds to Watch. The ICBP World Checklist of Threatened Birds*. ICBP, Technical Publication 8. 303 pp.

Collins, N. M., Holloway, J. D. and Proctor, J. (1984) Notes on the ascent and natural history of Gunung Api, a limestone mountain in Sarawak. *Sarawak Museum Journal* 33: 220–34.

FAO (1987) *Special Study on Forest Management, Afforestation and Utilization of Forest Resources in the Developing Regions. Asia-Pacific Region. Assessment of Forest Resources in Six Countries*. FAO, Bangkok Field Document 17. 104 pp.

FAO/UNEP (1981) *Tropical Forest Resources Assessment: Forest Resources of Tropical Asia*. Vol 3 of 3 vols. FAO, Rome. 475 pp.

Fox, J. E. D. (1978) The natural vegetation of Sabah, Malaysia. The physical environment and classification. *Tropical Ecology* 19: 218–39.

Hatch, T. (1982) *Shifting Cultivation in Sarawak – a Review*. Soils Division Research Research Branch, Department of Agriculture, Sarawak. 165 pp.

Hong, E. (1987) *Natives of Sarawak*. Institut Masyarakat, Malaysia. 259 pp.

Malingreau, J. P., Stephens, G. and Fellows, L. (1985) Remote sensing of forest fires: Kalimantan and North Borneo in 1982–3. *Ambio* 14: 314–21.

Phillips, C. (1984) Current status of mangrove exploitation, management and conservation in Sabah. In: Soepadmo *et al.* (eds), *loc. cit.* pp. 809–20.

Poore, D. (1989) *No Timber Without Trees: Sustainability in the Tropical Forest*. Earthscan Publications, London, UK. 252 pp.

Proctor, J., Anderson, J. M., Chai, P. and Vallack, H. W. (1983) Ecological studies in four contrasting rain forests in Gunung Mulu National Park. Sarawak, I. *Journal of Ecology* 71: 237–60.

Repetto, R. (1988) *The Forest for the Trees? Government Policies and the Misuse of Forest Resources*. World Resources Institute, Washington, DC, USA. 105 pp.

Sabah Forest Department (1984) *Annual Report*. State of Sabah. 31 pp.

Sarawak Forest Department (1987) *Annual Report*. State of Sarawak. 113 pp.

Scott, D. A. (ed.) (1989) *A Directory of Asian Wetlands*. IUCN, Gland, Switzerland, and Cambridge, UK. 1181 pp.

Soepadmo, E., Rao, A. N. and McIntosh, D. J. (eds) (1984) *Proceedings of the Asian Symposium of Mangrove Environment Research and Management*. University of Malaya and Unesco, Kuala Lumpur.

Thang, H. C. (1987) National report: Malaysia. In: Proceedings of the Ad Hoc FAO/ECE/FINNIDA Meeting of Experts on Forest Resource Assessment. *Bulletins of the Finnish Forest Research Institute* 284: 207–20.

Authorship

Mark Collins at WCMC with contributions from, Lee Hua Seng and Cheong Ek Choon of the Sarawak Forest Department, Daniel Hiong of the Sabah Forest Department, Clive Marsh from the Sabah Foundation, the Earl of Cranbrook in Saxmundham, UK, Barney Chan of the Sarawak Timber Association, Tim Hatch of Kuching, Robert Nasi of the CTFT in Paris and Liz Bennett of WWF – Malaysia, Kuching.

Map 24.1 Forest cover in Sabah and Sarawak

Sabah. The main source of forest cover data for Sabah is a full-colour 1:1,270,000 scale map *Sabah Malaysia, Natural and Plantation Forests*, published in 1984. This map is a useful representation of the protected area system and the gazetted forests in the Permanent Forest Estate, but it gives no indication of the extent (if any) of additional natural stateland forests. On request, the Sabah Forest Department provided a hand-coloured *c.* 1:2 million map *State of Sabah: Tree Crop Areas* dated 1988. This second map distinguished stateland forests and showed some areas where they have been converted to agricultural tree crops, but the remaining extent of natural forests indicated was not reconcilable with the available statistics and it has been assumed that virtually all stateland forests have now been cleared. Map 24.1 is therefore based only on the *Sabah Malaysia, Natural and Plantation Forests* map. Mangroves and rain forests were taken directly from this map, and montane forests were delimited from a 3000 ft (914 m) contour taken off JNC (Jet Navigation Chart) 54.

Sarawak. The most recent published forest cover map for Sarawak is the *Forest Distribution and Land Use Map* published in 1979 at 1:1 million. On request, however, the Forest Department prepared an unpublished hand-coloured 1:3 million map showing forest cover. This latter map was prepared from a set of 1:500,000 base maps drawn from satellite imagery at 1:250,000. The imagery dates from 1985 and was checked with aerial photographs and ground-truthing surveys. Unfortunately, however, the scale of this latter map and the level of detail proved unsuitable for this atlas, and we have used the 1979 map. Mangrove, swamp and other rain forests are conveniently demarcated on the map and the distribution of the montane forests conforms closely to the 3000 ft (914 m) contour used in Sabah.

The distribution of the Permanent Forest Estate and the protected area system are shown in two dyeline 1:1 million hand-coloured maps from the Sarawak Forest Department, *Permanent Forests in Sarawak* and *Existing and Proposed National Parks and Wildlife Sanctuaries in Sarawak*. The protected area system shown in this volume was extracted from these maps, with additional up-dates for recent changes.

25 Singapore

Land area	570 sq. km
Population (1989)	2.7 million
Population growth rate (1987–2000)	0.8 per cent
Expected maximum population (2050)	3 million
Gross national product (1987)	US$7940 per capita
Rain forest (see Fig 25.1)	c.1 sq. km
Roundwood exports*	315,000 cu. m
Sawlog and veneer log exports*	40,000 cu. m

* 1988 data from FAO (1990)

The tiny state of Singapore is a green garden city. Very little of the rain forests which once clothed the island, either in a natural or semi-natural condition, now remains. What does persist is legally protected but under continual threat by pressure on land and by human activity. Despite its isolation for a century, Bukit Timah, 71 ha in extent and the remaining rain forest fragment, is still a species-rich lowland evergreen dipterocarp rain forest, and appears to have its ecosystem functions still working. The isolated forest on Bukit Timah is of importance today because it may show us what many parts of the humid tropics will be like in the 21st century.

INTRODUCTION

The Republic of Singapore lies just north of the equator at the southern tip of the Malay Peninsula, from which it is separated by a shallow strait, 0.6 km wide at the narrowest point. The main island has an area of 570 sq. km (including 30 sq. km added by recent reclamation) and there are about sixty smaller islands with a total area of 48 sq. km. The highest point is only 163 m above sea-level. The climate is equatorial and one of the least seasonal in the humid tropics, with a mean monthly rainfall of at least 100 mm, and a mean annual rainfall of 2375 mm.

Neither the origin of human occupation in Singapore nor the impact of early settlers on the rain forest is known. Pre-European settlements seem to have been largely coastal and culminated in the rise of the town of Temasik at the mouth of the Singapore River on the south coast in the 14th century. However, when the British Colony was founded in 1819, the total population of the island (excluding boat dwellers) was said to be only about 150, and the forest cover seems to have been essentially intact.

Singapore is a garden city and the visitor cannot fail to be impressed by the leafy shade provided by the millions of trees planted since the late 1960s along roads and in all open places, but one soon realises that the same few species are planted everywhere (rain tree *Enterolobium saman* and narra *Pterocarpus indicus* are the most common). Tree planting has made Singapore a very pleasant place for humans but gives no hint of the high natural diversity and beauty of the original woody floras of the region – a great opportunity to restore some of these has not yet been grasped.

The Forests

Closed canopy forest once covered all of Singapore. From topography, soil patterns, and 19th century maps, it can be estimated that mangrove forests occupied about 13 per cent of the main island, freshwater swamp forest 5 per cent, and lowland dipterocarp evergreen forest the remaining 82 per cent. The floristic composition of the rain forest must have varied considerably with soil type and topography, as it does in Peninsular Malaysia, but extensive botanical collection did not start until the 1880s, when more than 90 per cent of the forest had been cleared, so we have little information on this variation.

Today, more than half the island is urban in character. Natural rain forest, disturbed to varying extents, is confined to the 71 ha Bukit Timah Nature Reserve (which is not all primary forest) and scattered patches of various sizes, totalling about 50 ha, in the adjacent Central Catchment Area (Figure 25.1), which includes about 15 ha of disturbed freshwater swamp forest. The 4 ha Garden's Jungle at the Singapore Botanic Garden is, in part, primary forest but now so degraded that it retains little of its original structure and species composition. There are, in addition, approximately 1800 ha of 50–100 year old plantation and secondary forests in the catchment area, on land cleared and cultivated in the 19th century. These have not been mapped in this atlas, but they may well have a growing value for conservation of biological diversity.

Deforestation

Most of the deforestation in Singapore took place between 1819 and 1900 as a result of clearance for cash crops, principally gambier and pepper (see box on page 123 and Figure 25.2). This was a form of shifting cultivation as plantations were usually abandoned after 15–20 years. There is little information available on the exploitation of rain forests for timber and other products, but this must have been substantial, given the proximity of a growing urban centre. One example that was recorded is the almost complete elimination from Singapore, in only four years during the 1840s, of the gutta percha tree *Palaquium gutta*. This was a result of the destructive extraction of its latex, which contains a thermoplastic polymer that was used for coating submarine telegraph cables. It is interesting to note that despite their severe impact on the rain forest, neither agriculture nor forestry formed a major part of Singapore's 19th century economy.

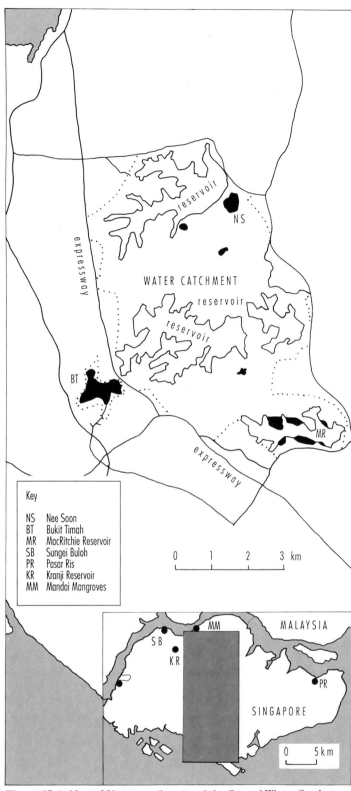

Figure 25.1 Map of Singapore (inset) and the Central Water Catchment Area, showing places mentioned in the text. *Source*: R. T. Corlett.

Dark shading shows approximate location of the major primary rain forest remnants. Dotted lines show reserve boundaries.

Key

NS	Nee Soon
BT	Bukit Timah
MR	MacRitchie Reservoir
SB	Sungei Buloh
PR	Pasar Ris
KR	Kranji Reservoir
MM	Mandai Mangroves

Mangroves

The original extent of mangroves was *c.* 75 sq. km (Corlett, 1987). Heavy exploitation from the 19th century onwards has been followed recently by elimination to provide more dry land for human settlement or to form freshwater reservoirs. At Sungai Buloh 85 ha of mangrove and abandoned prawnponds have recently been declared a sanctuary for migratory birds and 20 ha at Pasir Ris has been incorporated in a public park.

Biodiversity

Singapore, at the southern tip of the Malay peninsula, once had the same fauna and flora as persists today in parts of Peninsular Malaysia.

About 40 per cent of Singapore's pre-1819 terrestrial vertebrate fauna is extinct and probably about 20 per cent of the flora, as well as an unknown proportion of the invertebrates. Bird losses include all the trogons, hornbills and broadbills, all but one barbet, more than half the babblers and woodpeckers, and a variety of other species. Extinct mammals are mostly large and/or primary forest specialists, and include the tiger, leopard, clouded leopard, pig-tailed macaque *Macaca nemestrina*, sambar deer, barking deer and wild pig. It must be emphasised, however, that the immediate cause of extinction for the majority of the larger bird and mammal species was probably not deforestation *per se*, but hunting and trapping. Many fish species of forest streams have apparently also been lost. The majority of the remaining forest-dependent flora and fauna must be considered endangered. Naturalised exotics now feature prominently in the flora and fauna of the deforested areas (Corlett, 1988a).

Conservation Areas and Initiatives for Conservation

All the primary forest remnants are legally protected in nature reserves, run by the Parks and Recreation Department of the Ministry of National Development, on behalf of the Nature Reserves Board (recently re-named the National Parks Board). The 71 ha Bukit Timah Nature Reserve includes approximately 50, contiguous, hectares of mainly primary rain forest, while the 1800 ha Central Catchment Area, which is also a Nature Reserve, incorporates a similar total area in patches of various sizes, scattered in a matrix of secondary forest (Figure 25.1). The laws protecting these areas are probably adequate but are ineffectively implemented at present. The major weaknesses, apart from the tiny size of the rain forest remnants, are the unprotected margins and heavy human

Figure 25.2 Approximate extent of primary rain forest in Singapore, 1819–1987 *Source*: R. T. Corlett

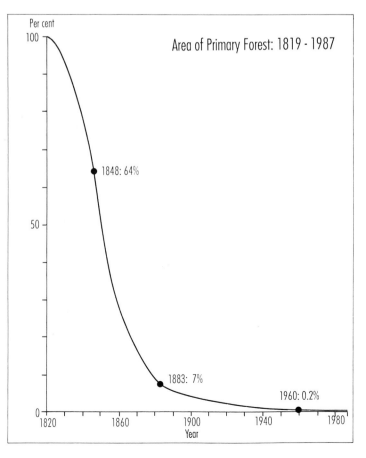

impact. The reserves are not fenced in most places, and are surrounded by roads, factories and residential areas, with no intervening buffer zone. Recreational pressure is greater at Bukit Timah and around MacRitchie Reservoir, while other parts of the catchment area are heavily disturbed by military exercises.

An additional weakness is the failure of the present protective legislation to distinguish between the primary forest remnants and the much more extensive but less diverse, secondary forests. These basic weaknesses reflect, in part, the lack of expertise in conservation biology and nature reserve management in the government authority responsible for the reserve system. The reserves are run principally as public parks rather than conservation areas.

Even in overcrowded Singapore there are still opportunities to improve the level of habitat conservation. The Malayan Nature Society is presently formulating an overall strategy for Singapore's protected areas. About 25 critical sites will be selected for potential reserve or sanctuary status. Two of the most important sites are wetlands in the north of the island, at Kranji Reservoir. A third site is in the Mandai mangroves, also on the north coast, and the last remaining mangrove habitat of any major significance. At present no mangroves are protected in Singapore and conservation of Mandai is considered to be a high priority. Conservation management in Singapore must also concentrate on minimising the extinction rate in the existing reserves and maximising benefits from man-made habitats. Three measures are most urgent: protection of the margins of existing reserves, restriction of military training in the reserves, and diversion of recreational pressure away from the most sensitive areas, ideally into the more extensive secondary forests. A more ambitious idea would be to accelerate succession in the secondary forests of the catchment area by assisting seed dispersal and planting primary forest species. It may also be possible to re-introduce locally extinct forest vertebrates, particularly birds, from Malaysia, now that hunting and trapping have been greatly reduced.

Increased public interest in environmental matters and a new government emphasis on the quality of life, rather than simply productivity, are reasons for optimism about the future of rain forests in Singapore. However, given the magnitude of the problems faced, a lot more than public goodwill will be required if much of Singapore's biological diversity is going to survive another century.

With so little rain forest left in Singapore, all remaining sites are critical. The most important areas, however, are the largest remnants: at Bukit Timah (see overleaf), around MacRitchie Reservoir, and around the Nee Soon (Yishun) firing ranges (Figure 25.1). All three areas have received some protection for at least 100 years and their floras are to some extent complementary. Bukit Timah includes species typical of coastal hills, MacRitchie is typical lowland forest, and Nee Soon includes a mosaic of freshwater swamp forest types. The international significance of Bukit Timah is argued in the review overleaf. Some of the same arguments apply to the other areas. In addition, Nee Soon supports the last surviving population of a leaf monkey, *Presbytis femoralis femoralis*, which may be an endemic subspecies.

There are three major threats to the future of the remaining rain forest.

• Firstly, there is a possibility that all or part of the existing reserves will be de-gazetted and developed. Many government departments still seem to view the reserves as a land bank and conservation has not been clearly established as a top priority. The primary forest remnants in the central catchment reserve are particularly vulnerable because they are mostly near the edges of the reserve. Two mangrove reserves established in 1951 were gradually reduced in area and then degazetted, in 1968 and 1971 respectively. The catchment area has also already lost a considerable area of mostly secondary forest to a golf course, public parks, roads and other developments.

• Secondly, the increasing recreational use of Bukit Timah and the MacRitchie Reservoir area, in particular, threatens the interior of the largest rain forest patches.

• Finally, the ultimate limit on the effectiveness of rain forest conservation in Singapore is the very small size of the remaining forest areas. Edge effects, isolation, and the small population sizes of all but the commonest species mean that continuing extinctions are inevitable.

GAMBIER AND DEFORESTATION

Gambier *Uncaria gambir* (Rubiaceae) is a woody rain forest climber grown for the astringent substances in the leaves. It has been used for chewing with betel nut, for medicinal purposes, for tanning leather, and for dyeing silk and cotton. Gambier was grown extensively by Chinese settlers on the island of Bentan (Bintang), south of Singapore, in the 18th century. In the early 19th century some of these gambier planters moved to Singapore and, when the British arrived in 1819, there were already about 20 gambier plantations established round the main settlement at the mouth of the Singapore River. In the next three decades, the cultivation of gambier, usually in association with pepper, expanded rapidly, spreading into the pristine forests of the interior of the island. The gambier from the earliest plantations was exported to China but later the British market became more important. By 1848, there was an estimated 100 sq. km of gambier on the island, about two-thirds of the total area under cultivation.

The disastrous impact of this crop resulted from the system of cultivation. Gambier grows on soil newly cleared of forest and each plantation required a roughly equal area of forest to provide the firewood needed to boil the gambier leaves (Jackson, 1965). The refuse from the gambier boiling was used as manure to enrich the smaller area of pepper vines. Within 15–20 years, the soil was exhausted and the fuelwood supply no longer sufficient. The Chinese cultivators, who rarely had any legal title to the land, then moved on to repeat the process in a new area. The practice spread north of Singapore island onto the southern part of the Malay peninsula.

Gambier continued to be a major crop in Singapore until the 1880s, when it was concentrated in the north and west of the island. Although many other crops were grown in the 19th century, with the exception of coconuts on the sandy soils of the east coast, these seem to have been largely on land previously cleared for gambier. Thus it is reasonable to attribute most of the 19th century deforestation to the gambier planters, rather than the effects of Singapore's success as a trading centre and the resulting growth in population. After 1890, the gambier area declined rapidly. Gambier cultivation continued longer in Johor, Malaysia, where the characteristic pattern of areas of secondary forest on the abandoned plantations, separated by strips of primary forest depleted by firewood extraction, can still be recognised. In Singapore, direct traces of gambier cultivation were erased by the subsequent rubber boom, but its effects are still evident in the absence of primary forest over most of the island.

View east from Bukit Timah. The forests in the foreground are pristine with secondary forest patches and plantations around the reservoir. N. M. Collins

BUKIT TIMAH NATURE RESERVE

The forest on Singapore's highest hill, Bukit Timah (163 m), first received protection in the 1840s, as a 'climatic reserve' (Corlett, 1988b). This reflected the widespread concern during the 19th century that destruction of forest, particularly on hilltops, would have detrimental effects on climate. In 1884, the Bukit Timah area became Singapore's first forest reserve. Since then it has never been legally logged, although timber thefts have often been a problem. The forest later sustained some damage in the Japanese invasion in 1942 during the Second World War, and the subsequent occupation. In 1951 Bukit Timah was finally declared a nature reserve, a role that it had in practice already fulfilled for more than a century.

Today, Bukit Timah Nature Reserve consists of 71 ha of forest, about two-thirds of which has never been cleared (Figure 25.3). An additional 10 ha of forest east of the summit is effectively part of the reserve, although technically part of the water catchment area. A recently completed expressway separates Bukit Timah from the remainder of the catchment area.

As a reserve Bukit Timah is far from ideal. The problems resulting from its small area and isolation are made worse by the irregular shape, exposed position, unprotected margins and penetration by a tarmac road and numerous walking trails. More than 78,000 people visited the reserve in 1987 and the number increases every year, attracted as much by the opportunity to climb Singapore's highest hill as by nature. However, despite all the problems, the reserve does fulfil an important conservation role.

Although about half of the original vertebrate fauna has been lost, the flora and invertebrate fauna still show no sign of the general collapse of biotic diversity predicted by many theorists. More than 850 species of vascular plants have been recorded from Bukit Timah in the last hundred years (Corlett, 1989) and there has been no significant invasion by exotic or non-forest plants and invertebrates, except along the margins of the road and other artificial openings. Superficially, the core areas of the reserve appear little different from undisturbed rain forest in Malaysia.

Although there are probably no endemic plant species at Bukit Timah, an estimated 15 per cent of the flora is at its southern limit and thus likely to be genetically different from other populations.

Forest clearance in the Malay peninsula is rapidly increasing the conservation importance of the reserve. There is now little rain forest left in adjacent parts of Johor, the southernmost Peninsular Malaysian state. The international significance has been further enhanced by the concentration of scientific studies carried out there over the past century. Few, if any, other areas of rain forest in Southeast Asia have been studied in such detail. Bukit Timah is the type locality for a number of plant species and many insects and other invertebrates; A. R. Wallace made major collections there during the last century. Apart from taxonomic studies, recent and current research projects at Bukit Timah include studies of plant reproductive phenology (Corlett, 1989), tree distribution patterns (Swan, 1989), tree diversity (Wong, 1987), macaques, insects (Murphy, 1973), ferns, bryophytes, mycorrhizal fungi, birds and freshwater crabs. A popular guidebook of the reserve is available.

The most urgently needed improvements at Bukit Timah are fencing of the margins (including the forested area north-east of the summit), and the control of visitors. Ideally, visitors would be divided at the entrance into those visiting the summit, who would be confined to the main road, and those entering the reserve proper, who would pass through an educational visitors' centre first. They would then be restricted to a small number of clearly marked trails, possibly on raised walkways to reduce trampling, and all other paths would be closed off. A larger and better-trained staff would be needed to enforce this policy.

In the long term, active management of some plant and animal populations will probably be necessary, but our current understanding of the dynamics of the reserve is insufficient to make any definite proposals at this stage.

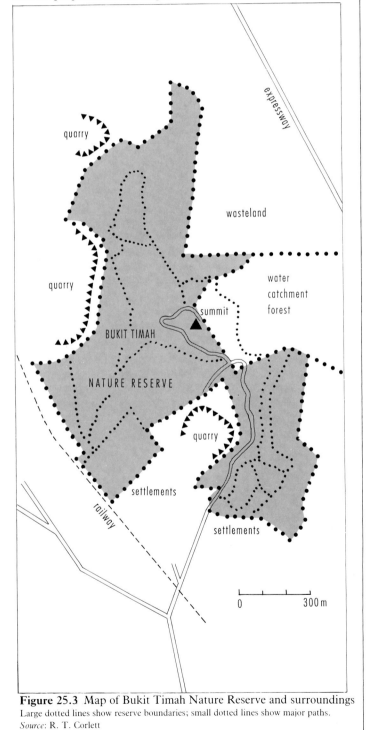

Figure 25.3 Map of Bukit Timah Nature Reserve and surroundings
Large dotted lines show reserve boundaries; small dotted lines show major paths.
Source: R. T. Corlett

References

Corlett, R. T. (1987) Singapore. In: *Mangroves of Asia and the Pacific: Status and Management* pp. 211–18. Umali *et al.* (eds) (*op. cit.*).

Corlett, R. T. (1988a) The naturalized flora of Singapore. *Journal of Biogeography* **15**: 657–63.

Corlett, R. T. (1988b) Bukit Timah: the history and significance of a small rain forest reserve. *Environmental Conservation* **15**: 37–44.

Corlett, R. T. (1989) Flora and reproductive phenology of the rain forest at Bukit Timah, Singapore. *Journal of Tropical Ecology*: in press.

Jackson, J. C. (1965) Chinese agricultural pioneering in Singapore and Johore, 1800–1917. *Journal of the Malaysian Branch, Royal Asiatic Society* **38**: 77–105.

Murphy, D. J. (1973) Animals in the forest ecosystem. In: *Animal Life and Nature in Singapore*, pp. 53–73. Chuang, S. H. (ed.).

Swan, F. R. (Jr) (1989) Tree distribution patterns in the Bukit Timah Nature Reserve. *Gardens' Bulletin, Singapore*: in press.

Umali, R. Zamora, P. M., Gotera, R. R., Jara, R. S. and Camacho, A. S. (eds) (1987) *Mangroves of Asia and the Pacific*. Ministry of Natural Resources, Manila, Philippines.

Wong, Y. K. (1987) Ecology of the trees at Bukit Timah Nature Reserve. *Gardens' Bulletin, Singapore* **40**: 45–76.

Authorship

Richard Corlett, formerly at the University of Singapore but now in Hong Kong, with a contribution from Cherla Sastry at the International Research Development Centre in Singapore.

26 Sri Lanka

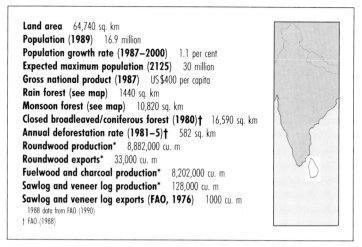

Land area 64,740 sq. km
Population (1989) 16.9 million
Population growth rate (1987–2000) 1.1 per cent
Expected maximum population (2125) 30 million
Gross national product (1987) US$400 per capita
Rain forest (see map) 1440 sq. km
Monsoon forest (see map) 10,820 sq. km
Closed broadleaved/coniferous forest (1980)† 16,590 sq. km
Annual deforestation rate (1981–5)† 582 sq. km
Roundwood production* 8,882,000 cu. m
Roundwood exports* 33,000 cu. m
Fuelwood and charcoal production* 8,202,000 cu. m
Sawlog and veneer log production* 128,000 cu. m
Sawlog and veneer log exports (FAO, 1976) 1000 cu. m
* 1988 data from FAO (1990)
† FAO (1988)

The past three decades have seen rapid depletion of Sri Lanka's forests, both in extent and quality. Forest land has been released to meet demands of an expanding population and timber has been harvested indiscriminately. The only guideline for harvesting of forests was the sustained yield regulation based on minimum felling girth, but even this was not stringently applied. Natural closed canopy forests were severely reduced in extent from 29,000 sq. km (44 per cent of land area) in 1956 to 16,590 sq. km (27 per cent) in 1980. The maps shown here indicate that by 1983 12,260 sq. km (19 per cent) remained, of which only 1440 sq. km was rain forest.

Recently the value of the tropical rain forest and the need to conserve it has been increasingly recognised by the Government. For example timber felling in the important Sinharaja forest was reduced in 1972 and stopped completely in 1978. In 1987 it was officially recognised that the few remaining lowland and montane rain forests should be completely protected.

A consensus has now been reached on how biologically valuable forest resources are to be utilised in the future. IUCN is helping with the environmental component of the Forestry Sector Development Plan and the concept of buffer zones, and integrated conservation management plans are being developed for the Sinharaja and Knuckles forests.

INTRODUCTION

Sri Lanka is 430 km from north to south and 224 km wide. The climate is strongly influenced by the monsoons, moderated by topography. The south-west corner has a rain forest climate, with up to 5000 mm mean annual rainfall; elsewhere the climate is seasonal, with mean rainfall declining towards the north-east.

Sri Lanka has a long recorded history. In 483 BC a series of dynasties of kings came from eastern or southern India. Portugal invaded in 1505 and was ousted by the Dutch in 1765. In 1815 the British overcame both the Dutch and the Sinhala kings, and declared the island a Crown Colony.

The Portuguese and the Dutch traded in spices and natural products including calamander *Diospyros quaesita* timber. The British were instrumental in building up the plantation economy based on coffee, tea, rubber and coconut.

Ceylon gained independence in 1948 and remained within the Commonwealth. In 1972, as a result of a constitutional amendment, Ceylon became a Republic and changed its name to Sri Lanka. The main ethnic groups are Sinhalese and Tamils; besides their languages English is widely spoken.

The Forests

Tropical rain forests are restricted to the wettest region, the south-west corner. Where rainfall is 3750–5000 mm per year lowland evergreen and semi-evergreen rain forests occur to 1000 m elevation. Dipterocarpaceae are locally important, with *Dipterocarpus hispidus*, *D. zeylanicus* and *Shorea* spp. common on alluvium. This is a species-rich forest with numerous Malesian genera, e.g. *Mangifera*, *Mesua*, *Palaquium* and *Vitex*.

Montane rain forest occurs above 900–1000 m. Major species include *Gordonia* spp., *Palaquium rubiginosum*, *Shorea gardneri* and *Stemonoporus* spp. in the lower montane, and *Calophyllum* sp., *Litsea* spp. and *Michelia nilagirica* in the upper montane formation.

Outside the south-west the climate is seasonal, in places strongly so (Figure 26.1). The original vegetation was monsoon forest, but thorn forest and scrub now occurs in the driest areas of the north, north-west and south-west. The long history of human intervention has led to all forest formations being extensively altered and degraded.

Forest Resources and Management

Various efforts have been made to assess the extent of the forests of Sri Lanka. Andrews (1961) estimated the total area of rain and monsoon forest (presumably including thorn forests) in 1956 as about 28,500 sq. km (44 per cent of land area). The UNDP/FAO inventory of 1982–6 reassessed the area (of closed forests) as only 16,590 sq. km (26 per cent of land area) (FAO, 1988). Another survey of rain and monsoon forests computed from Landsat imagery by the Centre for Remote Sensing in 1981 found a similar figure of 25 per cent, and recent unpublished data in the Government's Forestry Master Plan (FMP) give almost 27 per cent (Table 26.1).

Unfortunately the FMP does not distinguish between rain and monsoon forests on steep slopes and in nature conservation areas, so it is difficult to ascertain total figures for these formations. The monsoon and thorn forests included in this assessment were, in fact, widely degraded by slash and burn cultivators, even reducing the land to open woodlands. Much of the remaining intact dry forests are in the wildlife reserves in the drier parts of the country.

216

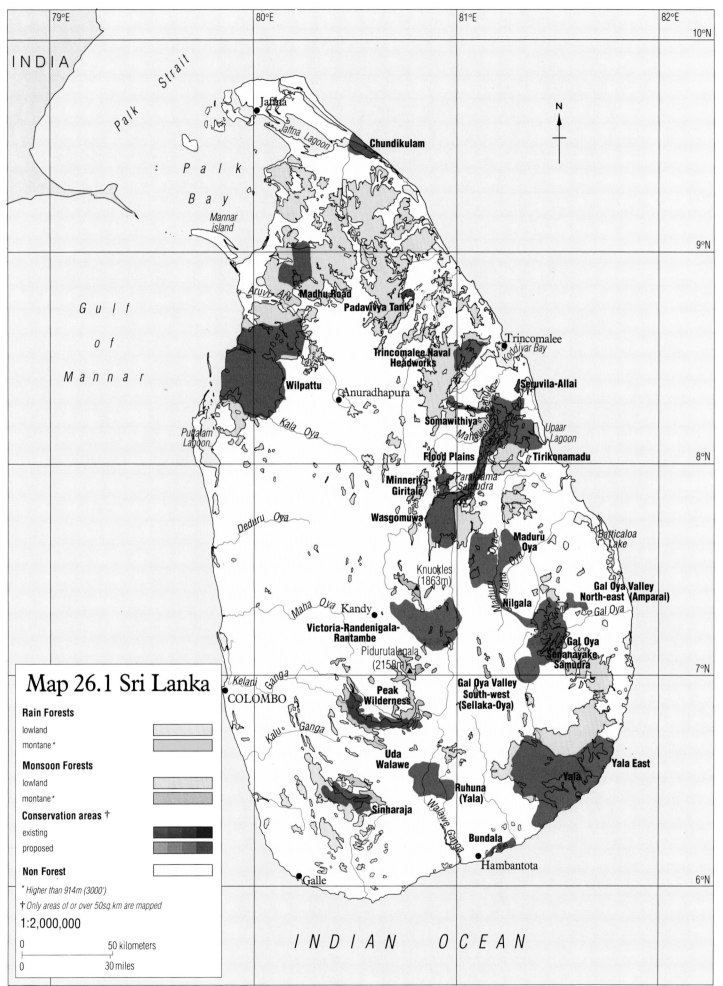

Map 26.1 Sri Lanka

Rain Forests

Monsoon Forests

Conservation areas †

Non Forest

* Higher than 914m (3000')

† Only areas of or over 50sq.km are mapped

1:2,000,000

0   50 kilometers

0   30 miles

Table 26.1 Extent of natural high forest lands in Sri Lanka, 1982–5

	Area (sq. km)
Closed forest in the lowlands	
Wet zone (rain forest)	1,200
Dry zone (monsoon and thorn forest)	9,550
Closed forest on steep slopes	1,750
Closed forest reserved for nature conservation	4,750
Total closed high forest	17,250

(Adapted from the Sri Lanka Forestry Master Plan, unpublished)

Map 26.1 shows the natural closed forests in Sri Lanka in 1983, based on data published in 1988 (see Map Legend). Table 26.2 gives a breakdown of the forest types, indicating that 10,820 sq. km of monsoon forest (16.7 per cent of land area), and a mere 1440 sq. km of rain forest (2.2 per cent of land area) remained at that time.

During the Second World War and shortly after, large timber demands were made on the rain forests for the first time. To meet the demand, selective felling began, mainly of medium hardwoods, but in due course extending to light hardwoods such as peeler logs for the plywood industry (which still today maintains two factories which are operating below capacity) (Perera, 1972). Evidence shows that application of felling rules has been lax (Gunatilleke and Gunatilleke, 1983). Shortage of trained staff, creation of many state agencies for timber harvesting, absence of a central record-keeping system to support field data and poor supervision are some of the reasons for poor application of felling rules. Some timber value has been maintained but the biological diversity of the forests has been reduced.

Felling was at first by axe and saw and extraction by elephant. Since 1972 it has become mechanised, using chainsaws, skidders and lorries that have greatly increased the damage. Skid trails now occupy 10–12 per cent of the extraction area. Recent mapping of the growing stock of 1190 sq. km of management areas identified only 480 sq. km suitable for future timber harvesting. It also indicated that nearly half of the earliest selectively felled areas would not be ready for recutting after the 20–30 years originally contemplated, but would require a much longer regeneration period.

Degraded or poorly structured areas have been subject to enrichment planting with mahogany *Swietenia macrophylla*, an exotic from Central America. Recently, greater attention has been given to the management of natural forests to conserve biodiversity. Emphasis has also been placed on the raising of industrial forest plantations and enhancement of tree cover outside the forest areas, in homesteads and village greens, to meet timber needs.

In the rain forest zone, policy changes in forest management date back to 1972. Harvesting of timber began in Sinharaja which was widely criticised and drew attention to the global significance of Sinharaja in terms of its biodiversity, as well as its role in water and soil maintenance. In response, the Government has placed more attention on the management of this and other rain forests for conservation purposes, and less on commercial timber extraction. The timber management area in the wet zone is now only 480 sq. km. National timber and fuel requirements are expected to be met from the dry zone forests, non-forest sources such as spice gardens (see next page), agricultural residue, forest plantations and imported timber.

Deforestation

Major causes of deforestation and forest degradation are fuelwood gathering (mainly for domestic use but also for the brickmaking industry), permanent agriculture, shifting cultivation (known locally as *chena*) tree plantations, fire, mining for gem stones, urbanisation and timber felling. The absence of well-defined forest reserve boundaries has exacerbated the problem.

The average loss of closed forests from 1981–5 was estimated by FAO to be 520 sq. km per year (FAO, 1988). There are no deforestation data differentiating between rain forests and monsoon forests, but most deforestation takes place in the more extensive monsoon and thorn forest zone. Nevertheless, as a proportion of the total, losses in the wet zone are undoubtedly very serious. Over two and a half years between 1981 and 1983 the Remote Sensing Centre calculated moist forest loss was 0.96 and 4.1 per cent of remaining forests in the lowlands and mountains respectively.

The Sri Lanka Forestry Master Plan (unpublished) gives deforestation statistics in natural forests over the longer term, citing 425 sq. km per year from 1956–83. This was considered to have fallen to 310 sq. km per year during the period 1981–3. These figures relate almost entirely to the dry forest zone.

Mangroves

Remnants of mangrove forests occur scattered around the coast, but in patches too small to figure on Map 26.1. They are an important resource for local inhabitants for many products but, as is common, land planners have failed to recognise this, or their importance as marine breeding grounds. Over-exploitation and attrition have occurred; for example satellite imagery showed two per cent were lost between 1975 and 1976. Recently a National Management Plan has been made for mangroves and other wetlands. IUCN has been asked to support survey and conservation activities (Jayewardene, 1987).

Biodiversity

Sri Lanka's great diversity of climate, geology, topography and soils is reflected in its flora, fauna and ecosystems. Over half of the species of amphibians and reptiles are endemic, as are over one-quarter of the fish, 14 per cent of the mammals and eight per cent of the birds. Of the estimated total of over 3000 species of flowering plants in Sri Lanka, some 830 are endemic; 94 per cent of which are concentrated in the rain forests. The remaining six per cent of endemics are spread over the large dry and intermediate zone land mass. The much higher endemism of the rain forests is shown in Table 26.3. Some rain forest species have very restricted ranges, and population density is characteristically low (Crusz, 1973; Erdelen, 1988).

Table 26.2 Estimates of forest extent

	Area (sq. km)	% of land area
Rain forests		
Lowland	740	1.1
Montane	700	1.1
Sub totals	1,440	2.2
Monsoon forests		
Lowland	10,640	16.4
Montane	180	0.3
Sub totals	10,820	16.7
Totals	12,260	18.9

(Based on analysis of Map 26.1. See Map Legend for details of sources)

Table 26.3 Tree diversity in samples of different forest formations in Sri Lanka

	Families	Genera	Species	% endemic species
Rain forests				
Lowland	31–41	65–88	101–136	59–67
Montane	26–38	37–65	54–96	44–50
Monsoon and savanna				
forests	21–34	41–67	47–75	13–18

(*Source:* Ashton and Gunatilleke, 1987; Gunatilleke and Gunatilleke, 1984)

Table 26.4 Degree of endemism among butterflies, fishes, amphibians, reptiles, birds and mammals observed in Sinharaja forest

	Species in Sri Lanka		Species in Sinharaja[1]	
	Total	Endemic	Total	Endemic
Butterflies	242	41	65 (27)	21 (51)
Fishes	64	17	10 (16)	7 (41)
Amphibia				
Tetropod	73	34	14 (19)	7 (21)
Others	38	19	19 (50)	8 (42)
Reptiles				
Snakes	90	39	29 (19)	14 (36)
Birds	384	20	141 (37)	19 (95)
Mammals	85	12	40 (47)	7 (58)

(*Source:* unpublished data from the Sri Lanka non-governmental organisation, March for Conservation)

[1] In brackets are the numbers of species present in Sinharaja forest expressed as a percentage of the total island species.

Working elephants in the tropical moist forests of Sri Lanka. J. A. McNeely

Surveys in rain forests have recorded over 170 threatened species of endemic plants. These include 29 species traditionally sought after by villagers for their daily medical and other needs. The botanic garden at Peradeniya near Kandi has a special medicinal plant garden. It also holds 71 species of lowland rain forest endemics which have been cultivated as individuals (Gunatilleke *et al.*, 1987).

The fauna of the lowland rain forests are less documented than the flora. However, a preliminary compilation of lists of butterflies, fishes, amphibians, reptiles, birds and mammals indicates a high degree of endemism in Sinharaja forest (Table 26.4).

THE SPICE GARDENS OF KANDI

The forested regions of Asia and the Pacific first attracted the interest of European traders and adventurers as a source of spices, the most valuable of which was cinnamon. Obtained by grinding the dried bark of the indigenous Sri Lankan *Cinnamomum zeylanicum*, cinnamon has been highly prized in Europe since Roman times. Throughout much of history its origin was shrouded in mystery. Transported by dhow to the west coast of India, it was then taken by a succession of Arab and African traders to the major cities of Europe. In London, in the early 19th century it fetched the fabulous price of £8 per pound.

The colonial powers attempted to monopolise and control the spice industry. During a period of Dutch control of Sri Lanka, contravention of laws governing cinnamon cultivation was punishable by death. It is recorded that the Dutch government in Amsterdam instructed its administration in the Dutch East Indies to suppress the cultivation of nutmeg and increase that of mace. Like many people today, they were not aware that both are produced from the fruits of the same tree, *Myristica fragrans*.

Many of the common spices are now grown throughout the tropics, and the relatively fertile soils of the Kandi region in Sri Lanka are particularly noted for the variety of spices that they produce. The so-called Kandi home gardens are considered by conservationists to be an example of ideal land use in the humid tropics. A large number of people attain a good standard of living by intensively cultivating a variety of high-value crops around their homes. Some of these gardens have become a major attraction for tourists on their way to visit the temples and palaces of the ancient capital, Kandi. Visitors can walk in the shade of the nutmeg (*Myristica fragrans*), clove (*Eugenia caryophyllata*), and tamarind (*Tamarindos*), all Indian trees. The South American vanilla orchid (*Vanilla planifolia*) grows as a climber on the larger trees, as does the black pepper (*Piper nigrum*). In the understorey, ginger (*Zingiber officinale*), turmeric (*Curcuma domestica*) and cardamom (*Elettaria cardamomum*) – all members of the ginger family (Zingiberaceae) – thrive in the partial shade. All are important ingredients of Asian and Middle Eastern cooking. A valuable export market for cardamom has developed as it is now a vital ingredient in Scandinavian breakfast pastries.

The Kandi gardens replicate many of the functions of a tropical forest. They have a high biomass and moderate the microclimate, and the diversity of their plant species means that scarce soil nutrients are used efficiently. Moreover, a greater variety of birds and insects occurs here than would do in a monoculture plantation. It would be a loss for conservation if commercial pressures led to intensive production of these products on industrial estates and the abandonment of the traditional home gardens.

Table 26.5 Conservation areas of Sri Lanka

Existing areas, 50 sq. km and over, are listed below. The remaining areas are combined in a total under Other Areas. Forest reserves are not included. For data on World Heritage sites and Biosphere reserves see chapter 9.

	Existing area (sq. km)	Proposed area (sq. km)
National Parks		
Flood Plains★	174	
Gal Oya★	259	
Maduru Oya★	588	
Ruhuna (Yala)★	979	
Somawathiya★	378	
Uda Walawe	308	
Wasgomuwa★	371	
Wilpattu★	1319	
Yala East★	181	
Strict Natural Reserves		
Yala★	289	
Nature Reserves		
Minneriya–Giritale★	75	
Tirikonamadu★	250	
Natural Heritage Wilderness Area		
Sinharaja★	76	
Jungle Corridor		
Nilgala	104	
Sanctuaries		
Bundala★	62	
Chundikulam	111	
Gal Oya Valley North-east (Amparai)★	124	
Gal Oya Valley South-west (Sellaka-Oya)★	153	
Madhu Road★	267	
Padavivya Tank	65	
Peak Wilderness★	224	
Senanayake Samudra	93	
Seruvila–Allai	155	
Trincomalee Naval Headworks★	181	
Victoria–Randenigala–Rantambe★	421	
Sub total	7207	
Other Areas	531	215
Totals	7738	215

(*Sources:* IUCN 1990, WCMC *in litt.*)
★ Area with moist forest within its boundary.

Conservation Areas

All natural forest is owned by the state, under many agencies and protected under several enactments, of which the oldest was the Land Order of 1873 prohibiting the clearing of forests above 1524 m.

To protect biological resources contained in other natural areas, National Parks, Strict Natural Reserves and Nature Reserves, Jungle Corridors and Sanctuaries have been declared under the Fauna and Flora Protection Ordinance and administered by the Department of Wildlife Conservation. The extent so protected is about 7800 sq. km or 12 per cent of the total land area. About 4750 sq. km of high forest is included within this (Table 26.5). Other remaining forests are categorised as Forest Reserves, Proposed Forest Reserves and Other State Forests – which add up to 9462 sq. km, or 14.4 per cent of the

land area for the country. The Forest Department is responsible for the management of all existing and proposed Forest Reserves. Other State Forests are administered by the Forest Department and the head of the particular district administration unit, namely the Government Agent. Generally, those over 40 ha in the wet zone are administered by the Forest Department and the remainder by the Government Agent of the particular district. Since 1950, Forest Reserves, Proposed Reserves, Other State Forests and wildlife areas have been subject to great pressure from the local population and some of the forests have been released either in full or in part for settlement purposes. The management of the remaining Forest Reserves and Proposed Forest Reserves is being continued by the Forest Department.

In 1975, 36 areas totalling 1270 sq. km were nominated as Biosphere Reserves under the Unesco/MAB programme (Sri Bharathie, 1979) of which 22, covering 536 sq. km, were in the rain forest. These, however, remained as proposals, but in 1988 76 sq. km of Sinharaja were protected under the National Wilderness Areas Act and given additional protection by being declared a World Heritage site.

The following areas are of particular significance for their rain forests and are deserving of careful management:

1 Peak Wilderness Sanctuary (224 sq. km, 700–1128 m). Habitat of *Stemonoporus* (Dipterocarpaceae), an endemic genus growing gregariously as a canopy tree at higher elevations (Greller *et al.*, 1987). In the inter-monsoonal period from mid-December to mid-May, nearly 900,000 religious pilgrims drawn from various parts of the island travel up to Sri Pada Peak (Adam's Peak, 2238 m), causing much disturbance of the forests. In addition, removal of fuelwood by labourers in nearby tea estates and unauthorised gem-mining aggravate the situation. Proposals are being considered to improve facilities for the pilgrims by supplying fuelwood and energy sources from outside the area. The Peak Wilderness remains biologically unexplored, and further scientific studies are necessary.

2 Kanneliya, **Dediyagala** and **Nakiyadeniya** (110 sq. km). These forests fall within the richest floristic area with 65 per cent of the endemic species of Sri Lanka (Ashton and Gunatilleke, 1987). They have been subject to timber harvest for two decades. Selective felling rules have not been enforced. It is planned to manage the whole forest as a reserve with minimal extraction of some forest products.

3 Hinidum Kanda (Haycock) Reserve (4 sq. km). A low hill, 668 m, within the rain forest. Two species *Diospyros oppositifolia* and *Schumnacheria angustfolia* are endemic (Gunatilleke & Gunatilleke, 1984).

4 Sinharaja Forest, (*c.*1110 sq. km), lies in the south-west lowlands at 300–1150 m. Established as forest reserve, some 89 sq. km were declared a Biosphere Reserve in 1978. In 1988, 76 sq. km of this was designated as a National Heritage Wilderness Area, and was inscribed on the World Heritage List in 1989. Sinharaja is of great biological importance, particularly for its high level of endemic plants (Ashton and Gunatilleke, 1987; Gunatilleke & Gunatilleke, 1984; Peeris, 1975). In 1986 the Forest Department helped by IUCN and WWF prepared a conservation plan (Forest Department, 1986), which led to a Sinharaja Conservation Project, developed since July 1988 with the assistance of IUCN. The objectives are boundary mapping, ensuring uniform legal status, socio-economic surveys, containment of human settlements, buffer zone management, awareness and training programmes, and building of infrastructure. A research and education centre is to be set up on the north-western section funded by WWF.

5 Knuckles Range Forests (217 sq. km). Located south of Kandi and north of the central massif, these forests have evergreen lowland, lower montane and upper montane forest formations. The flora and fauna have not been studied in detail. Cardamom cultivation in the middle and higher elevations presents a threat. A conservation project assisted by IUCN commenced in 1988; its objectives include boundary mapping, identifying critical conservation and management areas, and resolving socio-economic constraints to conservation. Scientific studies, and research and extension activities in the surrounding areas are to be carried out.

6 Horton Plains (MAB area 91 sq. km, National Park area 32 sq. km), designated as a Nature Reserve in 1969 and upgraded to a National Park in 1988. The Plains occupy the southern edge of the plateau of the central highlands at an altitude of 2100–2300 m. There are two peaks, Kirigalpotta (2394 m) and Totupola Kanda (2359 m), with the Adam's Peak Wilderness contiguous to the west. Tributaries of three main rivers originate here, and the plateau is covered by a vast expanse of undulating montane grasslands on wet black soils called 'patanas' associated with low stature upper montane forests. The vegetation of the area is unique – although floristically less diverse than the lowland rain forests there is about 50 per cent endemism amongst woody species. The Plains show a pattern of knolls and of swampy depressions. Between 1961 and 1969, part of the grassland was seriously disturbed when a potato seed station was set up by the State, and old ploughed areas and derelict buildings are still visible. Man-made fires are almost a yearly occurrence. Further scientific studies and control of outside interference are needed, and World Bank assistance has been sought to develop a Conservation Plan covering this area and the adjoining Adam's Peak sanctuary.

Initiatives for Conservation

The Sri Lanka Forestry Master Plan generated much controversy and it was criticised for failing to address environmental concerns. However, much progress has been made in building conservation

components into the projects which are implementing the Plan. The World Bank is now loaning money to help create an environmental management unit within the Forest Department. As a result, all the remaining moist forest areas are being surveyed and forest management plans will take account of the biological value of the areas. No logging will occur in areas of special conservation concern.

An FAO/UNDP funded mission to assist in the protected area component of the Master Plan recommended that Jungle Corridors between national parks and reserves, already instigated in Sri Lanka (see Table 26.5), should be extended. The existing Nilgala corridor extends south-east from Maduru Oya National Park (NP) to Gal Oya (NP). Further corridors have been recommended from Gal Oya south-east to the small Lahulgala NP, from there south to Yala East NP, and from the adjoining Ruhuna NP westwards through the proposed Lunungamvihira NP to Uda Walawe NP. These are important for the movement of animals, elephants particularly.

The Department of Wildlife Conservation is extending its programmes to improve management of protected areas and will receive international support for this.

One of the most encouraging new developments in Sri Lanka is the emergence of influential non-governmental conservation organisations. The Wildlife and Nature Protection Society has existed since the turn of the century and is a respected and active campaigning body on conservation issues. Other organisations have been established more recently, and this move reflects a growing awareness of conservation issues amongst the Sri Lankan public.

The universities, particularly Peradeniya, have active conservation research programmes and work on forest botany has helped give a sound scientific basis to conservation programmes.

References

Andrews, J. R. T. (1961) *A Forest Inventory of Ceylon.* Ceylon Government Press.

Ashton, P. S. and Gunatilleke, C. V. S. (1987) New light on the plant geography of Ceylon. *Journal of Biogeography* **14**: 249–85.

Crusz, H. (1973) Nature conservation in Sri Lanka. *Ceylon Biological Conservation* **5**: 199–208.

Erdelen, W. (1988) Forest ecosystems and nature conservation in Sri Lanka. *Biological Conservation* **43**: 115–35.

FAO (1988) *An Interim Report on the State of Forest Resources in the Developing Countries.* FAO, Rome, Italy. 18 pp. + 5 tables.

FAO (1990) *FAO Yearbook of Forest Products 1977–88.* FAO Forestry Series No. 23, FAO Statistics No. 90. FAO, Rome, Italy.

Forest Department (1986) *Conservation Plan for Sinharaja Forest.* Government of Sri Lanka publication. 87 pp.

Greller, A. M., Gunatilleke, I. A. U. N., Gunatilleke, C. V. S., Jayasuriya, A. H. M., Balasubramaniam, S. and Dissanayake, M. D. (1987) *Stemonoporus* (Dipterocarpaceae)-dominated montane forests in the Adam's Peak Wilderness, Sri Lanka. *Journal of Tropical Ecology* **3**: 243–53.

Gunatilleke, C. V. S. and Gunatilleke, I. A. U. N. (1983) Conservation of natural forests in Sri Lanka. *The Sri Lanka Forester* **16**.

Gunatilleke, C. V. S. and Gunatilleke, I. A. U. N. (1984) Distribution of endemics in the tree flora of a lowland hill forest in Sri Lanka. *Biological Conservation* **28**: 275–85.

Gunatilleke, C. V. S., Gunatilleke, I. A. U. N. and Sumithrarachi, B. (1987) Woody endemic species of the wet lowland of Sri Lanka and their conservation in botanic gardens. *Botanic Gardens and the World Conservation Strategy.* Academic Press Inc., London.

IUCN (1990) *1989 United Nations List of National Parks and Protected Areas.* IUCN Gland, Switzerland, and Cambridge, UK.

Jayewardene, R. P. (1987) Sri Lanka. In: *Mangroves of Asia and the Pacific.* Umali, R. *et al.* (eds). Ministry of Natural Resources,

Manila, Philippines.

Peeris, C. V. S. (1975) Ecology of the endemic tree species in Sri Lanka in relation to their conservation. Unpublished Ph.D. Thesis. University of Aberdeen, UK.

Perera, W. R. H. (1972) A study of the protective benefits of the Wet Zone Forestry Reserves of Sri Lanka. *The Ceylon Forester* **10**: 87–102.

Sri Bharathie, K. P. (1979) Man and Biosphere Reserves in Sri Lanka. *The Sri Lanka Forester* **14**.

Authorship

M. S. Ranatunga of IUCN Colombo with contributions from many of his colleagues in the Forest Department, Charles Santiapillai of WWF, Bogor and Jeff Sayer at IUCN, Gland.

Map 26.1 Forest cover in Sri Lanka

Data on the extent of natural closed forest in Sri Lanka were taken from *Sri Lanka: Chena Cultivation in the Dry Zone and Dense Natural Forest 1983,* published at 1:500,000 by the Survey Department of Sri Lanka (1988). Dense natural forest was mapped, and the boundary between the wet and dry zones shown on that map was used to delimit rain and monsoon forests respectively. There is some difficulty in distinguishing between the monsoon forest and the thorn scrub formations that eventually result from monsoon forest degradation. The latter are known to be rather widespread in the north, north-west and south-west, but no maps have been located. Even the *Maps of Series of Vegetation of Peninsular India and Sri Lanka* (Undated 1:2.5 million scale map by H. Gaussen, P. Legris V. M. Meher-Homji and collaborators), combines the vegetation of these regions into a single 'deciduous forest' formation, and the editors have been obliged to do likewise. Montane forests were delimited by a 3000 ft (914 m) contour taken from *Road Map Sri Lanka* (2nd edition) (1984), published at 1:500,000 by the Survey Department, Sri Lanka.

Protected areas were taken from *Directory of Protected Areas: Sri Lanka,* World Conservation Monitoring Centre, Cambridge (in press), which itself drew heavily upon the *Road Map Sri Lanka* cited above.

27 Thailand

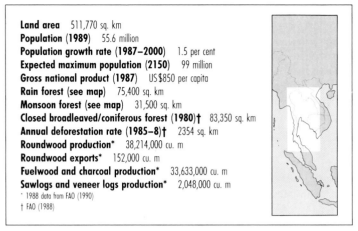

Land area	511,770 sq. km
Population (1989)	55.6 million
Population growth rate (1987–2000)	1.5 per cent
Expected maximum population (2150)	99 million
Gross national product (1987)	US$850 per capita
Rain forest (see map)	75,400 sq. km
Monsoon forest (see map)	31,500 sq. km
Closed broadleaved/coniferous forest (1980)†	83,350 sq. km
Annual deforestation rate (1985–8)†	2354 sq. km
Roundwood production*	38,214,000 cu. m
Roundwood exports*	152,000 cu. m
Fuelwood and charcoal production*	33,633,000 cu. m
Sawlogs and veneer logs production*	2,048,000 cu. m

* 1988 data from FAO (1990)
† FAO (1988)

Thailand, one of the wealthiest and most stable countries in Southeast Asia, was the first country in the world to ban all logging. The ban was a direct result of environmental disasters caused by logging and rubber plantation development. In November 1988, 359 people were killed and hundreds more made homeless by floods in the south of the country. Their houses were buried under an avalanche of logs and mud. The watersheds from where the floods had originated had been logged over and clear-felled for rubber plantations, and the steep slopes and friable soils were insufficiently stabilised. The Royal Decree to ban logging was issued in mid-January 1989 by the Prime Minister, Chatichai Choonhavan, and this was accepted by the House of Representatives in May. A second decree revoked all existing logging concessions.

That this should occur in Thailand is all the more surprising considering that, in the latter half of the 19th century, Thailand had been the first Southeast Asian country to begin managing its forests for a sustained yield. The decision to ban logging amounted to an official recognition that Thailand's timber must now be supplied by plantations and that natural forests will continue to exist only as isolated pockets in national parks, wildlife sanctuaries and some catchment protection areas. The Thai Government intends to allocate a total of 15 per cent of the country's land area for these.

The ban on logging has hit the timber industry hard and Thailand is now setting up trading links with its Indochinese neighbours to import logs and sawn wood.

INTRODUCTION

Thailand is a country of tremendous cultural and natural diversity. Its vegetation ranges from the upland pine forests on the Laotian and Burmese borders, to the lowland rain forests in the far south. The landscape has been moulded both by the original Malay population of the south, and successive waves of colonists who have moved into the country from the north over the past two thousand years.

The country divides naturally into six regions.

The Northern Highlands extend from the borders with Burma and Laos south to about 18° latitude. They are comprised mainly of ridges running north-east to south-east, reaching an elevation of between 1500 and 2000 m, and separated by wide valleys at between 300–500 m elevation. Originally the mountains above 1000 m were clad in evergreen montane rain forest, with mixed deciduous monsoon and dry dipterocarp savanna forests on their flanks. The valleys, however, have long been wholly cultivated. This region suffers from the steady southward push of hill tribes such as the Hmong and Yao, who cultivate upland rice and, at higher elevations, the opium poppy. Undisturbed forest is now restricted to a few scattered patches in remote areas.

The Korat Plateau covers the north-eastern bulge of Thailand. It forms a shallow saucer at 100–200 m, rimmed by the Petchabun Range in the west, and the Dangrek Range in the south. These reach 500–1400 m and meet in the highlands of the Khao Yai National Park. The plateau is now largely devoid of forest, but extensive areas still persist on the ranges. Dry monsoon forests on the lower slopes grade into evergreen rain forest on the hills and finally into pine woodlands on the ridge tops.

The Central Plain of the Chao Phraya River is now almost entirely under intensive rice cultivation and its original swamp and monsoon forest has entirely disappeared.

The South-East Uplands are an extension of the Cardamom Mountains from across the Cambodian border. Rainfall approaches 5000 mm in some areas. Small remnants of the once prevalent tropical rain forest still survive in protected areas.

The Tenasserim Hills extend south from about 18°N in the Northern Highlands, along the Burmese border to the Kra Isthmus, at about 10°N, rising steeply to about 1000 m. Since the Thai side of the Tenasserim lies in the rain shadow of higher hills on the Burmese side, it is relatively dry, but semi-evergreen rain forest persists at higher elevations along the border. The upper flanks are often precipitous, with bare rock. The slopes, once clothed in deciduous monsoon forest containing some teak and much *Shorea* spp., are now deforested, and covered with bamboo and grassland.

The Southern Peninsula extends to the Malaysian border from a line joining Chumphon to Ranong at 10°N. It is an area of heavy rainfall and was originally covered in rain forest. However, most forest in the lowlands has been lost to agriculture. Extensive tracts persist only on the hills, but during the last decade even these have come under assault, principally from rubber plantations, which have often been established with international aid.

The Forests

Lowland rain forest, shown on Map 27.1, comprises both evergreen and semi-evergreen formations. Evergreen rain forest occurs in the extreme south of peninsular Thailand, near the Malaysian frontier. This is the northern fringe of the great Malesian rain forests, which reach their northern limit at a line from Kangar to Pattani. This also occurs in the Chantaburi pocket, an isolated patch in the south-east, on the wet western slopes of the Cardamom Mountains.

Thailand's rain forests are rich in Dipterocarpaceae and other species associated with the forests of Malesia, but they also contain species with Chinese and Himalayan affinities. Many species from these major centres of plant diversity have their northern and southern limits respectively at the Isthmus of Kra. Semi-evergreen rain forest is Thailand's main forest formation. Its boundary with evergreen rain forest is fairly well known in the peninsula (see Whitmore, 1984), although not in the Chantaburi pocket where a complex mosaic results from the locally variable rainfall, soil and aspect.

Monsoon forest in Huai Kha Khaeng Wildlife Sanctuary, Thailand. WWF/ H. Jungius

Heath forest once occurred on some sandy soils in the south-east peninsula, but has now been degraded to open grass and shrublands.

Limestone with characteristic vegetation, occurs as karst towers in the south peninsula to about 9°N, and as islands off the south-west coast. There are also extensive limestone mountains in the north-west, and also to the west, north to *c.* 15°N latitude. Good examples of karst limestone vegetation are found in Ao Phangnga and Khao Sam Roi Yot National Parks and the Phu Luang Wildlife Sanctuary.

Freshwater swamp forest must once have existed along the major rivers, but it has now been entirely cleared to make way for irrigated rice cultivation. Swamp forests were the home of Schomburgk's deer (*Cervus schomburgki*), which became extinct in the 1930s. The only comparable formations to survive are the *Melaleuca* and *Alstonia* forests around Thale Noi in Phattalung Province, Bang Nara in Narathiwat Province in the southern part of the peninsula and the Pa Phiu Non-Hunting Area. This last is still extremely species-rich, and comprises 80 sq. km of peat swamp forest.

Beach forest with its typical Indo-Pacific flora, fringes sandy coasts of the mainland and offshore islands, but is now much altered by settlement and tourist development.

Montane forests in Thailand are difficult to define and map because distribution is dependent upon locally complex climatic and topographic variations. In Map 27.1 they have been delimited by a 914 m (3000 ft) contour. Montane forests contain strong temperate elements and are typically dominated by species of *Castanopsis*, *Lithocarpus* and *Quercus*. The higher forests at Khao Yai, at only 14°30′N, contain the Himalayan species *Betula alnoides*. Such temperate species become more frequent to the north, where Aceraceae, Lauraceae, Magnoliaceae and Rosaceae are abundant. Open stands of *Pinus kesiya* and *P. merkusii* occur as a fire climax formation on sandy soils on the hills of the north. A particularly good example occurs in the Phu Kradeung National Park and is visited by many thousands of people each year.

Deciduous monsoon formations were once much more extensive than rain forests, but have been widely deforested. The northern monsoon forests include commercially important teak, found mainly on well-drained soils derived from igneous rocks, and thriving under a regime of occasional ground fires which clear the undergrowth.

Extensive dry deciduous woodlands with some dipterocarp content also occur in the north and east but this open canopied formation has not been included in Map 27.1.

Forest Resources and Management

Table 27.1 is a summary of FAO data for forest cover of Thailand. FAO Rome estimated total natural forest cover at 156,750 sq. km in 1980 and predicted 137,800 sq. km by 1985 (FAO/UNEP, 1981; FAO, 1988). FAO Bangkok made a re-evaluation in 1987 and found slightly higher results for 1985 of 149,050 sq. km, but predicted 135,000 sq. km for 1990 (FAO, 1987). All these figures include open-canopied deciduous dipterocarp forests in northern Thailand, and it is of interest to note that this formation makes up a gradually larger proportion of the total (e.g. FAO (1987) shows 45 per cent open canopy forest in 1980 but 56 per cent in 1990).

Table 27.2, based on Map 27.1, is derived mainly from 1985 data (see Map Legend for details). It shows almost 107,000 sq. km of tropical moist forest in rain and monsoon forest formations. Open canopy dry dipterocarp forests have been excluded, but in the original maps about 43,000 sq. km of this formation was shown. The total for all forests is thus about 150,000 sq. km, in close agreement with the FAO assessment for 1985 (FAO, 1987). However it should be noted that there is some disparity between the totals for the open and closed canopy formations, with Map 27.1 showing more of the closed canopy rain and monsoon forests than FAO (1987) data would suggest.

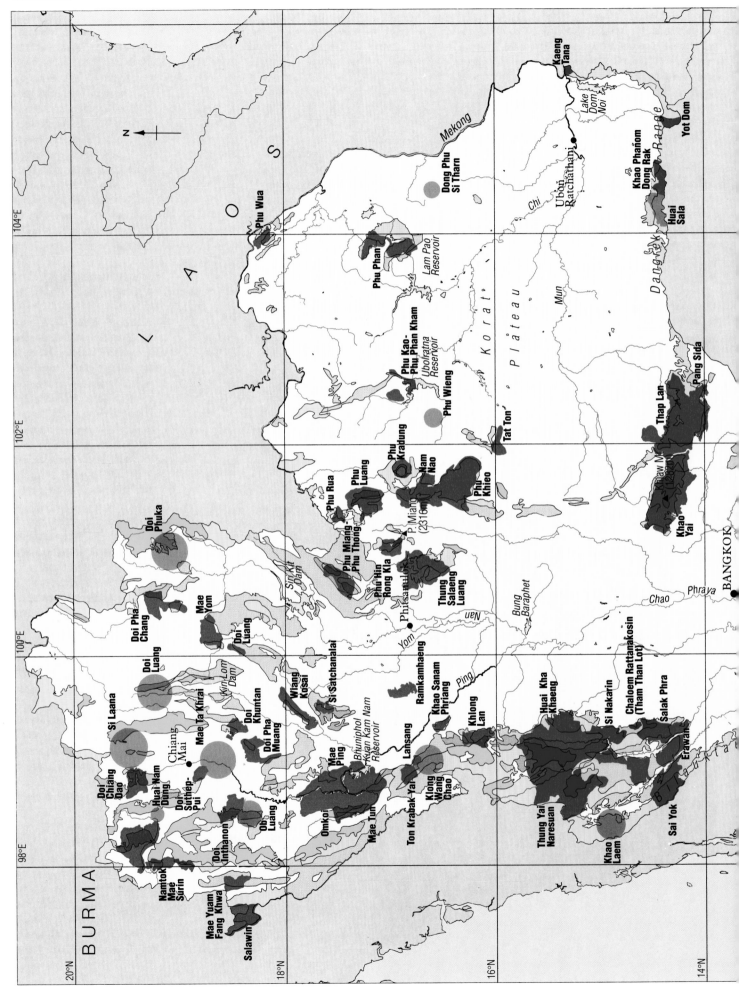

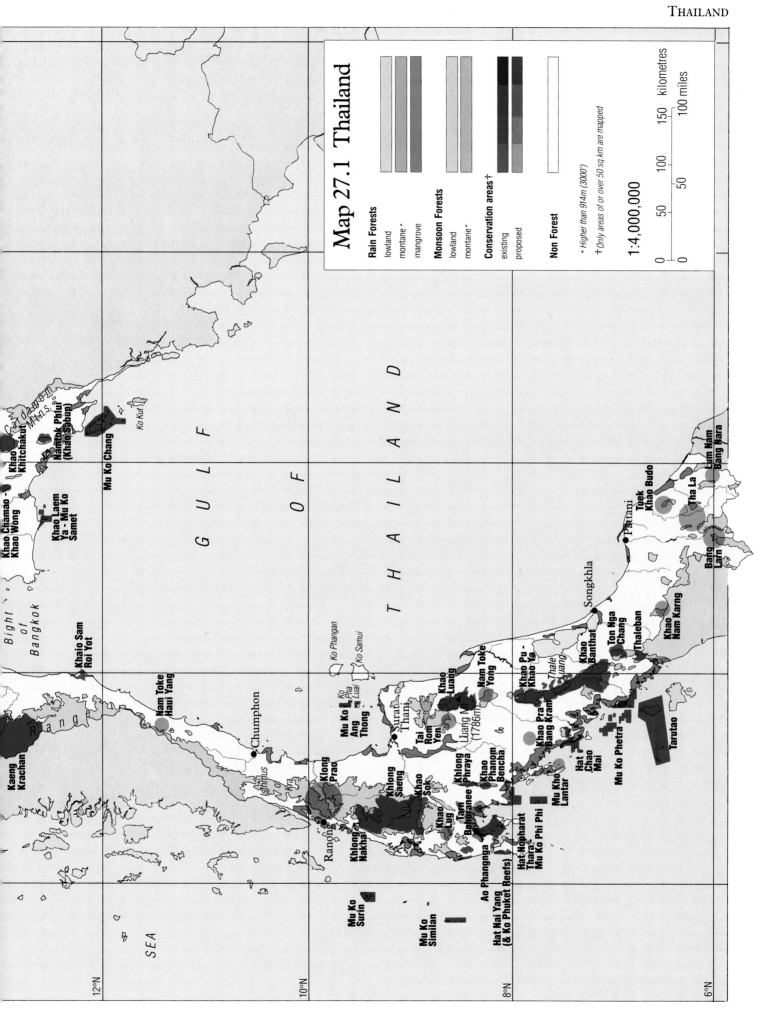

Map 27.1 Thailand

Rain Forests
lowland
montane *
mangrove

Monsoon Forests
lowland
montane *

Conservation areas †
existing
proposed

Non Forest

* *Higher than 914m (3000')*
† *Only areas of or over 50 sq.km are mapped*

1:4,000,000

0   50   100   150   kilometres
0   50   100 miles

Khao Khitchakut
Khao Chamao - Khao Wong
Namtok Phlui (Khao Sabup)
Mu Ko Chang
Ko Kut

Khao Laem Ya - Mu Ko Samet

Caldamon Mtns.

Bight of Bangkok

Khaio Sam Roi Yot

Kaeng Krachan

Range

Chumphon

Nam Toke Haui Yang

Ranong

Khlong Prao
Khlong Nakhai

Klong Saeng
Khao Sok
Tai Rom Yen
Khao Lug
Tarn Bojoranee

Khao Luang
Luang M (1786m)

Mu Ko Ang Thong
Ko Phia Luai

Surat Thani

Ko Phangan
Ko Samui

Nam Toke Yong
Khlong Phraya
Khao Phanom Bencha

Mu Ko Surin

Mu Ko Similian

Hat Nai Yang (& Ko Phuket Reefs)
Ao Phangnga
Hat Nopharat Thara Mu Ko Phi Phi

Mu Kho Lantar

Hat Chao Mai
Mu Ko Phetra

Khao Pra - Bang Kram
Mu Kho Lantar

Tarutao

Khao Pu - Khao Ya
Thale Luang

Khao Nam Karng
Khao Banthat
Thaleban
Ton Nga Chang

Songkhla

Pattani
Khao Budo
Tuek
Tha La
Cum Nam
Bang Nara
Bang Lam

THAILAND

GULF
OF
THAILAND

SEA

Isthmus of Kra

12°N
10°N
8°N
6°N

THAILAND

Table 27.1 Estimates of natural forest resources of Thailand (sq. km)

	FAO/UNEP 1981 report		FAO 1987 report			
	1980	*1985*	*1980*	*1983*	*1985*	*1990*
Broadleaved closed canopy	81,350	69,150	86,160	78,600	61,490	50,200
Bamboo	9,000	8,650	8,900	8,600	8,500	8,000
Coniferous	2,000	1,950	2,000	2,160	1,720	1,500
Sub totals	92,350	79,750	97,060	89,360	71,710	59,700
Broadleaved open canopy	64,400	58,050	79,540	78,630	77,340	75,300
Total, all natural forests	156,750	137,800	176,600	167,990	149,050	135,000

(*Sources:* FAO/UNEP, 1981; FAO, 1987; FAO, 1988)

Table 27.2 Estimates of forest extent

	Area (sq. km)	% of land area
Rain forests		
Lowland	54,900	10.7
Montane	14,800	2.9
Mangrove	5,700	1.1
Sub totals	75,400	14.7
Monsoon forests		
Lowland	29,500	5.8
Montane	2,000	0.4
Sub totals	31,500	6.2
Totals	106,900	20.9

(Based on analysis of Map 27.1. See Map Legend for details of sources)

Official statistics state that 28.8 per cent of the country is forest land (a total of 147,400 sq. km that accords quite closely with the data in Table 27.1). However, this includes both closed and open canopy formations and some areas legally gazetted as forest reserve, national park or wildlife sanctuary are in fact severely degraded, if not deforested. It is now officially recognised that total open and closed canopy forest cover may have fallen to 127,940 sq. km (25 per cent of national territory) and that much of this remaining forest may have been subject to considerable disturbance.

Foreign trading companies began the commercial exploitation of the northern teak forests in the middle of the 19th century. Several laws were passed between 1874 and 1896 to control this trade. In 1895 H. Slade, a British forestry expert, was hired from the Indian Forest Service by King Chulalongkorn to advise on the management of the teak forests. In 1896, the Royal Forest Department was established, with Slade as its first director general. Forest management techniques, developed under Brandis in the latter part of the 19th century in India, were then introduced into Thailand, forming the basis of its forestry programmes.

Ownership and control of all forests was transferred from the traditional local rulers to the government in 1895. Many laws were subsequently passed to control the exploitation of teak. However, the first comprehensive legal basis for forest conservation and management began with the Forest Care Act of 1913. Present forest programmes have evolved from the Protection and Reservation of Forests Act of 1938. This was revised in 1953 and 1954, and eventually repealed and replaced by the National Forest Reserve Act of 1964.

The northern teak forests continued to be the mainstay of commercial forestry until after the Second World War, when international markets in the light hardwoods from the dipterocarp rain forests of the peninsula began to develop. Exploitation was facilitated by the introduction of heavy logging tractors and later, in the 1960s, by the advent of portable chain saws. At the same time, the country's rapid economic growth began to create a strong domestic timber demand.

There are still about 30,000 sq. km of teak forest in northern Thailand, but much of it has been logged several times. Residual forests have been damaged by shifting cultivation and illegal logging, and their value greatly reduced in consequence (IIED, 1988).

By 1967, the effects of increased demand and declining resources were such that, for the first time, Thailand became a net timber importer, importing 38,410 cu. m. Between 1973 and 1984, imports grew from US$3.6 million (using an approximate conversion rate of US$1 = 25 baht) to US$57 million. During the same period, exports fell from US$52 million to US$4.1 million. In 1983 Thailand imported 614,000 cu. m of timber (Royal Forest Department, 1985).

During this period when Thailand went from being a net timber exporter to a net importer, major changes occurred in its forest industries. Under the original selection system, teak trees in natural forests were felled manually and then dragged by elephants to a river and floated to railways or ports (Marshall, 1959). Increased mechanisation and acute pressure of land led to the adoption of more intensive forestry practices; permanent roads were built into the forest and a broader spectrum of trees felled. Plantations were established on clear-felled lands to offset heavy investments in logging equipment and infrastructure. Most of these are teak plantations owned by the parastatal Forest Industry Organisation. In addition the Thai Plywood Company, privatised in 1985, operates 51 sq. km of teak, *Acacia*, *Eucalyptus* and *Leucaena* plantations (Thailand Development Research Institute, 1987).

Table 27.3 shows the extent of reforestation activity undertaken by the government. By 1985, 5400 sq. km had been reforested. The sixth national development plan (1987–91) proposes increasing the annual reforestation rate to 480 sq. km.

Parallel to this, a healthy development of private sector activity in forestry has taken place over the past 20 years. Royal Forest Department statistics (Royal Forest Department, 1985) show that planta-

Table 27.3 Reforestation by government agencies and concessionaires 1965–85 (sq. km)

	Up to 1980	1981	1983	1985	Total (including intervening years)
Forest villages	1,600	150	90	106	2,130
Watershed protection	630	140	75	101	1,120
Degraded forests	600	140	48	77	970
Concessions	480	110	150	110	1,181

(Adapted from Arbhabhirama *et al.*, 1985)

Working elephants in Thailand – out of a job since the logging ban? J. A. McNeely

tion rates grew from two ha in 1966 to 50 sq. km in 1985 when a total of 240 sq. km of forest plantations existed.

The 1989 logging ban was an inevitable consequence of the rampant, illegal exploitation and clearance of nearly all forests lying outside, and even inside, protected areas. Much of the logging was already at the limits of legality, and a great deal of illicit timber extraction was taking place in areas designated for watershed protection or nature conservation. The logging ban has impeded commercial logging inside protected areas and helped implementation of the wildlife protection and park acts. Imposition of the ban has also cleared the way for the gazettement of important new parks and reserves in some critical forest sites, hitherto subject to concession agreements (Round, 1989). These include important lowland rain forest sites in both the peninsula and the south-east of the country.

Government policy still allocates 25 per cent of land area for production forest. If the target is to be reached, it is probable that virtually all of this production forest will have to consist of plantations. At the current planting rate, this will take over a century to attain.

Deforestation

Official Thai government statistics state that 28.8 per cent of the country is forest land (including open canopy dipterocarp formations), a reduction from 53 per cent in 1961. An annual rate of encroachment on forest land of 5190 sq. km has been officially acknowledged for 1961–85. This annual deforestation rate is equivalent to the total area reforested during the last 25 years. A Royal Forest Department report published in 1989 gives an annual deforestation rate figure for 1985–8 of 2354 sq. km per year or 0.46 per cent of land area. Other observers fear continuing high rates of deforestation of between 5000 and 7000 sq. km per year, but these reports remain unsubstantiated.

All land which is not owned privately or by state corporations is legally classed as crown forest estate. However, a considerable proportion of this land has not had any forest cover for many years. At the time of the logging ban there were 163,256 sq. km of non-teak forest concessions, and at the same time it is officially acknowledged that only approximately 110,000 sq. km of potentially productive forest land remained (IIED, 1988).

The National Forest Policy (Royal Forest Department, 1985), as stated in the Fifth National Economic and Social Development Plan (1982–6), has a target of maintaining 40 per cent forest cover, comprising 15 per cent natural protection forest and 25 per cent production forest. But it makes no clear commitment to sustained yield management of natural forests, and present programmes favour the establishment of plantations on the production forest estate. It seems likely that, in the long term, the only natural forests will be those falling in the protection forest category. Over the past several years, 400 sq. km of forest plantations have been established each year, roughly half by the government and the rest by the private sector (Table 27.3). To meet the 25 per cent production forest target, it would be necessary to quadruple this to 1600 sq. km (1,000,000 rai) per year for the next 20 years (Arbhabhirama *et al.*, 1987).

Mangroves

Mangrove forests occur on both coasts (Arbhabhirama *et al.*, 1987; Aksornkoae, 1987; 1988; Kongsangchai, 1987; Piyakarncharna, 1987). They have been heavily exploited for fuelwood and timber, and as elsewhere converted to other land uses. Although Map 27.1 shows 5700 sq. km of mangrove, less than 2000 sq. km remains undegraded, and about 27 sq. km are lost annually. The Centre for Conservation Biology at Mahidol University estimates that only 6 per cent of mangroves are in protected areas, and that many of these are degraded scrub. Few areas of tall species-rich mangrove forests are protected; the best examples are found in Tarutao National Park.

Biodiversity

Thailand has a very diverse fauna and flora, with elements from different biogeographical regions, but since these are shared with neighbouring countries, endemism is relatively low. The birds and mammals of the Northern Highlands show affinities with those of western China, and many are not found elsewhere in Thailand. Conversely, the Southern Peninsula includes a number of lowland mammal and bird species that have extended northwards from the Sunda Shelf countries.

The size of Thailand's flora is not known precisely. Between 10,000 and 15,000 species are thought to occur, including more than 500 tree species and about 1000 orchids. The 858 recorded orchids are particularly threatened because many have restricted ranges and are subject to illegal collecting by horticulturists (FAO, 1981).

Over 900 bird species are found in Thailand (Lekagul, 1972), including 578 resident forest species of which 106 are thought to be endangered, threatened or vulnerable. Six species are now extinct (Round, 1988). Two hundred and sixty-five species of mammals (Lekagul and McNeely, 1977) and 100 amphibians (Brockelman, 1987) have been recorded.

Some key features of the fauna may be described region by region:

Northern Highlands Most of the large mammals originally found in this region have been eliminated by hunting, including elephant, banteng, gaur and tiger.

The Korat Plateau Thailand's most extensive areas of dry dipterocarp forest are found on the rim of this plateau. Larger mammals have disappeared from the plateau itself, but have survived in parts of the mountainous rim, making it one of Thailand's richest faunal areas.

Central Plain of the Chao Phraya River This formerly provided habitat for plain and swamp animals, such as Schomburgk's deer and hog deer *Cervus porcinus*, as well as for aquatic species such as the smooth and Asiatic clawless otters *Anonyx cinerea* and the Siamese crocodile, and for a variety of waterbirds. Much of the Chao Phraya

SHIFTING CULTIVATION

Shifting agriculture has been practised in Thailand for at least 3–4,000 years, and perhaps even longer (Spencer, 1967). Throughout nearly all of this period, it was the most rational and sustainable agricultural use possible in the uplands. The system began to deteriorate when large numbers of people from the hill tribes from Yunnan and Burma began to move into Thailand in the late 19th century. They continue to do so.

The term 'shifting cultivation' is now used to cover a multitude of activities. The original form of agriculture, which has evolved over the millennia, as an efficient and sustainable form of production on the nutrient-poor soils of the uplands, is now only carried out by a diminishing minority of Karen and Lua people in remote areas. These, and the other 500,000 ethnic hill tribe people, now compete both with displaced lowland Thais and private and state-owned corporations for land. The uplands are increasingly used to produce cash crops. The long rotation swiddens – where deep-rooted trees are preserved to enhance the nutrient status of the soils during the fallows – are becoming rare.

Shifting cultivation has become a major political and social issue in Thailand. This stems from the ethnic barriers which still persist between the hill tribes and the lowland Thai population. It is exacerbated by the fact that a minority of hill tribes are engaged in the cultivation of the opium poppy (*Papaver somniferum*). The poppy thrives above 1000 m and has traditionally been grown by the Hmong people. Unlike other upland peoples, the Hmong traditionally farm the same area until the soils are totally exhausted and then move on, leaving huge areas of barren grasslands behind them. Because of the large amounts of money to be made from opium and government efforts to prevent cultivation of the drug, a crisis has arisen in the remote border areas of Thailand, Burma and Laos (known as the Golden Triangle).

Moreover, many of the hill tribes are being gradually absorbed into the cash economy. This process is being encouraged by various government schemes which seek not only to introduce cash crops, establish small-scale industries, and support the rapidly growing tourism industry, but which also aim to establish the infrastructure necessary for gaining access to markets. Displaced lowland shifting cultivators are being settled into 'Forest Villages' under the Forest Industries Corporation. In these villages peoples are given title to plots of agricultural land. They also intercrop teak seedlings with rice and maize, a process that controls weed growth during the initial three to four years the teak seedlings need to become established. This agroforestry system is known as *taungya*, the Burmese name for forest fallow. The name came to be applied to the techniques used by the Burmese Forest Service in the 19th century for the restoration of teak forests on abandoned *taungyas*. (The term and the techniques are now employed throughout the tropics for the establishment of forest plantations on degraded land. See chapter 8.)

---

floodplain was still forested at the end of the 19th century and there are accounts of major elephant round-ups just north of Bangkok in the early years of the present century. Most of the wildlife has now disappeared, with only grassland, scrub or commensal species remaining.

The Tenasserim Hills Most of the larger mammals still survive, but they are coming under heavy development pressure, as dams and highways are constructed, particularly in Kanchanaburi Province.

The Southern Peninsula Rain forest species are most abundant and diverse in the Southern Peninsula. They include Malesian species, here at their northern limit, intermingled with Himalayan and Chinese species which are at their southernmost extent. However, most forest in the lowlands has been lost to agriculture and extensive tracts only persist on the hills. Even the latter have been under assault in the last decade, mainly for rubber plantations, often established with international aid. Species such as Gurney's pitta which are restricted to lowland forests are now close to extinction.

The Khao Luang National Park in Makhon Si Thammarat province protects good representative samples of the flora of the southern forests, including typical Malesian species of Dipterocarpaceae together with several species of northern origins.

South-east uplands The south-eastern rain forests have also been much reduced in extent. These are now restricted to a few hill areas where remaining forests are protected in national parks and wildlife reserves. The Khao Soi Dao Sanctuary, in Chantaburi Province, which includes some of the best forest areas, contains at least three endemics and a number of Yunnanese rain forest species.

The fauna of the south-east uplands is similar to that of the neighbouring highlands of south-west Cambodia. In addition some species occur which are otherwise restricted to the southern peninsula of Thailand, such as flying lemur (*Cynocephalus variegatus*), lesser long-tongued fruit bat (*Macroglossus minimus*), moustached hawk cuckoo (*Cuculus vagans*), buffy fish-owl (*Ketupa ketupu*), silver oriole (*Oriolus mellianus*), mountain fulvetta (*Alcippe peracensis*) and greater mouse deer (*Tragulus napu*).

Conservation Areas
The areas managed for conservation in Thailand are listed in Table 27.4.

In the north, a variety of upland rain forest types are well represented in several protected areas in the hills. Doi Inthanon, Thailand's highest mountain is protected as a national park. Its forests contain several endemic plants and animals. Doi Chiang Dao Wildlife Sanctuary contains a good example of natural montane scrub habitat and several endemic plants.

Several parks and sanctuaries, of which the Khao Luang National Park in Nakhon Si Thammarat province is a good example, protect samples of the flora of the southern forests, including typical Malesian species of Dipterocarpaceae, together with several species of northern origins.

To the south-east, the rain forests have also been much reduced in extent. They are now restricted to a few isolated mountains where remaining forests are protected in national parks and wildlife reserves. The Khao Soi Dao Sanctuary in Chantaburi Province, which includes some of the best forest areas, contains at least three endemic plants and a number of Yunnanese rain forest species.

In the west, Huai Kha Khaeng and the contiguous Thung Yai Naresuan Wildlife Sanctuaries in the Tenasserim hills together cover 5775 sq. km. Much of this is monsoon forest but it includes important areas of riparian rain forest.

The legal basis for nature conservation is provided by the Wildlife Protection and Reservation Act of 1960 and the National Parks Act of 1961. Khao Yai, established in 1962, was the first National Park. As of September 1989 a total of 59 parks had been gazetted, covering

Table 27.4 Conservation areas of Thailand

Existing and proposed areas, 50 sq. km and over and for which the editors have location data, are listed. The remaining areas are combined in a total under Other Areas. Forest reserves are not included. For data on ASEAN sites and Biosphere reserves see chapter 9.

	Existing area (sq. km)	Proposed area (sq. km)
National Parks		
Ao Phangnga★	400	
Bang Larn★		461
Chaloem Rattanakosin (Thame Than Lot)★	59	
Doi Inthanon★	482	
Doi Khuntan★	255	
Doi Luang★		1,170
Doi Phuka★		1,269
Doi Suthep-Pui	261	
Erawan★	550	
Hat Chao Mai★	231	
Hat Nai Yang (+ Ko Phuket reefs)	90	
Hat Nopharat Thara – Mu Ko Phi Phi★	390	
Huai Nam Dung★		179
Kaeng Krachan★	2,910	
Kaeng Tana★	80	
Khao Chamao-Khao Wong★	84	
Khao Khitchakut★	59	
Khao Laem★		814
Khao Laem Ya – Mu Ko Samet	131	
Khao Luang★	570	
Khao Lug★		150
Khao Nam Karng★		220
Khao Phanom Bencha★	50	
Khao Pu – Khao Ya★	694	
Khai Sam Roi Yot	98	
Khao Sok★	646	
Khao Yai★	2,169	
Khlong Lan★	300	
Klong Prao★		1,267
Klong Wang Chao★		779
Lansang★	104	
Mae Ping★	1,003	
Mae Ta Khrai		1,229
Mae Yom★	455	
Mu Kho Lantar★		125
Mu Ko Ang Thong★	102	
Mu Ko Chang★	650	
Mu Ko Phetra★	494	
Mu Ko Similan	128	
Mu Ko Surin	135	
Nam Nao★	966	
Nam Toke Haui Yang★		198
Nam Toke Yong★		202
Namtok Mae Surin★	397	
Namtok Phlui (Khao Sabup)★	135	
Ob Luang★		630
Pang Sida★	844	
Phu Hin Rong Kla★	307	
Phu Kao – Phu Phan Kham	322	
Phu Kradung★	348	
Phu Phan★	665	
Phu Rua★	121	
Phu Wieng★		324
Ramkamhaeng	341	
Sai Yok★	500	
Si Laana★		1,406
Si Nakarin★	1,532	
Si Satchanalai★	213	
Tai Rom Yen★		213
Tarn Bohoranee★		121
Tarutao★	1,490	
Tat Ton★	217	
Thaleban★	102	
Thap Lan★	2,240	
Thung Salaeng Luang★	1,262	
Ton Krabak Yai★	149	
Tuek Khao Budo★		293
Wiang Kosai★	410	
Wildlife Sanctuaries		
Doi Chiang Dao★	521	
Doi Luang★	97	
Doi Pha Chang★	577	
Doi Pha Muang★	583	
Dong Phu Si Tharn		250
Huai Kha Khaeng★	2,575	
Huai Sala★		444
Khao Ang Ru Nai★[1]	108	
Khao Banthat★	1,267	
Khao Harng Rue Nai★		1,019
Khao Khieo-Khao Chomphu	145	
Khao Phanom Dong Rak★	316	
Khao Pra Bang Kram		163
Khao Sanam Phriang★	100	
Khao Soi Dao★	745	
Khlong Nakha★	480	
Khlong Phraya★	95	
Khlong Saeng★	1,156	
Lum Nam Bang Nara★		201
Mae Tun★	1,173	
Mae Yuam Fang Khwa★	292	
Maenam Phachi★	489	
Omkoi★	1,224	
Phu Khieo★	1,560	
Phu Luang★	848	
Phu Miang-Phu Thong★	545	
Phu Wua★	187	
Salak Phra★	859	
Salawin★	875	
Tha La★		694
Thung Yai Naresuan★	3,200	
Ton Nga Chang★	182	
Yot Dom★	203	
Sub totals	46,615	13,821
Other Areas†	4,763	78
Totals	51,378	13,899

(*Sources:* IUCN 1990; WCMC data *in litt.*; Royal Forest Department, Thailand)
★ Area with moist forest within its boundary.
[1] extension by several sq. km is planned.
† Not including Non-hunting Areas.

The Klong-e-tow in Khao-Yai National Park – Thailand's first national park, established in 1962. J. R. Paine

31,505 sq. km or approximately 6 per cent of the country. Gazettement procedures are in hand for a further 21 areas covering an additional 11,121 sq. km or 2.16 per cent of the country. Of this, about 2000 sq. km comprise coastal sea areas. The National Park Act states that the objectives of these areas are educational and recreational, and the parks now receive over 4 million visitors a year – Erawan Park in Kanchanaburi Province alone receives over half a million visitors annually. However, it is widely recognised that the primary function of the national parks is the conservation of the natural environment.

Some 28 wildlife sanctuaries cover a further 21,594 sq. km or 4.2 per cent of the national territory. Seven further areas covering 2845 sq. km (0.55 per cent of national territory) are being gazetted. There is a good deal of overlap in the functions of the two categories of protected areas. Although wildlife sanctuaries have a more strictly 'conservation' function, many of them are in reality subject to considerable recreational use. Theoretically, this use is confined to 'Nature Education Centres' within the sanctuaries, and the bulk of the area within wildlife sanctuaries is supposedly protected from any human interference.

Forty-eight non-hunting areas covering 4023.5 sq. km (0.78 per cent of the country) have been gazetted. These are partial reserves, mostly in wetland areas. Totally protected areas therefore cover approximately 11 per cent of the land area. (A further 0.4 per cent is coastal/marine.) Additional areas, now being gazetted, will bring this total to approximately 13 per cent, which is well on the way to the ultimate goal of 15 per cent.

The protected area system is far from perfect. While a disproportionately large area of upland forest is protected, lowland evergreen forests are scarcely represented. The Conservation Data Centre at Mahidol University has estimated that only 4.7 per cent, at most, of the lowland rain forest of southern Thailand still remained at the end of 1985, and virtually none of this was protected. It is already too late to incorporate any significant examples of this habitat into the protected areas network, because those areas which do survive are small isolated patches. Moreover, much of the forest in Thailand's parks and sanctuaries has been subject to swidden agriculture or was logged before the areas were gazetted, and substantial numbers of people live in some protected areas in the north. Over a quarter of all the threatened birds in Thailand, as well as many mammals, occur in wetlands, but the vast majority of wetlands have been drained or seriously disturbed and few are included in the protected areas system. Wetland birds do, however, receive protection in several 'non-hunting areas'. Coastal ecosystems are reasonably well covered in theory, but in reality, fishing with explosives and mangrove exploitation has inflicted considerable damage on many potentially important coastal national parks and sanctuaries.

Initiatives for Conservation

The Royal Forest Department is now embarking upon the preparation of a national Forestry Master Plan. This will receive support from the Asian Development Bank and give special attention to ecosystem conservation issues.

In addition the Wildlife Conservation and National Parks Divisions of the Royal Forest Department are continuing to push vigorously for the expansion of the protected area network in line with the recommendations of a review by FAO (1981) and Kasetsart University (1987). The 1989 logging ban has cleared the way for the establishment of several protected areas which had previously been subject to concession agreements. Gazettement procedures are now in hand for 21 new national parks, six wildlife sanctuaries, and many more potential parks and reserves are under consideration. Among the most important for rain forest conservation is the Khao Pra Bang Khram in the lowlands of the peninsula. This is the only known locality for the endemic and endangered Gurney's pitta, and the site is to become a wildlife sanctuary. For the south-east there are plans to extend the Khao Ang Ru Nai Wildlife Sanctuary from its present 108 sq. km to include several hundred additional square kilometres of lowland semi-evergreen rain forest. This area contains elephant, gaur, pileated gibbons *Hylobates pileatus*, Siamese fireback pheasants *Lophura diardi* and other species which are threatened in Thailand.

The Forestry Department at Kasetsart University is active in research and planning for forest conservation and the main source of trained manpower for the Royal Forestry Department. Kasetsart also supports a strong social forestry programme which provides training for foresters and agriculturalists from the entire Asian region.

A Centre for Conservation Biology has been established at Mahidol University, with support from the World Wide Fund for Nature and Wildlife Conservation International (the conservation arm of New York Zoo). The centre maintains a computerised monitoring programme for Thailand's fauna and has been instrumental in drawing attention to many new sites which should be given protected status.

The National Environment Board is responsible for the environmental components of the National Economic and Social Development plans. It collaborated with IUCN in producing a draft national conservation strategy in the early 1980s.

A number of local non-governmental organisations are actively campaigning for forest conservation. A WWF affiliate organisation, Wildlife Fund Thailand, is active in public information and lobbying work and supports projects in some important protected areas.

References

Aksornkoae, S. (1987) Thailand. In: *Mangroves of Asia and the Pacific*, pp. 231–62. Umali *et al.*, (eds) (*op. cit.*).

Aksornkoae, S. (1988) Mangrove habitat degradation and removal in Phangnga and Ban Don Bays, Thailand. *Tropical Coastal Area Management*, **3**: 16.

Arbhabhirama, A., Phantumvant, D., Elkington, J. and Ingkasuwan, P. (1987) *Thailand Natural Resources Profile*. Thailand Development Research Institute, Bangkok.

Brockelman, W. Y. (1987) Nature Conservation. In: *Thailand's Natural Resources Profile* pp. 91–119. Arbhabhirama *et al.* (eds) (*op. cit*).

FAO (1981) *National Parks and Wildlife Management, Thailand. A Review of the Nature Conservation Programmes and Policies of the Royal Thai Forest Department*. FAO/UNEP, Bangkok.

FAO (1987) *Special Study on Forest Management, Afforestation and Utilization of Forest Resources in the Developing Regions. Asia–Pacific Region*. Assessment of Forest Resources in Six Countries. FAO Field Document 17. Bangkok, Thailand. 104 pp.

FAO (1988) *An Interim Report on the State of Forest Resources in the Developing Countries*. FAO, Rome, Italy. 18 pp + 5 tables.

FAO (1990) *FAO Yearbook of Forest Resources 1977–88*. FAO Forestry Series No. 23, FAO Statistics Series No. 90. FAO, Rome.

FAO/UNEP (1981) *Tropical Forest Resources Assessment* Vol 3 of 3 vols. FAO, Rome. 475 pp.

IIED (1988) *Pre-project Report: Natural Forest Management for Sustainable Timber Production*. IIED/ITTO London, UK.

IUCN (1990) *1989 United Nations List of National Parks and Protected Areas*. IUCN, Gland, Switzerland, and Cambridge, UK.

Kongsangchai, Jitt (1987) The conflicting interests of mangrove resources use in Thailand. In: *UNDP/UNESCO Regional Project RAS/79/002*, pp. 15–32. Report of Workshop for Mangrove Zone Managers, Phuket, Thailand, September 1986.

Lekagul, B. (1972) *Assessment of National Parks, Wildlife Sanctuaries and other Preserves Development in Thailand*. Faculty of Forestry, Kaselsart University; Royal Forest Department and Office of the National Environment Board, assisted by USAID, 30 pp. + maps.

Lekagul, B. and McNeely, J. A. (1977) *The Mammals of Thailand*. Association for the Conservation of Nature, Bangkok, Thailand.

Marshall, H. N. (1959) *Elephant Kingdom*. Robert Hale Ltd, London, UK.

Piyakarncharna, Twesukdi (1987) Multiple-use practices for establishing eco-development policies in Thailand. In: *UNDP/UNESCO Regional Project RAS/79/002*, pp. 47–9. Report of Workshop for Mangrove Zone Managers, Phuket, Thailand, September 1986.

Round, P. D. (1988) *Resident Forest Birds in Thailand: Their Status and Conservation*. ICBP Monograph No. 2. ICBP, Cambridge, UK.

Round, P. D. (1989) *The Implications of the Logging Ban for the Conservation of Thai Wildlife*. WWF Reports, October/November, Gland, Switzerland.

Royal Forest Department (1985) *National Forestry Policy*. Royal Forest Department Bangkok (written in Thai).

Spencer, J. E. (1967) *Shifting Cultivation in Southeast Asia*. University of California, Berkeley, California.

Thailand Development Research Institute (1987) *Thailand, Natural Resources Profile*. National Environment Board/Department of Technical and Economic Cooperation/United States Agency for International Development.

Umali, R., Zamora, P. M., Gotera, R. R., Jara, R. S. and Camacho, A. S. (eds) (1987) *Mangroves of Asia and the Pacific*. Ministry of Natural Resources, Manila, Philippines.

Authorship

Jeff Sayer in IUCN, with contributions from Jeff McNeely in IUCN, Phairote Suvannakorn, Prof. B. Klankamsorn, Suvat Singhapant, Sompon Tan Han, and Somthep from the Royal Thai Forest Department and Philip Round at the Centre for Conservation Biology Mahidol University, Bangkok.

Map 27.1 Forest cover in Thailand

Forest cover data for Thailand have been extracted from the 1:1 million *Forest Types Map* (1985) published by the Remote Sensing and Mapping Sub-Division, Forest Management Division, Royal Forest Department, Bangkok. This map was based on the interpretation of aerial photographs taken during 1972–7, and updated from Landsat imagery taken in 1985. The Royal Forest Department continues to assess forest cover from more recent imagery. A forest/non-forest map of Thailand in four sheets at 1:500,000 believed to date from 1988 imagery, while considered to be too detailed for the present purpose, was revised and taken into consideration in the final draft.

Data categories on the *Forest Types Map* have been harmonised with the mapped categories used in this atlas as follows (Thai forest types are in brackets): rain forest (tropical evergreen forest); monsoon forest (mixed deciduous forest and pine forest); mangroves (mangrove forest). The Thai categories of dry deciduous forest (an open woodland formation), scrub forest and rubber plantation have not been mapped. Montane forests were delimited using the 914 m (3000 ft) contour from 1:2 million Jet Navigation Charts JNC 37 and JNC 54.

Locations of protected areas were kindly provided by the Royal Forest Department. They are in the form of hand-coloured polygons distinguishing national parks and wildlife sanctuaries overlaid on to 1:500,000 Tactical Pilotage Charts (TPC) J–10C, K–98, K–9C, K–10A, L–10A and J–11D. Reserved forests are also shown, but have not been used in this exercise. Details of proposed national parks and wildlife sanctuaries were also provided by the Royal Forest Department, in the form of generalised locations overlaid on to the 1:2 million *Thailand Road Map* (1987) published by the Royal Thai Survey Department. These have been presented in the form of circles of an appropriate size.

28 Vietnam

Land area	325,360 sq. km
Population (1989)	66.8 million
Population growth rate (1987–2000)	2.4 per cent
Expected maximum population (2125)	168 million
Rain forest (see map)	37,170 sq. km
Monsoon forest (see map)	19,510 sq. km
Closed broadleaved/coniferous forest (1980)†	61,650 sq. km
Annual deforestation rate (1986–90)†	3110 sq. km
Roundwood production*	26,620,000 cu. m
Fuelwood and charcoal production*	23,248,000 cu. m
Sawlog and veneer log production*	1,626,000 cu. m

* 1988 data from FAO (1990)
† FAO (1987)

Originally almost entirely forested, Vietnam has now lost over 80 per cent of its original forest cover, a large proportion of it during the second half of this century. Losses caused by warfare, coupled with deforestation to make way for economic reconstruction since 1975, have left the nation with approximately 10–12 per cent cover of closed tropical forests, and less than one per cent in a pristine state. Because the country is in a weak economic position and still isolated from international economic and technical aid, it is unable to resolve its environmental problems. In addition, a high population density and birth rate are impeding efforts to regreen the countryside.

However, against these difficulties there are some positive signs for forest conservation in Vietnam. The Government is clearly well aware of the problems and is determinedly taking action. It has already succeeded in eliminating shifting cultivation in some areas through the use of agroforestry systems. Several ministries cooperate efficiently in promoting reforestation of areas devastated in the wars. Some of their reforestation programmes are among the best in the tropics. Mangroves, which were almost destroyed in the war, have been replanted and are now productive and well-managed.

Vietnam began to establish a system of protected areas in 1962, and recent proposals, once established, will include a total of 87 reserves. Maintenance of forest corridors between reserves remains an urgent priority if the biodiversity of tropical forest species is to be maintained.

A national Tropical Forestry Action Plan is currently being developed and the government is actively seeking external support for the management and conservation of forest resources. At the time of writing, many western countries are reconsidering the economic restrictions imposed on Vietnam because of its role in Cambodia.

INTRODUCTION

The Socialist Republic of Vietnam is situated along the south-eastern margin of the Indo-Chinese Peninsula, extending from latitudes 8°30'N to 23°30'N. Three-quarters of the country is hilly or mountainous, with the highest peaks rising to more than 3000 m in the north-west, but grading into rolling dissected plateaux in the south. The Annamite mountain chain forms the natural boundary between Vietnam, Laos and Cambodia. Land suitable for agriculture covers approximately 100,000 sq. km and is mostly situated in the larger fertile plains of the Nam Bo and Bac Bo, which include the Mekong and Red River deltas respectively (Vu Tu Lap, 1979). The climate varies from humid tropical conditions in the southern lowlands to temperate conditions in the northern highlands. Mean annual sea level temperatures correspondingly decline from 27°C in the south to 21°C in the extreme north. The approximate mean annual rainfall is 2000 mm but this increases in the narrow, central mountainous region to 3000 mm, sufficiently heavy to support tropical rain forest. There are three monsoon seasons, namely the north-east winter monsoon, and the south-east and western summer monsoons. Destructive typhoons sometimes develop over the East Sea during hot weather (Scott, 1989).

Vietnam is the most densely populated country in mainland Southeast Asia, with 66.8 million residents in 1989 and a mean annual growth rate of 2.4 per cent. Some 80 per cent of the population is rural, the biggest concentrations of population being in the Red River and Mekong deltas. The population is ethnically very diverse. The largest group is the Vietnamese (Kinh) with 54 million people. The largest minority groups, extensively spread over the Annamite mountain region, are the Tay, Khmer, Thai, Muong, Nung, Meo, and Dao although, in 1976, even the largest numbered fewer than one million people (Paxton, 1989). These hill tribes practise shifting cultivation, clearing the hillsides to plant hill rice and tapioca.

The Forests

The most comprehensive account of Vietnam's great diversity of forest types is that given by Rothe (1947). Lowland evergreen rain forest rich in Dipterocarpaceae is the natural vegetation of the plains in the south, while deciduous tree species occur more frequently towards the north, as the proportion of Dipterocarpaceae diminishes. Much of the uplands were previously covered by dense evergreen forests.

Above 1000 m, the Dipterocarpaceae are replaced by members of the Lauraceae, the Fagaceae (*Castanopsis*, *Lithocarpus*, *Quercus*) and the Magnoliaceae. Several conifers occur in these montane forests, including *Keteleeria roulata*, *Pinus* spp. *Podocarpus* spp. and *Taxus baccata*. Human disturbance, particularly that resulting from the use of fire, has created extensive areas of open park-like woodlands at higher elevations in which several species of *Pinus* occur.

Forest Resources and Management

An assessment of Vietnam's forest area was made between 1973 and 1976 with the aid of Landsat satellite imagery (FAO/UNEP, 1981). Estimated total closed broadleaved forest cover in 1980 was 74,000 sq. km (22.45 per cent of total land area), of which only 15,000 sq. km were in an undisturbed, natural state. Of this total cover 36,700 sq. km were considered productive forest, and 31,700 sq. km were considered as unsuitable for logging but potentially at risk from agricultural encroachment. Legally protected forest covered only 5600 sq. km. Figures published by FAO (1987) suggest that earlier estimates may have been exaggerated and that closed forest cover in 1980 was possibly only 61,650 sq. km. The same report estimated that closed forest covered 48,620 sq. km in 1985. Projections for 1990 suggest closed forest cover may fall to 34,060 sq. km, of which just 3000 sq. km will be undisturbed (FAO, 1987).

Unpublished information from the Ministry of Forestry in 1989 provides another set of statistics. Based on interpretation of 1987 Landsat imagery, it indicates that 87,254 sq. km of natural forest remain (26.4 per cent of national territory), 79,054 sq. km of which are closed broadleaved forest. 189,000 sq. km are classified as forest land (57.4 per cent of territory) and 24,200 sq. km of natural forest have been allocated as protection forest.

This estimate seems unduly optimistic in light of maps made available during the preparation of this atlas and believed to have their origin in the same 1987 interpretation. Table 28.1, based on Map 28.1, indicates rain forest cover of 37,170 sq. km and monsoon forest cover of 19,510 sq. km, a total of 56,680 sq. km. Clearly, in a nation where so little pristine forest remains, an extensive spectrum of degraded forests must exist. The variability of statistics is almost certainly due to differing interpretations of what constitutes a closed canopy forest.

The Ministry of Forestry has overall responsibility for forest policy, planning and research, including direct responsibility for 17,000 sq. km of forest land, 14,000 sq. km of which is actual forest. The remaining area of forests is under the control of local People's Committees. Both the national and provincial bodies use some 360 forest enterprises as their ultimate executive agencies. The Ministry

comprises a large number of institutes covering planning, administration, research, production and transport. The Forest Inventory and Planning Institute has a particular responsibility for surveying protected areas and preparing management plans for them. By 1989 management plans had been prepared for Cuc Phuong and Cat Ba National Parks and another management plan was being prepared for Nam Bai Cat Tien.

Deforestation

The population of Vietnam was originally centred on the Red River delta in the north but moved south during historical times, clearing and cultivating the coastal plains and valleys, and reaching the Mekong delta a few centuries ago.

By 1943 most of the forest in the Red River delta and drier parts of the Mekong delta had been cleared, together with the coastline, much of the lowland riverine forests and some uplands (Figure 28.1).

Table 28.1 Estimates of forest extent in Vietnam

	Area (sq. km)	% of land area
Rain forests		
Lowland	28,040	8.6
Montane	7,520	2.3
Mangrove	1,610	0.5
Sub totals	37,170	11.4
Monsoon forests		
Lowland	18,010	5.5
Montane	1,500	0.5
Sub totals	19,510	6.0
Totals	56,680	17.4

Based on analysis of Map 28.1. (see Map Legend for details)

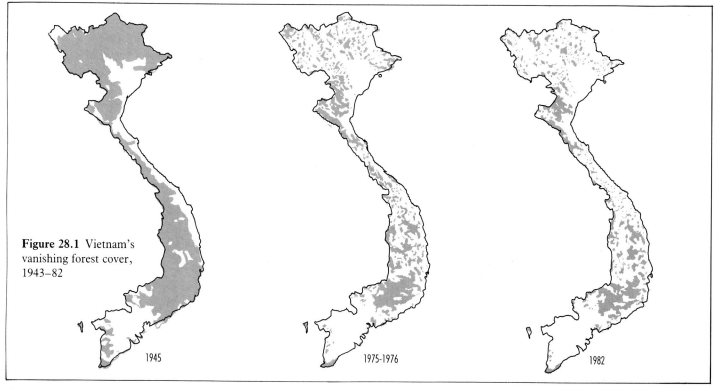

Figure 28.1 Vietnam's vanishing forest cover, 1943–82

1945   1975-1976   1982

(*Source*: Anon., 1985)

A firewood collector in Tam Dao forest, northern Vietnam. Fuelwood shortages cause overharvesting of forests in some parts. WWF/J. MacKinnon

Forests in the swamps and highly acidic areas of the Mekong delta remained untouched because their soils were not suitable for agriculture. At this time about 45 per cent of the country was still forested. During the French colonial period extensive areas of southern Vietnam were converted into industrial plantations – principally banana, coffee and rubber.

The period from 1945 to 1975 witnessed almost uninterrupted warfare, first against the French colonial administration (which ended in 1954) and then between the northern and southern parts of the country, causing death and suffering to millions of people as well as severe damage to natural resources. During the second war an estimated 22,000 sq. km of farmland and forest were destroyed, mainly in the south of the country, by intensive bombing, tactical spraying of 72 million litres of herbicides (12 per cent of the forests of South Vietnam were sprayed at least once), and mechanical clearance of forest. Direct attacks on wildlife that was potentially useful for war, such as elephants, also took place (Agarwal, 1984; Kemf, 1986; Vo Quy, 1985). In addition, a further 1170 sq. km of forest were destroyed by cratering from the 13 million tons of bombs dropped on Vietnam, and a further 40,000 sq. km by bombardment (United Nations data).

There were also indirect causes of forest loss, which were less obvious, but probably had greater negative effects. In order to produce enough food for the population, which nearly doubled between 1945 and 1985, as well as for the country's armies, large areas of forest were felled for agriculture. The area cleared was larger than would normally have been needed because vast quantities of food were destroyed by aerial crop spraying, and agriculture was destroyed by bombing of dykes and irrigation channels.

Despite the intensity of destruction during the wars, even more Vietnamese forests have been lost since hostilities ended in 1975. Driven by a need to reconstruct the country, and by the needs of a rapidly growing population, post-war lumbering operations were needed in order to rebuild homes, schools, hospitals, roads and irrigation systems. In addition there was relentless collection of fuelwood, and slash-and-burn agriculture continued. These factors, as well as forest fires, have all intensified the deforestation rate. it was estimated by FAO in 1981 that, each year, 450 sq. km of broadleaved forests were subject to timber exploitation and that 600 sq. km of dense broadleaved forest were destroyed by shifting agriculture (FAO/UNEP, 1981; FAO, 1988). By 1988 this estimate had increased to 3110 sq. km of forest lost annually, a figure far in excess of the current annual replanting of 1600 sq. km (FAO, 1987; Kemf, 1988).

The consequences of forest loss have been felt severely in Vietnam. Most deforested areas are now barren and almost 50 per cent of the country is unproductive wasteland. Increased flooding and damage from coastal typhoons, and problems of windblown sand ruining coastal agricultural areas have been attributed to deforestation, as has erosion. Severe erosion scars can be seen in many areas and heavy sedimentation has caused the failure of irrigation and hydropower projects. Erosion is further blamed for the loss of coastal forests. Deforestation has also resulted in fuelwood shortages in many areas and, combined with excessive hunting, led to a substantial decline in wildlife and other forest resources.

Mangroves

Extensive mangrove forests and associated brackish water forests of *Melaleuca* occur in the Mekong delta in the south. Small areas are also still found in the Red River delta and along the northern coast near the Chinese border. The Red River mangroves, once extensive, have been almost completely converted to agriculture, fisheries and forestry, and are now too small to appear on Map 28.1. An important site for nature conservation however, is an 11 ha block of mangrove in the delta at the mouth of the main branch of the Red River (Scott, 1989).

The Vietnamese mangrove forests were severely damaged in the war, with about half completely destroyed by aerial spraying with Agent Orange herbicide (Kemf, 1986). After the war the Vietnamese launched a massive replanting programme, which after initial setbacks has now led to successful re-establishment of many thousand hectares. These re-established mangrove forests are now supplying fuelwood, fish and prawns, and birdlife has returned. Nevertheless, the regreening of Vietnam still has far to go and more than 20 per cent of the tidal mangroves on the Camau Peninsula and 30 per cent of the *Melaleuca* forests have not recovered and remain wastelands (Kemf, 1986).

Biodiversity

The forests of Vietnam contain a great wealth of plants.
- Of 12,000 predicted species, over 7000 have been identified (Anon., 1985).
- At least 10 per cent of the estimated 8000 vascular species, are endemic to Vietnam (IUCN, 1986).
- Some 2300 species are known to be used by man for food, medicines, animal fodder, wood or other purposes (Anon., 1985).
- There are four distinct areas with high levels of endemism and many species are found in only very limited distributions and low densities (Anon., 1985).
- Most endemic species are found in the alpine zone of the Hoang Lien Son mountains.
- Other pockets of high endemism are the Ngoc Linh mountains, Lam Vien highlands and the rain forests of central Vietnam (Anon., 1985).

Twenty years after spraying with defoliants, the Mekong delta's war-torn mangroves remain heavily damaged. WWF/J. MacKinnon

Vietnam's fauna is also rich, with over 160 mammal species, 723 birds, 180 reptiles and 80 amphibians, in addition to hundreds of species of fish and an unknown number of invertebrates (Anon., 1985).

• Like the plants there is a high level of endemism amongst animals and many species are of great conservation interest.

• Some of the most spectacular species include Asian elephant, Javan rhinoceros, banteng, kouprey, tiger, snub-nosed monkey (*Rhinopithecus* sp.), red-shanked and black-shanked douc langurs (*Pygathrix nemaeus* and *P. nigripes*), black gibbon, black-necked stork (*Ephippiorhynchus asiaticus*), green peafowl and several rare pheasants, crocodiles and pythons.

Although there are now lists of protected species, there is no control over hunting and there is free access to firearms. The plight of wildlife in Vietnam looks bleak, unless efforts to save these valuable resources can be redoubled (Anon., 1985).

Conservation Areas

The government started to establish nature reserves as early as 1962 when it inaugurated the first national park at Cuc Phuong, about 130 km south of Hanoi. Further extension of the reserve system was postponed by the war but since 1980 has proceeded very quickly. The government recently approved the extension of the reserve system to include a total of 87 reserves and these will protect representative examples of most major forest formations in the country. These include seven national parks, 49 nature reserves and 31 cultural and environmental reserves although a lack of staff, resources and management experience prevents the protected areas system fulfilling its greatest conservation potential. Some cover substantial areas, such as the 450 sq. km Mom Ray nature reserve close to the Cambodian border, but many are much smaller, due to the highly fragmented condition of the remaining forest. However, forests retained to protect watersheds are also important for wildlife and as corridors between reserves and isolated forest patches. Table 28.2 lists the name, size and status of reserves.

It is highly desirable that a forest corridor should be created down the length of the Annamite mountain chain since this is an important habitat for elephant and other large mammals such as gaur, banteng and wild dog (*Cuon alpinus*). These corridors are probably also important for linking primate populations, especially the more arboreal forms such as gibbons and langurs.

The extensive wetlands of the Mekong delta are also of critical importance. Forest cover in this area is vital to ensure the proper flow of water through the delta's many small channels, for protecting its banks, fish and prawn nursery areas and providing refuges for waterbirds. The conservation of wetlands in the Mekong Delta, and in other parts of the country is discussed in detail by Scott (1989).

Spectacular forests survive in national parks. WWF/J. MacKinnon

NEW HOPE FOR THE KOUPREY

The kouprey *Bos sauveli* was unknown to science until 1937, a remarkable fact given that it is the size of a large cow (it is also known as the forest ox). There have been few observations since it was discovered, partly because the species is confined to the war-torn countries of Laos, Cambodia and Vietnam, with occasional wanderings into the Dongrak mountains of Thailand.

In 1986 a WWF project found evidence that the kouprey survived in its former haunts. In 1988 the Vietnamese government hosted a workshop on kouprey conservation which agreed several actions to save the species in the wild and explore its possible use for the benefit of the livestock industry. Proposed actions included surveys, establishment of protected areas, preparation of management plans, a captive-breeding programme, education and training.

Already, part of the plan has been put into practice. An initial survey by Vietnamese scientists has taken place in the Yok Don National Park in western Daklak Province, near the Cambodian border. Unfortunately, no koupreys were seen, but there was abundant evidence of gaur, banteng and buffalo. However, all the habitat requirements of the kouprey appeared to be met, and there is hope that it still survives in the region.

Sources: Laurie *et al.*, 1989; Stuart, 1988

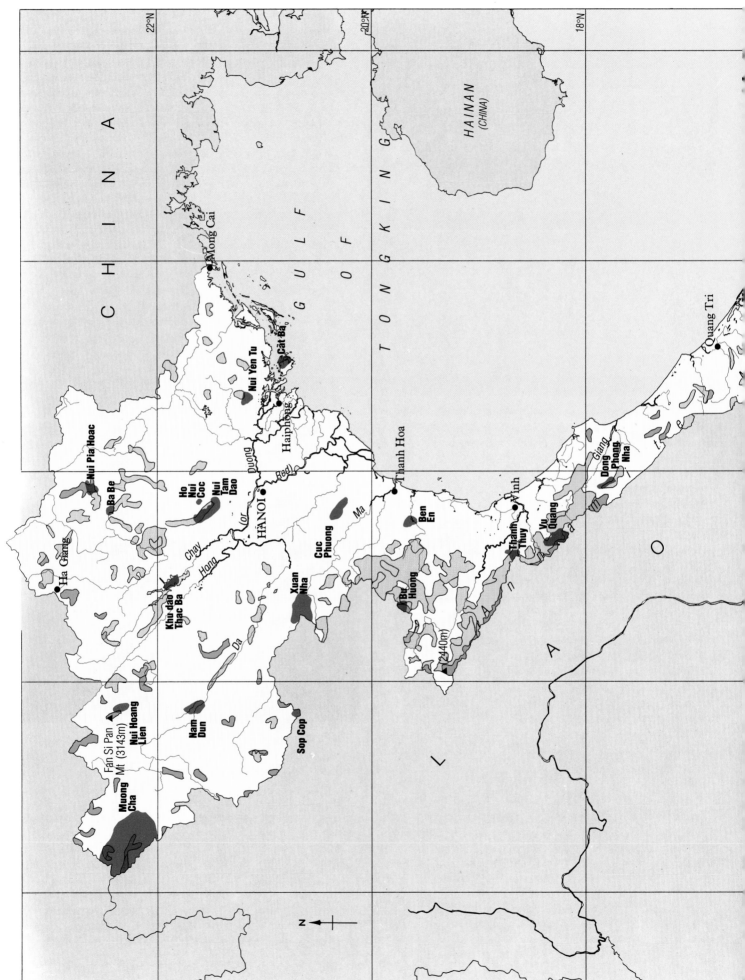

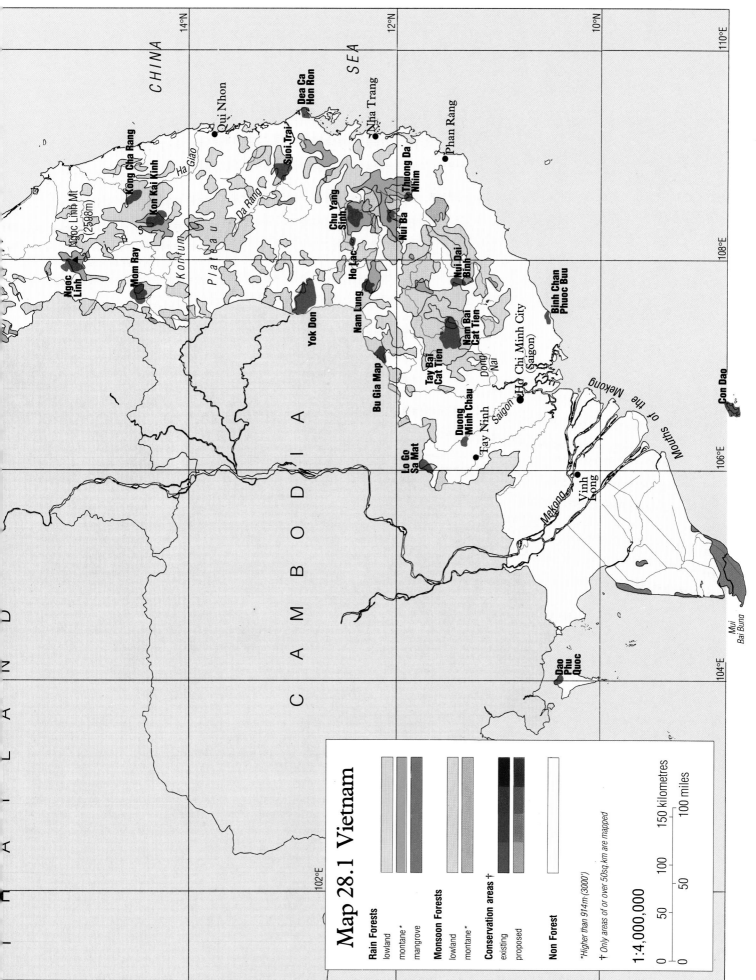

CHINA

SEA

Qui Nhon

Dea Ca
Hon Ron

Nha Trang

Kong Cha Rang

Suoi Trai

Phan Rang

Kon Kai Kinh

Ha Giao

Ngoc Linh Mt
(2598m)

Da Rang

Chu Yang
Sinh

Thuong Da
Nhim

Mom Ray

Kontum

Plateau

Ho Lac

Nui Ba

Ngoc
Linh

Nam Lung

Nui Dai
Binh

Yok Don

Bu Gia Map

Nam Bai
Cat Tien

Binh Chan
Phuoc Buu

Tay Bai
Cat Tien

Dong
Nai

Ho Chi Minh City
(Saigon)

Duong
Minh Chau

Saigon

Lo Go
Sa Mat

Tay Ninh

Mouths of the Mekong

Con Dao

C A M B O D I A

Mekong

Vinh
Long

T H A I L A N D

Mui
Bai Bung

Dao
Phu
Quoc

Map 28.1 Vietnam

Rain Forests

lowland

montane *

mangrove

Monsoon Forests

lowland

montane *

Conservation areas †

existing

proposed

Non Forest

*Higher than 914m (3000')

† Only areas of or over 50sq.km are mapped

1:4,000,000

| 0 | 50 | 100 | 150 kilometres |

| 0 | 50 | 100 miles |

Table 28.2 Conservation areas of Vietnam

Existing areas, 50 sq. km and over, are listed below. The remaining areas are combined in a total under Other Areas. Forest reserves are not included. For data on Ramsar sites, see chapter 9.

	Existing area (sq. km)	Proposed area (sq. km)
National Parks		
Ba Be★	50	
Bach Ma Hai Van★	400	
Cat Ba	277	
Con Dao	60	
Cuc Phuong	250	
Nam Bai Cat Tien★	365	
Nature Reserves		
Bana-Nui Chua★	52	
Ben En	120	
Binh Chan Phuoc Buu	55	
Bu Gia Map★	160	
Bu Huong★	50	
Chu Yang Sinh★	200	
Dao Phu Quoc	50	
Kon Kai Kinh★	280	
Kong Cha Rang★	160	
Lo Go Sa Mat★	100	
Mom Ray★	450	
Muong Cha★	1,820	
Nam Dun	180	
Nam Lung★	200	
Ngoc Linh★	200	
Nui Ba★	60	
Nui Dai Binh★	50	
Nui Hoang Lien★	50	
Nui Pia Hoac★	100	
Nui Yen Tu	50	
Sop Cop	50	
Suoi Trai★	190	
Tay Bai Cat Tien★	100	
Thanh Thuy★	70	
Thuong Da Nhim★	70	
Vu Quang★	160	
Xuan Nha	600	
Yok Don★	575	
Historic/Cultural Reserves		
Dea Ca Hon Ron	100	
Dong Phong Nha★	50	
Duong Minh Chau	50	
Ho Lac★	100	
Nui Tam Dao★	190	
Unclassified		
Ho Nui Coc	60	
Khu dao Thac Ba	50	
Sub total	8,204	
Other Areas	2,741	196
Totals	10,945	196

(*Sources:* IUCN, 1990 and WCMC data *in litt.*)
★ Area with moist forest within its boundary.

Initiatives for Conservation

Alarm at the degree of forest loss and its disastrous consequences for agriculture and national welfare has been felt at the highest government levels. Vietnam was one of the first developing countries to embark upon the preparation of a National Conservation Strategy (Anon., 1985). This outlines plans for limiting population growth, reforestation, the introduction of agroforestry and the establishment of nature reserves. Although the strategy has not yet been formally adopted by the Council of Ministers, it is hoped that the proposals will eventually be promulgated, probably with international assistance. Vietnam's international isolation, however, has severely curtailed the flow of aid and development resources, and conservation programmes are currently starved of funding.

There is hope that bilateral and multilateral development assistance may be renewed through the mechanism of the Tropical Forestry Action Plan (see chapter 10). With technical assistance to national foresters, a strategic plan that will embrace industrial forestry, fuelwood production, ecosystem conservation and institution-building is being developed. This will guide coordinated development assistance to Vietnam's forest sector in coming decades.

The national reforestation programme aims to increase forest cover to 57.4 per cent of the country's land area. In 1987, 1600 sq. km were replanted on a shoestring environmental budget, but the more ambitious goal is to increase the replanting to as much as 3000 sq. km each year. The Tet (lunar new year) Festival has now also become a traditional time for tree planting and in addition to Forest Department projects, tree planting is encouraged and organised in schools and at community level (Kemf, 1988). One problem with the tree planting programme has been the excessive use of species such as eucalyptus and pine. Planting mixtures of local species as an alternative is being encouraged by the National Resources and Environmental Protection Centre of Hanoi University.

Vietnam has pioneered techniques of restoring tropical forest cover after many years of experiment, often fraught with failure. The main testing ground was the Ma Da wood, 100 km north-east of Ho Chi Minh City. Once a thickly wooded tropical forest, the area was a stronghold for North Vietnamese soldiers and consequently subject to repeated defoliant and napalm attacks. Three-quarters of the trees died and the landscape reduced to barren hillsides and vast stretches of unusable *Imperata cylindrica* grasslands. Initial reforestation trials failed as saplings were burnt in grass fires ignited by the intense heat of the dry season. To overcome this a fast growing cover of exotic species such as *Indigofera tenemani*, *Acacia auriculiformis* and *Cassia siamea* was established. Subsequently native forest trees, including *Dipterocarpus alatus*, *D. dyeri*, *Hopea odorata* and *Anisoptera* sp. were planted under this canopy and are now surviving well. Although this preliminary trial covers just 300 ha it indicates that a degree of rehabilitation can be achieved.

Recent land reforms in Vietnam have given incentives to farmers to take better long-term care of the land they farm. Up to 20 per cent of the land can now be privately owned. Other land is allocated on long-term tenure with guarantees of transfer of land-use rights from father to son. A major new settlement programme is under way, directed primarily to the rehabilitation of previously cultivated and abandoned areas (see chapter 5).

Despite an impressive number of trained scientists, Vietnam urgently needs skilled personnel for forestry and conservation management. Hanoi University's National Resources and Environmental Protection Centre is training a cadre of professionals for the future and also offers high level advice to government in conservation matters.

THE VINH PHU PULP AND PAPER MILL

In the early 1970s public opinion in Sweden strongly opposed American involvement in the Vietnam war. So when the Paris peace accords were signed in 1975, the Swedish International Development Agency (SIDA) was among the first to offer aid to the victorious North Vietnamese regime. A major project was launched to help Vietnam achieve self-sufficiency in paper production. The Vinh Phu Pulp and Paper Mill was built 100 km north-west of Hanoi at Bai Bang. It had a capacity of 60,000 tons, modest by Swedish standards, but enormous alongside the 3,000 ton mills obtained from the Chinese and with which the Vietnamese were familiar. But no sooner was the mill completed, than it ran into serious difficulties. The 500,000 tons of bamboo and wood needed to feed the mill each year were not available. The Vietnamese estimation of these resources proved to have been widely optimistic and pulp had to be shipped from Sweden to make up the deficit. To make matters worse, Vietnam did not have enough qualified technicians and managers to operate such a large and costly venture. A small army of highly paid Swedish advisers had to be provided, complete with housing for their families, schools for their children and a hospital. Expensive imported spare parts and chemicals – which Vietnam could not afford – were also needed. Sweden responded by purchasing the paper and giving it as aid to strife-torn Ethiopia. Meanwhile, as waste discharged from the mill and polluted local rivers, the price tag for the project rose to an incredible half a billion dollars. Bai Bang seemed destined to join the ever-growing list of development assistance disasters.

Sweden, however, maintained its support, and as its foresters and aid workers gradually acquired greater knowledge of the country and its problems, so it was able to adapt the aid it provided. The Vinh Phu Pulp and Paper Mill has finally begun to make a major contribution not only to the Vietnamese economy, but also to the standard of living of the people in the project area.

The raw material for the mill now comes from plantations of *Styrax* and *Eucalyptus* and bamboo stands. These are owned by the 250 forest villages and 17,000 forestry workers in the area. Several cooperatives also organise plantations. The liberalisation of government economic policy has meant that producers can negotiate a fair market price for their wood. Houses have been constructed for the workers and there are clinics, schools and other child-care facilities.

Vinh Phu Mill is currently operating at 50 per cent of its capacity. The 30,000 tons production provides 50 per cent of all the pulp and paper used in Vietnam. As more plantations come into production, this percentage will increase.

Plantations for supplying the mill are being established on hill slopes with very poor soils. The silvicultural problems are far from solved, but since these soils have little or no agricultural potential, the deep ripping necessary to establish the plantations, is perhaps the best way of rehabilitating them.

The mill could not survive without continued Swedish support, and the paper it has produced so far could have been purchased on the international market for a fraction of the cost of the project. But the social benefits from the mill have been considerable, and the project itself has come to symbolise Vietnam's determination to rebuild its economy.   *Source*: J. A. Sayer

References

Agarwal, A. (1984) Vietnam after the storm. *New Scientist* **1409**: 10–14.

Anon. (1985) *Viet Nam: National Conservation Strategy*. Prepared by the Committee for Rational Utilisation of Natural Resources and Environmental Protection (Programme 52–02) with assistance from IUCN. WWF–India, New Delhi. 71 pp.

Eames, J. C., Robson, C. R., Wolstencroft, J. A., Ngnyen Cu and Truong Van La (1988) Viet Nam Forest Project Pheasant Surveys. Unpublished report to the International Council for Bird Preservation and others. 69 pp.

FAO (1987) *Special Study on Forest and Utilization of Forest Resources in the Developing Region. Asia–Pacific Region. Assessment of Forest Resources in Six Countries*. FAO Field Document 17. 104 pp.

FAO (1988) *An Interim Report on the State of Forest Resources in the Developing Countries*. FO:MISC/88/7. FAO, Rome, Italy. 18 pp.

FAO (1990) *FAO Yearbook of Forest Products 1977–88*. FAO Forestry Series No. 23, FAO Statistics Series No. 90. FAO, Rome.

FAO/UNEP (1981) *Tropical Forest Resources Assessment Project*. 3 vols. FAO, Rome, Italy. Vol 3 of 3 vols. 475 pp.

IUCN (1986) *Plants in Danger: What do we Know?* IUCN, Gland, Switzerland, and Cambridge, UK. 461 pp.

IUCN (1990) *1989 United Nations List of National Parks and Protected Areas*. IUCN, Gland, Switzerland, and Cambridge, UK.

Kemf, E. (1986) The re-greening of Vietnam. *WWF News* **41**: 4–5.

Kemf, E. (1988) Dance of a thousand cranes. *New Scientist* **8 October**: pp. 34–6.

Laurie, A., Duc, H. D. and Anh, P. T. (1989) Survey for kouprey (*Bos sauveli*) in western Daklak Province, Vietnam. Unpublished report to the Kouprey Conservation Trust. 34 pp.

Paxton, J. (1989) *Statesman's Yearbook 1989–1990*. Macmillan Press Limited, London, UK. 1691 pp.

Rothe, P. (1947) La forêt d'Indochine. *Bois et Forêts Tropicaux* **1**: 25–30, **2**: 18–23, **3**: 17–23.

Scott, D. A. (1989) (ed.) *A Directory of Asian Wetlands*. IUCN, Gland, and Cambridge, UK. 1181 pp.

Stuart, S. (1988) New hope for the kouprey. *Newsletter of the Species Survival Commission* **10**: 17.

Vo Quy (1985) Rare species and protection measures proposed for Vietnam. In: *Conserving Asia's Natural Heritage*. Thorsell, J. W. (ed.). IUCN, Gland, Switzerland, and Cambridge, UK. 251 pp.

Vu Tu Lap (1979) *Viet Nam Geographical Data*. Foreign Language Publishing House, Hanoi.

Authorship

John MacKinnon and Roger Cox in Cambridge and London, with contributions from Dinh Hiep in the Ministry of Forestry, Hanoi, Jan van der Heide in Groningen, Netherlands and Jeff Sayer at IUCN.

Map 28.1 Forest cover in Vietnam

Forest cover in Vietnam was taken from the 1:4 million forest map entitled *Cac Loai Thuc Vât bi de Doa Dien Hinh va Môt Vung Tâp Trung*, believed to be the result of a forest inventory in 1987. Also held is a simplified coloured version at 1:6 million, *Ban dô Hiên Trang Rung Nam 1987 (Forest Types Map)*. These maps show tropical rain, monsoon and the remaining Mekong mangrove forests. Montane forest was delimited from a 3000 ft (914 m) contour extracted from the Jet Navigation Charts, JNC 37 and JNC 54 at scale 1:2 million. Protected areas were mapped from various unpublished sources, held at WCMC including MacKinnon *in lit* and Eames *et al* (1988).

29
Western
Pacific
Islands

FIJI
Land area   18,270 sq. km •
Population (1987)   722,000
Gross national product (1987)   US$1570 per capita
Rain forest (see map)   6610 sq. km
Monsoon forest (see map)   360 sq. km
Closed broadleaved forest area (1980)†   8110 sq. km
Annual deforestation rate (1981–5)†   17 sq. km
Roundwood production   249,000 cu. m
Roundwood exports   4000 cu. m
Fuelwood and charcoal production   37,000 cu. m
Sawlog and veneer log production   205,000 cu. m
Sawlog and veneer log exports   4000 cu. m

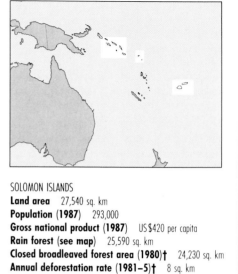

VANUATU
Land area   12,190 sq. km
Population (1987)   150,000
Gross national product (1988)   US$820 per capita
Closed broadleaved forest area (1980)†   2,360 sq. km
Annual deforestation rate (1981–5)†   39 sq. km
Roundwood production   63,000 cu. m
Roundwood exports   25,000 cu. m
Fuelwood and charcoal production   24,000 cu. m
Sawlog and veneer log production   39,000 cu. m
Sawlog and veneer log exports   25,000 cu. m
˙ All forest products are 1988 data from FAO (1990)
† FAO (1988)

SOLOMON ISLANDS
Land area   27,540 sq. km
Population (1987)   293,000
Gross national product (1987)   US$420 per capita
Rain forest (see map)   25,590 sq. km
Closed broadleaved forest area (1980)†   24,230 sq. km
Annual deforestation rate (1981–5)†   8 sq. km
Roundwood production   589,000 cu. m
Roundwood exports   160,000 cu. m
Fuelwood and charcoal production   210,000 cu. m
Sawlog and veneer log production   379,000 cu. m
Sawlog and veneer log exports   160,000 cu. m

From the Solomon Islands across to Vanuatu, Fiji, Tonga and the Samoas, the Pacific Ocean is flecked with tiny islands, many of which were once clothed in tropical moist forest, including rain forest on the higher islands. The major factors controlling the type of vegetation are topography and altitude and this is discussed further by Schmid (1989). Unfortunately, it is these forests that have been most affected by human activity, and on many smaller islands little or no lowland rain forest remains today. Long isolation has produced remarkable examples of endemism, especially in the birds. Loss of habitat and the introduction of predators by mankind have resulted in a large number of species being threatened with extinction. In the tropical western Pacific moves have been made to conserve remaining forest patches in Western Samoa (land area 2935 sq. km), American Samoa (200 sq. km), Cook Islands (240 sq. km) and Tonga (700 sq. km). However, even on these remote islands there has been widespread logging of rain forest with a substantial effect on, for example, Western Samoa (Anon., 1989; Paine, 1989 a,b,c).

This atlas only considers the three largest island groups in any detail, namely Fiji, the Solomon Islands and Vanuatu, which all have relatively extensive tropical rain forests. The tiny tropical rain forest areas of Micronesia and Polynesia are excluded since they are too small to map at the working scales used here. There are other islands in the Pacific with closed forest formations, notably New Caledonia and New Zealand, but these are subtropical and warm temperate, rather than tropical rain forests, and have therefore been omitted. As at the northern limits of the atlas the boundary is somewhat arbitrary, but has been guided by the purpose of this atlas, which is to demonstrate the distribution of *tropical* closed canopy forest formations.

INTRODUCTION – FIJI

Fiji comprises approximately 300 islands and islets scattered across an exclusive economic zone located between 10°–25°S and 173°E–176°W. The islands form several distinct groups: Rotuma; Vanua Levu and associated islands, including Taveuni and the Ringgold Isles; the Lau Group; the Lomaiviti Group; the Yasawas; Viti Levu and associated islands; and Kadavu and associated islands. Some 87 per cent of the land area of the main archipelago is accounted for by Viti Levu (10,386 sq. km) and Vanua Levu (5534 sq. km); other large islands are Taveuni, Kadavu and Ngau. The total sea area is estimated at 1,135,000 sq. km.

● The islands are composed mostly of igneous rocks, and the larger ones have rugged mountainous interiors, rising to 1324 m on Viti Levu and 1032 m on Vanua Levu.
● Fringing reefs, barrier reefs and lagoons with patch reefs constitute a significant physical and biological feature in Fiji (SPREP, 1980). A summary of principal physical features and coral reef formations of some 200 major islands is given in UNEP/IUCN (1988).
● The climate is hot and humid, especially in the summer. Annual rainfall is unevenly distributed, owing to rain shadow in high ground

areas. Typical rainfall figures are 3000 mm on east coasts and 1650 mm on the west. Up to six months of drought can occur in sheltered areas.

• Most of the population live on the coasts and along river valleys on Viti Levu and Vanua Levu. The major ethnic division is between Fijians (46 per cent) and Indians (49 per cent).

A general overview of Fiji, its natural resources and their conservation has recently been compiled (Paine, 1989d). The total area of tropical moist forest in Fiji is small on a global scale, but it harbours endemic plants and animals. There is some threat to the forests from conversion to other land uses, and pristine forests are also threatened by logging and conversion planting with mahogany. The rain forests are not at present adequately represented in conservation areas.

The Forests

Due to rain shadow effects rain forests in Fiji are found on the south and east sides of the main islands and seasonal forests, much degraded to scrub, savanna woodlands or to grasslands, are found on the western sides. Small limestone islands are still forested, but no forest remains on the small volcanic islands.

The higher mountainous areas have a low stature mossy upper montane rain forest, supporting a number of unique species, although the total area is small.

The seasonal forests of the northern and western parts of the large islands extend inland to 450 m elevation. Sugar cane is a major crop in this climatic zone. The boundary between rain and seasonal forests is a mosaic which includes patches of bamboo and grassland.

Highly localised landslides and cyclones are regularly occurring natural disasters. These have moulded the forests in such a way that secondary associations are a widespread and integral part of the Fijian forest ecosystems. This may mean that selected fauna have adapted to disturbed environments (Watling, 1988a). However, amongst the forest bird fauna eight species are wholly confined to undisturbed mature forest. Another 14 species are found in secondary forest habitat but may still require undisturbed forest for breeding. Schmid (1978) provided an account of the vegetation (after Parham, 1972) for Viti Levu and Vanua Levu. The freshwater wetland vegetation of Viti Levu has been described by Ash and Ash (1984).

Forest Resources, Management and Deforestation

The development of Fiji occurred in two broad phases, pre- and post-European contact. Prior to European influence, lowland rain forests and coastal beach forests were modified by swidden agriculture and exotic flora and fauna were introduced. Features of Fiji at this time included the extensive grasslands, formed deliberately by fires to facilitate wild yam harvesting in the drier western areas; terraced river valleys; and densely populated and heavily cultivated river deltas. European introduction of labour-intensive crops such as copra, cotton and sugar, centred mainly on the coastal zone, made a further and considerable environmental impact. The rugged interior of the main islands confines extensive agriculture to the coastal plains.

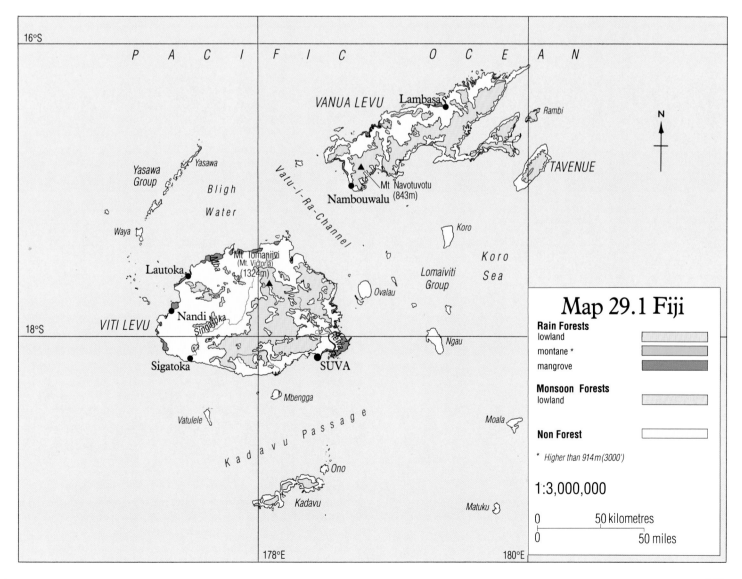

241

Natural rain and monsoon forests were estimated to cover 8110 sq. km in the early 1980s (FAO, 1988), or 44 per cent of the total land area. Map 29.1, derived from a Fiji Department of Forestry map dated 1985, shows 6970 sq. km of moist forest remaining at that time or 38.1 per cent of land area. The forests are confined to the larger islands of Viti Levu, Vanua Levu, Rambi and Taveuni, and consist mainly of lowland rain forests (see Table 29.1). Forest Department statistics supplied in early 1990 are very similar, they record 6814 sq. km of natural forest, representing 37.3 per cent of land area.

A timber inventory carried out in Fiji in the mid 1960s resulted in the classification of forests for commercial and non-commercial purposes. The Fiji Ministry of Forestry currently classifies 2288 sq. km as Protection Forest in areas where the slope exceeds 30°; a further 2250 sq. km is classed as Non-Commercial, and the remaining, 2276 sq. km Production Forest utilised for its timber. In 1986, 60 per cent of the Production Forest estate was under logging concession, and the figure is certainly higher now. On Vanua Levu, at least 50 per cent of forests have already been logged, and 90 per cent is destined for logging. About 313 sq. km of forest are protected in 19 Forest Reserves under the Forest Act.

Loss of natural forests is a serious environmental issue. They are disappearing at an annual rate of approximately one per cent. Since 1969 there has been a possible 30 per cent reduction in the area of non-commercial forest, a 5 per cent loss of production forests and an 8 per cent reduction in protection forests, although these are intended to remain under forest cover in perpetuity. There is no systematic monitoring of forest loss which varies greatly by district and is probably much worse on Viti Levu than elsewhere (Drysdale, 1988).

Selective logging in Fiji removes an unusually high number of trees, as many as 30 per hectare, and as much as two-thirds of the vegetation may be disturbed or damaged in some way. Despite the seemingly catastrophic effect, the ability of Fijian forest to recover if left alone is remarkable. The effects are to a large extent avoidable and are mainly caused by the management practice of mandatory extraction of a large number of species down to 35 cm diameter, insufficient control of logging operators, the employment of inexperienced contractors who frequently use inappropriate equipment, and the prevalence of uncontrolled repeat logging which negates any attempts at management (Watling, 1988a; 1988b).

Table 29.1 Estimates of forest extent

	Area (sq. km)	% of land area
FIJI		
Rain forests		
Lowland	6,070	33.2
Montane	20	0.1
Mangrove	520	2.8
Sub totals	6,610	36.1
Monsoon forests		
Lowland	360	2.0
Totals	6,970	38.1
SOLOMON ISLANDS		
Rain forests		
Lowland	24,810	90.1
Montane	780	2.8
Totals	25,590	92.9

Based on analyses of Maps 29.1 and 29.2 (see Map Legends for details).

Fiji has 900 sq. km of plantation forests, comprising 340 sq. km of hardwoods planted in logged Production Forest, and 560 sq. km of *Pinus caribaea* on grasslands in the drier rain shadow area.

The principal hardwood species planted is mahogany, *Swietenia macrophylla*, which is proving remarkably vigorous in some localities. The practice of establishing hardwood plantations after logging could lead to a high proportion (25–33 per cent) of Fiji's species-rich Production Forest being heavily altered, with the probable consequence of greatly reduced species diversity. From the point of view of biological diversity conservation, it would be preferable to log the Production Forests more lightly, as this would help to encourage natural regeneration, and make a point of targeting the hardwood plantations on forest lands that are already known to be degraded or in some other way non-commercial.

There are reports of unwise practices in the hardwood plantations, including planting on very steep slopes and right up to the edge of streams and rivers (Watling 1988a).

Mangroves

Fiji's mangrove forests are important economically for traditional fisheries, but they are under threat from wood cutting and reclamation for agriculture. Mangroves were removed from the Forest Reserve System in the 1970s, and while a mangrove management plan has recently been prepared, its implementation is uncertain. Map 29.1 (see page 241) indicates 520 sq. km of mangrove forests remaining in Fiji.

Biodiversity

A discussion summarising the state of Fiji's biodiversity is given by Paine (1989d). The flora is not rich by humid tropical standards, as is to be expected on a remote oceanic archipelago. There are approximately 1500 native vascular plant species, of which 40–50 per cent are believed to be endemic. Twenty-three of 28 native palms are endemic. There are eleven endemic genera, plus the endemic monospecific family Degeneriaceae.

The great majority of endemic plant species are totally dependent on the forest and many have very restricted ranges. This is amply illustrated by some of the endemic palms of Viti Levu. Of these, three have complete ranges of just a few sq. km, namely *Cyphosperma tanga*, *Gulubia microcarpa*, and *Neoveitchia storckii*.

In common with other Pacific islands, the mammalian fauna is very poor. There are no large native mammals. Six bats occur, including the endemic Fiji fruit bat *Pteralopex acrodonta*, restricted to Taveuni, and the long-tailed fruit bat *Notopteris macdonaldi*. Pratt et al. (1987) report the presence of up to 124 bird species, of which up to 87 breed in Fiji. At least 25 species are endemic.

Reptiles, amphibians and insects all include endemic genera and species. Many taxa are forest dwellers and may well be threatened by loss of cover.

Robinson (1975) found high levels of endemism amongst the 400 larger moths and butterflies of Fiji, but this was severely reduced in disturbed habitats. In primary montane forest 50 per cent of moths are endemic but in secondary forest and grassland the faunas are smaller and endemicity declines respectively to 35 per cent and zero. Four species are already believed to be extinct, and another is under threat.

Conservation Areas

Governmental economic and social policies are promulgated in five-year development plans. These have progressively addressed the problems of sustainable resource utilisation and environmental protection. The 1976–80 seventh plan states: '. . . during the plan period Government's fundamental goal will be to exploit Fiji's natural resources wisely, in a manner which is consistent with the maintenance of a healthy environment and with the generation of benefits for all the people today and in the future.' A number of objectives, covering issues such as mining, rural development, urbanisation, transport, resource surveys and unequal resource distribution, were established (SPREP, 1980). The objectives of the eighth development plan (1981–85) included the establishment of a system of regional and national parks and the promulgation of a National Parks and Reserves Act, as proposed by Dunlap and Singh (1980), although this was not implemented. The ninth development plan (1986–90) summarises the principal environmental threats to Fiji, noting the need for an effective institutional framework within the Government for the overall coordination and management of environmental matters.

Fiji now has 16 areas managed for conservation purposes. Six of these are Nature Reserves administered by the Ministry of Forests, while the others are designated as Forest Parks, Amenity Reserves, Wildlife Sanctuaries and National Parks administered by various organisations, including the National Trust for Fiji, the Department of Lands, the Native Land Trust Board and the Fiji Pine Commission. In total they cover only 66 sq. km, or 0.36 per cent of Fiji's land area. There are no areas over 50 sq. km in size and only two Nature Reserves, Ravilevu and Tomaniivi, exceed 10 sq. km. Montane rain forest, beach forest and limestone scrub are protected to some degree, but there are serious limitations or omissions in the coverage of lowland rain and monsoon forest, swamp and mangrove forests, savanna and grassland, sea turtle nesting areas and reefs.

In 1985 an Action Strategy for Protected Areas in the South Pacific Region recognised that Fiji's protected area system was inadequate in several ways (SPREP, 1985):

• No ecological or heritage considerations were involved in the selection of protected areas.

• Protection forests have no long-term conservation value, given their present inadequate legal status and management.

• Forest and nature reserves are under the management of departmental rather than national institutions.

• The rate at which reserved forests have been de-reserved has increased in recent years, and only requires ministerial approval.

• Reserves on native land without the approval or economic involvement of landowners have no practical long-term security.

• Planning, and the limited attempts at implementation of reserve establishment are being undertaken in a poorly coordinated manner.

Coupled with the inadequate legislative and institutional support, these difficulties present a gloomy picture for the future of protected areas in Fiji. Growing political and social pressures on the forests mean that the possibilities for establishing a system of protected areas, particularly for tropical moist forest, are likely to diminish rapidly as the resource becomes fragmented and degraded. The absence of a nationwide ecological survey prohibits the selection of representative areas, and the establishment of a protected areas system may be hindered by the existing land tenure system.

Recognising the shortcomings in the protected areas system, two New Zealand NGOs, the Maruia Society and the Royal Forest and Bird Protection Society, have now carried out an ecological survey of Fiji's forests. The survey was carried out at the invitation of the Native Land Trust Board of Fiji which is now considering recommendations arising from it for the establishment of 10 major and 24 minor protected areas. One of these – the Sovi Basin – is considered to be of World Heritage quality. The recommended reserves are located on customary land and attention is now focused on the best means of protecting areas within this framework. Economic incentives for landowners will be needed. The Native Land Trust Board is pioneering the development of village-based nature tourism enterprises at two locations as a basis for yielding economic benefits for customary landowners from protected areas. In the larger proposed reserves which have substantial merchantable timber volumes, international assistance will be necessary to support the establishment of protected areas.

Initiatives for Conservation

The ecological survey and associated recommendations for a representative protected area system for Fiji have laid the groundwork for conservation in Fiji. An appropriate legal framework for implementation on customary land now needs to be considered. This could take the form of either enactment of a National Parks and Reserves Act, or the establishment under existing law of a Conservation Trust which could act as a repository for leases with landowners, and a channel for international funding of the proposed protected areas system. Further work needs to be done in the development of nature tourism activity to build both village and governmental support for protected areas. Institution building to ensure an adequate management capacity will also be crucial. Individual protected area leases will have to be negotiated with landowners by the Native Land Trust Board, which has a statutory responsibility for such matters.

An important parallel development is the recent TFAP forest sector review by FAO. The recommendations of the review have yet to be considered by the Government of Fiji, but they would involve commitments to sustainable management of natural forests and the establishment of significant reserves for nature conservation, as well as a continued emphasis on establishment of plantation forests of exotic species in order to meet the demand for high quality timber.

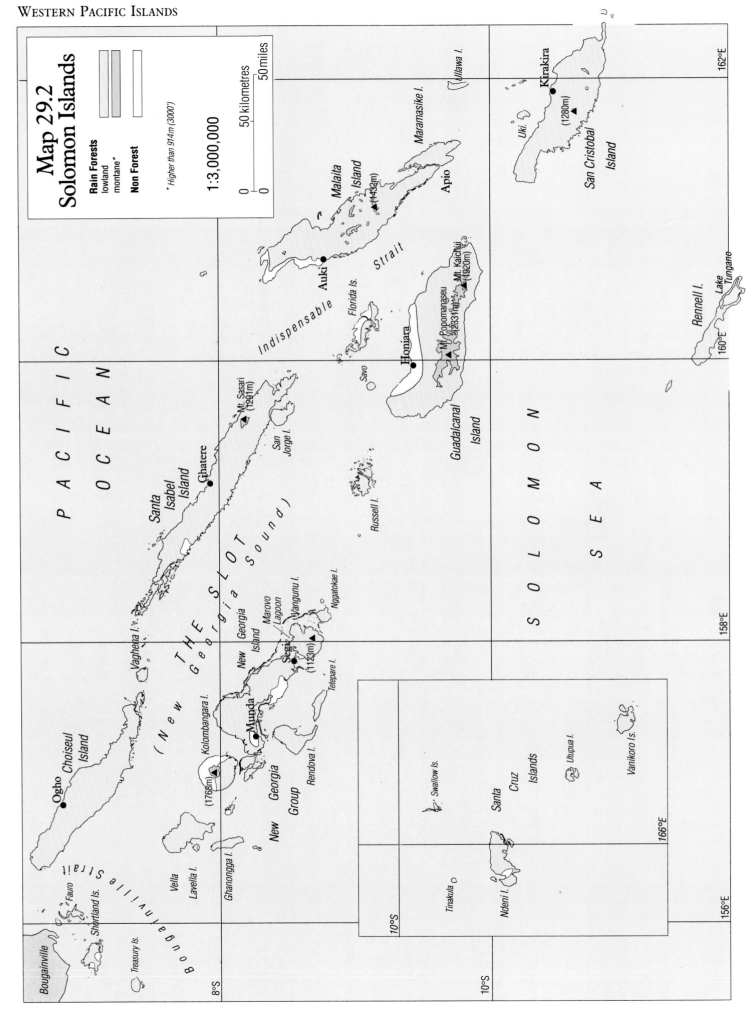

**Map 29.2
Solomon Islands**

Rain Forests
lowland
montane*

Non Forest

* Higher than 914m (3000')

1:3,000,000

50 kilometres
50 miles

Bougainville

Fauro
Shortland Is.
Treasury Is.

Bougainville Strait

Vella
Lavella I.

Ghanongga I.

New
Georgia
Group

Rendova I.

Ogho
*Choiseul
Island*

(1768m)

Kolombangara I.

Munda
Seo
(1123m)

*New
Georgia
Island*

Marovo
Lagoon

Vangunu I.

Nggatokae I.

Tetepare I.

(New Georgia SLOT Sound)

THE

Vaghena I. v.

Mt. Sasari
(1291m)

*Santa
Isabel
Island*

Ghatere

San
Jorge I.

PACIFIC

OCEAN

Russell I.

Savo

Honiara

Mt Popomangaseu
(2331m)
Mt. Kaichuj
(1920m)

*Guadalcanal
Island*

Florida Is.

Indispensable

Strait

Auki

*Malaita
Island*

(1432m)

Apio

Maramasike I.

Ullawa I.

Uki.

Kirakira
(1280m)

*San Cristobal
Island*

SOLOMON

SEA

Rennell I.

Lake
Tungano

Swallow Is.

*Santa
Cruz
Islands*

Utupua I.

Vanikoro Is.

Tinakula

Ndeni I.

8°S

10°S

10°S

156°E

158°E

160°E

162°E

166°E

INTRODUCTION – SOLOMON ISLANDS

The Solomon Islands comprise the whole Solomon archipelago, except the largest island Bougainville to the north-west which belongs to Papua New Guinea, plus the Santa Cruz archipelago to the south-east. The islands are steep and rugged with only limited coastal plains. The main islands form a double chain, Choiseul, Santa Isabel Malaita, and New Georgia, Guadalcanal and Makira (San Cristobal). There are also a large number of outlying small islands. The population is very largely rural, except in the capital Honiara. The people are Melanesian and, in common with many Pacific nations, over 87 per cent of land is owned communally.

The Solomon Islands have more tropical rain forest than any other western Pacific nation, and it also has a substantial logging industry. The export of hardwood logs provides a third of national export income, but the extent of loggable forest remaining is not large. There is strong pressure from timber interests because few Pacific countries still permit log exports. It is tempting for the customary owners to sell the standing timber in their forests even where the forests are essential to support village life, as on Rennell Island. Much of past logging has excessively damaged the forest and regeneration has been poor. A few timber plantations have been established. There is an urgent need to identify and create conservation areas to protect representative samples of the various forest types.

The Forests

With the possible exception of part of the northern coastal plain of Guadalcanal, which lies in a rain shadow and is regularly burnt, all the Solomon Islands have an extremely high rainfall with no dry season and would be naturally covered by rain forests. Indeed, even today most of the islands present a picture of dark green densely forested hills and mist covered mountains. It was this sombre appearance that may have been the origin of the name Melanesia: the dark islands (Walker, 1948; Whitmore, 1969).

The forest canopy is 30 to 40 m tall. The only emergents are *Terminalia calamansanai* and several species of strangling and banyan figs. Climbers and epiphytes are very abundant. Cyclones are the major influence on floristic differentiation, but humans have also had a strong influence on structure. Swidden agriculture is practised throughout the Solomons, although today people mainly live in coastal areas. Previously, when populations were larger, and distributed inland, larger areas were cultivated and subsequently valuable stands of timber developed when they were abandoned. There are about 60 common large trees, 12 of which are very plentiful and widely distributed.

The following points can be made about forest cover:

1 The Santa Cruz islands had forest dominated by the kauri pine *Agathis macrophylla* (Whitmore, 1966) but these are now almost completely logged over.

2 Rain forest is replaced on Guadalcanal around Honiara by a mixed deciduous forest which has been largely degraded to savanna woodland maintained by frequent dry-season fires. Here several exotic species have established themselves. The most prominent are *Leucaena leucocephala* and *Broussonetia papyifera*, the paper mulberry, both effective colonisers.

3 Small pockets of swamp forest occur mainly on the coast, on poorly drained sites. *Terminalia brassii*, an important commercial species, forms pure stands.

4 The Solomons are unusual in still retaining much beach forest fringing sandy shores, though as elsewhere many have been replaced by coconut plantations.

5 The most distinctive forest type is found on areas of ultrabasic rock. This forest is floristically poor and dominated by a few species. Ultrabasic forest has been reduced to scrub or fern thickets in some places, probably by man-made fires (Whitmore, 1969).

6 There is a strong compression of the vegetation zones on mountains and the flora is markedly impoverished.

7 Around villages, forests have been selectively harvested for the necessities of rural village life. Useful products include thatch from the Pacific sago palm *Metroxylon salomonense*; houseposts from *Securinega flexuosa*; floor, rafter, beam and wall material from various palms and the bamboo, *Bambusa vulgaris*, 'rope' from rattans, *Calamus* spp. and *Rhaphidophora* spp. and canoe boles from *Gmelina moluccana*. These areas of depleted forest have a rather open appearance with a degraded lower canopy. However, more specific and destructive forms of degradation can be identified.

Forest Resources and Management

The extent of closed canopy forest in the Solomon Islands was estimated to be 24,230 sq. km in 1980 (88 per cent of land area) (FAO, 1988). No forest maps have ever been published for the Solomon Islands and Map 29.2 is based on the knowledge of foresters working in the region. As Table 29.1 indicates, the area of forest shown on the map is 25,590 sq. km, or 92.9 per cent of total land area. Compared to the FAO figures this is somewhat optimistic, but it accords well with an estimate of 25,260 sq. km provided to the editors by the Ministry of Natural Resources (C. Turnbull, 20 June 1990).

The main agricultural development and logging activities take place in the lowland forests and in particular in the richer valleys and well-drained alluvial areas. Apart from Malaita and Guadalcanal most of the people live near the coast, for example not a single village is located inland on New Georgia. The beach forest is therefore under particular pressure, usually for conversion to coconuts and for forest products such as firewood and building materials. The mangrove forests are locally overexploited, but the freshwater swamp forests are inaccessible to commercial logging and often remain relatively undisturbed. A complete survey of the land resources of the Solomon Islands was made in the 1970s (Hansell and Wall, 1976). It included descriptions of forests and soils as well as a classification of the land into various degrees of suitability for agriculture.

Almost 90 per cent of the forest was considered by FAO to be unproductive of timber because of access problems on the steep ground (FAO, 1988). It is generally believed that at the current rate of exploitation, the timber resources in the remaining 10 per cent will last a maximum of 15 years. This has serious implications not only for the non-cash economy and environment but also on the national cash economy. Logging in 1987 provided the Government with a revenue of SI$33.4 million. The timber trade provides around a third of the total national export earnings each year. The Government hopes that revenue from the export of plantation grown trees will replace the earnings from logging once the natural forests have been worked out.

A proposal for a national forest inventory prepared in the mid-1980s with assistance from Australian aid (AIDAB) is now unlikely to go ahead due to a change in Government policy. However, forest policy is currently under review with assistance from FAO. Recently the Government has required 50 per cent of log processing (sawmilling) to be carried out in the Solomon Islands. The forest legislation was amended to a minor degree in 1987 and the overall objectives for the forest sector were outlined in the 1989 National Development Plan. Work continues towards the definition of a forest estate, to comprise those areas of government land where forestry has a primary interest, mainly plantation areas. Currently, the total area under proposal is about 1180 sq. km of which to date 230 sq. km have been planted.

Generally logging operations on their own do not cause deforestation. Where only logs over 55 cm diameter are removed damage is not excessive, but where all logs over 35 cm have been taken (locally called 'supersmalls') the forest has been utterly degraded, as is the case in Fiji. Areas that have been logged to this high intensity on Kolombangara from the 1960s onwards, developed climber tangles and small pioneer tree cover, and are only now, 20 years later, developing a forest cover. Where logging operations have been more selective and more closely controlled, the regeneration and restoration of a forest cover has been much quicker and may recover sufficiently for a further felling to take place after 15 years. Owing to the relatively low pressure on land, logging operations are rarely followed by farming. There are exceptions – for example limited areas of opportunistic farming are found close to the logging roads on Malaita and Guadalcanal. Most shifting cultivation is carried out in secondary forest near to villages.

There is increasing pressure on the remaining forest resource. One relatively small coralline island in the Roviana Lagoon, Ndova, is currently being considered by the traditional owners for a logging licence. In the future pressure may also develop to log above 400 m elevation.

As has already been described, depleted forests can be identified around villages. Nowadays villagers do not require the same mix of products and are less dependent on the forest. For example monofilament fish nets have replaced fishnets made from *Gnetum*. However,

the increasing population requires larger areas for shifting cultivation. The requirement for some products has increased and the long term resources are threatened. Supplies of *Securinega flexuosa* used for house posts are severely depleted on the north coast of Malaita and distant sources are being tapped. To a degree these local shortfalls can be remedied, and in some cases the situation can be totally reversed by, for example, the establishment of small plantations of *S. flexuosa* (Chaplin, 1988).

Since the 1960s areas of forest close to villages have been seriously degraded by commercial logging on many islands including Kolombangara, New Georgia, Gizo and Guadalcanal. The loss of areas of natural forest near to the village can be expected to have serious effects on the long term viability and quality of village life. Many communities have allowed logging to go ahead on customary land which they own, the motive being the short-term financial benefits and a general desire for the development that is expected to follow. Other communities, such as at Iriri on Kolombangara and the Kusaghe villages on north New Georgia, have resisted the temptation to allow logging. In the second example, major political tensions resulted between the local land-owners, government and the company involved.

While areas of forest around the village often become depleted by the removal of forest products for local use, it is also the case that in certain circumstances areas of forest are enriched or enhanced in their usefulness to the rural community. This occurs either directly or indirectly. Nut trees such as *Terminalia kaernbachii*, the okari nut, may be planted in old garden sites and later after the site is abandoned and secondary forest develops they are tended. Such trees are only associated with human intervention (Chaplin, 1985a). Regeneration of other useful species such as *Canarium indicum*, and *C. salomonense* which provide oil-rich kernels and the Pacific sago palm, may be encouraged and further enrich an area's productivity (Chaplin, 1985b). The very disturbed but intensively managed fruit and nut forests of the Reef Islands and parts of Santa Cruz are well-known examples (Yen, 1974).

Mangroves

Mangrove forests occur on most islands, but maps are lacking. They are relatively extensive on Santa Isabel, Malaita and in the New Georgia group. No large scale exploitation has taken place and

Marovo Lagoon in the New Georgia group, Solomon Islands. T. C. Whitmore

mangrove forests have legal protection. Two small scale threats can be identified. The beach forest, and often small areas of mangrove on the seaward side of coconut plantations, are usually, and generally unnecessarily, cleared. In the second instance mangroves are a source of firewood and building poles, and are under considerable pressure due to their coastal location near to the rural population.

Mangroves are believed to have an important role in the production of the small anchovy-type fish used as bait in the skipjack tuna pole-fishing industry. This industry is of crucial importance to the Solomon Islands' economy.

A significant threat to mangrove forests in the Noro area of New Georgia was averted when plans to use mangrove for industrial scale fish-smoking were stopped. An alternative source of suitable wood from the log yard of a logging company was identified.

Biodiversity

The lowland rain forest of the Solomon Islands is floristically relatively poor. This impoverishment is to a limited extent compensated by distinctive Melanesian and Pacific components in the flora. The flora is also remarkably uniform with few species endemic to individual islands or regions. The Solomons have a rich avifauna and this does show strong local differentiation (Mayr, 1945) and there is a high level of endemism. There are few reptiles, amphibians or mammals. The insects include several spectacular endemic birdwing butterflies (*Ornithopera* and *iroides*).

Conservation Areas

The existing system of protected areas is so weak that the Solomon Islands may be considered to have no effective conservation areas. Protected areas legislation is also weakened by not being applicable to land held in customary tenure. The Arnavon Wildlife Sanctuary was protected under a trespass law from 1975, and established in law as a protected area in 1980. However, the negotiations which led to its establishment did not take into full account the customary ownership claimed by a group from Choiseul and in 1981 they attacked and destroyed the research facilities in the sanctuary. There has been no subsequent attempt to re-establish a protected area there.

The area to the immediate south of Honiara around Mount Austin was designated as Queen Elizabeth National Park in 1954. Reduced from 61 sq. km to a little over 10 sq. km in 1973, no effective management was instituted and the forest, dominated by *Pometia pinnata* and *Vitex cofassus* has largely been replaced by severely degraded forest or open grassland as a result of shifting cultivation.

A narrow strip of unlogged forest on Kolombangara, home to a number of single-island endemic birds, ranging from the coast up to the areas of unlogged forest on the central mountain was to be reserved, but was subsequently selectively logged in the early 1980s.

To identify the critically important sites a national survey is required. Most of the land is under customary ownership and any measures to protect areas must take account of that. The principal objectives should be:
- Protection of internationally important areas such as Rennell, the Anarvons and the kauri (*Agathis*) forest in the Santa Cruz islands.
- Protection of coastal forests under particular pressure.
- Protection of all mangrove forests.
- Protection of all forest above 400 m.
- Protection of typical examples of the types of lowland forest.
- Continued protection of the Kolombangara Ecological Survey plots which were established in 1964 and are amongst the oldest in the humid tropics (Whitmore and Chaplin, 1986).

The following areas are of particular value and as such are strong candidates for protection in some form:
- Rennell Island (see case study), which is internationally significant.

- Parts of the natural kauri *Agathis macrophylla* stands in Santa Cruz.
- Selected coralline islands that will retain viable natural forest.
- Representative areas of rain forest on each of the major islands (as well as Rennell), to ensure the protection of the endemic flora and fauna. Ideally, a sizeable reserve embracing the full ecological transition from the mountains to the coast should be sought in each case. Lowland forest such as the customary owned land at Iriri on Kolombangara is an example of such areas.
- All forest above 400 m is protected from logging, but this must be strengthened, in anticipation that the lowland forests will be logged-out in 10 to 15 years' time.

Initiatives for Conservation

Reports to Parliament by the Solomon Islands Ombudsman (OSI) have drawn attention to the disastrous effects which essentially uncontrolled logging is having on rural people and their resources. These reports have highlighted issues and are beginning to lead to reform.

It is clear that large scale export logging operations are still rapidly depleting the lowland forests of the Solomon Islands. During the 1980s reported annual log exports averaged 300,000 cu. m in addition to up to 40,000 cu. m felled for domestic consumption. Licences have been issued to allow harvesting to rise to 460,000 cu. m per annum, which gives the remaining potentially exploitable forests a lifetime of 10–15 years.

Eighty-five per cent of logging is carried out on customary land. This has proved to be very difficult to control, as the Conservator of Forests states in his 1987 Annual Report:

'The Forest Policy states clearly the concept of sustained yield, however landowners have exclusive rights on the use of their land and timber resources. This arrangement severely restricts the ability of the Forestry Division to issue licences according to a planned strategy in the best interests of the nation as a whole. If correct procedures are followed by landowners and companies, Forestry Division has little option but to issue the licence requested.'

In a special report to Parliament (OSI, 1989) the Ombudsman states that under the present legal and political system it is practically impossible for rural people to stop the entry of foreign logging companies into their forests; there is widespread opposition to logging; and the logging is bringing little benefit to the country or the landowners. He concludes:

'In 20 years' time we shall look back on the activities of these logging companies with the same horror with which we now regard the selling of valuable coastal land for shell money and sticks of tobacco, or the "recruiting" of labour for foreign owned plantations . . .'

In 1989 a reviewed forest policy was adopted and a new Forest and Timber Act was drafted. The 1989 policy requires forests to be managed on a sustained yield basis, and calls for a reduction in the rate of felling and the creation of a reforestation agency for customary land. Already a moratorium on logging licences has been imposed. According to the policy, a forest planning unit is to be established, a forest inventory has been approved, a forestry sector plan is to be produced, timber operations and sales are to be controlled and forest reserves and protected areas are to be set aside.

The flora and fauna of the Solomon Islands is very special and in some cases unique. It is very closely linked to a way of life that will need to maintain that link, indeed dependence, into the 21st century. Maintaining the viability of this natural resource is a national priority for the Solomon Island, but it will be impossible unless protected areas are established. During 1990 an ecological survey will define a representative system of sites. International funding is then to be sought for the leasing of these areas from customary landowners.

Many other positive developments are beginning to take place. As well as the forest policy review and the moratorium on logging licenses, companies are under pressure to process logs locally; there has been success with enforcing selective logging; a forest estate is being established and the plantation programme is being expanded. All of these factors will tend to increase the prospects for the acceptance of more positive practices with regard to forest industry, forestry plantations and conservation.

However, in view of the current vigour and expansionist aims of the logging industry. Several matters (in addition to the establishment of protected areas require attention:

● Forest plantations are currently confined to government land. Means of establishing plantations on custom-owned land need to be identified and put into practice.

● An inventory of the remaining natural commercial forests is urgently needed to enable rational planning to take place.

● A review of all natural resources, both flora and fauna, and including the inshore marine resource, is required.

RENNELL ISLAND

Rennell is the largest raised coral atoll in the world, 86 km long and over 15 km wide, with an area of 825 sq. km, and is the most isolated of the larger islands of the Solomons. It lies 170 km west of Makira, 180 km south of Guadalcanal and 1600 km north-east of Queensland. It is inhabited by people of Polynesian origin and has little dependence in the outside world.

Unlike most of the larger Solomon Islands, Rennell is a 'low' island. Its surface consists of exposed cavernous pinnacle limestone, which has eroded and now forms a typical karst landscape. Lake Tungano, 29 km by 10 km, is the largest enclosed body of water in the Pacific. An endemic banded sea snake *Laticauda crockeri* occurs in the slightly saline waters of the lake.

The island is mostly covered by dense forest with a canopy averaging 20 m tall with numerous larger emergent trees. The particular nature of the forest is not well documented but it is likely to be unique. It may well be heavily disturbed due to the activities and needs of the Rennellese.

As many as 43 per cent of Rennell's breeding birds are endemic and include:

● White ibis   *Threskiornis mollucus* subsp. *pygmaeus*
● Australian dabchick   *Tachybaptus novaehollandiae* subsp. *rennellianus*
● Rennell fantail   *Rhipidura rennelliana*
● Rennell white-eye   *Zosterops rennellianus*

Dendrobium rennellii is a stunningly attractive and rare endemic endemic orchid, found on small islands in the lake. During a recent study the number of known orchid species was raised from four to 22 in five days (Cribb, 1989).

The above examples serve to illustrate the unique nature of the Rennellese flora and fauna and therefore the general importance of the island both nationally and internationally. The inscription of Rennell on the Unesco World Heritage List has been suggested by IUCN but this has not yet been accepted.

During the 1960s proposals were made to mine bauxite on Rennell. More recently a logging company has offered infrastructural developments and cash royalties for logging rights and this proposal is being considered (Cribb, 1989).

The cataclysmic short-term changes that are usually associated with logging or mining operations are not appropriate to Rennell, and will not benefit the islanders in the long term. They would be very damaging to the forests and their component plant and animal life and would threaten the soil and ground water resources that are essential to the viability and quality of life on Rennell. They would jeopardise and destroy the very resources that could be used to develop the long-term prosperity.

Clearly the Rennell life-style is as much under threat from mining and logging operations as from lack of development and progress. Therefore positive long term sustainable development utilising, but not destroying, the natural resources is required. Possible options include the development of a specialist tourist industry based around Lake Tungano.

VANUATU

Three-quarters of the total land area of Vanuatu is still covered with natural vegetation, including lowland rain forest and some montane rain forest. Pressure on the land has been low but is increasing rapidly. Much of the forest has low commercial potential because of cyclone damage. The most valuable timber species, kauri (*Agathis macrophylla* and *A. silbai*) was almost completely logged out under the previous colonial administration, leaving small primary stands in central Erromango and Espiritu Santo. There has never been a forest inventory, although one is now planned. There are thus no good maps of forest cover or other information on areas of greatest natural interest. Land use and agronomic potential have, however, been assessed (Quantin, 1982).

In the 1980s the annual forest cut has ranged from 19,500 to 38,000 cu. m with up to two-thirds being exported. Export logging permits may be phased out by the early 1990s. The major threats to the forest are from extensive development projects, such as for pasture and cocoa which require the clearing of thousands of hectares, particularly on Espiritu Santo and Malakula. The construction of new roads on Espiritu Santo will open substantial areas of pristine forest to development. There are also still occasional pressures from outside to log large areas of forest.

Plantations have been developed to meet local needs, and industrial forestry plantations are expanding. It is intended eventually to meet most local wood requirements. The Forestry Department is developing and implementing plans for sustainable forest use, but it still lacks an adequate database on which to formulate planning decisions. There are at present no terrestrial protected areas in Vanuatu, but one is planned for the remaining kauri forest on Erromango. It is now time to identify those forest areas requiring protection from development. Plans to prepare a National Conservation Strategy are under way, and this should provide the Government and people with an opportunity to consider the long term future of their land and forests.

Quantin (1982) includes maps of potential agronomic land-use, at 1:100,000 for Espiritu Santo, Malakula, Efate and Tanna (5 sheets) and at 1:500,000 (2 sheets) covering the entire country. A general discussion of location, population, economy, geology, topography, climate, soils and land use and a detailed treatment of soils and potential crops is given. However, no maps of the distribution of natural forests on Vanuatu have been located.

References

Anon. (1989)   Rain forest echoes. *News from Le Vaomatua 22.* Pago Pago, American Samoa.

Ash, J. and Ash, W. (1984)   Freshwater wetland vegetation of Viti Levu, Fiji. *New Zealand Journal of Botany* 22: 337–91.

Chaplin, G. E. (1985a)   A potentially useful nut tree, *Terminalia kaernbachii* Warb. *Forest Research Note* 17 4/85. Forestry Division, Honiara, Solomon Islands.

Chaplin, G. E. (1985b)   Indications of the potential fruit and kernel yields of *C. indicum* and *C. salomonense* in Western Province Solomon Island. *Forest Research Note* 19 6/85. Forestry Division, Honiara, Solomon Islands.

Chaplin, G. E. (1988)   The status of *Securinega flexuosa* in Solomon Islands – an appropriate species for small scale community forestry. *Forest Research Note* 46 14/88. Forestry Division, Honiara.

Cribb, P. J. (1989)   Desert island discoveries: orchid hunting on a coral island. *Orchid Revue and The Orchadian.* Royal Botanic Gardens, Kew, UK. (In press.)

Drysdale, P. J. (1988)   Rain forest management and conservation in Fiji: a prescription for action. In: *Proceedings of Second National Conservation Congress 9–10 June. Vol 2,* pp. 1–264. National Trust for Fiji, Suva, Fiji.

Dunlap, R. C. and Singh, B. B. (1980)   *A National Parks and Reserves System for Fiji.* Report to the National Trust for Fiji. 3 Volumes.

FAO (1988)   *An Interim Report on the State of Forest Resources in the Developing Countries.* FAO, Rome, Italy. 18 pp. + 5 tables.

FAO (1990) *FAO Yearbook of Forest Products 1977–88.* FAO Forestry Series No. 23, FAO Statistics Series No. 90. FAO, Rome.

Hansell, J. R. F. and Wall, J. R. D. (1976)   Land resources of the Solomon Islands. *Land Resources Study* 18.

Mayr, E. (1945)   *Birds of the South West Pacific. A Field Guide to the Birds of the Area Between Samoa, New Caledonia and Micronesia.* Macmillan, New York, USA.

Ombudsman of the Solomon Islands (OSI) (1989)   Can rural people say no to foreign logging? *Ombudsman's Report to Parliament.*

Paine, J. R. (1989a)   Western Samoa, an Overview of its Protected Area System. World Conservation Monitoring Centre, Cambridge, UK. Unpublished report.

Paine, J. R. (1989b)   Tonga, an Overview of its Protected Area System. World Conservation Monitoring Centre, Cambridge, UK. Unpublished report.

Paine, J. R. (1989c)   Cook Islands, an Overview of its Protected Area System. World Conservation Monitoring Centre, Cambridge. Unpublished report.

Paine, J. R. (1989d)   Fiji, an Overview of its Protected Area System. World Conservation Monitoring Centre, Cambridge, UK. Unpublished report.

Parham, J. W. (1972)   *Plants of Fiji Islands.* Government Press, Suva.

Pratt, D. H., Bruner, P. L. and Berret, D. G. (1987)   *The Birds of Hawaii and the Tropical Pacific.* Princeton University Press, Princeton, New Jersey, USA.

Quantin, P. (1982)   *Vanuatu: Agronomic Potential and Land Use maps.* (Includes seven folded maps.) ORSTOM/Ministry of Land and Natural Resources, Paris. (French/English text.) 49 pp.

Robinson, G. S. (1975)   *Macrolepidoptera of Fiji and Rotuma: a Taxonomic and Biogeographic Study.* E. W. Classey, Faringdon, UK. 362 pp.

Schmid, M. (1978)   The Melanesian forest ecosystem (New Caledonia, New Hebrides, Fiji Islands and Solomon Islands). In: Unesco/UNEP/FAO; *Tropical Forest Ecosystems.* Unesco, Paris.

Schmid, M. (1989)   The forests in the tropical Pacific archipelagoes. In: *Tropical Rain Forest Ecosystems.* pp. 283–301. Lieth, H. and Werger, M. J. A. (eds). Ecosystems of the World 14B. Elsevier, Amsterdam, The Netherlands.

SPREP (1980)   *Fiji.* Country Report No. 4. South Pacific Commission, Noumea, New Caledonia. 31 pp.

SPREP (1985)   *Action Strategy for Protected Areas in the South Pacific Region.* South Pacific Commission, Noumea, New Caledonia.

UNEP/IUCN (1988)   *Coral Reefs of the World.* Vol. 3. *Central and western Pacific.* UNEP Regional Seas Directories and Bibliographies. IUCN, Gland, Switzerland and Cambridge, UK, and UNEP, Nairobi, Kenya.

Walker, F. S. (1948)   *The Forests of the British Solomon Islands Protectorate.* Forest Record No. 1, Forestry Division, Ministry of Natural Resources, Honiara, Solomon Islands.

Watling, D. (1988a)   The effects of logging on Fijian wildlife. A Paper presented at the National Trust for Fiji's Second Conservation Conference, June 8–9, 1988.

Watling, D. (1988b)   The Forestry Sector Development Study. FIJ/86/004. Report of the environmental scientist. Unpublished Report. Suva, Fiji.

Whitmore, T. C. (1966)   The social status of *Agathis* in a rain forest in Melanesia. *Journal of Ecology* 54: 285–301.

Whitmore, T. C. (1969)   The vegetation of the Solomon Islands. *Philosophical Transactions of the Royal Society* **B** 255: 259–70.

Whitmore, T. C. and Chaplin, G. E. (1986)   The Kolombangara ecological survey: Review 1964–1986 and proposals for the future. *Forest Research Note* 27–8/86. Forestry Division, Honiara.

Yen, E. E. (1974)   Arboriculture in the subsistence of Santa Cruz, Solomon Islands. *Economic Botany* 28: 247–84.

Authorship

James Paine of WCMC, Cambridge covered Fiji, with contributions from A. M. Ravuvu of the Ministry of Forests in Suva, Birandra Singh of the National Trust for Fiji in Suva, Michal Fromaget of ORSTOM, Noumea, and Bill Howard of ODA, London. Arthur Dahl of UNEP, Nairobi covered Melanesia with contributions from Guy Salmon of the Maruia Society in Auckland. Graham Chaplin of the Oxford Forestry Institute covered the Solomon Islands with additional data from C. Turnbull, Senior Forest Officer in Honiara.

Map 29.1 Forest cover in Fiji

The remaining indigenous forest in Fiji was extracted from a 1:500,000 forest cover map, prepared by the Ministry of Forests, Fiji, from a 1985 survey. Forest types were added with the help of the Maruia Society, Auckland, New Zealand, whose staff generously prepared a summary forest map based on the Fiji Forest Inventory carried out in 1966–9 and published in 1972, in 29 map sheets at 1:50,000 by the Directorate of Overseas Surveys, London. Protected areas information and maps were also prepared by the Maruia Society.

Map 29.2 Forest cover in the Solomon Islands

There are no published maps of existing vegetation in the Solomon Islands. Map 29.2 is based on a hand-coloured map prepared by the Forestry Division, showing plantation forests, logged forests and logging concessions overlain onto the published 1:1 million scale map *Solomon Island*, Edition 2, revised and published by The Survey and Mapping Division, Honiara, in two sheets. Additional information was added by G. Chaplin, based on his personal experience of the region. Difficulties were experienced in discovering the total land area of The Solomon Islands; FAO uses 27,540 sq. km., but other sources give figures 1000–2000 sq. km larger.

Acronyms

Apia Convention Convention on the Conservation of Nature in the South Pacific
AIDAB Australian International Development Assistance Bureau
AsDB Asian Development Bank
ASEAN Association of South East Asian Nations
AVHRR Advanced Very High Resolution Radiometry
BAKOSURTANAL National Centre for Coordination of Surveys and Mapping (Indonesia)
BARC Bangladesh Agricultural Research Council
BIOTROP Southeast Asian Regional Centre for Tropical Biology
BP British Petroleum
CITES Convention on International Trade in Endangered Species of Wild Fauna and Flora
CMC IUCN Conservation Monitoring Centre (now WCMC)
CNPPA Commission on National Parks and Protected Areas (IUCN)
CPA Construction and Planning Administration (Ministry of Interior, China)
CSIRO Commonwealth Scientific Industrial Research Organisation, Australia
CFDT Committee for Forest Development in the Tropics (FAO)
CTFT Centre Technique Forestier Tropical (Paris)
DANIDA Ministry of Foreign Affairs, Department of International Development
dbh Diameter at breast height
DENR Dept of Environment and Natural Resources (Philippines)
DoT Department of Trasmigration (Indonesia)
ECAN Environmentally Critical Areas Network (Philippines)
ECE Economic Commission for Europe (UN)
EEC European Economic Community
ELC Environment Liaison Centre
ESCAP Economic and Social Commission for Asia and the Pacific (UN)
ESRI Environmental Systems Research Institute
FAO Food and Agriculture Organisation of the United Nations
FELDA Federal Land Development Authority (Malaysia)
FINNIDA Finnish International Development Agency
FRIM Forest Research Institute, Malaysia
FSI Forest Survey of India
GEMS Global Environment Monitoring System (UNEP)
GIS Geographic Information System
GRID Global Resources Information Database (UNEP/GEMS)
GTZ Deutsche Gesellschaft für Technische Zusammenarbeit
HELVETAS Switzerland Development Agency
HIID Harvard Institute for International Development
IBM International Business Machines
IBP International Biological Programme
IBPGR International Board for Plant Genetic Resources
ICBP International Council for Bird Preservation
IDRC International Development Research Centre (Canada)
IIED International Institute for Environment and Development
ILO International Labour Organisation (UN)
ISFP Integrated Social Forestry Programme (Philippines)
IPT Asian Wetland Bureau
ITTA International Tropical Timber Agreement

ITTO International Tropical Timber Organisation
IUCN International Union for Conservation of Nature and Natural Resources – The World Conservation Union
IUFRO International Union of Forestry Research Organisations
IWRB International Waterfowl and Wetlands Research Bureau
JNC Jet Navigation Charts
MAB Man and the Biosphere Programme (Unesco)
MNS Malayan Nature Society
NARESA National Resources Energy and Science Authority (Sri Lanka)
NCC Nature Conservancy Council (UK)
NCS National Conservation Strategy
NGO Non-governmental Organisation
NRMC Natural Resources Management Centre (Philippines)
OCA/PAC Oceans and Coastal Areas Programme Activity Centre (UNEP)
ODA Overseas Development Administration (UK)
ODNRI Overseas Development Natural Resources Institute (UK)
ONC Operational Navigation Charts
ORSTOM Institut Français de Recherche Scientifique pour le Developpement en Cooperation
OSI Ombudsman of the Solomon Islands
POSSCEP Project on Study Survey and Conservation of Endangered Species of Flora (India)
Ramsar Convention Convention on Wetlands of International Importance Especially as Waterfowl Habitat
RePPProt Regional Physical Planning Programme for Transmigration (Indonesia)
SACEP South Asia Cooperative Environmental Programme
SAM Sahabat Alam Malaysia (Friends of the Earth, Malaysia)
SAR Synthetic Aperture Radar
SIDA Swedish International Development Authority
SKEPHI Sekretariat Kerjasama Polestarian Hutan
SLAR Side-looking Airborne Radar
SPOT Systeme Probatoire d'Observation de la Terre
SPREP South Pacific Regional Environment Programme
SSC Species Survival Commission (IUCN)
TFAP Tropical Forestry Action Plan
TPC Tactical Pilotage Charts
UN United Nations
UNCTAD United Nations Conference on Trade and Development
UNDP United Nations Development Programme
UNEP United Nations Environment Programme
Unesco United Nations Educational, Scientific and Cultural Organisation
UNIDO United Nations Industrial Development Organisation
UNSO United Nations Sundano-Sahelian Office
US–AID US Agency for International Development
US–NPS US National Park Service
WCED World Commission on Environment and Development
WCMC World Conservation Monitoring Centre
WCS World Conservation Strategy
WEI Wau Ecology Institute
WFP World Food Programme
WRI World Resources Institute
WWF World Wide Fund for Nature

Glossary

accretion *See* LAND ACCRETION.
agroforestry Interplanting of farm crops and trees.
anthropogenic Produced as a result of human activities.
arboreal Tree-dwelling.
arboretum Place where trees and shrubs are grown for study and display.
aseasonal Without clear seasons.
avifauna Birdlife of a region or period of time.
biodiversity Richness of plant and animal species and in ecosystem complexity.
biogeographical province Area defined by fauna and flora it contains.
biomass Amount of living matter in a defined area.
Biosphere Reserve Concept introduced by Unesco's Man and Biosphere Programme. A reserve including zones with different degrees of land use. *See* CHAPTER 9.
biota The flora and fauna of an area.
biotic Relating to living things.

bole Trunk of a tree.
broadleaved (tree) Any tree belonging to the subclass Dicotyledonae of the class Angiospermae (flowering plants).
buttress Flange at base of a tree bole (qv); common in rain forests.
canopy The whole of a forest from the ground upwards. Some scientists use canopy to mean just the top of the forest.
catchment A river basin, sometimes referring only to its upper part.
clear felling Complete clearance of a forest, as opposed to selective fellings. *See also* monocyclic/polycyclic systems.
climax The final stage in the natural succession reached by a community of organisms, especially plants, in equilibrium with existing environmental conditions.
closed canopy Canopy (qv) which is effectively complete, rather than consisting of scattered trees; in practice, canopy cover of 40% or more.
commensal species Different species that associate, bringing benefit to one of the species and harming none of them.
concession Block of forest granted for exploitation over a specified period to a firm or person, the concessionaire.

250

cordillera Chains of mountain peaks.

corridors of forest Strips or belts of forest running through non-forested land, joining larger forest blocks.

coupe A technical forestry term referring to the amount of forest cut in a specified period.

creaming Light exploitation of a forest (removal of the most valuable trees).

crown canopy Cover formed by the top branches of trees in a forest.

crown cover Coverage of ground by tree crowns.

cytology Study of cells.

degazette an area, degazettement Rescind the legal demarcation of an area.

desertification Expansion of deserts by climatic change or by overgrazing and clearing of vegetation in adjacent areas.

desiccation Removal of moisture; drying out.

dipterocarp Member of the Dipterocarpacae, a family of old-world tropical trees valuable for timber and resin.

ecological niche The functional position of an organism within an ecosystem.

ecosystem A natural unit consisting of organisms and their environment.

endemic Native or confined to a particular area.

endemism Noun from endemic.

epiphyte A plant which uses another for support, not for nutrients.

escarpment Long cliff or slope separating two more or less level slopes, resulting from erosion or faults.

estuarine Living in an estuary.

faller Person who fells trees.

fauna Wildlife in a particular area or time.

felling cycle Time period between successive forest harvests.

feral Referring to animals or plants that were once domesticated but have escaped to the wild.

fire climax Synonym: pyroclimax. Regions of plant life, e.g. forests, grassland, where fire plays an important role in suppressing some plants and encouraging the growth of others. *See* CLIMAX.

flora Wild plant life in a particular area or time.

floristics The plant species composition of an ecosystem.

friable (soil) Crumbly.

frugivorous Fruit-eating.

germplasm The genetic diversity of a group of organisms.

Gondwanic Pertaining to Gondwanaland, the southern super-continent which has disintegrated from the early Tertiary onwards.

granodiorite Coarsely crystalline acid igneous rock.

hardwood Wood of a flowering plant, technically recognised by its possession (with rare exceptions) of vessels. Hardwoods range from hard and dense (e.g. *Lignum vitae*) to soft (e.g. balsa).

Imperata cylindrica Aggressive stoloniferous (qv) creeping grass which forms fire climax vegetation after forest destruction.

inflorescence Flowering shoot.

karst Cavernous and deeply eroded limestone.

land accretion Fixation of land.

lateritic (acid l. soil) Hard impermeable soil unsuitable for cultivation.

littoral Situated near a (sea) shore.

massif Large mountain mass.

monoculture Cultivation of a single crop.

monocyclic system Synonym: uniform system. Removal of all saleable trees at a single operation. The length of the cycle corresponds roughly to the rotation (qv) period of the trees. Damage to the forest is more drastic than under a polycyclic system.

monotreme Egg-laying order (Monotremata) of Mammalia with many primitive reptilian features.

monotypic Having a single representative (used of a biological group).

monsoon forest Closed canopy forests in seasonal tropical climates (*see* CHAPTER 1).

montane Growing or living in mountainous areas.

morphology Study of the form of animals and plants.

multistorey *See* STOREY.

niche *See* ECOLOGICAL NICHE.

open forests *See* WOODLANDS.

peelers, peeling *See* VENEER LOGS.

perhumid Permanently humid climate with no dry season.

photosynthesis Process by which green plants use sunlight to build complex substances from carbon dioxide and water.

physiognomy External features.

physiographical Describing natural phenomena.

phytochemistry Chemistry of plants.

poison girdling Poisoning of unwanted trees and climbers to enable nearby trees to develop.

polycyclic system Synonym: selection system. Systematic repeated removal of mature trees to encourage growth of young ones. *See* CHAPTER 6.

polymer Chemical compound consisting of repeating structural units.

primary forest *See* PRISTINE FOREST.

pristine forest Forest in a primary, virgin or undisturbed state.

production forest Forest designated for the production of goods, usually timber.

propagules Any part of a plant capable of forming a new plant when separated from the parent.

rain forest Closed canopy forests in aseasonal climates; may be found in tropical and temperate latitudes. *See* CHAPTER 1.

refugium, plur. refugia Region where biological communities have remained relatively undisturbed over long periods.

residual stand The number of trees left standing after logging.

riparian Land bordering water.

riverine Living or growing on a river bank.

rotation Length of time needed for a stand of commercial timber trees to reach a suitable felling size.

sawlogs Logs which are to be sawn lengthwise for the manufacture of sawnwood.

scaling (logs) Use of a pre-determined measure (scaling stick) to determine the number of board feet ($12' \times 12'' \times 1''$) per tree.

sclerophyll Plant with tough evergreen leaves.

secondary forest Forest containing fast-growing trees which flourish after disturbance.

selection system *See* POLYCYCLIC SYSTEM.

shifting cultivation System of agriculture that depends on clearing and burning an area of forest for farming over a temporary period. *See* SWIDDEN AGRICULTURE.

silvicultural treatment Treatment often involving removal in a natural forest of unwanted climbers, damaged trees or uncommercial species. Replanting is rare.

silviculture The cultivation and management of forests and woodland.

sinker Logs that are denser than water and thus cannot be rafted down river. Antonym: floater.

skid track, skid trail Track caused by logs being dragged or skidded.

skidder Vehicle used to haul logs from the forest.

skyline working Skyline cable logging, overhead logging.

slash and burn *See* SHIFTING CULTIVATION.

softwood Wood from a conifer, technically recognised by the absence of vessels. Softwoods have abundant fibres and make good paper.

stand *See* RESIDUAL STAND.

stoloniferous Describes a creeping plant which throws out runners.

storey Layer or stratum of a forest.

swidden agriculture Shifting agriculture carried out in the traditional, sustainable way, i.e. with periods of fallow to restore soil fertility.

taxonomy Classification of plants and animals based on natural relationships.

tetrapod Vertebrate with two pairs of limbs.

thermoplastic Capable of softening or melting when heated and hardening when cooled.

transfer pricing The price at which intra-company trades are consummated e.g. from a firm's sawmill to a company-owned wholesale warehouse.

ultrabasic rocks Igneous rocks almost entirely composed of ferromagnesian minerals.

understorey *See* STOREY.

ungulate Hoofed mammal.

uniform systems *See* MONOCYCLIC SYSTEMS.

vascular Used to describe channels carrying fluids in plants (and animals).

veneer logs Logs from tree that are good 'peelers', i.e. relatively easy to cut into thin veneers for making plywood.

vessel Continuous tubular structure in a plant used for the longitudinal conduction of materials from roots to leaves.

virgin forest *See* PRISTINE FOREST.

woodland Woody vegetation formations with scattered trees, generally with less than 40% crown cover. Also known as 'open forests'.

Index of Species – Plants

Page numbers referring to Tables are given in **bold**.

Index of Species – Animals and Birds

General Index

The page numbers of Tables are denoted by **bold** type. Map page numbers are preceded by (*M*). Both Map and Figure page numbers are given in *italic* type.